LAND OF GIANTS

LAND

OF GIANTS

The Drive to the Pacific Northwest
1750-1950

By DAVID LAVENDER

This edition published in 2001 by Castle Books,
A division of Book Sales Inc.
114 Northfield Avenue, Edison, NJ 08837

Published by arrangement with Doubleday, a division of The
Doubleday Broadway Publishing Group, a division of Random House
Inc.

Library of Congress Catalog Card Number 58-12049

ISBN 0-7858-1348-9

For MY MOTHER

Contents

Book One: THE SEA PEDDLERS

   1. Short Cut to Cathay   1

   2. The Track of the Bear   7

   3. The First American   16

   4. Ledyard's Heirs   23

   5. Nootka Sound and the Fury   31

   6. Columbia's River   39

Book Two: THE WARS OF THE BEAVER KINGDOMS

   1. To Claim a Continent   53

   2. "Ocian in View"   63

   3. The Star Man   76

   4. Astor's Threat   82

   5. The Beginnings of Disaster   92

   6. "A Dagger to My Heart"   98

   7. Doldrums   107

   8. Persons of the Great Drama   114

   9. To Strip the Country Bare   123

   10. Accidental Greatness   130

Book Three: OREGON FEVER

1.	Prophet without Honor	141
2.	The Fruit of Failure	148
3.	The Cry from the Wilderness	153
4.	Portents	163
5.	The First Women	174
6.	The Opening Wedge	182
7.	The Vineyards of the Lord—and Others	189
8.	The New Order	200
9.	Conflict and Tragedy	209
10.	Way Station	215
11.	"May We Not Call Them Men of Destiny?"	223
12.	Substitutes for Anarchy	237
13.	Decision	249
14.	An Era Ends	257

Book Four: THE PANGS OF ADJUSTMENT

1.	The Magic Wand	269
2.	Assorted Frankensteins	274
3.	Oregon's Rambunctious Stepchild	281
4.	"A Real Go-ahead Man"	287
5.	"I Wonder If the Ground Is Listening?"	296
6.	Whose War Is This?	303
7.	Exit Goliath	315

Book Five: EXTRAVAGANZA

1. Stampede 327

2. Law and Disorder 336

3. How to Build an Empire 343

4. "Coarse, Pretentious, Boastful, False and Cunning" 356

5. The Bones of Their Mother 364

6. The Railroad Rush 374

7. Mineral Boom—and Bust 387

8. One More Merry-go-round 400

Book Six: FOR THESE BLESSINGS

1. The Trees 415

2. The Fish 425

3. The Water 433

BIBLIOGRAPHY 447

INDEX

MAPS FOLLOWING PAGE

1. The Sea Routes of Early Pacific Exploration 36

2. The Area of the Fur Trade of the Northwest 108

3. The Missions and Early Settlements of the Northwest 180

4. The Routes of the Explorers, Early Forts, and Trading Posts of the Northwest 276

5. The Mining Camps and Indian Settlements of the
     Northwest   348

6. The waterways, Dams, and other Natural Resources
     of the Northwest   420

LAND OF GIANTS

Book One

THE SEA PEDDLERS

1. Short Cut to Cathay

SPAIN was frightened. For almost a century, ever since Pope Alexander's bull dividing the New World, she had considered the Pacific as her private lake. And then suddenly, in the Year of Salvation 1579, red-bearded Francis Drake of England materialized—no Spaniard knew how—off the western coast of South America.

Helplessly the dons watched his single ship, the *Golden Hind*, raid their ports at Valparaiso and Callao de Lima. Next the Englishman seized a treasure galleon bound for Panama, and from her stripped strongboxes full of emeralds and pearls, thirteen chests of coined silver, eighty pounds of gold ingots, twenty-six tons of silver bars. Glutted with plunder, the *Golden Hind* then vanished toward the north.

North!

What attraction, the ravaged Spaniards wondered, could lie in that direction . . . unless it was the Strait of Anian, western end of the supposed Northwest Passage through America? Had Drake found the seaway? Was he planning to escape through the same channel by which he had come?

Other circumstances added to the fear. As Spanish agents in London were aware, a reformed semi-pirate named Martin Frobisher had already made two trips across the North Atlantic, hunting among the icebergs beyond Greenland for the eastern end of the passage. Was it only coincidence, then, that shortly before Drake's raids Frobisher had embarked on a third expedition? To be sure, his ostensible purpose was to dig for arctic gold. But what of the inlet whose mouth Frobisher had discovered on his earlier trips, an inlet reputedly pointing straight in the direction of Spain's Southern Sea? Did he and Drake plan to meet and concoct more devilment somewhere up in those bleak waterways?

The Spanish were, of course, jumping at bogies. Drake had entered the Southern Sea through the Straits of Magellan. He had, however, no intention of returning that way. On his outward journey Cape Horn's "hell-darke nightes and the mercyless fury of tempestuous storms" had swallowed one of his accompanying ships while sending another scudding in terror back to England's green and pleasant land. Only the *Golden Hind* was left, and now the aroused Spaniards, as well as the wind-racked seas, awaited any attempt to retreat via the south. Escape to the north was preferable—if a navigable northern waterway back into the Atlantic indeed existed.

Drake tried to learn. Quite probably his own desires were fortified by secret orders he carried, enjoining him to search for the far end of Frobisher's inlet. We cannot be sure, for no record remains beyond Drake's own enigmatic remarks. But we do know that something prompted him to sail doggedly northward for more than three thousand miles and so become the first white man to glimpse the lower reaches of what we today call the Pacific Northwest.

The landfalls he made dismayed him. Although his means for determining longitude were crude, they nonetheless showed him that he had gone far to the west. Central America might be relatively narrow, but this part of the continent was enormous. Frobisher's inlet lay thousands of miles off, and the likelihood of a strait spanning so tremendous a distance was remote indeed.

Equally discouraging was the weather: "extreame gusts and flaws . . . most vile, thicke, and stinking fogges." Their tropic-thinned blood chilled by one of the Northwest's infamous mists, the English buccaneers decided to abandon the search for the passage, particularly since they now possessed captured Spanish charts showing the way to the Philippines.

Yet Drake could not ignore his secret orders without giving good cause. Voicing those causes became the work, in part, of Parson Francis Fletcher, the ship's chaplain. Piously Fletcher wrote that when the *Golden Hind* gave up her northward cast and turned south, seeking a bay where the men could careen the ship before tackling the open ocean, every hill they passed "though it was June . . . [was] covered with snow"—this in a California spring! Only fools, of course, would push ahead under such circumstances. And as for the Strait of Anian, "wee conjecture that either there is no passage at all through these Northerne coasts (which is most likely) or if there be, yet it is unnavigable."

Having thus invoked weather and probability to witness the correctness of his actions, Drake refurbished his leaky vessel in a pleasant California haven just north of San Francisco Bay. Naming the land New Albion in defiance of Spain's prior claims, he sailed on around the world toward home. Nearly two hundred years—years which saw the rest of America's geography take shape—would pass before other men of European stock looked again on the Northwest.

Though Drake might doubt the existence of the Strait of Anian, Martin Frobisher never did. Today we know that Frobisher's inlet, discovered in 1576 during his first North Atlantic journey, opens into a deep bay and that the marching icebergs at which he marveled were floating on the tide rather than on an ocean-to-ocean current. To Frobisher, however, the chill white parade brought kindled anticipation. The fabled short cut to the Orient lay at his fingertips!

The season being late, he hurried back to England to report and to prepare for further exploration the following spring. Unfortunately he took with him a heavy piece of black rock that one of his men had picked up near the entrance to his inlet. This rock fell into the hands of Michael Lok, Frobisher's spokesman at court.

Lok, about fifty years old at the time, was a merchant-adventurer in the full, stirring Elizabethan sense of the term. He had sailed over much of the known world, spoke most of its major languages; as a director of the Muscovy Company he traded with mysterious Russia through the far-off White Sea. In spite of his experience, however, he remained so gullible that he spent much of his lifetime fooling himself. As soon as he saw Frobisher's black rock he became convinced that it was loaded with gold.

His fixation was part of a yearning that filled all Europe. Bullion from Spain's American colonies was ballooning prices; the only answer jealous non-Spaniards could offer to the resultant economic chaos was an attempt to find still more gold somewhere else. Although several London assayers told Lok that Frobisher's ore was iron pyrites, the stubborn merchant kept on shopping around until he turned up an alchemist who told him what he wanted to hear.

Gold! Promptly the Company of Cathay was chartered, Michael Lok as governor. Though the organization's name implied that the company would press the search for the Northwest Passage, Frobisher's next two journeys dwindled, to his disgust, into gold-digging expeditions. To complete the anticlimax, the ore he brought back from the trips proved worthless, the Company of Cathay went bankrupt, and Michael Lok spent most of the rest of his life petitioning the court for relief.

During one of his stays in debtors' prison, Lok whiled away the time completing a map of the world. On it he clearly showed Frobisher's passage lying north of a curiously misshapen North America. Since Lok presumably believed his own fantasy, he naturally was ready to believe the tales of any mariner who wanted to claim first-hand knowledge of the route.

In 1596 such a man appeared. Lok was in Venice at the time, trying to collect certain monies he felt were due him. Through an English friend he met a Greek pilot—bronzed, long-bearded, sixty years old, and a competent liar—who professed to have passed much of his life in the service of the viceroy of Mexico. The fellow's real name, so he told Lok, was Apostolos Valerianos, but for the sake of his Spanish masters he had invented the pseudonym Juan de Fuca.

The viceroy of Mexico, according to Juan de Fuca, was convinced that Drake had sneaked into the Pacific by a secret route north of California. Accordingly he had sent three ships, with Juan as pilot, "to discover the Straits of Anian . . . and to fortifie in that strait, to resist the passage and proceedings of the English Nation." The attempt collapsed "by reason of a mutinie which happened among the Souldiers, for the Sodomie of their Captaine." Juan, however, refused to give up. Off he had gone again, Anno 1592, in command of "a small Caravela and a Pinnace." This time, he claimed, between 47° and 48° north latitude, he had found the strait. Furthermore, and his fabrications were obligatory to the times, "he saw some people on Land, clad in Beasts skins; and that the Land is very fruitfull, and rich of gold, Silver, Pearle, and other things, like Nova Spain."

For twenty days, said he, he had sailed in the strait, reached the North Sea, and returned to Mexico, "hoping to be rewarded greatly of the Viceroy." Both in Mexico and in Spain, however, he had been welcomed "in wordes after the Spanish manner" but with nothing else. The reason for the indifference, De Fuca hazarded to Lok, was that Spain now believed England had not found the passage after all.

Well, Juan de Fuca was the man to shake such complacency. Through Lok he appealed to Queen Elizabeth, guaranteeing with his life that he could quickly relocate the passage. Excited, Lok wrote eager letters to England's Lord Treasurer, to Sir Walter Raleigh, and to "Master Richard Hakluyt that famous Cosmographer," urging that they bring Juan to England. The court, however, was used to the extravagant tales of self-seekers, and nothing came of the plan.

Nothing official, that is. Unofficially, the tale found its way into *Hakluyt Posthumus or Purchas His Pilgrimes, Containing a History of the World in Sea Voyages and Lande Travells by Englishmen and Others.* There it stayed, fascinating the curious and beclouding the advance of geography. It is but one of history's many ironies that the prevaricating old Greek was more right than he realized. Between Vancouver Island and the Olympic Peninsula, frequently shrouded by fogs so dense that the first authentic explorers never guessed its presence, lies a true strait at almost the exact latitude where Juan de Fuca said a strait did lie. And so perhaps it is appropriate that his name should have been given, as it was nearly two hundred years after his invention, to the lovely passageway that leads into the rich empires and deepwater ports of today's Pacific Northwest.

For decades after Juan's death men continued to dream of a short cut to Cathay, manufacturing whatever myths were necessary to fit it into their legendary geography. In time all these vaporings were gathered together in the fertile imagination of one Arthur Dobbs, who devised the theory that the only reason a sea passage through North America had not been discovered was the negligence of the Hudson's Bay Company. So shrill did Dobbs's trumpetings become that finally the Hudson's Bay Company in 1737, and the English Admiralty itself in 1742, were roused to dispatch naval expeditions to search once again for a shipway through northern Canada. The negative reports of the explorers simply led Dobbs, one of the world's most unconvincible men, to counter with charges of lies and bribery.

Under his repeated needling Parliament in 1745 offered a reward of twenty thousand pounds to any private person locating the passage. Promptly the Dobbs Company was formed and sent two ships forth to find the unfindable. One vessel was named the *Dobbs*, though the guiding genius himself was present only in the person of his agent. The other ship was called the *California*, a name that must have sounded to the disturbed Spanish like unconcealed imperialism—which it was, for the company proposed to form settlements on the western coast of America as soon as the way to get there was determined.

No such way was discovered, of course. Yet still Arthur Dobbs was not through. Transferred to America as colonial governor of North Carolina, he encountered Major Robert Rogers, fabulous hero of the French and Indian Wars, who had come down from the north to quiet the Cherokees. To Rogers, Dobbs passed on his will-o'-the-wisp of a water passage to the Pacific.

Rogers added refinements of his own, emerging eventually with the idea of a river route across the continent. This concept he gained partly from ill-understood geography picked up in Detroit and in Michilimackinac, where he served as commander; and partly from one Jonathan Carver, who in 1766 explored as far westward as the vicinity of present St. Paul, Minnesota. On Carver's return, both men sought the help of the English government in pushing from the headwaters of the Mississippi (and later from the Missouri) across a negligible height of land to a great River of the West, called by Rogers Ouragan or Ourigan, and by Carver Oregon.

Where the name came from is unknown, though various ingenious suggestions have been offered. Equally uncertain is the germinal point of the mythical River of the West, for Carver's travels did not bring him within a thousand miles of any such stream, or even of Indians who could have told him about it. The fact that the Columbia actually does lie in the approximate vicinity of his river Oregon is a coincidence comparable to that which led Juan de Fuca to locate a fanciful strait in the vicinity of a real one. And, just as Juan's name stuck, so did Oregon, though not to the river. For this carry-through the Northwest can thank young William Cullen Bryant, who relished the sound of the word and so wrote into his precocious poem *Thanatopsis* the resonant phrase:

> *. . . in the continuous woods*
> *Where rolls the Oregon . . .*

The very fact that Rogers and Carver could dream up their schemes of pushing west with government help underlined what had become a poignant new worry to Spanish policy makers. This was England's emergence, after the 1763 Peace of Paris, as the dominant force in North America. By terms of the treaty, French Canada and Spanish Florida were handed outright to the spreading British Empire. As a sop for the loss of the Floridas, Spain was then repossessed of Cuba and given Louisiana. The gift, its extent largely unknown, was not entirely welcome, for it created in the Mississippi Valley a common boundary with England, a mortal enemy that at any time might cast covetous eyes toward the silver mines of Mexico. Or perhaps the expansion to the Pacific would come farther north, through Canada.

This last danger, however, was in 1770 still somewhat dimmed by distance. The immediate threat that finally aroused Madrid to take a closer look at the New World's long-neglected Northwest coast was a challenge from a most unmaritime and hitherto ignored quarter—Russia.

2. The Track of the Bear

WITHIN the space of a man's lifetime, in a land occupation as extraordinary as Spain's in America, the Russians swept eastward from the Urals to the Pacific. The headlong push was initiated by a river pirate named Yermac. Driven from his favorite fields beside the lower Volga by soldiers of Ivan the Terrible, Yermac led nearly a thousand Cossacks north along the western slope of the Ural Mountains to salt mines being operated by the Stroganov family. Uneasy in the company of such uninvited guests, Grigor Stroganov got rid of them by telling them of rich fur grounds beyond the mountains.

In 1581, the year after Francis Drake brought his treasure-laden *Golden Hind* back to England, Yermac crossed the Urals and fell ferociously on the Tatars of Khan Kuchum. Utterly overwhelmed, Kuchum abandoned his capital, the city of Isker, sometimes called Sibir.

Within fifty years the name of that little city—Sibir—had spread across the entire continent. In the van of this wild rush went the incredible *promyshleniki*, the more than half-wild, fanatically reckless Siberian counterparts of the American mountain men. Close behind came the fur merchant. With him, invariably, rode the gatherer of *yassack*, annual tribute in furs for the czar. Separately and in concert this threesome—hunter, merchant, and tribute gatherer—subjected the natives to a merciless grinding. If a tribe's quota of furs was not met, hostages were killed, chiefs tortured, villages put to the torch by forerunners of a people who later cried shame over the Americans' treatment of the Indians. Resistance brought decimation to entire groups. Humbly, therefore, the precious sable and marten and ermine furs were delivered; and as fast as the animals were exterminated in one district, the exploiters hurried on to the next.

Southward the insatiable promyshleniki ran into resistance from the Chinese in Outer Mongolia. One countermeasure used by the Orientals was the stopping of all shipments of tea, silk, and medicinal herbs into Russia. Quickly the tea-thirsty Russians pulled the promyshleniki back behind the border and negotiated a treaty that designated an official boundary point where Russian traders would be allowed to meet Chinese caravans from beyond the Gobi Desert. Since by Chinese law only silver or fur could be received in exchange for the caravans' goods, fur became the principal—almost the sole—base of Siberia's silverless economy.

Meanwhile the eastern wilderness of Siberia, including the gigantic peninsula of Kamchatka, remained mysterious land. The primitive Chukchi of the northeast Asian coast, for example, did not seem to know that a continent reached its end in their territory; and so long as the promyshleniki found a profitable supply of sable, they did not care where they were, scientifically speaking.

The Russian throne, however, had passed, toward the close of the seventeenth century, into the hands of a man who did care. He was Peter the Great, Westernizer of his nation and almost the first Russian to have any interest in creating a workable navy.

One of Peter's last acts, as he lay dying in agony from the effects of his mammoth debaucheries, was to call out of self-imposed retirement, late in 1724, one of his sulky foreign naval officers, a methodical, heavy-set, forty-four-year-old Dane named Vitus Bering. Bering was ordered to go across the almost trackless continent to Kamchatka, build a vessel where neither shipways nor supplies existed, discover whether a land bridge linked Asia to America, and then explore the coast of the neighboring continent. If the Dane chanced to find the Northwest Passage along the way so much the better; for the dying Peter was tantalized by the possibility that his non-seafaring nation might accomplish what had eluded the great maritime countries of the world.

Nearly three and a half years of staggering labor and dreadful suffering passed before Bering at last launched his sixty-foot vessel, the *St. Gabriel,* from the eastern coast of Kamchatka, and bore northward, hugging the shore line. One month and a dozen degrees later, the hitherto north-trending coast swung sharply westward. Bering now guessed that he had passed the farthest reach of Siberia. But it was a guess only. To quiet his scientific conscience he sailed northward two more days, to 67° 18'. No land was visible. Afraid to continue lest unfavorable winds result in fatal delay, he jumped to the conclusion that America and Asia were not joined, then turned back. Though on the return journey he reportedly stayed well out to sea, he failed to detect, in the dense mists, the new continent he was supposed to examine. [1]

[1] History has been kind to Vitus Bering. Bering Strait was probably discovered by a Cossack, Simon Dezneff, who embarked from the Arctic coast in 1648, eighty years before Bering's trip. Bering's was the official venture, however, and so it is by his

On March 1, 1730, five years after his departure from the capital city, Bering returned to St. Petersburg. There the academicians pointed out from the comfort of their studies how inconclusive his findings were. Intensely annoyed, the Dane stubbornly demanded that a second expedition be dispatched to check on what he said.

Surprisingly enough, his record considered, Bering was given charge not only of this expedition but of three more interlocking ones as well. Before he had time even to be bewildered, he learned that he was now supposed to study the natural resources of Siberia, chart the entire Arctic coast, explore from Kamchatka southward toward Japan and eastward toward the mythical continent of Gamaland. Finally, he was directed to look into the matter of America.

Five hundred and eighty laborers, mechanics, priests, soldiers, traders, scientists, and what not were assigned to him. Many, Bering included, took along their wives and children. Out in the wilderness more hundreds of reluctant natives had to be impressed for transporting the melange's food and clothing, books and instruments, necessities and trivia. Scores of barges had to be built at each waterway, thousands of pack horses readied at each portage. Local officials, appalled at the requisitions placed upon them, had to be won or forced to complaisance. Bering's own men bickered and dueled among themselves, built up resentments among the natives, bore tales to their commander, sought his favors, and then intrigued behind his back.

Not until 1741, eight years after leaving St. Petersburg, was the Dane able to cross the Sea of Okhotsk to the new port of Petropavlovsk on the eastern coast of the Kamchatka Peninsula, jumping-off point for America. Along the way one of his supply barges ran aground, losing its cargo. As a result Bering in the *St. Peter* and his lieutenant Alexei Chirikov in a companion vessel, the *St. Paul*, left Avancha Bay with only five months' supply of food aboard instead of the two-year quota on which they had counted.

Aboard Chirikov's vessel was Louis Delisle de la Croyère, one of two map-making brothers in the Russian Academy of Sciences. The maps prepared by this pair showed (as did other maps of the period) a continent known as Gamaland. Whether or not Gamaland was a separate land mass or an extension of America was hotly debated. One of Bering's assignments was to find out.

---

name that the strait is known. Also, immediately after Bering started home for St. Petersburg, an untrained army officer named Michael Gvozdev took the *St. Gabriel* within sight of Alaska. But again the trip was unofficial; again there was no proper credit.

Southeast the two vessels sailed, to latitude 47°, or approximately even with the mouth of the Columbia River. About the time that even Delisle was being forced to admit that Gamaland did not exist, a storm separated the *St. Peter* and the *St. Paul*. For a few days, while short supplies and shorter water dwindled still lower, the two captains beat back and forth, looking for each other. Then, taking responsibility into his own hands, Alexei Chirikov dismissed Gamaland as impossible and sailed northeast.

On July 15, near present Sitka, he sighted land. Two days later a watering party was sent ashore. The men vanished. Another party rowing out to investigate likewise disappeared. Probably these first white men to set foot on the soil of northwestern America were slain by Indians, although Russian fable later told of redheaded, light-complexioned descendants of the lost sailors being found along the coast.

Possessing no more small boats in which to hunt for the men, Chirikov sailed on. Storms and fogs enmeshed the *St. Paul;* supplies gave out. When at last Kamchatka was sighted, Chirikov had to fire a distress signal to summon enough able-bodied rescuers from land to bring the ship in. Louis Delisle, whose dream of Gamaland was partly responsible for the debacle, expired before he could be carried ashore.

Meanwhile Bering, too, was trapped in the uncharted seas. After their separation he, like Chirikov, had borne northeast. On July 16, a day later than Chirikov's landfall, he detected through a rift in the clouds an unbelievable snow peak towering above a wonderland of islands, inlets, forests, and gleaming icebergs. To this monstrous mountain he gave the name it still bears, St. Elias. But he could not share the elation of the scientists aboard his vessel—scientists he had labored so strenuously to bring so far. Vitus Bering was sixty years old now, thick-bodied, flabby-fleshed. The Siberian crossing had exhausted him. He was suffering, moreover, from the lassitude and the terrible sense of depression that accompany the initial stages of scurvy. Glumly he hove to and watched his naturalist, Georg Wilhelm Steller, leave for shore with a watering party.

Suddenly, while half the water casks remained unfilled and Steller was grubbing joyously through an abandoned Aleut fireplace, Bering gave orders that the ship weigh anchor. Dumfounded, Steller asked whether ten agonizing years of preparation were going to dwindle off into less than ten hours of exploration. Bering ignored him. Unspeakably disgusted, the naturalist gathered up such artifacts as he had had time to collect and returned aboard—but not before he had left his name to the striking dark blue, high-crested jay of western North America, Steller's jay.

Fog closed in as the ship crept westward behind the uncharted swell of the Aleutian chain. The sea seemed haunted. Strange bird and animal voices wailed through the gray wrack. Then rain turned to sleet; rotten rigging began to snap. The dread specter of scurvy stalked unchecked; nearly every day someone perished in his fouled hammock, until a dozen men had died.

Finally, early in November, bitter weather cleared the skies and a cry of land went up. "It would be impossible," Steller wrote later, "to describe the joy created by the sight of land; the dying crawled upon the deck to see with their own eyes what they would not believe; even the feeble commander was carried out of his cabin. To the astonishment of all a small keg of brandy was taken from some hiding place and dealt out in celebration of the supposed approach to the coast of Kamchatka."

But it was not Kamchatka. As the desperate knowledge began to dawn, a gale struck. Long combers rolling before the arctic wind parted one of the ship's anchor cables, then another. A foaming breaker picked up the vessel and hurled it, with a dismal crunching of the hull, into a quiet cove. Here, willy-nilly, the crew would spend the winter.

While preparations were being made for a landing, Steller led out a scouting party. Blue foxes swarmed everywhere. Offshore in the kelp beds grazed monstrous, now vanished animals that, like the jay, would be named for the scientist, *Rytina stelleri*, or Steller's sea cows, twenty-five feet long and up to three tons in weight. But not a tree was to be seen. Adding to the desolation was inescapable proof that the party had been marooned on an absolutely unknown stretch of sand and rock, since called Bering Island.

Returning to the cove, Steller started the men digging pits in the sand. These were lined and covered with driftwood and sailcloth, chinked with moss, mud, and fox skins. As fast as the shelters were completed, the sick were carried to them. Nine of the men were so far gone that they did not survive the transfer.

The blue foxes were a maddening nuisance. They had to be driven from the corpses. They bit the invalids, scattered provisions, carried off hats and boots. They were so unawed that during the first day of work on the huts Steller and another man killed sixty with their axes. Carcasses and skins were useful for food and clothing, though later on better furs were obtained from sea otters and seals, better provender from the sea cows and from a dead whale cast up on the beach.

Before the huts were completed a hurricane broke. For three weeks it roared so furiously that men could venture forth only on hands and knees. The *St. Peter* was driven ashore and demolished. Fine sand sifted endlessly into the huts. Steller tried to keep it brushed away from Bering, but the commander whispered to let it be; it kept him warm. On December 8, 1741, about the time when Arthur Dobbs was tuning up to full voice in England, Vitus Bering died.

Twelve of the original seventy-six crewmen had perished before the landing, nine during it. Ten more, including Bering, succumbed by the first of the year. Mysteriously then the others improved; by spring everyone was up and about. The problem now was to escape. The *St. Peter* was wrecked beyond repair; the crew's carpenters were dead. But a Cossack was found who had once labored in a shipyard, and under his uncertain supervision work began on a new vessel. There were few tools, no wood but wreckage, no rigging but rotting hemp. Nonetheless, by mid-August the survivors had floated a clumsy craft forty feet long, thirteen of beam, six deep. Its upper part was calked with tallow from the sea cow, its under with tar salvaged from the hull of the *St. Peter*. It wallowed. It leaked. But it held together long enough to reach Avancha Bay on Kamchatka.

Although the miraculous return occasioned rejoicing in Petropavlovsk, the Russian court remained indifferent. The enthusiasm that had launched the expedition had died with the ascension of a new empress. Worse, very few of the scientists who had made the different voyages remained alive to press for publication in the face of current inertia and anti-foreign bias. (Steller, for one, died while crossing Siberia.) Such news of their findings as did leak out was largely unofficial and disclosed against the wishes of the government.

In eastern Siberia, however, there was one item of information that could not be suppressed. This was the knowledge that the survivors had brought back with them nine hundred sea-otter skins.

Bobri morski, sea beaver, the Russians called the five-foot-long, web-toed animal. The fur is a dark, dark brown, almost ebony in the water, but with enough underlying silver to impart an unmatchable sheen when it is stroked. The underfur, so dense it sheds water, is silky soft. For such a pelt the Chinese merchants at the edge of the Gobi Desert were willing to pay up to one hundred gold rubles.

The news spread like wildfire. The promyshleniki stampeded for Bering Island as once Yermac's men had stampeded after sable. Their first craft, modeled after the barges employed on the rivers, were the "woven" boats, the *shitika,* mere flat-bottomed log frames covered with green planks held together by deerhide thongs and willow withes, calked with moss and tallow. The men who risked their lives to these unseaworthy vessels could scarcely reef a sail or plot a course. It is said that, of every three crews that embarked during the early days of the rush, only two came back.

Results, however, were sometimes fabulous. The first man out after the return of Bering's crew, a Cossack sergeant named Basov, sailed into Petropavlovsk with a cargo worth 112,000 rubles—in today's currency not much less than a million dollars. This was just the beginning. A decade later a single ship reputedly grossed nearly two and a half million dollars.

The exploitation that resulted was as brutal as any the world has known. First the bobbing ships put in at Bering Island, where the gentle sea cows were slaughtered and cured as supply of meat, with such ruthless efficiency that soon the animals were extinct. Next the hunters steered for the Aleutians. As fast as one island was stripped the men moved on to the next. As they ventured farther and farther east ships of necessity grew larger and piloting better. No surveys were made, however, and few records kept. The promyshleniki and their savage commanders were interested only in furs—and in women.

At first the Russians did their own hunting. Soon, however, they learned that the amiable Aleut natives would do it for them, in sea-tight little skin *bidarkas*, in return for the cheapest trinkets. When at last the Aleuts grew less ingenuous and more demanding, the promyshleniki invoked refined methods of persuasion originally developed among the natives of Siberia. Hostages, principally young women, were seized and held on shipboard as an incentive to production. Obediently then the husbands went forth to hunt. The safe way was for them to use Russian-supplied traps for foxes, nets across tidal channels for otter. Another way, but slow, was for a ring of bidarkas to surround an otter and keep it diving until its supply of oxygen ran out and it could stay beneath the surface no longer. But the most productive way was to wait until one of the inevitable hurricanes drove the otter herds onto the reefs for shelter. The Aleuts then followed through the tumult of white water, clubbing the animals if possible from the pitching bidarkas, or, more often, disembarking and running up on them undetected in the crashing surf. Casualties were high, but that did not bother the Russians, snugly ensconced with the waiting women.

Outrage followed outrage. Massacre Bay on Attu received its name when Russian hunters killed all fifteen males of a small settlement in order to make off with the women. On another occasion, after some female hostages had committed suicide rather than endure further oppression, the commander tied up the rest of the group and threw them overboard to drown rather than leave witnesses alive to talk. Eventually, on the island of Unalaska in 1764, the Aleuts struck back, killing in a series of winter-long skirmishes most of the hunters from five different ships. It was a useless spasm. In retribution trader Ivan Solovief wiped out settlement after settlement, even those offering no resistance. Once, so it is said, Solovief bound a dozen Aleuts in a row and fired into them merely to see how many persons a single musket ball could kill. Eight men sagged dead; the bullet stopped in the body of the ninth.

Gradually echoes of the wanton cruelties reached St. Petersburg, and a few perfunctory gestures were made toward reform. More important to America's Northwest coast, however, was the decision of Catherine II to resume the exploratory work started by Peter the Great.

Immediately Spanish secret agents in St. Petersburg forwarded garbled word of the projected expeditions to Madrid. By letter of January 23, 1768, to Mexico City the *visitador-general* of New Spain, José de Gálvez, was ordered "to observe such attempts as the Russians may make there, frustrating them if possible." This suited Gálvez. Well-educated, unscrupulous, vindictive, and insatiably ambitious, he had already determined to foster his personal glory by colonizing California. Now he had official sanction. Promptly he sent out several expeditions by land and by sea. None of these got very far northward, but they prepared the way for more sweeping efforts under the direction of Gálvez' successor, Antonio Bucareli. When fresh alarms about Russia reached Mexico in 1773, Bucareli directed the founding of San Francisco as a defensive outpost for New Spain's northern flank. He also ordered that a naval survey of the Northwest be made during 1774, by Juan Pérez, onetime commander of the Manila galleon and veteran of earlier California experiments.

Pérez was supposed to sail as far north as 60°, landing here and there along the way to take possession of the best places for settlement. Actually he made no landings, missed both the Columbia River and Juan de Fuca Strait, and at 55° turned back because of scurvy and bad weather. On his way south he anchored by chance on the west coast of what is now called Vancouver Island, in a lovely, mountain-girt sound that he named San Lorenzo. When he did not offer to come ashore, several canoes loaded with curious natives paddled out to greet him. Some of these Indians soon grew bold enough to board his vessel, and one of them stole from the ship's pilot, a man named Estévan José Martínez, two silver spoons. Neither Martínez nor Pérez could foresee, of course, that in fifteen years those spoons would become a matter of international concern or that another name for their remote little anchorage—Nootka—would reverberate angrily through the courts of Europe.

Pérez had scarcely reached Mexico when he was ordered to pilot his same ship, the *Santiago*, back into the same northern waters, this time under the command of his superior officer, Bruno Heceta. Accompanying the *Santiago* went a tiny thirty-six-foot schooner, the *Sonora*, captained by a charming and uncommonly persistent don named Juan Francisco de Bodega y Cuadra. On July 14, 1775, these two vessels anchored some distance apart off the coast of present Washington, within sight of the majestic white peaks and dense rain forests of the Olympics. Each commander sent landing parties ashore, Heceta's to take formal possession of the Pacific Northwest for Spain, Cuadra's to get water.

Indians massacred the watering party, and from then on the effectiveness of the expedition was at an end. A timorous council of officers aboard the *Santiago* ordered Cuadra to take the now undermanned *Sonora* back to Mexico. Refusing to obey, Cuadra slipped northward on his own. The *Santiago* ventured cautiously in the same direction but was soon frightened back by bad weather and scurvy.

Either in fog or darkness the lookouts once more missed the entrance to Juan de Fuca's strait (as did Cuadra in the *Sonora*), but just north of 46° Heceta came to the threshold of an equally significant find. Strong currents of discolored water clutched at his ship—surely the discharge from a river of more than ordinary moment.

He named it the San Roque. Excitement filled him. If he entered the bay that must lie beyond the breakers, anchored for the night, and the next day explored . . .

Pérez and the other officers objected, saying that so many men were sick they could not lift the anchor again if once they let it go. Reluctantly Heceta gave in. And so that chance was lost; the actual sight of the Columbia River would have to wait for another man. (Parenthetically it might be noted that Juan Pérez had reason to fear scurvy: before the *Santiago* reached Mexico, he was dead of it.)

Scurvy was Cuadra's demon also, stopping his venturesome *Sonora* at the southern tip of present Alaska. There he again landed and took possession for Spain. Now let the Russians or the English come. Spanish sovereignty was at last solidly rooted.

Unknown to Cuadra, the Russians were nearby, out in the Aleutians, and the English were making plans. Thus, in 1775, the year of Lexington and Concord and Bunker Hill, three European powers were either extending or were about to extend their American claims in a race for empire on the far-off shores of the Pacific.

3. The First American

IN ENGLAND, dispute about a Northwest Passage still lingered. Finally, in 1776, the Admiralty determined to settle the matter. The twenty-thousand-pound reward for discovery which Parliament had authorized in 1745 was extended to include naval as well as private personnel. Once again a ship was sent across the Atlantic into Baffin Bay to explore possible northeastern approaches. Then, as capstone to the effort, Captain James Cook was delegated to examine the American Northwest with his famous ship *Resolution* and an attendant sloop, *Discovery*.

That name—Cook—shows how seriously the Admiralty took the venture. England had no finer navigator. Cook's painstaking work in charting the St. Lawrence River (he was with Wolfe at the capture of Quebec) and his surveys of the Newfoundland coast had led to his being sent on his first great voyage, a trip into the South Pacific to observe the transit of Venus. While there, he had developed, though he was no physician, revolutionary plans for controlling the dread killer of the seas, scurvy. On his second voyage he finished the charting of the southern oceans. He also proved his dietary and sanitation theories, defeating scurvy in spite of objections by his sailors against staying alive at the cost of eating sauerkraut, drinking broth, and airing their bedding.

Shortly before sailing on his expedition to the Northwest, Cook signed on as a corporal of his marines a Connecticut-born Yankee who was in some ways as remarkable as his commander. This was fortune's favorite fool, John Ledyard. Fatherless at ten, Ledyard had been raised by an incompatible grandfather, then had passed under the aegis of an equally unsympathetic uncle, and finally had been invited by Eleazar Wheelock to attend newly opened Dartmouth College, there to learn to be a missionary to the Indians. Ledyard liked Indians well enough— at one point he disappeared from college to live with some of them

—but he chafed under discipline. Money trouble completed the conflict. Headstrong, emotional, athletic, and charming, he persuaded several friends to help him chop down a tree and hollow it into a clumsy fifty-foot dugout. Alone in this oversized creation, he fled Dartmouth by sailing down the Connecticut River to a job as a common sailor with a shipload of mules bound for Africa. Seafaring brought him to London, aged twenty-four. There he enlisted with Cook, about the time of the Declaration of Independence but well before news of that event had reached England.

On March 7, 1778, the *Resolution* and *Discovery* raised the coast of Drake's New Albion but were prevented by contrary winds from seeing either the mouth of Bruno Heceta's river or Juan de Fuca Strait. Then, on March 29, beating landward after still another storm, Cook sighted two deep inlets, separated by several miles of mountainous, heavily wooded shore. As he later discovered, these sea arms, embracing triangularly, formed a small island tucked snugly into what he thought was the mainland. Actually it was the coast of Vancouver Island, though the geography would not be straightened out for several years. The southern inlet (which Juan Pérez four years earlier had designated as San Lorenzo) the English mariner at first called King George's Sound. Later, because of some mistaken notion rising from the gabble of the natives, he changed the name of both the small island and the sound to Nootka, though actually there was no such word in the language of the local Indians.

As the storm-buffeted ships drew in toward Nootka Sound, three canoes approached, the occupants flinging out feathers, red dust, and occasionally bursts of oratory by way of welcome. More canoes followed, until there were thirty-two, loaded with both men and women. They were singular craft, light of weight and instantly maneuverable, though some were as much as forty feet long and seven wide, each manufactured with infinite labor, fire, and steam, from the trunk of a single huge cedar tree.

The rowers were equally singular. Such men as were dressed at all sported blankets woven of dog's hair mixed with the inner strands of cedar bark, the whole skillfully decorated, Corporal Ledyard noted, with paintings of whale hunts or other aquatic scenes. Over these blankets, many edged with fur, the wearers negligently draped priceless robes of ill-treated fox or sea-otter skin.

Both the men and the women had daubed themselves with red clay mixed in whale oil. They wore their black hair long, soaked it in fish oil, sprinkled it with the white down of birds. Their bodies were short and stocky, their legs malformed from continual crouching in their seatless canoes. The uplifted faces were broad and dull-looking, the peering eyes small and black. Pendants of bone or horseshoe-shaped bits of metal hung from the Indians' pierced ears or from their flat pug noses. A few wore masks carved from wood, bizarrely painted and so ingeniously constructed, Ledyard saw with amazement, that the eyes and mouths could be made to move.

Anchoring in a deep cove, the English moored their ships stern and bow to pine trees on the precipitous shore. Instantly the natives swarmed aboard, showing neither surprise nor awe, though Cook interpreted their gestures to mean that they never before had encountered European vessels. (Yet what of Pérez?) Indeed, the only thing that ruffled the Indians during the white men's stay was the firing of a musket through six folds of the heavy leather garments they used as protective armor in warfare.

On a bit of flat ground near the cove the English sailors found a curious, semimobile village. Each communal house had a long, permanent roofbeam supported by heavy wooden posts seven or eight feet tall. The roof itself and the wall sidings were made of broad, loose planks that could be dismounted, piled on the big canoes, and floated off to another streamside site whenever the exigencies of village economics, principally fishing, so demanded.

Each house sheltered several families. Inside, each group had its own fireplace but otherwise made little attempt at private living. Slightly elevated platforms covered with mats or furs served for sleeping. Furniture consisted of storage boxes, wooden dishes, fishing implements, and weapons, all strewn about in complete confusion. The disorder was increased by racks of drying fish and by the family's totems, painted wooden images four or five feet tall. Scant effort was made to dispose of excrement, fish intestines, or other debris, so that, in Cook's words, "the houses are as filthy as hogsties, everything in and about them stinking of fish, train-oil, and smoke."

Although Cook believed that the Nootkas had never before encountered Europeans, they were nonetheless familiar with certain articles of European origin. They had chisel-ended bits of strap iron that they inserted into wooden handles and pounded with stone mallets. They possessed copper for ornament—they were wild to obtain the brass button rings off the sailors' clothes for nose bobs—and one native was found wearing two silver teaspoons on a cord around his neck. The spoons, Cook decided, were of Spanish origin—and he caused future trouble for England by noting the fact in his journal.

The other metal, he concluded, must have followed aborigine trade routes across Canada from Hudson Bay, a notion he clung to even up in Alaska amidst signs of Russian penetration. Ledyard, too, believed the same thing, and the notion planted a daring seed in his mind. If a white man's goods could cross America, why couldn't a white man?

To obtain more metal from Cook's ships the natives tried first stealing and then trade, offering in barter everything they had: garments; bags of red ochre; carved wooden masks; female slaves they had captured by raiding other coastal tribes; even roasted, half-eaten human hands. But furs were what the sailors wanted most. Knowing they were bound for the Arctic, they asked eagerly for "the skins of various animals, such as bears, wolves, foxes, deer, racoons, pole-cats, and martiens, and, in particular, that of the sea-otter," planning after they had used the articles to sell them at the first civilized port the ships reached. The pelts selling cheaply, trade grew brisk. "Whole suits of clothes were stripped of every button, bureaus of their furniture, and copper kettles, tin cannisters, candlesticks and the like, all went to wreck, so that our American friends here got a greater medley and variety of things from us than any other natives we had visited in the course of our voyage."

After nearly a month in Nootka, Cook bore northward again, through squalls and misty weather that prevented more than occasional glimpses of the mainland. When opportunity presented, he landed to claim sovereignty for England; and in Prince William's Sound his men were able to trade more iron and beads for sea-otter cloaks. The broad expanse of Cook's Inlet delayed them several days— they thought perhaps they had discovered a Northwest Passage until the inlet's upper end pinched off the hope—and it was mid-August before they had threaded a way through the Aleutian Islands, passed Bering Strait, and so reached latitude 71°. There the ships ran into ice. Turn and twist as he would, even "in shoal water, upon a lee-shore, and the main body of the ice to windward, driving down upon us," Cook could find no way through. Finally, after two weeks of probing and in apprehension of the onset of "frost," he bore south, pausing at Unalaska Island long enough for Ledyard to find the Russian settlement and guide its commandant back to the *Resolution* for a polite conference in sign language.

From Unalaska, Cook sailed south to the Sandwich Islands. When he put ashore he was greeted by a tremendous concourse of Hawaiians as their god Lono, returned from a long visit to distant lands. The delusion did not last, however. Quarrels soon boiled up, reaching a climax over the theft of the *Discovery's* cutter. When Cook went ashore to seize the king as a hostage for the boat's return, violence erupted. During it the navigator was stabbed from behind, "fell with his face in the water and instantly expired." Four marines were also slain, but the others involved, including Ledyard, fought clear and swam to safety.

Command now devolved on Captain Clerke, a career officer who once had had the unique battle experience of standing on top a mizzen-mast when it was shot from underneath him, plunging him into the sea. He took the fleet north again, found nothing, contracted consumption, and died just outside Avancha Bay, Kamchatka. Turning homeward at long last, the two hard-used ships paused for supplies in the Macao Roads below Canton, China. Acting through the good offices of the East India Company, Lieutenant James King of the *Discovery* went upriver to the forbidden city of the mandarins to see what he could find. By chance he took with him twenty sea-otter skins.

The effect on the Cantonese was electric. Hitherto they had seen only such otter pelts, invariably damaged in transit, as had trickled past the other teeming cities of China down the long inland route from Siberia. Now here was a new source. To King's amazement he was paid eight hundred dollars for twenty low-quality pelts and besieged with requests for more.

His sailors, he said, might have a few. Promptly, through the medium of the English merchants in Canton, arrangements were made for an auction on shipboard in Macao.

The affair almost ended in mutiny. The few prime skins available brought $120 each, an exorbitant price in terms of today's currency. Men who had sold their furs in Kamchatka—and the number of pelts disposed of there amounted to at least two thirds of the original total—groaned with hindsight. Two English sailors deserted, presumably to try to find some way of getting back to America. In wildest excitement the rest demanded that the ships return to the Northwest coast.

After quelling the uproar King wrote in the official journal he had been keeping since Cook's death, "When . . . it is remembered, that the furs were at first collected without our having any idea of their real value; that the greatest part had been worn by the Indians, from whom we purchased them; that they were afterwards preserved with little care, and frequently used for bed-clothes, and other purposes, during our cruise to the north; and that, probably, we had never got the full value for them in China; the advantages that might be derived from a voyage to that part of the American coast, undertaken with commercial views, appear to me of a degree of importance sufficient to call for the attention of the public." He thereupon proceeded for two and a half pages to direct attention to his views of how the trade could best be pursued.

Meanwhile Corporal John Ledyard was developing his own variations on the same theme. Nothing could be done at the time, of course. Ledyard was almost penniless, and his enlistment had three more years to run. Furthermore, the explorers now knew that war was raging between England and her American colonies, supported by France. Though each belligerent had issued orders that Cook's ships were not to be molested, the officers prudently added more armament before beating on around the Cape of Good Hope to England.

In England Ledyard managed to sit out all but the tag end of the war. When at last he was sent against the land of his nativity his transport anchored off Long Island. Promptly Ledyard deserted, made his way to a boardinghouse run by his mother, and then fled to Connecticut. There, buried in his uncle's law office during the greening April days of 1783, he scribbled off at white heat his own story of Cook's third voyage—an account which beat the Admiralty's official publication off the presses by nearly a year.

How much of what he wrote was the fruit of retrospect cannot now be said. Exactly five years had passed since his first sight of Nootka Sound. In those five years Yorktown had ripped the British Empire apart; and although the formal terms of peace remained to be announced, there was no doubt that a new nation had risen in the New World.

How big was that nation? To Ledyard's war-weary Connecticut neighbors, the Appalachian Mountains, or at most the Mississippi, were far enough. The Pacific, if they thought of it at all, was a Spanish ocean, too remote for meaning. Ledyard, however, alone of all his countrymen, had stood on that distant shore. Southward, as he knew, Drake had taken possession for England. North and south, as perhaps he did not know, Cuadra and Heceta had erected crosses and buried bottles for Spain. Northward, too, a Russian fur trader named Grigorii Shelekhov was already talking to his empress about Russian colonies, Russian sovereignty. But these men were outsiders. Only Ledyard had returned home to "the shores of that continent which gave me birth."

Always he was a romantic and highly emotional man. As his pen paused over the paper and his mind cast back to that exotic day when the welcoming savages had flung out their handfuls of feathers and red dirt, his remembered feelings became inextricably mixed with his feelings here on the Eastern seaboard, so that with complete conviction he could write of that distant day, ". . . though [I was] more than 2000 miles distant from the nearest part of New-England, I felt myself painfully affected. [1] All the affectionate passions incident to natural attachments and early prejudices played round my heart, and I indulged them because they were prejudices. I was harmonized by it."

Harmonized in Nootka—for the first time continental unity as an emotional as well as a geographic fact had entered an American's thinking. The Pacific was not something apart. Its shore, too, was America.

On that shore, moreover, a new source of wealth awaited the man bold enough to seize it. For the unabashed sake of patriotism and profit, John Ledyard hoped to be that man.

He spent the rest of his life trying—and failing. He almost talked Robert Morris of Philadelphia into promoting an expedition, but the postwar depression had left American merchants chary of untried ventures. Unable to secure additional financing, Morris switched his interest to the tea trade with China. In disgust, Ledyard went to Europe. For a time John Paul Jones flirted with the idea but that hope, too, collapsed. Once Ledyard actually boarded a ship bound for Nootka, but revenue cutters brought her back with attachment orders from her creditors. Thomas Jefferson, the United States representative in France, now helped the onetime corporal further a wild scheme whereby Ledyard proposed to cross Siberia to Kamchatka, catch a ship from there to the Northwest coast, and then hoof across America, even as he supposed trade goods crossed the continent from tribe to tribe. It was a fantastic idea, fantastically begun. After a series of exhausting ordeals, including a fifteen-hundred-mile hike in the dead of winter around the Baltic Sea, Ledyard reached east central Siberia, only to have the suspicious Russians drag him back. Brokenhearted then, he turned to African exploration. In Cairo, aged thirty-seven, he died.

He should have come home. As he lay mortally ill in Egypt, two Boston ships, whose captains had each read his journal, were wallowing through stormy seas off Cape Horn. Their destination—Nootka Sound.

---

[1] Actually, as Ledyard should have known from Cook's calculations, he was more than three thousand miles away.

4. Ledyard's Heirs

IN 1785 there arrived in New York with a profitable cargo of tea and silk the *Empress of China,* a ship that might have been Ledyard's had not the caution of Robert Morris and her other backers shifted her from Nootka to Canton. One year later the *Grand Turk* of Salem returned to New England with an equally exotic and even more remunerative lading. To traders struggling out of the doldrums left by the Revolution the effect of these arrivals was galvanic. The only limit to the new commerce, apparently, was what the Orientals would accept in exchange. Silver was one medium; ginseng was another (aging mandarins had a notion that a powder from ginseng's bifurcate root would restore virility), but American supplies of both commodities were small. A more likely possibility, as revealed in the recently published journals of James Cook and John Ledyard, was sea-otter fur.

Promptly the alert imagination of merchant Joseph Barrell added up the various elements into what soon became the famous three-cornered trade of the Yankees: Massachusetts gimcracks to the North-west; Northwestern furs to Canton; and Chinese goods on around the world to Boston. It was a sound plan—but late in developing. English traders in the Orient had long since learned of the dazzling prices which Lieutenant King's sailors had received from the Cantonese for their sea-otter pelts. Already several merchants were hurrying toward the Northwest coast, and in case of conflict with interlopers they would inevitably appeal for help to the full power of the British Empire.

None of this was known to Joseph Barrell. Convinced that he had hit upon an original, foolproof idea, he asked five other Yankee merchants for support. Together the six men subscribed fourteen shares of stock, each share worth thirty-five hundred dollars. With the proceeds they outfitted two ships. One was the fourteen-year-old *Columbia Rediviva,* eighty-three feet long, 212 tons burthen, mounting ten guns and manned by thirty men. The other was a 90-ton sloop named the *Lady Washington.* Almost immediately the sailors contracted the names to *Columbia* and *Washington.*

No precedent other than Cook's brief account existed to tell the owners what sort of goods would most appeal to the Nootka Indians. As a result the ships were filled with quantities of such unlikely objects as snuffboxes, rattraps, and jew's harps, together with items favored by East coast savages—pocket mirrors, iron tools, and cooking utensils.

The familiar custom of striking off medals to impress local chieftains was also followed; several of these, bearing likenesses of the *Columbia* and *Washington* on one side and the names of the proprietors on the other, were issued.

To command the expedition the owners selected John Kendrick. He should have been a good choice, for he had been on the sea for a quarter of a century and had commanded, during the Revolution, three different privateers. He was a huge man, tempestuous, brave, persuasive. But he was forty-seven years old, almost ancient for those times and that trade; and age may help explain the strange indolence, even lethargy, that so often sapped his effectiveness. Age alone, however, can hardly explain the dishonesty which later closed his career.

As Kendrick's subordinate, in charge of the sloop *Washington*, the proprietors placed an obscure captain named Robert Gray. Like Kendrick, Gray was rough, hot-tempered, and brave to the point of foolhardiness. There resemblances end. Fifteen years younger than his superior, Gray possessed a restless, driving energy and, so far as his employers' interests were concerned, a scrupulous honesty.

Not until the first day of October 1787 were the two ships able to cast off on the initial step of their journey, a month-long crossing to the Cape Verde Islands. There they paused to fill their water casks and take on fresh food in the form of live cattle, hogs, and a milk goat named Nancy. It should not have been a lengthy job, but Kendrick's dilatoriness made it so. Sourly Gray wrote to Barrell, "We lay forty one days, which was thirty six more than I thought was necessary." Meantime Kendrick was at complete loggerheads with his crew. The *Columbia's* first mate resigned in a huff and the doctor deserted. Later the captain came to outright blows with his second mate, nineteen-year-old Robert Haswell, and at the Falkland Islands shifted that angry young man to Gray's *Washington*.

Because of the delays, the two ships approached Cape Horn at the worst season of the year. On April 1, 1788, huge seas and a blinding snowstorm separated them. As Gray dryly put it in his report to Barrell, "I had the good luck to part Company . . . and I made the Coast six weeks sooner by being alone."

The landfall came on August 2. Though several of the crew were in an advanced state of scurvy, the skipper refused to pause so long as wind and weather favored. Northward he drove along the present Oregon coast, which to Robert Haswell's land-starved eyes was "a delightfull Country, thickly inhabited and Cloathed with woods and verdure with maney Charming streems of water gushing from the vallies." Often Indians launched canoes and paddled after them, waving skins, or ran along the shore "with great swiftness keeping abreast of us for many miles."

Finally, on August 14, Gray sighted what was probably Tillamook Bay and consented to stop. As the anchor plunged down, curious natives swarmed out to the ship. Many of them were loaded with berries and ready-boiled crabs, manna to the scurvy-stricken crew. Though a brisk trade in skins sprang up, Gray's main concern was taking on wood and water for the men, grass and "shrubbs" for the livestock. In pursuit of the latter occupation, First Mate David Coolidge and young Haswell landed a boatload of men and then wandered up to the village to see what they could see. It wasn't much—just a haphazard jumble of small wooden huts, "intolerably filthy."

A dance began, which young Haswell described in his log as "long and hideous accompanyed with frightfull howlings. It Chilled the bludd in my veins." Uneasy now, the mates walked back along the beach to where the men were cutting grass.

Suddenly one of the workers, a Cape Verde Island Negro named Marcus Lopius (as Haswell spelled Lopez), let out a yell and began to chase an Indian who was making off with a cutlass. Coolidge, Haswell, and a sailor pursued the runners on foot while the remaining men piled into the boat and followed along the shore. Nearing the village, the horrified whites saw several Indians "drench there knives and spears with savage fury in the body of the unfortunate youth. He . . . stagered toward us but having a flight of arrows thrown into his back," he collapsed.

At this Haswell and his companions began wading out to the boat. Until now the mates, who alone carried weapons, had held their fire because of Gray's strict orders to avoid bloodshed. But when the shrieking savages splashed into the water after them, hurling spears and arrows, they figured enough was enough. Each shot, killing a man. This slowed the others sufficiently for the whites to climb into the boat, though not unscathed. The unarmed sailor with them was critically wounded and each mate was nicked. As they pulled for the ship, the Indians launched their own canoes, but two or three shots from the swivel guns on the *Washington* soon routed the pursuit. An abortive attack later that night was easily dispersed, and the next morning the *Washington* warped out of the harbor.

In the fog Gray missed the mouth of the vast river which Bruno Heceta had sensed thirteen years before and had named the San Roque. Though the Americans saw the Strait of Juan de Fuca (discovered and named a year earlier by an English trader, Charles Barkley), they sailed on by, coasting Vancouver Island. Nearing the latitude of Nootka, they turned toward the rocky shores, hunting landmarks which would identify the sound. A rolling swell almost threw the *Washington* onto a reef. As the frightened men groped away from it, they were surrounded by huge native canoes, some of whose occupants cried up words of English. Yielding to gestures of friendship, Gray let the canoes help tow the *Washington* into a nearby harbor —it was Clayoquot Sound—and there, to their deep chagrin, the Yankees found a native chief named Wicananish incongruously "dressed in a genteel sute of Cloths."

Gray was late on the scene. To his growing mortification he learned that for no less than four years an increasing number of ships, principally English, had been beating back and forth off the coast. The parade had started with James Hanna, who had sailed from China in 1785 with a diminutive 60-ton brig and after killing a few Indians had netted $20,600 worth of pelts during a six-week stay. Reports of his luck initiated a stampede of sorts. The year before the *Washington's* arrival there had even been a white woman about, Frances Barkley, the seventeen-year-old bride of Captain Charles W. Barkley of the 400-ton merchantman, *Imperial Eagle*, who astounded the Indians into probing her with dirty forefingers to see if she was real.

Other English ships pausing at Clayoquot shortly before Gray's appearance had drained off the best skins. Acceptable ones could still have been purchased, however, if the Americans had possessed suitable goods. But the Indian taste, unpredictable at best, had been rendered completely capricious by the dazzling trinkets offered by these strange, pale sea peddlers for what seemed to the savages a very ordinary sort of commodity indeed, mere furs. Disdainfully they rejected Gray's ill-chosen gewgaws. With more than a little foreboding the empty-handed captain left Clayoquot to search for Nootka, his appointed rendezvous with the *Columbia*.

On September 15 he descried a longboat under sail putting out of an inlet. Its crew boarded the American ship and the next day helped tow the *Washington* into Nootka Sound and around the southwestern tip of Nootka Island. There, in a semicircular harbor called Friendly Cove, Gray anchored beside a pair of two-masted, square-rigged brigs flying what Haswell called "Portogees Coulers." The flags were a blind, however. As Gray soon learned, actual command resided in a former officer of the British navy named John Meares, as engaging a scoundrel as ever sailed the Northwest coast.

After resigning his lieutenancy in 1783, John Meares had learned in India of James Hanna's phenomenal luck in the sea-otter trade. Somehow obtaining a ship, the ex-officer hurried recklessly across the bleak waters of the North Pacific and eventually, in the fall of 1786, had poked his way into the chill beauty of Prince William Sound, Alaska. There he had determined to winter.

It proved a disastrous decision. By the following May, twenty-three men had died, most of them from scurvy, and had been dumped unceremoniously through groaning cracks in the ice. The rest quite probably were saved only through the fortuitous arrival of two more English traders. These not very obliging countrymen loaned Meares the supplies and help he needed to get afloat again—then exacted from him a promise, guaranteed by a bond of two thousand pounds, that he would immediately leave the coast without indulging in further trade. Seething helplessly, Meares limped back to the Orient.

In Portuguese Macao he somehow secured enough financing to buy two more ships, the *Felice Adventurer* and the *Iphigenia Nubiana*. The *Iphigenia* he put under command of Captain William Douglas, in the spring of 1788, with orders to take her on a trading trip along the coast of Alaska, then rendezvous with Meares and the *Felice* in Nootka Sound. To gain preferential port charges in Macao and to avoid clashes with the South Sea and East India companies, Meares meanwhile raised the Portuguese flag above the vessels, having registered both under the name of the Portuguese firm of Cavalho & Company—an unfortunate subterfuge, as matters developed.

He was filled with a ferment of new ideas. One scheme involved building at Nootka a small sloop that could be easily maneuvered into and out of the tortuous inlets of the coast. Framework and supplies for the vessel were in the *Felice's* hold. Also aboard were fifty or so Chinese laborers, hired because they were faithful workers—and cheap. Another odd passenger was a petty Nootka chief named Comekela, who had been taken on a visit to Macao by another trader in an effort to secure his good will.

As the *Felice* dropped anchor in Nootka's rock-girt Friendly Cove and the natives flocked out to greet the newcomers, Comekela decked himself in all his finery. On went a scarlet coat with brass buttons. To his queued hair he attached a clanging cluster of copper kettles stolen from the *Felice's* galley. In his hand as he mounted to the railing he brandished a huge metal roasting spit. Utterly bedazzled, his countrymen welcomed him back with a shattering howl. But if Meares had expected Comekela to prove useful as an interpreter, he was soon disillusioned. The wandering Indian's talk had become such a mélange of Nootka, Chinese, and English that the homefolk could no longer understand him.

The next day the principal chief, Maquinna (or Maquilla), appeared with a great parade of war canoes, his oily hair white with bird down, his face daubed with ocher. From him Meares purchased for two pistols—or so the Englishman later claimed—a plot of ground near the village. Since most Indians had not the foggiest grasp of any such abstraction as the private ownership of land, Maquinna was probably being no more than agreeable when he nodded acquiescence to Meares's pointing finger. Nonetheless he made no objection when the English landed their goods on the plot, built a flimsy two-story house of logs protected by a breastwork, and then constructed shipways on which the Chinese promptly laid the keel of the sloop. Indeed, the Indians even helped build the house, receiving their pay in beads or iron each evening at the ringing of a bell.

Assured that the construction work was going well, Meares left on a trading trip. By late summer he was back at Nootka. William Douglas joined him in the *Iphigenia*, and after an uproarious holiday all hands turned to in eagerness to complete the sloop and depart the sound before the onset of winter. They had almost finished when a cry of "Sail!" went up. Quickly Meares dispatched a longboat to investigate.

The newcomer, Robert Gray's *Lady Washington*, promised competition from a source the Englishman had not hitherto contemplated —the infant United States of America.

Gray was in a quandary. By now Kendrick should have overtaken him—unless the *Columbia* had foundered. Meanwhile Meares and Douglas were warning him not to tarry in Nootka. They swore that there was no trade (actually 750 skins were stored in the *Felice's* hold), that the natives were hostile, the winters unendurable. Gray suspected that the English captains were exaggerating in an effort to scare off competition. Still, there might be virtue in sailing to Macao, where he could buy the proper sort of trade goods to appeal to the Indians. Yet had he the right to take so drastic a step on his own authority?

As he wandered about, postponing decision, he found plenty to absorb his attention: formal dinners exchanged with the English, the strange Indian village, and above all the trim sloop on the stocks. On September 20, four days after the Yankee's arrival, the new vessel was ready for launching. At the appropriate moment she was christened *North West America*, the guns of the larger brigs roared in salute, and the vessel shot from the ways—almost from the harbor, for Meares in his exuberance had forgotten to provide either anchor or cable. The ship was soon retrieved, however, and the English settled down to a day of festivity. The Americans went back to loading wood and water.

A day or two later Meares left for China with the season's furs. Busily Douglas in the *Iphigenia* and Robert Funter, who had been placed in command of the *North West America*, cleared up the last loose ends preparatory to wintering in the Sandwich Islands. Quite possibly Gray would have followed them, had not the *Columbia* suddenly appeared, her topsails reefed and her topgallant masts down on the deck. Alarmed by these indications of trouble, Gray boarded the ship to hear Kendrick's tale of woe.

Ever since the two vessels had separated off the Horn, the *Columbia* had been in jeopardy. Desperate, Kendrick had at last put in at the island of Juan Fernandez. There the Spanish commandant, Blas Gonzales, had succored him with food and water—a kindness, it later developed, for which Gonzales was sacked as soon as his superiors heard of it. But the help had not sufficed. As the *Columbia* toiled on northward, scurvy had killed two of the crew and, as Gray could see, had crippled most of the rest.

At once Gray proposed that both ships repair to China. Kendrick overruled him. The reason the natives would not trade, the commander said, was that the English had ordered the Indians not to. They feared Meares, who during the summer had forced compliance with his wishes by firing on their villages and canoes. As soon as the English left, matters would improve; and to speed the departure Kendrick ordered his seamen to help the rivals make ready.

Apparently he had guessed correctly. Once the English were gone, the natives flocked about to trade fish, whale oil, and venison. With their pelts they were more chary; only when the Americans refashioned some of their iron tools into "chisels"—bits of iron about eight inches long and one inch wide, with one end drawn down to a cutting edge—were the whites able to obtain many skins. Nonetheless Kendrick determined to winter in the sound.

He escaped the freezing Meares had predicted. Very little snow fell, but rains were incessant and brought their own penetrating chill. To this the Indians seemed inured. They paddled unconcernedly about in ankle-length, broad-belted mantles of cedar bark, their heads covered with conical bark hats decorated by tufts of feathers or tassels of hide. And of course there were always the magnificent cloaks of otter, handled with an infuriating negligence. One vexing native custom, for example, was to toss a cloak over a pot in which food was being boiled. The steam and heat brought swarms of vermin out of the seams for the owners to catch and eat.

Pettifogging details of daily living, broken by the brief excitement of a fire on the *Columbia* and thefts by the Indians, were enough to satisfy Kendrick. Gray, however, champed with impatience. At the first faint show of spring in mid-March he put out on a trading trip to the south. When he returned six weeks later, he found that Kendrick had sailed the *Columbia* a total of four miles up the inlet to a cove where he had built a small hut for sheltering a blacksmith forge. That was all, in spite of the fact that William Douglas had returned in the *Iphigenia* from wintering in the Sandwich Islands. Soon Funter appeared with the *North West America*, took on supplies, and headed north. Still Kendrick made no move, though by now he was rapidly losing whatever advantage might have accrued by being first on the scene. Furious, Gray left him and on May 3 started his own cast to the northward.

As he cleared the headland, he encountered a vessel from still another restive nation, the 26-gun Spanish warship *Princessa*, commanded by Don Estévan José Martínez. Politely Martínez summoned the American captain aboard, spun a tale which Gray recognized as not completely candid, and asked searching questions about the other ships in the sound. It was all very mysterious—even ominous—and became more so when Gray learned that the 16-gun *San Carlos* under Gonzalo López de Haro was somewhere behind Martínez. Well, if it added up to trouble, let Kendrick worry. Gray had been sent here to trade, and trade he would. Accepting gifts of brandy, wine, and ham from the Spaniard, he sailed on northward.

Eventually he reached the maze of islands off the southeastern coast of present Alaska. There his recklessness in pressing too close to shore nearly brought disaster. A sudden gust hurled the little *Washington* onto the rocks. Jib boom and bowsprit were carried away. "The next surf," wrote Robert Haswell in his log, "took us far up into a nook in the rocks where we ware surrounded with huge craggy clifts nearly as high as our mast heads." Some of the seamen jumped wildly for the slippery ledges. Finding footholds, they made fast ropes so that the heaving ship could not warp about. They then hoisted out the boat and dragged her free. She was still tight, but so battered that Gray decided to return to Nootka for repairs. Along the way he had his first stroke of trading luck—two hundred prime pelts for one chisel each.

When he reached Nootka on June 17, Kendrick was still there. So were Martínez and Haro and with them a strange English ship, the *Princess Royal* commanded by Captain Thomas Hudson. From the slopes of Hog Island a Spanish fort and three smaller buildings scowled out over Friendly Cove. Although the surface of things seemed cordial, Gray soon learned that commercial rivalries had taken on national colorings and that very real trouble was most likely on its way.

5. Nootka Sound and the Fury

TODAY it is possible to unravel the sequence of those distant events. But it is not always possible to reconstruct motives. The actors were passionate, autocratic men, far from home. None of their orders had been designed to meet the situations that developed. They improvised as they went; and as a result their deeds seem more frequently the result of caprice than of plan. Surely they would not have behaved as they did if they could have foreseen the international complications which their whimsies would later produce in the startled courts of London and Madrid.

Key man in the situation was Estévan José Martínez—the same Martínez who had anchored in Nootka Sound with Juan Pérez fifteen years before and from whom two silver spoons had been stolen. As had been the case with that earlier voyage, suspicion of the Russians lay behind Martínez' present sailing. Three years before, in 1786, a French admiral, returning from an examination of the North Pacific, had put into Monterey, California, with reports of Russian expansion toward the American mainland. This word was relayed to Mexico City, and in 1788 Viceroy Flórez dispatched Martínez and López de Haro to investigate. What the two Spaniards heard from the Russians on Kodiak and Unalaska Islands sent them hurrying home in high excitement. The Empress Catherine, it was said, planned to send four frigates south to occupy Nootka.

Actually this was a garbled rumor of an entirely different expedition recently authorized by the Russian empress, but Flórez had no way of knowing that. Not daring to wait until he could receive instructions from Madrid, the viceroy ordered Martínez and Haro to take over Nootka ahead of the Russians. Nor was this to be a mere token occupation. Martínez carried with him, as Spanish colonial expeditions always did, priests for converting the Indians, as well as the artisans and soldiers necessary for establishing a garrison. A supply ship was to follow shortly; and as soon as possible (indicative of Spain's ignorance of the coast she claimed) a land force would march along behind! If foreign ships did put in at Nootka, Martínez was to show them, politely but firmly, the superior claims of Spain to the district. He was also "to prevent as far as possible their intercourse and commerce with the natives."

So much for the immediate threat. There was a more distant one. With a flash of prescience it was recognized by Flórez, who had recently removed the commander of Juan Fernandez Island for aiding Kendrick in the *Columbia*. Writing his home government on December 23, 1788, the viceroy said, "We ought not to be surprised that the English colonies of America, being now an independent republic, should carry out the design of finding a safe port on the Pacific and of attempting to sustain it by crossing the immense country of the continent. . . . It is indeed an enterprise for many years, but I firmly believe that from now on we ought to employ tactics to forestall its results." Lewis and Clark, Astoria, the Oregon Trail—all are immanent in those words. And that, too, is another reason why Spanish armor was sent to Nootka, where Americans already had arrived in the persons of Robert Gray and John Kendrick.

Though Flórez might be suspicious of the Americans, Martínez was not—at least not when it came to making common cause against the English. From his meeting with Gray outside the sound, the Spanish commander had learned that one sizable English vessel, Douglas' *Iphigenia*, was already in the harbor, that Funter's schooner *North West America* was coasting around the neighborhood, and that at least one more ship was due shortly from China with supplies. Meanwhile Martínez was alone, his consort vessel not yet having come up. Consequently he entered Friendly Cove all smiles. He wined and dined both the English captain, William Douglas, and the American, John Kendrick, on his ship; and each returned the favor. Soon Kendrick was won completely—or perhaps it was the other way around. The Yankee captain had no love for the English, against whom he had helped fight a war not long before, and he could hardly be expected to grieve if an English rival now ran afoul of the Spanish. Indeed, there were ugly whispers later among the English that Kendrick's gloved hand pushed Martínez into some of the radical moves the Spaniard made. But none of that can be proved.

At last Martínez' supporting vessel, the *San Carlos*, appeared. Kendrick being safely neutralized, Martínez now demanded the *Iphigenia's* papers, kept them overnight for translation, and then peremptorily ordered Douglas and Viana, the *Iphigenia's* ostensible captain, aboard his ship—for Douglas was still pretending to be operating for the firm of Cavalho & Company. Flinging the Englishman's instructions on the desk, Martínez demanded explanation of a clause which his interpreter had translated as follows: if any Russian, Spanish, or English vessel tries "to divert you from your voyage . . . resist by force. . . . If, perchance, in such conflict you should have the superiority, you will take possession of the vessel and its cargo, conducting them, with the officers, to Macao in order that they may be condemned as legal prizes and the officers and crew punished as pirates."

Martínez' lip curled. He was a pirate, was he? Or would it not be more accurate to say that Douglas, operating under such orders, was the one open to the charge? Furthermore, what about these false Portuguese colors and registration papers?

Squirming, Douglas said that the translation presented matters in a false light, that——

Interrupting contemptuously, Martínez ordered Douglas and his officers imprisoned.

A few days later the Spaniard abruptly switched. Admitting that perhaps the translation had been inaccurate, he freed the English officers. But lest he be rebuked by Viceroy Flórez for having let a legitimate prize slip through his fingers, he required Douglas and Viana to sign a bond agreeing that Cavalho & Company would pay the full value of the vessel and its cargo in case Flórez declared the *Iphigenia* should have been held. Two Americans, Kendrick and his mate Joseph Ingraham, having witnessed the bond, Martínez now entertained Douglas at a sumptuous banquet aboard the Spanish flagship, then escorted the *Iphigenia* out of the harbor and politely told the English captain to go straight to China. Douglas agreed, but as soon as darkness cloaked his movements he turned north to trade.

Later Martínez stated that he had not held the *Iphigenia* because he lacked crew enough to man her. The truth may be, however, that he devised the maneuver as one whereby he could retain, through the bond, the fruits of the seizure without having to worry about countermoves by the English if they were imprisoned. In any event, no *Iphigenia* was on hand to interfere on June 8 when Robert Funter sailed the tiny *North West America* back into the sound with 215 skins aboard. Promptly Martínez pounced on her, rechristened her *Gertrúdis,* and then tried to inveigle the outraged English into continuing their trading trip under Spanish colors! When they refused, Martínez turned to the Americans. Blandly agreeing to go into a trading partnership with the Spaniard, Kendrick sent over the first mate of the *Washington*, David Coolidge, to take charge of the appropriated ship.

While this was going on, another English ship appeared, commanded by Thomas Hudson. She was the *Princess Royal*, owned by a new company recently formed in Macao by the ever resilient John Meares. Behind the *Princess Royal*, Hudson said, was another Meares ship, the *Argonaut* under Captain Colnett. Aboard the *Argonaut* were supplies for three years, the frame for another small schooner to be constructed in Friendly Cove, and two dozen additional Chinese laborers. Although Meares had remained in Asia, it was obvious that he planned grandiose developments for Nootka—more grandiose than Spain's newly aggressive Northwest policy could allow.

Thus the situation stood when Gray sailed the *Lady Washington* to anchorage under the guns of the new Spanish fort.

Martínez' counter to Hudson's appearance was an attempt to nail down, for all the world to see, his country's claims to Nootka. With John Kendrick sitting in as witness, the natives were asked to describe the clothing and flag of the first Europeans they had seen. Spanish! And what about the passage in Cook's *A Voyage to the Pacific Ocean* —an English account—that described an Indian wearing two spoons on a cord around his neck? Those spoons had been stolen from Martínez himself, years before any Englishman had come within hundreds of miles of Nootka.

Besides all that, had not Alexander VI's papal bull of 1493 awarded the entire Western world to Spain?

These points made, Martínez staged a triumphant pageant of possession. While his soldiers and sailors knelt with him on the beach, the friars sang *Te Deum Laudamus*. After this Martínez announced in a loud voice, "I take, and I have taken, I seize and I have seized, possession of this soil . . . for all time to come." As he spoke he pointed his sword at various trees, distributed stones, then hoisted a cross on his shoulders and led a chanting procession along the sandy shore. Afterward he served a great banquet aboard his ship (attended by the Americans Gray and Kendrick, and a somewhat bewildered Hudson) and closed the day with a twenty-one-gun salute from the fort.

What the Indians thought of all this to-do over land rights is not on record.

A few days later Hudson sailed away on the *Princess Royal*. As he left the sound, a sail showed on the horizon. For some reason he did not stop, although it marked the arrival of Captain Colnett in the *Argonaut*.

According to Colnett's subsequent accusations, he was lured into Friendly Cove by Martínez' solemn promises of immunity and then was refused permission to depart. Be that as it may, a violent quarrel soon developed in Martínez' cabin aboard the Spanish frigate. During the altercation Colnett perhaps drew his sword, as was charged, and threatened Martínez. Colnett later denied it, and says he was struck unconscious to the cabin floor by men slipping secretly up behind him. Martínez denied the Englishman's accusation. Whatever happened, it left Colnett in such a passion that he went temporarily insane. Imprisoned, he jumped from his cabin window into the sea and was saved from drowning only after considerable difficulty.

Though Martínez asserts he had earlier let the *Iphigenia* go because he lacked enough sailors to man her, shorthandedness no longer deterred him. He seized first the *Argonaut* and then the *Princess Royal* when Hudson returned a few days later, seeking his consort. With the English crews imprisoned below decks, Spanish sailors then took both vessels to Mexico as prizes.

The drama of Nootka so fascinated John Kendrick that he could not tear himself away. Gray, however, grew restive. At last he must have got on Kendrick's nerves, for abruptly the superior officer ordered that they switch vessels. Such supplies as remained were placed aboard the *Washington*; the furs were loaded on the *Columbia*. Gray was ordered to sail the latter ship to Canton, sell the pelts, buy tea, and continue to Boston. He must have been surprised. The management of the business in Canton and the eventual accounting with the owners at home would seem the duty, even the privilege, of the senior officer. But evidently John Kendrick, who was his own man out here in the middle of nowhere, did not want to go home, although a wife was waiting for him in New England. He told Gray that he would stay behind with the *Washington*, trade as long as supplies held out, and then follow along to Canton later in the year.

Possibly because of lack of space Martínez had not sent the English crew of the schooner *Gertrúdis*, nee *North West America*, to Mexico with the other prisoners. Now he proposed that Gray carry the stranded Englishmen to China. The Yankee agreeing, Martínez gave

Gray enough skins to pay their passage and their wages for the time they had been sitting idle in Nootka; he also entrusted to the American, for safe delivery to Meares, the 215 pelts which he had confiscated during the seizure of the *North West America*. An enigmatic man, at times, was Estévan José Martínez.

On July 30, Gray sailed the *Columbia* out of Nootka. Four weeks later, in Hawaii, he picked up two young natives eager to see the world, Opie and Attoo, the latter of whom would be called by the Boston newspapers the crown prince of the islands. Reaching Macao in November, Gray disembarked the English sailors and went on up the river to Whampoa, fantastic anchorage of foreign ships. Thousand-ton East India merchantmen towered over the weather-ravaged *Columbia*. Lacquered tea boats drifted by under square brown sails. There were flower boats, intricately carved; tiny sampans whose owners cried exotic wares in singsong tones; haughty mandarin boats with bright pennants, driving serenely by under double decks of oars.

Harbor officials came aboard, collected "gifts," and measured the *Columbia* for duties. Chopboats ferried the pelts twelve miles upstream to storage in one of the factories, or hongs, on Jackass Point. Then the dickering began. Robert Gray was a green hand in the devious ways of the China trade. Though he sold his skins and pieces of skins for $21,404.71, he had to pay out nearly half the sum for fees, bribes, and repairs to his ship. The $11,241.51 remaining to him he invested in 21,462 pounds of Bohea tea. Unfortunately 12,000 pounds of this would be damaged on the way home.

As he was preparing to sail for Boston near the end of January 1790, he received a letter from Kendrick, who had just put into Dirty Butter Bay near Macao. The captain had finally roused himself for a trading trip north of Nootka and actually had some skins aboard the *Washington*. By return letter Gray advised him to hold onto the pelts, as the market was depressed. Sailing down the river, Gray then passed within sight of Kendrick's anchorage, but the two men did not meet. Bad weather prevented, or so Gray later told the owners.

All in all, the single returning ship did not bring a profitable return on the owners' original forty-nine-thousand-dollar investment. Still, there was prestige. The *Columbia* was the first American ship to circumnavigate the globe. When she entered Boston Harbor on August 9, 1790, the fort on the hill gave her a federal salute of thirteen guns, and "three huzzas" rose from a "great concourse of citizens assembled on the various wharves." Governor Hancock held a reception to which the leading men of Massachusetts came. Gray went in state, marching

MAP I

The Sea Routes of Early Pacific Exploration

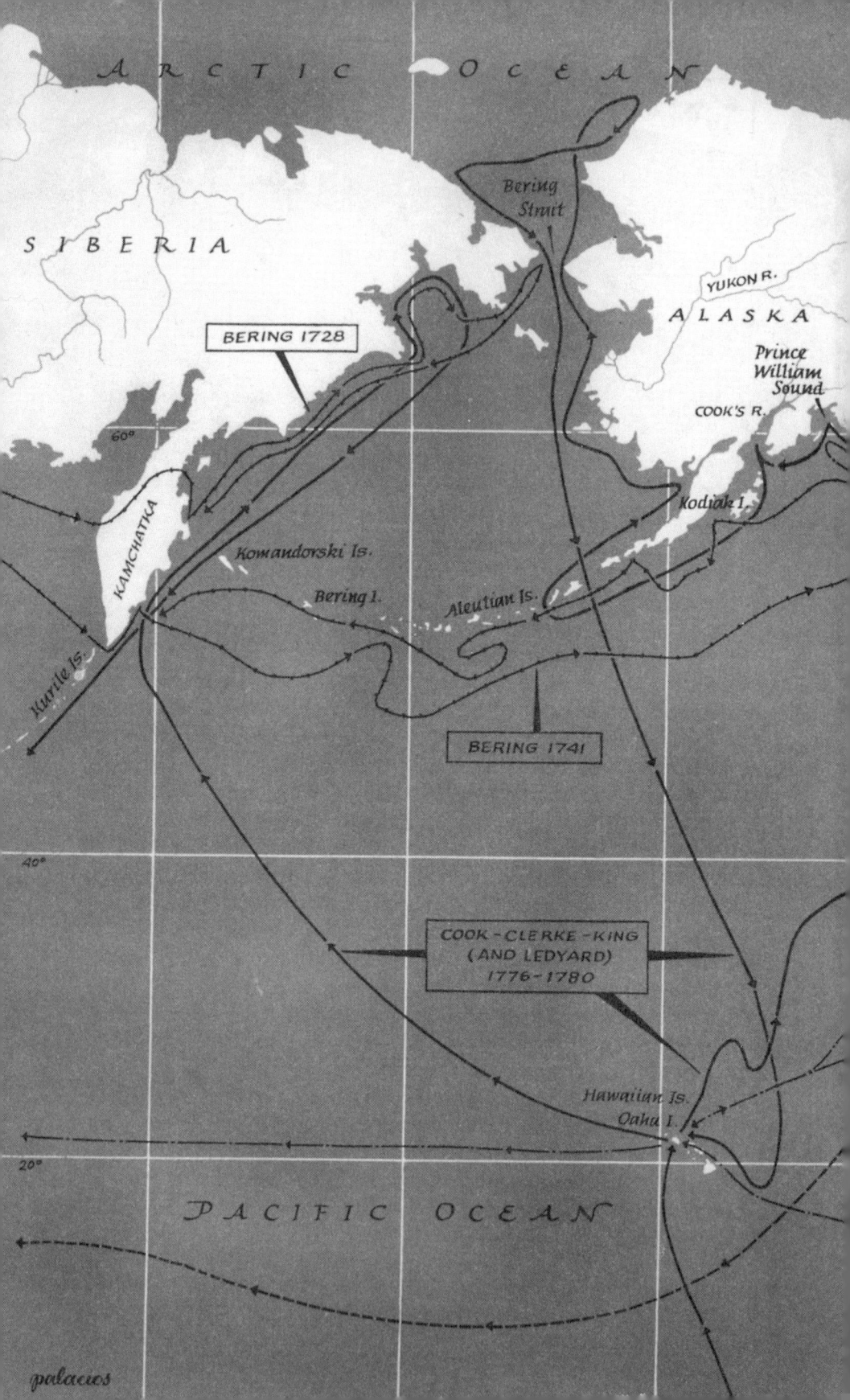

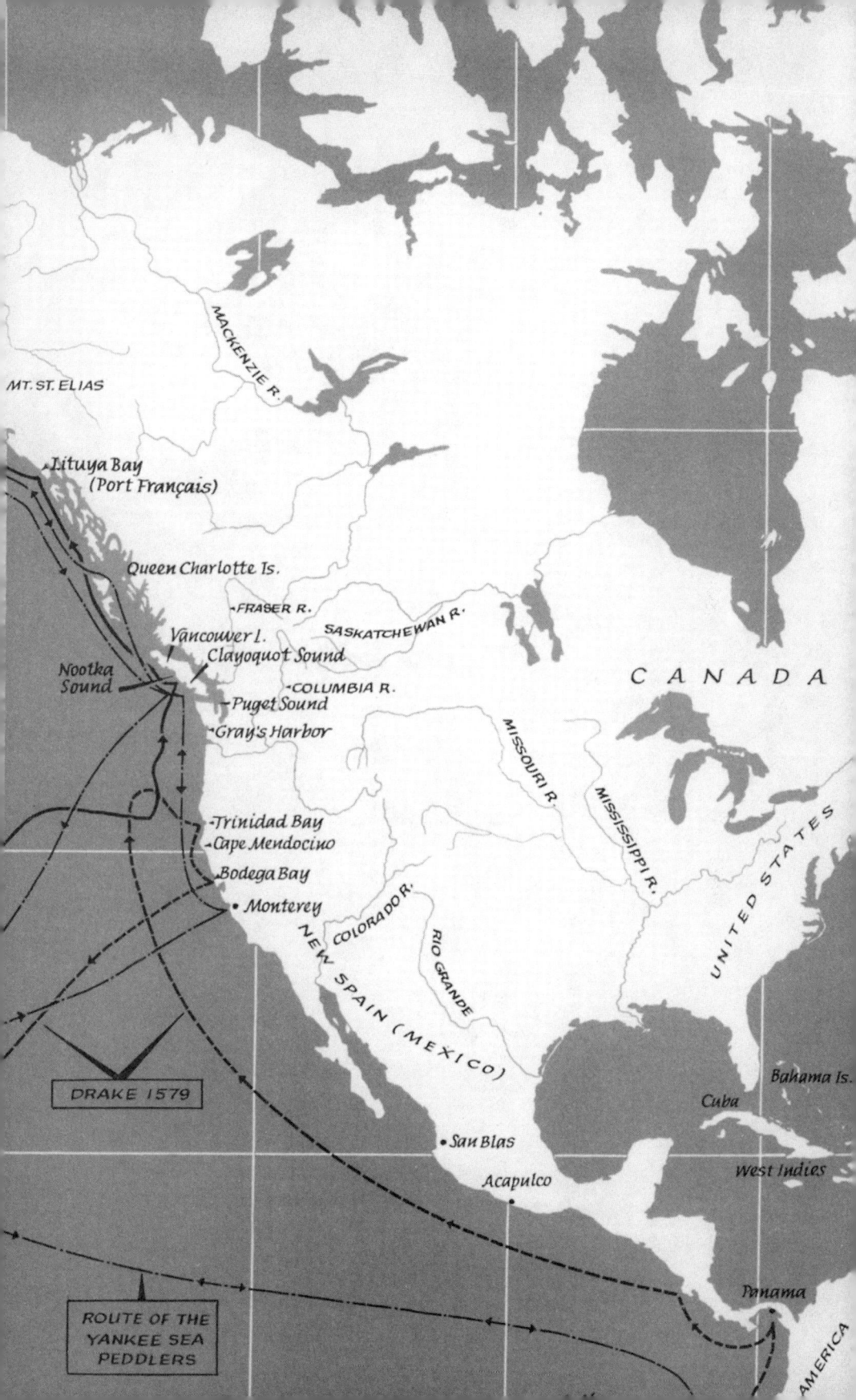

MT. ST. ELIAS

MACKENZIE R.

•Lituya Bay
(Port Français)

Queen Charlotte Is.

FRASER R.

SASKATCHEWAN R.

Vancouver I.
Clayoquot Sound

Nootka
Sound

•COLUMBIA R.

•Puget Sound

•Gray's Harbor

CANADA

MISSOURI R.

MISSISSIPPI R.

•Trinidad Bay
•Cape Mendocino
•Bodega Bay
• Monterey

DRAKE 1579

NEW SPAIN (MEXICO)

COLORADO R.

RIO GRANDE

UNITED STATES

Bahama Is.

Cuba

West Indies

•San Blas

Acapulco

ROUTE OF THE
YANKEE SEA
PEDDLERS

Panama

AMERICA

down the middle of the street, followed closely by "Crown Prince" Attoo, who was described as a living flame, clad in a crested feather helmet and a feather cloak of golden suns set in scarlet.

The seafarer had many a tale to spin at that reception. To his listeners not the least interesting was his eyewitness version of the squabble at Nootka.

Because of that squabble the Western world was on tenterhooks. Seven or eight months before Gray's arrival in Boston, Viceroy Flórez of Mexico had written to Madrid a somewhat inaccurate account of Martínez' seizure of British property. Picking up rumors of this, the outraged British chargé d'affaires in Madrid communicated with Prime Minister Pitt. Promptly there followed an exchange of stiff notes between the powers, but the bristling was done in diplomatic privacy until all at once egregious John Meares interjected himself into the furor with his famous *Memorial* of April 30, 1790.

The first inkling that something might be amiss in Nootka had been brought to Meares in Macao by William Douglas of the *Iphigenia*. The sailors of the *North West America*, returning to China on the *Columbia*, added the rest of the details. In fury and alarm Meares rushed to London to try enlisting the support of his government. Sanguine though he was, he nonetheless must have been surprised to find the Foreign Office already carrying a huge chip on its shoulder, and to be ushered straightway into the presence of no less a personage than Pitt himself.

The basic issue, of course, was not over one sea peddler's tubs in the distant Pacific. Rather it was over the right of the Spanish to claim that whole ocean on the basis of a papal bull three hundred years old and to exclude, or try to exclude, ships flying the English flag. At stake also was the definition of what constituted effective discovery. With a confident show Spain trotted out indisputable evidence, including Martínez' silver spoons, that her mariners had visited Nootka at least four years prior to Cook. But England had published the results of Cook's explorations; Spain had kept her information largely secret. In open dispute before the world, which gave the stronger right?

Angrily Spain called on Louis XVI of France for help under terms of the Family Compact between the two nations. Pitt countered by evoking the new Triple Alliance between England, Prussia, and the Netherlands. At this point Meares arrived, to have his private woes ballooned into public ones when the government issued his *Memorial*, the story of the ship seizures, as a propaganda device for stirring up popular indignation. Amazed by the *Memorial's* success, Meares immediately rushed to press with a travel book called *Voyages Made in the Years 1788 and 1789 from China to the North West Coast of America*. To its royalties he hoped to add substantial sums collected in damage suits against Spain for his lost ships and their presumed profits. Growing as the international tension grew, the amount he demanded soared to an astronomical £469, 865—more than two and a quarter million dollars.

By now Spain had ordered her fleet to mobilize and had received from Louis XVI a promise of fourteen ships of the line. The English Parliament reacted by voting a war chest of a million pounds and dispatching troops to the West Indies, close to Spain's rich colonies. Prussia promised to stand by the Triple Alliance, and Holland sent ships to join the most formidable assemblage of naval armament the world had yet seen. In America, President Washington and his Secretary of State, Thomas Jefferson, watched with alarm, wondering what would happen to their unprepared little country if Spain and England took to fighting each other in the Floridas and up and down the Mississippi Valley.

At this point one of history's big "ifs" intrudes. If the French Revolution had not been gathering headway . . . but it was. The States-General, scowling on Louis XVI's offer to help Spain, began a long debate on whether the right to make war lay with the people or with the king. As the summer passed and the rush of events in France made it obvious that no aid could be expected from that source, Spain took another look at the massed English fleet and began to back down. England, likewise worried by the happenings in France, decided to be gracious. Finally, on October 28, 1790, the Nootka Sound Convention ended the dispute—and, in effect, Spain's pretensions as a colonial power in North America.

Though nowhere explicitly stated, the Nootka Convention's most important point was the tacit abandonment by Spain of her former claim to exclusive control of the Northwest coast. For in granting the right of British subjects to trade or settle on lands not currently occupied by Spanish subjects, Spain also granted by implication the same right to the peoples of other countries. England's signature to the convention also held the same implication. Sovereignty, in other words, became a matter of occupancy—the hinge on which, before another half century was out, the whole Oregon question between the United States and Great Britain would swing.

None of this was lost on Thomas Jefferson. Always he had been keenly interested in the West. Now he became convinced that to keep the United States from being drawn into European wars this country must drive a wedge between the quarrelsome neighbors on her flanks. In short, the west bank of the Mississippi, at the very least, must become American. And so far-off Nootka planted one of the seeds, though only one, that shortly would blossom into the Louisiana Purchase.

And, finally, the convention assured Meares's company of restitution of its seized property, plus damages eventually arbitrated at $210,000. This represents some deflation; but considering the negligible returns garnered by the Yankee merchants who had sent out Gray and Kendrick, Mr. Meares did very well for himself with his one-man war.

6. Columbia's River

ROBERT GRAY'S stay in Boston lasted only seven weeks. Even before settlement of the Nootka controversy he was again sailing the *Columbia* toward the Northwest in an effort to recoup the losses of the first voyages and stir the dilatory Kendrick to action. [1] This time he was equipped with more suitable trade goods: woolen cloth; trousers, pea jackets, and shoes; racks of ancient muskets and blunderbusses; 14,000 nails, 143 sheets of copper, 4261 quarter-pound "chissells."

Eight months and five days out of Boston, the *Columbia* reached Clayoquot Sound, a quicker trip by nearly four months than the one under Kendrick had been. There'd been trouble, nonetheless. Violent storms off the Horn had helped kill Nancy, the Cape Verde Island goat who had circumnavigated the globe with Gray; and on April 23, 1791, at 5 P.M., she was committed to the deep, "much lamented," wrote the new fifth mate, sixteen-year-old John Boit, "by those who'd got a share of her milk." Scurvy grew acute. As soon as the *Columbia* limped into Clayoquot the sick were hustled ashore and buried in earth up to their hips. According to Boit, the treatment helped, though perhaps the "greens" the men devoured and the berries they bought from the Indians were even more beneficial.

There was no word of Kendrick at Clayoquot, and because Gray did not know what the situation might be in Nootka, he stayed away

[1] In even less time Gray's ex-mate, Joseph Ingraham, had been employed by rival New Englanders and had hurried back toward Nootka in the tiny 70-ton brig *Hope*.

from that strife-torn sound. For a time trade went well. Then Attoo, the "crown prince" of Hawaii, tried to desert to the Indians. (The other Hawaiian boy, Opie, was with Ingraham on the *Hope*.) Duty-bound to return Attoo to his home, Gray took severe measure to get the boy back. Luring one of Clayoquot's principal chiefs aboard, he imprisoned the man and threatened him with death unless Attoo was returned. The chief's frightened people complied, whereupon Attoo was publicly flogged—to the Indian mind an unheard-of and abhorrent punishment. Gray then announced that if any more of his men deserted they must straightway be returned by the natives; otherwise he would flog, in the deserter's stead, the first Indian chief he caught.

The whole performance bewildered the savages. In time the animosity it aroused would bear dangerous fruit, but the Indians' initial reaction was simply to turn sullen and quit trading. Finding business slow, Gray quit the harbor and beat haphazardly up and down the coast, bearing at length for the Queen Charlotte Islands, where he had so successfully traded chisels for furs two years before. The natives here had peculiar customs. For one thing, the women bossed the men. For another, the softer sex cut incisions into their underlips and by inserting labrets, pieces of wood as large as goose eggs, "boomed" the mutilated member as much as two inches out from their chins. They were not, young Boit confided to his log, "very Chaste, but their lip peices was enough to disgust any Civilized being; however some of the Crew was quite partial"—an intercourse Gray endeavored without success to restrain.

Cruising about, the *Columbia* fell in with Joseph Ingraham's tiny *Hope*. Ingraham, it developed, was turning into one of the canniest traders on the coast. Finding that the Indians, well supplied by now with unadorned cloth, turned up their noses at his offerings, he sewed brass buttons on his goods and got rid of every stitch. When Gray's free-handed bargaining depreciated the value of chisels, Ingraham converted his iron into seven-pound collars, somehow made the monstrosities fashionable, and peddled them at the rate of three skins for a single collar. In forty-nine days he collected fourteen hundred sea-otter pelts, one of the most successful ventures, day for day, on record.

Leaving Ingraham, Gray threaded the complex islands off southeastern Alaska, lost his second mate and three hands to Indians, and on August 29, 1791, returned to Clayoquot. A strange log house stood on the shore and in the bay rode a strange brig . . . no, not strange. It was the *Lady Washington*, transformed from a sloop into a brig. Leaning over the rail, watching as the *Columbia* hove to, was her former master, John Kendrick.

Kendrick had a depressing saga to tell. Shortly after Gray's departure from Nootka he had taken the *Washington* north into Barrell Sound (now Houston Stewart Channel). There Indians had stolen some clothing from the ship. In retaliation Kendrick strung up two chiefs in such wise that he could thrust a leg of each Indian into a cannon barrel. Terrified by his threats to fire, the tribesmen frantically produced the stolen goods. This was not enough. As a further condition Kendrick demanded every skin in the village. These he paid for "at the regular price" and sailed away, reaching Dirty Butter Bay just as Gray had been leaving for Boston.

For more than a year Kendrick had stayed in Macao. Part of the time he had been desperately ill; part he had spent refitting the *Washington* as a brig. He had also sold the ship to himself, a sham transaction, he explained unconvincingly, to avoid Chinese commercial regulation. Gray noticed, however, that Kendrick treated the vessel as if it really did belong to him. As for returns to the owners from either the sale of his ship or from his pelts, there were none. The expenses of refitting the *Washington* had been high, the pelt market low, and the officials difficult. Before Kendrick could dispose of all his skins he had been arrested (for reasons no longer apparent) and ordered out of Macao. Taking two hundred prime furs with him, he had gone to Japan in company with the ship *Grace*, the first American to enter that forbidden country. The Japanese not caring for otter pelts, the furs still remained in the *Washington*'s hold.

Returning to the Northwest, Kendrick had again visited Barrell Sound, scene of his previous tussle over the stolen garments. The natives appeared to have forgotten, and trade droned along as usual— until a sudden rush by the Indians captured the deck and its arms chest. As the sailors tumbled down the companionways, searching for more weapons below, the Indians closed about Kendrick. "Put me in your cannon now," a chief snarled, and lunged with a dagger. The blade ripped through Kendrick's shirt, nicking his belly as he jumped backward. At this juncture the sailors returned with firearms. At the first volley the Indians melted away, save for one shrieking female who clung howling to the chains until cut loose with a cutlass. As canoes and swimmers struggled to reach shore, a barrage of grape killed forty or more without loss to the defenders.

Yes, Kendrick continued in answer to Gray's questions, the Spaniards still held Nootka, though Martínez himself had been summoned home on his wife's complaint of non-support. From Maquinna, Kendrick had purchased, without Spanish objection this time, a piece of land near Friendly Cove; and in Clayoquot he had secured two more parcels of real estate. The land might be useful for a trading post. Not this season, though. He was going back to China as soon as he graved the brig. But sometime . . .

Gray left him, still dreaming, and traded southward for two weeks. When he returned, Kendrick was still there and did not leave until September 26.

Deciding to winter in Clayoquot, Gray located a landlocked cove, had his men chop out a clearing on its shores, and there built a two-story log fort eighteen feet wide by thirty-six feet long. Aping Meares, he now set up shipways, blacksmith forge, and saw pits for building a seventy-five-foot schooner, the *Adventure,* whose frame he had brought with him from Boston.

The Indians seemed amiable. Dusky maidens supplied berries, salmon, and other comforts; Gray cured a sick chief. On Christmas the whites amazed the Indians by bedecking fort, shops, and ship with evergreen boughs. Twenty geese were roasted on spits before a huge fire, and the local dignitaries and their ladies were invited to a feast on the ship. (Rather than board the *Columbia,* the women sat outside in their canoes, waiting for whatever their lords tossed down.) Chief Wicananish repaid the compliment by inviting some of the whites to a name-giving dance, during which he handed on his name to his son and assumed a new one. The native singing interested young John Boit, Jr., but, he added in his journal, "the *Smell* was too strong for my Organs."

In spite of the festivities, ill will yet lingered because of Gray's rough-handed treatment first of Attoo's desertion and, later, of a case of stealing. One day various Indians were noted talking too long and too earnestly to the Hawaiian "prince." On being grilled, Attoo confessed that the Indians had promised to make him a big chief if he smuggled them ammunition and, at a designated moment, wet down the whites' powder. The savages would then attack the *Columbia*—an easy matter, for the vessel had recently been moored alongside a cliff and her guns unshipped preparatory to her being hauled ashore and graved.

Forewarned, the whites had no difficulty frustrating the attack. But either the pressure of the alarm or the long, rainy winter or just too much living on the uncivilized side of the world turned Gray irascible. Mercilessly he drove the workers to launch the *Adventure,* repair the

Columbia, and quit the sound as soon as possible. By the end of March he was ready to leave, but not before he let the natives feel his displeasure. On his way down the sound he bore in toward the Indian village. The inhabitants fled. John Boit, Jr., was then ordered out with a landing party to burn the entire settlement: houses, fish-drying racks, totems, everything.

When the ships separated outside the sound, the *Adventure* turning north and the *Columbia* south, Gray seems to have been actuated by a desire to find something more permanent than the haphazard trade that had satisfied him on earlier journeys. On this trip he kept trying to poke his way into various havens along the present Washington-Oregon coast. He couldn't manage. "Currents and squally weather hindered," young Boit wrote in his log, ". . . however Capt. Gray is determined to persevere in the pursuit."

The reason for the perseverance is not known. Perhaps Kendrick's talk of buying land had made Gray feel that he too would like a cove where he could set up a factory unhampered by outside interference. Nootka would not do, being a bone of international contention; and Kendrick had first claim to Clayoquot, even if Gray's treatment of the Indians had not ruled out that sound. Northward the weather and the Russians offered obstacles. Southward, however, lay . . . what? Probably Gray knew that in that direction armchair geographers had long since placed Jonathan Carver's Oregon, the great River of the West; and by now he had been trading off those coasts long enough to have perhaps picked up from the Indians an inkling that the stream existed in more than fancy. If it did, its estuary would be virgin ground for the first trader to reach it. Too, there might be prestige connected with the discovery, though in other cases Robert Gray's cool Yankee blood seems not to have been unduly heated by the prospect of uncommercial exploration.

All this is speculation. It is known, however, that at latitude 46° 10′ he found an alluring entry but could not breach it because of its strong "reflux" and the tumultuous wall of breakers extending across it. Abandoning the attempt until weather and tides were more favorable, he drifted northward, anchoring finally off a village called Kenekomitt. There, toward sunset on April 28, the lookout descried two sails.

They were English ships, the 340-ton, copper-sheathed *Discovery* under Captain George Vancouver and the smaller armed tender *Chatham* under Lieutenant W. R. Broughton. From the *Discovery* a boat bearing Lieutenant Peter Puget and surgeon-naturalist Alexander Menzies crossed to the *Columbia*. From the two Englishmen Gray learned that Spain had abandoned her claims to Nootka and that Vancouver had been appointed Britain's representative to accept the restitution of the land which John Meares still said he had bought from Maquinna. More important, Vancouver was also to complete the exploratory work of the Northwest coast begun by Captain Cook, with whom Vancouver had sailed as a midshipman. In the process he was to conduct still another search for the Northwest Passage.

The Passage! That ghost was walking again, thanks partly to John Meares's high-blown guesses, in his recently published *Voyages*, about the eastern limits of Juan de Fuca Strait. (Its "extremity," he wrote, ". . . could not be at any great distance from Hudson's Bay.")

Eager to learn what they could about this alluring waterway, Vancouver's men pumped Gray for such information as he possessed. It was not much. Although he had once penetrated nearly fifty miles into the strait, he had no definite knowledge about where it ended; and because he had been avoiding Nootka, he did not know that the Spanish had recently been pushing explorations in those waters. So he mistakenly said that the region around the strait was untouched. To this sparse data he added word of a river at $46°$ $10'$.

When the latter information was brought to Vancouver, he brushed it aside. He had seen the shoals and breakers and discolored water that Gray described. But he believed the discoloration resulted from spring freshets, and he had not learned from his master, Cook, that great rivers characteristically pile up vast sand bars across their mouths. The unexplored Strait of Juan de Fuca, with its potential passageway through the continent, sounded far more exciting. Off he sailed.

Gray tagged after him for a ways, then swung south again. At $46°$ $58'$ he saw another promising but difficult-to-reach harbor. "Stubbornly"—the word is Boit's—he pushed through crashing breakers and over dangerous shoals into a commodious roadstead. This he named Bulfinch's Harbor, after one of his backers. (Today it is more appropriately called Gray's Harbor.) A river was there, but of no particular consequence.

Astounded by their first sight of a white man's ship, the local natives flocked about in their canoes. They were fat, naked, unhandsome, and heavily armed. Though they were eager to trade, the whites remained cautious. It was well they did. There was a monstrous uproar on the beach that evening—war dances, probably—and shortly after midnight several canoes took off across the moon-silvered water. Gray ordered a cannon fired over the heads of the paddlers. The craft kept on. One large one, holding at least twenty warriors, pressed within half a pistol shot of the *Columbia*. Exasperated by the Indians' refusal to heed his warnings, Gray ordered a nine-pounder and ten muskets loaded with buckshot to fire point-blank. "We dash'd her all to pieces and no doubt kill'd every soul in her." At that the other canoes retreated. Amazingly enough, the Indians resumed trading the next day without apparent rancor.

Whatever doubts Gray may have had about a huge river to the south of him were dissipated by the information he now gleaned from the Indians. He does not say so in his log. Yet he must have been looking for something definite. On the evening of May 10, 1792, he hurriedly quit the harbor and bore south, missing in the darkness the entrance to Willapa Bay. The next morning at 4:00 A.M., so he noted in his log, they "saw the entrance of our desired port." Out went a pinnace, groping for a way through the tumult of white water. Under short sail the *Columbia* followed into "a large river of fresh water, up which we steered. At one P.M. came to with the small bower, in ten fathoms, black and white sand. . . . Vast numbers of natives came alongside."

For eight days the ship lingered inside the huge estuary of the mythical river that was no myth. During that time Gray shifted anchorage once. Even the cutter which explored the channel traveled no more that thirty or thirty-five miles upstream. If the exploration seems strangely niggardly after so much perseverance, trade is the reason. In Boit's words, "The Canoes that came from down river brought no Otter Skins . . . [and so] we contented ourselves in our present situation which was a very pleasant one."

Still, though trade was Gray's primary aim, he was not unaware of the significance of what he had done, especially since he had learned from Vancouver that Spain was relaxing her pretensions. If Spain didn't own the country, who did? Landing, he declared that the territory now belonged to the United States of America, three thousand miles away. Because he had run out of names, having applied those of his backers and of current politicians to other landmarks up and down the coast, he decided to call this majestic new river after his ship— Columbia's River, a spelling form which did not long survive.

Gray's thoughts about the countryside did not escape into his laconic log. Fortunately seventeen-year-old John Boit was more articulate:

This River in my opinion, wou'd be a fine place for to sett up a *Factory*. The Indians are very numerous, and appear'd very civill (not even offering to steal). during our short stay we collected 150 Otter, 300 Beaver, and twice the number of other land furs. [The whites bought four otter skins for a single sheet of copper, a beaver pelt for two spikes, other furs for one spike each. A single "board nail" would purchase two salmon.] the river abounds with excellent Salmon, and most other River fish, and the Woods with plenty of Moose and Deer, the skins of which was brought us in great plenty, and the Banks produce a ground Nut [probably the wapatoo root] which is an excellent substitute for either bread or Potatoes, We found plenty of Oak, Ash and Walnut trees, and clear ground in plenty, which with little labour might be made fit to raise such seeds as is necessary for the sustenance of inhabitants, and in short a factory set up here and another at Hancock's River in the Queen Charlotte Isles, wou'd engross the whole trade of the NW Coast (with the help of a few small coasting vessels).

[May] 20. This day left Columbia's River and stood clear of the bars, and bore off to the Northward. The Men at Columbia's River are strait limb'd, fine looking fellows, and the women are very pretty. they are all in a state of Nature, except the Females, who wear a leaf Apron (perhaps 'twas a fig leaf), but some of our gentlemen that examin'd them pretty close, and *near*, both *within* and *without*, reported that it was not a leaf but a nice wove mat in resemblance.

The rest of Gray's trip was, in a sense, anticlimax, though perhaps it did not seem so at the time. There were more prowlings in and out of inlets, two more brutal fights with the Indians, and in July, north of Vancouver Island, a shattering crash on a reef that split the *Columbia's* keel, smashed her stem, and stripped away much of her sheathing. Plugging the leak with a topsail, Gray limped back to Nootka for repairs.

Friendly Cove had changed considerably since his last visit. Several ships of various nationalities were in the harbor, including Ingraham's diminutive *Hope*. The Spanish settlement now numbered sixteen buildings, presided over with courtly charm by Juan Francisco de Bodega y Cuadra, the fiery don who had sailed these waters seventeen years before with Bruno Heceta.

The friendship that had marked American relations with Martínez continued with Cuadra. The Spaniard offered Gray, free of charge, every resource at hand, had the Yankee captain live with him while the ship was out of commission, and invited the rest of the *Columbia's* officers to a dinner that all but popped young John Boit's eyes from his head: "Fifty four persons sat down . . . and the plates, which was *solid silver*, was shifted five times, which made 270 Plates!" Real warmth must have lain beneath the formality, for after Gray had returned to Massachusetts and married, he named his first-born son Robert Don Quadra Gray.

Shortly Vancouver's two ships joined the assemblage. By doggedly prowling the maze of channels opening off Juan de Fuca Strait and after almost losing both vessels on the rocks, the English had completed the first circuit of what would shortly be known as Vancouver Island. Along the way they had initiated a magnificent survey of the Northwest's spectacular harbor systems (but had missed the mouth of the Fraser River, discovered a year earlier by Spaniards working out of Nootka) and had given to a multitude of landmarks names they still bear—Puget Sound and Mount Rainier, for example.

In Nootka, Vancouver asked Cuadra for restitution of the land Meares supposedly had bought from Maquinna. Gray and Ingraham, however, had told Cuadra that no such sale had ever been consummated. The Spaniard accordingly declined to hand the land over, and a mild dispute developed. During it the English and Spanish commanders entertained each other at dinner and named Nootka's parent island after themselves—Cuadra and Vancouver Island, a name which usage soon cut in half. After several weeks of pleasant bickering the captains agreed to refer the quarrel to their governments.

The restless Gray meantime had sold the sloop *Adventure* to Cuadra for $4125, paid in otter skins. Sailing to Canton, he exchanged his year's take of furs for tea, nankeens, sugar, and porcelain. Though the trip enabled the owners to recoup their earlier losses, they did not send their diligent captain back to the Northwest and Gray sank into obscurity. Supposedly he died of yellow fever at sea in 1806. Some years later his widow appealed to Congress to rescue her from poverty.

At least he returned home. His onetime superior, John Kendrick, never did—and never returned a solitary dime to the owners. In 1793 and again in 1794 he was back on the coast in the *Lady Washington*, apparently trading for himself in his usual unhurried fashion. China-bound late in 1794, he stopped at Hawaii and with a Captain Brown of the ship *Jackal* meddled in an intra-island feud. Their faction being successful, Brown and Kendrick proposed to salute each other. By oversight one of the *Jackal's* guns was not unshotted. Its load of round and grape pierced the side of the *Washington*, wounded several of the crew, and blew off Kendrick's head as he sat at his table.

All this was learned by John Boit, Jr., shortly after the accident. At the ripe age of nineteen Boit had signed on as commander of a sixty-foot, 89-ton sloop, the *Union*, and had sailed her back to the Northwest. In Puget Sound he had fought a bloody but successful battle with several hundred savages; and later he had tried to enter Columbia's River but had been baffled by wind and breakers. At Hawaii native canoes ("the females were *amorous*") greeted him with hogs, pineapples, and gossip of Kendrick's demise. On July 8, 1796, having attained voting age the previous October, he sailed the *Union* into Boston Harbor.

After talking with Gray at Nootka in the fall of 1792, George Vancouver decided he had better look in at the great river he had missed, but the Columbia's treacherous bar gave his ships rougher treatment than he anticipated. Tumultuous waves broke completely over Lieutenant Broughton's tender, the *Chatham*, smashing one of her smallboats. Nonetheless Broughton got through. Vancouver in the larger *Discovery* never did. Fearfully battered, he gave up trying and continued alone to rendezvous at Monterey.

Inside the estuary the *Chatham* discovered the fur-trading schooner *Jenny*, whose Captain Baker had also learned of the river from Gray in Nootka. [2] Nothing about the Columbia, so far as Broughton could see, matched Gray's terse descriptions. Without taking into account the fact that the Yankee had entered during spring floods and the *Chatham* during a season of low water, Broughton voiced a doubt that Gray had ever got out of the estuary into the river itself. Hoping to capitalize on the fact, he hoisted out a longboat and rowed ninety miles or so upstream. Landing in full view of a majestic peak he called Mount Hood, he took possession of the country in the name of King George.

Later, Broughton was sent home with dispatches; and when Vancouver resumed his explorations in 1793 it was James Johnstone who commanded the *Chatham*. Patiently the two ships poked in and out of the intricate channels north of Vancouver Island, unaware that Alexander Mackenzie with a single canoeload of frightened *voyageurs* had already crossed the Continental Divide and was gingerly approaching the very inlets they were mapping. By the next summer Vancouver had at last nailed the ghost of the Northwest Passage firmly in its coffin; and there is appropriateness in the fact that the first land crossing of the northern part of the continent should coincide with the end of the search for a usable seaway.

Putting back into Nootka for the last time on September 2, 1794, Vancouver learned that Cuadra had died in Mexico and that no instructions had yet arrived as to what to do about their dispute. After

2 It was for Captain Baker that Broughton named Baker Bay on the north shore of the broad river mouth, a designation it still bears.

waiting vainly for six weeks, he sailed home. Meanwhile representatives of the two powers, conferring in Europe, had agreed on mutual abandonment of the district. Pursuant to this accord, two commissioners met in Nootka on March 23, 1795, destroyed the decaying houses of the already deserted settlement, and turned the sound back to Maquinna's people.

By now the sea-otter trade was slowly destroying itself. Because of England's involvement in the Napoleonic Wars, the commerce was falling by default largely into the hands of the Yankees. Ruthless exploitation by them and by the Russians quickly thinned the Northern otter herds to such an extent that a hardheaded, hard-drinking captain called Honest Joe O'Cain contracted with Baranov, the Russian governor, for Aleut hunters to poach along the forbidden coasts of California. This was in the fall of 1803. In the spring of that same year another Yankee captain named John Salter paid full price for the wrongs inflicted by all the peddlers who had preceded him into Nootka Sound.

Sailing his ship *Boston* five miles or so up the channel beyond Friendly Cove, Salter anchored where he thought his crew would be undisturbed while taking on wood and water. The Indians promptly followed and were soon clambering at will about the ship. One day Maquinna came aboard from duck hunting in a sulky mood. A lock on a double-barreled shotgun given him by Salter had broken. Contemptuously he said the gun was *peshak* (bad). Salter took umbrage. Not only was Maquinna looking a gift horse in the mouth, but also his own stupidity was probably the cause of the damage. With various slurs on Indians in general and Maquinna in particular, the captain tossed the gun for repair to the ship's armorer, a twenty-year-old youth from Hull, England, named John Jewitt.

Maquinna knew enough English to follow the drift of the insults. Outraged, he went ashore. As he brooded, he recalled how James Hanna, on the whites' very first trading trip to Friendly Cove nearly twenty years before, had killed a score or so of his tribesmen; how the Spaniard Martínez in a fit of temper had slain Maquinna's friend and fellow chief Callicum; how, more recently, another trader had dared enter Maquinna's own house during the chief's absence, frighten his nine wives, and make off with forty choice skins. And now this!

Normally thirty armed whites were enough to insure respect, but Maquinna had a stroke of inspiration. Cleverly he divided the enemy forces by telling Salter that salmon were running and persuading the captain to send out nine men on a fishing party. Next the chief, wearing a grotesque wooden mask, led aboard the *Boston* what purported to be a group of merrymakers. Scores of other Indians floated idly about in their canoes. While Maquinna piped a tune on a sort of whistle, his people went into a ludicrous dance that soon had the sailors in stitches.

Working below decks, armorer Jewitt heard the dance give way to a confused uproar. Curious, he ran up the steerage steps. As his head appeared, an Indian caught his hair and swung an ax. Luckily the savage's hold slipped on Jewitt's short hair, and the ax struck him only a glancing blow. Stunned, he tumbled backward to the foot of the stairs.

When he revived, Maquinna offered him his life if he would become the chief's slave and serve also as tribal blacksmith. A glance showed the wounded youth that the ship was in the hands of the Indians. Arranged neatly along the quarter-deck were the severed heads of Captain Salter and the crew, including the nine fishermen. Dumbly Jewitt nodded agreement.

Under his direction the Indians clumsily raised anchor, set sail, and took the *Boston* to Friendly Cove. There they beached her while the excited villagers drummed triumphantly upon the resonant plank roofs and walls of their houses. The captive was then taken to Maquinna's house, where he set about gaining good will by cutting the metal buttons off his coat and making a necklace of them for the chief's eleven-year-old son. This recognition of the warm father-son relationship prevailing in the tribe soon paid dividends, for during the night a great racket was occasioned by the discovery that the *Boston's* sailmaker, an elderly man named Thompson, was still alive in the ship's hold. By pretending to be Thompson's son, Jewitt managed to save the old man's life—though there were times later on when Thompson's cantankerous temper almost made him wish he hadn't.

News of Maquinna's unprecedented victory drew from all over Vancouver Island a concourse of natives eager to see the prize. The strutting chief decided on a ceremony of welcome. His warriors bedecked themselves in whatever loot from the *Boston's* cargo struck their fancy—ruffles, women's smocks, stockings drawn over their heads. They thrust circles of daggers into their belts, strung staggering weights of shot pouches and powder horns around their necks. With loaded muskets and blunderbusses, they squatted in a line on the beach, the butts of the guns pressed against the sand. Thompson packed a huge charge of powder into a cannon brought from the ship. Maquinna and Jewitt climbed onto a housetop and began a thunderous drumming with sticks. When the proper frenzy had been reached, Maquinna howled a signal. Thompson fired the cannon; the Indians pulled the triggers of their guns. Awed by the roar of their own volley, the savages fell flat. Then, springing erect and facing their guests, they began a savage song of triumph.

Their prize did not long survive. A plundering savage prowling the *Boston's* hold set the ship afire with his torch, and it vanished in a spiral of greasy smoke. Nor did it seem that other vessels would ever appear. News of the massacre reached potential traders through the Indian grapevine, and most of them gave Nootka wide berth; when two ships did approach, the cocky Indians drove them off by firing on them with the stolen cannon.

In despair, Jewitt wrote out, with materials previously salvaged from the *Boston*, several letters detailing his plight. As opportunity presented, he smuggled these out with visiting natives in the hope that somehow, sometime one would fall into the hand of a wandering trader. Beyond that there was nothing to do but wait and work. At Maquinna's insistence he took a native mate. He passed the time blacksmithing, making weapons, learning the language, and doing such odd jobs as filing the teeth of a disgruntled husband who wanted to bite off the nose of a newly purchased wife who declined to sleep with him. And always there was the problem of fishing Thompson out of the embroilments into which that surly individual's temper was forever landing him.

One year passed, another. A profound melancholy was settling on Jewitt when unexpectedly the brig *Lydia* of New York appeared at the entrance to the harbor. Her captain, Samuel Hill, had picked up one of Jewitt's letters.

Maquinna was suspicious. But he was also greedy. For more than two years he had been without trade, and he knew that the massacre was the reason. Before the *Lydia* ventured into the cove her captain would undoubtedly demand word about the *Boston* and its survivors. What could be better, the chief reasoned slyly, than to have the survivors themselves provide an answer? He ordered Jewitt to write the captain of the brig a letter giving Maquinna a clean bill of health.

Producing a raven-quill pen and ink mixed from powdered charcoal and blackberry juice, Jewitt turned out a letter of somewhat different tenor, then blandly outfaced the chief's searching questions. Satisfied at last, Maquinna went aboard with the missive. Following Jewitt's recommendations, Hill promptly clapped the Indian into irons.

From that point on, it was simply a matter of negotiating an exchange with the wailing tribesmen.

The release was effected in July. Four months later in November 1805, Captain Hill took the *Lydia* across the foaming bar of the Columbia River and dropped anchor off the northern shore. He knew the district. The previous April he had anchored there for a month while taking a small boat upriver as far as, or perhaps farther than, Broughton had gone a decade earlier. Now he was back to cut some spars and to pick up whatever trade he might have missed.

The Indians who visited the *Lydia* brought with them medals stamped with a likeness of President Jefferson. They said they had got the objects from two captains named Clark and Lewis, who recently had come downriver with several men from the United States, wherever that was.

Jewitt understood from the broken talk that Lewis and Clark had just departed the estuary on their return journey overland. For reasons never divined, however, the Indians were not telling the truth. Only a few days before, the expedition had left this exposed northern shore for the sheltering woods on the south bank. They were over there at that very moment, out of sight in the trees, seeking a site for miserable winter quarters they would name Fort Clatsop. They would much rather have gone home by ship. They certainly could have used supplies.

The *Lydia* never knew this. Without having noticed in the gray mist the smoke from his countrymen's fires, Captain Hill put back to sea, unaware that he had missed a rendezvous with history.

Book Two

THE WARS OF THE BEAVER
KINGDOMS

1. To Claim a Continent

THE notion of a land passage across America was almost as old as the hope of a seaway through it. The search had even been mandatory for the French traders working out of Montreal; one provision under which they held their licenses was a promise that they would try locating a route to the Western Sea. That man-made requirement ended in 1763, when the Peace of Paris handed Canada to England. But in the place of royal decree came a sterner taskmaster—practical necessity. The American continent, as men were learning through incredible toil, was altogether too big to be economically supplied by canoe from the East.

It was a time of explosive energy. Into the vacuum left by the removal of the French fur monopolies rushed a mélange of opportunists, principally colonists from New England and Scots from the Highlands. Contemptuously called "Pedlars" by the long-established Hudson's Bay Company, these indefatigable newcomers drove themselves staggering distances through hellish difficulties to reach the Indians ahead of their competitors. Among them were two colonials who had first reached Canada with Jeffrey Amherst's army. One was Alexander Henry of New Jersey; the other, violent Peter Pond from Connecticut. Both helped pioneer the unstable amalgam of traders that named itself the North West Fur Company and became the Hudson's Bay Company's most formidable opponent. And both were among the first to realize that in the developing struggle victory could best be achieved by better transportation.

The Bay Company's initial advantage was enormous: it could bring its goods by ship to the western shore of Hudson Bay, whose longitude approximates that of Minneapolis, and then move a relatively short distance by canoe and portage into the fur-rich lands of the Athabaska district, in midwestern Canada. The port of the Nor'Westers, on the other hand, was Montreal, which lay as far east as New York City. From Montreal, goods had to be wrestled westward in huge freight canoes of four tons burden, up the twisting rivers, across ninety portages, along the windy north shore of Lake Superior to Grand Portage. At Grand Portage the ninety-pound "pieces," or bales, of goods and unprofitable provisions were back-packed nine miles, then reloaded into smaller, ton-and-a-half canoes, and taken to the winter depot at Rainy Lake. The next summer the *engagés* drove on through bogs, mosquitoes, rapids, and endless miles of flooded river to the Athabaska district. Only the French and the half-breeds—the ignorant, gay, enduring *voyageurs* of Canadian legend—could furnish the sinew that made the trade possible. And it began to look, when the routes grew longer, as if even their efforts would not be enough.

Attempts were made both through the government and through direct proposals to the Hudson's Bay Company to water down the latter's monopoly at least to the point of leasing to outsiders transit rights across the bay. These overtures were rebuffed. Meanwhile, far up by the turbid rivers and broad lakes of the Athabaska country, Alexander Henry and Peter Pond, of the North West Company were hearing from the Indians tantalizing rumors of navigable streams leading to salt-water seas. The geography that the men attempted to reconstruct from this welter of aborigine gossip was completely confused. They pointed rivers in the wrong direction and minimized the chill magnitude of the Canadian Rockies; and because they could not compute longitude, they thought they were farther west than they really were. Yet despite their mistakes they evolved a basic idea which, with variations, would guide nearly all future efforts to tame the Northwest, from John Jacob Astor's grandiose schemes to the Panama Canal: use the Pacific for supplying the new land.

Henry seems to have been the first to suggest, in 1781, the establishment of Pacific depots for facilitating the beaver trade of the interior. Three years later during a trip to Montreal Peter Pond picked up a copy of Cook's *Voyage*, together with rumors of Ledyard's attempts to reach Nootka and word of the Russian thrust across the North Pacific. Tremendously excited, he became obsessed with the idea of capturing a share of the sea-otter trade for his own company and of combining the Pacific trade to China with new supply lines to the interior. He even dropped hints, as did Henry, that Yankee ships and Yankee financing would be welcome (and it is not beyond possibility that these proposals became one more item in the Western thinking of

Thomas Jefferson). Nobody rose to the bait. The plans involved more cash than war-impoverished American merchants could produce, more risk than the cautious North West partners were willing to take. Disconsolately Pond went back to the wilds to ask more questions of the Indians, to draw more speculative maps on birch bark, to corral whoever would listen and then talk the long nights through in his bombastic, arrogant, electrifying way.

One of his listeners was a young Scot named Alexander Mackenzie.

Years later Mackenzie became Sir Alexander. He grew rich and correct. He commissioned a formal portrait of himself in impeccable broadcloth and starched linen, his wavy hair combed neatly back from a high, handsome forehead. He looked—and was—aloof, reserved. Because of these transformations it is difficult to picture him as ardently young, dreaming new adventures under the star-jeweled arctic night; bewhiskered, in greasy capote and moccasin pacs, licking bear fat off his fingers, roaring through drinking bouts when rare occasion presented.

He had been born in 1763 or 1764 at Stornoway in the bleak island of Lewis, one of the Hebrides. The family migrated to New York about 1774. When the Revolution erupted, the father joined the British navy and young Alexander was sent to Montreal. After a brief period of school he entered the employ of a firm that tried to buck the North West Company. Soon Mackenzie was dispatched by this firm to Detroit and from there to the interior, where he participated in a ruinous trade war that ended with the absorption of his organization by the North West Company. The gauge of his ability lies in the fact that his former competitors took him, aged twenty-three, into their hierarchy as a full partner and sent him with Pond to the man-killing Athabaska Department.

If fifty-year-old Peter Pond held any hope of finding the way to the Pacific himself, the chance vanished when his men became involved in a murder and he, as their bourgeois in charge, was recalled. Immediately Mackenzie picked up the torch.

On June 3, 1789, he left the new fort that he and his cousin Roderick had just completed on the shore of Lake Athabaska. In his canoe were five voyageurs and the squaws of two of them. In accompanying canoes were more Indians and a trader bound for Slave Lake. Though travel was laborious because of rains and rapids, the tiny fleet nonetheless reached Great Slave Lake within a week, just as the ice was breaking. Spring gales blowing across the three-hundred-mile expanse of water whipped up oceanlike waves; ice floes heaved and split. In spite of it Mackenzie inched a way around the shore to a huge outlet river. It pointed due west, the direction it must go to reach the Pacific at Cook's Inlet in present Alaska, as Pond believed it surely must. Leaving the trader at the lake, Mackenzie pushed down the strong current.

For three hundred miles it carried them west. Then dead ahead a white range of mountains rose across the horizon. The stream swung north, swollen to gigantic size by flooded tributaries and flowing at such headlong pace that it hissed like a boiling kettle. Northward, ever northward it rolled, until it split into the channels of its delta. Perplexed, Mackenzie took the middle way and on July 12 reached a broad, shallow body of water that at first he thought was a lake. Actually he had reached the Arctic Ocean.

For five hazardous days the men prowled the bay, touching at islands, dodging ice, even giving chase to a whale. They had coursed the second largest river on the continent to a hitherto unknown spot. What Mackenzie thought of the accomplishment is reflected in the name he gave the river as he turned toward home—the Disappointment. Other geographers approved a different name for the stream, for the territory through which it flows and the bay it enters, for the mountains that border it. All are now called Mackenzie.

Back at Fort Chipewyan on Lake Athabaska the young Scot shook off his discouragement and began to plan again. Another possibility remained. This was the Peace River, which flowed from the west to meet the Slave a few miles north of Lake Athabaska. Perhaps a canoe could be pushed up the Peace to its source, portaged across the height of land, and refloated on the far side in some stream that by all logic must reach the Western Sea. This time, however, Mackenzie was determined to travel better prepared. On his dash to the Arctic he had lacked not only proper instruments but the knowledge of how to use them, so that he could not draw a scientifically acceptable map of where he had been. This next exploration must be definitive.

For two years he labored doggedly to put his Athabaska Department in shape to leave. Then in the spring of 1791 he went with the furs down the interminable rivers, across the lakes, over the portages. In Montreal he took ship for London. It was his first visit to civilization in six grueling years; yet he did not, could not, relax. He was a man possessed. Into the few months available he must cram all the learning he would need. Avidly he pored over everything about the Northwest he could find—the guesswork of the maps, the myths of Jonathan Carver, the more factual accounts of Cook and Meares. He bought instruments, taught himself to make astronomical observations and calculate the results.

In April 1792 he boarded ship for Montreal. In a special canoe he pushed on ahead of the Nor'Westers' supply fleet and by August—incredible time—had reached Fort Chipewyan. The winter he passed three hundred miles up the Peace River (near the site of the present settlement of Peace River, Alberta), where two men dispatched during the previous summer by his cousin Roderick had started building a trading post.

By mid-April the prairies were greening. Gnats and mosquitoes began to swarm, and clerk Alexander McKay, out wandering with spring fever, picked a bouquet of pink and yellow flowers. When the river ice broke on April 25, an eager bustle commenced. Six canoes laden with furs and dried meat were sent downstream to Fort Chipewyan. At seven in the evening on May 9 another canoe, twenty-five feet long and loaded with three thousand pounds of food and equipment, was pointed up the Peace. In it with Mackenzie were a dog, six voyageurs (two of whom had gone with him to the Arctic), a pair of Indians to hunt and interpret, and clerk McKay.

Though the water was high, the first week's travel was ordinary enough. On May 17, much sooner than expected, the Rocky Mountains came into sight. The lift this gave the men's spirits disappeared two days later when the canoe nosed into Peace River Canyon.

For twenty miles the contracted flood howled between banks a thousand feet high. The men poled, towed, unloaded, portaged. They leaped from boulder to boulder where a misstep meant drowning. Rocks rolling down hillsides threatened to crush them. When snags punched holes in the maltreated canoe, they found dangerous perches on infinitesimal footholds, patched the hard-to-handle vessel, went on, broke it again, and once more patiently repaired the damage. If progress on one side of the flood was blocked, they somehow traversed to the other side while white cascades snarled at their heels. After two days of the most excruciating labor they called it quits, cut a kind of stairway up the green-timbered mountainside, and with the help of rope belays dragged the canoe out of the canyon. More days were spent hacking a roadway along the top of a ridge bordering the river, part of it through a dense growth of briars that had sprung up in an old burn.

On May 24 they were able to return to the river. The snow peaks of the Rockies loomed on either hand and the air was bitter. A week later the river forked. Acting on the advice of an old Indian who had visited the Peace River post during the winter, Mackenzie took the left-hand branch toward the south, now called the Parsnip. The voyageurs grumbled at the choice and felt their judgment vindicated when the Parsnip, too deep for poling, grew too swift for paddling and for nearly one whole day they had to drag themselves forward by clutching at branches overhanging from the banks.

Gradually they neared the headwaters, where any tributary might lead to a portage. Anxiously Mackenzie watched for Indians who could show him the proper route. Finally, on June 9, he caught up with three men, three women, and half a dozen children. The males were short-statured and round-faced, their long black hair hanging in wild disorder. The females, very dirty, wore as decoration a painted black stripe running under their eyes from ear to ear. They were timorous, never having seen white men before. But they had heard of white men, and they possessed iron points on their weapons.

Through his interpreters Mackenzie asked eagerly where the metal originated. Far to the west, he was told—an eighteen-day walk. There dwelt a tribe who obtained metal from a people living still farther to the west.

Mackenzie's heart sank. His party could not back-pack enough supplies for an eighteen-day walk through the dense forests; nor would his river-bred voyageurs listen to such a proposal. Besides, a land traverse that long would be useless as a supply route from the Pacific.

There *had* to be a westward-flowing river. He told the interpreters to ask the natives again.

The Indians just kept shaking their heads.

After a sleepless night he tried once more. Again the answers were negative and he was almost in despair until by chance he thought that perhaps the emphasis on "west" was the stumbling block. So now he had his interpreters ask simply about streams. Oh yes, the natives said, there was a river but not one that went west. The one beyond the mountains flowed south and did not enter the sea.

Mackenzie was elated. Not flow into the sea? Nonsense! Eventually any river on the far side of the mountains must turn west to the Pacific. These poor creatures had never traveled far enough along it to know. But they could show him how to reach its upper tributaries.

Inducing one of the natives to serve as guide, the whites crossed a portage 817 paces long between two small lakes and so reached a south-flowing stream that turned into pure hell. Waist-deep in icy water the men dragged the canoe over gravel bars, chopped out fallen timber, and at length lost the bulk of their ammunition and almost their lives in a wild wreck. The voyageurs balked. Warming them with food, rum, and appeals to their pride, Mackenzie charmed them into continuing. With a little poor bark they found nearby, with pieces of oilcloth and liberal applications of gum, they managed to repair the shattered canoe. By now it was so heavy from its layers of patches that two men could carry it no more than a hundred yards at a stretch. And devilish stretches they were—swarming mosquitoes, windfallen trees, morasses of mud tangled with roots.

At last the sweating travelers emerged from the tributary onto the main river. Later the stream would be called the Fraser, but Mackenzie used its Indian name, Tacoutche-Tesse. It was brownish-colored, sliding powerfully between monotonous banks of spruce and jack-pine forest. For a distance it encouraged the explorers by bearing west, but soon veered due south into the roaring water of Fort George Canyon.

Again they were traveling blind, for the guide had deserted one night when clerk Alexander McKay, the man assigned to watch him, had fallen asleep. Now, as the river kept stubbornly south, Mackenzie wanted to find more Indians possessed of local information. Occasionally the canoe passed deserted wooden houses different from anything east of the mountains, but no people appeared. When at last a meeting did occur it was almost disastrous. Sweeping around a bend, the canoe came suddenly on a group of Carrier Indians who were startled into letting fly a volley of arrows.

Appealing to Indians on hair trigger with alarm offered its peril, but Mackenzie directed his men to put him ashore. While one of his hunters slipped through the trees to cover him, he walked along the bank, displaying beads and mirrors. Finally he enticed two bolder souls to approach and through them reached the others.

The group spoke a language his interpreters could handle after a fashion, but the information was discouraging. The lower river was said to be unnavigable; the tribes along its bank were wickedly hostile. The way to reach the sea was to go overland, straight west.

Mackenzie refused to believe the reports. On down the river he drove, meeting more Indians who told him the same thing. At last acknowledgment overcame desire. His supplies of pemmican, powder, and ball were dangerously short. So was time. If he continued much farther he would not be able to buck a way back upstream before winter. And by now he was beginning to fear that the Tacoutche-Tesse reached far to the south, just as his first despised informants had said. Perhaps it might even be a tributary of the River of the West. [1] Yet he would not abandon his dream. The way to the sea described by the Carriers might never do as a supply route, but at least he could dip his hand into the ocean that by now had become a mania.

To reach the westward trail he had to return upstream and find a tributary known today as the Blackwater. The about-face perplexed the first group of Carriers the party had met. The strange white man had said he would not change his course and go overland, yet now he was coming back. Why? Alarmed afresh, the savages hurled new threats, then melted out of sight. This in turn dismayed the voyageurs, whose morale in no wise improved when Mackenzie was forced to cut rations to two meals a day.

The true measure of the twenty-nine-year-old Scot lies in the fact that during those uncertain days he kept fear from melting the party into disintegration. One method he used was to give the voyageurs something to do—building a new canoe to replace the hulk that had brought them here. In spite of indifferent bark, the replacement turned out to be better than its predecessor. This stirred the men's pride, and spirits lifted again as they pushed up the Blackwater.

Reaching the limits of navigation on July 4, they cached their canoe and such goods as they could not carry. Under loads approaching a hundred pounds per man, they slogged westward through timber and marsh and brawling streams. Rates varied from twelve to more than thirty miles a day. Drenching rain was a daily discomfort, the danger of getting lost in the tangled woods and mountains a continual worry.

After crossing a cold, barren pass and threading a way through the most enormous trees Mackenzie had ever seen, the party reached a village on the Bella Coola River. Here Mackenzie obtained canoes and paddlers. At first the change was exhilarating: the Indians were more superb navigators than even his voyageurs, and at night there was salmon to eat instead of niggardly bits of pemmican. But the respite was short. As the whites neared the sea the mountain-girt river divided into a bewildering series of channels. The natives grew poorer, less friendly. At one village an ax was stolen, and when Mackenzie as a matter of principle insisted on its return there was a moment of ugly tension before it was produced.

Late in the afternoon of July 19, so he later wrote without apparent emotion, "I could perceive the termination of the river, and its dis-

---

[1] Not the Columbia, of whose discovery by Gray the year before he was unaware, but the mythical stream. Mackenzie's recent studies of theoretical geography had led him to believe implicitly in the mapmakers' logic-bred River of the West.

charge into a narrow arm of the sea." That was all. The goal of prodigious effort, including a false cast clear to the Arctic; the consummation of man's westering drive—whatever it meant to him he does not say. He was a dour person, but surely not that dour. . . . On the twentieth, having borrowed another, leakier canoe, the little party rowed under leaden skies, at low tide, onto salt water. They fired guns at sea otter, missed. Tossed about by high swells, they landed on a dismal shingle. Another guide deserted; their spirits sank again. Glumly Mackenzie estimated the moment of their triumph: "twenty pounds weight of pemmican, fifteen pounds of rice, and six pounds of flour, among ten half-starved men, in a leaky vessel, and on a barbarous coast."

Nonetheless he pressed on, skirting inlets and islands. Along the way the party encountered fifteen Indians in three canoes. One savage was particularly insolent, grumbling that white men in a large canoe had lately been in the bay "and that one of them, whom he called *Macubah*, had fired on him and his friends, and that *Bensins* had struck him on the back, with the flat part of his sword." Though Mackenzie had no way of identifying the pair then, he later learned that "Macubah" and "Bensins" were Vancouver and his naturalist, Menzies, who had visited the vicinity less than two months before. And now Mackenzie's party must pay for the pique occasioned on that earlier visit. Reinforced by ten canoeloads of Indians from the village of the stolen ax, the truculent savages dogged the whites to an eventual camping place in a sort of natural fort scarcely large enough to hold them. At dark, after stealing various small articles, the natives withdrew.

By this time the voyageurs and the two Indian interpreters were in a gray funk, but their leader would not withdraw before he had made exact observations. Then, methodical even in his vanity, he mixed vermilion in melted grease and used it to inscribe in large letters on a bold rock, "Alexander Mackenzie, from Canada, by land, the twenty-second of July, one thousand seven hundred and ninety-three."

He almost didn't get back. From crisis to crisis he worked his way up the swift-flowing river. He outbluffed a press of dagger-armed savages in the village of the stolen ax, nursed a sick guide back to reliability, faced down and calmed the almost daily panic of his voyageurs. At last the Bella Coola pass dropped behind. On the Fraser, routine asserted itself, and the trip sank into the anticlimax of all exploration—the long slog home.

Two tremendous voyages . . . all they brought the North West Company was knowledge. Since it was not the sort of knowledge that buys beaver pelts, Simon McTavish and the other partners ignored it. For six years Mackenzie tried to fight their lethargy, tried to make them see that though his trips had not turned up an easy route to immediate riches the seed was there and with further exploration might be made to flourish. McTavish would not heed. Bitterly Mackenzie resigned, as other disgruntled partners were doing. He was not yet ready, however, to join in opposition to the North West Company. Rather, he went to England in the hope that there he might find means to implement his goal of claiming the entire Northwest for Britain.

By now he knew that Robert Gray had discovered the mouth of the Columbia River. Overlooking Vancouver's references to the Spanish discovery of another great river emptying into an arm of Juan de Fuca Strait, the Scot jumped to the very natural conclusion that the Columbia and his Tacoutche-Tesse were one and the same. With this misapprehension fixed in his mind, he set about writing an account of his journeys. To the book he appended a carefully matured plan for the future expansion of the fur trade. First of all, he wrote, Great Britain must secure the river approaches to the Western interior by establishing a boundary line "south of the Columbia." To stimulate trade on the Pacific coast existing monopolies must be relaxed: the East India and South Sea companies must permit other merchants access to the Pacific littoral and to China; and the Hudson's Bay Company must be urged to join other Canadian traders in a "commercial association" to develop the interior. If the Hudson's Bay people declined to associate, then at least the company must grant all comers transit rights across the bay, so that goods could be disembarked at the bay's western rivers and from their headwaters carried across to the "Saskatchiwine."

The latter river, the Saskatchewan, was now a paramount factor in Mackenzie's planning. The Peace River, as he had found, offered no easy way to the Tacoutche-Tesse; but surely exploration farther south via the Saskatchewan would reveal a usable route. This was to be a route not merely for travel but for binding the northern continent together. Bluntly he declared, "By opening this intercourse between the Atlantic and Pacific oceans and forming regular establishments through the interior and at both extremes, as well as along the coasts and islands, the entire command of the fur trade of North America might be obtained, except that portion of it which the Russians have in the Pacific." Before this iron grip American "adventurers" on the West coast "would instantly disappear."

Mackenzie meant to practice what he preached. In January 1802, shortly after the publication of his book, he formally laid the scheme before the Colonial Secretary, Lord Hobart. But the proposal was too bold, too injurious to established patterns. There were hemmings and hawings and the sop of fancy honors. In February Mackenzie was knighted by King George and lionized by London society, to the sour jealousy of Nor'Wester Simon McTavish back in Montreal. But nothing was done about the plan. Forced to let it lie in abeyance, Mackenzie returned to Canada. There he became the dominant figure in the new opposition popularly known as the XY Company, which was doing its best to crush McTavish and the North West firm.

Meanwhile his book was finding readers he knew not of. One was Thomas Jefferson, inaugurated only a few months before as President of the United States. Another was Jefferson's young secretary, Meriwether Lewis. They were disturbed. A boundary line for Britain *south* of the Columbia, south of Robert Gray's river . . . This needed watching.

2. "Ocian in View"

IN A secret message to Congress on January 18, 1803, Thomas Jefferson gave his answer not only to Mackenzie's proposals but also to America's increasingly obvious need to obtain more information about the far reaches of her continent. Let Congress, the President urged, appropriate twenty-five hundred dollars for an expedition that would ascend the Missouri and cross from its headwaters to those of the Columbia. While exploring the latter river the expedition would also be re-establishing the claim of the United States to Robert Gray's great discovery.

Twenty years of interest in the unknown West lay behind Jefferson's appeal. As far back as 1783 rumors of British colonial designs on the Pacific littoral had fired him to suggest, without avail, that George Rogers Clark hurry ahead of the recent enemy with an expedition. Three years later, while minister to France, Jefferson had listened sympathetically to John Ledyard's chimerical schemes; and in 1792 he had supported what turned out to be an ill-judged, ill-prepared transcontinental fumble by one André Michaux, a French botanist (and, as matters developed, a French secret agent).

By the time of his election to the presidency the problems of Western expansion had grown acute. Restless Americans were pouring across the Alleghenies into the Mississippi Valley. Friction with Spain on the far bank had produced increasing irritations, even though Spain at the turn of the century was too weak to pose a formidable threat. Napoleon, however, was something else; and one of Jefferson's first presidential crises came when he learned that France had wrested from Spain, at the secret Treaty of San Ildefonso, the entire Far Western territory known as Louisiana.

Napoleon's design was double-pronged: to re-establish France as a colonial power and, simultaneously, to deal England a mortal blow by seizing what was left of her New World territories, notably Canada. As a first step in the plan a French army sailed to the West Indies, ostensibly to crush rebellious Toussaint L'Overture. Jefferson, guessing the real purpose of the move, reluctantly contemplated a defensive alliance with England. Before the fear could take substance, however, yellow fever in Santo Domingo crippled the invading army. That disaster, plus other considerations beyond the scope of this work, led Napoleon to abandon his New World gamble. Surmising the change, Jefferson hurried envoys to Paris in hopes of buying New Orleans and, if luck broke right, the Floridas. There seems no reason to assume he counted as yet on acquiring Louisiana. Still, he was an opportunist, and beyond Louisiana (which ended at the Rockies) there remained Britain's threat to the Columbia basin. And so, after telling his private secretary, Meriwether Lewis, to brush up on such unsecretarial matters as natural science and the use of astronomical instruments, the President asked Congress for funds to send an exploring party into the Northwest.

Even in his secret appeal to the lawmakers Jefferson could not be completely candid. He labeled the project as "literary," that is, geographic and scientific. Having set up this window dressing for the courts of Europe, the President then faced squarely toward the harder-to-fool British fur traders in the upper Missouri Basin. If his proposed expedition found easy water transportation from western Canada into the Mississippi Valley, Jefferson told Congress, then much of the Northern trade in peltries could be diverted into American hands. Nor was this all. If the Missouri proved navigable within easy portaging distance of the Columbia and if American claims to the farther river were strengthened by overland exploration, then Mackenzie's grandiose scheme of cornering the fur trade of the Pacific would collapse. Even more important, the finding of a usable water route across the continent would place mankind's long-desired short cut to Cathay firmly in the grasp of the United States.

It is quite likely that the germ of all this had been in Jefferson's mind long before Napoleon's threat to Louisiana brought matters to a head. Otherwise, why had he, even before his inauguration, reached into the ranks of the army to hire Meriwether Lewis as his private secretary? As Jefferson well knew (for Lewis had been brought up on a plantation near the President's Virginia home), the young man had not been trained for paper work. As a boy Lewis had reveled in lonesome hunting and camping trips. When scarcely eighteen he had vainly tried to join André Michaux's abortive transcontinental venture. At twenty he had marched with the militia in a bloodless campaign to suppress a "rebellion" of whiskey-making farmers in western Pennsylvania. Entranced by the brisk maneuvering, he had then switched to the Regular Army and more serious maneuvers against the Indians in Ohio. He was a withdrawn, rather moody person, given to inward-looking agonies of self-analysis. But he was remarkably self-disciplined; and above all he was discreet—useful qualities for a secretary . . . or for a man about to be sent on a secret mission. In any event Jefferson went to more than ordinary lengths to locate the young army officer and bring him to Washington. For two years Meriwether Lewis lived as a member of the President's household. Thus when Congress acceded to Jefferson's request for an expedition to the Northwest the ex-lieutenant knew exactly what his mentor had in mind.

Always moodily thorough, Lewis at once faced the possibility that he might not survive the trek and would need a companion to finish the work. Various names occurred to him. The one he finally settled on was William Clark, a bluff, redheaded army captain under whom he had briefly served in Ohio. Though the association had lasted only a matter of weeks, it had fathered mutual respect. Promptly Clark accepted Lewis' offer of joint command.

Except in the matters of rugged health, army background, and love of the outdoors, the two captains were totally different. Four years the elder, redheaded William Clark was gregarious and matter-of-fact, whereas Lewis was reserved and idealistic. Though not as well educated as Lewis, Clark possessed perhaps an even greater fund of plain horse sense. Completely generous, he had no envy in him. For that matter, neither had Lewis. During the ensuing three years of enforced propinquity, much of it spent in extreme discomfort, the two men maintained extraordinary equanimity; they apparently never quarreled about anything whatsoever.

Well before the two captains and their hand-picked party were established in their first winter camp on the east bank of the Mississippi, directly across from the boiling discharge of the Missouri, astounding news reached them. Napoleon had sold not just New Orleans but all of Louisiana to Jefferson's envoys. Now the captains' mission assumed double import. All along the way the Indians they met must be made to understand the significance of the change in sovereignty.

In mid-May 1804 the party started up the Missouri. Five months of grueling labor with oars and cordelle brought them sixteen hundred miles upriver to what is now central North Dakota. Here, near the earthen villages of the sedentary Mandan Indians and of the Mandans' more widely roving neighbors, the Minnetarces, the whites would winter. Here, also, they found two Montreal squaw men, René Jessaume and Toussaint Charbonneau. Both voyageurs were promptly hired by the Americans as interpreters, though only Charbonneau would go on to the Pacific.

More French—this time a group of North West Company traders under François Laroque—appeared almost before the explorers had finished building their winter quarters of cottonwood logs. Relations between the parties were cordial but not entirely frank. Blandly, in an effort to find out what these Columbia-bound Americans were up to, Laroque asked if he could go along with them to the Pacific. With equal blandness Lewis and Clark said no. Then in February Laroque took a hurried trip to Fort Assiniboine in Canada. Ostensibly he went for supplies; undoubtedly he also wanted instructions about what to do next.

On his return the Frenchman had interesting news to impart. Simon McTavish, he said, was dead—jealous, grasping Simon McTavish, erstwhile head of the North West Company and Alexander Mackenzie's most bitter enemy. Now the Nor'Westers and Mackenzie's competing XY Company were going to amalgamate.

These bare facts Lewis noted in his journal. Unfortunately no word escaped through his pen about whatever speculations he and Clark indulged in on learning the surprising items. Yet they must have recognized some of the implications. With Mackenzie's star on the rise again, the Nor'Westers' push toward the Columbia would be resumed. Indeed, even under McTavish, there had been a start of sorts. In 1800–01, Duncan McGillivray, in conjunction with the company's great geographer, David Thompson, had made a futile attempt to cross the Rockies. Thompson's name, at least, was familiar to Meriwether Lewis. The Nor'Wester had visited the Mandans in 1797, and Lewis had just had the satisfaction of correcting the man's erroneous calculation of the villages' latitude and longitude. Whether or not Lewis also knew, through gossip with the Canadian voyageurs, of Thompson's abortive cast at the Rockies cannot be said. Probably he did, for the American was an indefatigable question-asker about the West. In any event, both he and Clark surely realized, on the cold February day when they heard Laroque's news, that finding a short, commercially feasible route to the ocean was now even more immediately urgent than when they had left St. Louis. [1]

About this time it dawned on the captains that they possessed an unguessed asset in the second wife of one of their interpreters, lecherous old Toussaint Charbonneau. The girl was sixteen, perhaps seventeen, years old. Her name, to use one of the variant spellings in the journals, was Sah-cah-gar-we-ah, later refined to Sacajawea. She was a Shoshone. Five years before Minnetaree raiders had surprised a camp of her people near the three forks of the Missouri River, at the foot of the mountains. As Sacajawea scampered wildly through a "Shole place" in the stream, hoping to find refuge on the far bank, a mounted warrior had swooped her up. During the next five years she had been passed from brave to brave, until Charbonneau had won her in a gambling game. Now she was about to bear her first child. When the delivery proved unusually painful, Lewis sent her, on René Jessaume's advice, some crumbled rattlesnake rattles to be swallowed in water. Whether or not the medicine helped, Lewis wrote, "I shall not undertake to determine, but I was informed that she had not taken it more than ten minutes before she brought forth."

For the young mother the meeting with Lewis and Clark was an introduction to immortality. Mountain peaks have been named for her; statues carved. No other Indian woman, Pocahontas not excepted, has been so romanticized. As debunkers tirelessly show, little of the adulation is deserved. Though the captains hoped she might serve as a guide, her knowledge of geography, even that of her own homeland, proved almost non-existent. Such usefulness as she possessed arose largely from the accident of her language and her sex; she could interpret, and her presence convinced suspicious tribes that the whites were peaceful or they would not have brought a woman along. Yet the acknowledgment of these limited functions does not hide a winsomeness and fortitude, a wide-eyed wonder in the unfolding world that lets Sacajawea emerge through casual references dropped by the expedition's various journal-

---

[1] One fact perhaps unknown to Lewis and Clark should be noted: Alexander Mackenzie was excluded from active management of the new company formed by the union of the North West and XY firms. But so far as broad policies were concerned this exclusion was immaterial. Mackenzie's demand for expansion would be heard through the voice of his disciple, Duncan McGillivray, a rising power in the new firm.

ists as a more definite personality than do some of the shadowy males who made the great trek with her.

Slowly the Mandan winter dragged by. The captains collected numerous botanical, zoological, and geologic specimens to send to Jefferson in the spring, along with detailed ethnological reports and geographic notes. The enlisted men hunted, built cottonwood dugouts for use on the upper river, and operated a blacksmith shop where they made iron implements that could be traded to the agricultural Mandans for corn. For diversion they danced to the fiddle of one-eyed Peter Cruzat, whose music enthralled every Indian tribe the party encountered between the Mississippi and the Pacific. And, of course, there was dalliance with the "handsome tempting" light-skinned, venereal-infected Mandan squaws. The fascination exerted on the curiosity-loving damsels of the wilderness by the shiny black skin of big York, William Clark's slave, has long since become a staple of Western folklore.

At last spring opened the river. On Sunday afternoon, April 7, 1805, the party's six homemade dugouts and two pirogues pushed against the swollen current. In addition to the two captains there were twenty-six soldiers, two interpreters, a Negro, an Indian squaw and her infant, and Lewis' huge Newfoundland dog Scammon. A year of hard discipline and shared accomplishments had welded the group into a tight, smooth-functioning, amazingly compatible unit. In the zest of their release, the men and captains thought they could cross the Divide, reach the ocean, and return to the Mandan villages by the following winter.

All too soon the estimate had to be revised. Nearly a month was spent dragging the boats and goods eighteen miles around the thundering Great Falls of the Missouri. Right there one of Jefferson's principal hopes collapsed. The river above the falls was mountain-swift and treacherous. When the weary men stumbled ashore to haul on the cordelle ropes, the flinty ground and endless cactus lacerated their feet. Continual falls on slippery stones resulted in painful sprains. Mosquito bites bloated wrists and faces. To make matters worse, the valley beyond the Great Falls bent south instead of continuing west, and the men's prodigious labor seemed to be bringing them no nearer their goal. In short, the upper Missouri was not practicable for commercial navigation, though inexplicably enough Lewis and Clark denied the unwelcome fact both in their journals during the trip and later in their reports.

Where the brawling stream split into three forks, the expedition turned up what the captains named the Jefferson River. Progress slowed to a snail's pace. Though Sacajawea was now recognizing landmarks, she still could not tell the worried leaders where to find a pass over the looming mountains. Worse, the whites had not yet glimpsed any sign of her people, the horse-owning Snake, or Shoshone, Indians.

Without horses the party could not cross the mountains before snow fell. And that meant disaster. On August 9 Lewis pushed desperately ahead with one of the interpreters, Drewyer (as the journals spell Drouillard), and with Privates Shields and McNeal. Behind him Clark, half crippled with a raging carbuncle on his ankle, kept the dugouts creeping onward among boulders, over gravel bars, through the willow-tangled channels of endless beaver swamps.

Two days later, deep in the mountains, Lewis spotted a lone, mounted savage. Lifting his blanket in the peace signal of the mountain Indians and calling *"Ta-ba-bone, Ta-ba-bone* [White man, white man]," he endeavored to entice the rider close. Private Shields, off to one side, did not notice the parley and blundered too near with his gun. The Indian bolted.

Wearily the four whites walked on. The next day they crossed a dividing ridge now known as Lemhi Pass and descended, Lewis wrote, to "a handsome bold running Creek of cold Clear water, here I first tasted the water of the great Columbia river"—a blithe assumption, since he had no way of knowing at the time where the handsome creek would lead him. And still there were no Indians.

That came the next day, August 13, when finally the quartet overhauled three terrified females. Through the women Lewis made contact with a migrating band of Shoshones under a chief named Cameahwait. Greetings were friendly, the Indians hugging the whites until "we were . . . all besmeared with their grease and paint." But when Lewis endeavored to persuade the band to take horses across the divide to the main party, the Indians grew frightened. It was all a trick. The white men were in league with the Pahkees (the Blackfeet) and were trying to lure the outnumbered Shoshones into ambush.

If the transcontinental venture had any single crisis, this was it. Shrewdly Lewis surmounted it. With just the right amount of insult he impugned Cameahwait's courage. He appealed to the greed of all the Indians by mentioning presents. But his most adroit weapon was curiosity. The whites east of the divide, he said, had with them a Shoshone woman and, even more amazing, a man whose skin was pure black. Finally he got the group strung out behind him. To encourage the starving Indians still more, he ordered Drewyer and Shields out to find meat. This aroused fresh alarm, and wary young warriors dashed after the men to make sure the whites really hunted. Fortunately Drewyer managed to kill two deer, and Shields an antelope. The hungry Indians attacked the raw meat "like a parcel of famished dogs," but even then Lewis could not subdue fresh outbursts of suspicion until he had handed his own gun to Cameahwait as an earnest of good faith.

By extraordinary coincidence Cameahwait turned out to be Sacajawea's own brother. No doubt the emotional impact of the famous meeting increased the whites' favor in the eyes of the chief. But it did not, as is sometimes said, prove decisive in persuading the Shoshone to hand over precious horses to the explorers. That motive came from Lewis and Clark, who promised that, if the expedition succeeded, other Americans would follow with trade goods, including guns to help the Shoshone fight off their mortal enemies, the Blackfeet.

That clinched it. Unfortunately most of the Indians' horses were at a village back on the west side of the divide and would have to be sent for. On hearing this the captains decided to split their group. Clark and eleven men went ahead to establish relations and to see whether the river below the village (the Salmon) was really as unnavigable as Lewis had already heard. Meanwhile Lewis and the other men stayed east of the pass to build pack saddles, cache the canoes and some of the goods, and conduct the interminable dickering for the vital animals.

Not until August 29 did the parties rejoin in the valley of the Salmon. Lewis' exertions had produced only twenty-nine horses—for baggage carrying and not, save in the case of the two captains, for riding. By this time Clark's laborious explorations had convinced him that the canyon of the Salmon, its waters "foaming & roreing through rocks in every direction," afforded no passage for canoes. Many miles to the north, however, as each leader had separately learned, was a trail used by the "Pierced nosed indians" in journeying to the Missouri. So northward the party bore, guided by a Shoshone Indian whom the men called Toby, and by Toby's son.

A short, rough passage through a dismayingly early snowstorm brought them from the Salmon watershed into the lovely, mountaingirt valley of the north-flowing Bitterroot. Here the whites met a band of amiable Flatheads (who, in spite of their name, did not follow the coastal practice of deforming their skulls). From these Indians they purchased several more "ellegant" horses. The captains also learned of trails leading directly across the Rockies to the Great Falls of the Missouri, only five or six days' march away. This information buoyed them afresh. Their own circuitous route from the falls to the Bitterroot had devoured nearly two months, an impossible handicap for transcontinental transportation. But perhaps these other trails . . . Exploration, however, would have to wait. Right now the party must drive desperately on to the West. Already ice was forming at night on quiet water; the frosted aspens gleamed gold. And the Pacific still lay an unguessable distance ahead.

The Lewis and Clark expedition has on occasion been dismissed as undramatic—nothing happened. One wonders if the men who spent the next ten days fighting the choked windfall of the Lolo Trail across present Idaho; who camped some nights without water and ate precious horseflesh in lieu of anything else; who struggled to retrieve pack animals that had rolled down the craggy mountainsides; who floundered in snow until even the uncomplaining Clark could write, "I have been wet and as cold in every part as I ever was in my life"—one wonders whether those men would agree that nothing happened. When at last they reached a Nez Percé village near the forks of the Koos-koos-kee River (the present Clearwater), they fell ravenously on Indian gifts of dried salmon and camas root. The new diet completed their debilitation. An acute dysentery laid nearly every man flat, despite Clark's dynamite doses of each purgative in his medicine kit.

Now that the explorers were again on navigable water, they were as anxious to be rid of their troublesome horses as once they had been to obtain the animals. Between violent attacks of cramps, they felled trees and burned out the interiors of five large dugouts. They branded and turned over to the safekeeping of the Nez Percés their thirty-eight remaining horses. On October 7, after caching their saddles and a bit of ammunition, they struck out for the great river that the Indians said led to the stinking lake. Two volunteer guides went along. Other red emissaries were dispatched ahead to spread word of the whites' coming, so that unprepared natives would not be startled into shooting. The flashing news brought continuous troops of savages riding down to both banks of the stream to watch the cavalcade and to follow along for miles, whooping and conversing happily.

The dugouts were moving now into a huge, melodramatic country. Beds of lava two thousand feet thick underlay the austere landscape. Vast, terraced canyons opened a way for the rivers—the Clearwater, then the powerful Snake (which Clark with amazing geographic acumen recognized as the parent stream of the distant Salmon). Finally the tiny fleet swung into the foam-flecked, green-tinted Columbia itself —a mighty expanse of bare hill and glaring water so enormous that one anticlimactic by-product was the fact that the sun-squinting natives whom the party met were nearly all subject to sore eyes that often turned blind.

The staple diet item of the Indians was salmon—fresh salmon, dried salmon, pounded salmon stored in pyramidal piles of rush baskets and traded to other Indians who came from hundreds of miles away. Flyblown salmon hung everywhere on ramshackle drying racks; decaying salmon stank to high heaven at the entrances to the long plank houses. Heartily sick of it, the whites bought from the villages they passed as many dogs as they could afford, a dish Clark never did learn to relish.

In part because the wayfarers were lucky but more because they were always careful, they lost only one canoe and no lives as they threaded the lava-pinched rapids of the Snake and portaged around the thundering Dalles of the Columbia. Below the Dalles their Nez Percé guides turned back and the last touch of familiarity went with them. The Indians they met next were squat, thieving, sullen, vermin-infested, often with malformed legs and flattened heads. There was also evidence of contact with white traders to the west—a brass kettle, blankets, sailors' pea jackets.

On November 7, 1805, Clark wrote exuberantly in his notebook, *"Ocian in view! O! the joy."* Actually he was looking at the yawning estuary of the Columbia rather than at the Pacific itself. The joy, too, was short-lived. Ever since passing the ferocious rapids where the Columbia broke through the big-timbered Cascade Mountains, the men had been soaked by fog at night and rain by day. More rain and more wind pinned them against the impenetrable underbrush and steep cliffs of the river's north shore, their wet beds spread on a rocky shingle scarcely large enough to hold the huddled party. Waves, tide, and drifting trees two hundred feet long threatened to crush the dugouts. When the miserable group tried to move camp, more waves overwhelmed them and they retreated into a dismal cove. There the only camping place they could find was on driftwood logs that at night went afloat on the rising tide.

Waves did not bother the Chinook Indians who inhabited the northern shore of the river. They paddled up in their high-prowed canoes through the worst of weather, gossiped, left fleas, stole trinkets, and casually paddled away again, "the best Canoe navigators," Clark admitted in his journal, "I ever saw." Among them was a one-eyed chief named Comcomly, eventually to become famous in the annals of the Northwest.

The sign talk and the garbled, sailor-taught English of the oil-smeared visitors seemed to indicate that a settlement of whites lay around the northern point. Hoping for supplies and perhaps ship passage home, Lewis went exploring. No settlement existed, of course, nor did additional searching of the exposed north shore reveal a suitable spot where the expedition could establish winter quarters of its own. On November 25, accordingly, the men crossed to the densely wooded southern bank. They were still prowling the swampy lowlands and tidal creeks, looking for a dry site, when the brig *Lydia*, with rescued John Jewitt aboard, put into the river mouth. The landfarers never knew of the ship's presence, though one of the reasons they had determined to stay near the coast rather than seek a more temperate camp farther inland was the hope of meeting a trading vessel. Why the Indians kept silent about the *Lydia*—and, indeed, why Jefferson sent no ship to meet his explorers—remain enigmas.

On December 3, while awaiting Lewis' return from a scouting trip, Clark recalled the words that the first crosser of the continent had printed on a cliff far to the north: "Alexander Mackenzie, from Canada, by land, the twenty-second of July, one thousand seven hundred and ninety-three." Moving out of the wind-lashed rain to the sheltered side of a huge tree, the American drew his knife. In the rough bark he carved, perhaps with conscious challenge, "William Clark December 3rd 1805. By Land from the U. States in 1804 & 1805."

Some distance south of that tree and within hearing of the breakers pounding the beach to the west, Lewis found, near a sluggish creek now called Lewis and Clark, enough high ground for a fort. The party floundered up to it through "bogs which the wate of a man would Shake for ½ an Acre." The men were racked with colds, stiff joints, boils. Yet in spite of their aches and the incessant, gale-driven rain, they were able to complete by New Year's Day, 1806, eight small cabins. These faced inward, their back walls joined by a strong stockade. Because the post was located in the land of the Clatsop tribe, the leaders named it Fort Clatsop.

The Indians promptly gathered around. To forestall the pilfering of useful trade goods for purchasing favors, the captains "divided some ribin between the men of our party to bestow on their favourite Lasses" —and then spent a good deal of time doctoring the boys for venereal diseases. There was no other diversion. Idleness, fleas, wretched weather, tasteless elk meat brought with great labor through the swamps and trees . . . the days stretched endlessly. One party went to the coast to make salt. Another group, including Sacajawea, accompanied Clark to the ocean in hopes of securing blubber from a dead whale stranded on the beach. In March the last of the tobacco was gone. Dismally the men ground up bark to smoke, and even shredded and chewed the tobacco-impregnated handles of their pipe tomahawks.

As morale and health declined and the hope of meeting a vessel died completely, the captains determined on an early start home. After leaving with the Indians several papers announcing their crossing (one of which shortly reached the *Lydia*, which had been trading along the coast all winter); and after purchasing a superb Indian canoe in return for Lewis' gold-laced officer's coat ("I think the U' States are indebted to me [for] another Uniform coat"), the party on March 23, 1806, pushed upriver. A short delay occurred while Clark examined the lower Willamette, whose island-hidden mouth the explorers had missed on their downward trip. More serious delays were occasioned by the spring floods and by the thievery of the Indians.

Salmon had not yet started to run and food was desperately short. At one point Clark had to frighten a huddled band of Indians into trading edible wapatoo roots by dropping a bit of sputtering fuse into their fire. For several days the whites camped on an island, drying enough venison to last until they reached the Nez Percés. Rain droned as they moved upstream, dripped as they made the grueling portage around the Cascades. Here a howling eddy sank one of their two priceless Indian canoes.

When they neared the Dalles, Clark and a small party went ahead to trade for horses. The Indians scornfully fingered the pathetic dab of trade goods the redheaded captain offered and then, as Clark put it in his journal, "tanterlized me." Grimly he persisted. By traveling from village to village, shivering blanketless throughout the cold nights in flea-ridden huts; by using lies, blandishments, and especially the crude doctoring of his medicine kit, he at last secured enough miserable plugs to start the party overland toward the friendly Nez Percés of the Clearwater.

The Nez Percés had kept reasonable care of the horses and goods left in their charge the previous fall. Although the whites now had the livestock necessary for pushing on toward home, deep snow on the upper Lolo Trail held them back for more than a month. On June 15 they tried to force a crossing, failed. A week later, helped by three

Indian guides, they made it, and on June 30 were once again camped in the Bitterroot Valley, eventually to be the western boundary of Montana.

Here Lewis and Clark split forces. Lewis was to test the transportation possibilities of the direct route between the Bitterroot and the Great Falls of the Missouri. Clark meanwhile was to retrace their outward journey's roundabout route as far as certain caches, then cut overland to the Yellowstone and examine that great river.

It was on Lewis' venture that the only serious violence of the expedition occurred—a violence whose inadvertent aid to the North West Company the American never knew. The trouble erupted on the Marias River, east of the Continental Divide. After crossing the mountains, Lewis took three of his small force northward to determine whether the headwaters of the Marias interlocked with the Saskatchewan and so would provide a canoe route for diverting Canadian furs to the Missouri. The Marias, he found, did not. Disappointed, he turned back toward the Missouri. Along the way a small party of the Piegan tribe of Blackfeet Indians endeavored to steal the whites' guns and horses. In the ensuing scuffle two warriors were killed, one by Lewis. Fearing that the surviving Indians would bring reinforcements, the Americans fled by forced marches to the Missouri.

There was no immediate pursuit. But as word of the killings spread among the confederated tribes of Blackfeet, the Indians grew enormously excited. That winter while women relatives of the slain warriors wailed in the lodges, the chiefs passed pipes back and forth around the council fires. War drums throbbed. Passion fed on itself, and when the trails opened in the spring the Blackfeet surged southward to watch the Missouri, hoping to find Americans and wreak vengeance. And so it happened that the route along the North Saskatchewan to the mountains was left open.

For more than a year now David Thompson of the North West Company had been planning to further his company's new policy of western expansion by making a second attempt to cross the Rockies. One of his principal obstacles had been the Blackfeet. The Blackfeet had no intention of letting British goods—especially British guns—reach the Indians beyond the mountains. But this summer the Blackfeet were watching the Missouri. Smiling dourly, Thompson pushed unmolested up the North Saskatchewan, bound for the land that drained into the Western Sea—a rich and varied land that might be held by those who occupied it first.

Land that could be occupied and held—the bringing of this awareness to the United States was Lewis' and Clark's enduring accomplishment. Their immediate objectives, other than valuable scientific findings, had not been realized. There was no riverway for diverting the fur trade into American hands. There was no practical water route to speed commerce across the continent and on to China. But although exploration had ended those dreams, the two captains had planted a more permanent reality in the nation's consciousness. From now on no American would ever forget the exhilarating sweep of the continent on which he lived. The Northwest would no longer be pictured merely as a dim coastline offering a few savage ports of call for a handful of sea peddlers. It was land, huge and varied and rich. As such, it would henceforth always be, in one way or another, desirable.

3. The Star Man

EVEN today, a century after David Thompson's death, men still argue about his accomplishments. He left one superlative monument, a topographical map of the Canadian West that prepared the way for countless settlers. Yet some Canadian detractors have insisted that the political map of their country would be far different if David Thompson's timidity and dilatoriness had not let British control of the Oregon country slip through his fingers. With equal ardor, admirers retort that Thompson's aim in Oregon was beaver fur, not territory. And still others, discounting both trade and patriotism, insist that the man's sole mistress was science, beloved with a passion so pure that even the Indians recognized it and named him Koo-Koo-Sint, The Man Who Watches Stars.

Product of a London charity school, apprenticed at the age of fourteen to the Hudson's Bay Company, David Thompson had little background for so abstract a love. Most of the mathematics he needed he taught himself. The rudimentary techniques of the craft—the handling of sextant, chronometer, compass, and artificial mercury horizon —he learned one winter on the icy Canadian prairies from the Bay Company's head surveyor.

Some ungaugeable yearning found its fulfillment in the clean precision of those simple instruments. Night after night, while his companions slept off the fatigue of the day's journey, Thompson was awake, sighting the stars and jotting down the inarticulate figures which somehow told what he had seen. When winter immobilized his travels he made his computations and roughed out his maps. To obtain more freedom for his beloved work, he left the Hudson's Bay Company for the more aggressive Nor'Westers. In 1804, aged thirty-four, he became a full partner in the latter company, a recognition of both his abilities as a trader and of the almost incalculable miles he had surveyed from the Mandan villages on the Missouri northward into the tangled waterways of Athabaska.

That same year—1804—the Nor'Westers ended their feud with Mackenzie's XY Company and began thrusting westward. Simon Fraser in 1805 moved far up the Peace River and established the first British post beyond the Rockies. The next year, in 1806, Thompson was ordered to open up still more trading territory by crossing the range somewhere beyond the headwaters of the North Saskatchewan, scene of his abortive 1800–01 explorations with Duncan McGillivray.

The Piegans, who might have stopped him, were busy watching the Missouri for Americans; and on July 25, 1807, after an uneventful winter of preparation, Thompson led his tiny party, including his half-breed wife and three small children, into a peak-surrounded gap atop the Continental Divide. In his journal he was content to call the spectacularly beautiful spot by the unimaginative name of Mountain Portage. [1] Yet poetry enough, of his own sort, filled him at that climactic moment. The Pacific slope! As he looked down the green hills at Blaeberry Creek, foaming steeply westward, he wrote in his journal, "May God in his mercy give me to see where its waters run into the ocean" —a prayer he did singularly little, during the next few years, to fulfill. And therein lies the strangeness of the man: the split between desire and doing.

Blaeberry Creek led the wayfarers to a huge river surging northwest. Since Thompson knew that the Columbia flowed into the sea far south, not north, of where he then stood, he had no reason to guess that he had reached the great River of the West. Moreover, as he had learned from Kootenay Indians slipping fearfully across the Divide to trade for guns with which to fight the Blackfeet, the river at his feet headed in two beautiful lakes a hundred miles to his left, or south. A scant mile beyond the upper of those lakes was another huge stream. This second stream flowed due south; and by logic should be the Columbia. (Actually it was the Kootenai.) In any event the Indians whose trade he wanted to develop lived in that direction. Up the Columbia he went, to a magnificent site near the outlet of the lower of the river's headwater lakes.

---

[1] Later it would be named Howse Pass after a Hudson's Bay man who in 1809 crossed it in a belated effort to spy on Thompson's activities west of the mountains.

There, where lush meadows break the dense forests that roll between the Rockies and the tumultuous snow peaks of the Selkirks, he built a post called Kootenae House. [2] He had only eight French-Canadian workers with him; and, as clerk, a violent, red-whiskered six-foot four-inch mountain of man named Finan McDonald. Their hands were full. Between hewing timbers and digging foundations, they had to run down wild horses for food. That fall they were also forced to outlast a siege by angry Piegan Indians, who swarmed revengefully across the pass after learning that Thompson had slipped west behind their backs and was selling guns to enemy tribes beyond the mountains.

Another, less immediate threat came from what is still one of the unsolved mysteries of the Northwest. In the fall a grinning Kootenay Indian handed Thompson a letter dated Fort Lewis, Yellow River, Columbia, July 10, 1807. Signed by a Captain Perch and a Lieutenant Roseman, the missive sternly laid down what purported to be United States regulations Thompson must follow in his trading. During Christmas week another letter of similar tenor arrived by Indian hands from a Lieutenant Jeremy Pinch at Poltito Palton Lake. The first note Thompson ignored. The second he answered via Indian bearer, saying that he would pass Pinch's letter on to the North West Company's directors. Mildly he added, "If prior discovery forms any right to a country, Lieut. Broughton of the British Navy many years ago explored the Columbia for 120 miles."

Nothing more was heard of the matter. Investigation by curious historians has turned up in United States records no such names as Fort Lewis, Yellow River, Poltito Palton Lake, Roseman, Perch, or Pinch. One explanation suggests that American trappers, learning of Thompson's approach, devised the names and the letters in an effort to bluff him out of the country. If this is true, then a small facet of our history needs revising. So far as records show, the first American to cross the Divide after Lewis and Clark was Andrew Henry, who in 1810 built a short-lived post fifty miles west of the Teton Peaks, on Henry's Fork of the Snake, in present Idaho. Yet in 1807, three years before Henry's advent, someone who must have been west of the Divide knew exactly what David Thompson was up to.

In the spring of 1808 the Canadian made his first attempt to unravel the bewildering geography of the area—as complex as any on the continent. After threading the lakes above Kootenae House (today they are called Windermere and Columbia Lakes) he and his voyageurs

---

2 Kootenae is Thompson's spelling. Canadians use Kootenay; United States geographers prefer Kootenai.

portaged across the topographically strange, mile-wide flat that separates the north-flowing Columbia from the south-flowing river of which the Indians had told him. (Eighty years later a steamboat canal would connect the two rivers at this point.) This new stream, the Kootenai, led into what is now the northwestern corner of Montana, bent west through a rugged canyon—and suddenly swung north. Mystified, Thompson left part of his men at a temporary trading camp near the site of present Bonners Ferry, Idaho, and pushed downstream to Kootenay Lake. There he learned from the Indians that the river broke tumultuously through the lake's mountainous west border and soon joined another vast river flowing . . . south again!

Another southbound river! Was it Mackenzie's Tacoutche-Tesse? Or had the north-flowing stream on which he had built Kootenae House somehow got itself pointed south after hundreds of miles of flowing north (as is the case)? Or was he now faced with a hitherto unsuspected river?

He made no attempt to learn, partly because of circumstances and partly because of lack of time. Far and wide the swollen Kootenai had broken out of its banks. Indians whom Thompson had counted on meeting for trade were "unable to come here on account of the flooding of the country and thus all my fine hopes are ruined." Furthermore, it was time now to send what furs he had secured to the company's central depot at Rainy Lake House, near present International Falls, Minnesota. Though one of his men might have done the job, Thompson decided to go himself. It was an arduous trip thousands of miles long by horse and canoe, and he had to drive remorselessly in order to be back at Kootenae House by fall. No doubt the effort was good business, but it took him across land he knew like the palm of his hand. Meanwhile the Columbia flowed on unexplored.

Far to the west, gloomy Simon Fraser was making his own attempt to solve the puzzle of the Northwest's erratic rivers. Uninterested in geography except as it related to trade, the squat, bushy-haired trader was being purely utilitarian about it. Transportation difficulties were swallowing the profits of the three posts he had opened since 1805 in New Caledonia, as he called the wildly beautiful lake region beyond the headwaters of the Peace River. As he brooded over the problem, his thoughts kept turning to the old dream of supplying these Western lands via the Columbia or, as he thought, the Tacoutche-Tesse.

In Fraser's jealous mind (his journals are peppered with slurs on Mackenzie's abilities) the great Sir Alexander had been too easily frightened off the Tacoutche-Tesse, or, as it is currently called, the Fraser. Now that Lewis and Clark had reached the Western Sea, it was high time that some Britisher completed the record of the great river, and who better than Simon Fraser?

In late May 1808, after building Fort George at the confluence of the Tacoutche-Tesse and Nechaco, he began his journey with a far stronger party than the company had ever granted to Mackenzie or Thompson. Twenty-four men rode the four canoes: two Indian interpreters, nineteen voyageurs, and three "gentlemen"—Jules Quesnel, from whom both a town and a river in British Columbia would take their names; wasp-tempered John Stuart, who in later years would be the exasperation and galvanizer of New Caledonia; and Fraser himself.

In triumph they passed the southernmost point reached by Mackenzie. Exultation faded, however, when the canoes slammed into frantic rapids, report of which had helped turn Mackenzie back. Some of this white water the voyageurs ran—"a desperate undertaking!" in Fraser's own words. Other sections they portaged around along canyon slopes so steep that at one point they had to plunge daggers into the ground for handholds. Finally they abandoned the canoes altogether and struggled ahead on foot under ninety-pound packs.

Temporary relief came when they emerged into a beautiful valley where a huge blue-green river from the east was swallowed by the muddy current of the main Tacoutche-Tesse. Mistakenly thinking that his partner David Thompson had built Kootenae House on the headwaters of this tributary stream, Fraser gave it the name it still bears, the Thompson.

At the junction of the Thompson and the Fraser, the foot-weary voyageurs secured Indian canoes and took to the river again. Almost at once the canyon deepened; the water grew wilder than any they had yet seen. In mounting fear they dragged their canoes along a fantastic Indian trail that zigzagged from ledge to cliff, climbing tree trunks and frail ladders of willow withes. Then, sooner than Fraser had anticipated, the river bent west. The land smoothed to a heavily forested valley where hostile savages, massed in their plank villages, pounded drums and brandished war clubs. Even more dismaying, the river now split into a maze of channels—obviously a delta. Fraser calculated his latitude. He was just north of 49°. The mouth of the Columbia, he knew, lay close to 46°. Bitterly he wrote, "This river is, therefore, not the Columbia. If I had been convinced of this when I left my canoes, I certainly would have returned."

Not the Columbia . . . and definitely not suitable for transport. Where, then, was the Columbia? Could it be one of David Thompson's discoveries? If so, would it furnish the desired opening to the sea?

Strangely and inexplicably, Thompson still made no effort to learn. This does not mean he was idle. Quite the contrary. Following paths scouted out by Finan McDonald and a volatile half-breed named Jacques Finlay (whose nickname Jocko is still borne by a Montana valley), he pushed south from the horseshoe bend of the Kootenai River to Pend Oreille Lake in today's northern Idaho. After building Kullyspell House on the lake's eastern shore, he turned eastward up Clark Fork River and in present-day western Montana built Saleesh House.

Thus anchored, his life settled into arduously routine trading ventures. After all, trading was his company's business. He possessed the kind of iron conscience that drives a man harder than can any outside monitor; and when he found himself buried in the wilderness, far beyond any voice that might say him nay, he perhaps felt doubly bound to hew close to the money-making duties that meant so much to the partners in Montreal. Perhaps, too, as middle age settled on him, he no longer felt the yearning need to drive on and on and on—though each summer he imposed on himself the exhausting, familiar trip over Mountain Portage to Rainy Lake and back. Between these eastern trips he could assuage such old stirrings as he did feel with minute data about the land and weather around his mountain posts. While traveling one thirty-six-mile stretch of the Kootenai River, for example, he recorded in his notebook no fewer than eighty observations.

He seems to have been reasonably content. Certainly he enjoyed the Indians among whom he was now located, particularly the misnamed Flatheads, or Salish. They were like the nomadic tribes he had known as a young man on the plains, colorful in beaded, quilled, and fringed buckskins and shaggy buffalo robes. Meticulously clean, their persons and their mobile leather tepees were free of the ravening swarms of vermin that plagued the sedentary Indians of the lower Columbia and the coast—Indians, to be sure, whom Thompson had not yet seen. Their moral standards he admired: "[They] set a high value on the chastity of their women," he wrote approvingly; "adultery is punished by death to both parties." True, they joyfully tortured Blackfoot prisoners when occasion offered, but otherwise were amiable, truthful, upright—"a fine race, the finest I had seen."

These were traits that would appeal to David Thompson. The debauchery of the Indians which he had witnessed, while still in his teens, at the bleak posts beside Hudson Bay had sickened him; and he had resolved never to traffic with liquor in any form. When ordered to stimulate trade by importing alcohol among the mountain tribes, he had loaded the liquor on a notoriously fractious horse and soon had the satisfaction of seeing the kegs smashed among the trees. The cynicism and atheism of many of his fellow traders disturbed him. Deeply devout, he regularly penned in his journal, often with fingers stiffened by below-zero cold, his thanks to God for each day's favors. Whenever circumstances allowed, he seated his voyageurs on a convenient bank and in barbarous French read to them from his Bible, "adding," one listener remembered, "such explanations as he thought appropriate."

He was solid, stolid, dependable. And yet . . . for three years this seemingly dedicated geographer stayed away from the riddle of the Columbia. When he did push a short distance down the Clark Fork below Pend Oreille Lake, his motivation was not discovery but the locating of a route—he didn't find it—whereby he could avoid his old enemies, the Piegans.

The Piegans had known what they were about when they tried to keep the Kootenays from getting guns. For as soon as the Kootenays were armed they had gone on the warpath, triumphantly slaughtering several of their hereditary foe. Blaming Thompson, the Piegans revengefully crossed the mountains again, searching for him. When the trader started his annual trip east in May 1810 he missed them by a hair's breadth, at the portage between the Kootenai River and Columbia Lake. The respite was temporary. Well enough he knew that when he returned he would find them waiting for him at the paths leading up to the portage across the Divide.

4. Astor's Threat

AT RAINY LAKE HOUSE, which David Thompson reached that year on July 22, he picked up word of a far more dangerous threat to his company than angry Piegans. A German-born American named John Jacob Astor was preparing to invade the Northwest.

Although Astor had done extensive business with Thompson's company, it is unlikely that the geographer knew the American personally. Yet surely Thompson had heard of Astor's phenomenal career: how, after fleeing his father's butcher shop in Waldorf, Germany, and tarry-ing briefly in an uncle's music store in London, he had reached New York City at the age of twenty with a stock of musical instruments to sell on consignment; how he had tramped New York State with a pack of trinkets on his back to buy furs first from farmers and then from the Iroquois; how gradually he had begun purchasing pelts in Montreal and disposing of them through English connections even more advantageously than could the London agents of the North West Company. The former German's touch was magic. His music store became a general store, where he dispensed, among other things, oriental silks, nankeens, tea, fans, cloves, nutmeg. Soon Astor had his own ships plying to China. Concurrently he formed the American Fur Company, and then extended his influence into the Great Lakes region by taking over a Canadian firm in which several North West partners had been interested. Inevitably his gaze had reached from there on across the continent to the shores of the ocean his ships were already sailing.

The Canadians themselves may have given shape to his ideas. On his annual buying trips to Montreal, Astor often stayed at the home of Alexander Henry the elder, pioneer Nor'Wester who, with Peter Pond, had first envisioned expediting the Western fur trade through Pacific ports. Undoubtedly Astor also knew of Mackenzie's elaborations on the plan; and when the first reports of the Lewis and Clark expedition were published the canny merchant saw how a transcontinental fur monopoly could be implemented through American as well as through Canadian rivers. Furthermore, Astor could take beaver pelts and sea-otter skins directly into Canton and swap them for tea, whereas the Nor'Westers could trade there only under license from the East India Company—an expensive stricture that Mackenzie, now living in England, was earnestly trying to remove.

To all this Astor added an idea new to the Canadians—the Russian trade in Alaska. For an appropriate fee Astor ships would first haul goods to the Russian-American Fur Company settlements near the Arctic and then transport Russian skins to Canton, a port from which citizens of the czar were still excluded. The Russian consul general in New York had already acceded to the plan in hope that Astor would freeze out the fly-by-night coastal peddlers who smuggled arms and liquor to the murderous Alaskan natives. In return Astor was to receive a free hand on the Columbia. This was no empty consideration; Nikolai Rezanov, governor of the Russian-American Company, had already advocated seizing the river. Indeed, only the inability of Rezanov's scurvy-ridden crew to cross the Columbia's treacherous bar in the summer of 1806 had kept the governor from personally selecting a site for his proposed post. Already, too, Ivan Kuskov was snooping about northern California and soon would start building Fort Ross a short distance north of San Francisco Bay. A Russian move to absorb the fur trade of the entire Northwest coast of America remained, in short, a possibility Astor dared not ignore.

Meanwhile Fraser and Thompson had crossed the Rockies. In an effort to neutralize the Canadians, as he had the Russians, Astor now suggested that the North West Company join him in his grandiose scheme.

Join *him* in *their* plan! Contemptuously the Nor'Westers refused. Undeterred, Astor went ahead on his own, forming a corporation which he called the Pacific Fur Company. To man his proposed fort on the Columbia, he brazenly hired away from the North West Company some of its best voyageurs, brightest clerks, and even partners or erstwhile partners—notably David Stuart and his nephew Robert Stuart; Duncan McDougal; barrel-bodied Donald McKenzie (a cousin of Sir Alexander's, though the names were spelled differently); and Alexander McKay, who had gone on Mackenzie's great trip to the Pacific.

When David Thompson arrived at Rainy Lake in July 1810 the defecting Nor'Westers were already preparing to start for the Columbia. Huge Donald McKenzie was recruiting voyageurs to cross overland along Lewis and Clark's old trail. The Stuarts and Duncan McDougal were heading south with a party of clerks and voyageurs to New York, there to embark on Astor's ship *Tonquin* for a sea trip around the Horn. Belatedly alarmed, the Nor'Westers in both Montreal and London were now trying to block the threat by hurrying letters to their government, protesting that the Columbia country belonged to Britain by virtue of Mackenzie's crossing, Vancouver's survey, and Broughton's examination of the lower river: "No establishment of the States . . . should therefore be sanctioned."

It is inconceivable that David Thompson, a wintering partner of the company and the man closest to the scene of the developing conflict, did not pick up word of these developments at Rainy Lake. But whether or not he was instructed to race the Astorians to the mouth of the Columbia and set up an establishment before they could arrive is something else. As the Nor'West partners well knew from the posts they had defiantly built cheek by jowl against competing forts of the Hudson's Bay Company, prior occupancy of itself guaranteed nothing. Government, not individual, action would ultimately settle title to the

Columbia. Still, a log house on the river might prove useful by providing a bargaining point during coming negotiations; and so Thompson may have been ordered to hurry. Today there is no way of telling. Besides, the question is immaterial. Even if his crossing did start out as a race with the Astorians, the Piegans soon spoiled it.

He began vigorously, though perhaps he was mainly interested in outpacing winter. By mid-September his four heavily laden canoes had pushed up the North Saskatchewan as far as Fort Augustus (near present Edmonton, Alberta). Here, while the canoes went ahead, Thompson paused to visit his family.

Several miles above the uppermost fort of Rocky Mountain House, Piegans caught up with the laboring canoes and turned them back. Word of the blockade missed Thompson, who was riding horseback along a short cut to an appointed rendezvous with the voyageurs. Fortunately he discovered what had happened just before the Indians discovered him. Pell-mell he galloped away to a hiding place in a dense copse of trees—the principal source of later accusations of cowardice, though under the circumstances the episode might well be justified as discretion.

Finally, after an involved comedy of errors, a confederate at Rocky Mountain House got the Piegans roaring drunk, thus enabling the voyageurs to slip past and rejoin their bourgeois. By now Thompson had had enough of the Saskatchewan. He decided to strike northward through heavily timbered country, where plains-bred Indians like the Piegans rarely ventured. His goal was the Athabaska River. By following this stream into the mountains he could reach an unguarded pass which Nipissing and Iroquois trappers had recently discovered.

Extra men, twenty-four horses, and several "leather tents" (tepees) were hurried to him from Rocky Mountain House. For a month the reinforced party wearily chopped passageway through old burns, windfall, and tangled scrub. On November 29 they reached the Athabaska River and ascended it to the vicinity of Jasper Lake, in what is now Jasper National Park. Though temperatures reached thirty-two degrees below zero, there were as yet only six inches of snow on the ground.

Finding a good meadow, the voyageurs built huts for shelter and settled down for what seems a leisurely month while they assembled dogs and prepared snowshoes and a few small sleds. Records are not clear, but it seems that some of Thompson's men deserted him. In any event he was not able to move his full stock of goods across the mountains but was obliged to leave part behind in charge of a clerk named William Henry.

With a hand-picked crew, fortified by what today seems foolhardy confidence, Thompson set out to cross the Canadian Rockies in the bitter-cold month of January 1811. Four days of brutal toil brought the small party to timber line. Ahead, pinched between a green-tinted glacier and an ice-toothed peak, a desolate swell of snow rose to the glittering Divide. In dismay the voyageurs pointed out that they could not possibly cross that horror in a single day's run. Ignoring the plaints, Thompson ordered them to pile firewood on the sleds and keep going. Not until the Northland's early winter dusk began to close in did he stop for the night.

As soon as camp was pitched he slogged ahead to examine the morrow's route. Returning, he found the voyageurs trying to learn the depth of the snow by probing with a twenty-foot pole. Sarcastically he asked them what good the knowledge would do them; they would be better off resting. But there was little rest that night. The firewood thay had packed with them (including the pole) proved insufficient, and long before dawn they were shivering forlornly under the diamond brilliance of an unclouded sky.

Early the next morning they crossed the Divide to a downslope so steep that the sleds broke out of control and piled with the dogs against trees and rocks in dismaying tangles. A week of such rigorous travel brought them to the confluence of the Wood and Canoe rivers with the Columbia. At this point the Columbia, after flowing northward for nearly two hundred miles, makes an abrupt horseshoe bend around the Selkirks—the first of its so-called Great Bends—and plunges south.

By deductions he never divulged Thompson had at last decided that this river *was* the Columbia. But though he knew the sea-borne Astorians must be nearing its mouth, he decided (so he wrote later) that his party was too small to attempt journeying down the winter-locked river just then. Upstream he went, planning to engage more personnel at his trading posts in Idaho and Montana.

The wet snow was hip-deep; the dogs could scarcely travel. When five days' desperate effort took them practically nowhere, the men mutinied. Helplessly Thompson returned to the mouth of the Wood River and announced they would wait there until travel conditions improved. During the night several of the men deserted and slipped back over Athabaska Pass. Seeing that he was in for a long stay, Thompson sent two more out with a message written on boards, asking William Henry to forward supplies. Meantime the bourgeois and his two remaining voyageurs waited out the dreary days in a twelve-foot hut constructed of cedar shakes. Their time was spent in hunting and in splitting pliable laths of cedar wood for building a canoe twenty-five feet long. Not the weather or the loneliness oppressed Thompson most. Rather it was the enormous size of the trees that turned winter daylight into perpetual dusk. "We were pygmies," he wrote; "in such forests what could we do with Axes of two pounds weight?"

In mid-April, though three feet of snow remained on the ground and he had but one dog left, he determined to make another attempt to reach his posts. The next two months are staggering even to imagine. Slowly the men toiled up the rapids, sometimes wading beside their canoe in "excessive cold Water" and sometimes towing it from the bank on snowshoes. Generally they camped on snow. They were always hungry. Spring rains chilled them; one man was afflicted with snow blindness. Helped by the dog, they portaged two and a half miles across the rotten ice of Kinbasket Lake amid some of the loveliest scenery on the continent . . . which they did not notice. In May matters eased when they met a few Nipissing and Iroquois trappers whom Thompson was able to hire. But as the snow receded the water rose and mosquitoes came out in swarms.

At the Kootenai the battered canoe was abandoned for horses. These presented their own difficulties as the party floundered through swamps and spring freshets to Saleesh House on Clark Fork. To their dismay they found the post abandoned. After leaving notes for Astor's overland party in case the Americans came that way, Thompson turned downstream. Kullyspell House at Pend Oreille Lake was also empty. Finally, in mid-June, the vanished hunters were located at Spokane House, a new fort built during the winter by Jocko Finlay and Finan McDonald nine miles below the present city of Spokane.

For three days Thompson rested at Spokane House, approving the fort's location at the junction of the Spokane and Little Spokane rivers, where multitudes of Indians came to catch and dry fish. Then, borrowing horses, he rode northwest to an even more famous fishing spot, Kettle Falls on the Columbia (now submerged under Franklin D. Roosevelt Lake). Here Indian fishermen hung kettle-shaped baskets on the end of poles close to the falls; salmon trying to jump the thundering cataract fell back in incredible numbers into the primitive traps.

At Kettle Falls, Thompson built another cedar canoe. On July 3 he and eight men at long last cast off for the mouth of the Columbia. As he traveled through the dwindling pines into the vast barrens, as he fought through the lava rapids and portaged around the occasional boiling cascades, he did not act like a man in a hurry. Rather, he acted like a canny trader building good will for the future. Whenever he encountered Indians he stopped, sometimes in the face of hostile demonstrations, passed out British flags, and added eloquent harangues about what the North West Company was soon going to bring the savages . . . if they were good.

At the mouth of the Snake (Sawpatin, in Thompson's phonetic rendering of the Indian name) he set up a small wooden post and attached to it a half sheet of paper bearing a sweeping declaration:

Know hereby that this country is claimed by Great Britain as part of its territories and that the N.W. Company of Merchants from Canada . . . do hereby intend to erect a factory in this place for the commerce of the country around. D. Thompson. Junction of the Sawpatin River with the Columbia. July 9, 1811.

Well, at least it was a gesture. Yet he must have realized that more than paper gestures would be necessary to forestall men who had been trained along the same hard trails that had trained him.

A week later, on July 15, wind-whipped waves on the broadening Columbia forced the group to land and portage across a narrow, rocky peninsula known even then as Tongue Point. From its far side Thompson detected, against the green wall of forest two or three miles ahead, the rude beginnings of a settlement, named Astoria after the man who envisioned but never saw it. With thoughts he did not trouble to record the Canadian spruced up his clothes, made sure that the British flag was flying from the stern of the canoe, and had his voyageurs sweep him smartly to the dock.

A heterogeneous crowd ran to the river edge to see the newcomers: Scottish clerks, their native burr still strong on their tongues; French Canadians, whooping their patois; brown Kanakas, imported as workmen from the Sandwich Islands; bandy-legged Chinooks, peering curiously out beneath deformed, sharply sloping foreheads. Three erstwhile Nor'Westers stood at the front of the throng: Duncan McDougal, David Stuart, and David's nephew, Robert. Old friends, former partners—they welcomed Thompson boisterously and hurried him into their private quarters, where his own abstinence probably did not prevent a bottle's being broken out to toast his arrival.

As the excitement wore away a note of discouragement crept into the Astorians' voices. Things had not gone well since they had joined the American company. The captain in charge of the ship *Tonquin*, which had transported the sea-borne detachment of Astorians around the Horn, was mad; nothing else could account for some of Jonathan Thorn's actions. Oh, no doubt Thorn was a brave seaman; Stephen Decatur had commended him for gallantry against the Tripolitan pirates. But trying to impose wartime naval discipline on lordly North West partners and their ebullient clerks had led to repeated clashes. The climax had come at the Falkland Islands, where Thorn had actually sailed away from a shore party that had failed to heed (because they had not heard) the captain's signal to return to the ship. Only Robert Stuart's forcing Thorn at pistol point to heave to had saved the men from being marooned.

At Hawaii, where the *Tonquin* had stopped to take on fresh food and to hire twenty-four native workmen, Thorn in another outburst of temper had beaten a belated sailor almost senseless and then had thrown the man overboard. As the ship steered on toward the Columbia, fresh quarrels arose over who had ultimate control of the trade supplies: Thorn, in charge of bartering along the coast; or Duncan McDougal, the factor in charge of land operations. Nerves were further strained when the clerks took to talking Gaelic and the voyageurs their patois merely to annoy the captain, who was sure that plots were being hatched against him.

And then had come the murderous bar of the Columbia. Unable to detect from the masthead any channel through the crashing surf, Thorn had ordered a boat crew to explore, in spite of their anguished protests. The small vessel disappeared, never to be seen again. During the following days three more men died in similar efforts—eight lives lost, all told—before the *Tonquin* finally heeled shudderingly across the bar into the estuary.

After considerable waste motion exploring the river's north shore (and more near drownings, averted when Chief Comcomly's Chinook Indians fished McDougal and his men from a swamped boat), a site for the fort had been selected on the south bank. It was not an ideal location, but Thorn had refused to explore any farther. So the land party had set about clearing away the rocks and brush and the fantastic trees, some of which reached fifty feet in girth. Four axmen working simultaneously on scaffolds eight feet high had had to hack for days to bring a single monster down. Then the trunks and vast stumps had to be blown apart by gunpowder so that the pieces could be hauled away—all on an enervating diet of boiled salmon and in perpetual rain and chill fogs that kept half the workers, the Kanakas particularly, on the sick list all the time.

At length enough space had been opened for a warehouse sixty by twenty feet. To find sufficient small logs for constructing the building, the men went deep inland, harnessed themselves in teams of eight, and like oxen dragged the timbers to the site. As the building took shape, Thorn had rushed ashore an insufficient dab of goods; and on June 1, taking partner Alexander McKay with him as supercargo, he had sailed away to trade around Vancouver Island. Since then work had gone slowly, both on the fort and on a small schooner named the *Dolly*, whose keel stood on stocks at the water's edge.

Hoping to turn the discouragement to his own ends, Thompson painted a gloomy picture of the poor trade along the upper river. But the Astorians recognized a North West wile when they heard one. Matters would pick up, they retorted, when the ship *Beaver* appeared with more supplies and when reinforcements crossing overland arrived. Besides, the Astorians knew more of the upper country than Thompson might think. A month before, two Indians, ostensibly man and wife, had appeared at Astoria with a letter from Finan Mc-Donald at Spokane House, addressed to John Stuart at a post in New Caledonia. On reaching the Columbia and hearing of white men at the river's mouth, the messengers had gone downstream instead of up. Their reports of the upper river were considerably different from Thompson's. In fact David Stuart was even then making preparations to take a trading party upstream under the pair's guidance. If Thompson thereupon demurred and told his rivals of the claim notice he had posted for Great Britain and the North West Company at the mouth of the Snake (no record suggests that he did), the Astorians simply grinned the threat aside. Blandly Stuart went on with his work.

When Thompson saw the two Indians from Spokane he was dumfounded. Man and wife, nothing! Both were females, despite the "man's" bow and quiver. Three years before this masquerader, a Kootenay squaw, had been living with one of his voyageurs, until Thompson had run her off for loose morals and troublemaking. Now she was posing as a great prophetess, frightening the Chinooks with threats of smallpox (a disease they had become all too familiar with during virulent epidemics in the Willamette Valley a few years before Lewis and Clark) and with tales of two giants who were approaching, overturning the ground, burying whole villages. Indeed, the "man" talked too much. If Thompson had not calmed down one angry delegation of Chinooks, the Indians would probably have murdered the pair.

With this fine twosome traveling sometimes with him and sometimes with David Stuart's party, Thompson started back up the river. For nearly two hundred miles the American and Canadian groups stayed close together, but at the Dalles, or "Long Narrows," the Canadians began to pull ahead in their lighter, more easily portaged canoe. At the mouth of the Snake, where earlier he had left the claim notice, Thompson found a huge gathering of Nez Percés. In an effort to protect the north country, he asked the Indians to divert the Astorians up the Snake, which he followed himself as far as the Palouse before securing horses and riding overland to Spokane House. Stuart, however, detected the maneuver and kept straight up the Columbia to the Okanogan with his homosexual guides, who startled twenty-six horseloads of gifts out of the ingenuous Indians they encountered along the way.

The rest of David Thompson's career is, in a sense, anticlimactic. Returning from Spokane House to Kettle Falls, he built another canoe, pushed upstream, and so completed surveying the entire length of the Columbia—which he might have done at least three years earlier. The winter of 1811–12 he spent trading in western Montana among his favorite Indians, the Flatheads. In the spring he gathered together from his various posts a rich 122 packs of beaver pelts and headed out via Athabaska Pass (which for the next several decades would be, despite its northern location, the principal route of the Western fur trade). With Thompson on this eastern journey went wiry John George McTavish, who the previous fall had led in a large party of men, just in case they were needed against the Piegans . . . or the Astorians.

When Thompson and McTavish reached Fort William on Lake Superior they learned that war had broken out between the United States and Great Britain. Thompson, however, was destined to play no part in the hostilities; instead, the company put him to work on his cherished dream, a map of the Canadian West. That done—we are casting ahead now—he worked for ten years on the commission that delineated the boundary between the United States and Canada. For another thirty years he eked out a living as a private surveyor. In 1857, half-blind and poverty-stricken, he died, a forgotten man—until J. B. Tyrrell, a locating engineer for the Canadian Pacific Railroad, discovered that yellowed copies of a certain unidentified map of the Columbia River were more accurate than anything else the government or railroad possessed. Curious, Tyrrell began the studies which at last rescued the Star Man from oblivion.

Meanwhile another almost forgotten man was traveling furiously back over those carefully mapped trails. He was John George Mc-Tavish, and he carried with him to the brigades west of the mountains word that war had been declared in June of 1812. Should opportunity afford, the Nor'Westers could now legitimately seize the American post at the mouth of the Columbia. But it would not be wise to act too precipitately. Reinforcements might have arrived at Astoria either overland or by ship, and McTavish's first move was to approach his old partners as a friend while he felt out the enemy's strength. If he could not act with the men he had, he was to wait for reinforcements of his own.

5. The Beginnings of Disaster

A FULL year before the outbreak of hostilities the Astorians had begun to fret over the weaknesses of their position. David Stuart's departure upriver with Thompson had left fewer than three dozen persons, one third of them Sandwich Islanders, to man unfinished Astoria. This reduction of itself was enough to inflame the natives. In August 1811 further tinder was supplied by Puget Sound Indians drifting southward to fish for the huge sturgeon of the Columbia. The Astorians' ship *Tonquin*, these visitors whispered to the natives around the post, had been destroyed in one of the rugged coves of Vancouver Island. The outlanders were not invulnerable!

Although the Astorians soon picked up vague rumors that something had happened to the ship, months passed before the dismayed whites learned the full details of the tragedy. These were supplied at last by a native interpreter who had been aboard the *Tonquin*. According to this Indian, the trouble had started when Captain Thorn had insulted a local chief. The next day, despite warnings by Alexander McKay, large numbers of vindictive savages were allowed to board the ship. Suddenly they struck. Only survivors of the onslaught were the interpreter, who was spared by the Indian women, and five of the crew, who barricaded themselves below decks. Of these five, one was so sorely wounded that he could not go along when the others slipped away during the night. (Later the fleeing quartet were captured and tortured to death.) The next morning this wounded man lured a swarm of Indians onto the vessel. Vanishing below, he then touched off the four and a half tons of powder in the *Tonquin's* hold, blasting himself and an unguessable number of savages to kingdom come.

Even before the full story was known at the post, the Astorians had sensed the trouble it was brewing. Inspired by the rumors, the natives along the Columbia had begun making strong talk: if the white man's ship could be captured, could not a similar coup be counted on his fort?

Luckily a secondary chief sounded a warning. The alarmed Astorians threw up a log palisade around their warehouse, dragged cannon into the corner bastions, instituted drills and watches. Remembering the terror which the man-dressed Kootenay prophetess had inspired with her talk of smallpox, gloomy Duncan McDougal next sought to strengthen these defenses still more by a bluff that years later would backfire against his successors. After inviting several chiefs inside the fort, he closed the doors and held up a small bottle. If he pulled the cork, he said, the smallpox inside would escape. Appalled, the Indians promised to behave. But they did not forget the white man's claim of being able to control disease.

The respite produced scant satisfaction. The *Tonquin* disaster had left the Astorians without one of their best partners, Alexander McKay. Irreplaceable trade goods, the means of prosecuting the all-important coastal trade, the psychological advantage of having an armed vessel at their backs—all were gone. Glumly the whites finished their fort and launched their little schooner *Dolly*—too little and too unwieldy a ship, they immediately learned, to be useful for much more than running errands along the river.

In the fall their spirits lifted with reports that David Stuart had found a prosperous site for a post where the Okanogan River ran into the Columbia, and with the return of young Robert Stuart from a successful venture into the beautiful Willamette Valley, hardly a hundred miles away. Pessimism soon crept back, however, as the rain-swept year dragged to its end with no word from the reinforcements crossing overland from St. Louis.

Then on January 18, 1812, a shout went up. Two canoes carrying white men were approaching. Duncan McDougal being ill, historian-clerk Gabriel Franchère hurried out to do the offices of welcome.

For a moment Franchère could only stare in shock. Were these the long-awaited reinforcements? The emaciated arrivals scarcely resembled men. Even massive Donald McKenzie, described as normally weighing three hundred pounds, was drained down to a hide-covered skeleton. Those with him—partner Robert McClellan, clerk John Reed, and eight Canadians—were in equally bad shape.

Franchère hurried them inside; McDougal rose from his sickbed. What had happened? Where was the rest of the party?

It was a harrowing tale, though it began routinely enough. More than a year before, in the fall of 1810, Donald McKenzie and an inexperienced partner of Astor's named Wilson Price Hunt had started up the Missouri with fifty-odd voyageurs, plus hunter Pierre Dorion, his squaw Marie, and Dorion's two children. Also along were three more of Astor's American partners: Robert McClellan, Ramsay Crooks, and hot-tempered Joseph Miller.

At this point in the telling Donald McKenzie's voice grew bitter. He had assumed he was to share command with Wilson Hunt, but letters from Astor to their winter camp had put the American in top place. A slap in the face, that. New Jersey-born Hunt's trade experience had been limited to a St. Louis shop, while McKenzie was *un homme du Nord*. Such things a man does not forget.

During the spring of 1811 the party ascended the Missouri as far as the mud villages of the Arikara Indians, just below the present southern boundary of North Dakota. There Hunt, made cautious by reports of hostile Blackfeet farther upstream, had decided to strike overland. From the Arikaras and later from the Cheyennes, he secured a total of 118 horses and with them wound an uncertain way across western South Dakota and Wyoming. Near the stupendous peaks of the Tetons the party detached four trappers, then, in October, crossed a majestic pass into today's Idaho. Time was running out. Stinging pellets of snow lashed the party as they hurried across lovely meadows to the straggle of deserted log huts that had been built the previous fall by Andrew Henry.

Near these buildings—the first American post west of the Continental Divide—flowed a considerable stream, now called Henry's Fork of the Snake River. There the saddle-galled voyageurs spent nine days hollowing sixteen canoes out of cottonwood trees. Four more hunters were detached to try their luck; and in a fit of temper partner Joseph Miller withdrew from the company to join the quartet.

On October 19, after caching their saddles and entrusting the horses to two young Indians, Hunt's overland party embarked on Henry's Fork. Soon they ran into the green-tinted principal branch of the Snake. With increasing velocity the current swept them into the great semicircular curve by which the river courses southern Idaho. The land grew barren. Treeless cliffs of black lava two and three hundred feet high pinched tight on the boiling water. Canoes began to founder; precious goods were lost. Finally, in a dreadful cascade, Ramsay Crooks's canoe smashed on a rock, drowning one man.

Scrambling to the gorge top, Hunt went ahead to reconnoiter. He returned dismayed, with reports of thundering cataracts (since named Shoshone and Twin Falls, each two hundred feet or so high). Sixteen men nevertheless tried to force a passage through the canyon with the best canoes. The effort failed. Abandoning their craft, the sixteen voyageurs struggled back upriver through a pelting rain to the main group.

Drenched, lost, desperately short of food, and bereft of transportation, the party now broke into fragments. After helping cache the trade goods in several huge pits, Ramsay Crooks led a handful of men on foot back toward Henry's Fort to secure the horses left there. Though Hunt and the bulk of the personnel stayed by the caches, waiting for Crooks's return, some of the men were more aggressive— or more foolhardy. McClellan and three companions went downstream along a route already taken by a small scouting party under indefatigable John Reed. McKenzie and four more men angled northward in the general direction of what they hoped was the main branch of the Columbia.

By sheerest chance McKenzie's party came together with Reed's and McClellan's. None of the men had found game or Indians. Some wanted to return to Hunt at the caches. McKenzie stopped them. Why add their hungry mouths to the desperate main party? Better to go on alone—and he made them believe it. Resolutely then he led them northward through one of the most rugged sections of the United States. The vast canyon of the Snake, in places more than a mile deep, yawned to their left; timber-choked mountains towered ahead and to the right. During long stretches when they could not reach the river the thirst-crazed Canadians took to drinking their own urine. Food had dwindled to broiled strips of beaver skin when at last McClellan managed to kill a mountain sheep. Temporarily braced by the meat, the men clawed on across mammoth ridges, through dense forests, past the gorges of the Little Salmon and the Salmon. Finally they reached the navigable Clearwater and there obtained canoes from the Indians. The rest had been comparatively easy.

Hunt and Crooks? McKenzie shrugged. Snow had been falling in the mountains when his party reached the Clearwater, and spring might arrive before the rest of the party managed to break through.

He reckoned without the others' doggedness. McKenzie had scarcely left the caches when Ramsay Crooks returned to Hunt with word that it would be impossible to cross the desert to Henry's Fort and return with horses before winter blocked the trails. There was no choice but to divide forces in order more easily to secure food, and go on afoot. Crooks and nineteen men tried the south side of the river; Hunt and nineteen more, plus Marie Dorion and her two children, took the north.

A month of brutal toil brought Hunt's group to today's aptly named Seven Devils Mountains. Floundering one snowy morning down to the river, they were hailed, to their astonishment, from the other side by Crooks's famished, utterly fatigued group. Using the skin of a horse recently purchased from the Indians and butchered for food, Hunt constructed a canoe on which meat could be sent to the starving men. Crooks and one voyageur then returned on the frail vessel with hopeless tales of impassable cliffs farther down the river, of equally impassable snowdrifts in the mountains.

The parties began a disorganized retreat, hoping to find Indians with whom they could winter. One man drowned while trying to cross the river to friends who had killed game. Hunter John Day, a long-time associate of Crooks's collapsed. Loyally Crooks determined to spend the winter there in the wilderness with him, as did a Canadian named Dubreuil. Leaving the trio two live horses and the carcass of a third, Hunt regrouped the remainder of the party and, following Indian suggestions, struck northwest through the Blue Mountains of eastern Oregon. Three men dropped out to live with the Indians; one more wandered off and disappeared. The rest, including Marie Dorion's two children and Marie herself, who paused along the way to give birth to a short-lived baby, struggled through and on February 15, 1812, reached Astoria.

Joyfully they were welcomed with cannon fire and a rattle of musketry. Dispatches announcing their arrival were started back overland to Astor in charge of John Reed, who had just completed the westward ordeal with McKenzie. At one of the portages in the Cascades, however, Indians fell on the party Reed was with, wounded him, and made off with the bright tin box containing the messages. Abandoning the cross-country effort, Reed went on upriver to David Stuart's post at Okanogan. In May both groups returned to Astoria. Along the way, in another of the Northwest's extraordinary coincidences, they picked up Ramsay Crooks and John Day (but not the Canadian Dubreuil, who, falling ill, had been left with friendly Indians). After fantastic hardships Day and Crooks had managed to follow Hunt's trail as far as Celilo Falls on the Columbia. There the ever pestiferous savages of the portages had robbed the pair even of their clothing. Utterly dispirited, the two then heeled about and were contemplating a desperate return journey to St. Louis when they were rescued.

On May 9, 1812, just before the returning parties reached Astoria (and a month before the United States' declaration of war against Great Britain) the supply ship *Beaver* edged across the treacherous bar with fresh workers, eager clerks, and one more partner, tall, handsome, vainglorious John Clarke, still another ex-Nor'Wester. Spirits soared at last. The one interior post so far established, a sixteen-by-twenty-foot hut, which David Stuart had built of driftwood near the mouth of the Okanogan, had succeeded spectacularly. There clerk Alexander Ross, with no more company than a dog, had, in his words, "procured 1,550 beavers, besides other peltries, worth in the Canton market £2,250 sterling, and which stood the concern . . . in round numbers, £35!" David Stuart meanwhile had pushed on north from Okanogan to the forks of the Thompson River in present British Columbia and had returned with glowing accounts of the trade possibilities there. Donald McKenzie, bounding back fast from the ordeal of his overland crossing, had followed Robert Stuart's trail up the fertile Willamette to the Oregon river now called McKenzie and had started another promising post.

Inspirited by all this, the reinforced Astorians laid their plans. It was decided that, while Hunt sailed to Alaska on the *Beaver* to corner the sea trade with the Russians, the other partners would throw out a cordon of forts around the northern reaches of the Columbia, thus blocking any advance down the river by the North West Company. And finally young Robert Stuart was delegated to finish Reed's interrupted journey, carrying dispatches across the continent to Astor.

The one sour note came from the American partners Crooks and McClellan. Like Joseph Miller before them, they were sick of the adventure. Resigning from the Pacific Fur Company, they started east with young Stuart along a route which, with modifications, would later become famous as the Oregon Trail. [1]

Even before reaching St. Louis in the spring of 1813, after terrible hardship, the wayfarers learned out on the plains what John George McTavish of the Nor'Westers had been told the previous summer at Lake Superior: Great Britain and the United States were at war. His sympathies sorely mixed by the information, Robert Stuart

[1] By still another extraordinary coincidence, they found along the way ex-partner Miller and his trappers starving in the wilderness, and took them back to the States.

hurried on east to meet with Astor. He was a loyal young man, and he knew that the post so laboriously established on the Columbia was in no shape to withstand a determined assault by the Nor'Westers, let alone by the British navy. Loyal, yes—but Robert Stuart was also a Scot, a former Nor'Wester. So were the uncle and the other companions he had left at Astoria. In the case of armed conflict between their employer's country and their own, where would their duties lie?

6. *"A Dagger to My Heart"*

STILL completely unaware of the war, several parties of Astorians in the summer of 1812 started up the Columbia to wage their private economic feud with the North West Company. Competition was instantaneous, vigorous—and friendly. After all, most of the men were former associates; their new contracts said nothing about bloodshed. When David Stuart built Fort Kamloops on the Thompson River, a party of Nor'Westers promptly moved in beside him but challenged him with nothing more deadly than price quotations. At almost the same time Astorian John Clarke built an American post within a hundred yards of the Canadians' Spokane House, held amiable horse races with the opposition, and in the fall dispatched trading brigades to undercut the Nor'Westers among the Kootenays and Flatheads. Here occurred the sole violence of the campaign—a pistol duel between two clerks, who succeeded only in aerating each other's trousers.

Southward, in the Snake country of today's Idaho, the Americans were bothered by no opposition whatsoever. Returns, however, were slim. Huge-bodied Donald McKenzie established a ramshackle post at the foot of the heaving, tawny hills where the Clearwater runs toward the Snake and then spent his time grumbling about the refusal of the Nez Percés to strain themselves trapping for the scattered beaver of their homeland. Nor did the other Astorian bourgeois operating in the vicinity succeed much better. He was indefatigable John Reed, to whom had fallen the arduous task of retracing the overland party's outward trail and salvaging the goods Hunt had been forced to cache. In addition Reed was also to pick up the trappers whom Hunt had detached along the way.

By some wilderness legerdemain Reed did locate most of the wandering trappers in the midst of an unmapped tumble of desert and mountain. He also found that the men had rifled the caches. Perhaps the robbery had justification. The hunters had endured desperate hardships. At least one had been slain by Indians; another, ugly whispers said, had been eaten by his starving companions. Only the goods in the caches had enabled the survivors to pay friendly Indians for succor and to keep going. In their far-flung wanderings some of them had set their traps southward along Bear River Valley as far as today's Utah. Others had traveled northeastward to the headwaters of the Missouri. All had been repeatedly robbed by various bands of savages, so that they had nothing to show for their fantastic peregrinations. Yet they were still willing to keep on trapping.

Reed took them north with him to McKenzie's post on the Clearwater. The big Scot was still grumbling, and Reed's experience did nothing to cheer him up. Leaving Reed in charge of the post, McKenzie went dourly up to Spokane to discuss with his partner, John Clarke, the advisability of pulling out of the Snake country entirely.

Next door to Clarke's post, at the North West Company's Spokane House, McKenzie found John George McTavish, freshly arrived across the mountains from Rainy Lake with devastating news. War, McTavish said—one can imagine how the Scottish burr rolled—and warships to batter down the Americans' post at the mouth of the Columbia. The North West Company's ship, *Isaac Todd*, was due off the river by the end of March 1813, armed with letters of marque to legalize the seizure of Astoria.

Precipitately McKenzie hurried back to the Clearwater. Assembling Reed and his men, he cached the post's goods, then in mid-January 1813 fled down the Columbia to warn Duncan McDougal of the enemy's approach.

None of this—his indolence as a trader or his panic as a fighter—sounds like the man McKenzie would later show himself to be. Perhaps, disgruntled still at having been outranked on the westward trip by Hunt, he had no desire to further Astor's interests. Perhaps he had not yet been in the Northwest long enough to visualize, as soon he would, the one plan by which profits could be wrung from the enormous reaches of the interior. Or perhaps his conduct was as deliberately treacherous as Astor and Astor's historian, Washington Irving, always believed.

Whatever his motives, McKenzie found at Astoria a man constitutionally prone to see the darkest side of any picture. This was Duncan McDougal, factor in charge. Stampeded by the first hint of trouble, McDougal called a frightened meeting. Even the resident clerks were assembled, though they had no vote in policy decisions. After pessimistic hand wringings the two Astorian partners determined to leave the country for St. Louis on the first of July. In view of McKenzie's recent overland ordeal, the decision suggests desperate sincerity rather than unadulterated treachery.

Since more furs were already on hand than could be conveniently carried overland, Duncan McDougal stopped all trade in pelts and began stockpiling provisions instead. McKenzie and Reed hurried back up the river to raise their caches and to start bartering for the three or four hundred horses that would be necessary for transporting the huge cavalcade to St. Louis.

Straightway they ran into trouble. Indians had pilfered the caches. When villagers who the whites knew were guilty denied the thefts, the recently panicked McKenzie determined on a reckless stratagem. Stalking angrily from tepee to tepee, Reed and he slashed open potential hiding places with their daggers. Taken completely aback by the audacity, the Indians promised to produce the stolen articles if the whites would stop their destruction.

Grimly McKenzie acceded (although only a portion of the goods was returned), and then sent far-wandering John Reed on to the interior posts to acquaint the partners with the plan for abandoning the country and to urge their help in procuring horses. Rendezvous was appointed for June 1 at the junction of the Walla Walla with the Columbia, where the parent stream makes the last of its great horseshoe bends and sweeps starkly westward between the majestic buttes of Wallua Gap.

McKenzie's own horse trading started slowly. The Indians, resentful of his highhanded tactics about the stolen goods, declined to barter. Exasperated, McKenzie took to pointing toward whatever animal he wanted, offering a fair price, and then, on being refused, shooting the horse dead. Though he always paid (after which his men ate the carcass), the Indians found it a disconcerting way to deal. At one point they drove the whites to shelter on an island; but when phenomenal shots continued to bring down livestock, the red man at last consented to do business.

Clarke, too, built up ill will. At one of his camps on the way to the rendezvous, an Indian stole a silver goblet; in retaliation Clarke hanged the culprit in front of his shocked tribesmen. Word of the unprecedented punishment flashed from village to village, and as the trappers gathered at the rendezvous, so did a huge concourse of threatening natives. Warned by an agitated chief, the whites broke camp during the middle of breakfast, abandoned such horses as they had secured, and paddled for Astoria.

There they found that John George McTavish and twenty Nor'-Westers had come down from Spokane ahead of them and were camped outside the stockade, waiting for the *Isaac Todd* to seize the place. The ship, however, was long overdue. Perhaps something had happened to it or perhaps the whole story was a bluff. Moreover, trade had been excellent—seventeen packs of prime beaver from the Willamette, a hundred and forty from Okanogan, Spokane, and the farther posts. Reluctant to abandon returns like those on the strength of McKenzie's and McDougal's spur-of-the-moment decision, Clarke and David Stuart began to raise objections. For one thing, they pointed out, adequate numbers of livestock could not be obtained from the aroused Indians in time for the Astorians to cross the mountains before winter. The company had better stay put.

McKenzie and McDougal retorted with telling points of their own. Why hadn't Wilson Price Hunt returned in the *Beaver* on schedule from Alaska? Where was the annual supply ship from New York? Even granting that the *Isaac Todd* did not appear, Astoria could not survive without supplies, and beyond doubt England was now blockading the East coast to American shipping.

In the end Stuart and Clarke agreed to a compromise. The Astorians would trade for one more year and then, if succor had not appeared by July 1, 1814, they would leave the country. To neutralize McTavish in the interim the partners relinquished to him Astor's Pacific Fur Company posts at Spokane and among the Kootenays. In return the Nor'Westers promised the Astorians a year's free hand at Okanogan and among the Flatheads. The Astorians also sold the Canadians (with whom they were theoretically at war) merchandise billed at $858. With these goods loaded in canoes, the enemy obligingly returned upstream to Spokane.

In order to make the most of the year's grace, David Stuart hurried back to Okanogan, Reed to the gloomy barrens along the Snake, Clarke to the Flatheads. To feed McDougal's force at Astoria, McKenzie set up hunting camps in the Willamette and also beat back and forth along the river bartering for fish.

Eager for still more defensive strength, Duncan McDougal sought the good will of the neighboring Chinooks by wooing the head-flattened, oil-anointed eldest daughter of crafty Comcomly, the tribe's one-eyed chief. The price was high—fifteen guns, fifteen blankets, and assorted small trinkets. But McDougal was either tired of celibacy—or afraid. He agreed to pay on the installment plan. Details settled, a gay fleet of high-prowed canoes escorted the bride-to-be across the river to the fort, and once the marriage had been fittingly celebrated nothing remained but to wait out the uncertain days there on the fog-shrouded mouth of the river.

Throughout the records, by implication in the minutes left by the partners and with outspoken acerbity in later books by some of the scribbling clerks, runs the theme of abandonment. Astor, they felt, had forsaken them.

Actually the merchant was playing every angle he could in an effort to supply his Pacific post. When he was unable to secure from the American government an escort vessel to defend his regular supply vessel from British seizure, he sent to his agents in London £12,000 to buy and outfit the brig *Forester*, and sail her to the Northwest under British colors. When chaos in England's war-harassed ports delayed the *Forester*, he boldly outfitted the 300-ton *Lark* in New York; then on March 13, 1813, sprang her through the British blockade by means of a sailing permit which the Russian consul obtained from the English admiral on the pretext that the *Lark* was going to Alaska.

Late that same month a heavily escorted convoy left England for the Pacific. In it were the North West Company's oft-delayed *Isaac Todd*—and Astor's *Forester* sailing under a British flag. [2] Learning of the convoy's warships almost simultaneously with their sailing and suspecting that the Columbia might be their destination, Astor on April 4, 1813, wrote in agitation to the Department of State: ". . . even yet it is not too Late to Do good if aur Government would act with promptness. . . . Good god what an object is to be securd. . . . There are 12 or 13 American [trading] ships on that coast all of which might be Safd if Steeps ware naw taking. . . . I have not time to point out all the advantages that would result from the Securing the River to us."

To this letter Astor added a pointed remark that he was about to meet Secretary Gallatin and discuss lending the goverment two and a half million dollars for war expenses. Taking the hint, the government offered the frigate *Adams*, and Astor hurriedly outfitted still another supply ship, the *Enterprise*. Then a sudden crisis in the Great Lakes diverted the *Adams'* crew, and that hope died.

---

[2] The *Forester* became separated from the convoy in the Pacific and went to the Sandwich Islands. Trouble with the crew and uncertainty among the officers about her anomalous position as a British ship carrying American goods led her to by-pass the Columbia in favor of trade with the neutral Russians and Californians.

Disaster meanwhile was plaguing the *Lark*. Near the Sandwich Islands a hurricane rolled her on beam-ends. By cutting away the masts, the crew righted the ship, but she was now a waterlogged hulk, her decks awash in the heavy seas. Volunteers diving into the flooded cabins salvaged a small sail and twelve bottles of wine. Rigging the sail on the bowsprit and subsisting on a gill of wine per day, the men floundered northward until finally the *Lark* grounded on a reef off the island of Maui and there was pillaged by the natives.

Astor's chief agent on the coast, Wilson Price Hunt, was having no better luck. At first, to be sure, matters went well. After leaving Astoria in August 1812, Hunt had sailed to New Archangel. There, at heavy cost to his stomach, he had concluded a profitable agreement with hard-drinking Governor Baranov, in pursuit of which he sailed his ship *Beaver* on to the Aleutians and put aboard her nearly seventy-five thousand seal and otter skins. During the process storms battered the *Beaver* so badly that her captain refused to return Hunt to the Columbia, of whose murderous bar he was deathly afraid, until he had been to the Sandwich Islands for repairs. Disembarking at Oahu to await the annual supply ship for Astoria, Hunt sent the *Beaver* on to Canton with the furs. There her captain heard of the war and decided to sit tight in China.

No supply ship reached Hawaii, but rumors of hostility did. Apprehensively Hunt chartered the ship *Albatross* and stood out for the Columbia. Arriving on August 20, 1813, more than a year after his departure, he learned of the decision to abandon the post if help did not arrive from the East by the following July. Convinced it would not arrive, McDougal and McKenzie were already making plans for their departure.

For six days Hunt protested, but finally the other two wore him down—with this modification: rather than risk the furs to overland transport Hunt would go outside again and charter another ship for carrying the pelts to market. (The *Albatross*, already under charter by a different company for the fall season, could not wait while furs and men were assembled.) It was further agreed that if British attack threatened Astoria before Hunt returned with the new ship McDougal was to improvise whatever steps seemed necessary.

McKenzie started upriver to apprise the interior forts of this latest change. Along the way he met the first of the Canadian reinforcements dispatched across the mountains by the confident North West Company—seventy-five singing, beaded, belled, and fringed voyageurs who, upon reaching Spokane House, had been put under the command of John George McTavish. With McTavish was Astorian John Clarke, bluffed completely out of his Flathead post. McKenzie decided that he too might just as well go back down the river with frightened Clarke.

On October 7 the cavalcade reached Astoria. Raising the Union Jack defiantly near the Stars and Stripes, the Canadians went into camp under the guns of the fort—meantime having bought provisions from the Americans. A few days later the Nor'Westers were reinforced by John Stuart's exploring party from New Caledonia, the same Stuart who had been with Simon Fraser on the first water-torn traverse of the Tacoutche-Tesse. To the Astorians, Stuart's very presence was alarming: he had been dispatched to locate a transport route from New Caledonia via the Fraser River and Lake Okanagan to the sea, just as though the Columbia were already in British hands.

Still more Nor'Westers under partners Alexander Stuart and Alexander Henry the younger were scheduled to arrive, so McTavish said, within a month.[3] But perhaps the most upsetting threat of all was contained in a letter McTavish produced. Dated from London the previous May, it announced the belated sailing of the *Isaac Todd* "accompanied by a Frigate, to take and destroy every thing that is American on the N.W. Coast."

In spite of these piling alarms, most of the Americans at Astoria, some of the Canadians, and many later historians have felt that the Americans should have put up a fight. Counting their Chinook allies, the Astorians' force was as strong as that of their rivals, who were short of food. As for the British warship, the faultfinders say, it could have been evaded by the partners' loading their furs into canoes and retreating to some unnavigable side stream.

Such recommendations ignore the fact that the Astorians were on the Columbia to trade, not fight. Already their debts were mounting astronomically, and if they defied the Nor'Westers there was no telling when business might be resumed. The British traders likewise had no desire to fight; such an eventuality would see Astoria battered into uselessness by the *Isaac Todd* and its movable property seized by the navy as a prize of war. Both trading companies would benefit by a more peaceable solution. Thus, whether it was the Nor'Westers' McTavish or the Astorians' McDougal who first broached the idea of a sale, each found the other a ready listener.

Under the circumstances, the bargain seems fair enough. The North

[3] This Henry, who did arrive at Astoria on schedule, was a nephew of the pioneering Nor'Wester of the same name, Alexander Henry the elder.

West Company agreed to pay for the trade goods on hand in the fort a price approximately ten per cent above cost. The salaries of the Astorian workers would be assumed and places provided for those men who decided to switch allegiance to the Nor'Westers. For the Pacific Fur Company's seventeen thousand pounds of beaver and two thousand other skins McTavish offered forty thousand dollars. [4]

On October 16, 1813, the deal was closed. And still no *Isaac Todd* appeared. Uncertainty now began to afflict the Canadians. Suppose American ships had swept the sea! When a sail was sighted beyond the bar on November 30, McTavish hastily loaded furs and supplies into several canoes and scuttled out of sight behind Tongue Point. But the vessel was HMS *Raccoon*, commanded by a Captain Black and carrying as passenger a North West Company partner, John McDonald. The *Raccoon* had lost the *Isaac Todd* in a storm off South America and after a fruitless wait at rendezvous at Juan Fernandez Island had come on alone.

Captain Black was disgusted. He thought he had rounded half the world to reduce a stronghold. Instead, here was a stick-palisaded collection of log houses he could have blown off the map with a single salvo. But he determined to give the affair such panache as he could, once the miserable weather quit pinning him against the north shore.

After two weeks' wait the fort's little *Dolly* was able to ferry him across the river with an escort of sailors and marines. Landing in the dark, the men stumbled profanely over stones and driftwood, through puddles of rain water. The next day, December 13, everyone assembled under arms around a newly erected flagstaff in the square—voyageurs, Kanakas, traders, and military. Up went the Union Jack. Black then broke a bottle of Madeira against the flagstaff, announced in stentorian tones that he was taking possession of the country for Britain, and changed the name of Astoria to Fort George. Three rounds of artillery and musket fire punctuated the huzzahs. Afterward clerk Franchère endeavored to explain the ceremony to the mystified Chinooks.

As the rainy month wore away with no sign of the *Todd*, Captain Black lost patience and departed, satisfied his duty was completed.

---

[4] These furs, Washington Irving grumbles in *Astoria*, would have been worth a hundred thousand dollars in the market . . . but the market was several thousand hostile miles away. No doubt McDougal and McKenzie, in advocating the sale, were not distressed by the fact that the purchasers were former colleagues and natives of the same country. But to jump from there to a conclusion of treachery or even of cowardice seems an unnecessarily long leap.

Actually, as we shall see, he had done his country a greater disservice than he knew.

On the last day of February 1814 Hunt appeared in the chartered brig *Pedlar*. While searching for a ship in Oahu, he had learned of the wreck of the *Lark*. Rushing to Maui, he had picked up the survivors. Though no record says so, he may even have received via the *Lark's* captain a water-stained letter Astor had dispatched to him with the ship:

Our enterprise is grand, and deserves success and I hope in God it will meet it. If my object was merely gain of money, I should say, think whether it is best to save what we can and abandon the place; but the very idea is like a dagger to my heart.

Well, there was little Hunt could do now to retrieve Astoria. Hounded by misfortune, worn out by four years of worry and unbelievable hardships on land and sea, he gave in to what his partners had done. On April 3 he left the Columbia for home with such men as chose to depart by ship. Two days later ninety overlanders, both Nor'Westers and Astorians, started for Athabaska Pass.

As their ten canoes toiled past the mouth of the Walla Walla, an Indian woman's voice crying in French checked them. It was Pierre Dorion's wife, Marie, and from her came the last grisly tale of the ill-fated venture. Down at the mouth of the Boise River, in southwestern Idaho, Indians had fallen on John Reed and his nine men, including Pierre Dorion, as they were scattered among their traps. Only Marie had escaped with her two children. All winter she had stayed hidden in the snowy Blue Mountains, subsisting on the smoked meat of two horses she had killed. In March she had crossed to the Columbia and had found succor with local Indians. Iowa was her home, but how was a lone widow to get back among the Iowas? Disconsolately she turned downstream with her children toward such friends of Pierre's as might still be at Astoria . . . or—what was the strange name these men used?—Fort George.

So ended the war in the Northwest. It had spilled not one drop of blood. But the savage land and its peoples, the merciless rivers and storms—these had demanded at least sixty-one lives from the Astorians. In 1814 they must have seemed wasted lives. The brave claims to Oregon established by Robert Gray and by Lewis and Clark were shadowed now by the Union Jack flying unchallenged beside the dripping forests that lined the vast River of the West.

7. *Doldrums*

VICTORY over the Astorians brought no satisfaction to those Nor'Westers who were delegated to remain on the Columbia. Rather, morale collapsed completely. After watching the overland brigade paddle upriver toward the East, Alexander Henry, the partner left in charge of Fort George, mourned to his journal, "Here we are at the mercy of chance on a barbarous coast, among natives more inclined to murder us for our property than to assist us."

Like his men, Alexander Henry hated everything about Fort George: the wallows of winter mud and the dank green moss that insinuated damply even into the billets; the filth of the neighboring Indian villages and the gross displays of the females. Venereal complaints were hospitalizing so many of the crew that finally Henry ordered time lost from such causes to be deducted from the men's wages; and in exasperation he personally drove from the fort's gates one "canotée of prostitutes under threat of putting them in irons."

Into this unhappy situation, late in April 1814, sailed the long-overdue *Isaac Todd*, bearing the new head of the Columbia Department, irascible old Donald McTavish. A poorer choice could hardly have been made. McTavish, lured from retirement in England by the offer of this choice position, was determined to bring with him what he considered the comforts of civilization—among them an ample supply of strong waters and a white mistress: rosy Jane Burns, reputedly a Portsmouth barmaid. [1]

The effect was devastating. The little schooner *Dolly*, named originally for Astor's wife, was promptly rechristened *Jane*. Henry, capitalizing on Jane's boredom from the long ocean voyage, offered her what he termed in his journal "protection"; Donald McTavish, after a few sharp words, contented himself with a Chinook consort incongruously known as Mrs. Clapp. Chief Comcomly's son, even more electrified, rushed emissaries across the river with an offer of a hundred choice sea-otter skins for Jane's plump hand. But the comedy did not last. At five o'clock on the windy afternoon of May 22, Henry and McTavish, intending to lighter in some goods from the *Isaac Todd*, put out from the fort with a crew of six in a single-sailed, split-cedar boat ballasted with stones. A heavy surf was running. Legend adds, perhaps unjustifiably, that the men were in their cups. In any event the boat swamped and only one of the hands managed to swim ashore.

---

[1] Burns in Alexander Henry's journal; Barnes in Ross Cox's account.

Late in the summer Jane sailed back into obscurity, on either the *Isaac Todd* or the company's supply vessel *Columbia*, and Fort George returned to lethargy. Half a globe away the War of 1812 came to an end with the Treaty of Ghent, an inconclusive document that called for *status quo ante bellum*. Points in dispute, including the boundary of the Oregon country, were handed over to various commissions for settlement.

In July 1815, Secretary of State Monroe advised the British chargé d'affaires that the United States intended to reoccupy the Columbia. The British replied that the *status quo* doctrine did not apply, since Astoria had been transferred by sale, not by seizure. Splitting hairs, Monroe retorted that the actions of Captain Black of the *Raccoon* in running up the Union Jack and announcing that he was taking possession of the country constituted seizure and the property must be restored.

Scenting victory, Astor proposed that the United States establish a military post on the Columbia, manning it with fifty men—and give him a commission as lieutenant. This was a stronger step than the government was prepared to take. Monroe did, however, appoint Commissioner J. B. Prevost to receive restitution of the post. After a flurry of paper exchanges, Britain conceded Astoria, with the reservation that the act in no way prejudiced her claims to all Oregon.

Prevost arrived at the Columbia on October 1, 1818. Like Captain Black, he must have found the post an insignificant goal for so long a journey. Less than a year before, Captain Corney of the North West Company's brig *Columbia* had described the settlement as a range of low buildings inside a picket-protected square of about two hundred yards. By hacking desultorily at the forest the inhabitants had managed to clear some two hundred acres, "20 of which is planted to potatoes for use of the gentlemen. They have twelve head of cattle, with some pigs and goats imported from California. The stock does not increase for want of proper care. Wolves often carry off goats and pigs."

Prevost was graciously received by Factor James Keith, was fed potatoes perhaps, and on October 6 watched the British flag go down, the United States flag go up. For the sake of the record Keith then asked, in writing, whether the North West Company was likely to be ejected from the fort, and, if so, what compensation could be expected. Prevost replied with such diplomatic vagueness that Keith construed the answer as permission for his company to continue occupying the buildings until such time as Astor chose to return.

MAP 2

The Area of the Fur Trade of the Northwest

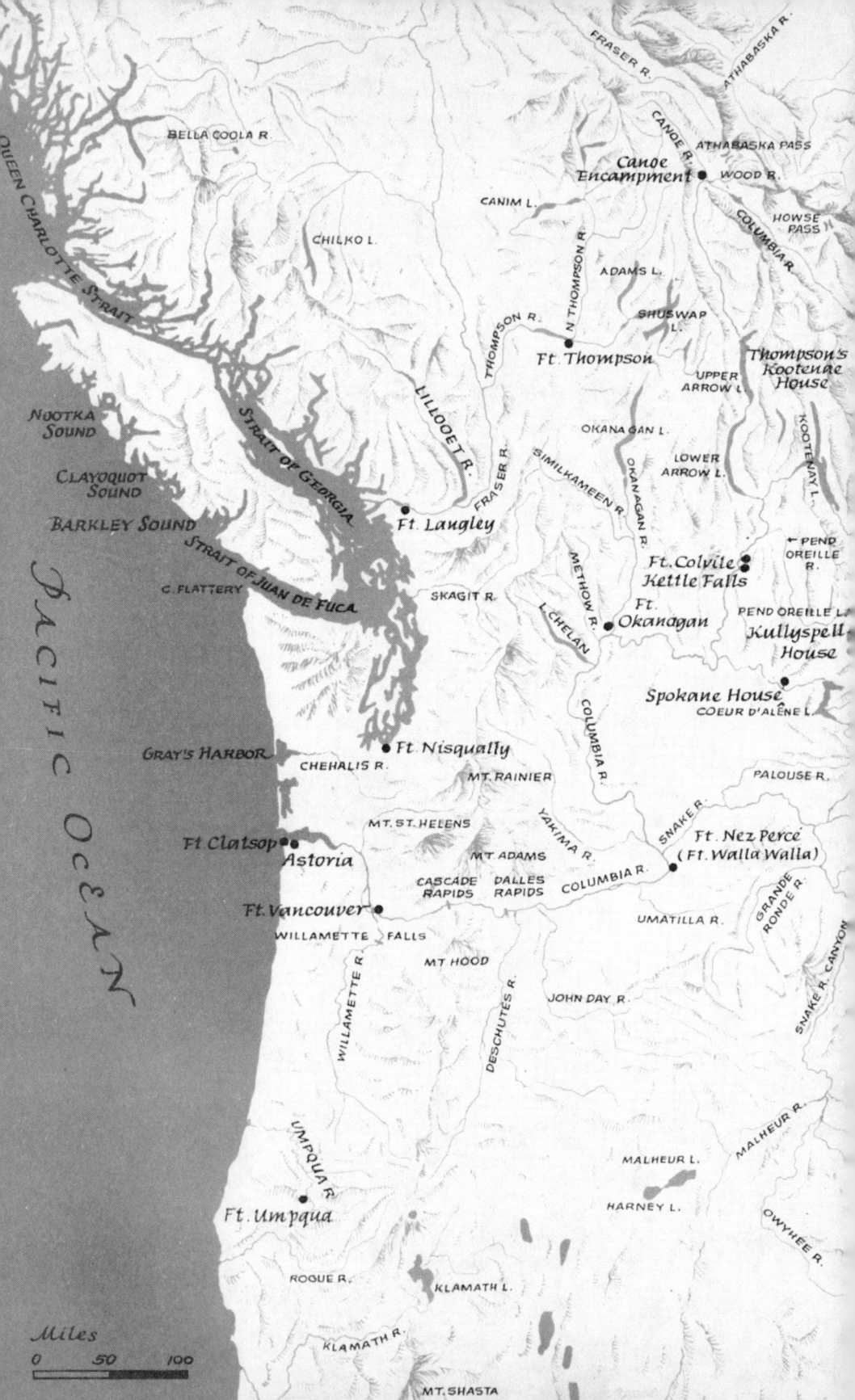

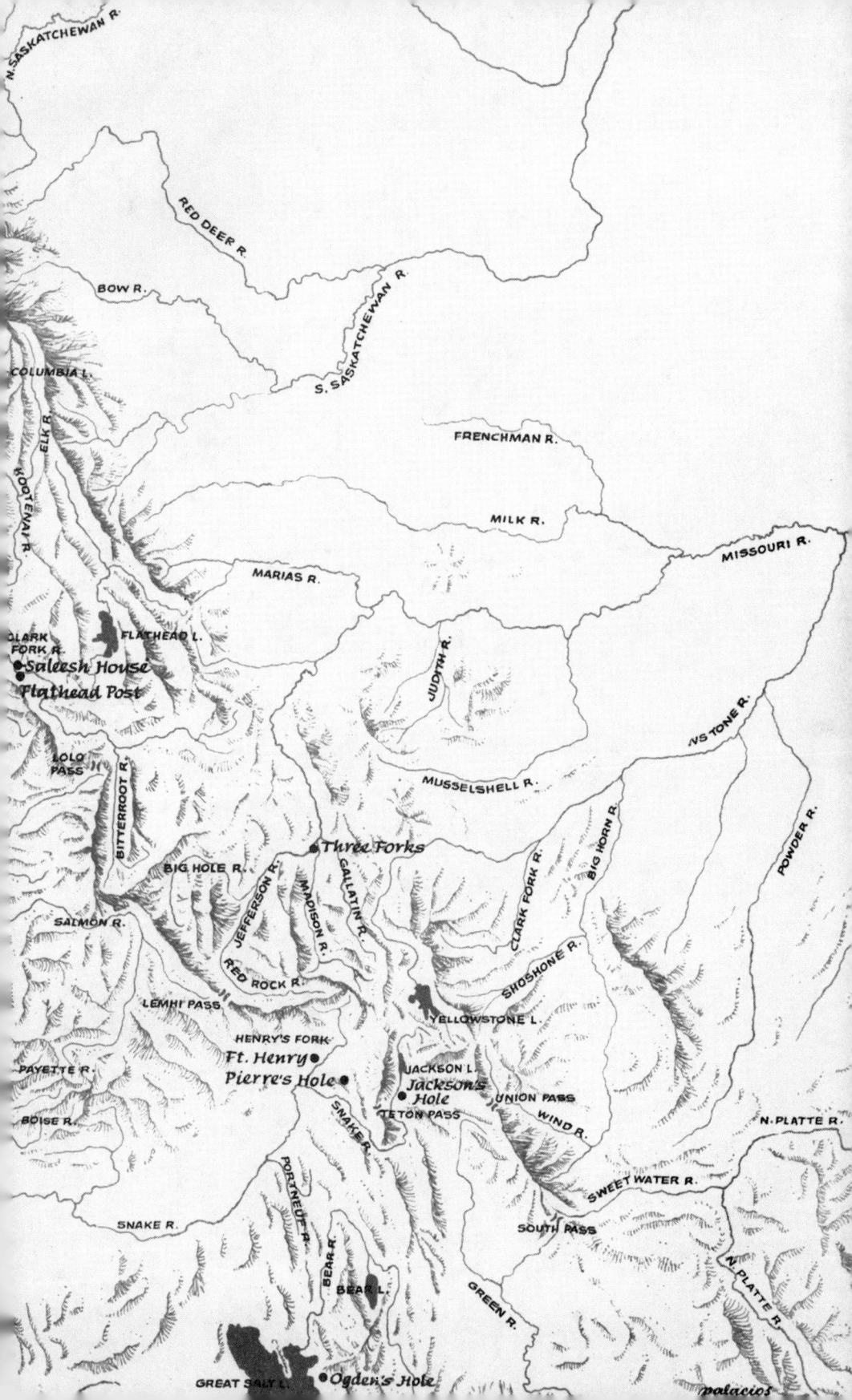

The time never came. The commission appointed under the Treaty of Ghent to determine the boundary could reach no compromise between the extremes of the British claim south to California and the American claim north to Alaska. Weary of dickering over a wilderness, the diplomats on October 20, 1818, signed a convention of joint occupancy that gave citizens of each country for the next ten years equal rights of trade or settlement. To Astor a mere right, unbacked by government aid, looked like a tenuous weapon for unseating the now firmly established North West Company. He decided to let matters ride.

James Keith and the other North West traders stationed at Fort George would happily have enlarged the political *status quo* to embrace all other activities in their district. The prospect of disturbing changes was everywhere gnawing at their positions. Even holding a port on the Pacific had brought the Nor'Westers little tangible gain. The East India Company had imposed so many restraints on trade in Canton that to avoid the strictures the Nor'Westers finally were forced into an agreement with a Boston firm, Perkins & Co., whereby the Yankees carried Columbia pelts to China, swapped them for oriental goods, and took these back to Massachusetts for marketing on account or for transshipment to London. On the face of things profits seemed high; but when charges and divisions were in, the balance sagged. And who got the blame? Why, the Columbia Department did, along with pointed remarks about harvesting more pelts.

Still more damaging to morale was the life-and-death struggle being waged east of the mountains with the Hudson's Bay Company. As Keith well knew, the trouble had started in 1811, when Lord Selkirk, by purchasing control of the Hudson's Bay Company, had been able to obtain in fee simple 116,000 square miles of land centering on the Red River in what is now southern Manitoba, northern Minnesota, and North Dakota. Onto this land and under auspices of the Hudson's Bay Company, Selkirk had moved Scottish tenant farmers displaced from the Highlands by the spread of large-scale sheep raising.

To this agricultural invasion of the Red River district the North West Company reacted furiously. Selkirk's colony lands not only lay athwart the Nor'Westers' transportation routes but also occupied the heart of the buffalo range on which they depended for vital supplies of pemmican. Prompted by the more hotheaded of the Nor'Westers, the half-breed hunters, the *métis*, began a reign of terror culminating, in 1816, in the murder of twenty-one Red River colonists, including their governor, Robert Semple.

Competition between the two fur companies now exploded beyond all sanity. Bloodshed, the debauchery of the Indians, and a frantic stripping of the country of every possible fur-bearing animal became integral parts of the struggle for supremacy. Although the Columbia lay far from the actual conflict, repercussions inevitably reached across the mountains. On the Pacific watershed, as everywhere, discipline crumbled; extravagance became rife.

The warfare kept the best of the voyageurs east of the Divide. In their places the Columbia Department received more and more Iroquois and Abenaki Indians from the St. Lawrence. Undependable at best, these trigger-happy Eastern Indians caught the taint afloat in the air and responded in kind. Their wanton horse stealing and rape so inflamed the natives of the Willamette region to the south and the Cowlitz to the north that both these rich valleys had to be written off the books for the next few seasons as potential fur grounds.

Meanwhile the partners at Fort William, the Nor'Westers' headquarters post on Lake Superior, continued to demand results. To stimulate action they dispatched across Athabaska Pass in the fall of 1816 that huge Scot of the Astorian sellout, Donald McKenzie.

It was a strange return. McKenzie had left the Columbia with the first east-bound brigade in April 1814. In New York he had asked Astor for a position in the American Fur Company and had been angrily rejected because of his actions on the Pacific. In spite of this disappointment, finding a job by going back to the West coast, where he had failed so miserably, was certainly no part of McKenzie's desire. But the Nor'Westers startled him by offering the then princely salary of five hundred pounds a year to see what he could do about increasing the Columbia's inland trade, and the price was more than he could turn down.

At Fort George he was met with jealousy and suspicion. His plan of splitting the Columbia Department into inland and coastal districts would water down the prestige of James Keith. The exploitation of the Snake country, to which McKenzie had been specifically directed, would drain manpower and goods from Fort George. And for what? Who knew better than McKenzie himself the difficult nature of the upheaved Snake watershed, the scattered location of the beaver colonies, and the sullen reluctance of the Indians to do what they considered the slave work of trapping? Why, so argued James Keith, the whites would find nothing in the interior to trade with the Indians but bullets. The partners must be insane even to consider the move.

Patiently McKenzie heard the objections out. Then, taking the men

Keith gave him—a dismaying gang of Iroquois, Sandwich Islanders, and castoff voyageurs—he spent two years reassessing the country he had once considered as profitless. Along the way he sedulously sought the good will of the thievish natives of the portages and carefully placated the hostility of the more distant Nez Percés and Snakes—a hostility he himself had helped create years earlier when trying to buy horses for abandoning Astoria.

On June 5, 1818, he returned downriver with a plan that brought howls of outrage from the hidebound factor at Fort George. Since the inland savages could not be persuaded to trap, McKenzie had determined to take his own hunters into the field, a revolutionary procedure which, though tried sporadically in other sections, had never become standard policy in any responsible fur company. Furthermore, the Scot proposed to establish, as a base of operations, a new post at the mouth of the Walla Walla River, surrounded by the most unfriendly of the inland natives.

To Keith the plan seemed, in Alexander Ross's words, "full of folly and madness." Yet the factor had to accede; crisp orders to that effect had just arrived from Fort William. With monumental ill grace he handed over to McKenzie the almost unheard-of force of one hundred men, together with mountains of supplies. When the United States commissioner, James Prevost, arrived four months later to raise the American flag, the thought may well have touched Keith's mind that it would not be amiss if Astor did reoccupy the fort. The Columbia seemed hardly worth all this trouble.

McKenzie's new fort, named Nez Percé, stood on a treeless plain overlooking a broad curve of the sun-struck, green-shimmering river. Northward and eastward rolled gaunt flatlands; southward rose a pair of striking buttes and beyond them the swell of the Blue Mountains. It was a barren, discouraging prospect. Not even building materials were visible. In order to secure the huge planks necessary for the fort's stockades, armed parties had to go a hundred miles back into the hills for pine logs that could be floated down to the site.

The sudden activity of the whites attracted great concourses of natives who demanded exorbitant toll for the materials being used in the construction. After endless palavering McKenzie made peace with the Nez Percé and associated tribes, and won their promise that they would conclude similar treaties with their hereditary enemies, the Snakes. This waving of the olive branch, however, brought little reduction in the post's armament; no Indian could withstand too much temptation. Fort Nez Percé was protected not only by an outer wall nearly twenty feet high but by an inner one twelve feet tall as well. To the usual bastions were added galleries and loopholed balustrades. Two large water tanks guarded against assault by fire. Except for special councils Indians were not allowed inside; trade was conducted through a wicket cut in the ponderous outer gate.

"Perpetual Motion," Ross called McKenzie. Vast, tireless, and insatiably curious, the Scot was discontented only when sedentary. "To travel a day's journey on snowshoes was his delight, but he detested spending five minutes writing in a journal. His traveling accounts were often kept on a beaver skin, written hieroglyphically with a pencil or piece of coal." [2]

For history it was an unfortunate aversion. When McKenzie moved deep into the Snake country in the fall of 1818, after putting Ross in charge of the new fort, he was reshaping an industry. In order to help maintain discipline and to convince suspicious natives of his peaceful intent, he took along with the brigade the Indian wives of many of his men. It meant more mouths to feed, more horses to worry about. Children had to be provided for—many were even born on the long marches. But in compensation the squaws set up the lodges, attended to the domestic chores, and dressed the furs, leaving the men free to fan out along the streams, each armed with six traps. As long as the majority of the hunters produced beaver, the camp remained stationary; otherwise down came the lodges and on went the cavalcade to the next valley. If the Indians they met chose to trade, fine: there were goods for that; but now the main dependence was on the brigade itself.

The Iroquois who made up a large portion of each brigade were not reliable. On one occasion a handful of them, smarting under McKenzie's peremptory discipline, decided to murder him—a temporary ruffle he calmed by flattening two of them with a tent pole. More troublesome was their complete lack of responsibility. Once a group of them pestered him to turn them loose along the Boise River. As soon as he was out of sight they found a party of Snakes and promptly swapped guns, horses, and traps for women.

The temper of the native tribes was equally uncertain. Though a full brigade was seldom attacked, stragglers were always in danger. A particular sufferer was brash William Kittson, McKenzie's over-

---

[2] Not only McKenzie's but most traders' field journals were tightly written with quill pens on small sheets of beaver skin bound together with thongs, and the accounts obviously presented extraordinary problems in deciphering to the clerks back at headquarters who were faced with transcribing them.

confident lieutenant, whose columns were frequently bled as they were strung out through the defiles while carrying supplies to McKenzie or transporting furs back to the fort. McKenzie himself had his own close calls. Once when he and three men were alone in one of the camps, a band of Snake Indians started to swarm across the whites' small breastwork. By rolling out a keg of gunpowder, lighting a spill, and threatening to blow them all up, himself included, the Scot bluffed the Indians off. On another occasion the slaying of two Sandwich Islanders beside a stream along what is now the southern part of the Idaho-Oregon boundary gave the river the name it still bears, the Owyhee (an early spelling of Hawaii.)

During the winter of 1818–19 McKenzie pushed the brigade as far as the hairpin bend of the Bear River in southeastern Idaho. After settling the main party there under charge of Michel Bourdon, he led half a dozen scouts northward to the sources of the Snake. Traveling often on snowshoes, he re-examined the Jackson Hole and Teton country he had first seen in 1811 with Wilson Hunt. It was a gigantic effort, but scarcely winded him. Returning to Fort Nez Percé in April, this once indolent partner of the Astorians checked the navigation possibilities of the lower Snake, then cut restlessly southward to the Boise River. There he received reinforcements from Kittson and once again invaded, during the winter of 1819–20, the valley of the Bear River.

Results on the Bear were spectacular. One hundred and fifty-four horses had to be rounded up for carrying the furs back to Fort Nez Percé. As the homeward-bound brigade crossed the Blue Mountains, a band of Cayuse Indians, five hundred horses strong, fell in with them; and in what must be one of the more flamboyant scenes of the Northwest's saga, a chanting, bespangled savage column two miles long rode down from the hills to the station.

For twelve days McKenzie stayed there, readying the transport for Fort George and no doubt joining the men in drinking the regale, as the mass intoxication preceding a brigade's departure was called. Then back he went, this time as far as the Green River in present Wyoming. When he returned in July 1821, his five-year contract was up. Rather than start for Athabaska Pass at that late season, he spent the winter at Fort Nez Percé with Alexander Ross, and then left the country forever.

He had wrought great changes. But while he had been buried in the interior even greater changes were taking place outside. In 1820 those implacable antagonists, Lord Selkirk of the Hudson's Bay Company and Alexander Mackenzie of the North West Company, died. Moderate counsel by men sick of bloodshed and violence now prevailed; and in a move that left the veteran traders of both organizations shell-shocked with incredulity, the firms combined under the name of the elder concern. The Hudson's Bay Company now stretched unchallenged from coast to coast.

8. Persons of the Great Drama

IN SPITE of Donald McKenzie's herculean efforts, mismanagement on the lower river still reddened the books of the old North West Company's Columbia Department. After casting up accounts in London, the all-powerful governor and committee of the expanded Hudson's Bay Company gloomily wrote to George Simpson, their new field manager in Canada, "Should the result of all your enquiries be unfavorable to the plan of continuing the trade of the Columbia, it will be proper to consider" withdrawing into New Caledonia, as British Columbia was then called.

George Simpson did not withdraw. He was not the kind ever to retreat. More importantly, the Columbia became, even while he was investigating its potentials, the target of international dispute. Once again the Americans were aiming political and economic shafts at the Northwest; and with a quiver felt as far away as London, the Hudson's Bay Company awoke to the fact that the Columbia's significance might lie not in mere profit but in the protection it could give their entire fur preserves west of the Rockies.

The American political barrage had begun as early as 1819. Perhaps the most vigorous attack was that launched by Thomas Hart Benton. An opportunistic Missourian, Benton sought frontier approval by denouncing the joint occupation treaty and advocating in his St. Louis newspaper a chain of government-supported posts stretching across the continent to the mouth of the Columbia, where a base could be built to control the maritime trade with Asia. Elected senator, Benton carried the theme to Washington. There he gathered more ammunition from a chance meeting with two of Astor's erstwhile Pacific Fur Company partners; and at the same time he attracted the attention of his future uncle-in-law, John Floyd of Virginia. [1] Though in later

[1] John Floyd's interest in the West stemmed from his cousin Charles Floyd, a sergeant with the Lewis and Clark expedition who died of illness near present Sioux City, Iowa, and thus achieved a negative sort of fame as the only casualty of the historic crossing.

years Benton would make a somewhat undeserved name for himself as a leading proponent of annexation of the Northwest, it was Floyd who launched the congressional sorties. In 1821, partly to embarrass the Administration, he launched the first of a series of bills looking toward the establishment of "the territory of Origon"—the initial American application of the name to land instead of just to the river.

A bored Congress shelved the bills for a variety of reasons. One of them sounds strange indeed to modern ears: "Nature has fixed limits to our nation; she has kindly interposed as our Western barrier, mountains almost inaccessible, whose base she has skirted with irreclaimable deserts of sand. This barrier our population can never pass—if it does, it becomes the people of a new world, whose connexions, whose feelings, and whose interests, are not with us, but with our antipodes."

But if Congress was indifferent, the American Department of State was not. By a treaty ratified in February 1821 the United States acquired, as lagniappe to a five-million-dollar bargain purchasing the Floridas, Spain's ancient claims to the Northwest—"the only European power," said John Quincy Adams, forgetting both Cook and the Russians, "who prior to the discovery of the [Columbia] River, had any pretensions to territorial right on the Northwest Coast of America."

Russia immediately reminded Adams of her pretensions by a ukase of September 1821, extending Alaska to the fifty-first parallel. The American retort to this and to European meddling in Latin America became known to history as the Monroe Doctrine. Defiantly the young nation told the world "that the American continents, by the free and independent condition which they have assumed and maintain, are henceforth not to be considered as subjects for future colonization by any European powers"—in spite of the fact that the joint occupation treaty specifically gave both Great Britain and the United States equal right of settlement in Oregon.

Faced with this nation's and Britain's vigorous objections, the Russian czar pulled his sights back to the present southern terminus of Alaska, 54° 40'. Britain then decided that she too should seek a compromise with the aroused Yankees, and offered to relax her claim to all of Oregon if the Americans in turn would accept the Columbia River as the international boundary. George Canning, Foreign Secretary, notified the Hudson's Bay Company of the proposal and added a recommendation that Fort George (nee Astoria), which stood on the south bank of the Columbia, be abandoned in favor of a settlement farther north, perhaps on the Fraser.

The Hudson's Bay Company thus knew that eventually it would lose its trapping rights east and south of the Columbia. The difficulty lay in not knowing when. The Americans were not disposed to accept Britain's compromise offer. By now the State Department in Washington was aware that the Columbia's ever dangerous bar ruled out the river as a dependable harbor for sailing vessels, and hence the Yankees were eager to secure the only other first-class Pacific anchorage available, Puget Sound. (Mexico, of course, still held San Francisco and San Diego.) Though the Americans, for bargaining purposes, talked boldly of rights extending to 54° 40′, it was surmised that they would compromise at the forty-ninth parallel—the boundary line between Canada and the United States east of the Rockies. This supposition Britain was reluctant to heed, and it began to look to the Hudson's Bay officials as though years might pass before a solution was reached. In other words, the joint occupation treaty might remain in force long beyond the decade originally comtemplated when the document was signed.

Such a stalemate had been ideal so long as the supremacy of the Company in Oregon remained unchallenged. Those palmy days, however, were passing. Once again American trappers were pointing toward the Far West. For years they had been held back, first by the War of 1812, then by government strictures on their trade, and finally by the fury of the Blackfeet. By 1820, however, the United States Government had relaxed its regulations and was extending military protection toward the frontier. Thus encouraged, strong bands of trappers began once again working up the Missouri. Inevitably the drive would soon break across the Rockies toward the Columbia. If by that time diplomacy had not established the river as a boundary (and such establishment seemed remote), the Americans would then have every right to swarm on northward across present Washington into the fabulous fur grounds of New Caledonia, the richest territory the Hudson's Bay Company possessed.

In London the company's governor and committee sifted the problem down to two knotty lumps: first, a way had to be found to keep the Yankees back from the Columbia for as long as possible; and secondly, preparations had to be made for abandoning the country east and south of the Columbia when and if that river became the international boundary. In order to keep the stockholders happy, both goals had to be achieved with maximum economy.

Implementation of these policies fell to George Simpson, another of the wildly incongruous figures of the fur trade. Though in the mid-

1820s Simpson held the destinies of the world's greatest fur company in his palm, he had not so much as seen a beaver until he was approaching the age of thirty. An illegitimate son, born in one of the most remote parts of Scotland, he had been raised in the home of his grandfather, a minister. From there he had gone to London, where an uncle had employed him as clerk in a firm of West India merchants. One of the partners of this firm, Andrew Colvile, was also a director of the Hudson's Bay Company. The connection assumed startling import in 1820, when the Bay Company's governor in Canada, bluff William Williams, was threatened with jail on charges brought by the North West Company. In order to have a substitute on hand in case of necessity, the London directors turned, at Colvile's recommendation, to George Simpson, twenty-eight years old and inexperienced beyond his clerk's stool in the London countinghouse.

Perhaps the selection came about because Colvile knew the clerk to be discreet, energetic, personable—an attractive figurehead for a temporary post. But Simpson was also intensely ambitious. On reaching Canada and learning that Williams was not going to be arrested, he might have returned home. Instead he volunteered to take over the remote, harshly difficult Athabaska District, which had been unexpectedly left without supervision.

It was a masterly stroke of opportunism. While Simpson was in the wilderness, toughening his soft London muscles and learning some of the practical aspects of the trade, the once warring Hudson's Bay and North West companies worked out their peaceful merger. Almost the first search of the new board of directors was for a business-trained diplomat, unscarred by the hatreds of the recent competition, who could reorganize the overlapping, demoralized units in the field. Again the choice fell on George Simpson.

He had maneuvered his way into no sinecure. During three years of tireless canoe voyages he swept his new broom into nearly every post, large and small, east of the Rockies. On his journeys he was demoniac—and as regal as a pharaoh. At two o'clock every morning camp was struck. A voyageur carried the governor (and, indeed, any traveling person of importance) pickaback to his canoe, deposited him gently in the middle, handed him a lighted pipe. Sternman, bowman, middlemen took their places; red-painted paddles flashed, until finally at eight o'clock there was a short halt for breakfast. Shortly after noon there came another pause while the men gulped a few mouthfuls of pemmican, Simpson's servant meanwhile serving him a cold cut and a glass of wine. Then on again until 8:00 P.M., the brigade often covering a hundred watery miles in the eighteen-hour day. Under pressure the hours were extended—and Simpson's traveling was always under pressure. One bit of apocrypha says that an exasperated voyageur once dragged the governor from the canoe and held him under water until Simpson promised to slow down.

Nor was style sacrificed for speed. The governor (and all chief factors in permanent posts) dressed every day, one observer relates, "in a suit of black or dark blue, white shirt, collars to his ears, frock coat, velvet stock, and straps on the bottom of his trousers . . . a black beaver hat worth forty shillings . . . and over his black frock . . . a long coat made of Royal Stuart tartan lined with scarlet." As the governor's brigade approached an important post, a special piper taken along for just this purpose unlimbered his instruments. Bugles answered, the voyageurs struck up a chant, and antiphonal musket shots echoed between canoes and bastions. Landing, Simpson was carried ashore and then strode to the gates, preceded by his bagpipes.

By the spring of 1824, after unguessable thousands of canoe miles between Hudson Bay and the Rockies, Simpson felt he had affairs flowing smoothly enough that he could go to England and get married. His request for leave was peremptorily denied, however, and he was ordered to the Columbia, to initiate, with appropriate economy, the company's new policies. First he was directed to deter the advance of American land trappers by hunting bare the approaches to the Columbia, thus removing the enemy's incentive. Concurrently he was to drive away Yankee sea peddlers by building up the maritime trade, long neglected by the Nor'Westers. Finally he was to supplant Fort George by locating a temporary post on the north bank of the Columbia and by building a permanent central depot somewhere near the mouth of the Fraser, safely beyond the forty-ninth parallel.

Replanning the economy of the far-off Northwest was one thing. Finding a man capable of keeping it functioning once the start had been made was something else. As Simpson searched for possible resident managers, his mind kept returning to a man whom he did not like and whom he would eventually hate with virulent intensity—towering white-haired John McLoughlin, a former Nor'Wester.

Legend in Oregon has inclined to hallow John McLoughlin almost beyond humanity. The portrait needs adjustment. An autocrat of violent prejudices and flaring temper, he was considerably less than a saint—yet at the same time he possessed an impulsive generosity that lifted him far above the level of just another able fur trader. Though he was by no means a great man, destiny made him, even more than it did Simpson, the central figure in the twenty-year drama to control one of the richest sections on our continent.

Born of French, Irish, and Scottish stock in 1784 in Rivière du Loup, Lower Canada, John McLoughlin was articled at the age of fourteen to a Quebec doctor. Five years later he went to the North West Company's headquarters post, Fort William on Lake Superior, as an apprentice surgeon, at a salary of twenty pounds a year. He soon abandoned medicine. Except for a few brief weeks during the summer, when Fort William swarmed with transport brigades and rendezvousing partners, there was little doctoring to do. Besides, the six-foot four-inch, big-handed youth was not an adept physician. He preferred the fur trade, and soon showed an astonishing capacity for managing Indians.

Through some unrecorded liaison in the wilderness he acquired a half-breed son, Joseph. A year or so later and perhaps because the boy's mother was dead, McLoughlin entered into his more famous union with Marguerite Wadon McKay, half-breed daughter of a Swiss trader and a Cree Indian mother. Marguerite was thirty-five when Mc-Loughlin appeared, eight years older than he. Decorous convention in the Northwest refers to her as Alexander McKay's "widow." This is straining the word. Marguerite McKay and John McLoughlin began living together several months before word of Alexander McKay's death in the Pacific aboard Astor's ill-fated *Tonquin* could possibly have reached them. [2] Yet if the union was as careless of formalities as were most fur-trade marriages, it proved as enduring as the best of them—as David Thompson's, for instance.

In 1814, aged thirty, McLoughlin became a full partner in the North West Company. Arrested on a flimsy pretext during the Red River troubles, he was dispatched in a canoe across Lake Superior for trial in Montreal. A storm swamped the craft; nine of its twenty-one occupants were drowned and McLoughlin was dragged ashore unconscious. Fable says the experience turned his great halo of silken hair snow white. Probably the change came more naturally; but whatever the cause, the premature graying contributed no little bit to the patriarchal reputation that gradually began to grow up around the man.

The jury that eventually tried him acquitted him in less than an hour. Disheartened by the experience and by the internecine violence

---

[2] Fourteen-year-old Thomas McKay, Alexander and Marguerite's son, escaped the *Tonquin* disaster by having stayed behind at Astoria. He spent the rest of his life in the Northwest, becoming, while in the employ of his stepfather, Dr. John, one of the country's renowned trappers and scouts.

that had brought his firm to the edge of bankruptcy, the ex-doctor now spearheaded a drive to talk peace with the Hudson's Bay Company. The wintering partners listened to him and gave him their proxies to carry to London. There, according to another revered legend, he was a dominant figure in working out the details of the amalgamation. Actually the city slickers of both firms elbowed him aside and his voice was seldom heard. But his trading talents were recognized and he was taken into the expanded company as a chief factor, a shareholding position analogous to his former status as a wintering partner among the Nor'Westers.

Returning to Canada, McLoughlin assumed charge of the border post of Lac la Pluie. His two-year success in undercutting American competition may have been one reason why Simpson suddenly selected him to head the vast Columbia and New Caledonia districts.

On July 27, 1824, three months short of his fortieth birthday, John McLoughlin left York Factory on the west coast of Hudson Bay for his distant post on the Columbia. This was a twenty-day start on Simpson, who was also heading for the Columbia. Lulled by this, although he knew the pudgy governor's reputation for speed, McLoughlin fondly supposed he could cross the Rockies and forge far down the Western river before his superior overhauled him. It was an embarrassing mistake, and one McLoughlin probably never forgot.

At 7:00 A.M. on September 27, long before he had reached even the Athabaska River east of the Rockies, he heard the triumphant skirl of Simpson's bagpipes. To complete his mortification, he was still sitting in camp when the governor swept up—all of which Simpson dryly noted in the official journal he was keeping for the directorate in London. To this self-satisfied account the governor then added his famous description of the Columbia's new resident manager:

He was such a figure as I would not like to meet in a dark night in one of the bye lanes in the neighborhood of London, dressed in Clothes that had once been fashionable, but now covered with a thousand patches of different Colors, his beard would do honor to the chin of a Grizzly Bear, his face and hands evidently Shewing that he had not lost much time at his Toilette, loaded with Arms and his own herculean dimensions forming a tout ensemble that would convey a good idea of the high way men of former Days.

There were no more late starts for John McLoughlin. During the next month the combined parties toiled with twenty-one horses across

Athabaska Pass, "Wild & Majestic beyond description," fought through quagmires and brush to the Columbia, and in rain, snow, and fog swept four hundred miles down the river to the mouth of the Spokane. Meeting a supply brigade bound for Spokane House, they rode sixty miles eastward over rolling hills to inspect the post. There Simpson's Scotch frugality exploded with outrage.

Because supplies for the Columbia District were shipped around the Horn and there was room in the holds for what the governor called "European luxuries," the Western traders had fallen out of the habit of living off the land. Though in Simpson's opinion two boatloads of supplies should have sufficed for Spokane, he discovered that five or six craft were annually hauled up the river from the ocean, "loaded with Eatables, Drinkables and other *Domestic Comforts.*" Well, there'd be no more of that. The rivers teemed with fish; the soil would grow potatoes. Those were good enough for any man.

More stops farther down the Columbia brought more outbursts. At Okanogan he found the traders (who seemed to him to spend undue time worrying about the faithfulness of their Indian wives) "not satisfied unless they have a posse of Clerks Guides Interpreters and Supernumeraries at their disposal"—but a posse not employed in farming. Farming, the field men protested, was no part of the fur trade. Coldly Simpson retorted, "Every pursuit tending to leighten the Expence of the Trade is a branch thereof." This opinion was in no wise altered when he reached Fort Nez Percé and discovered that its men had, in three years, purchased from the Indians seven hundred horses to use for food. "The river," he warned, "with a potatoe Garden will abundantly maintain the Post," then pushed furiously on through the roaring gorges of the Cascades to a final shock at Fort George: the traders there were "amusing themselves Boat Sailing."

Despite side trips and inspection stops the implacable little dynamo had covered the distance between Hudson Bay and the Pacific in eighty-four days, twenty less than it had ever been done before. Vast changes came with him. Promptly he ordered the abandonment of Fort George and dispatched a party to the Fraser to locate a new site for the company's principal Western depot. It was a strange decision. Although Simpson had never seen the northern river and must have known of Simon Fraser's ordeal in its canyons, he nonetheless blandly described it to the London directors as "formed by nature as the grand communication with all our Establishments on this side of the mountain." Meanwhile he relegated the man who would ultimately be responsible for running the post, Chief Factor McLoughlin, to locating a subsidiary fort somewhere along the north bank of the Columbia.

A hundred miles above Fort George and a half dozen above the confluence with the Willamette, McLoughlin found a spot where beautiful meadows broke through the interminable forests. There, on a swell of land inconveniently far from the river but safely beyond reach of floodwaters, he began work on a small stockade. No description of the post remains, probably because no one deemed it would amount to much.

As soon as enough bark roofs had been placed to afford shelter, Fort George's movable goods were ferried upstream, including thirty-one head of cattle and seventeen hogs riding a specially constructed barge. At sunrise on March 19, 1825, Simpson wrote, he "baptized [the post] by breaking a Bottle of Rum on the Flag Staff and repeating the following words in a loud voice: 'In behalf of the Hon'ble Hudson's Bay Co'y I hereby name this Establishment FORT VANCOUVER. God save King George the 4th!' with three cheers." He had chosen the post's name carefully as a pointed reminder to the United States that the first man to penetrate this far up the river had been Lieutenant Broughton, exploring under orders from Captain George Vancouver.

By now McLoughlin had full instructions: stop all traffic in alcohol; develop the long-neglected coastal trade; open business, if possible, with the Russians; finish building Fort Langley on the Fraser; sweep clean of fur-bearing animals the country between the Columbia and United States territory; send other brigades south toward California; plant gardens—and keep those expenses down! With a boom of salutes ringing in his ears, Simpson waved farewell and headed east, taking with him for transplanting to the Red River colony several dozen superannuated voyageurs pared from the pay rolls.

On the way upstream he decided that Spokane House was too expensive and too isolated to maintain any longer. Selecting a more economical site near the foaming ledges of Kettle Falls on the Columbia (and personally stepping off the bounds for a potato garden), he ordered a new post built and named Fort Colvile after his benefactor. He also summarily demoted, as brigade leader of the trappers working the Snake country, Alexander Ross, who had first come to the Northwest with the Astorians. In Ross's place, to supervise the creating of a fur desert between the river and the Rockies, Simpson appointed another of the giant figures of Western history, barrel-chested Peter Skene Ogden, of whom more will be noted later.

Satisfied that the Columbia would now function efficiently, Simpson resumed his headlong course back to the East. He ran the legs off his companions. When the entire group finally collapsed about him out on the central prairies, he galloped on alone through the night to the next fort. So impressed were the governor and committee in London with his whirlwind accomplishment that they voted him a bonus of five hundred pounds and a salary increase of two hundred pounds a year. The Western fur preserves, the company felt, had been saved.

9. To Strip the Country Bare

THE weapon which Simpson aimed at the American trappers was the Snake country brigade, forged by Donald McKenzie less than ten years before as the sole means by which profits could be wrung from the vast drainage of the Snake River. And it was from McKenzie himself, now serving as governor of the once turbulent Red River colony, that Simpson had learned the strengths and weaknesses of these wandering bands of trappers who moved erratically through the country with their wives and children and obstreperous herds of horses. They were, the governor said in his journal, "the most unruly and troublesome gang to deal with in this or any other part of the World. . . . They therefore require superior management." Yet superior management was exactly what the brigades had not had since McKenzie's departure from the country.

Root of the trouble lay in the so-called freemen. These were half-breeds, Iroquois, and French-Canadian laborers (but mostly Iroquois) whose term of service with the company had expired but who preferred to remain in the wilderness with their native families rather than return east. To earn their precarious livings they bought scanty supplies from the company, operated under a company-appointed bourgeois, and then paid off their store bills by turning into the company warehouses whatever furs they caught.

They were utterly irresponsible. Even when they knew Blackfeet lurked in the vicinity, they often refused to guard their horses and as a result lost many animals. They were prey to sudden panics, weird fancies, and explosive resentments. At the nicker of a stallion they would stop work to race horses with visiting Indians. Every bourgeois sentenced to work with them seethed about their indolence and lack of loyalty. Yet what motive was there to command loyalty? The company held them in economic thralldom, selling them goods at exorbitant markups and buying their beaver at rock-bottom prices. It was such cheap hire that even George Simpson could overlook their in-efficiency.

So long as the Hudson's Bay Company was the freemen's only source of livelihood, the system worked. But trouble came with the approach of competing Americans—difficulties which the company itself inadvertently hastened by shifting, in 1821, the departure point of the brigades from Fort Nez Percé on the Walla Walla to Flathead Post on the Clark Fork River in western Montana, near David Thompson's old Saleesh House.

The reason for the shift was sound: as the relocated brigades moved southward from Flathead Post to the waters of the Snake, they could add to their harvest by trapping along the shoulders of the Continental Divide, which there bulges erratically westward. But the route also brought the trappers near to—at times even onto—American territory. The very first year the Hudson's Bay Company tried the new trails, fourteen Iroquois deserted and wandered eastward with their women and furs in hope of encountering Americans with whom they could make a better deal. [1]

The move to Flathead country also brought the brigades close to the relentless Blackfeet, who slashed murderously at the 1822-23 out-fit led by Finan McDonald, a red-whiskered giant who had been with Thompson on the 1807 discovery of the upper Columbia. Six of Finan's men died. Furiously he struck back. Sixty-eight of the enemy, he reported after the battle, "remane in the Planes as Pray for the wolves . . . they will not be so radey to atack People another time." But Finan wasn't ready to tackle Blackfeet again, either. Before he went out with another Snake brigade, he vowed, beaver would have to grow golden skins.

And so, in 1824, it became Alexander Ross's turn. By then Simpson knew that the advancing Americans had reached as far as the upper Missouri and in all probability would soon cross the Divide. Accordingly he warned Ross to have no association whatsoever with any alien trappers he encountered. Ross, however, was not remarkable for his adroitness.

---

[1] It was an ill-judged venture. Out on the plains Crow and Cheyenne Indians killed several of the deserters, robbed the rest of their women, children, and furs. Reaching Fort Atkinson, near present Omaha, the survivors waited there while the American military made a perfunctory and fruitless effort to recover their wives for them. Some of the men then accompanied Santa Fe traders to New Mexico and with trappers working out of Taos eventually re-established contact, near Great Salt Lake, with Hudson's Bay people coming down from Flathead Post. As Dale Morgan remarks in his biography of Jedediah Smith, a firsthand journal of the wanderers' experiences "would be one of the immortal narratives of Western history."

While trapping in what is now southern Idaho, he infuriated certain Snake Indians with his highhanded tactics. Seeking revenge, these Snakes fell on a detached portion of Ross's Iroquois, robbing them of everything they possessed save certain furs *en cache*. At this juncture seven Americans appeared, led by twenty-five-year-old Jedediah Smith. To the terrified Iroquois, who momentarily expected a return of the Snakes, the whites looked like salvation. Eagerly they gave Smith 105 beaver pelts for necessary supplies and for guarding them on their perilous journey back to the camp of their bourgeois. When the Americans appeared, grinning complacently, Ross suspected them of using the opportunity to spy out the land. But he did not know how to get rid of them. Instead, he let them tag along with him back to Flathead Post on the Clark Fork. Quite naturally, they used their eyes as they went.

That finished Alexander Ross on the Columbia. Unceremoniously Simpson took him back to Red River, where the erstwhile brigade leader became a schoolteacher and later wrote the books on which much of our knowledge of the early Northwest rests. Moving up to replace him, as already noted, came imperious, wild-humored Peter Skene Ogden, notoriously capable of physically manhandling any would-be troublemaker in the entire Hudson's Bay Company.

Thirteen or so years before, at the age of sixteen or seventeen, Ogden had quit the lawbooks thrust on him by his jurist father, a colonial loyalist originally from New York, and had entered the North West Company as a clerk. Assigned to the factory at Ile à la Crosse, he and another clerk had straightway created a monstrous hubbub by assaulting a Hudson's Bay trader inside his own post and then swaggering away untouched by the victim's own gape-mouthed voyageurs. When the clash between the companies reached open warfare Ogden captured the Bay Company's Ile à la Crosse fort and used it for imprisoning twenty men, more than a hundred women and children, and "dogs innumerable." This stroke of law defiance was too much even for the Canadian wilderness. The authorities moved in and Ogden was ordered to flee across the mountains to Fort George. When the firms merged, the Hudson's Bay Company directors gagged at swallowing so violent a former rival. Ogden was fired, but in 1823 Simpson reinstated him as chief trader. Now the governor was exacting payment: the Snake country brigades.

On December 20, 1824, Ogden left Flathead Post for the Snake. All told there were sixty men in his party, the erratic freemen outnumbering his more stable engagés four to one. A thin, crusted snow gleamed under the winter sun; the spruce stood black and stiff along the ridgetops. Horses pranced in the cold; squaws shrilled and dogs ki-yied. In the midst of the confusion Jedediah Smith and his half dozen Americans were scarcely noticeable. Ogden was nevertheless uncomfortably aware of them as they trailed along, back toward their own countrymen, living off supplies the Hudson's Bay Company had grudgingly sold them at Flathead Post.

In journeying toward the Snake, Ogden's brigade, like its predecessors, took a shortcut by crossing a bulge of the Continental Divide. This brought them onto the headwaters of the Missouri. Here the bourgeois let his restless freemen trap without regard for the fact that they were on territory belonging to the United States. At the time, neither Smith nor his Americans protested. But they did not forget the incident.

From the Missouri the hunters crossed back to the Pacific slope in Lemhi Valley. There they were snowbound for seven weeks before they could break out to the south. They lost horses, fought with Blackfeet. In the spring, as the trail-hardened trappers moved into what is now southeastern Idaho, Smith's Americans annoyed the Canadians by working the streams just ahead of them. Then one morning Jedediah's party vanished into the tangle of hills along the upper Bear River. Thinking himself free of interference at last, Ogden pressed on toward the Great Salt Lake and the site of the Utah city that today bears his name. He trapped ruthlessly as he went. Normally the Hudson's Bay Company conserved enough game to keep a region profitable, but this country had already been written off as lost. For once exploitation, leaving nothing to lure the Americans westward, would be good business.

The bourgeois knew that sooner or later he would meet the enemy, but he was not prepared for the clash that developed. On the morning of May 23, 1825, a man named Etienne Provost rode into Ogden's camp at the head of a motley gang he had brought up from Spanish Taos. Provost was hostile. The previous fall several of his men had been massacred by the very Snake Indians whom Alexander Ross had aroused. Furiously, Provost blamed all Canadians indiscriminately for the bloodshed.

Before Ogden could even start to pacify Provost, up rode twenty-five Americans, the flag of their country ostentatiously displayed. Riding with the invaders, Ogden saw to his dismay, were fourteen of his freemen. The Americans had met the Iroquois and French Canadians working the neighboring streams and had persuaded them to desert.

Jedediah Smith was not in evidence. Nevertheless Ogden felt that Jedediah had triggered the trouble, on meeting his countrymen, by telling of the trespass on the upper Missouri. If there'd been no Smith, there'd have been no clash, he thought, and railed in his journal about "that dam'd all cursed day that Mr. Ross consented to bring the 7 Americans with him to the Flat heads." Actually the collision had been inevitable. American trappers had recently reached the Salt Lake region in swarms. They had expected to find virgin country, and the unwelcome advent of Hudson's Bay men in country that Yankee propaganda said belonged to the United States was regarded by the majority of them as a personal affront.

Truculently their leader, one Johnson Gardner, planted his camp within a hundred yards of Ogden's. Announcing loudly that this was United States land and that all hands were free to deal as they liked, he offered to buy beaver for $3.50 a pelt and to sell the freemen goods cheap in proportion—so cheap that Ogden's hands at once figured they could improve their economic position eightfold by shifting allegiance. Before nightfall twenty-three more of his men—over half his force—had melted away, taking seven hundred skins over to the Americans. When Ogden and his clerks endeavored to interfere, Johnson's men cocked their guns and poured out obscenities. Their purpose, Ogden felt, was to provoke an incident that would justify their slaughtering the outnumbered Britishers. Accordingly he choked down his wrath and made his men hold their fire.

Even more galling was the Americans' threat, as Ogden reports it, "that you will See us shortly not only in the Columbia but at the Flat Heads & Cootanies as we are determined you Shall no longer remain in our Territory."

It seems not to have occurred to either party that the soil where the incident took place belonged to Mexico.

With so many of his men gone and the temper of the rest uncertain, Ogden retreated northward along the route by which he had come. Beyond the Divide, on the headwaters of the Missouri, he wrote out a long report of the affair for the company's governor and committee in London. Injudiciously he dated his tale of woe at the point where the letter originated, the "East Fork of the Missouri." Because of that place name, the London directors jumped to the conclusion that the desertion had taken place within United States territory. Promptly a chill rebuke went to Ogden's superior, John McLoughlin. Henceforth Hudson's Bay trappers were to stay "within the limits of the

Company's territories on the Neutral Ground till the boundaries of the two Powers are defined, and any inattention to this instruction . . . will be attended with our serious displeasure." That, too, was a bitter pill to swallow when it came. Yet there was no choice but to obey, and the Hudson's Bay trespass of strictly American territory was not repeated—a restraint which United States representatives in Congress would overlook during the tub-thumping that eventually developed.

None of this was an auspicious beginning to the attempt to hold back the Americans. Only time seemed to oppose the realization of their threat to invade the Northwest—the time it would take the Yankees to learn the trails of the vast country and to bring up supplies along the backbreaking overland route from St. Louis. None of the time, however, was either Ogden or McLoughlin prepared to concede. Veterans of a harsher trade war than this one, they immediately prepared to carry the fight back to the scene of Ogden's previous defeat.

The first step was to restore the shattered morale of the freemen. In a blunt letter to the governor and committee in London, Ogden pointed out the grinding economy under which the men toiled: " . . . it was almost impossible however industrious a man might be to clear his annual expenses, in fact his four horses and traps alone cost him One hundred fifty large beaver . . . and seldom could a Trapper return to the depot without being obliged to renew both."

A copy of this letter he sent to McLoughlin at Fort Vancouver. Without waiting for London's permission, McLoughlin on his own responsibility lowered the prices charged against the freemen for supplies and raised the payment for furs. But Ogden hadn't delayed even to learn this. Within twelve days of his return to Flathead Post, and before he heard of McLoughlin's decision, he was on the move again.

Following Simpson's instructions, he shifted the departure point of the brigades back to Fort Nez Percé at the junction of the Walla Walla and Columbia. From there he drove southward across the Blue Mountains toward the great horseshoe bend of the Snake River in what is now southern Idaho. The men worked well, partly because he had stabilized the personnel of the brigade by the inclusion of more French Canadians and fewer Iroquois, but more because the trappers knew that Ogden had gone to bat for them. Yet even Ogden was amazed at what they endured that winter; " . . . almost half froze," he wrote in his journal, "naked as the greater part are, and destitute of shoes . . . two-thirds without a blanket or any shelter, and have been so for the last six months . . . it is surprising not a murmur of complaint do I hear."

On April 9, 1826, he met the Americans again. They had already pushed almost entirely across what is now the southern part of Idaho, and they were astonished when the Canadians suddenly appeared in front of them. Having once driven Ogden out of the country, the mountain men were smugly confident he would not dare risk another debacle in furs and men by returning. Yet there he was.

Ogden himself, as his journal shows, gloomily expected the worst. But when the showdown came his men stood staunch, resisting the blandishments of the opposition. Meanwhile he discovered that some of the deserters of the previous year were with the Americans. By skillfully playing on their erratic tempers—they had not found the grass beyond the fence so green after all—Ogden managed to collect old company debts from some of them and actually succeeded in luring a few of them back into his fold.

By this time the Snake country had been pretty thoroughly despoiled by the competing trappers. Just beyond it, however, in what is now southern Oregon and northern California lay virgin ground. Fearful lest the Americans open a way into the untracked region, find it profitable, and then swing north along the coast to the Columbia, McLoughlin and Ogden determined in 1827 to move in ahead of them. From Fort Nez Percé the stocky bourgeois hurried almost directly south across the high, gray sage deserts of western Oregon, penetrated illegally into northern California, found and named a gigantic mountain (Mount Shasta) which the *Californios* did not know they possessed, and came back with a wealth of both skins and geographical knowledge.

With that flank protected, he returned to the Snake during the winter months of 1827–28. It was a terrible time. Bitter cold and towering drifts locked him in his camp on the Portneuf River, in the southeastern part of present Idaho. He lost contact with some of his men. He succored various Americans who were unable to get back to their own camps. But though he kept the wanderers alive, he declined to help them on their way, forbidding his voyageurs to sell them snowshoes even when the Yankees offered as much as twenty-five dollars for a single pair. His reasons were pragmatic enough: he feared that his competitors, having spied him out, would return with reinforcements to beat him to the nearby streams as soon as the weather opened—or, worse, would return with liquor, for which the American traders were notorious, and shatter the discipline he had so laboriously created.

In the end he outdid the opposition completely. For each of the four key years of the struggle, 1825 through 1828, he brought back to the Columbia upwards of three thousand skins. Presumably the Americans harvested almost as abundantly, though not because of any conscious policy. Strident individualists, they were competing among themselves as well as with the British monopoly; and besides, they had never been trained in conservation: when you saw a pelt you took it, and let someone else worry about tomorrow. Thus within four years the Bay Company's plan had been realized. The southwestern approaches to the Columbia had been made so unprofitable that during the next decade only stragglers would venture across it into the heartland of Oregon. If the Northwest was to fall to the United States, it would not be because of the American mountain men.

10. Accidental Greatness

WHILE these relatively negligible numbers of trappers were jockeying for position along the cold, unmapped tributaries of the Snake, starched diplomats once more carried their own form of jockeying to the international conference tables, trying to settle what by this time seemed as perennial a question as death or taxes: Who owned the Pacific Northwest? The claims of each nation were shined up again, refuted, fortified, disdained. Wasted breath. Britain still insisted on the Columbia as a boundary; the United States, eying Puget Sound, still demanded the forty-ninth parallel.

In 1827 the area in dispute (it boiled down to approximately what is now the western two thirds of the state of Washington) was no better known than it had been during the skirmishes preceding the first treaty of joint occupation. Since neither claimant was willing to grow belligerent over so dubious a piece of real estate, the weary conferees at length decided to extend indefinitely the stopgap convention of 1818—with this difference: either power could cancel the agreement for joint occupancy by giving the other signatory a year's notice of intent.

Knowledge of the extended *status quo* went west with George Simpson when he left York Factory, on Hudson Bay, July 12, 1828, for another lightning trip across the continent. Four years had passed since Simpson's first visit to the Columbia. The international uncertainties which had determined his policies at that time had now become, paradoxically, as permanent as uncertainties can be. The Snake brigades would have to go on holding the Americans at bay; activity against the Yankee sea peddlers on the coast would have to be stepped up; and, in particular, the new central depot Simpson had ordered built on the Fraser would have to be given more attention than Dr. John McLoughlin, still stationed at Fort Vancouver, seemed willing to give it.

McLoughlin's attitude annoyed Simpson. Though a crew dispatched by the massive chief factor had obediently built Fort Langley thirty miles upstream from the Fraser's double-pronged delta, McLoughlin himself declined to visit the new post. Worse, he refused to use the Fraser for supplying the rich forts of New Caledonia. Instead, the goods still came in over the ship-crippling bar of the Columbia, were painfully hauled five hundred miles upstream to the Okanogan, then were laboriously ferried up that river to the horseback trails John Stuart of the Nor'Westers had blazed fifteen years before. McLoughlin's sole excuse for the negligence, so he wrote the directors in London, was that he had heard that the Fraser was "difficult and dangerous and Great part of it in the Summer Months unnavigable."

To George Simpson hearsay evidence was not enough. Nor was he swayed by reminders of Simon Fraser's experiences in the river's canyons. Fraser had made his wild dash during the season of the spring floods; at later seasons the river might be much more amenable to navigation. Anyway, it was a thing someone should check.

With characteristic impulsiveness Simpson decided to do the checking in person. Complete with pipes, tartan, and tall beaver hat, he led eighteen men in two canoes up the Peace River with its terrible portages, crossed overland through central British Columbia to visit Fort St. James on Stuart Lake, and in late September began his exploration of the river. The hideous tumult of white water he ran into both along the Fraser and in an alternative cast through the howling lower part of the Fraser's chief tributary, the Thompson, turned him into a believer. "I . . . consider the passage down," he wrote to the committee, "to be certain Death, in nine attempts out of Ten." Graciously then he ate crow: "I shall therefore no longer talk of it as a navigable stream."

Fort Langley, in short, could not serve as a center of the Northwestern fur trade. The Columbia would have to remain the company's highway to the interior. Consequently Fort Vancouver, on the river's north shore, was pushed willy-nilly into a position of greatness that its founders had never envisioned. One necessary corollary followed: in so far as the Hudson's Bay Company could influence international politics, its potent directors would try to make Great Britain deafer than ever to American talk of a boundary along the forty-ninth parallel.

After building more boats at Fort Langley (his party had now grown to thirty-three men), Simpson steered out of the Fraser into the Gulf of Georgia, threaded the lovely San Juan Islands, and so reached the southern end of Puget Sound. There he burned his boats to keep them from the Indians, portaged to the Cowlitz River, and descended that stream to the Columbia. Late on the night of October 25, 1828, still indefatigable, he was pounding on the gates of McLoughlin's fort.

The gigantic factor had wrought well. His fields had produced, during the season just past, 4000 bushels of potatoes and more than 3000 bushels of various grains. The cow-herd had grown from 31 head to 153; pigs from 17 to 200. He had built a sawmill four or five miles up the river from the fort, and was exploring the possibilities of exporting lumber and salmon to California and the Sandwich Islands. Simpson's economical soul glowed. Nonetheless there would have to be radical changes. The fort stood too far from the river docks and from a suitable supply of domestic water to meet the increased burdens soon to be imposed upon it. The entire establishment would have to be uprooted and moved to a new location three quarters of a mile farther downstream and within two hundred yards of the riverbank.

Work was begun in the spring of 1829 on a timbered stockade 318 feet square. Inside were the multitudinous buildings necessary for carrying on the trade: warehouses, shops, offices, commissaries, kitchens, dormitories, trash pits, privies, even a jail and, later, a church. McLoughlin and his family were to be housed in a forty-by-seventy-foot residence of massive square-hewn timbers; eventually the dwelling would contain such unfrontier-like pretensions as a huge central fireplace and french windows that opened onto a vine-covered porch approached by two curved staircases. Water for the fort was provided by a pair of rock-lined wells fed through seepage from the river. As usual, small cannon guarded the corner bastions, and by 1832 powder was stored in a special brick and stone magazine.

Behind the north stockade were small log houses for married men, pens for livestock, fields and orchards. Legend says that the first apple trees had already been planted in 1826 from seeds slipped by a sentimental London belle into the waistcoat pocket of the captain of one of the company ships—a date which seems to clash with the subsequent transfer in sites.

The start of this construction with all that it implied took place under the coolly appraising American eyes of ubiquitous Jebediah Smith. No longer was Smith the mere wandering trapper whom Alexander Ross had injudiciously brought among the Flatheads; by 1828 he had risen to full partnership in the aggressive firm of Smith, Jackson & Sublette. As such he possessed a competitor's keen interest in the developments taking place on the Columbia and the threat they might pose to every beaver stream in the West.

At the time of Simpson's arrival Smith was, to be sure, in no condition to act on his newly acquired information. Only the bounty of the Hudson's Bay Company was keeping him alive after the most tragic year in his tragedy-studded career.

Though one of the most skilled, humane, and religious of the American mountain men, Jedediah Smith seemed ironically doomed to violence. During the previous summer of 1827, while crossing the fierce deserts of the Southwest to California, he had lost more than half of his men to attacking Mojaves. Outfitting his party afresh on the coast and trapping as he went, he had worked north during the rainy months of early 1828. With him he drove a burdensome three hundred head of horses which he planned to sell at the annual rendezvous of the American fur hunters in what is now Wyoming.

After incredible toil in the storm-swept forests and abysmal canyons of northwestern California, the wayfarers had at last reached Oregon's Umpqua River. There they offended the Indians by threatening to hang a pilfering chief if he did not return a stolen ax. The man brought it back—and then bided his time. On July 14, 1828, while Smith and two men were off exploring for a pass into the upper Willamette, the Indians fell on the camp. Fifteen whites perished; only one escaped. Separately this lone survivor and Smith's trio fled to the sanctuary of Fort Vancouver, arriving destitute and exhausted during the second week of August.

McLoughlin responded immediately. Scouts were dispatched to examine the situation, and the fort's annual Umpqua brigade under Alexander McLeod was ordered to hurry its preparations for departure. On September 6 it started south, Smith accompanying it to see what could be done about recovering his property.

When Simpson arrived at Fort Vancouver in October, he wholeheartedly commended McLoughlin's decisive action in behalf of a potentially troublesome rival. Partly the approval was dictated by philanthropy—and partly by policy. Indians must not be allowed to attack any whites, even Americans, with impunity.

In pursuit of the company's iron policy of keeping the savages in hand McLoughlin had, a few months earlier, sent this same Alexander McLeod to Puget Sound on a bloody punitive expedition against Indians who had killed five men returning from Fort Langley. On the Umpqua, however, McLeod was less rigorous. Feeling that Smith's men had provoked the outbreak, he did not punish the savages. But he did demand the return of the plunder, now scattered far and wide. For nearly three patient, rain-soaked months he pressed every lead, finally salvaging several hundred skins, a paltry thirty-eight horses, and odds and ends of goods.

When Smith returned to Vancouver in December, Simpson extended the company's generosity still further, but did it with a top-lofty condescension that must have been hard to swallow. McLeod's search, the governor told Jedediah in writing, "has occasioned the loss to us of the Services of this Expedition for the whole Season thereby subjecting us to an expense of exceeding £1000 independent of the loss of Profits." Even so the company would make no charges and would also purchase Smith's livestock "at 40/Stg p. head, which is a higher price than we ever pay for horses. . . . Your Beaver which is of very bad quality the worst indeed I ever saw . . . I am willing to take off your hands at 3 Dollars p. skin." He also urged Jedediah not to risk journeying back to American territory until his small group could be escorted safely by a company caravan. In the meantime he urged upon the stranded trappers the full hospitality of the fort.

Jedediah repaid the generosity with the only currency he possessed —information. On the strength of his reports about California, Simpson and McLoughlin determined on even deeper penetrations to the south before more Americans began threatening from that direction —and never mind the fact that California belonged to Mexico.

Smith also told his hosts, as Simpson later reported to the committee in London, "that the flattering reports which reached St. Louis of the Wilhamot Country, as a field for Agricultural speculation, had induced many people in the States to direct their attention to that quarter; but he has on his present journey, discovered difficulties which never occurred to their minds. . . . Mountains [the Sierra Nevada] which even hunters cannot attempt to pass, beyond which [to the east] is a Sandy desert of about 200 miles, likewise impassable, and from thence a rugged barren country of great extent. . . . And the other route by Louis's River [the Snake], Settlers could never think of attempting.

So that I am of the opinion, we have little to apprehend from Settlers in this country."

Even granting that the remark about the Snake River route was Simpson's conclusion rather than Jedediah's, the overall impression Smith gave the governor about the approaches to the Columbia was far different (as we shall see) from the data he later passed on to the United States Government about the ease with which Oregon could be reached. Why he switched stories so radically is hard to say. Jedediah Smith was not a hypocrite. But in so far as international politics was concerned, he was misinformed. He sincerely believed that the Columbia River belonged to the United States and that the joint occupation convention simply granted to British subjects certain temporary trading concessions. The new Fort Vancouver being laid out under his eyes that spring of 1829 most obviously was not temporary. It was designed to be as permanent as if the Hudson's Bay Company owned the land in fee simple, and the unruffled assumption of sovereignty, completely unwarranted in Jedediah's estimate, rankled his patriotism. His contradictions may have sprung, perhaps subconsciously, from that sore.

During that same spring of 1829 more Americans invaded the disputed territory, both by sea and by land. The land groups, two of them, struck into the Flathead country of Montana, the only section where the Hudson's Bay Company had suffered marked loss of trade to competitors. One of these two groups was headed by Smith's partner, David Jackson. As soon as Jedediah learned of it, he hastened out with two of his men to join it. (The fourth survivor of the Umpqua massacre, John Turner, chose to stay with the Hudson's Bay Company and was employed by the company as a guide for the expeditions working into California.) This much gratitude Jedediah did show for Simpson's generosity: he hurried David Jackson's trappers back across the mountains; never again during the short remainder of his life did men of Smith, Jackson & Sublette re-enter the Columbia watershed.

The second land party was the ragtag remnant of a bankrupt group led by a man named Joshua Pilcher. In a final desperate effort to keep solvent, Pilcher proposed to Governor Simpson a joint British-American expedition to the headwaters of the Missouri. The illegal group he offered to lead under his own name so as to circumvent United States embargoes against trapping by foreigners. Peremptorily Simpson refused the bait. That sounded Pilcher's death knell. Most of his men joined David Jackson's brigade; their former leader repaired to

Fort Colvile at Kettle Falls. He too kept his eyes open, and when he returned to the United States he, like Jedediah Smith, offered useful but highly prejudiced testimony about the Columbia to his government and, through the government, to prospective settlers.

The chain of circumstances that Smith's and Pilcher's testimony would help to forge was still obscured in the future. Of more immediate concern to Simpson were two American trading brigs, the *Owhyhee* and the *Convoy*, both of which appeared in the mouth of the Columbia shortly before Jedediah Smith left newly building Fort Vancouver. The ships' pugnacious arrival sharpened Simpson's longstanding worries about the neglected maritime trade. To the governor's disgust, nothing had been done to challenge the Yankee sea peddlers. Nor'Westers under indolent James Keith had ignored the coast; McLoughlin had been hamstrung by inefficient captains on inefficient vessels. The only company ship that had so much as tried to help the chief factor was a 70-ton schooner, energetically commanded but so diminutive that, in Simpson's disgruntled words to the committee, "there are hundreds of War Canoes, on the Coast, longer and higher out of the Water than she is."

By 1829 the sea otter had been all but exterminated. To replace that branch of the commerce the Yankees began to bid for inland furs, luring beaver-trapping Indians to the coast with promises of rum and guns. In retaliation Simpson had envisioned locating forts at strategic spots from Alaska to California, so as to cut off the flow of furs before they reached the American ships. So far, however, only Fort Langley existed to block the draining away of vital pelts, and now the emboldened Yankees on the *Owhyhee* and the *Convoy* were carrying their drive into the very heart of the company's bailiwick.

Simpson's instructions from the governor and committee in London specifically directed, "If the American Traders settle near our Establishments, they must be opposed, not by violence, which would only be the means of enabling the Traders to obtain the interference of their Government, but by underselling them." In order to carry out this underselling the governor ordered McLoughlin to open wide the Vancouver warehouses, confident that the company's annual supply vessel would soon arrive to replenish the stock. But when the ship tackled the Columbia's deadly bar early in March, she struck and careened, her cargo a total loss. The crew took to lifeboats but perished in the raging surf.

Meantime the trade war was stripping McLoughlin bare. Prices tumbled fantastically: blankets from five beaver to one; guns (which the company for security reasons liked to keep expensive) from eighteen skins each to six. At that point, on March 26, 1829, Simpson departed for the East, leaving his sore-pinched chief factor to make out as best he could.

Fortunately another supply vessel arrived in the proverbial nick of time, and matters leveled off into a good-natured tug of war. As always, an ungrudging friendliness was one hallmark of John McLoughlin's nature. He gave Captain Dominis of the *Owhyhee* potatoes, sold him needed lumber, treated a sick mate, and, legend adds, forestalled an Indian attack on the vessel.

For seventeen months one or the other of the American ships remained in the Columbia, trading as far upriver as the Dalles. Finally, in July 1830, they moved to Puget Sound, cut briefly into Fort Langley's trade, and at last departed with twenty-nine hundred pelts—a mediocre return for a year and a half's effort, but a serious loss to McLoughlin. (Captain Dominis, it is worth noting, also carried with him to Boston fifty-three barrels of pickled Columbia River salmon. He sold them for fourteen dollars a barrel but had to pay import duty because of the Revenue Department's insistence that the fish had originated in foreign territory—a somewhat ironical stand in view of cries currently being sounded in Congress concerning American ownership of the Northwest.)

Although this too close contact with American shipping made McLoughlin more anxious than ever to establish the coastal forts Simpson had directed, disaster again delayed him. This time it was a devastating plague that broke out in October 1830. It was an intermittent fever, malarial in character; and though it would linger for several years, the first months of the onslaught were the worst. Along the lower Columbia, where alcohol and venereal diseases had long since undermined resistance, nine tenths of the native population were swept away amid scenes of indescribable filth and misery. The Chinooks, remembering Duncan McDougal's threat at Astoria to open a vial of smallpox among them, blamed the outbreak on "bad water" let loose by the American brigs. Other Indians, plus several whites, attributed the outbreak to miasmas arising from newly plowed ground near Fort Vancouver.

Though not mortal to whites, the disease was painfully incapacitating. At one point seventy-five of Vancouver's employees were on the sick list. Work came almost to a standstill; McLoughlin, irritably recalling his almost forgotten medical lore, was forced to take personal charge of the improvised wards.

Only the trapping brigades to the south continued to function with anything like normal vigor. Stimulated by Jedediah Smith's stories, Peter Skene Ogden drove through the wastes of the Great Basin to the lower reaches of the Colorado River, used short wooden spears to fight off attacking Mojave Indians—his Canadians killed twenty-six of them—and then set traps all the way down the river to the Gulf of California before turning back. Details of the epic journey are only sketchily known. After reaching Fort Nez Percé with his catch, Ogden started down the Columbia in a canoe. At the Dalles it capsized; nine lives, five hundred furs, and all of Ogden's records were lost.

The Snake brigades meanwhile had been turned over to John Work. Floods, Blackfeet, and years of ruthless trapping sent him home almost empty-handed. Day after day, he complained, his men had set 150 or more traps but garnered from them a dozen or fewer pelts. From now on future expeditions to the Snake country would eke out their profits by carrying trade goods. These were swapped at exorbitant prices to the Americans, who were now deep in a cutthroat war among themselves for what beaver remained in the Rockies.

Ogden's second trip into California made more evident what was already patent: here was the man to get things done. When the abatement of the plague in 1831 released workers for the oft-delayed expansion program, McLoughlin chose the blocky little trader to take charge of the northern push. With two ships Ogden beat as far toward the Arctic as the mouth of the Nass River. There he founded Fort Simpson and proposed to the Russians that they use the Hudson's Bay Company rather than the fly-by-night American traders as a source of goods and farm produce for the Alaskan settlements. The Russians playing coy, Ogden in 1833 pushed boldly north from Fort Simpson into the Stikine River, whose mouth the Muscovites held, and promptly stirred up a hornets' nest that would buzz angrily for the next half dozen years. Meanwhile other coastal forts were brought into being: Fort McLoughlin on Milbanke Sound off the coast of central British Columbia, Nisqually at the southern tip of Puget Sound in present Washington, and Umpqua near the coast of central Oregon. American competition, McLoughlin might well have supposed, had at last been swept out of the entire Northwest.

At this point something new in his experience appeared—eleven bedraggled men led by a thirty-year-old Bostonian named Nathaniel Wyeth. Obviously Wyeth was no experienced trapper, nor did he claim to be. "He says he came," McLoughlin wrote the committee on October 29, 1832, the very day of Wyeth's arrival, "to ascertain if possible to make a business of curing Salmon in this River, & at the same time to supply [with trade goods and equipment] the American Trappers in the Rocky Mountains."

There the chief factor quite likely paused in thought. He was not without information. In addition to regular dispatches from the company headquarters, there were American newspapers brought by each ship that rounded the Horn. McLoughlin was in the habit of reading these from end to end—and remembering what he read.

His pen flowed on. ". . . though it may be as he states, still I would not be surprised to find that his views are in connexion with a plan which I see in a Boston newspaper of March 1831 to colonise the Willamette. . . ."

No, Nathaniel Wyeth was not the problem. His green little band could be easily shunted aside. But handling the forces that had called that band into existence might be something else entirely.

Book Three

OREGON FEVER

1. Prophet without Honor

I AM Hall J. Kelley; that is my name; am what education, habits, and the *grace* of God have made me." So he wrote in 1867, once again seeking help from his government. He was always writing, pouring out memorials, petitions, "histories," all bearing the same theme: "The colonization of Oregon was both conceived and achieved by me."

Delusion triumphant—or so the Congress thought, and turned down his appeals. Oregon would have been settled if Hall Jackson Kelley had never uttered a sonorous line. And yet . . . the first thin strands of Manifest Destiny did twine together in his frantic, half-crazed hands. His influence did draw the first handful of American farmers to the deep-soiled plains of the Willamette Valley. In the long story of our nation's westering there are few adventures more curious or more difficult to assess.

Born in New Hampshire in 1790, Kelley was manually dexterous but given to solitary dreams rather than to gregarious handicrafts. He injured his eyes, he says, through studying Virgil by moonlight. His mother so inculcated him "with the love of truth, that not a single doubt as to the divine authenticity of the scriptures, ever profaned the sanctuary of my heart." He knew early that he was marked for great things: "In my youth the Lord Jesus revealed to me in visions the lonely, laborious, and eventful life I was to live."

For thirty years that life was commonplace enough. After graduating from Middlebury College, Vermont, Kelley set up as a schoolteacher in Boston, married the daughter of a minister, lost her, and took a second wife in 1822. He authored several profitable elementary textbooks, claims to have started the first Sunday school in Boston, and devised, by his own account, an improved system of land surveying. In short, he was talented. But he was also humorless, self-centered, inflexible, and cursed with an unfortunate propensity for grating on the nerves of everyone with whom he came in contact.

In 1823, for undisclosed reasons, he was summarily fired from the Boston school at which he was teaching. Undismayed, though he had a growing family to support, he flung himself into what had become to him a mania: Oregon.

The sources of his inspiration are obvious: the Lewis and Clark journals, the Astorian adventure, the joint occupation treaty and the debates it occasionally caused in Congress, and the tales of Boston mariners who had been on the Northwest coast. Even the idea of colonizing the Columbia was not as original with Kelley as he later insisted. At least twice before he felt the call, government aid had been solicited for Oregonian schemes: in 1819 by a company from Virginia and in 1823 by "eighty enterprising farmers" of Maryland—though there is no proof that Kelley had heard of either proposal.

His own grandiose scheme, first submitted to Congress in the form of a memorial in 1828, stated that the signers of his petition and "three thousand others" were prepared to take the long trail to Oregon as soon as the government lent a helping hand by financing the emigration and promising to protect the new settlements.

While waiting for Congress to seize on the opportunity, he formed, in 1829, the American Society for Encouraging the Settlement of the Oregon Territory. In 1831 he incorporated the organization under the laws of Massachusetts. Meantime, through a florid series of "General Circulars," "Geographic Sketches," "Manuals of the Oregon Expedition," and letters to newspapers throughout New England he endeavored to sign up his three thousand emigrants.

Every scrap of material he could find about the Northwest was turned into ammunition. The 1831 publication of Ross Cox's two-volume *Adventures on the Columbia* furnished several salvos, as did the reports which Jedediah Smith and Joshua Pilcher had sent to the Secretary of War and which had been made available as a congressional document. From Pilcher's account in particular Kelley drew arrays of data about climate, resources, soil, and what not. [1] Of even

---

[1] Kelley also followed Smith and Pilcher into the common American error of supposing that the United States held indisputable claim to Oregon and that the joint occupation treaty merely ceded certain temporary privileges to Great Britain. Both fur traders grumbled that Fort Vancouver was not temporary and that the Hudson's Bay Company was spreading unchecked into United States land south of the Columbia, "while no American," complained Smith, "has ever gone, or can venture to go on the British side." Actually, of course, sovereignty had not been established and there were no legal "sides." The misunderstanding would, during the

more moment were the statements by both men that Oregon was easily accessible from the United States. According to Pilcher, although "the Rocky mountains are deemed by many to be impassable, and to present the barrier which will arrest the westward march of the American population . . . [actually] wagons and carriages may cross them in a state of nature and without difficulty." Smith's firm of Smith, Jackson & Sublette added specific evidence: in 1830 their men had taken ten wagons and two dearborns to the annual trappers' rendezvous near the head of Wind River, and "the ease and safety with which it was done prove the facility of communicating over land with the Pacific ocean"—quite a different story from Smith's earlier statements to George Simpson at Fort Vancouver.

Fearful that Kelley's repeated siren songs might lure workers from the already tight labor markets of New England, certain Boston newspapers opened their columns to counterarguments by a man named W. J. Snelling. Since Snelling had seen no more of Oregon than Kelley, he perforce drew his material from the same sources; and Massachusetts was presented with the edifying spectacle of two humorless debaters quoting identical scriptures for antagonistic purposes about a country neither had visited. In the derangement of his later years Kelley would multiply Snelling into a shadowy army of Hudson's Bay agents and Yankee sea peddlers bent on destroying him lest he ruin their trade. Actually it is doubtful if the sum total of all the oratory changed half a dozen minds. Certainly no more than one per cent of Kelley's wishful figure of three thousand emigrants ever signed up with the American Society for Encouraging the Settlement of the Oregon Territory.

One mind which Kelley did excite was that of twenty-nine-year-old Nathaniel J. Wyeth, then engaged with Frederic Tudor in devising ways to ship Massachusetts ice to tropical ports. Forsaking Tudor's bizarre business (though eventually it would make fortunes for both of them), Wyeth borrowed books from Kelley, futilely ransacked the local libraries for more, and in the end came up with a fur-trade plan basically similar to the one Astor had devised a quarter of a century before. To this concept he added Captain Dominis' abortive idea of shipping Columbia River salmon to New England. Oddly, the entire plan seems to have been developed with only the scantiest information about Astor's experiences and none at all about the fur trade emanating from St. Louis. Had either Kelley or Wyeth got in touch with Astor's

___

next several years, poison many American minds in addition to Kelley's toward England in general and the Hudson's Bay Company in particular.

New York offices or with the fur traders working out of St. Louis, they might have saved themselves endless grief.

Kelley's motives in going to Oregon were philanthropic and patriotic. Wyeth's were commercial. When the iceman realized, in the fall of 1831, that Kelley's idealistic nonsense was tangling the colony plans beyond all practicability, he pulled out of the movement and went his own way. Alarmed, Kelley rushed to Washington in the hope that personal interviews might stir laggard congressmen into voting him aid. This failing, he returned to Boston. There he learned that Wyeth had already left for the West with twenty-four men.

Frantically Kelley spent the summer of 1832 trying to clothe his own dreams with equal substance. He engaged a ship, rented warehouse space, scheduled weekly meetings, and bombarded the newspapers with letters rehashing all his old arguments and adding a new one (again not original) which very shortly, in different hands, would have powerful appeal—the sending of missionaries to the Columbia to convert the Indians.

As he flew wildly about, he was arrested. Probably the detention was for debt, but as Kelley told it later, the attack was instigated by "wicked adversaries in high places"—that is, agents of the Hudson's Bay Company or the American Fur Company or the sea traders, who put into motion "an unscrupulous hireling, in the shape of a lawyer, living in a dark alley in the city of Boston." Harassment piled on harassment. "They [the adversaries] watched every movement of mine, pursuing me from city to city, laying every plan to vex and worry me. By falsehoods and calumnies . . . I was made the object of scorn and contempt. . . . Such vile sayings as these . . . panic-struck my followers and turned them back."

Very well, let the faint of heart quail. He would go without them. After telling his estranged wife good-by ("She probably felt sad, though her affectionate regards had been somewhat alienated by deceiving monsters") he left Boston on November 1, 1832. In New York he somehow obtained credit, plus contributions, Bibles, and tracts for uplifting the Indians. Via Washington, where he picked up passports, he went to New Orleans. There he joined a shadowy handful of followers who had come by ship. Unidentifiable now, they were probably opportunists looking for a way to the Pacific. Almost immediately disaffection set in. Some sued Kelley for misrepresentation, some stole from him, the rest grew downcast. "Gladly I dismissed them all."

In Vera Cruz he lost more property through graft and exorbitant customs duties, then pushed on to Mexico City. There, while recuperating in a hotel run by Americans, he learned a little Spanish, tried to interest President Santa Anna in building a railroad, and suggested himself as just the man to lead colonizing expeditions into California. These evanescent schemes fading, he secured pack stock and journeyed, often alone, across bandit-infested mountains to San Blas on the Gulf of California. Crossing to the peninsula of Lower California, he turned northward through country that even today is hazardous to travel away from its poor highways and eventually reached Puebla, near San Diego.

At Puebla he fell in with one of the unsung giants of Western pioneering, far-ranging Ewing Young. As usual, Kelley launched onto his now standard sales talk about Oregon. Oddly, the mountain man listened to the neophyte.

Perhaps Young was tired. For the past thirteen years he had been living a life right out of legend. Among the first to travel the Santa Fe Trail, he had sought beaver and fought Apaches throughout the Southwest. In the winter of 1829–30, with young Kit Carson in his train, he had made the dreadful crossing of the Mojave Desert to California. There he had dreamed up a plan of driving Spanish mules across half the continent for resale in Missouri. Later men would benefit from the scheme, but Ewing Young never did. Although he hurried to Santa Fe in 1831 to implement the scheme, his company's first venture was disappointing. Rather than return east with the paltry six hundred head of livestock acquired, Young went back to California's vast central valleys, trapped northward into Oregon, swung restlessly south again, and eventually landed in San Diego. He was thinking of settling there—he had even ordered equipment for a grist mill—when Hall Kelley appeared.

Young knew something about Oregon. In his trapping he had encountered Hudson's Bay brigades under Peter Skene Ogden or rollicking Michel Laframboise, and had got along famously with the Britishers. A settler might do well along the Columbia, better perhaps than in backward San Diego. Yet this wild-eyed Kelley somehow wasn't the sort to win a mountain man's confidence. Young held fire.

Alone Kelley pushed on to San Francisco. There for the first time he faltered. The ways to the north looked "dark and threatening. . . . To penetrate that trackless region alone seemed too hazardous. In hope, therefore, of collecting a party of emigrants to travel with me . . . I preached Oregon." No one listened. Disconsolately he drifted from town to sleepy town. As he was about to give up, Young suddenly appeared with seven men. The erstwhile trapper had thought things over and had decided to go to Oregon, after all.

On July 8, 1834, the party started northward, driving with them about one hundred head of horses and mules, seventy-seven of which belonged to Young. As they were working their way around the waterlogged deltas where the great rivers of the central valleys pour into San Francisco Bay, they were overtaken by horse thieves driving fifty-six head of stolen stock. If Kelley's memory runs true, the newcomers were a rough lot indeed. They ravished the women of one small Indian camp and later, at another camp, shot down in cold blood some inoffensive red males who had offered no threat whatsoever. Young did not protest and Kelley dared not—according to Kelley's recollections, the only account we have.

Naturally the author does not say that by this time he had become a colossal irritant to his traveling companions. Yet that is the impression one gains, even reading between Kelley's own lines. For example, as the emigrants were passing the sky-shouldering bulk of Mount Shasta, Kelley was stricken with the intermittent fever that for the past few years had been plaguing the coast. No one, he says, paid his sufferings the least heed. When finally he fell from his saddle in a faint, he might have been abandoned where he lay if his companions had not halted to look for some strayed horses.

During the delay up came the Hudson's Bay California brigade under Michel Laframboise. Here was another of the West's unsung giants. A master hand with Indians, partly because of his uncanny prowess with a rifle and partly because he had a wife in nearly every coastal tribe, Michel Laframboise had first seen the Columbia aboard Astor's *Tonquin*. Since then each succeeding firm had bought his services. Though he was no gentleman in the Bay Company's caste-ridden sense of the word, he had risen to be *partisan* in charge of the southern brigades. McLoughlin might rule at Vancouver and the Mexicans at Monterey; but throughout the wilderness in between, Michel's was the word which men heeded.

Laframboise dosed Kelley with quinine and then transported him by muleback and canoe to Fort Vancouver. There McLoughlin, his heavy features more than usually sullen, ordered the invalid outside the stockade into a lean-to hut of one of the company's Canadian servants—"extremely filthy" quarters, Kelley says, which had long been used for the dressing of fish and wild game. There the prophet of Oregon spent the winter of 1834–35, fed by dishes McLoughlin ordered sent from the kitchen, but unvisited by any of the fort's officials.

For the rest of his life Kelley fumed over the treatment. Yet there was some justice on McLoughlin's side. Just before Kelley's appearance Nathaniel Wyeth had been at Vancouver—Wyeth's second visit to the Columbia since he had been set in motion by Kelley's proselyting nearly four years earlier. From Wyeth and from ship-carried Boston newspapers McLoughlin had learned of Kelley's excoriations of the Hudson's Bay Company and of his plans to drive the British out by colonizing the country. Moreover, McLoughlin had just received from the governor of California a letter stating that one "Joachim" Young and certain adventurers had "committed the crime of robbing upwards of two hundred head of horses belonging to various Mexican citizens . . . and I doubt not but that you will in case these marauders should make their appearance in your quarter take such measures as will be efficient to apprehend them and either chastise them or dispoil [sic] them of their booty."

Kelley, of course, was guilty only by association. So too was Young. Yet Young was treated even worse than Kelley. McLoughlin turned him away from the fort and then compounded the insult by posting the neighborhood with warnings to the people to have nothing to do with the newcomers, thereby building up in Young a fury that in time would play its own odd part in the history of the Northwest.

Because he was sick, Kelley was at least fed and sheltered. Had he been less prickly by nature he might eventually have been one more recipient of McLoughlin's famed hospitality, for the factor soon realized that the strange American, whatever else he might be, was no horse thief. Unfortunately, instead of appreciating the fact that he was dependent on the fort's charity for his very existence, Kelley began peremptorily demanding his rights, in his own words, as "an American on American soil . . . pursuing the avowed purpose of opening the trade of the territory to general competition." So shrill did he become that by the time he could move around again even his own countrymen shunned him.

During part of the winter there were at least seven Americans at the fort—two scientists and five missionaries. A score or more of other United States citizens were at work on Wyeth's fort on Wapatoo Island, at the mouth of the Willamette, or on farms above the Willamette Falls. Yet, of them all, only missionary Jason Lee seems to have given Kelley more than a nod. Even Wyeth, coming down the Columbia in February from a trapping trip west of the Cascade Mountains, paid his onetime mentor only the most perfunctory of visits.

Completely isolated, broken in spirit and health, obsessed with fantasies that would bedevil him the rest of his life, Kelley gave up. In March 1835 he accepted from McLoughlin a gift of seven pounds and passage to the Sandwich Islands on a Hudson's Bay ship. The rest is a bleak story of small failures. He never achieved reconciliation with his family, never pulled himself out of debt, never succeeded, during thirty years of trying, in convincing Congress or the nation that his Oregon efforts were worth a grant of land to help out his old age.

Yet the adventure was not entirely without effect. When Caleb Cushing of Massachusetts was collecting material for Congress on the Northwest in 1839, he received no more lucid account than Hall Kelley's. And whenever a list of pioneer American residents of Oregon is tabulated, there at the top stand the names of men who arrived with Wyeth or who came with Ewing Young. No doubt the itch was in their feet already. But the fact remains that Hall Jackson Kelley was the one who set both parties into motion. That much, at least, cannot be taken from him.

2. The Fruit of Failure

IT IS necessary here to backtrack briefly to Nathaniel Wyeth's first journey to the Columbia in 1832, after he had split with Hall Kelley in Boston. For the Northwest the trip was portentous. But for Wyeth and his two dozen associates, loosely bound together in a joint-stock company, the venture was a continuing debacle.

The first shock came in St. Louis. There the tenderfeet learned that the Western mountains swarmed with competitors against whom Wyeth's untutored preparations would be ludicrously inadequate. Dismayed, three of the company promptly resigned. Wyeth, however, was a man of boundless optimism and compelling charm. Holding the rest of the company in line, he calmly set about rectifying his mistakes, and even persuaded mountain man William Sublette to let the tenderfoot group tag along with the supply caravan which Sublette was conducting to the trappers' rendezvous, held that year in Pierre's Hole (now Teton Basin, eastern Idaho). [1] One still admiring follower of

[1] Although William Sublette was one of the signers of his firm's 1830 letter to the Secretary of War, describing wagon travel to the West, he decried wheeled vehicles to Wyeth, and in 1832 was himself using pack animals. One reason was speed: on the way to the rendezvous the Sublette-Wyeth caravan easily passed and left far behind the twenty toiling wagons of Benjamin Louis Eulalie de Bonneville, onetime army captain on extended leave to catch furs for himself and look over Oregon geography for the War Department. Bonneville's twenty wagons were the first actually to cross

Wyeth could even declare in a letter home, "He goes ahead in every thing, is a good hunter, fertile in expedients, and will mend a gun or a wagon . . . with no other implement than his jack knife."

Not all of the "partners" possessed comparable resiliency. Under the plains' normal torment of gnats and bad water, sun glare and blowing sand, three more men burned out and quit. Arrived at the rendezvous, half of the remaining men, including Wyeth's own brother and a cousin, measured the opposition around them and bitterly tossed in their hands, not without recriminations against the erstwhile iceman.

And still Wyeth's charm held. Eleven stalwarts stayed with him through the wild roister of the rendezvous, shared somewhat ingloriously (except for Wyeth) in a bloody trappers' battle against Gros Ventre Indians, hunted beaver in the scraggly hills along the present Utah-Idaho border, and then hurried northward ahead of winter to the Hudson's Bay Company's Fort Nez Percé on the Columbia, a post more commonly called Fort Walla Walla by the few Americans who visited it. At Walla Walla, or Nez Percé, Pierre Pambrun, the trader in charge, gave Wyeth a new suit of clothes, agreed to care for the party's horses until spring, and put the men aboard a downriver barge.

Eleven days later, after portaging around the roaring sluices at the Dalles and the Cascades, after gaping at the vast cone of Mount Hood —"a more stupendous pile than any of the Rocky Mts"—and, most particularly, after studying the ways of the river Indians, Wyeth reached Fort Vancouver. McLoughlin made him welcome, at first through innate courtesy and later because Wyeth's magnetic charm won the factor completely—an admiration the American returned in full.

The ship *Sultana*, which Wyeth's company had sent around the Horn with their heavy equipment, was not in evidence. On a visit to the mouth of the river, where he encountered a Hudson's Bay vessel inbound from the Sandwich Islands, the ex-iceman learned the brig had been wrecked. Completely disheartened, the last of his partners now asked to be released from their contract. Wyeth acceded and wrote equably in his journal, "I am now afloat on the great sea of life without stay or support but in good hands i.e. myself and providence and a few of the H.B. Co. who are perfect gentlemen."

Too restless to stay quiet for long, he persuaded two of his former associates, Abbot and Woodman, to accompany him on an explora-

---

the Continental Divide and reach Green River, but he did not repeat the experiment. Wagons, as will be shortly seen, were unadulterated hell on the dry sagebrush plains and in the gullied mountains.

tion trip up the Willamette. For twenty-odd miles the narrow, steep-sided, heavily forested valley struck him as uninviting; but as his canoe rounded a bend and he saw the river's white-smoking falls pouring in three thunderous jets over the basalt ledges ahead of him, his Yankee eyes gleamed. "The scituation for mill priviledges," he told his journal, "is beyond anything I have ever seen."

Some four years earlier John McLoughlin had recognized the same potentials and had started to establish claim both to the eastern river-bank and to an island at the brink of the cataract. Today it is not clear whether the factor was acting primarily for himself or for the British company. In any event, objections by the Indians and interruptions by intermittent fever had precluded more work than the building of three small huts, the hewing of timber for a sawmill, the planting of potatoes, and sporadic digging at a millrace. Well, there was no hurry. Or so it seemed then.

Twenty miles above the falls the Willamette Valley opened onto broad prairie lands interspersed with groves of timber. The soil, Wyeth saw with exact prescience, was "extremely rich. . . . If this country is ever colonized this is the point to commence."

The beginnings of settlement, he noted further, were already taking shape. French Canadians retiring from the service of the Hudson's Bay Company were locating farms in the valley, hoping to stay in the West rather than return across the mountains to the main colony at Red River. Official company policy frowned on the effort. In the eyes of the London directors, farming and the fur trade did not go together; furthermore, the firm's government license forbade leaving discharged servants in the Indian country. There was, however, no practical way short of violence by which McLoughlin could compel the men to leave. After the American brigs *Owhyhee* and *Convoy*, under Captain Dominis, appeared on the scene, the factor could not even wield the bludgeon of supplies. If he did not furnish what the freemen wanted, they would buy from the Americans, who would thus be encouraged to return more and more frequently.

Rather than throw the Canadians into the arms of potential op-ponents, McLoughlin worked out one of his typical compromises. If a would-be settler was married and had fifty pounds credit on the company books—in other words, if the farmer was solvent enough not to be easily tempted by the sea peddlers' offers—McLoughlin would loan him enough equipment and livestock to get his farm started and would guarantee him a market for his produce, principally wheat. It was an arrangement George Simpson never liked, but there was very little the governor could do about it—except store up one more black mark against the Columbia's self-sufficient chief factor.

By the time of Wyeth's arrival, nine families had started tilling widely separated farms on what would soon be known as French Prairie. One great doubt plagued them. Everyone, including McLoughlin, felt that when the joint occupation treaty was ended the land south of the Columbia would go to the United States. What then would happen to their claims?

The French Canadians besieged Wyeth with questions. Would the United States Government let them keep their land? Would they have to pay for it? How much? If they were ordered off as non-citizens, could they collect reimbursement for their improvements?

Wyeth did not know. But he promised that he would try to find out. [2]

The knowledge of those deep-soiled holdings spread among Wyeth's stranded ex-associates, and several of them drifted up the Willamette to French Prairie for their own fling at farming. Others, marrying Indian wives, wandered seaward toward agriculture on the Clatsop plain. Two at various times taught Oregon's first schools, at Vancouver and among the French Canadians. Eventually most of the company returned to the States. But at least two (the tracks are hard to follow) stayed in one capacity or another. And so, forty years after Robert Gray's discovery of the great River of the West, the Columbia received, as the fruit of Wyeth's failure, its first permanent American citizens.

By February 1833, after casting a professionally approving eye on the brief ice of the Columbia, Wyeth was chafing for action. Signing on the same two men who had accompanied his exploration of the Willamette, he headed with Francis Ermatinger's brigade for Flathead post in present Montana. As the travelers gossiped away the desolate miles Wyeth learned that Ermatinger the year before had taken trade goods into the Snake country to swap with the American trappers. To Wyeth it made good sense. He had watched William Sublette's supply caravan toil up the Platte River and over South Pass; and it struck him that a similar operation, working out of Fort Vancouver with cheap Nez Percé horses and cheap Canadian labor, could reach the rendezvous in less time and at less expense than was entailed on the long route from St. Louis.

[2] Back in Cambridge a year later, he wrote Jackson's Secretary of War, Lewis Cass, asking for an opinion. Whether or not Cass's reply reached him before he started west again in April 1834 is unknown.

Fired with the notion, he wrote out a proposal for Simpson. Let him buy goods at Fort Vancouver, take them on pack trains to the rendezvous, collect furs from the trappers by underselling the American supply companies, and return the pelts to the Hudson's Bay depot at a guaranteed price. (Simpson would like the idea until the London directors' roar against intruding Americans reached him.) The letter dispatched and a copy sent to McLoughlin (who also thought the idea sound), Wyeth settled down with Ermatinger at Flathead post —"the most romantic place imaginable," he declared in his journal— to learn how the Hudson's Bay Company ran its business.

Still learning, he joined Ermatinger's handful of Canadians on a slow drift through the chill Montana Rockies. Soon the hunters fell in with a nomadic village of perhaps a thousand Flatheads and allied Indians. Like most whites, Wyeth admired the mountain savages: they were cleanly, honest, handsome, and amiable. They were also protection against Blackfeet. The trappers stuck close to their red allies as the village crossed the Divide to hunt buffalo on United States territory, then swung erratically back to the headwaters of the Salmon River in central Idaho. There they picked up nine more whites traveling with a band of Nez Percés.

In incredible confusion the twelve hundred Indians, driving nearly two thousand horses, wandered southward into Snake country. Out of the swarming mob Wyeth picked up two savages who would play their own accidental but significant part in the history of the United States. One was a twenty-year-old Nez Percé whom Wyeth employed as a sort of roustabout; by portentous chance this Indian had a slightly deformed skull. The other acquisition was an alert, shiny-eyed little Flathead-French-Canadian half-breed named Baptiste, twelve or thirteen years old, whom Wyeth determined to train as an interpreter.

By fits and starts the cavalcade moved toward rendezvous, held this summer of 1833 near a new fort which Captain Bonneville had built in the valley of the Green River. Accretions and fragmentations were continuous. Bonneville's own brigade joined up; Ermatinger turned back. Wyeth's plan underwent similar fluctuations. He at first agreed to undertake a trapping expedition in California for Bonneville, then changed his mind when he saw the reckless prices the trappers at the rendezvous were paying to get foofaraw for their women, alcohol and a few bare necessities for themselves. Convinced afresh that fortune lay in supplying the trade from the Columbia, Wyeth decided not to wait for Simpson and the Hudson's Bay Company to play ball with him, but to drum up his own financing in Boston, send a shipload of goods around the Horn, meet the brig in the river, and load her with salmon and furs. As an added fillip he secured, either at the rendezvous or on the caravan trail to the Big Horn River, a contract for freighting out from St. Louis the Rocky Mountain Fur Company's 1834 requisition of supplies.

His trip home was fantastic. Part of the way he traveled with the roistering fur carriers, by horse at first and then down the Midwestern rivers in cranky "canoes" made of bent willows and tallow-smeared buffalo hides. After a month of frantic difficulties and incredible luck along the Missouri, he put his rotting craft in at the army's newly built Fort Leavenworth. Obediently complying with regulations, he herded his Nez Percé and Flathead Indian boys into the office of the post surgeon to be vaccinated. There the pair stood transfixed, scarcely noticing the needle, for the doctor's wife and another woman were present. Released, the two rushed outside to tell their companions, little Baptiste jabbering in ecstasy. "He had seen a white squaw," Wyeth wrote, "white as snow and so pretty."

In Boston, Wyeth was engulfed in a wonder of his own. A tall, bearded, electrically excited man solicited him for an interview. Introducing himself as Jason Lee, the stranger asked breathlessly whether it was true, as newspapers said, that Mr. Wyeth had recently brought two Flathead Indians from the Columbia.

Two Indians, yes. One was a Nez Percé. The Flathead was a half-breed.

Ah, but a Flathead! Could—would Mr. Wyeth bring the Indians to a missionary meeting at the Bromfield Street Church on Friday evening, November 29, 1833?

3. The Cry from the Wilderness

JASON LEE'S fervor sprang from what has since been called the "Macedonian cry" of four Indians who in 1831, two years before Wyeth's return, had made an unprecedented journey from the Rockies eastward to St. Louis. This far-wandering quartet, so Wyeth's audience in the Bromfield Street Church believed, had left their homelands in search of religious teachers to take back to their people. And indeed that probably was the Indians' motive, though hardly in the sense the good Christians of the Eastern seaboard supposed.

By 1831 the Indians of the Northwest were fairly conversant with Christianity, or at least with its more showy symbols. Much of their information had come from eastern Iroquois. From the time of David Thompson on, these Indians, who were Catholic, had been employed west of the mountains by the North West and Hudson's Bay companies; and inevitably some of them, marrying local squaws or fleeing the bondage of their employers, had settled among the mountain tribes.

Like all Indians, the Iroquois loved pomp and storytelling. In the lodges and around the campfires they awed the simple mountain listeners with marvelous accounts of the Black Robes, amazingly celibate; of crucifixes, chants, and of the Great Prayer, or mass. Further evidence came from the whites. Devout David Thompson often read from the Bible to his voyageurs, and other traders added their own forms of Sunday observance. To the watching Indians, who regarded all forms of written communication as extraordinary magic, the traders' frequent reference to one particular set of "talking papers" naturally invested the Bible with tremendous interest.

In due time a pair of their own teen-age boys secured a Bible. This came about when George Simpson took the lads, one a Kootenay and one a Spokane, east with him in 1825—as a matter of policy and not, as is sometimes said, as the result of missionary zeal. Simpson was not a religious man. When he had first assumed his governorship in Canada he had been exasperated by the importunities of the missionary then stationed at York Factory. In his annoyance he had injudiciously written to Andrew Colvile, his patron and one of the directors of the Hudson's Bay Company, that in his opinion an enlightened Indian was a spoiled Indian; educating the savages served only to fill the pockets and bellies of hungry preachers and schoolmasters.

Colvile's answer was chill. The recent struggle with the North West Company had put the fur trade in bad odor in missionary-conscious England. Hence, "It is incumbent on the Company . . . to allow missions to be established at proper places for the conversion of the Indians, indeed, it wd be extremely impolitic . . . to show any unwillingness to assist in such an object."

Further caution came from Donald McKenzie, founder of the Snake brigades, now stationed at Red River. This was the era of conciliation; the Scottish, the Irish, the English, the French, the Indians, the clergy —all had to be placated. "Therefore," McKenzie wrote, "with faces long and minds most pure and delicate shall you and I regularly attend the chapel. . . . With the Priests we will hold discussions . . . ever mindful of giving no kind of umbrage to their dearly beloved bigotry."

Thus beset, Simpson felt a new light dawn. When he was planning his first trip to the Columbia and was asked to bring back two coastal

Indians to the missionary school at Red River, he obediently agreed. Once in the West, however, he seems to have forgotten. At least he made no effort to secure any of the distinctive, head-flattened Indians of the coast. He was homeward bound and on a hurried side trip to Spokane House before he picked up two local lads. One of the pair he named Kootenay Pelly, the other Spokane Gerry, thus combining the names of their tribes with those of two company directors.

Both Indian boys apparently revisited their people in 1829. Returning to Red River, Pelly fell off a horse and was killed, but in 1830 or 1831 Spokane Gerry came home permanently. He could read and write—great magic—and had his Bible with him. Zealous to share his knowledge, he persuaded his tribe to build a little wooden schoolhouse where the city of Spokane now stands. Though enthusiasm and novelty soon faded for both Gerry and the Spokanes, the initial impression throughout the region was very real.

Because of all these influences the mountain Indians by the 1830s were definitely, if erratically, observing the Sabbath. [1] But as both Francis Haines in *The Nez Percés* and Bernard DeVoto in *Across the Wide Missouri* have emphasized, these ceremonies were "medicine." The Indian prayed for triumph today, not salvation tomorrow. "Medicine" was power, to be wooed by incantations and such charms as feathers, hair balls, magic stones, or whatever else struck the individual's fancy.

To the Indian mind it was quite clear that the white man's guns, knives, cloth, burning glasses, and talking paper were the product of extra powerful medicine. Mastering the white man's medicine, it followed, would lead to mastery of the white man's power.

On impulse probably and no doubt after long periods of desultory campfire talk, several Nez Percés decide to go to St. Louis and see what they could pick up. They chose St. Louis because they knew it to be the home of William Clark, a tribal folk hero ever since the days the great expedition had suddenly appeared in the Nez Percé homeland. Another motive for the trip was simple curiosity. The Indians wanted to see where the whites were coming from.

The delegation started out in 1831. On the headwaters of the Missouri they met more Nez Percés and Flatheads hunting buffalo. Discussions, normal Indian vacillation, and sudden fears changed and

---

[1] From Nathaniel Wyeth's journal, May 12, 1833: "Sunday . . . long prayers in form as usual at some lodges the Inds. are singing as an act of devotion.

May 19. "Being Sunday the medicine chief had devotional exercises with his followers. he formed them into a ring men women and children and after an address they danced to a tune . . ." And so on.

shrank the personnel of the pilgrims. In the end only three Nez Percés and one Flathead joined Lucien Fontenelle's American Fur Company caravan and went with the white traders down the river to civilization.

In St. Louis the Indians sought out Clark, with whom they could converse only in the universal sign language of the North American aborigines. Leaving him, they wandered forlornly through the hot, humid city, eating strange foods, experiencing unguessable shocks to their nervous and physical systems. Two of them fell mortally ill. Before they died they somehow reached Catholic priests and were baptized. The crosses and black robes stirred recognition of Iroquois tales, and they made gestures of familiarity, duly reported by Bishop Rosati in a letter suggesting that priests be sent among the tribe. Nothing developed, however, and the next spring the survivors started home. One died en route; the other reached a camp of his people hunting buffalo along the Missouri but was soon killed in a battle with Blackfeet.

About the time the delegation was in St. Louis, an educated, Christianized, American half-breed named William Walker chanced to be in the city. Walker did not see the Western Indians, but he heard of them, perhaps from Clark, whom he visited on business. The story stuck in Walker's mind—and grew. On January 19, 1833, several months after his return to his home in Ohio, he wrote a letter about the episode to one G. P. Disosway, a New York businessman interested in promoting Indian missions.

Desirous, even as you and I, of making a good story better by personalizing it, Walker said that he had witnessed things which in truth had reached him only by hearsay. He told of interviewing the delegation and learning of their epic journey for "a book containing directions how to conduct themselves." He said that Clark had given the Indians "a succinct history of man," an exposition of the Decalogue, and a briefing on the doctrines of salvation—something of a feat in sign language. Walker also added a drawing of the visitors' heads, malformed so as to slope backward from their eyebrows to a peak above their ears. This typical Pacific coast deformation he could have derived from various sources—but not from the Indians he said he saw. Their heads were normal. [2]

[2] The Nez Percés and Flatheads, of course, did not pierce their noses or flatten their heads. The names resulted from clumsy European translations of the sign-language gestures for the tribes. Further evidence that the craniums of the St. Louis delegation were not deformed comes from sketches of the two survivors painted in the spring of

Completely enthralled, Disosway fired Walker's letter to the Methodist *Christian Advocate*. It was printed, together with Disosway's editorial exhortation: "Let the Church awake from her slumbers and go forth in her strength to the salvation of these wandering sons of our native forests."

The appeal was familiar to the Church. For ten years word of the benighted Indians of the Northwest coast had been coming back to the Atlantic seaboard via the Sandwich Islands, where the American Board of Commissioners for Foreign Missions (then supported jointly by the Presbyterian, Congregational, and Dutch Reform churches) had established a station in 1820. In 1829 the island mission had dispatched the Reverend Jonathan Green on a trading ship to explore possibilities. Although bad weather on the Columbia had kept the ship from entering the river itself, Green picked up considerable information about the district from ubiquitous Captain Dominis of the brig *Owhyhee* and from the skippers of Hudson's Bay ships putting in at the Hawaiian Islands. All this was incorporated in his report, portions of which were serialized in the *Missionary Herald*. His poverty-stricken home station in the islands felt, however, "that the indications of providence . . . are not sufficiently plain to warrant this Mission to take any direct steps" without help from America. No help came. The home board was having trouble enough financing those stations it had already established.

The point kept intruding, however. Ross Cox's newly published *Adventures on the Columbia* remarked that Columbia missions were desirable. This led Hall Kelley to include the point in his Oregon sales talks, and roused the editor of the *Methodist Magazine* to use a review of the book as a springboard for demanding action. Still nothing happened. Indians were too close to home, too unglamorous to stir the imagination—until the dramatic appearance in the *Christian Advocate* of March 1833 of William Walker's letter to G. P. Disosway. Hundreds of readers felt their pulses quicken. The heroic transcontinental trek, the cry for help, the flattened heads—something had to be done for the poor, innocent, wistful, mutilated, lost creatures!

In an answering letter to the *Christian Advocate*, Dr. Wilbur Fisk, new president of Wesleyan University in Middletown, Connecticut, cried excitedly:

. . . Let two suitable men, unencumbered with families, and possessing the

1832 by George Catlin. Additional evidence about Walker's fabrication can be found in Francis Haines, "The Nez Percé Delegation," *Pacific Historical Review*, March 1937.

spirit of martyrs, throw themselves into the [Flathead] nation. Live with them—learn their language—preach Christ to them and, as the way opens, introduce schools, agriculture, and the arts of civilized life. . . . Money shall be forthcoming. I will be bondsman for the church. All we want is men. Who will go? Who? I know of one young man . . . of whom I can say, I know of none like him for the enterprise. . . .

The young man was Jason Lee, a native of the border village of Stanstead, Quebec. At the age of twenty-three Lee had been converted during a backwoods revival. Three years later he had decided to supplement his meager education by enrolling in the Methodist Academy at Wilbraham, Massachusetts, where Dr. Fisk was then serving as principal. The over-age applicant impressed Fisk. Lee was six feet three inches tall and iron-hard from years of dawn-to-dusk farm labor. More important, his spiritual and intellectual determination were as tangible as one of his great, knotted fists. Promptly Fisk put the convert in charge of one of the dormitories. Though Jason Lee was able to stay at Wilbraham less than a year, he and his erstwhile principal afterward maintained an intermittent correspondence.

As Fisk knew, Lee wanted to be a missionary, but appointments eluded him. Then came the Macedonian cry. In June 1833, on a wave of enthusiasm engendered by Fisk's letter to the *Christian Advocate*, the tall, hand-callused, earthy preacher was launched toward his desired goal. As his associate for the labor in the Northwestern vineyards he chose his favorite nephew, Daniel Lee, a man only three years younger than himself.

Summer sped by in preparations and in stumping the East for contributions. In November the two Lees held a farewell service in New York City, then read in the next morning's newspaper that Captain Nathaniel Wyeth had just returned to Boston from Oregon with two Flathead Indians. Excited by this stroke of providence, uncle and nephew hurried north to consult with the mountain man.

They gained even more than they had dared hope for. Sanguine and persuasive, using his goods-carrying contract as a lever, Wyeth had already raised capital for a second trip to the Columbia. The missionaries, he said, could send their heavy equipment around the Horn on his new ship, the *May Dacre*. The Lees themselves could travel overland from St. Louis with his spring caravan. And as a crowning joy, though Wyeth himself was confessedly an infidel, he agreed to go to a hastily arranged meeting at the Bromfield Street Church, there to answer questions about the Northwest and to show off his Indians.

The Bromfield Street meeting and another held two evenings later in a different church were sensational successes. The Indians were responsible. To be sure, the little one's head appeared normal, as was to be expected in a half-breed. The taller one, however—a Nez Percé? —ah, but see the malformation of the skull! Definitely a Flathead!

Wyeth seems not to have disabused the enthusiasts. He even allowed the Lees to borrow the Indians for further fund-raising meetings throughout the East, saying he would pick up the young redskins at the home of his brother Charles in Baltimore when he started for St. Louis in the spring. Indeed, Nathaniel was feeling affable toward all sorts of non-commercial wayfarers that winter. Before starting for St. Louis he also added to his expedition Thomas Nuttall, the shy, parsimonious, self-educated curator of Harvard University's Botanical Garden (for whom Wyeth had gathered seeds during his first trip and who resigned his Harvard post to go on this new expedition); and Nuttall's twenty-five-year-old protégé, John Townsend, a Philadelphia surgeon and ornithologist.

The trip west struck Jason Lee as uneventful. He enjoyed it, although his small party of two missionaries, one teacher, and two hired hands spent most of their time eating dust with their cattle at the rear of "the most profane company I think I was ever in." Lee, however, knew that kind of reality. Farm-bred, powerful, relishing the buffalo hunts and the exhilaration of the wilderness, he got on well with the trappers, so that even his expostulations about their language brought no resentment—and, naturalist Townsend adds, no effect.

The rendezvous, however—held this year in the sun-blasted wastes along Ham's Fork of the Green—was a shock. Six hundred or more whites cavorted in fantastic fur caps and greasy black buckskins through the year's great holiday of raw alcohol, complaisant squaws, fights, shooting matches, horse races, and hair-raising hunts—one grizzly bear and one buffalo were even chivied through the camp itself.

Hordes of savages milled drunkenly in every direction. Among them were several score Cayuses, Nez Percés, and Flatheads, arrived to trade horses and perhaps to learn if their white teacher was on hand. Lee could see nothing abnormal about the shape of their heads; and at this point he could hardly have expected to. During the thousand-mile trip Wyeth had certainly told the tyros something of the facts of Indian life and probably had pointed out the handicaps in the way of the proposed mission. It wasn't safe: Blackfeet were forever raiding through Flathead lands. Furthermore, the establishment would be arduous to supply with goods hauled first by boat hundreds of miles up the Columbia and then by horse across killing deserts to the mountains. The land, though good for grazing, was, in Wyeth's opinion, worthless for farming. Lastly, the tribes Lee hoped to work with were completely nomadic—and how was one to seize a soul if the body was continually on the move?

The valley of the Willamette, on the other hand, offered easy access to shipping, fertile plains, sedentary if disease-ridden savages (who were also true flatheads), and the protection of Fort Vancouver. These considerations, added to the drunken milling of the Indians at the rendezvous, sounded the death knell of the Flathead mission even before its builders had seen the country. Instead, the Lees decided to travel on to the Willamette, where they had to go anyhow to pick up the goods being shipped on Wyeth's brig, *May Dacre*.

Wyeth, meanwhile, had run head-on into harsh realities of his own. William Sublette, the normal freighter of goods for the Rocky Mountain Fur Company, had beaten the Bostonian to the rendezvous by two days. By bribery, so Wyeth thought, Sublette persuaded the Rocky Mountain Company to repudiate its contract with the Johnny-come-lately. So there Wyeth sat amidst the revelry with more than a hundred rejected horseloads of red- and yellow-edged blankets, red-handled butcher knives, vermilion, looking glasses, lead, powder, coffee, bales of tobacco, and metal canisters of alcohol.

To many men it would have been a demoralizing blow. Wyeth, however, with characteristic resiliency, determined to use the goods for stocking a new trading post on the Snake River, which he would thereafter supply via the Columbia. This fort, he thought, would absorb the trade of the mountain Indians and show the contract breakers that even a green hand could slip a few jokers into the deck.

Still traveling together, Wyeth and the missionaries moved on from Ham's Fork toward the Snake. They had company—a small band of Nez Percés and Flatheads, and an English sportsman, Sir William Stewart, who was so enthralled with mountain life that for years he would stay in the wilds. The cavalcade soon acquired more associates —the Hudson's Bay Snake brigade under Tom McKay, McLoughlin's rambunctious stepson.

As had been the case with Francis Ermatinger two years before, McKay was prepared to trade with Americans or Indians as well as to trap, and he carried with him a full complement of goods. As soon as he realized what Wyeth was up to he promptly swung around with him, to checkmate whatever move the American made. As the combined parties rode through the glades of Bear River and down the Portneuf, the two leaders became warm friends, for that was Wyeth's gift. But friendship, as the American had learned, was no protection against the economic throat-slitting of the fur trade.

On a grassy meadow near the confluence of the Portneuf and the Snake in what is now southeastern Idaho, Wyeth began constructing his fort. It was an idle time for the missionaries, broken by McKay's unexpected request, one hot Sunday, that Jason Lee conduct religious services. Though feeling unwell, the rawboned preacher repaired with some thirty whites and as many Indians to a shady spot under rustling cottonwoods. There he read a psalm, sang a hymn, and delivered an exhortation. "The Indians," Townsend wrote, "sat upon the ground like statues. Although not one of them could understand a word that was said, they nevertheless maintained a most strict and decorous silence, kneeling when the preacher kneeled, and rising when he rose, evidently with a view of paying him and us a suitable respect."

Afterward there was horse racing. In a violent collision one of McKay's French Canadians was mortally hurt. That night he died. "Service for him," Wyeth noted in his journal with customary lack of punctuation, "was performed by the Canadians in the Catholic form by Mr. Lee in the Protestant form and by the Indians in their form . . . he at least was well buried."

When McKay's brigade started west the next day the Lees and Sir William Stewart decided to go with it. Wyeth stayed behind for another week to complete his post. He christened it Fort Hall after one of his backers, "manufactured a magnificent flag from some unbleached sheeting a little red flannel and a few blue patches, saluted it with damaged powder, and wet it in vilanous alcohol." Miserably hung-over, he then pushed north with his men across the harsh lava deserts of the Snake plain and over the Sawtooth Mountains at no great distance from where Sun Valley now stands.

At Fort Walla Walla (originally Fort Nez Percé) he found the missionaries camped in their white tents just outside the post's stockade. But "Mr. McKay," he wrote in puzzlement in his journal, "for some reason remained in the mountains."

The reason, it developed, was deadly enough. Near one of the twin mouths of the Boise River, in a decaying horse pen where first John Reed of the Astorians and later Donald McKenzie of the Nor'Westers had tried to establish posts, McKay built a hutch of crooked cottonwood poles. Here he set about undermining Fort Hall's trade, and did it so well that soon his ramshackle hut was replaced, on a slightly different site, with a more imposing adobe structure called Fort Boise. What neither Wyeth nor McKay realized in the heat of their rivalry was the fact that in creating the forts they were really delivering one more blow to the dying fur trade: within a decade both Fort Hall and Fort Boise would be wayside havens not for trappers but for thousands of emigrants driving their prairie schooners across the fading game trails of the West.

At Fort Walla Walla, Jason and Daniel Lee gave final token that they no longer intended to settle among the mountain Indians. They handed over to the trader at the fort their ten horses, four mules, and three cows in exchange for other livestock and goods to be picked up at Fort Vancouver. Then on a hired barge, with Wyeth's trappers following in three canoes (two of which smashed up), they ran through buffeting head winds and drenching rain to a hearty welcome by John McLoughlin.

Always McLoughlin would believe and say that it was his advice which settled the missionaries in the Willamette. Actually he simply confirmed a decision already reached. But he did furnish the canoes and guides that took the travel-worn party to Tom McKay's farm on French Prairie. There they secured horses for exploring the fifty-mile-broad valley.

One day's ride out of McKay's farm they were overtaken by Wyeth. He too was in search of farm land. Fresh disaster had just struck him. He had intended that his brig *May Dacre* should reach the Columbia while the salmon run was still on. Instead she had been so delayed in Valparaiso by damages resulting from a lightning bolt that she had warped into the river only a single day before his own arrival, long after there were any fish to be caught. As a result he could count on no quick cash income from pickled salmon to compensate for his lost freight contract.

Making the best of matters, Wyeth took the brig around to the southwestern side of long, timbered Wapatoo, or Sauvie, Island, still a cherished hunting spot whose upper end masks the double mouths by which the Willamette debouches into the Columbia. There, some eight miles from John McLoughlin's huge headquarters, he began a competing post which he named Fort William, using such assorted labor as his trappers, the brig's sailors, and twenty Kanakas whom the captain of the *May Dacre* had brought from the Sandwich Islands. The work satisfactorily launched, he hurried up the Willamette, intent on finding a farm. If Nathaniel Wyeth failed on this, his second invasion of the Northwest, the crash would not result from any lack of brashness or of whirlwind effort.

4. Portents

SOME sixty miles above the Columbia, near the present town of Salem, on oak dotted plains looking toward Mount Hood, brilliantly white against the eastern sky, the exploring missionaries and the restless iceman found farm sites that suited their fancy. Straightway they returned to Fort Vancouver, their thoughts diverging now to their own private urgencies—the Lees toward borrowing winter supplies from McLoughlin, Wyeth's toward keeping economically afloat in this alien ocean.

He was extraordinarily buoyant. To McLoughlin he proposed a trade agreement similar to the one he had suggested by letter, the previous winter, to Simpson: let him buy Hudson's Bay goods for bartering with the Americans in the Rockies and sell the furs he garnered to the company; let him pickle, for export, salmon he caught in the river or traded from the Indians; and in return he would promise not to trap within a hundred miles of any Hudson's Bay post.

The trapping threat did not worry McLoughlin. His brigades could easily outmaneuver the American. The real danger lay in the possibility that a rebuff might lead Wyeth to counter with cheap goods or, most damaging, alcohol imported from outside sources. Moreover, the factor was certain that Wyeth's scheme would in time fail through its own inadequacies. Seeing no need to grind down a man whom he liked, McLoughlin agreed to the proposal, providing confirmation could be received from his superiors. [1]

On paper the agreement was sound, but Wyeth had no chance to explore its possibilities. Even sooner than McLoughlin anticipated, the American's affairs collapsed. At Fort Hall in Idaho several of his men deserted; Blackfeet stole horses and equipment, killed various trappers; an irresponsible clerk squandered goods in drunken mismanagement; and Tom McKay's Fort Boise absorbed the trade that might have

---

[1] The confirmation never materialized. George Simpson, taking his cue from the London office's rejection of Wyeth's first proposal, upbraided McLoughlin for giving aid and comfort to the enemy. Mortified, the chief factor retorted with an array of affidavits from other personnel at Fort Vancouver, supporting his action. These demurrers struck Simpson as presumptuous, and added one more canker to the growing malignity between the trigger-tempered governor and his self-assertive subordinate.

come from the west. Wyeth's own hunting venture east of the Cascade Mountains in the winter of 1834–35—dismal marches through the bleak, storm-bound gorges of the Deschutes River—brought him practically nothing. His brig, *May Dacre*, spent the winter hauling an unprofitable cargo of lumber to the Sandwich Islands, then returned to the Columbia to find that her salmon-catching equipment was inadequate for the job and that the Indians (as McLoughlin had surmised they would) went right past the ship and past Fort William on Wapatoo Island to trade their fish at the Bay Company's more familiar depot.

To top the ill luck, Wyeth and most of his men were stricken during the summer by the same intermittent fever that was depopulating the Willamette of Indians and that had flattened Wyeth's original catalyst, Hall Kelley (whom the trader encountered briefly, to his astonishment, while Kelley was querulously moping around Fort Vancouver). It had been a "sickly" season, Wyeth wrote his wife on September 22. "We have lost by drowning and disease and warfare 17 persons to this date and 14 now sick." But the ingrained optimism of the man could not completely tarnish: "Keep up good spirits my dear wife . . . altho I shall be poor yet we can always live."

Stark failure . . . and yet the stuff that had gone into the making of his dreams was solid enough. All over the continent, welling up from God knew where, the same magnetism was beginning to catch the needle of man's desire and point it toward the land's farthest reach. Portents of the tug were reaching the Columbia even before Wyeth left; and, since he was nobody's fool, it is barely possible that he recognized some of the harbingers for what they were. . . .

Down in California, for instance, John Turner was talking Oregon to a handful of dissatisfied trappers. Turner had lived an epic life; after surviving the massacre of Jedediah Smith's party on the Umpqua River, he had joined the Hudson's Bay Company as guide of their southern brigades. On one of his California trips he met, during the spring of 1835, various Americans, some of whom had been associated with Ewing Young—the same Young whom Hall Kelley had lured to Oregon, even as Kelley had lured Nathaniel Wyeth. Young, Turner told his new American friends, had settled on a farm in the Willamette, where the soil was fat and the winter mild. Oregon . . . even on John Turner's whiskered lip the name could beguile. Seven men, including a dissipated, ship-jumping young English doctor named William J. Bailey, decided to ride north with the trapper to see the fine new land.

Only half of them arrived. Just beyond Mount Shasta, Rogue River Indians killed half of the party. The survivors, again including Turner, groped northward, living on roots. They were hideously injured, William Bailey in particular, his half-severed face tied together with a handkerchief. It would heal repulsively distorted and scarred, so that no one seeing him later, after he had become one of Oregon's leading citizens, would ever doubt the price he had paid to reach the territory. Bailey would not forget the ordeal, nor would his companions; and in time those bleak memories would breed their own ghastly repercussions.

Far eastward, meanwhile, an even more incongruous follower of the needle's tug was moving toward land's end. He was Samuel Parker, a fifty-six-year-old preacher and scholar who, among other things, had once served as the headmaster of a girls' boarding school. In October 1835, with no more company than three half-naked Walla Walla Indians, Parker was picking his way along the flinty portages where the Columbia bursts through the Dalles. At the foot of the compressed torrent he met Nathaniel Wyeth, journeying toward Fort Hall to rescue what he could from the crash of his hopes.

Trader and divine paused long enough for Wyeth to write out for Parker a basic vocabulary of the Chinook language. During the process they certainly talked; for Parker was by nature garrulous, curious, alert, and Wyeth had a genius for drawing men out. What he heard was, in its own way, one of the incredible sagas of America's westering. More importantly, though Wyeth had no way of recognizing the fact, it forecast the doom of British aspirations in the Northwest.

It is necessary to leave the men at the Dalles working over the Chinook vocabulary for Parker, and to backtrack again to the Macedonian cry of the Indians for religious teaching. More than just Lee's Methodists had been set into motion by that misunderstood appeal. The Presbyterian and Congregational churches' American Board of Commissioners for Foreign Missions had in 1834 dispatched Samuel Parker and two companions to St. Louis to catch one of the fur caravans bound for the West. The would-be missionaries arrived too late, learned they could not reach Oregon for another year, and faced the unhappy fact that their funds would not tide them over so long a delay.

Parker's two associates contented themselves with establishing a mission among the Pawnees in eastern Kansas. Parker himself returned to his home at Ithaca, New York, determined to raise funds and find helpers for another effort to reach the land of the benighted Flatheads. Alone, driving a light buggy through the stiff cold mud of late November, he toured the little towns west of the Finger Lakes in western New York, speaking wherever church meetings could be arranged.

At one of these meetings, in Prattsburg, he was approached by a chunky, craggy-headed country doctor named Marcus Whitman, thirty-two years old. For the time and area, Whitman was well educated, having learned his trade, in the idiom of the day, by riding with a local practitioner and later attending two sixteen-week sessions at medical college. Of strongly religious bent, he had, a year or so before, offered his services to the American Board as a medical missionary but had been turned down because of ill-health. Since then, he assured Parker, he had recovered and would like to go to Oregon.

Parker urged him to apply again to the Board, then drove on through spats of rain and sleet to a hamlet some fifty miles away. There he struck another spark, this time in a woman named Narcissa Prentiss.

Somehow Narcissa did not seem quite like missionary material. She was full-bodied, with a lovely, disturbing voice, copper glints in her blond hair, and wide eyes of sparkling vivacity. Yet she remained unmarried, though she was almost an old maid of twenty-six and did not lack admirers.

After the last hymn, which she led as usual, Narcissa asked Parker whether unmarried females would be acceptable for mission work in Oregon. Dubiously Parker said he would check.

Back in Ithaca he was visited, in January 1835, by Marcus Whitman, whose application the American Board had just reconsidered and accepted. During the planning that followed, the elder man mentioned Narcissa Prentiss. Whitman, it developed, had once attended a prayer meeting at the Prentiss home, but whether he had met Narcissa herself does not now appear. Anyway, off he rushed to see her for a single weekend. When he departed, they were engaged—hardly an impetuous courtship, however, for the contract was qualified by an unromantic proviso that marriage should wait until the feasibility of the Oregon mission had been determined.

To investigate those feasibilities Parker and Whitman in mid-May joined the American Fur Company's westbound supply caravan. Immediately they were greeted with catcalls and even rotten eggs hurled by mountain men who wanted no longfaces spoiling their fun or sending back protests to the newspapers about their dealings with the Indians. That sort of treatment, however, was part of a missionary's cross and could be endured. Far more insidious was the pair's own ineptitude. Parker, remembering how desperately he had worked to raise money, refused to part with enough cash to buy adequate equipment. What livestock he did purchase the two greenhorns could scarcely handle. Nearly every day, while the mountain men hooted in delight, the tenderfeet's ill-balanced loads either fell off the mules or were bucked off. Retreating into the ivory tower of his superior age and education, Parker consigned more and more of the camp chores to Whitman, then shuddered fastidiously when the overworked doctor cooked their meals while reeking of mule sweat and ate the ill-prepared dishes with his knife.

Soon enough these contretemps were swallowed in a graver danger. Before the caravan was well started cholera brought it to a dead stop. As the men began falling sick the partisan in charge sent a frantic call for help to the tent where Whitman and Parker were camped by themselves, beyond the unfriendly pale. Though the doctor was in misery from a chronic ache in his side, he crawled out of bed to see what he could do.

Medically it was not a great deal. Morale-wise, the value of his common-sense nursing was inestimable. He moved the stricken camp into high, clean ground, kept the men warm and fed and encouraged. After twelve exhausting days he had the caravan back on the trail. From that point on there was no more jeering at the missionaries—until they reached the hectic, alcohol-sodden rendezvous in the desolate valley of the Green.

Several hundred thirsty whites and thousands of mercurial Indians gyrated about on the redolent sagebrush flats. Utes were there, Snakes, and large bands of handsome Nez Percés and Flatheads in their gaudy finery. Word of the missionaries' coming had preceded the caravan. The Indians, already titillated by the brief passage of the Lees the year before, grew highly excited. Taking cynical advantage of the red men's credulity, the more rowdy of the trappers sold them decks of cards as Bibles and said that the way to win the Great Spirit was to hand over females for certain introductory rites.

It was not a situation conducive of good will. Yet the missionaries surmounted it, Parker with a naïveté so total that it was invulnerable, Whitman with rough-and-ready medical treatments that included slicing a three-inch arrowhead from Jim Bridger's horny back.

From Hudson's Bay voyageurs out of Forts Walla Walla and Boise, from Wyeth's Fort Hall crew, and particularly from Sir William Stewart, that footloose English adventurer whose peregrinations weave so curious a thread through the Western fur trade, Parker and Whitman learned that the Lees had gone straight past the Nez Percé land to the Willamette. The Macedonian cry remained unanswered, though the eagerness of the Indians at the rendezvous left the two men with no doubt that it needed answering at once. Yet delay there must be. To explore the homeland of the Nez Percés and Flatheads for mission sites and then return east for workers would devour at least two years' precious time.

Blandly and incredibly, Parker volunteered to cut the delay in half by doing the exploring alone while Whitman fetched in supplies and personnel. The two men would meet again at next year's trapper rendezvous, and Parker would guide Whitman's party to whatever site God's will and his own judgment pointed out.

The suggestion put the doctor in a cruel dilemma. No affection bound him to Parker: the elder man's toplofty assumption of perquisites that have no place on any camper's trail had grated his nerves, just as Whitman's crude ways had irritated Parker. Moreover, Whitman was in a hurry to get back to New York. He had seen the fur company take its wagons as far as Fort Laramie in what is now eastern Wyoming; he knew that three years before, in 1832, Captain Bonneville's men had driven twenty laden vehicles over South Pass to this very valley of the Green. In the exuberance of his burgeoning plans, he saw no reason why wagons could not roll on to the land of the Nez Percés. Wheels, household comforts, Narcissa . . . There in the sun-smitten desert, surrounded by the wistful gazes of the savages whose salvation from the Pit would give meaning to his life, he was overwhelmed with the vision of her bright gold hair forever at his side.

But if going for her meant leaving the fumble-handed Parker alone in a hostile wilderness . . .

He would not be alone, Parker retorted, if divine Providence was with him. And without divine Providence even two of them could not succeed.

Finding the argument unanswerable, Whitman consented. The Nez Percés, thrown into a boil of ecstasy by the decision, promised to take good care of their new medicine man. Charles Compo, a French Canadian with a Nez Percé wife, was hired to go along as interpreter. Parker also appropriated the pack mules, leaving Whitman five dollars to buy a scarecrow horse which, the doctor wrote the Board, "was a disgrace to any man to pack on account of his extreme sore back." With him Marcus took east two Indian boys to train as interpreters and perhaps to use, as the Lees had used Wyeth's Indians, in appeals for support.

On August 22, 1835, the men separated. For a week Parker and his attendant savages traveled with Bridger's trappers northward past the towering Tetons and over the glorious saddle that leads into Pierre's Hole. There the trappers went about their business, leaving Parker to make his way on west with his Indians and his rather ineffectual interpreter.

No bashfulness restrained the explorer. He hinted broadly for special food and treatment, and got them from his solicitous guardians, so that later he could boast he was never reduced to eating horse or dog—though at times his companions were. When he encountered new bands of Indians, the entire group would line up single file, chiefs first and on down to the littlest children, to shake his hand in excited welcome. They gratified his vanity by building shady bowers for him to preach in, then touched his heart by listening with utter absorption to his explanations of original sin, salvation, resurrection, and judgment.

No triumphant potentate ever had a more devoted retinue. And in spite of their help his journey remains an almost unbelievable feat. He was fifty-six, trained to a scholar's study, helpless in woodcraft. The mountains of central Idaho were vast, the canyons awesome. Faith could not soften the gait of a Nez Percé pony or warm the frosty nights. He fell ill, but rode doggedly on, clumsily bleeding himself as Whitman had taught him. One day, clinging dizzily to the saddle horn while his horse minced over breathless slopes between mazes of windfall, he thought he would surely die, but consoled himself with the thought, so he wrote, that "I needed the trial to lead me to an examination of my spiritual condition."

Sick though he was, he never left off taking copious notes about everything he saw—geology, botany, natural resources, local customs. He was a shrewd observer; when published, his account would add immeasurably to America's knowledge of the land beyond the Rockies. But in one respect he was innocence distilled. Patiently he taught the Indians the Lord's Prayer and the Ten Commandments until the savages could repeat the words letter perfect; and he thanked his God for his success, never dreaming that in the neolithic minds of his charges the chants were a new magic, an incantation for producing not spiritual grace but materialistic gratification.

And so he came down through the tall clean timber to the Clearwater River, where Lewis and Clark had obtained succor after their own ordeal. Liking the countryside, he noted it as a possible site for a mission. Though the Indians wanted him to linger, he pressed on to

Fort Walla Walla. In that vicinity too, he decided, a station might thrive. He paid off his interpreter with a niggardly eighteen dollars' worth of poor quality trade goods, promised the Nez Percés that he would return in the spring, and confidently embarked on the surging Columbia in a canoe manned by three strange Walla Wallas.

Approximately seven weeks after leaving the rendezvous he skirted the Dalles and there encountered Nathaniel Wyeth.

The Chinook vocabulary copied, the two men parted, Wyeth to spend a drear winter at Fort Hall, Parker to enjoy McLoughlin's hospitality at Fort Vancouver. In the British post the missionary passed a comfortable winter, teaching hymn singing at the fort's school, working up his notes, visiting the rainy mouth of the Columbia, and even venturing up the Willamette to pay a call on Jason Lee.

At the Methodist station he found much to admire. Though plagued by bad weather, inexperience, and ill-health, the pioneer missionaries had, in little more than a year, built a sound house and barn close to the riverbank, had cultivated thirty acres of virgin soil, and had established a school where frail Cyrus Shepard, who had come with Jason Lee from the East, was teaching reading and salvation to nineteen listless Chinook children. To these good works Jason Lee added, about the time of Parker's visit, a temperance society, and on February 11, 1836, persuaded three of the Willamette settlers to sign the pledge. This war against trade-disrupting rum so won John McLoughlin that he sent to the mission, which he had already aided with loans of livestock and tools, a contribution of twenty-six pounds raised among the "principal gentlemen" of Fort Vancouver.

In spite of these accomplishments, Jason Lee was discouraged. On March 15 he wrote a gloomy letter to Wilbur Fisk, wherein he confessed that the crushing physical labor of housekeeping in the wilderness had kept him from "attending to spirituals"—"we have no evidence that we have been instrumental in the conversion of one soul." But the school might prepare the way if only help could be obtained for "attending to temporals," that is, to the farm chores. "I do not speak of money, but of *men* and *women*," the latter request underlining a cry he had initiated a year before when writing Fisk on February 6, 1835: "I have requested the Board not to send any more *single men*, but to send men with families. . . . A greater favour could not be bestowed upon this country, than to send to it pious, industrious, inteligent females."

Parker recognized the same need and noted in his journal, "There is yet one important desideratum—these missionaries have no wives. Christian white women are very much needed to exert influence over Indian families." Well, in the American Board's mission, the problem would be met, provided of course that Narcissa Prentiss carried out her contract with Marcus Whitman.

Great areas where still more missions might be located remained to be explored. When winter relaxed its grip in mid-April, Parker resolutely journeyed back up the river with a Hudson's Bay brigade to Fort Walla Walla. There he secured horses and an Indian guide, rode hundreds of rolling miles to the ruins of Spokane House, swung westward to Fort Colvile and on to Fort Okanogan, threading on his way the vast, hushed ditch of Grand Coulee, and then returned to Walla Walla.

Originally he had intended to travel from Fort Walla Walla to the Green River rendezvous with Nez Percé Indians, who he thought would follow the direct trail across the Blue Mountains and on by the wilderness hostelries of Forts Boise and Hall. At the fort, however, he learned that the Indians wanted to hunt buffalo en route, and so had decided to strike across the uninhabited wastes of central Idaho. On hearing this, Parker's heart failed him. He had just finished a grueling ride, and the path of the wandering buffalo hunters would add unguessable hundreds of miles to what lay ahead. In addition trappers told him that the deep snow in the mountains would mean long delays—perhaps so long that he could not reach the rendezvous in time to meet Marcus Whitman. Nor could he forget that during his outward journey he had nearly died in the very mountains the Indians now proposed to recross. How much easier it would be to float down the Columbia to Fort Vancouver, sail on a Hudson's Bay ship to the Sandwich Islands, and there board a vessel bound for the United States.

He entrusted the Indians with a letter for Whitman. Another missive went by Tom McKay. Why Parker could not also travel with a Hudson's Bay brigade bound for the Green does not appear. Conflicting timetables may be one explanation. Or perhaps it was simply the timetable of age. Samuel Parker, fifty-seven years old this spring, was just plain tired out.

Back to Vancouver he went, to still another harbinger of the future —the Hudson's Bay Company's new hundred-foot-long, stubby-bowed, square-sterned, black-hulled steamship named *Beaver*. She had arrived on the river shortly before Parker's departure for the upper Columbia, having come from England around the Horn under sail during the winter. (She could not steam around, lacking storage capacity for fuel.) During his explorations she had been refitted with brick furnaces, a low-pressure iron boiler, and side-lever engines to drive the paddle wheels she had carried into the Pacific aboard her own decks. On May 2, 1836, she had been launched; and by the time Parker returned in June she had been put through her shakedown runs along the river and was now ready for an excursion trip up the Willamette. The fort's gentlemen and their Indian wives went aboard with picnic lunches; there was singing and gaiety and talk, so Parker reports, of "coming days . . . when cities and villages shall spring up on the west, as they are springing up on the east of the great mountains, and a new empire shall be added to the kingdoms of the earth."

Chief Factor John McLoughlin did not share the gaiety. The steamship represented a denial of his policies. The fur trade, he believed, could be better carried on from fixed posts commanding the routes by which pelts came from the interior and by which trade goods flowed back. Under his direction a chain of such coastal forts had been built from the Umpqua River in southern Oregon to Russian Alaska. The establishments were, he felt, cheaper than ships, for they needed no insurance; they were more easily manned, for they needed no trained crews; they exerted stronger influence over the Indians, for they stayed permanently among the fickle savages. When the company had sent him an extra trading ship in 1834 he brusquely ordered her to turn around and go home; and when he had heard of the original plans for a steamship he objected vigorously. The *Beaver*, nevertheless, had appeared on schedule, along with a stinging letter of censure concerning the vessel he had ordered back to England. He was not king of Oregon yet, the letter implied; henceforth he would do as he was told.

Parker seems not to have detected the split between McLoughlin and his superiors. Nathaniel Wyeth, who was much closer to the chief factor, probably did. For one thing, Wyeth's repeated attempts to intrude himself into the company's monopoly had helped deepen the breach. He kept right on digging at it. On returning from Fort Hall in the spring of 1836 (he passed Parker on the way and at Vancouver witnessed the launching of the *Beaver*), he resumed his efforts to become middleman between the company and the American fur gatherers, even agreeing, in return for the concessions he wanted, to surrender Fort Hall to the Hudson's Bay Company and confine his own trapping parties to the Colorado River and the Great Salt Lake basin.

Once more McLoughlin tentatively agreed, thus inviting another acrimonious rebuff from Simpson. Heartened by the factor's consideration, Wyeth next hurried east, via the rendezvous, in an effort to raise capital. He failed. He arrived in Boston just as the depression of the late 1830s was beginning to paralyze trade, and his backers refused to listen to his pleas. Completely beaten at last, he arranged to sell Fort Hall, its goods and equipment to the Hudson's Bay Company for a paltry $8179.94. Fort William on Wapatoo Island he put in charge of Courtney M. Walker, one of the lay assistants who had come to the Columbia with Jason Lee in 1834. Walker was instructed to lease or sell Fort William on the best terms obtainable, but no takers appeared at any price—not with the place lying so close to the overwhelming bastions of Fort Vancouver. Finally Walker abandoned the structure. McLoughlin moved in then, establishing a dairy farm under Jean Baptiste Sauvié, who lived there so long that today the spot is known as Sauvie's or Sauvie, Island. [2]

Before the abandonment, bits of Fort William's equipment were peddled, either by Wyeth himself or by Walker, to the Willamette settlers. One significant copper kettle, used originally for pickling salmon, went to Ewing Young and so touched off, as we shall see, the farthest-reaching chain of consequences ever initiated by one humble pot. For Young, still smarting under McLoughlin's ostracism, planned vengeance by using the kettle as a whiskey still that quite conceivably could blow the economy of the entire Northwest to smithereens.

Long before the threat developed, Wyeth had started east on his last futile effort to raise money. Behind him he left several ex-employees who would become permanent settlers, vocal Americans in a wilderness dominated by a British trade empire. And ahead of him, as he rode with Tom McKay's brigades through the molten heat of July into the barren valley of the Green, he saw proof that despite-his own bankruptcy his countrymen would succeed. There in the midst of the hurly-burly of the rendezvous sagged a hard-used wagon. Beside the wagon stood a tent housing something utterly new to the interior West—two white women, the wives of Marcus Whitman and a fellow missionary, Henry Spalding.

The effect of these two females on the nation's thinking lies beyond

[2] Even after the sale of Fort Hall and such other assets as he could scrape together, Wyeth ended with a net loss of twenty thousand dollars for his five-year effort to invade the Northwest. Re-entering the ice business with Frederic Tudor, he paid off his debts and made a handsome competence for himself in a trade that the two men spread almost around the globe. Many of the mechanical devices used in today's ice business are direct descendants of inventions by Nathaniel Wyeth; even so, it is probable that his "failure" in the Northwest turned out, in the long run, to be of more worth to his country.

calculation. Here at the rendezvous every Indian squaw, having learned the trick from white men, saluted the pair with noisome kisses. Looking at Narcissa Whitman, mountain man Joe Meek remembered that for nine years he had not tasted bread; footloose Sir William Stewart felt his first pang of dissatisfaction with his wandering life; and a dozen trappers, pretending awakened interest in Bibles, bobbed into the tent to see something they had almost given up hope of ever seeing again. Oregon, farms, wives . . . the thought rippled through a world of lonely men. Oregon—it ran back over the passes to the depression-ridden Mississippi Valley. The Pacific Northwest was not isolated, after all, but was a place a wagon could reach, a woman . . .

In that moment Hall Kelley's fantasies became reality. Forevermore that reality would be part of a young nation's consciousness. Women had crossed the continent . . . and what had been done once could be done again.

That fact, not copper kettles or intruding sea peddlers or trade agreements with foreigners, was the irresistible force that would at last break the iron grip of the Hudson's Bay Company and make the land American.

5. The First Women

NOT the least remarkable of the Northwest's far-reaching coincidences is the one which made Henry Harmon Spalding and his wife Eliza the reluctant subordinates of Marcus and Narcissa Whitman. An illegitimate child, obsessed with shame and a feverish desire to right himself by righting the world, Spalding some years before had proposed to Narcissa and had been rejected. Later the tall, dour youth had married Eliza Hart, as dark and scrawny as Narcissa was golden and buxom, and had offered himself and his bride to the American Board for missionary work.

As soon as the Board received Whitman's request for workers to go with him to the Columbia, the Spaldings were mentioned. But by then Eliza was pregnant and the two were passed over on the reasonable grounds that the effort was too great for a woman with a newborn child. Other couples were proposed instead. For one reason or another, however, all proved unavailable.

By February 1836, Whitman was desperate. His wedding was set for the eighteenth, his departure for the end of the month—but only if one more husband-and-wife team could be secured to travel with him and Narcissa as fellow workers. At that juncture he learned Eliza Spalding's child had been born dead and she was therefore free to travel. Unfortunately the Spaldings had just left for a mission among the Osage Indians in Missouri.

Whitman determined to overhaul them and change their destination. Whether he knew of Spalding's rejection at Narcissa's hands cannot now be determined, though apparently he was aware that the two were acquainted. In any event his own marriage now depended on the compliance of the unsuccessful suitor. Urgently he set out on horseback and after two days' hard riding overtook the pair.

At some time or another—perhaps at this very time—Henry Spalding blurted, loudly enough for busybodies to hear and to carry the words back to Narcissa's home town: "I will not go into the same mission with Narcissa, for I question her judgment." In spite of this, however, he suddenly agreed to give up his own mission and go west as his rival's underling.

Building on Whitman's experience of the previous year, the incongruous quartet spent upwards of thirty-two hundred dollars to provide themselves with cattle, mules, horses, Indian trade goods, camp equipment, medicine, and two wagons. One of these wagons the women loaded, against Whitman's cautions, with what seemed a bare minimum of household goods. Along the roadless way there would be continued, heartrending disposals of more and more "necessities," until finally the vehicle itself would be abandoned at Fort Laramie in eastern Wyoming, hundreds of miles short of its destination.

The other wagon was a small, springless dearborn with yellow wheels. Originally Spalding had intended it for his Osage mission. Now it was dedicated to carrying the women. Actually Narcissa preferred horseback riding, even on an insecure sidesaddle. This feat Eliza Spalding, still wasted from the stillbirth, never quite mastered and insisted on staying in the jolting wagon—or so one reads, meanwhile wondering if deeper incompatibilities might not have underlain the choice.

Confusions and delays kept the party from leaving the frontier with the American Fur Company's annual caravan. During a frantic effort to overhaul these indispensable protectors, Spalding was dragged from a ferryboat by a cow, and shortly thereafter was further chilled by an icy rainstorm that blew down his and Eliza's tent. The cold he contracted clung so persistently that the bulk of the work fell, as it had the year before with Parker, on Marcus Whitman. The doctor had help. The American Board had sent along sour-natured William Gray as the mission's lay assistant, and in Missouri Whitman had hired two teen-age youths to attend to the chores. The livestock was handled by the Indian boys whom he had taken east and by a third Nez Percé unaccountably picked up on the frontier. But the responsibilities, the decisions, the placating of everlastingly ruffled tempers were Whitman's. With anxiety for his great venture burning even into his sleep, he soon worked himself to the raw edge of exhaustion.

Eliza, too, stayed sick, so that only Narcissa, unfolding in marriage, seems to have enjoyed the trip to the rendezvous. After that, even her spirits flagged. Parker's failure to appear bred an uneasiness that was not allayed by his letters, or by the assurances of Nathaniel Wyeth, or even by a providential escort in the form of the Columbia-bound Hudson's Bay brigade. The desert miles grew longer, hotter. Food deteriorated. In place of fresh buffalo steak, which Narcissa had loved, the wayfarers now lived principally on flyblown jerky purchased from the Indians. "I can scarcely eat it," she wrote her mother, "it appears so filthy." And though her record never speaks of quarrels, the constraint with which she mentions the Spaldings bears out others' reports of angry flare-ups along the way.

Apex of the misery was the yellow-wheeled dearborn. The abandonment of the larger farm wagon at Fort Laramie had made Whitman all the more determined to drag this sole remaining vehicle on to Oregon. The struggle worried his wife. After the arduous descent into the valley of the Bear she wrote, "Husband has had a tedious time with the waggon today. Got set in the creek this morning while crossing, was obliged to wade considerably in getting it out. After that in going between two mountains, on the side of one so steep that it was difficult for horses to pass the waggon upset twice. . . . It is not very greatful to my feelings to see him wear out with such excessive fatigue and I am obliged too. He not as fleshy as he was last winter. All the most difficult part of the way he has walked in his laborious attempt to take the waggon over."

Three days later an axletree broke and she rejoiced, thinking that now the vehicle would be abandoned. But no—"they are making a cart of the hind wheels this afternoon and lashing the forward wheels to it, intending to take it through in some shape or another." On it jolted, after a brief respite at Fort Hall, into the gully-riddled desert south of the Snake River. There, to lighten the strain on the precious running gears, Whitman abandoned the wagon box. Now only the wheels and axle remained. Even that was too much. When he drove the cart into a deep ford over the Snake the vehicle capsized. The mules, Narcissa wrote later, "would have drowned, but for a desperate struggle to get them ashore. Then after putting two of the strongest horses before the cart & two men swimming to steady it, they succeeded in getting it over."

An accursed thing! One of the hired hands had quit at Fort Hall because of it. The Hudson's Bay trappers, for all their courtesy, began chafing at the delays it caused. At Fort Boise the traders assured the stubborn doctor that the Blue Mountains, lying ahead, were utterly impassable to wheels. Narcissa importuned. Exhausted and racked by rheumatism, Whitman finally agreed. But after so many wrenching miles the abandonment came like a physical pang. He never forgot it. Later, when another chance came to take wagons all the way, he would not give in so easily.

After the party had forded the Snake again and were toiling toward the Blue Mountains, it was decided to split forces. The sore-footed cattle could no longer keep pace with the impatient escort of trappers. Accordingly the Spaldings, accompanied by a guard of Nez Percé Indians, were delegated to drop behind with the animals. Meanwhile the Whitmans and sour William Gray were to hurry ahead with the trappers to Fort Vancouver in an effort to catch Samuel Parker before his departure for the Sandwich Islands, and also to secure winter supplies.

A sense of release sings through Narcissa's account of the hard, forced ride to Fort Walla Walla. To be sure, Gray was along with his acid conceits, but at least the newlyweds were, for the first time, free of Eliza's plaints, of Spalding's brooding eyes. And by now Narcissa knew she was pregnant. Loitering behind the caravan, she and Marcus stole brief moments together. And each noon there was a blessed hour of relief from the heat and the pounding saddle: "My Husband who is one of the best the world ever knew is always ready to provide a comfortable shade with one of our saddle blankets, spread upon some willows or sticks placed in the ground. . . . Here we recline & rest untill dinner is ready."

Except for these private gains, the ride produced nothing. The overloaded bateaux that took the furs from Fort Walla Walla to Vancouver could not accommodate the missionaries and they had to wait for another boat to be made ready. During the delay the Spaldings arrived with the cattle, which were left at the fort, and in resumed constraint the reunited party journeyed to Fort Vancouver. There they learned that Parker had long since departed by ship for home and that all future decisions were up to them alone.

Somewhere along the trail the incompatible couples had agreed that one mission station could not house both families. At Vancouver, therefore, they planned for separate locations, spending a busy ten days gathering necessary supplies and information from ever obliging John McLoughlin. Then, with grumpy William Gray in tow, the husbands retraced their way up the river, intending to work together only until they could establish their individual sites. As soon as shelters were erected they would return for their wives.

The weeks passed pleasantly for the women. There were comfortable quarters to sleep in, good things to eat. They were lionized. Narcissa in particular soon became a favorite of the half-breed wives of John McLoughlin and James Douglas, his second in command, and of the fort's children, whom she taught to sing. She and Eliza visited a company sailing ship, and at least once a week rode horseback around the environs, marveling at the orchards and vineyards, the rolling grain fields and the dairy, the sawmills and grist mill.

Flourishing changes had occurred in the eight years since Jedediah Smith had witnessed the start of the original 318-foot-square stockade. Another similar compound had been added, creating a rectangle 638 feet long. Dominating the two dozen buildings inside the twenty-foot pickets was McLoughlin's imposing residence, and work was just about to commence on a bachelors' dormitory 153 feet long. The schoolhouse doubled on Sundays as a church (later, church buildings would be erected both inside and outside the stockade), and although Narcissa does not mention the fact, there was also a jail. [1]

Outside the stockade, in untidy clusters, sprawled fifty or so double-family log huts to house the establishments of thirty European mechanics and a hundred or more French-Canadian and Iroquois farm laborers. Two dozen Kanakas felled the great trees and ran the sawmills. Most of these assorted workers had Indian wives, and most of them owned from two to five slaves each, a matter on which Narcissa was again silent, probably through ignorance. Thus the total population of the place probably reached seven hundred and fifty, not counting transient trappers, sailors, and handlers of the bateaux that brought in furs from as far away as British Columbia. Their common

[1] Additions during the 1840s extended the fort's stockaded length to 733 feet. For a discussion of the many buildings inside and outside the stockade, their numbers increasing with the years, see Lewis R. Caywood, *Final Report, Fort Vancouver Excavations* (United States Department of the Interior, San Francisco, 1955).

language was the Chinook trade jargon that had been developing since even before the days of the first sea peddlers.

To the two American brides the fort was a haven of luxury. To two other white women recently arrived by different ships from England, the outpost was considerably less desirable. One of the unhappy pair was a Mrs. William Capendale, who had arrived with her husband the previous March to run the dairy. Narcissa had heard of her as far away as Green River, had met her as anticipated on arrival—and never spoke of her again. Mrs. Capendale was not mingling. As McLoughlin dryly reported the affair, "Things [were] different to what she expected." She sulked in her quarters, badgered her husband, and finally drove him home on the fall fur ship.

The other woman Narcissa saw more frequently. She was the wife of the Reverend Mr. Herbert Beaver—"an appropriate name for the fur trade," wrote Peter Skene Ogden, in charge by this time of all New Caledonia and distinctly unimpressed by the numbers of clergymen invading the headquarters post. "A perfect nuisance," he called them and had a point. Herbert Beaver, though of the Church of England, had arrived only a week before the American missionaries to care for the spiritual needs of the fort's several hundred French Canadians, who were Catholics. A more egregious choice could hardly have been made. Beaver and his wife at once offended McLoughlin by demanding better quarters than he could provide. The quarrel intensified when the Beavers plied evening visitors with more wine and brandy than the teetotaling factor thought was fitting, and finally reached white heat when the clergyman began sniffing about morals.

Beaver had discovered that most of the traders had married their Indian wives by contract, without blessing of the clergy. Worse, he somehow learned that McLoughlin and Marguerite had begun living together before Alexander McKay's death, and in a letter to the governor and committee in London he referred to the woman, to whom McLoughlin was devoted, as "a female of notoriously loose character . . . the kept Mistress of the highest personage in your service at this station."

The slur came back to McLoughlin. Furiously he descended on Beaver as the latter was walking toward his house, where his wife was standing in the doorway. As the clergyman reported the event:

. . . this monster in human shape . . . came behind me, kicked me several times, and struck me repeatedly with his fists on the back of the neck. Unable to cope with him from the immense disparity of our relative size and strength, I could not prevent him from wrenching out of my hand a stout stick with which I was walking, and with which he . . . inflicted several severe blows on my shoulders. He then seized me from behind, round my waist, attempted to dash me on the ground, exclaiming "you scoundrel, I will have your life." In the meantime, the stick had fallen to the ground; my wife on impulse . . . picked it up; he took it . . . very viciously out of her hands and again struck me with it severely. We were then separated by the intervention of other persons. . . .

All this developed after Narcissa and Eliza had left. On October 18, less than a month after the two husbands had gone upriver in search of mission sites, Spalding was back with word that locations had been found. Whitman and Gray were already building a house at Waiilatpu, "the place of rye grass," in the broad valley of the Walla Walla River, twenty-five miles upstream from the fort of the same name. Spalding's own site lay a hundred and twenty-five miles farther east, at Lapwai, or "butterfly valley," where a small stream broke through the tall brown hills into the Clearwater, ten miles above its junction with the Snake. As soon as the building at Waiilatpu was finished, Gray would go to Lapwai to help Spalding build a house. Meanwhile both men were anxious for their wives to join them.

Reluctantly McLoughlin sold them clothing, household furniture, provisions, farming supplies. Winter, he felt, was no time for untrained white women to risk the interior and he urged them to stay at the fort. They refused, Narcissa because she wanted her baby, due in March, to be born in her new home. On November 3 they loaded their goods into two boats he loaned them and were rowed by his crews to Fort Walla Walla.

Almost immediately the Spaldings left for Lapwai, but Narcissa stayed at Walla Walla until her home was more nearly suitable. On December 10, Marcus finally took her to it: "a house reared & the lean too enclosed, a good chimney & fire place & the flour [floor] laid. No windows or door except blankets. My heart truly leaped for joy as I alighted from my horse and entered and seated myself before a pleasant fire." The long trip was ended. Soon other wives of discontented men throughout the United States would know it and take courage.

McLoughlin anticipated censure for his generosity, and in his annual report justified his actions on the grounds that if the company did not supply the missionaries the newcomers would import goods from

MAP 3

The Missions and Early Settlements of the Northwest

PACIFIC OCEAN

QUEEN CHARLOTTE STRAIT

BELLA COOLA R.
CHILKO L.
FRASER R.

Canoe Encampment • WOOD R.
CANIM L.
ATHABASKA R.
CANOE R.
ATHABASKA PASS
HOWSE PASS
COLUMBIA R.

THOMPSON R.
N. THOMPSON R.
ADAMS L.
SHUSWAP L.

Ft. Thompson

LILLOOET R.
FRASER R.

UPPER ARROW L.
COLUMBIA

OKANAGAN L.
SIMILKAMEEN R.
OKANAGAN R.
LOWER ARROW L.
KOOTENAY L.

NOOTKA SOUND
CLAYOQUOT SOUND
BARKLEY SOUND

STRAIT OF GEORGIA

Ft. Langley

Ft. Victoria
C. FLATTERY
STRAIT OF JUAN DE FUCA

SKAGIT R.
METHOW R.
L. CHELAN

Ft. Colvile
Kettle Falls
PEND OREILLE L.
PEND OREILLE R.

Ft. Okanagan
Kullyspel Hous

Seattle

YAKIMA R.

Tshimakain Mission
Spokane House
COEUR D'ALÈNE L.
Cataldo Mission

Olympia • Ft. Nisqually
GRAY'S HARBOR
Tumwater
CHEHALIS R.
MT. RAINIER

COLUMBIA R.

PALOUSE R.
SNAKE R.

Cowlitz Farms

MT. ST. HELENS
MT. ADAMS

Lapwai Mission

Ft. Clatsop
Astoria
COLUMBIA R.

Ft. Nez Percé
(Ft. Walla Walla)
Waiilatpu Mission

WAPATOO I.
CASCADE RAPIDS
DALLES RAPIDS

Ft. Vancouver
WILLAMETTE FALLS
Champoeg
Portland
The Dalles Mission
UMATILLA R.

GRANDE RONDE R.

Oregon Trail

Lee's First Mission
Oregon City
MT. HOOD
SNAKE R. CAN.

FRENCH PRAIRIE
Salem
(Lee's Second Mission)
DESCHUTES R.
JOHN DAY R.

WILLAMETTE R.

MALHEUR R.
Ft. Boise

UMPQUA R.

Ft. Umpqua
MALHEUR L.
HARNEY L.
OWYHEE R.

ROGUE R.
KLAMATH L.

KLAMATH R.

Miles
0   50   100

MT. SHASTA

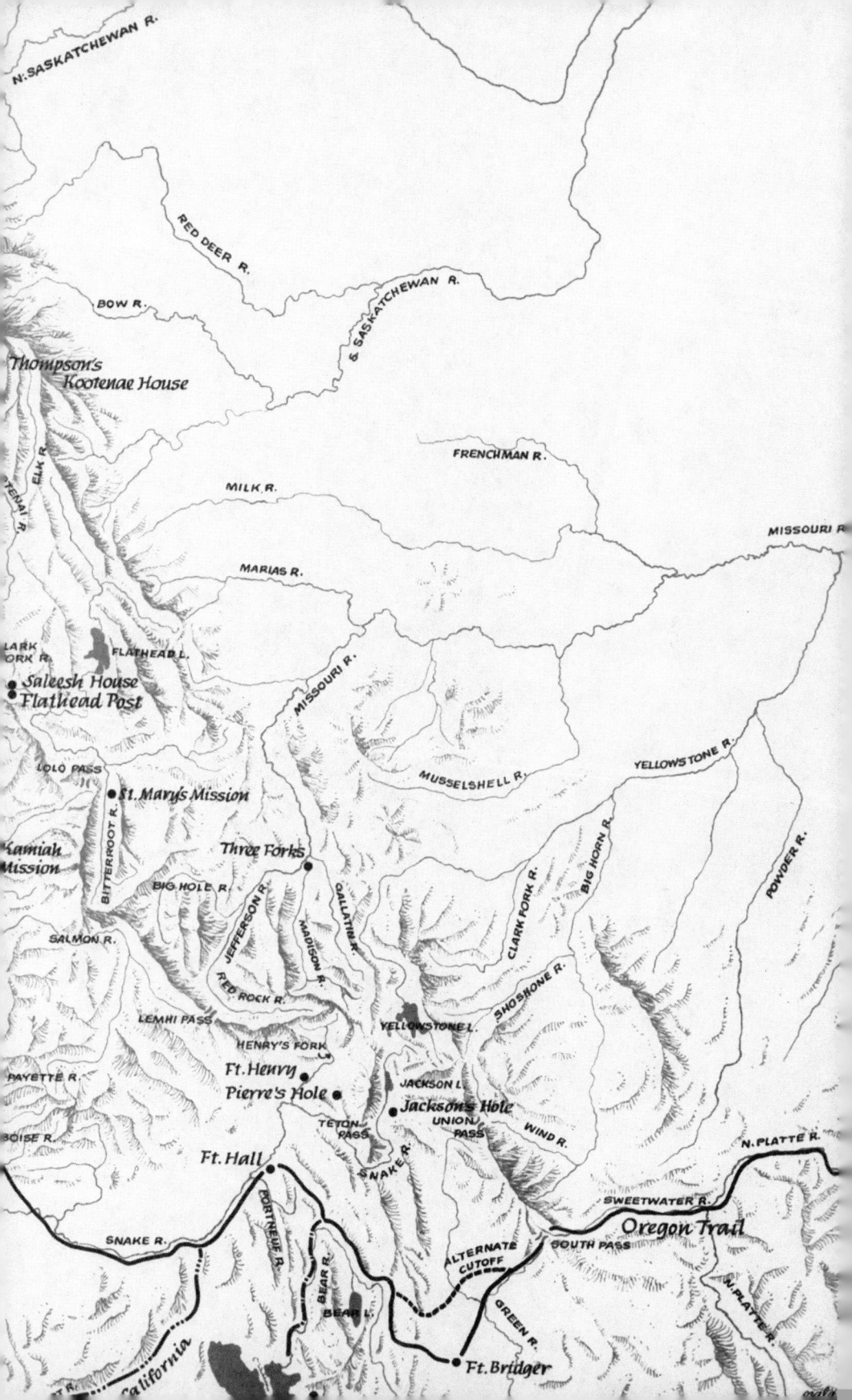

the Sandwich Islands. This in turn would attract "Adventurers . . . [to] open shop in opposition to us. . . . We ought in policy to secure their Good Will and that of those who support them in their Laudable Endeavor to do Good."

If only Jason Lee's station in the Willamette and Whitman's and Spalding's in the interior had been involved, the directors might have agreed. But what London knew, though McLoughlin as yet didn't, was the disturbing fact that in June 1836 eight more earnest souls—two married men with their wives and children, one bachelor, and three unwed females—had sailed from New York via the Horn and the Sandwich Islands to reinforce Lee's mission in the Willamette. The next January four more adults, accompanied by their children, had sailed from Boston, also bound for Lee's establishment.

To the English this looked like an excessive number of missionaries for the disease-decimated tribes of the lower Columbia, and led to their answering McLoughlin's remarks with a worried warning:

Were we satisfied that the sole object of those Missionaries, were the civilization of the Natives and the diffusion of moral and religious instruction, we should be happy to render them our most cordial support and assistance, but we have all along foreseen that . . . the formation of a Colony of United States citizens on the banks of the Columbia was the main or fundamental part of their plan, which, if successful, might be attended with material injury, not only to the Fur trade, but in a national point of view.

Long before that letter reached the Columbia something else occurred to give still more body to the directors' uneasiness. In the closing days of 1836, less than two months after Henry Spalding had started up the Columbia with his and Whitman's wives, a strange brig felt her way across the bar. Cautiously she tacked up against the current to Fort Vancouver's docks. Her name was *Loriot*. She carried almost no cargo. Her sole passenger was an inquisitive American named William Slacum.

Disembarking, Slacum presented himself to McLoughlin as a private merchant bent on gaining commercial information about the Northwest. Vaguely he mentioned a party that was supposedly coming overland from the States. McLoughlin pretended to believe it. Privately, however, he pegged William Slacum for exactly what the man was, a secret agent of the United States Government. More than missionaries, it would seem, were at last becoming concerned about the state of affairs on the Columbia.

6. The Opening Wedge

TO PRESIDENT ANDREW JACKSON the Northwest in 1836 was of interest primarily as that far-off land might affect Texas, then in revolt against Mexico. Great Britain might be tempted to intervene, and that might mean further exacerbations anywhere that Americans and Englishmen came into contact. Accordingly the President began casting for information about Britain's potentials all along the frontier from the Great Lakes to the Pacific. And those, by and large, were synonymous with the potentials of the Hudson's Bay Company.

For some years the War Department had been collecting reports from various fur traders, most of whom were not overcome with affection for their British rivals. Jackson received additional information directly from Captain Benjamin L. E. de Bonneville, just returned to Washington from his profitless trapping ventures around the periphery of the Oregon country—and furious at the Hudson's Bay Company for refusing to sell him supplies he needed. At about the same time Hall Kelley returned from Fort Vancouver and sought the public prints with bitter diatribes about McLoughlin's treatment of American citizens—that is to say, about McLoughlin's treatment of Hall Kelley.

All these views—the trappers', Bonneville's, Kelley's—were intensely personal. Wanting a more dispassionate estimate, Jackson asked his Secretary of State to send a man to the Columbia.

The person chosen was William Slacum. Slacum was not a top-drawer spy, for this was not a top-drawer job. His background is vague. He is said to have been a purser in the United States Navy. He may have done some prior snooping for the Administration in the Southwest and perhaps had loose threads to wind up in that direction. In any event he traveled to Guaymas, on the Mexican side of the Gulf of California, before starting for the Columbia.

He was an extraordinary optimist. He first prepared to ride, in midsummer, across the ferocious deserts of California to his destination. Dissuaded by saner heads, he sold his saddle horses and pack mules and bought instead a remodeled, 12-ton longboat. This diminutive craft he proposed to sail to the Columbia. Quickly chastened by one of the gulf's wild storms, he embarked on a normal ship for the Sandwich Islands. There he chartered the brig *Loriot*, and on January 2, 1837, warped up to the Vancouver docks, his eyes and pencil busy.

McLoughlin blandly answered the American's questions (perhaps not truthfully [1]) and then enlisted his help in solving an embarrassing

[1] Slacum's report to the government curiously overestimated Fort Vancouver's productivity. For example, he stated that 3000 acres were under cultivation in 1836. Two

predicament. Two and a half years before, so the chief factor told Slacum, another American named Ewing Young had led into the district a small party of men driving a herd of horses reputedly stolen in California. Acting impulsively, McLoughlin had ordered the Canadian farmers in the Willamette to have no dealings with Young, and himself refused to accept, in exchange for needed supplies, some furs Young had sent to Fort Vancouver with another man. Since then McLoughlin had come to the conclusion that perhaps he had acted hastily, that probably Young wasn't a thief. In the meantime, however, the American and a partner named Lawrence Carmichael, infuriated by their treatment, had decided to turn the wheat of their Chehalem Valley farm (near present Newberg) into a commodity whose marketing would not be dependent on the Hudson's Bay Company—into alcohol. They were brewing their hell's fire in a salmon pickling kettle of Nat Wyeth's, and unless they were stopped there was no telling what kind of havoc they might wreak.

Slacum, already feeling benignly paternalistic as an agent of the United States Government, was pressed into service as an emissary. Up the Willamette he went with the company's tacit apology: if Young would abandon the still he would not only be allowed to trade at the company's store but would be granted a loan for purchasing whatever he needed.

Six voyageurs rowed Slacum's canoe. For twenty-two unbroken hours they cheerfully bucked the current, portaged around the falls, and above the cataract swung west for twenty miles along the great curve of the river. Their destination was an ancient Indian camp ground called Champoeg—an open, sandy peninsula on the south side of the river. Because the Canadian farmers of French Prairie could trundle wheat down to Champoeg in their homemade carts and there load the grain in the Bay Company's flat-bottomed freight bateaux, McLoughlin had built a warehouse on the peninsula. In time, ironically enough, incoming Americans would use the building as a meeting place for asserting their independence of him and his monopoly.

It was dark as Slacum's canoemen groped uncertainly along the bank, looking for a landing place. A sudden voice calling through

---

years later trader James Douglas, in an official report to the company directors, said only 861 acres were available for farming. Slacum estimates that a total of 28,500 bushels of wheat, barley, oats, and peas were raised in 1836. Narcissa Whitman, who presumably got her figures from the same source, estimated 11,000. Slacum said there were 1000 cattle; McLoughlin's report for 1841, after five years of increase, put the figure at between 400 and 500. Perhaps the Britishers were stuffing the American; or perhaps Slacum wanted to enhance the importance of the place he had been sent so far to examine.

the night told them where to turn. Stepping ashore, Slacum met tall, bearded Jason Lee, who somehow had learned of the agent's projected visit and had ridden from the Methodist mission, eighteen miles farther upstream, to meet him.

The next morning the two men, no doubt accompanied by residents of the vicinity, rode horseback to Lee's station. Several more people were waiting there, ready to pour out their troubles to the first official of the United States who had ever bothered to come their way.

Most of their grievances had to do with the Hudson's Bay Company. True, McLoughlin was kind. He had willingly loaned tools and seed, horses and cows to everyone who needed them. He would not sell the animals, however, and asked that all increase be turned back to the company. His stated reason was that he needed to build up Fort Vancouver's jealously nurtured herd. In the opinion of the settlers, however, he was trying to keep the entire Willamette Valley, newcomers as well as retired Canadians, in economic subservience. Look how it worked: a man could not have a cow except on McLoughlin's terms; had no place to sell his wheat or furs except the company warehouse, no place to buy goods except at the company store. He could not even repair a broken tool without taking it to the company forge. If this area really was going to fall under United States sovereignty, as everyone seemed to believe, could not Congress do something to help—at least establish laws so that a citizen could have some guarantee that his person and property would be respected? Thus reassured, other settlers and merchants would come, and the hold of the Hudson's Bay Company would gradually be broken.

The best Slacum could advise was that the settlers draw up a petition stating their case and send it to Washington.

Next he turned to the matter of Young's and Carmichael's disruptive whiskey still. The settlers were as disturbed about it as McLoughlin was. Shortly before Slacum's arrival Jason Lee's temperance society had sent to the two men an agitated request that they desist and had pledged fifty-five dollars and twelve bushels of wheat to reimburse them for labors and materials so far expended. Slacum now added word of the fort's relenting. With their point made and popular opinion solidly arrayed against them, Young and Carmichael agreed to drop the project "for the present." But what were they going to do to make a living? They were still too stubborn to deal with McLoughlin.

At this point either Slacum or Young or both of them together had a dazzling inspiration. The settlers needed cattle but could buy none.

California abounded in cattle. Young, an ex-mountain man, was familiar with the trapper trails between Oregon and the Mexican province. Furthermore, he wanted to go there to clear his name once and for all of the horse-thief charges. If enough Willamette settlers would chip in to buy a herd and go along to help drive it back, Young would assume the leadership of the venture. In fact he would put in a thousand dollars himself to start things going. (His contribution eventually worked out at $1119.27½). Further inducement came from Slacum who, as representative of the United States Government, offered the drovers free passage to California aboard his chartered brig *Loriot*.

Two French Canadians and nine Americans promptly agreed, scraping together about two thousand dollars, partly in cash and partly in credit due them for wheat delivered to the Hudson's Bay Company . . . if they could collect the money. Slacum loaned Lee enough so that the Methodist was enabled to invest $624 on behalf of the mission. The agent contributed another hundred dollars or so on his own account.

When the adventurers reached Fort Vancouver and diffidently asked McLoughlin for the sums owed them, he not only obliged but added $558 in his own name and $300 in the names of two of his traders. In his report to the government Slacum does not mention the support, although the additional fund obviously reduced the price per animal delivered in Oregon. [2]

Eleven men and three hired Indian hands started the epochal trip—destined to be the West's first great cattle drive. From beginning to end it was unalloyed misery. At the storm-tortured mouth of the Columbia a gale snapped the *Loriot's* anchor cables and drove the brig ashore, from which predicament the ship was rescued by Hudson's Bay Company help. One man dropped out and went home. After three rain-drenched weeks the *Loriot* at last escaped across the Columbia's thunderous bar. (Reflectively Slacum advised his government, "I beg leave to call your attention to 'Puggit's sound' and urge,

---

[2] Slacum's report evinced throughout a strong anti-Hudson's Bay slant. He charged that the company made no effort to check Indian slavery; blamed its brigades for excesses among the Indians that resulted in retaliatory attacks on less well-equipped parties of Americans; said that McLoughlin had spread rumors among the Indians that Captain Dominis of the *Owhyhee* had spread the intermittent fever that was depopulating the region. "Some steps," he added piously, "must be taken by our government to protect the settlers and traders, not from the hostility of the Indians, but from a much more formidable enemy . . . the Hudson Bay Company." When copies of the report, later printed as a congressional document, reached McLoughlin, he was understandably outraged.

in the most earnest manner, that it should never be abandoned.")

The open sea brought no relief. As the battered *Loriot* neared California, Philip Edwards, the twenty-four-year-old treasurer and diarist of the party, moaned to his journal, "What a repulsive passage. Tempestuous and cold! sick and melancholy! Perhaps no period of my life had been less calculated to give happiness. But peace! God is merciful and I am safe!"

The drovers safely deposited in California, Slacum sailed on home to report. Behind him, the Oregonians found jobs to support them while Young began the nerve-fraying process of wheedling government permission for taking cattle out of the province. For three months he was shunted back and forth—from San Francisco to Monterey, south to Santa Barbara, north again and across the Golden Gate to Sonoma—before finally he was allowed to purchase eight hundred cattle at three dollars a head. And such cattle! Because the Mexican officials pocketed Young's money, the missions and ranchos which were ordered to furnish the stock naturally palmed off on the foreigners their wildest, most undesirable animals. Mercilessly these varicolored, lean-hipped beasts, blood cousins to the fabled Texas longhorns of a later era, were hazed out of the brush into corrals to wait for the Americans. There some of the animals stayed as long as seven days without food or water.

Young was moving as fast as he could. He bought forty riding horses, augmented his crew with five more footloose Americans, and began throwing the rebellious cattle together into a trail herd. Painfully the drovers crept around the southern tip of San Francisco Bay and then turned north to their first obstacle, the San Joaquin River. This the cattle refused to cross.

One expedient after another failed. First the men dragged calves across behind their saddle horses. Only a few mother cows followed. Next the crew built a pen at the water's edge, jammed it tight full of bawling beasts, and by brute pressure tried to squeeze the herd into the river. Instead the animals broke down the fence and stampeded. The cursing men rounded them up and tried again . . . and again . . . and again. On one occasion they succeeded in getting the herd into the water, but in mid-river a panic seized the animals and they broke back, seventeen of them drowning during the frantic melee.

Finally, after heat-seared, mosquito-tormented weeks of this, the crew hit on the idea of building rafts of bulrushes. Three or four men boarded each raft. Half of them held a lassoed cow which was belabored from behind by riders. The other half hauled the raft forward by pulling hand over hand on a rope stretched across the river. And so, one by one, the herd was towed across, the labor doubling with the necessity of guarding a starving, fractious herd on either bank.

When finally the crossing was finished Edwards wrote wearily, "Another month like the last, God avert! Who can describe it?" And still he had not seen the worst.

At snail's pace in the parched August dust the footsore herd dragged out of the Sacramento Valley into the maze of high ridges, precipitous ravines, and impenetrable brush bordering Mount Shasta. Each day the thirst-crazed animals broke out of control and plunged for water into the bottom of dead-end gullies, from which only physical violence could dislodge them. Each evening the sullen men had to go back and pick up the day's strays one by one. The exhausted riding horses gave out, so that at times the weary men had to night-herd the weary cattle on foot.

Tempers snapped, quarrels flared. Only Young's iron discipline averted open battle, and as they neared the Rogue River of southern Oregon even his control was not enough. This was the point where Rogue River Indians two years before had killed half of John Turner's party on their way toward the Willamette. Three survivors of that massacre were with Young now—Turner himself, George Gay, and William Bailey, his brooding fingers rubbing back and forth across the frightful scar on his lower face.

One day an adult Rogue River Indian wandered into the camp, accompanied by a boy. Without warning, Gay and Bailey opened fire. The man dropped, riddled with bullets. The boy darted out of range. Young flew into a passion, but weakening his force now by ordering Gay and Bailey out of camp would do no good. He let them stay, sympathizing perhaps with their motives if not with their judgment. Throwing out flankers to guard against the inevitable retaliatory attack, he started the herd along the trail once more. His alertness forestalled the ambushes the Indians tried to spring. It was a running three-day fight, nevertheless, with sudden flights of arrows humming from the brush just when the men were too entangled with the cattle to fight back. Several horses were hurt, several cattle killed; but only George Gay among the men was wounded. And there, with exasperating abruptness, Philip Edwards quit writing his journal.

By unrecorded stages the herd crossed the Rogue and reached safer, greener pastures. Fed and rested, they quickened their pace and in mid-October, some seven hundred miles and eighteen or nineteen weeks from their starting point in San Francisco, the drovers reached Lee's mission. Six hundred and thirty animals remained alive. After the herders had been paid in cattle at the rate of twenty dollars a month, the remaining stock was prorated among the investors. A large proportion of them found their way across the Columbia to the Fort Vancouver herd, for McLoughlin agreed to accept these wild, trailgaunt animals in lieu of the trained, gentle milk cows and work oxen which he had loaned the settlers. In his generosity the factor even agreed to count a lean, red-eyed Spanish calf as a full-grown animal.

The effect on morale was tremendous. Until this moment the thirty-odd settlers in the Willamette had possessed almost nothing they could call their own. The titles to their land were clouded, since no sovereignty yet existed. Their crops had value only if the Hudson's Bay Company chose to buy. These stringy, fence-breaking cattle, however, were something on which a man could stamp his brand and say, "This is mine!" As such Young's epic drive had a significance far transcending its size or its monetary value; for it was the Northwest's first gleam of independence, the first crack in the Bay Company's benign but hitherto invulnerable monopoly.

Other boosts to morale appeared. During the drovers' absence the Willamette had welcomed the handful of missionaries from Boston and New York whose sailing had so worried McLoughlin's London directors. Among the newcomers was a doctor, slim, blue-eyed, officious Elijah White and his wife, who performed perhaps their greatest service to the community by ferreting out scar-faced William Bailey's medical background and inducing him to resume his studies and, eventually, his practice.

Also included among the immigrants were four intensely devout, unwed females. One of them was the fiancée of Cyrus Shepard, the mission's frail schoolteacher. Another, Anna Maria Pittman, had been dispatched by the mission society in the East with the understanding that, if matters proved agreeable, she was to wed Jason Lee.

Between spells of nursing a mission full of sick Indians, Lee did what he could to oblige—and evidently did it well. Scarcely a month after Miss Pittman's arrival the Northwest's first all-white wedding was solemnized in a grove of firs. Shepard and his fiancée were wed on the same day and in the same spot.

As might be expected, the double ceremony attracted considerable attention to the two remaining unmarried females. One soon found a husband. The other, Margaret Smith, held out three years before succumbing to William Bailey's blandishments and marrying him. It was an unfortunate mistake. Within three weeks some bristling incompatibility between the vindictive Indian slayer and his pious bride led him (by her account) to try strangling her. Later he fell off the wagon with a resounding crash, slept openly with every Indian squaw he could entice into bed, and finally bedeviled his wife into obtaining one of the Northwest's first divorces. Community sympathy, however, seems to have attached to Bailey. He would be in time a member of various legislative bodies and even a candidate for governor. As a divorcée, meanwhile, his ex-wife was, in her own words, "shunned and slighted and regarded with suspicions in every place, till my life is more burdensome than death would be." She sought solace in writing a novel, published in 1854. Civilization had indeed come to the Columbia.

7. The Vineyards of the Lord—and Others

CATTLE, farms, women: no one sensed their implications more surely than did towering, white-haired John McLoughlin. The fur trade could not survive civilization, and now civilization was singing hymns at his doorstep.

Statistically, the threat was not yet evident. In 1837, the year that the California cattle and the American females reached the Willamette, McLoughlin's Columbia Department sent a bumper pelt crop worth £26,735 to the company's London showrooms. Naturally the English stockholders, who in 1837 and again in 1838 received dividends of twenty-five per cent, visualized a beaver-filled wilderness reaching unbroken from the Rocky Mountains to the sea.

McLoughlin did his best to dispel the notion. Readers of his annual reports must have realized that for some years now Fort Vancouver had ceased to be the center of either the fur or the Indian trade. Rather, it was a distribution point. Into it poured furs gleaned from as far away as California on the south, Wyeth's old Fort Hall and the Montana posts on the east, New Caledonia and Russian Alaska on the north. In return Vancouver sent back toiling brigades laden with English trade cloth and English hardware—and with boatloads of flour, dried peas, potatoes, smoked meat, dried salmon, and cheeses produced on the ever growing farms outside the stockade.

McLoughlin was no farmer, but the way fruit, vegetables, grain, and livestock thrived on these virgin fields would have caught even a less agricultural eye than his. Unlike most pioneer agriculturists, moreover, he could sell his surplus. The Russian-American Fur Company's inefficient Fort Ross in California had proved unable to supply the growing settlements in Alaska, and the Northern traders were eager to buy all the grain McLoughlin could offer. The implications were obvious, even to a man primarily interested in beaver pelts.

Other agricultural possibilities kept suggesting themselves. British and Boston mariners, as McLoughlin's ship captains well knew, had recently opened a booming hide-and-tallow business with the California *ranchos*. There seemed no reason why a similar trade could not succeed at Vancouver—a consideration which played no small part in McLoughlin's support of Ewing Young's cattle drive. Inspired by the success of that drive and by the knowledge that livestock could be pried loose from the Mexican governors of California, he next ordered his brig *Nereide* to import, during the summer of 1838, eight hundred head of sheep from San Francisco.

All this took land, and by 1837 most of the suitable acreage in the vicinity of Fort Vancouver had been utilized. Expansion into the Willamette was inadvisable, since the country south of the Columbia might go to the United States. Accordingly McLoughlin turned his attention northward. Good pasturage was found for the new sheep at the southern tip of Puget Sound, where Fort Nisqually had been built as a fur and trading post less than half a dozen years before. Farm land was located on the Cowlitz Plains, a projection into present Washington of the great trough whose southern extension forms the Willamette Valley. Here a rival settlement to those in the Willamette was designed. Its first settler was Simon Plomodon and his singularly pretty Indian wife, retiring in 1837 after sixteen years' service with the company and grandly equipped by McLoughlin with seed, livestock, tools, and promises of protection. To encourage other settlers to join Plomodon, McLoughlin prevailed on the company to send in Roman Catholic priests, something the Willamette did not have. Two of them, Fathers Blanchet and Demers, arrived the following year.

The London directors' co-operation in these civilizing pursuits was dictated in part by political considerations. The company's license was coming up for renewal in 1838, and the directors needed to justify themselves before Parliament. One method, of course, was to show that the interests of England and of the Hudson's Bay Company were identical.

As early as February 1837, Simpson showed the drift. Writing Governor J. H. Pelly in London, he stated that the company hoped to strengthen England's claim to the country north of the Columbia "by forming the nucleus of a colony through the establishment of farms." Pelly, in his turn, blandly told Parliament, during the hearings about the renewal of the company's license, that the Columbia Department's thousand employees, twenty-one trading posts, six vessels, and two migratory trading and trapping brigades really produced no great profit but were useful to England in that they "compelled the American adventurers, one by one, to withdraw [Wyeth and Dominis, for example] and are now pressing the Russian Fur Company so closely that . . . [we] hope at no very distant period to confine them to the trade of their own proper territory."

The point, though not entirely candid, was effective. Relying almost entirely on the Bay Company's own description of its proposed farms and of its impregnable trade position, Parliament renewed the license. More pertinently, English diplomats stiffened their demands that the Columbia and not the forty-ninth parallel be made the international boundary, and American negotiators seemed further than ever from gaining the coveted harbors of Puget Sound.

Governor Pelly, perhaps, was talking agriculture for effect. McLoughlin wasn't. More and more the factor was seeing, partly with the help of William Tolmie, the fort's canny Scots doctor, the dazzling possibilities inherent in setting up a subsidiary corporation to coordinate and direct the farming ventures so haphazardly begun.

Farming in a fur preserve! The more conservative of the London stockholders were certain to object. But if a full prospectus were drawn up and presented—why not do it himself, in person, when he went to London on his long-deferred furlough?

At exactly the same time Jason Lee was planning to hurry east to further an expansion plan of his own.

A curious dichotomy was disturbing the Methodist's thinking. As yet he had not dared voice it to his fellow missionaries—perhaps not even to himself. Nonetheless he sensed that a decision was staring him squarely in the face. Where, exactly, did his duty lie? To the Indians, almost none of whom he had been able to convert? Or to the encroaching whites whose arrival meant extinction to the tribes he had come here to save?

The Indians still seemed to absorb him. Even his honeymoon was apparently devoted to studying their needs. In August of 1837, not long after the double ceremony at the mission, he and Cyrus Shepard took their brides on a wedding horseback trip southward through the

Willamette Valley and then across the coastal mountains to the sea. Ostensibly the quartet were exploring for additional mission sites, although by now Lee knew that the Stone Age minds of the Indians were incapable of receiving the doctrines he was trying to impart. The savages needed time to adapt—more time than they were likely to get. Already the population of the coastal tribes had dwindled, in places, by three quarters or more; and the apathetic, fish-smelling, disease-ridden remnants could not survive much longer. Meanwhile one saw on every hand rich foundations for white civilization: fertile prairies; towering stands of timber; and, across the misty expanse of the Pacific, the limitless trade of the Orient. To the Indians such change would be tragic. Yet could not that tragedy be lightened? Could not Methodism serve both the dying savages and the about-to-be-born whites? Lee determined to try.

In March 1837 he had sent his nephew Daniel and one of the new arrivals up the Columbia to the Dalles. At that spot, too, there were Indians in need of salvation . . . and it also happened to be a place through which future immigration was bound to pass. Other equally strategic stations took shape in his mind: one at the mouth of the Columbia; another south on the Umpqua; a third north on Puget Sound, near the Bay Company's Fort Nisqually; and, most significantly, a key establishment at the falls of the Willamette, priceless with water power. (By coincidence, at exactly this same time McLoughlin decided he had better renew his own claim to the Willamette site. Workers were dispatched to the falls to square timbers and build a little house to replace one the Indians had destroyed a few years earlier.)

To insure the scores of helpers and the tens of thousands of dollars needed for his new mission stations, Lee determined to present the case in person to his church's board—just as McLoughlin was planning to visit his board of directors.

Their plans matured simultaneously. McLoughlin set his departure for March 22, 1838, planning to travel with the annual express across Athabaska Pass. When Jason Lee heard of it he asked if he might go along.

There is no written proof that McLoughlin knew anything definite about Lee's intentions. Yet it seems he must have had at least a premonition, for with uncharacteristic lack of generosity he turned down the request. This, after all, was a matter of empire.

Undeterred, Lee summoned a meeting at the mission house on March 16, 1838. It was attended, in addition to the resident missionaries, by more than a dozen American settlers and by nine French Canadians. Their purpose, as they knew in advance, was to approve a petition to the Congress of the United States, written by young Philip Edwards along lines suggested more than a year ago by William Slacum.

"We flatter ourselves," the petition read, after urging Congress to extend its jurisdiction over an Oregon whose boundaries the document did not venture to define, "we flatter ourselves that we are the germ of a great state."

Then the signing began, names for most but marks for John Deportes and Joseph Gervais, former Hudson's Bay employees who, along with Etienne Lucier, were the district's first settlers. All ten mission members added their names. So did John Turner, who had arrived in 1828 with Jedediah Smith; and Solomon Smith and Calvin Tibbetts, who had come with Wyeth's first expedition; and Ewing Young, who more than anyone else had produced the material support for these dreams.

Solemnly Jason Lee placed the document in a small tin box he would carry strapped to his saddle across the continent. Solemnly he kissed his pregnant wife good-by. The trip meant that Anna Maria would bear her first child while her husband was far away, but she made no protest. This was the Lord's work—and destiny's. If Methodism could presume to help destiny.

With Lee when he started east were a mysterious Mr. Ewing, who had somehow landed in Oregon a year earlier for his health, and young Philip Edwards, who had come west with the missionary in 1834 and was now returning to Missouri. Also along, for proselyting purposes, were two appealingly peak-headed teen-age Chinook Indian boys who had been rechristened William Brooks and Thomas Adams, after two famed divines of the day. At Fort Hall, Lee was to pick up three more traveling companions—the half-breed sons of Thomas McKay— and take them east to be educated.

The canoes slid into the water four days after McLoughlin had started his own journey east. The missionary made no attempt to overhaul the trader; neither man had any sense of being in a race.

Lee paid a leisurely visit at his nephew Daniel's new station at the Dalles, then moved on to Fort Walla Walla, where he intended to join the annual brigade bound for the rendezvous. Learning that the trappers would not leave for five more weeks, he passed the time by visiting his Presbyterian counterparts at Waiilatpu and Lapwai. To each he revealed, during the long nights of talk, the expansion he envisioned for Methodism in Oregon.

Whitman and Spalding, grievously overworked in a far more rigorous section than Jason Lee knew, could not repress unchristian pangs of envy. The only help they could expect was whatever sour William Gray might bring in during the summer—and even that help would not be produced with Whitman's full blessing.

Gray's venture requires a digression. Restless and dissatisfied, he had left his superiors early in 1837 and with Francis Ermatinger's Flathead brigade had started for Montana, hoping to find a field for a mission of his own. Along the way, in the snowbound land of the Spokanes, he re-encountered Henry Spalding, plowing through the drifts from Lapwai with some Nez Percé Indians to visit Fort Colvile on the Columbia.

While waiting for the trails to open, the reunited missionaries met Spokane Gerry, one of the savages whom George Simpson had taken across the mountains to be educated at Red River. Gerry fed Gray and Spalding native-grown potatoes, showed them the log schoolhouse his tribe had built under his tutelage, and translated when Spalding delivered a sermon. Tremendously impressed, Spalding and Gray decided that the country of the Spokanes was a propitious spot for Gray's mission. They further decided that Gray should go east to present the case to the American Board in person, taking some Indians along with him to strengthen his arguments. More practically, he would also drive along a herd of cheap Nez Percé horses and trade them in Missouri for cattle to bring back with him.

Word of these decisions did not reach Whitman, the mission's head, until Gray had gone on beyond reach to Montana. Marcus was annoyed. He did not believe Gray was proper material to head up a mission. He also felt they should strengthen their current establishments before trying to expand.

And now here came Jason Lee with plans that made even Gray's scheme look picayune. Carried away by their envy, Spalding and Whitman addressed an almost frantic letter to the American Board—a letter which Lee himself agreed to carry east. In it, the Presbyterians asked for two hundred and twenty helpers—missionaries, teachers, physicians, laborers, and their wives—plus a flour mill, "several tons of iron and steel," bales of hardware and trade goods. At the very moment of the writing, though they could not know that, William Gray was starting back toward the Northwest not with two hundred helpers but with eight, and with no more equipment than could be packed on horseback. It was all the assistance the beset American Board, responsible for three hundred and sixty stations throughout the world, would ever be able to dispatch to Oregon. Whitman realized the presumption of his appeal almost at once. But it was too late to stop it. Lee had already left for the rendezvous.

This year the shrunken bacchanal of the American fur trade had been moved east of the Continental Divide to the Popo Agie River. The business was dying. Over the cups of raw alcohol rumors were rife that this would be (as it proved to be) the last of the exuberant trade councils which for one wild, free decade had been the pulsebeat of the West. The last . . . and into it came Jason Lee, time's errand boy, riding eastward with dreams of a new civilization burning behind his high-domed forehead.

William Gray was there, too, after a blood-spattered trip that had made his name anathema throughout the mountains. The year before he had been in such a hurry to promote his Spokane mission that he had left the rendezvous without waiting for the protection of the fur traders' Missouri-bound caravan. Accompanying him were half a dozen Indians and two or three impulsive whites. At Ash Hollow, in present Nebraska, their recklessness caught up with them. A fight flared between the eastbound party and a band of Sioux Indians accompanied by a white trader. The horses Gray was taking to Missouri for barter were lost, his Indians killed. Afterward Gray insisted—and his account is the only one we have—that the intercession of the trader saved him and the other whites. But in the mountains men always believed that William Gray, would-be servant of God, swapped his Indians' lives to the Sioux in exchange for his own.

Now he was on his way back. He had secured one bachelor and three married couples as helpers, plus a wife of his own. It was an ill-assorted, contentious group. After a month on the trail one of the women, Mary Walker, admitted to her diary, "We have a strange company of missionaries. Scarcely one who is not intolerable on some account." (And most intolerable of all was William Gray. By the time the bickering group reached Whitman's station the newcomers were so enraged at him that not one would inhabit the same district with the man. As a result the Spokane mission, established at Tshimakain, about thirty miles northwest of modern Spokane, was assigned to Elkanah Walker and Cushing Eells; a second new station, Kamiah on the Clearwater, went to rasp-natured Asa Smith. Gray himself, promoter of the expansion, was shunted off onto Spalding at Lapwai.)

At the rendezvous Gray read the letter Lee was carrying to the

American Board. From his own experience he knew that no such quantities of aid would be forthcoming. He may even have observed to Lee, as in effect the Board had observed to him, that the West was trying to get too big too fast. If he did speak, his pessimism failed to dampen Lee's ardor.

Even personal tragedy failed. At the Missouri border Lee was over-hauled by the last of a relay of messengers bearing word that his wife and his first-born son had both died. But Lee was hurrying now and there was no time for grief. Changing horses for canoes, he swept down the Missouri River, into the Mississippi. Somehow he learned that Illinois Methodists were in conference at Alton, on the river's eastern bank. Landing, he marched in his buckskin clothes up the street and into the church, his peak-headed Chinooks trailing behind.

It was the beginning of an indefatigable series of dramatic personal appearances. Without consulting his Board, Lee spent the early part of the fall stumping Illinois to raise money for his proposed but still un-authorized expansion. In Peoria the Chinook boy named Thomas Adams fell ill and was left behind under the care of sympathetic townspeople. Thomas was no mean proselyter himself. Convalescent and homesick, he took to hanging around a local wagon shop, where he spun exotic yarns in broken English about the farms and furs and the great salmon of the Willamette. Fired by the tales, eighteen young men led by Thomas Jefferson Farnham headed west the following spring, determined to wrest the land from the Hudson's Bay Company. Dissension soon shredded the group. Only a few of them reached Oregon. Though some stayed, to become influential in the new ter-ritory's affairs, Farnham himself soon returned home. There he wrote a book about his travels, adding one more bit of easily available infor-mation to the slowly growing store of public knowledge about the Northwest.

Lee meanwhile was adding potent bits of his own. In November 1838 he appeared before the Board of Managers of the Missionary Society of the Methodist Church, overbore the objections of the more conservative members, and won an unprecedented grant of forty thousand dollars. To help raise the sum he launched a six-month lecture tour, during which he addressed, counting his Illinois appear-ances, no less than eighty-eight audiences. At one of them, in Philadel-phia, he shared the platform with his old friend William Slacum, for-mer agent of the United States Government.

Still more currency was given his views by his contacts with the Congress of the United States. In January 1839, Senator Linn of Missouri introduced to the Upper House the petition which Lee had brought from the Willamette settlers. Caleb Cushing of Massachusetts asked the House of Representatives to listen to "Professor Lee" speak on Oregon; and although the request was denied, Lee gained approximately the same ends by writing Cushing a vigorous letter in which he declared, as had the petition, ". . . rely upon it, *there* is the germ of a great State." This letter, together with voluminous matter gathered from Slacum, Wyeth, Kelley, and others, Cushing presented to the House early in 1839. Impressed, the representatives ordered ten thousand copies of the report printed for distribution throughout the country. [1]

One of Lee's missionary appearances took place on January 25, 1839, before a highly enthusiastic audience in Lynn, Massachusetts. Lynn was the home of Lee's lay assistant, Cyrus Shepard, and of Shepard's wife—the couple with whom the Lees had shared their bridal tour and, beyond doubt, their excited honeymoon dreams of a white, Christian society burgeoning on the Willamette.

By coincidence, or perhaps because of inspiration found in letters from the Shepards, there had recently been established in Lynn an organization called the Oregon Provisional Emigration Society. The intent of this society, which published an official organ called *The Oregonian and Indian's Advocate*, was to send forth into the Western wilderness two hundred Christian families to civilize the savages, clinch title to the Northwest for the United States, and form colonies for subsequent thousands of settlers. Obviously the society had more than casual interest in Lee's visit, and its handful of members turned out to hear the missionary speak.

By still another coincidence, George Simpson of the Hudson's Bay Company chanced to pass through Boston on his way to New York shortly after Lee's tour of the region. He of course heard both of Lee's efforts and of the Oregon Provisional Emigration Society. Not unnaturally he confused the two, thinking that the missionaries whom Lee purposed to lead to Oregon were members of the society. His confusion seems never to have been resolved, even though he apparently talked to Lee himself and also received, from the secretary of the Emigration Society, a letter asking what help the colonist could

[1] Cushing took his own report seriously: in 1840 his family firm sent their brig *Maryland* to the Columbia to trade for salmon. Though the venture failed, the *Maryland's* captain, John H. Couch, prevailed on the owners to send him back in another ship, the *Chenamus*, loaded with goods for trade with the settlers. He set up shop in 1842, and so delivered the coup de grâce to the already faltering economic monopoly of the Hudson's Bay Company.

expect from the Hudson's Bay Company in return for a promise to stay out of the fur trade.

The developments could hardly have come at a more unwelcome time. Only a few months before the Hudson's Bay Company had nudged the British Foreign Office into an extraordinary diplomatic victory over the Russians in Alaska. To exploit this triumph Simpson wanted to make sure that British, not American, rights became paramount along the Columbia.

The British victory was the outgrowth of an 1834 clash between Peter Skene Ogden and the Russian-American Fur Company. According to treaty, British subjects had the right to navigate the streams of the Alaskan panhandle in order to reach what is now northwestern British Columbia. But when Ogden had endeavored to assert this privilege by sailing up the Stikine River to build a post in the interior, he had been stopped by a Russian fort at the river mouth, by Russian gunboats in the harbor. Ogden had referred the matter to the company, which in turn had passed it on to the Foreign Office.

Out of the diplomatic jockeying emerged an agreement whereby the Russian-American Fur Company leased the mainland portion of the Alaskan panhandle to the Hudson's Bay Company for an annual rent of two thousand land-otter skins. The Russians further agreed to purchase through the Bay Company specified amounts of trade goods and agricultural products deliverable in Sitka—wheat, flour, dried peas, barley, pork, salt beef, butter. The latter was no one-sided bargain, for it enabled the Russians to abandon their own expensive and illegal agricultural establishment on Mexican territory, Fort Ross in California.

Simpson had signed the accord in Germany on February 6, 1839, and then had hurried to London to consult with his directors and with McLoughlin about implementing it. The upshot, built on McLoughlin's earlier suggestions for increased farming, was the Puget Sound Agricultural Company.

Theoretically separate from the Hudson's Bay Company, the Puget Sound Agricultural Company was actually controlled by the same board of directors. It was to start business by absorbing all of the farming enterprises (except those adjacent to Fort Vancouver) which formerly had been conducted by the fur company—the Cowlitz farms, to which Catholic priests had recently been dispatched in an effort to encourage settlement; and Fort Nisqually on the sound, where McLoughlin's sheep had been landed the summer before. McLoughlin himself, while still retaining his title of chief factor of the Columbia

District, had been appointed manager of the new concern at an additional generous salary.

The establishment of the extensive farms envisioned, of course, land titles based on English sovereignty—which in turn would be based on settlement by English farmers. Thus Simpson was considerably dismayed to hear that American colonists were also on the move—two hundred of them, he mistakenly thought on the basis of the letter from the Emigration Society.

Presumably the American emigrants would gravitate toward the Willamette, south of the Columbia. But one could never be sure, particularly since the United States Government showed no evidence of relaxing its insistence on having the forty-ninth parallel as the country's northern boundary. In short, the Puget Sound Agricultural Company's colonizing program must not be suffered to lag.

Lagging was exactly what it was doing, however. In England, where Simpson had hoped prospective settlers could be found, the Pacific Northwest was regarded (if the average worker considered it at all) as a howling wilderness to which no proper person would dream of moving. No adequate sources of information existed to dispel the impression. In America matters were different. Congressional documents like Cushing's report, books like Farnham's and Samuel Parker's, and papers like *The Oregonian and Indian's Advocate* were already, or soon would be, chipping away at the nation's ignorance about its Western coast. Moreover, when a would-be colonist did chance to appear at the Bay Company's London offices, he was chilled by the terms offered him: a tenant could only lease, not own, his farm in the Northwest and had to agree to assign at least half of each year's products to the company, no matter what other markets might appear. The predictable result was that London signed up, during the spring and summer of 1839, exactly no settlers whatsoever.

This news Simpson learned just about the time Jason Lee sailed from New York aboard the chartered ship *Lausanne*, Captain Josiah Spaulding commanding, in October 1839. With Lee were his new wife, his one surviving Chinook, Thomas Adams, and fifty other men and women. They had been recruited entirely through the Missionary Society of the Methodist Church. The Oregon Provisional Emigration Society had not contributed a single colonist—and never would, for the organization shortly thereafter went out of existence. Nor did Lee have any idea, during the uneventful trip to Oregon or while founding his new missions in the summer and fall of 1840 (including one near

Nisqually), that he might be racing the Hudson's Bay Company or anyone else.

Such a thought, nevertheless, was in Simpson's mind. On November 15, 1839, a month after Lee's sailing, he switched recruiting efforts from London to Red River, ordering an agent there to encourage "steady respectable halfbreeds and other settlers" with small families to migrate overland to Oregon. He wanted the transplanting to take place during the summer of 1840. But the same niggardly terms that had repelled prospective settlers in England also repelled them in Canada. Not until Simpson's agent promised that the company would sell the settlers their land as soon as sovereignty was established did a scant twenty-three families agree to move west in 1841.

By this time Simpson, too, was on his way across the continent. He traveled with more splendor than ever. The winter before he had been knighted in London for his help in putting down the Canadian rebellion of 1837 and for his promotion of arctic explorations. Fittingly accoutered, he swept out of London in March 1841 for a two-year circuit of the world, via Canada and Siberia. Along the way he intended to inspect everything the Hudson's Bay and Puget Sound Agricultural companies had wrought on the two-thousand-mile stretch of coast between California and Alaska, between the Rockies and the sea. From those works England would send down her roots into the Northwest, and George Simpson, for the sake of his companies, meant to be the gardener.

8. The New Order

JASON LEE, who had left his Willamette station four days behind McLoughlin, returned to the Columbia a full half year after the factor. Once the *Lausanne* had put across the river's stormy bar, however, the impatient Methodist set vigorously about making up for lost time. In an Indian canoe he pushed ahead of the slow-tacking ship to arrange for food and shelter at Vancouver, swept up the Willamette to announce his arrival, hurried back to the fort, and there gathered together his fifty wide-eyed newcomers while he disposed of their futures.

Mechanics were sent to Chemeketa (modern Salem), there to build a grist mill and a sawmill—and there the main mission station would shortly be moved. A farmer and his family reinforced Daniel Lee's branch station at the Dalles. Other recruits were delegated to open stations at the mouth of the Columbia, at Puget Sound, and at Willamette Falls. Those who went to Puget Sound survived mainly by drawing on the Hudson's Bay store at Fort Nisqually; and at Willamette Falls the Reverend A. F. Waller built his mission house out of lumber McLoughlin had prepared for establishing his own claim to the site (or his company's claim; the matter is not clear).

The rest of the recruits went with Lee to the original station. There one change had occurred. The autumn before, frail, devoted Cyrus Shepard had fallen ill with a "scrofulous" infection of the leg. Scarfaced William Bailey and Dr. Elijah White had amputated the member, but on New Year's Day, 1840, Shepard had died. For all practical purposes the mission's Indian school died with him; no successor was able to approach his results.

The amputation also marked Elijah White's last major work at the mission. He and Lee fell into a squabble, and White sailed away on the *Lausanne* for the Sandwich Islands. (Soon he would return, to cause more uproar.) For the Hudson's Bay Company it was an unfortunate departure. First White and, later, Captain Josiah Spaulding of the *Lausanne* would visit Congress with scurrilous tales about the British monopoly—tales hard to reconcile with the hospitality both men had seen accorded to the new American arrivals, yet tales that were nonetheless pregnant with future mischief.

John McLoughlin, meanwhile, was busy with his own affairs. Almost immediately on his return from England he had taken a flying trip to Cowlitz, Nisqually, and Fort Langley on the Fraser River, to acquaint the local managers with the revolution being effected by the Puget Sound Agricultural Company's supply contracts with Russians.

The next step involved ironing out details with the Russian commander at Sitka, alerting the Hudson's Bay coastal forts about the rental of the Alaskan panhandle, and establishing additional stations to exploit the newly available trade routes to the interior. These prime assignments fell to James Douglas, another of the Northwest's towering figures.

Tall, slim, and regally erect, James Douglas was so swarthy that men occasionally called him after a famous Scottish namesake, the Black Douglas. Most of his apprenticeship had been served in the remote stations of New Caledonia. There he had endured, not always in true epic style, the usual Indian turmoils and the bone-cracking journeys. There, too, he had married Amelia Connelley, the handsome half-breed daughter of his immediate superior. In 1830, aged twenty-seven, he had been shifted to Fort Vancouver as a clerk. Austere, intelligent, conservative, he soon won McLoughlin's confidence and rose fast. During the factor's absence in England it was Douglas who was put in charge of the Columbia. And now, in the spring of 1840, it was Douglas who was entrusted with implementing the Alaskan contracts.

In Sitka he held his own with the hard-drinking Russians, danced correctly at a lavish ball with the beautiful blonde Finnish wife of Governor Etholin, and, clear-eyed the next morning, outdickered the opposition in its home bailiwick.

These details completed, he next sailed to the mouth of the Stikine River, where Peter Skene Ogden had been turned back six years before. The crude Russian fort which he took over needed strong leadership to keep it in hand: those fog-shrouded barrens were depressing, the neighborhood Indians unpredictable, the laborers sullen about their assignment. Instead of strength, however, Douglas could leave at Stikine, thanks to McLoughlin's nepotism, only weakness—William Glen Rae, McLoughlin's unstable son-in-law, and young John McLoughlin, Jr., the factor's even more unstable son.

John, Jr., had been raised by relatives in the East. Nearing maturity, he had been sent to Paris for a medical education under McLoughlin's surgeon brother. The arrangement failing, the youth had been shipped back to Montreal, where he ran up extravagant debts. At loose ends in 1836, he signed up with several other wastrel half-breeds in the filibustering expedition of one John Dickson, who proposed to drive the Mexicans out of the Southwest and set up an Indian nation in California. The harebrained plan soon collapsed, but not before young John had alarmed Canadian authorities by trying to enlist additional recruits among the *métis*, or half-breeds, in the Red River colony. To oblige the authorities and get the boy out of harm's way, George Simpson had hired him at an outrageously high salary and had sent him across the mountains to the Columbia. For the next three years the young man had functioned with reasonable diligence under his father's watchful eye. Now he was to be rewarded by being made his brother-in-law's chief assistant at Fort Stikine.

If Douglas had forebodings, he kept them to himself as he sailed northward another hundred miles to the neighborhood of the Taku River. There, near the site of present Juneau, he built still another fort, then sailed homeward, reaching Fort Vancouver in October. In his report on his trip he recommended that the company establish still more forts along the coast. To McLoughlin this was good news, for it furnished him with additional ammunition in his running argument with George Simpson about the best way to conduct the coastal trade—by fort or by ship. Passing on Douglas' suggestion to the governor would be a pleasure indeed.

Douglas, too, found good news at Fort Vancouver. During his absence he had been elevated to the rank of chief factor, an office equal in every respect except seniority to McLoughlin's. And the Black Scot had achieved it at the relatively young age of thirty-seven.

His travels were not yet done. A year earlier in London, McLoughlin had proposed to the directors a trading post in San Francisco Bay. Such a station, he had argued, would facilitate the supplying of Laframboise's California trapping brigades, would be useful in developing markets for Oregon lumber, wheat, and salmon, and would help keep the Puget Sound Agricultural Company supplied with California sheep and cattle. Though George Simpson objected vehemently to establishing a purely mercantile post on foreign soil, the London directors agreed with McLoughlin. He was given free rein to investigate further and then, if he felt justified, to go ahead with building the California fort.

Once again James Douglas was delegated to do the spadework. Once again he succeeded brilliantly. He purchased cattle and sheep, and landed crews in San Francisco Bay for driving the animals back to Oregon. He gained trading privileges for Hudson's Bay ships under the proviso that their captains go through the formality of taking out Mexican citizenship papers. He persuaded the governor of California to modify John Sutter's order that British trappers keep out of the Sacramento Valley; and he secured in what is today the heart of the San Francisco business district a sandy piece of real estate on which to erect the company's new post. [1]

In February 1841 he returned to Vancouver with word of what he had done. Delighted, McLoughlin summoned his son-in-law, William

[1] This California excursion by the Hudson's Bay Company came at a time when certain American expansionists were excited over strictly unofficial British proposals that Great Britain accept California in lieu of Mexico's unpaid debt. Such gossip, together with private talk among visionary Englishmen of utopian British colonies in California, may have been in Douglas' mind when he wrote concerning his trip: "We have also other objects of a political nature in view." From such evidence, none of it official, some California historians have concluded that the Hudson's Bay Company was an agent in a plot to grab the province. Actually no Hudson's Bay document mentions the possibility. Furthermore, official British foreign policy at the time was adamantly opposed to annexation of California, partly for fear it would bring on war with the United States. (See W. Kaye Lamb, introduction to *McLoughlin's Fort Vancouver Letters, Third Series*, p. xxix; also Ray Billington, *The Far Western Frontier*, pp. 147-48.)

Glen Rae, down from Fort Stikine to take charge of the operations in California. The move was injudicious. Rae, as time would show, was not the sort of man to be turned loose among the petty intrigues of California politics. And John McLoughlin, Jr., not yet thirty, was definitely not the sort to leave in charge of explosive Fort Stikine.

Two months after Douglas' return, and well before tragedy could develop at either Stikine or San Francisco, the United States made its first openly official appearance in the Northwest since the inauguration of the treaty of joint occupation. The occasion was a visit by a naval expedition under Charles Wilkes—the self-sufficient martinet who twenty years later, during the Civil War, would precipitate the *Trent* crisis with Great Britain by whisking two Confederate commissioners off an English mail steamer. Ostensibly Lieutenant Wilkes's mission in 1841 was non-political. After exploring the Antarctic coasts and the South Seas for the benefit of the American whaling industry, he was to drop in on the Northwest for a purely scientific bit of map making. Meanwhile, however, he was also quietly to size up, for future congressional consideration, the value of the disputed area between the Columbia River and the forty-ninth parallel.

Two of the expedition's ships were still in the South Seas when Wilkes with the remaining three approached, in April 1841, the crashing bar of the Columbia. Even though he had an experienced pilot with him (Josiah Spaulding, who a year before had brought in Lee's missionaries aboard the *Lausanne*), Wilkes declined to risk, in his own words, "the terror of the bar . . . one of the most frightful sights that can possibly meet the eye of the sailor." Instead, he sought easier anchorage in Puget Sound. These island-studded roadsteads, overlooked by the stupendous bulk of Mount Rainier, were more to his liking. In his official report he wrote, "There is no country in the world that possesses waters equal to these"—a remark which had no little effect in hardening the State Department's determination not to yield its demand for a boundary at least as far north as the forty-ninth parallel.

From Nisqually, where he enjoyed the full hospitality of the Hudson's Bay Company, Wilkes dispatched exploring parties to examine the interior. He himself went via the Cowlitz to Astoria, where he was supposed to rendezvous with his two South Sea ships. They were not in evidence. Leaving a watcher at the river mouth, he worked his way back up against the current to Fort Vancouver. There, as befitted his position, he was sumptuously entertained by McLoughlin, who was under no illusions whatsoever as to the real nature of the visit.

Like Slacum before him, Wilkes found occasion, as a representative of the United States Government, to intercede in the affairs of the American colonists. The first opportunity came in helping a group of young men launch a tiny, homemade, forty-eight-foot schooner. The motives of these would-be navigators, only one of whom had ever been on the ocean, were not clear. At first they told Wilkes that they were tired of Oregon; there were no white women there to marry and they wanted to go to California. Earlier, however, they had told McLoughlin, when buying supplies from the Vancouver store, that they were building a ferryboat to ply the Willamette. On still other occasions they had talked of going to California for cattle that would further weaken the economic dominance of the Hudson's Bay Company; and it may have been fear of McLoughlin's disapproval that had led them, shortly before Wilkes's arrival, to ask certain French Canadians to front for them at the store in buying the cordage and canvas they needed.

The devious approach was a mistake. Discovering it, McLoughlin decided that the group could not possibly be up to anything good and sent them word that henceforth they could not get so much as a piece of string from him. The interdict brought one of the shipbuilders storming into the fort. Angrily he shouted that his rich uncle would soon appear on the Columbia and take over the whole Hudson's Bay Company. Pressed for the name of this amazing relative, the American is supposed to have thundered, "Uncle Sam, that's who!"—an incident which, when McLoughlin cooled down enough to reflect on it, is said to have amused him considerably.

At this point Wilkes arrived. From his own supplies he furnished the adventurers with a flag, compass, anchor and anchor chain, spyglass, and even ship's papers authorizing the *Star of Oregon* to sail along the coast "to the ports of California for the purpose [still another one!] of hunting Sea Otter." To McLoughlin, the whole business was folly, for he was convinced that the neophyte sailors would surely drown in their contrived craft. With Wilkes's example before him, however, he relented and opened his store to the men.

Leader of the group and only seaman of the lot was Joseph Gale, a onetime sailor who had quit the sea to trap with Ewing Young in California in 1831. With Young and Kelley, Gale had migrated to Oregon, then had gone to work for Wyeth at Fort Hall. When the fur trade slumped he had joined other disgruntled mountain men in taking up a farm at the edge of the Tualatin hills, near Young's homestead. Perhaps the life was too quiet for him. In any event he let the shipbuilders persuade him to sell his claim, leave his family with friendly neighbors, and lead the expedition to California.

Amazingly, Gale succeeded. During most of the trip his crew of four landlubbers and one Indian boy were too sick to do more than groan, yet at each emergency he somehow pummeled enough of them onto their feet to scrape through. Arrived at San Francisco, the mariners swapped the *Star of Oregon* for 350 cows—which may have been their intent all along. To increase the size of the herd they worked all winter in California, invested their pay in more livestock, and in the spring persuaded an indeterminate number of men, women, and even children to accompany them back to Oregon. With them the party drove 600 horses and mules, 1250 cattle, 3000 sheep—a potent addition to the independent population and wealth of the Northwest.

Wilkes's other intervention in the affairs of the American colonists was less positive. The lieutenant did not like the Willamette. After the ordered might of Fort Vancouver, the valley settlements seemed slipshod and wasteful. The members of the Methodist mission, he sniffed, were more interested in developing commercial pursuits than in saving the Indians—some of them, for example, had begun their long quarrel with McLoughlin over possession of the waterpower sites at the Willamette Falls—and his general opinion of them was in no wise improved when Jason Lee, instead of dropping everything to entertain him as McLoughlin had done, hurried on down to Clatsop on mission business.

While Wilkes was in this negative frame of mind, a committee of five waited on him to ask his opinion about forming a provisional government until the United States extended its jurisdiction to them. It was a radical step. For some years the Willamette settlers had lived in an unruffled state of Arcadian anarchy. During the previous February, however, a situation had arisen that baffled them. Ewing Young had performed his last signal service to Oregon by dying insane—and intestate. Because Young had been the region's most prosperous and influential citizen the entire community had turned out for his funeral. So far as anyone knew he had no heirs; and after the services his neighbors began wondering what disposition should be made of his choice farm, mill, and the extensive herd of cattle that had grown up out of the animals brought from California in 1837.

One upshot was the appointment of Dr. Ira Babcock of the Methodist mission as a judge with probate powers, assisted by a clerk of court and public recorder, a sheriff, and three constables. The primary duties of these officials was to liquidate Young's estate, and they set about it with a vim that leads to an almost unavoidable digression. Three public auctions, stimulated by the stentorian voice of mountain man Joe Meek, netted almost four thousand dollars. Later, after a provisional government had been established, the early officials paid themselves out of this fund and used the surplus for financing Oregon's first public building—a jail. Then, in 1854, a young man suddenly appeared from Taos, New Mexico, claiming to be Ewing Young's son. He bore affidavits from such New Mexican notables as Charles Beaubien and Kit Carson, who attested that Ewing had lived in Taos as the common-law husband of one Maria Josefa Tafoya and that the claimant, José Joaquin Young, was their son. Ewing's former compadre, Joseph Gale of the *Star of Oregon*, supported the contention, and finally there were copies of the Taos parish records, which stated that the four-day-old natural son of Maria Josefa Tafoya had been baptized in that town on April 12, 1833. Overwhelmed by the evidence, the Oregon courts awarded the boy the proceeds of the estate, plus accrued interest. All very curious—especially since every available record of Young's movements indicates that he left New Mexico permanently in September 1831, nearly nineteen months before his "son's" birth. The matter has never been clarified.

In 1841 no formal government existed in Oregon to give sanction to Judge Ira Babcock and his cohorts. This bothered the legal minds in the colony. Accordingly a committee was appointed to fill the vacuum by framing a constitution and drafting laws. In order to enlist the support of the numerically superior French Canadians, their priest, Father Blanchet, who recently had moved over from the Catholic mission on the Cowlitz, was named committee chairman.

McLoughlin disapproved. Exasperated by his water-rights quarrel with the Methodists, who dominated the committee's membership, and fearing that the proposed government would furnish malcontents with a sounding board for impugning the Hudson's Bay Company, the factor quietly let the priest know he wanted matters dropped. Blanchet acceded by calling no meetings of his committee, and as a result nothing happened.

At this juncture Wilkes arrived in the valley. A committee of settlers promptly appealed to him for advice. They might have spared themselves the trouble. It was Wilkes's private opinion that the agitators wanted a government mainly so that an appearance of stability would attract immigrants and raise property values. He therefore took as his text one old trapper's pragmatic statement that if everyone behaved himself there would be no need for laws. Was not the mission providing an adequate moral code? Would not the district's French-Canadian majority and, through them, the Hudson's Bay Company soon take control of whatever legislative body was set up? Would it not, in short, be safer and wiser to let sleeping dogs lie until the United States extended its jurisdiction over the Northwest—a recommendation he was going to urge on Congress in his report?

Completely flummoxed by his glibness, the committee withdrew. Their ardor was so dampened that nearly two years passed before another move for self-government gathered headway.

Wilkes went back to Nisqually, worried now about the non-appearance of the two ships from the South Seas that were supposed to have met him at Astoria. When word at last did arrive from the belated vessels, it was bad. One of the ships, the *Peacock*, had run aground on the Columbia's bar. Though Chinook Indians rescued the crew, the vessel herself was a total loss.

If Wilkes needed further evidence to convince him that the Columbia would not serve as the United States' main outlet to the Pacific, this disaster was it. When the time came for him to pen his report, he would go whole hog and urge that his government, as a matter of economic necessity, claim the entire coast between California and the Russian boundary at 54° 40′.

Meanwhile he had to make some sort of arrangement about the *Peacock's* men. Boarding another of his ships, the *Porpoise*, he risked his own skin to the bar and hurried to Vancouver, to see what he could do.

For a time he contemplated discharging the shipless sailors in Oregon. The thought of so many uncontrollable men loose in the district thoroughly alarmed McLoughlin, and he cast about for some way to get rid of them. Luck was with him. An old coaster named Thomas Varney had brazenly brought into the Columbia the previous May a brig loaded with trade goods. To get rid of his competition McLoughlin had bought Varney's cargo for forty-five hundred dollars, payable in salmon. At this point Wilkes offered twelve thousand dollars for Varney's brig, to replace the wrecked *Peacock*. Varney said he would sell if he could get rid of his cargo of salmon. Immediately McLoughlin took the fish back, though it meant clogging his own vessels, which he had planned to load with lumber for the Sandwich Islands. He also collected a five-hundred-dollar forfeit from Varney, resold Varney's trade goods to Wilkes, and best of all, he provided an exit for the unwanted sailors.

A good bargain, he thought. But he reckoned without George Simpson, who at about this time came sweeping splendidly up to the Vancouver docks on his trip around the world. Simpson was not pleased about the Varney deal—or, for that matter, about anything else McLoughlin did.

9. *Conflict and Tragedy*

SIR GEORGE'S 1841 crossing of the continent was as headlong as his earlier journeys had been. This time, however, he devoured the miles mostly on horseback rather than in a canoe. Far east of the Rockies he overhauled the creaking cavalcade of his Red River emigrants, bound for the Cowlitz and Nisqually farms of the Puget Sound Agricultural Company, and for a day condescendingly plodded beside their dusty cattle and canvas-covered, two-wheeled carts. The Rockies he crossed at a hitherto untrod pass, then led his small party along David Thompson's old Kootenay and Pend Oreille trails to Fort Colvile on the Columbia. There the entourage transferred at last to boats. At dusk a few days later the most powerful man in Canada stepped ashore at the Vancouver docks.

He paused scarcely long enough to wash away the dirt and weariness of the trail—though he did take time to entertain Lieutenant Wilkes at a stiffly formal dinner. Pumping the American explorer's injudicious subordinates for information, he learned of Wilkes's intention to recommend that the United States press its claims north to 54° 40'. The area, of course, embraced the very region where Simpson's companies were busily engaged in putting down their newest roots. With Wilkes's no longer secret purpose now coloring his observations, the governor hurried northward to see how those roots were taking hold—the farms, the coastal trade, the Russian transactions. When he returned to Vancouver a few weeks later, on October 22, he had, in his own mind, determined the future of the entire Pacific Northwest.

Some of his opinions he put into a memorandum that he knew would reach the British Foreign Office. Let the Americans have the land south of the Columbia. That area, "so much spoken of in the United States as the Eldorado of the shores of the Northern Pacific, must from the dangers of the Bar and impediments of the navigation, together with its unhealthfulness, sink in public estimation." Not so the lands he had just visited in what is now western Washington— lands the Puget Sound Agricultural Company hoped to exploit. Harbor-studded and rich with natural resources, "the intermittent fever being unknown . . . there is no doubt that that country will, in due time, become important as regards settlement and commerce." The directors, he went on, should "urge H.M. government not to consent to any boundary which would give to the United States any portion of the Territory north of the Columbia River."

One potentially powerful instrument for clinching H.M. government's claims lay at Simpson's fingertips. This was the Red River colony. One hundred and seventeen souls in all, old women and small children included, they had reached Fort Vancouver while Simpson was in the North. Chief Factor James Douglas had already taken out a vanguard of them to look over a possible site for their new homes. It was a majestic spot, the snow cones of Mount St. Helens and Rainier rising grandly above the tree-girt parks. But the colonists had not come for scenery, although scenery seemed about all they were going to get out of the company. They grumbled unhappily, and the grumbles reached Simpson. Strangely he did nothing to allay the dissatisfaction. As a result, within a year the immigrants deserted the farms on which they were placed and, alleging that the land south of the Columbia was superior, moved to the Willamette.

Not soil but possessory rights were the Willamette's real attractions. Here, south of the Columbia, a man might someday be able to point at his farm and say, "This is mine." It was a prospect no English citizen could be sure of realizing within the vast perimeter of the company's monopoly.

The difference was profound. As the Red River immigration proved, English colonists could have reached the Northwest despite the difficulty of the Canadian mountains. Indeed, another year would pass before a comparable group of would-be homemakers arrived from the United States. But American colonists kept coming; Britishers did not, mainly because the directors of the Hudson's Bay Company never realized how fiercely the hunger for land can gnaw at a poor man's vitals. Annoyed by the attitude of the first Red River colonists, the company abandoned plans to promote an annual movement from outside and instead recruited their farm laborers among the maturing children and retiring servants of Fort Vancouver. These proved numerous enough to grow crops. But they were not numerous enough to nurture empire.

Simpson's views on protecting the empire already in existence were equally expedient. He carped at McLoughlin for buying Varney's cargo of trade goods with salmon and then taking the fish back so that Wilkes could buy Varney's ship. That sort of improvident dealing, the governor snapped, would encourage other American adventurers to bring goods into the Columbia in hope of making the factor pay to get rid of the competition. Indeed, McLoughlin was too soft with everyone. For example, a Frenchman named De Morfas had arrived at Fort Vancouver during Simpson's absence and was being royally entertained even though he was obviously a French spy. De Morfas could hardly have gleaned vital information at the fort, but that wasn't the point. Policy in such situations dictated aloofness rather than friendliness, and Simpson drove the point home by treating De Morfas with a calculated incivility that not only offended the Frenchman but embarrassed McLoughlin, to whom hospitality was a basic tenet of the wilderness code.

These quarrels were trivial compared to their explosive differences over basic policy. For years Simpson had argued that the coastal trade should be served by ship; McLoughlin that it should be handled by forts. At first the signing of the Russian contracts had seemed to favor McLoughlin's thinking, especially when James Douglas recommended posts instead of vessels. Abruptly, however, Simpson swept the plans aside. During his trip to Sitka the governor had become convinced that the country between the Alaskan panhandle and the Rockies was not as extensive as supposed. Ships calling at the annual salmon-catching fairs of the natives would be adequate, in his opinion, to handle the trade. Peremptorily, therefore, he ordered McLoughlin to cancel preparations for additional posts and to start abandoning the ones already established.

Nor was that all. The governor had long felt that Fort Vancouver's position on the Columbia was too exposed for safety, and on his way north he had taken time to investigate a substitute site on the southern tip of Vancouver Island. First discovered by the captain of a company ship and later commended by James Douglas, the place offered a fine harbor, open fields, and readily available timber. "It will," Simpson wrote the committee, "doubtless become, in time, the most valuable section of the whole coast above California." To speed that time he forthwith directed McLoughlin to locate a new post on the site —not a mere coastal trading stockade but a fort designed to supersede the great bastion of Fort Vancouver. (Belatedly begun in the summer of 1843 and named Fort Victoria, the new establishment was the precursor of modern Victoria, capital of British Columbia.)

To McLoughlin these directives were a repudiation of nearly twenty years' struggle to make Fort Vancouver the paramount power of the Northwest and to extend the sway of the company so powerfully northward that American vessels scarcely dared risk competing anywhere in the area. Moreover, Simpson had not even bothered to consult McLoughlin about the changes—although McLoughlin would be responsible for their success or failure. It was a bitter insult. Not for thirteen years had Simpson set foot in the Northwest. Yet on the strength of one characteristically headlong trip he presumed to wave aside the painfully garnered experience of the fort's veterans and substitute his own impulsive plans instead.

Still, Simpson was boss. Imperious and stubborn though McLoughlin could be in his own turn, he seems to have swallowed his wrath for the time being. He and his daughter sailed on the same ship with Simpson to San Francisco Bay, there to inspect the company's newest post, in charge of William Glen Rae, McLoughlin's erratic son-in-law.

Although in London Simpson had reluctantly consented to McLoughlin's plans for expanding the company's business into California, he now flew into a passion about the scheme. Mexican red tape exasperated him. California beaver prospects were disheartening. And, finally, he did not like the post's location. Yerba Buena, as the town on the bay was called, was in his words "a wretched place . . . least adapted in point of situation & climate for an Establishment." Brusquely he directed McLoughlin to wind up the California business within two years.

From Yerba Buena the badly strained party sailed to inspect the company's store and warehouses at Honolulu. There the two men boiled over, each sending off to London a blistering report in support of his own policies. Then they separated, not speaking, McLoughlin returning to the great fort on the Columbia which he thought Simpson was destroying, and Simpson sailing northward for further consultation with the Russians.

In London the directors decided to mark time. They did not wish to dispense with either man, and apparently the committee hoped that separation would result in enough cooling off that workable business relations could be re-established. Unfortunately, however, a tragedy was shaping up at Fort Stikine which would make impossible any sort of adjustment.

On his previous visit to the North Simpson had removed from Stikine its one strong man, Roderick Finlayson. The move had left young John McLoughlin, Jr., in unsupported command of twenty ill-disciplined Iroquois and French-Canadian half-breeds at an isolated station surrounded by unruly Indians. John had a poor opinion of his own chances. Gloomily he wrote to a friend, shortly after Simpson's departure, "I am still amongst the living of this troublesome post though report says that I am going to be dispatched to the *Sandy Hills*."

He spoke with accurate prescience. When Simpson, swinging north again, neared the fort on April 25, 1842, he found the flag at half mast. John McLoughlin, Jr., had just been murdered by his own men.

Simpson conducted a hasty investigation and reached exactly the conclusion that the men at the fort wanted him to reach. In a letter of April 27 to the boy's father he wrote brutally, "From all I can collect, the whole conduct & management of Mr. McLoughlin was exceedingly bad, and his violence when under the influence of liquor, which was very frequently the case, amounting to insanity. . . . The occurrence having taken place within Russian Territory, no legal steps against the parties can be taken by me; but my belief is, that any Tribunal by which the case could be tried, would find a verdict of 'justifiable Homicide.' " A subsequent letter intensified the condemnation. Young McLoughlin "had become a slave to licentiousness and dissipation. . . . His treatment of the people was exceedingly violent & Opressive . . . the business intrusted to his charge was entirely neglected. . . ."

The grief-stricken father, who knew that his son's accounts were in order, refused to accept the charges. He put James Douglas on the trail of more information; and through a series of lucky chances the Black Scot won a confession from one of the participants, an Iroquois named Pierre Kanaquasse. No, young John had not been given to drink or licentiousness. But he had been weak. In open defiance of his orders his men had repeatedly brought Indian prostitutes into the barracks at night and had stolen wares from the storehouses with which to pay them. When McLoughlin had threatened them with exposure the crew had inveigled him into one of his rare bouts with the bottle and had provoked a drunken brawl as a cover for killing him.

The son triumphantly vindicated, McLoughlin now threw his full energies into two related purposes: punishing the perpetrators and crushing Simpson, whom he blamed for the murder on the grounds that if Finlayson had been left at Stikine the tragedy would not have occurred.

Justice proved expensive and elusive. Men like James Douglas and Chief Trader Donald Munson wasted company time on McLoughlin's private investigations. Not only the suspects but the key witnesses had to be jailed and fed. When the Russians refused to accept jurisdiction of the case and it looked as if the murderers might go free, McLoughlin at his own expense sent the two chief suspects and eleven witnesses across the mountains to drawn-out hearings in Lower Carada. Those courts, too, decided they had no jurisdiction, censured some of McLoughlin's extralegal actions in the affair, and decreed that a trial, if any, could take place only in England—the expenses to be borne by the bereft father. His finances already strained to the breaking point, McLoughlin at last gave up.

He fared no better with Simpson. The company was averse to washing its dirty linen in public, and, furthermore, their pudgy Canadian governor was all but indispensable. The directors accordingly kept trying to tone McLoughlin down, then lost patience as the factor grew more and more intemperate. Page after page of his reports, which should have been confined to company business, were filled with virulent charges against Simpson and with plaintive rehashings of the most minute aspects of the affair. These reports of course passed through Simpson's hands, and it did McLoughlin's case no good when the governor discovered amidst the verbiage what seemed to him some questionable, or at least careless, bookkeeping. Viciously Simpson pounced, and now there were protracted arguments over accounting methods to tax the patience of the committee in London.

And finally there was McLoughlin's fatal disobedience about the post at Yerba Buena. He had not closed it as ordered and the neglect resulted in the death of his own son-in-law, William Glen Rae.

Remote from Vancouver, often lacking the detailed instructions his vacillating nature craved, Rae had taken to drink. He had let his accounts become involved. He had squandered company money, so legend says, on a Spanish beauty and then had injudiciously supported, with lances and ammunition, a rebel faction that failed in its attempted coup. Fearing that the government would retaliate by executing him and expropriating his warehouses, Rae on January 19, 1845, committed suicide.

Word of the tragedy reached London at a time when the company was wondering whether even Fort Vancouver could be long maintained. During the three years between Simpson's visit to the coast and Rae's death, an incredible horde of Americans had struggled across mountains and deserts and down the wild gorge of the Columbia into the Willamette. McLoughlin had opened wide the company storehouses to them, extending thousands of pounds' credit on almost negligible security. One did not like to question his loyalty, but still . . .

It might have been kinder to fire him outright. Instead, the company came up with an expedient—a triumvirate in which he was henceforth to share authority with two former subordinates, James Douglas and Peter Skene Ogden. Perhaps the directors hoped he would be stung into resigning. In any event the scheme seemed to guarantee that there would be cool heads nearby to help him make decisions.

Certainly cool heads were needed. After a slow and erratic start the Americans were on the march, and how far or with what violence the swelling tide would carry, no man could yet be sure.

10. Way Station

DURING the first years of the American immigration the key point on the long trail was a station whose founding McLoughlin himself had furthered with supplies during the fall of 1836. This was Marcus Whitman's mission at Waiilatpu on the Walla Walla River, a score or so miles above the Columbia.

The years had not been easy. Brutal labor had stooped Marcus' square back. Loneliness had corroded the sparkle with which Narcissa had once so unsettled the mountain men at the rendezvous. Grief had paid its visits. One June afternoon in 1839 the couple's only child had fallen into the river and drowned.

Often when the pair most needed companionship they had found themselves wrangling bitterly with their brother missionaries, Spalding and Gray at Lapwai; Asa Smith at Kamiah; Walker and Eells at Tshimakain. There were hot words about the location of the community sawmill, about the amount of education an Indian needed before he could be received into church membership; about the advisability of shifting Whitman, the group's only doctor, to a more central location—trivial quarrels, it seems, but the bitterness they caused was far-reaching. Unable to vent sufficient spleen among themselves, all but Spalding fired captious letters about his fellows to the American Board for Foreign Missions in the East. Ironically, it was Spalding at whom most of the ill-natured remarks were leveled, principally by

Gray and Smith, but on occasion by Whitman as well, for the doctor could be overbearing when the temper was upon him.

The faultfinding, added to worries the Board already had about the expenses of the Oregon mission and its meager results, soon led those gentlemen to question the value of the experiment. Before long the doubts would become momentous.

In spite of all these shadows, however, there had been progress at Waiilatpu. Aided by a succession of outlandish helpers—a Negro trapper, several Kanakas, Indians, and stranded adventurers—Whitman had broken out fields for grain and potatoes, had fenced pastures, had erected a mill and shop and buttery. His original cabin, called the mansion house, was eventually supplemented by a T-shaped building that was a combination Indian school, hospital, church, and free hotel. He had acquired cattle, horses, pigs. A handful of sheep imported from the Sandwich Islands had multiplied until they numbered more than eighty head. A few Cayuse Indians (though not as many as the Nez Percés Spalding had gathered at Lapwai) were settling along the thin green line of the stream and were scratching out gardens with crude hoes or even with nails in the ends of crooked sticks. In the schoolhouse a handful of savage children were learning to read and pray in English; and during evenings and on Sundays occasional adults would gather with them to follow Narcissa's sweet, full voice in favorite hymns.

It was a tiny oasis, overwhelmed by the immensity of the brown wilderness surrounding it. Yet its effect on travelers riding down the lonesome hills was enormous. Here at last a man could foresee the end of his road. Here at last his weary wife, resting again in a civilized kitchen, could believe that life in Oregon might be possible, after all.

The tide grew slowly—occasional adventurers or random groups of ill-supported missionaries, sent out by earnest congregations. Occasionally a man would come along with no attachments whatsoever, except the Word that burned in his bosom. Both Spalding at Lapwai and Whitman at Waiilatpu gave work and shelter to several of these destitute wayfarers, including one crazed fanatic who grew embarrassing when visions told him he owned Waiilatpu and who later, in the Willamette Valley, in an ecstasy of self-immolation, fatally cast himself into his own forge.

And then, almost imperceptibly, the first avowed immigrants began to trickle by. The original group, its numbers and even its destination obscure today, was a handful of men, women, and children led by Joel Walker. Joel was the brother of one of the greatest of the mountain men, Joseph Reddeford Walker, and perhaps Joseph's tales of green lands beyond the mountains had excited Joel to move his household west during the summer of 1840. With prodigious effort he and his companions pushed one, perhaps two, wagons as far as Fort Hall. There, having been told wheels could go no farther, they switched their goods to pack horses, swung northward into Oregon, wintered there, and the next fall went on down to California with Lieutenant Emmons of the Wilkes expedition. At the end of the great loop Joel's wife discovered that she was the first American woman to reach California by land.

It seems uncertain whether any of the Walker party stayed behind in the Northwest. If so, they were the first white families to cross the continent for the sole purpose of a farm in Oregon. Almost immediately, however, others took their trail. Walker was only a few days out of Fort Hall when in came mountain man Robert "Doc" Newell, shepherding three families of missionaries. They, too, were advised to shift their goods to pack horses; and in order to pay Newell for his services the missionaries gave him their discarded wagons and harness.

Times were hard in the Rockies that year. Beaver pelts were almost worthless. The great fur companies had pulled back onto the prairies, where buffalo robes became their main source of business, and the mountain rendezvous was forever ended. The trappers who still roamed the far trails were in desperate condition. A few turned to pillage. One group rode to California to steal horses from the Mexicans; another pair raided the herd at Fort Hall—an incident which in no wise lessened McLoughlin's wariness of American frontiersmen.

Doc Newell was too honest for such recourses, and too much in love with the West to drift back penniless to the stodgy towns of the Mississippi Valley. Yet he had to stay alive somehow. And now he owned some wagons. The connotation was inevitable—farming.

He talked the idea over with his two brothers-in-law, Joe Meek and Caleb Wilkins—the trio had married Nez Percé sisters—and in the end they decided to settle with their families in the Willamette. What's more, they'd take the wagons with them—the one Joel Walker had abandoned and the two that Newell had obtained from the missionaries. (Because of involved swappings back and forth at Fort Hall the exact ownership of the historic vehicles is now difficult to ascertain; one at least seems to have ended up belonging to Francis Ermatinger of the Hudson's Bay Company, who wanted it delivered to Fort Walla Walla.)

Four or five more displaced trappers joined the party, and in late September 1840 the cavalcade began its "impossible" journey. The wagons caused the same unmitigated hell that Whitman's cart had occasioned in 1836. The travelers had to make wheelway by chopping trees, rolling boulders, digging down the banks of ravines. Even more troublesome was the sagebrush. The only way through its knotted branches was to smash through. In time the effort drained the strength of the draft animals. To lighten the loads the men put more and more goods on pack horses, then at last threw away the wagon boxes entirely, so that only the running gears reached Waiilatpu.

There the party broke up. Two of the mountain men, William Craig and John Larison, drifted over near Lapwai on the Clearwater in order to be near their wives' people. There Craig caused considerable trouble for Spalding by undermining the missionary's work among the Indians; there, too, he added a small footnote to history: when the Idaho land office was opened years later, his farm became the first piece of patented land to be recorded in the territory.

Back at Waiilatpu, meanwhile, it had become apparent that Doc Newell's small half-breed son and Joe Meek's youngest daughter, emaciated, vermin-infested Helen Mar Meek, were too ill to travel farther. Both were left for Narcissa to clean up and care for during the winter. The rest of Helen Mar Meek's short life would be spent at Waiilatpu, where soon she would be joined by the half-breed daughter of another famed mountain man, Jim Bridger, and by other small strays that one way or another the trail was beginning to cast up at the Whitmans' compassionate door. The next summer, however, Newell returned for his son—and for his wagon. The vehicle he took apart and floated down the Columbia in a bateau, hiring gangs of Indians to help him carry the parts across the portages. And so, in 1841, as incidental to the making of a farm, the first wheels had spanned America.

The other two wagons apparently stayed on the Walla Walla. And their portent stayed with them, growing slowly in Marcus Whitman's mind. As he told Newell, the way had been opened. Inevitably other wagons would follow—wagons bringing white settlers.

The thought was a necessary antidote to his growing discouragement. Each year he seemed to make less progress with the Indians. The great bulk of them did not want to farm. Those who once had enrolled their children in the school now began to withdraw them, fearing that the missionaries would put the young ones to work. They turned their horses into the mission cornfields; they demanded pay for the land on which the station stood. One of them even dared strike the doctor during a quarrel.

These trials Whitman could have borne—if he had seen an end. But five years of selfless labor had brought him to the reluctant conclusion already reached by Jason Lee: the completely materialistic minds of the Indians were not yet capable of absorbing Christian grace. Nor were the savages likely to be granted the time necessary to make the growth: civilization was spreading too fast. And so, as a corollary, his life had failed . . . unless destiny had brought him to this strategic point not so much for the salvation of the Indians as for the succor of his own race.

The thought was forced into the open by a crisis resulting from the continued animosity of his fellow missionaries. At their annual meeting in 1841 they fell into particularly virulent quarrels and afterward dashed off vituperative letters to the Board. Harassed by falling receipts and mounting expenses, the Board's response was a general house cleaning. Not only Henry Spalding but Spalding's chief detractors, Asa Smith and William Gray, were to be fired. Whitman was to move to Tshimakain, and the Lapwai and Waiilatpu stations were to be closed.

At the time of making this drastic decision, early in 1842, the Board of course did not know that only a few months earlier thirty-one weary American immigrants had found refreshment at Waiilatpu on their way to Oregon, [1] or that more than a hundred Red River colonists from Canada had at about the same time passed down the Columbia on their way to the tenant farms of the Puget Sound Agricultural Company. Even if the Board had known, probably they would not have understood the implications. So far as they were concerned, the missionaries had been sent west to Christianize the Indians, nothing more.

Meanwhile, in the spring of 1842, the missionaries set about cleaning their own house. Waspy Asa Smith was encouraged to resign, and the others held an emotional love feast. Letters announcing the rapproachement were immediately sent east, but it was too late. The

[1] These thirty-one were part of the cross-country group known as the Bidwell-Bartleson group. As far as Fort Hall the party had traveled with Pierre-Jean de Smet's Catholic missionaries bound for the Flatheads of Montana under the guidance of mountain man Thomas Fitzpatrick. At Fort Hall the Catholics turned north, and the emigrants split. The Bidwell-Bartleson section made history by breaking out the first emigrant trail to California. Their Oregon-bound counterparts, however, following more familiar ways northwest, sank into the Willamette with scarcely a ripple.

order of closure was already in the hands of Dr. Elijah White, the United States' new Indian agent for the Pacific Northwest.

Elijah White, it will be recalled, had been a member of the Methodist mission in the Willamette until difficulties with Jason Lee had sent him huffily home aboard the ship *Lausanne*, captained by Josiah Spaulding. Like nearly every American visitor to Oregon, Josiah Spaulding had presented a report on the region to Congress. In this document he repeated garbled tales about the early troubles which Jedediah Smith, William Bailey, and John Turner had experienced with the Indians of southern Oregon. According to Spaulding, the massacres had been the fault of the Hudson's Bay Company. Excesses committed by the company's brigades "upon the poor, defenceless, and peaceful Indians, living within the defined and acknowledged jurisdiction of the United States," led to savage reprisals against less powerful parties of Americans who later happened along the trail.

The charges were almost wholly false, but they gave Senator Linn of Missouri reason for popping into the congressional hopper still another of his premature bills to organize Oregon Territory. Linn also demanded that the government appoint an Indian agent for Oregon—a move of questionable legality, since sovereignty of the district remained in abeyance (in spite of Spaulding's remarks about "acknowledged jurisdiction"). The agency was nevertheless created, though the bill for territorial organization was voted down.

As the only experienced Oregon hand available in the East, Dr. Elijah White was nominated to fill the post.

Slight of frame, springy-heeled, with exuberant blue eyes and a facile tongue, White seems to have understood that part of his job was to encourage emigrants to go west with him. Rushing to Missouri in the spring of 1842, he began an enthusiastic publicity campaign by way of newspaper announcements, street-corner talks, and speeches in churches. Families totaling more than a hundred persons (the figure varies with different accounts) signed up to travel with him, but probably most of them had reached their decision before his appearance—there just wasn't time enough for the average mover to have sold out his business and assembled an outfit in the interim between White's arrival and the train's departure. The agent did, however, lay valuable groundwork for the following year's caravan. Stirred by his assurances that the government was going to act on the Oregon question, several men told White that in 1843, after they'd had time to get ready, they, too, would hit the trail. Thus when the doctor led his column out of Missouri he was convinced that he was the precursor of still greater caravans—a persuasion that would prove crucial to Marcus Whitman.

Most of White's troubles en route were self-made. He proposed too many elaborate trail rules; the caravan voted them in—and then with typical frontier intransigency declined to obey their own laws. White was elected captain and then was demoted following a furious to-do over his proposal that the caravan's dogs be slain lest their barking attract Indians. About half the hounds were killed before the women flew to arms and stopped the slaughter. Nor did the surviving dogs draw Indians. The sole encounter with savages was a bloodless affray involving Lansford Hastings, White's successor as captain, and a traveler named A. L. Lovejoy. Sioux Indians surrounded the pair as they were carving their names on Independence Rock in present Wyoming, the great register of the westward movement. Before anything serious resulted, however, the caravan's guide, Thomas Fitzpatrick, rode up and rescued the frightened tenderfeet.

Once past the Green River and out of range of hostile natives, the quarrelsome train broke into fragments. As the different sections creaked into Fort Hall, the trader in charge advised the wayfarers to abandon their wagons, as the travelers of the previous years had done. There seems no reason to consider the advice as a willful attempt by the Hudson's Bay Company to discourage American immigration, although anti-British propagandists soon took up the charge. The trader was a new man, fresh from the plains of Canada. He probably did not know of the vehicles Meek and Newell had taken through, and in any event the mountainous horse trails he had recently followed from Fort Walla Walla certainly did not look like a wagon road to him. Better go the rest of the way with pack stock, he said.

White, as usual, was the first to go. Traveling fast with a small group of well-equipped horsemen, he reached Whitman's mission at Waiilatpu early in September 1842. There, as his eager listeners pressed their good food and warm comforts on him, he told of the hundred people toiling down the Fort Hall trail behind him, of the greater numbers who would come in 1843—all of them eager for the sustenance they would find here at the mission, the sole American station between the Rockies and the coast.

He then handed over the letters from the American Board, ordering the station closed, and rode on.

Deeply agitated, Whitman sent Indian runners to the other stations, summoning the members to an emergency meeting at Waiilatpu. The first order of business was to accept the resignation of William Gray, who wanted to go to work for the Methodists—and who had been fired by the Board's letter anyway. The other directives from the East were not so easily solved, however. Should the missionaries obey? Should they defy? In their agony of indecision all but Whitman were disposed to wait and see what resulted after the Board received their own letters about the rapport of the previous spring.

Whitman rejected the shilly-shallying. The stakes were too great. For one thing, there was the matter of the Catholics. He knew that Pierre-Jean de Smet had taken a group of Catholics among the Flatheads the year before; he had learned that the Canadian priests stationed at the Cowlitz planned to establish missions at Forts Walla Walla and Colvile on the Columbia. Only days before White's arrival Marcus had written to the Board with the full intolerance of the times, "Romanism stalks abroad on our right hand and on our left hand and with daring effrontery boasts that she is to prevail and possess the land. I ask, must it be so?" Closing the Presbyterian missions, he felt, would help make it so.

Beyond that was his responsibility not to the Indians alone but also to the white settlers who in increasing numbers would be depending on the foodstuffs and repair shops at Waiilatpu. Were they to be left bereft by the Board's decision?

Letters would not be adequate to explain the full import of these new developments. The statements would have to be expounded in person—and he, Marcus Whitman, was willing to make the long ride to do it.

Immediately there were objections. At least a year would pass before he could return, and the wives of the other missionaries recoiled at the thought of being left so long without a doctor. Furthermore, who would manage Waiilatpu during his absence? And dared he start so desperate a ride alone so late in the year?

After long hours of argument Whitman finally won a qualified approval of the plan, and the meeting broke up so that the others could return to pressing chores at their own stations. The agreement was that each man would, as soon as he had time, write to the Board a letter that Whitman could carry east with him in support of his contentions.

Considering how essential time was, the arrangement seems strangely haphazard. Nor did Whitman let himself be bound by it. There was, at Waiilatpu, a belated immigrant who said he was willing to turn around and ride back east. This was A. L. Lovejoy, one of the two men who had been surrounded by Indians at Independence Rock.

Lovejoy's proffer of companionship was all the incentive Whitman

needed to forget the uncertain letters of his fellow missionaries. Away
the two galloped on October 3, aboard fast horses and carrying the
barest minimum of supplies.

At Fort Hall word of Sioux war parties along the Platte trail swung
them south through Colorado and New Mexico. It was an almost disastrous detour—poor guides, shrieking snowstorms, fatigue, starvation, frostbite. Worn out by the ordeal, Lovejoy collapsed at Bent's
Fort on the Arkansas River. Alone, Whitman hurried to overtake a
Missouri-bound party of mountain men and rode with them to the
settlements.

11. "May We Not Call Them Men of Destiny?"

STILL wearing trail-blackened buckskins under a buffalo
overcoat, his face and hands still mottled from frostbite, Whitman
paused in Washington, where legend says (probably incorrectly) that
he talked to no less a personage than President Tyler, and in New
York, where he did talk to Horace Greeley, who one day would make
current a famous phrase about the West. Then on he went to Boston.
With an ease that suggests letters might have sufficed after all, he
persuaded the American Board to reinstate Spalding and to revoke
the order closing Lapwai and Waiilatpu. His mission accomplished, he
made a hurried visit home. There he adopted a motherless thirteen-
year-old nephew named Perrin Whitman, and with the lad in tow
again faced toward the frontier. By the middle of May 1843 he was
moving in amazement through the crowded streets of Independence,
located where the Missouri River makes its great bend toward the
north.

Part of the town's turmoil was normal: the annual spasm of men
and livestock that each spring sent the vast, canvas-topped caravans
of the Santa Fe trade lurching toward New Mexico. But this year
a new element had been added. These were "the movers," bound for
Oregon.

Few of the migrants had exact ideas about how best to reach their
promised land. Most were relying on a mythical entity to be known
as the company, a hoped-for pool from which each man could somehow draw the knowledge and support he would need.

It was an indigenous optimism. During the winter, self-generating
emigrant societies scattered throughout the Mississippi Valley had
been enrolling, in companies, the names of correspondents who professed an interest in traveling to the Columbia. Other organizational

beginnings sprang from newspaper advertisements. For example, a man named Lindsay Applegate, of a large and stalwart family in Missouri's Osage Valley, announced in print his and his brothers' intention to go west, and invited men of similar bent to join them. (The very name Applegate was enough to persuade several hesitant Missourians to enroll.) And, finally, other groups were boomed into existence by ambitious men hopeful of creating a following that might be politically useful in the new territory—men, for example, like Peter Burnett, an unlucky storekeeper and self-taught lawyer of Platte County, Missouri, who had spent the snowy months extolling to cold listeners the perpetual greenness of the Pacific coast, where fevers and agues were reputedly unknown. (The harangues were good practice: for a brief time Burnett would function as captain of the 1843 caravan; he would hold political office in Oregon; and still later, after following the lure of gold southward from the Columbia, he would become the first governor of the new state of California.)

By the middle of May nearly a thousand men, women, and children had poured into Independence, seeking their still unformed companies. And the wonder of it, even after the explanations are in, remains— why? Why were they taking this enormous risk?

Not many of them needed to. As yet the westward tide had washed up very few of those misfits to whom any change is a good change. That kind of mover and his fellows—the adventurer and the parasite —would come later, with the gold rushes. These early migrants were mostly family men, prosperous enough to buy substantial outfits or else sound enough of character that backers were willing to finance them, as debt-ridden Peter Burnett was being financed. In order to go west, many of them had sold at a sacrifice better farms than the ones they would find in Oregon. For that matter, if virgin land was all they wanted, for a paltry $1.25 an acre they could have bought, in adjacent Iowa and newly opened Wisconsin, all the fat-soiled acres any one family could handle. Yet they were passing that up and going two thousand laborious miles to the unknown x of Oregon.

Why?

Back of it was a yeast as old as America. Something new beyond the hills. A promise, a fulfillment—a westering bent so strong among the bulk of the movers that it amounted almost to an instinct. In colonial times their Scottish and Irish and English progenitors had settled restlessly in the hills of Virginia and North Carolina, then had sent equally restless sons across the Alleghenies into Kentucky and Tennessee, and grandsons beyond the Mississippi into Missouri and

Arkansas. Now the newest generation was straining at the edge of the longest jump yet.

Some of them, suckled on tales of whipping the British at Cowpens in 1781 and at New Orleans in 1815, sincerely believed that they were needed to down the enemy once more in the Northwest—a prejudice inflamed by tales of Great Britain's rumored meddling in California, and actual meddling in Texas. Other men were driven by a deeper pride. Slaveowning neighbors had moved in beside their small farms in the hills of Kentucky or southern Missouri and had scorned them for working their ground with their own hands. Nigger jobs —well, now they were going where that stigma would never again attach. No niggers whatsoever (the word is theirs)—whether free or slave—would be allowed inside the new territory if the more rabid of the migrants had their way, as for a short time they would.

There were crasser motives, of course. Always the West has dazzled itself with land speculations, and Oregon was no exception. Land there, instead of costing $1.25 an acre, would be completely free, even if getting to the Columbia did drain a man's pockets. The preceding February, Senator Linn's latest bill to extend United States jurisdiction over the disputed territory had squeaked through the Senate by a vote of twenty-four to twenty-two; and if it also passed the House, as the West was mistakenly sure it would, every white male in the Northwest could claim 640 acres in his own name and generous additional allotments in the names of his wife and children. Moreover, it was land which (the movers thought) would immediately rise in value. Lack of markets and poor transportation would not (they told each other) hamper a farmer as he was hampered in the almost roadless, thinly populated Midwest. The Hudson's Bay Company, which some chauvinists proposed to drive out of the Northwest as soon as they arrived, was represented in the next breath as eager to purchase every bushel of grain the settlers could raise. In addition the navigable Columbia would open cheap shipping to the unlimited markets of Alaska, California, the Sandwich Islands, and teeming Asia. A man in on the ground floor could (they said) choose his own way of making a fortune—farming, selling lands to late-comers, developing timber claims, establishing townsites.

All this, plus romance. Bigger bears than any hunter had ever seen at home. Taller pine trees, fatter fish. Snow peaks incredible against the sun. And something more than romance: there in the greener grass a man's dream of himself—and of all mankind—could somehow come true. It was their job to make it true, their duty to carry the blessings of the American way of life to lands otherwise stifled under the heavy hand of foreign powers.

Two years later a name would be invented for the feeling—Manifest Destiny. As a synonym for aggrandizement the term has since taken on ugly connotations. But whatever it added up to, and the strands of idealism and opportunism were inextricably intertwined, the convictions were very real during those decisive years in Independence. Northward, in a Canadian jumping-off point called Red River, there were no such convictions. The lack is not without its import in our history.

And so, for whatever reason, destiny flowed into Independence that spring of 1843, complete with milch cows and crated chickens, washtubs and churns. The movers had equipment to spare. But not knowledge. They overloaded their wagons with heavy plows they should have shipped around the Horn and with family furniture they would chop up for fuel long before they reached the westward-flowing streams. They did not know the trail—its fords, its hazards, its techniques. They did not know how to deal with Indians or kill buffalo or jerk meat; how to cook over buffalo dung or protect their horses' legs from cactus.

They did not even know, in 1843, whether they could get their wagons through to Oregon.

Philip Edwards of the California cattle drive, who had returned east with Jason Lee in 1838 and who lived across the river from Independence in the town of Liberty, said emphatically that wagons could not travel more than two-thirds of the way. He also said that, for ease in securing game and pasturage, parties should be limited to one hundred and fifty persons each.

Chill words. Almost a thousand people had gathered at the rendezvous outside Independence. They did not want to split up with their fears and uncertainties. And they had to get their wagons through. So many things they'd need in Oregon . . .

Harassed committees called on Whitman. They left no record of their talks, but later developments make it almost certain the doctor said wagons could get through—if the vehicles were sound, if the drivers carried extra parts, if there were plenty of tools for building road as the caravan went.

And so, through trial and error, the once mythical company began to take on substance. Committees were formed to inspect the vehicles and enforce regulations. Other committees met to decide on rules of organization borrowed largely from the Santa Fe traders and from the trapper caravans—methods of trail discipline, division into messes, night corraling, guard duty, and so on. The election of officers, it was decided, should wait until the men had had a chance to see each other in action.

On May 22, in a massive hubbub, the cavalcade started out. Vexations were instantaneous. Unadjusted livestock recently bought in Independence broke loose and ran home—or just ran. Children were lost, possessions mixed. In the mornings there were sharp jockeyings for the less dusty positions at the front of the sprawling caravan; at night, for preferred campsites. There were wrangles over wood, over water holes. Truculent individuals bent on proving their manhood engaged in clamorous fist fights. Exuberant men wasted their animals' strength and risked their wagons in exhilarating races across the prairies. The rules of procedure they had been quick to vote into effect they were equally quick to ignore.

They were a strange breed—nimble-fingered, hardheaded, aggressive, and opinionated. Above all else, they were touchy to the point of explosiveness. A reading of their journals leaves one wondering how they ever hung together as far as the so-called Coasts of Nebraska, let alone the coast of the Pacific. Yet one of their number, Jesse Applegate, who would come to know their intractability well, could write of them:

No other race of men with means at their command would undertake so great a journey—none save those could successfully perform it with no previous preparation, relying only on the fertility of their invention to devise the means to overcome each danger and difficulty as it arose. . . . They have undertaken to perform, with slow-moving oxen, a journey of two thousand miles. The way lies over trackless wastes, wide and deep rivers, rugged and lofty mountains, and is beset with hostile savages. Yet . . . they are always found ready and equal to the occasion, and always conquerors. May we not call them men of destiny?

The shakedown part of the trip culminated at the swollen Kansas River, near the site of present Topeka. Finding the ford too swift for swimming, the emigrants built two crude boats and laid a platform of poles between them. One by one the wagons were rolled by hand onto the improvised ferry, which was then hauled across the stream by gangs of chanting men pulling on ropes.

On the far bank, in what became a tradition of the trail, the group gathered to elect a permanent captain, a sergeant, and a council of ten. Democracy in the raw attended the voting. Candidates for the council of ten made their promises, then lined up abreast, and at a given signal walked off across the greening prairie. Balloting consisted of having each man's supporters fall in behind him. To boost enthusiasm and perhaps to confuse the counters, the lines pranced and serpentined with loud howls through the camp, and the affair degenerated into a good-natured uproar. Meantime, in more orthodox fashion, young J. W. Nesmith and florid Peter H. Burnett were elected sergeant and captain respectively.

Burnett, who was going west partly for his wife's health and partly for the baronial acreage he hoped to claim through his numerous children, did not hold his captaincy long. The caravan was scarcely under way again when violent quarrels broke out between those emigrants who owned sizable herds of livestock and those who possessed only a cow or two for milk. Men without cattle refused to help guard their fellows' animals by night and protested the herd's slowness by day. Unable to force a solution and plagued by ill-health of his own, Peter Burnett resigned.

The caravan now split. Sixty-one unburdened wagons moved on ahead. Approximately an equal number of livestock owners formed themselves into what they called the cow column and elected as their leader one of the notable figures of Western history, Jesse Applegate.

Kentucky-born, lean, more than six feet tall and so homely he avoided mirrors all his life, Applegate moved with an effortless, loose-swinging stride that enabled him to walk, when need arose, upwards of threescore miles a day. Unlike most of his rawboned constituents, he had been well educated. As a young man he had studied briefly in the St. Louis law office of Edward Bates, who one day would be nominee for the presidency of the United States and Lincoln's Attorney General, and whose esteem Applegate commanded throughout their widely divergent careers. In spite of Bates's friendship, young Jesse left the law to become deputy surveyor for the sparsely settled counties of southern and western Missouri. He did not go to seed, as he so easily might have. Even in the wilderness he never lost his taste for reading, and somehow he developed, beside his lonely campfires, a lucid prose style that would leave its mark on the principal legislation of early Oregon.

Marrying, he broke out a new farm in the Osage Valley but could find no satisfactory market for his corn and cotton and fat steers. Meanwhile slaveowners were moving in beside him. Hating their competition, Jesse decided abruptly to move to Oregon. His brothers Charles and Lindsay joined him with their wives and children; and because word had somehow got abroad that Oregon was a stockman's paradise, the trio invested the money they raised from the sale of their farms in a herd of several hundred head of breeder cows.

Other men added more animals—a dozen, a score, a hundred—until the trail herd numbered, quite apart from draft animals, well into the thousands. [1] Onto this relatively homogeneous group Applegate was able to impose a cohesion that eluded the advance column. Defections, to be sure, would develop. Even so, under Jesse Applegate's persuasive hand the ponderous cow column plodded safely through a far longer and in some respects far more amazing march than the storied drives that would be made years later by the vaunted trail herders of Texas.

The cow column tried to (and did) stay close enough to the advance group so that the parties could render mutual aid in case of need. This meant that the stars were still shining when Applegate's shivering night guards woke the camp with a salvo of rifle shots. Cook fires sent thin tendrils of smoke into the dawn as half a hundred riders jogged out to contract the vast herd toward the circle of white-gleaming wagons.

Inside that circle pandemonium erupted with daylight. If a man was late getting started he would have to eat dust all day long at the end of the line. Oaths and cuffs hurried stubborn draft oxen and sleepy children into place. Tents were struck, wagons loaded. Bugles trumpeted the start, and by seven o'clock the train was swinging slowly into line, in platoons of four whose position in the column was varied from day to day so that none except confirmed laggards had to endure the tail-end place for more than his fair share of time. Behind the wagons or sometimes on a slightly different line of march, filling the air with their unhappy bawling, plodded the cow herd.

Northwestward across Kansas the days were a storybook adventure, a loose, winding line over rolling hills spangled with wild flowers. Occasionally there were Indians to stare at. More spectacular were the violent thunderstorms—such rain, as one later emigrant put it, that a man could not lie down for fear of drowning or stand up for

[1] As usual, contemporary "evidence" varies widely about the size of the 1843 emigration, called the Great Emigration because of its importance to Northwestern history rather than because of its size. Estimates of the number of men, women, and children involved range from five hundred to more than a thousand, of animals from seventeen hundred to five thousand. Median figures would probably be approximately correct.

fear of being struck by lightning. While the women struggled with collapsed tents, sodden fires, and crying children, the men rode wildly about the more exciting work of preventing stampedes.

The next day the sun was out again. On the wagons trundled, draped with drying blankets. Boys and girls romped across the prairies or raced their ponies as the slow miles drifted past—ten, fifteen, sometimes even twenty a day. At dusk the circle formed again, the wagons facing outward with the tongue of each chained to the rear wheel of the one ahead. Tents went up; campfires bloomed. While the elders gossiped a violin stirred a brief dance among the younger people. Soon, however, weary bones sought rest and the guards were left alone under the enormous heavens, to listen to the howl of wolves and the monotone of teeth on grass, fearful that each break in the sound might mean that Pawnee Indians were slipping up to steal the horses.

Marcus Whitman was not with the column during these early stages of the journey. He had stayed behind at the Shawnee mission just beyond Westport (within the limits of present Kansas City) and had noted with some envy that the methods and equipment available to his brother Presbyterians seemed to elicit better response from the displaced Indians of the East than did his own efforts among the wild Cayuses of the Walla Walla. When at length he started after the caravan with his nephew and a handful of belated emigrants, he overtook another man of destiny—or at least a man who, seizing the coattails of expansion, would endeavor to make himself destiny's darling. This was John Charles Frémont, bound for Oregon with a government exploring party that was designed to link its investigations with those recently completed by Lieutenant Wilkes.

Frémont's trip was the brain-baby, in part, of Missouri's two stentorian senators, Thomas Hart Benton (the explorer's father-in-law) and Lewis Linn. Both legislators, correctly gauging the restless mood of their frontier constituents, felt that Western expansion would be stimulated if exact geographical knowledge of the trails and of the West's resources was made readily available to would-be emigrants. They picked the right man to implement the hunch. Frémont examined accurately, wrote clearly. When the report of his two expeditions— to South Pass in 1842 and to Oregon and California in 1843–44—was issued as a congressional document in 1845, it instantly became the primary guidebook for untold thousands of Oregon farmers, Utah Mormons, and, shortly thereafter, California gold-rushers.

Whitman of course could not foresee all this. But he did realize that the government was at last becoming openly interested in a land whose sovereignty could not stay in abeyance much longer. For a night he camped with Frémont, answering the explorer's questions as fully as he could. The next morning, astride a fast-stepping mule, he hurried on after the caravan with his laggard companions. June was well underway before he overtook it.

He and his adopted nephew were not universally welcomed. Totally devoid of worldly goods, they sponged unabashedly and so incurred the annoyance of several reluctant hosts. To Jesse Applegate, however, and to the caravan's guide, mountain man John Gantt, Whitman was worth all the handouts he cost.

The doctor had gained, during the past years, a command of wilderness living that bred, by force of example, more assurance than all the guidebooks ever written. With a word or a gesture he could convince stubborn greenhorns that certain rules about caring for themselves and their equipment were, after all, wise rules. As a medical man he could bring faith to those who were ill and to those who feared that they might be. Most especially, he was always on hand to din into the train's reluctant ears the one stark bit of advice which might spell salvation for them all: "Travel, travel, travel!" He had seen how snow piled up in the mountains at the end of the trail. He had watched the Columbia grow turgid with autumn rains. Travel! "Nothing"—so Applegate later reported his words—"nothing is wise that does not help you along. Nothing is good for you that causes a moment's delay."

Travel they did, into increasing desolation. Wind scoured; sun pounded. Skin cracked and chapped. Alkali dust reddened their eyes and rasped their throats. Alkali water and unaccustomed meals of fresh buffalo meat brought on cramping attacks of dysentery, for whose embarrassing miseries the barren valley of the Platte often provided not even a willow bush for privacy. Tempers grew edged. Men snarled as they crowded into the watering places, boys as they gathered the sackfuls of buffalo chips that were their only fuel, women as they crouched over stingy fires in shallow trenches.

When they reached the forks of the Platte they found a brown flood rolling down the southern branch, which they had to cross. The advance column paused in dismay. The cow column caught up and there was a tangle of dejection. (During it Whitman inspirited everyone by successfully delivering a baby.) Should they wait—— No! "Nothing is wise that does not help you along." They killed several buffalo and improvised boats by stretching the green hides across dismantled wagon boxes. These clumsy craft were loaded with goods and manhandled through the flood by men wielding hand-hewn oars and pulling on ropes. Then the empty wagons were drawn into the stream at an angle so that the current would not strike the wheels broadside. Men wading or swimming downstream of each yoke of oxen pounded the dumb, frightened beasts back into line whenever they threatened to swing around.

Five days the crossing took. But there was no time afterward to rest. Dry out, load up, go on. On through the deep-gullied sand hills to what then seemed the terrifying precipices of Ash Hollow on the North Platte in Nebraska; on past the eroded fantasies of Chimney Rock and Scott's Bluff. Buffalo disappeared. Some said the Sioux Indians had driven the herds out of reach. Others said, with acid anti-British oaths, that Sir William Stewart's party of sportsmen, traveling just ahead, had frightened all but occasional beasts away from the trail. In any event there was no fresh meat. Prodigal cooks who two weeks ago had been throwing away bacon rind and leftover biscuits counted the days ahead and took to hoarding every scrap.

In what is now eastern Wyoming, at Fort Laramie and its adjacent posts, there was a brief pause to buy skimpy supplies at outrageous prices, to tighten loose wagon tires, to hammer bent wagon hounds back into place. But there was no pause for rest. They had left Missouri late; they were averaging less than fifteen miles a day. Travel! On they pushed. The dust grew thicker, the winds more parching. If we could heal our sores; if— No! "Nothing is good for you that causes a moment's delay." But the oxen—so thin, the grass so sparse . . . No! And now attrition of nerves was added to exhaustion of body. Would the animals last? Could the failing train continue to march as fast as the onrush of winter?

On the Sweetwater, feeling that Indian danger was past, the caravan broke into fragments, partly because of accumulated cabin fever and partly because smaller groups would have better luck finding desperately needed game and pasturage. Over South Pass the sections crawled, disgusted that its low sage swales looked so little like the Continental Divide of imagination. Slowly the Green River and its blistering deserts dropped behind. Painfully they climbed the first real mountains they had yet encountered and with frightful creakings and groanings from the wagons they dropped down to the lush meadows along the Bear River, in eastern Idaho. Travel—but not today. Flesh can stand just so much. On the Bear they collapsed.

There Frémont, fresh from scouting alternative routes through Colorado, overhauled them, and in his journal reported an idyllic picture that would breed false confidence in later travelers—"a picture of home beauty that went directly to our hearts . . . smokes were rising lazily from the fires, around which the women were occupied in preparing the evening meal, and the children playing in the grass; and the herds of cattle, grazing about in the bottom, had an air of quiet security and civilized comfort that made a rare sight for the traveler in the remote wilderness."

Whatever quiet security the emigrants may have felt on the Bear disappeared at Fort Hall. Trader Richard Grant treated them as kindly as his means allowed and then devastated them by saying their wagons could not go through. This was desperate. Not enough horses were available at the fort for carrying the women and children, let alone the baggage. What were they going to do?

At a frightened conference Whitman (who had just received from Waiilatpu four or five horseloads of flour to distribute among the most destitute immigrants) insisted that wagons *could* go through. To be sure, he had failed to push his two-wheeled cart past Fort Boise; to be sure, Newell's mountain men had not been able to break out a way with loaded vehicles. But this group possessed an asset its predecessors had lacked: enough able-bodied men to build road as they went.

The immigrants agreed—they had little other choice, actually—and hired Whitman at a reputed fee of four hundred dollars to go ahead with a small party and blaze the way. (Gantt, the original pilot, left the main group at this point with sixteen or twenty people bound for California.)

Beyond Fort Hall the train was split into still smaller sections by the heat, the knotted sage, the lacerating lava stones. It strung out for miles, and through most of September Whitman wasted endless energy riding back along the exhausted line, trying to hurry his charges forward.

At the first ford of the Snake, where the trains cut off an arc of the river to save miles on the way to Fort Boise, a man named Miles Eyres was dragged underneath the water and drowned by a heavy money belt around his waist. To his despairing wife and three children Whitman promised haven for the winter at Waiilatpu—the first of a years-long series of heart-weary persons who would try to put their lives back together again at the mission that so nearly had been abandoned.

In the circular, beautiful valley of Grande Ronde, doubly lovely after another grueling ford of the Snake and a long pull through the fire-killed timber of Burnt River, a messenger met the train. He brought an urgent summons for the doctor. Henry and Eliza Spalding were both ill and needed him at once. Leaving the train under the guidance of a Christianized Indian named Stickus, who had ridden out to meet him, Whitman cut across country to Lapwai, found the Spaldings recovering, and then was summoned a hundred and forty miles to Tshimakain by word that Mrs. Eells's baby was imminent.

And so he missed bringing the train into the station he had saved. Before he had returned from Tshimakain; before he had fetched Narcissa back through the gray November rains from the Methodist mission at the Dalles, whither she had fled because of Indian alarms at Waiilatpu, the bulk of the immigrants had passed on by. But the long ride overland with them had given him a totally new concept of his mission, so that by the next spring he could write in retrospect to Narcissa's parents, "As I hold the settlement of this country by Americans rather than by an English colony to be most important, I am happy to have been the means of landing so large an emigration on to the shores of the Columbia. . . . I have no doubt our greatest work is to be to aid the white settlement of this country to found its religious institutions."

And the Indians? They had caused Narcissa trouble during his absence; they had been sulky since his return. They were given, he was now convinced, to "indolence, violence & blood shed." They could not be civilized "before the white settlers will demand the soil and seek the removal of both the Indians and the Mission. . . . It is equally useless to oppose or desire it otherwise."

Oh, he kept on working with them, as was his Christian duty. But they sensed the change. They knew they were no longer his children, as once he had said.

He had been right about the wagons. With the Indian Stickus pointing the way, a crew of forty axmen spent four days chopping and grading a "road" across the Blue Mountains. A fall of October snow terrified the caravan but did not last long enough to be dangerous. Safely down on the Umatilla River at last, the migrants found thickets of ripe berries on which they gorged and mission-trained Indian farmers from whom they obtained fresh vegetables in exchange for old clothing. More supplies were available at Waiilatpu, but the prices quoted by the man Whitman had left in charge seemed fantastic—a dollar for a bushel of wheat, forty cents for a bushel of potatoes. The figures were almost double Missouri prices, and some of the immigrants (who were traveling to Oregon in order to command high returns for their crops) cursed Whitman bitterly, saying he had brought them this way—Waiilatpu was a little off the most direct route—so that he could sell them his produce.

At Fort Walla Walla, where the overwhelmed Hudson's Bay trader did all in his power to help the exhausted travelers, the last semblance of organization vanished. Some cattle owners, afraid that they could not drive their animals to the Willamette over the heavily timbered Cascade Mountains, traded good-blooded but trail-gaunt Missouri stock for scrubby Spanish cattle that they could pick up from the company herds at Fort Vancouver. Others, determining to risk the mountains, traded their wagons for pack animals and started their herds along breakneck trails far above the river. A few, hearing that routes were better along the north bank of the Columbia, swam their animals across the river two at a time, tied behind rented Indian canoes.

Immigrants without cattle took directly to the river. Early arrivals, like Peter Burnett, were able to buy, at Fort Walla Walla, the few available Hudson's Bay bateaux. Travel in these was relatively easy: the roomy craft were forty-five feet long by five broad, yet light enough so that gangs of Indians could carry them across the portages. Late-comers, however, found no boats. A few wracked their wagons on to the Dalles, where they hired small Indian canoes for the rest of the journey. Soon even the canoes were gone, and the last arrivals had to build their own transport.

The more reckless of the builders tied together clumsy rafts onto which they wheeled their wagons. Ankle-deep in the icy water, with chill November winds blowing on them through the canyon, they floated, lined, and portaged a dangerous way down the stream. Others, fearing to trust their goods and lives to such uncertain craft, laboriously gathered together drift logs, dug pits for whipsawing the timber into planks, and hammered together rowboats that they hoped would be safer than rafts. Safety, however, is a relative situation.

In two such homemade craft the combined Applegate families and their hired hands embarked, having made arrangements to leave their cattle near Fort Walla Walla during the winter. At first the change from wagons was exhilarating. The current carried them effortlessly; the scenery was austere and majestic. Even their guide was amusing, a weathered Indian with a dirty red handkerchief around his head and long black hair hanging down his back.

Imperceptibly the current strengthened. Suddenly, one morning, it leaped under them more wildly than they could manage. A shout came from the rear boat, occupied by three of the children and three older men. The parents in the lead boat looked back just in time to see the spinning craft drop out of sight under a foaming surge. Instinctively the fathers started to their feet. The mothers pulled them back. Their own boat was running uncontrolled straight for the rocks.

Somehow they fought clear and managed to land. Frantic with grief, Lindsay Applegate jerked a rifle from the baggage to kill the Indian pilot. Luckily the man disappeared before Lindsay could shoot. Meanwhile the stark-eyed mothers were clambering back along the rocky bank. One swimmer appeared and clawed free of the water. Another man floated into sight on a featherbed tick. And then one boy bobbed by, battered but safe. But the bodies of the third man and of two ten-year-old cousins, one Jesse's son and another Lindsay's, were never found.

In rain-swept coves throughout the beautiful, terrible gorge the families were huddled, hungry, cold, destitute. They clogged up at the portages, pleading with the Indians for help, trading loved possessions for bits of flyblown salmon. Stronger or luckier men hurried ahead for assistance. Settlers in the Willamette responded with some supplies. But the difference between disaster and salvation was John McLoughlin, who sent not only Hudson's Bay Company food but also boats for transport.

One of these supply boats was rowed upstream by a crew under an immigrant named James Waters. Among the first to reach Vancouver, Waters had appealed to McLoughlin for provisions, assuring the factor that the stranded wayfarers would be glad to pay any fair price. McLoughlin assented, furnishing crew and boat, and asking in return the same price on the goods that his own laborers would have had to pay at the store at the fort. Eagerly the starving fell on what Waters brought them. Then, feeling comfortable again, many of them abused him and McLoughlin for trying to cash in on their misfortune. Few ever kept their promises to pay; and Waters and McLoughlin had to make good the losses out of their own pockets.

For Waters it was an isolated experience. For McLoughlin, however, variations on the theme became standard procedure, not alone in 1843 but during subsequent years as well. Yet he was not soured, even though he must have foreseen that Simpson would censure the generosity as careless business, as indeed the governor did. But Simpson had not stared into those hungry eyes, had not seen the desperation that would seize by violence what it could not gain in peace. In addition, McLoughlin sensed, as Simpson did not, that the immigration of 1843 was the precursor of larger influxes in 1844, in 1845, in . . . who knew for how many years? How could such numbers possibly be fed except on crops grown by the newcomers of '43? And how could those destitute men of '43 plant the essential foodstuffs unless the Hudson's Bay Company made loans of tools and seed? And so, each day during the closing months of 1843 and again during the late months of the next two years, McLoughlin mingled generosity with what he considered sound policy until the worthless debts owed his company totaled between sixty and eighty thousand dollars. Unquestionably the largess saved lives. But it did not improve the chief factor's position in the eyes of the directors.

Unlike many of their luckless fellows of '43, the Applegates remained solvent. At the Dalles they bought supplies from an old friend, Robert Shortess of the ill-fated Peoria party of 1839, and then floated on down to the Willamette. In drenching rains they dragged themselves up that river to shelter in an abandoned cabin at Lee's old mission. (A new Methodist mission had been built a few miles farther south, within the limits of modern Salem.) While Charles and Lindsay took such odd jobs as they could find, Jesse rode westward to the base of the coastal mountains. There he saw a spot he liked. On ground no government could yet legally give him he filed three claims for the three brothers and, on his own holding, tossed together a temporary shanty.

For miles up and down the fog-shrouded valley other soaked men were erecting similar shanties on similar claims. Now and then as their axes rang they smiled to themselves. God knows why . . . except that no fog lasts forever. Already in their minds they could see the sheen of August sun on their wheat—American wheat. Already they could hear themselves saying to their wives, "Here. Here's the place where we'll put the new house." This was trail's end. This was home.

12. Substitutes for Anarchy

THE immigrants of 1843 had scarcely time to draw their breaths when they found themselves buttonholed by candidates for political office. An interim government for Oregon was in the throes of birth. A constitution had been promulgated, and elections were scheduled for the following May. Somewhat bewildered by the tumult, the more civic-minded of the newcomers asked for copies of the legislation they were now supposed to live under and promptly decided they did not like it. Yet when faced with the story behind the amateur state making, they were forced to admit that some sort of action had been necessary to relieve the growing tensions of the Northwest.

Two years earlier the disapproval of John McLoughlin and the deprecations of Lieutenant Wilkes had been enough to dampen the political stirrings that followed the death of Ewing Young. But as the population of the valley grew the yeast kept bubbling.

Divisions along national lines had been inevitable. Intensifying these were religious cleavages. When the Catholic immigrants from Red River deserted the Puget Sound Agricultural Company in order to establish squatters' right claims in the Willamette, they completely undid the numerical superiority the Methodists had achieved through Jason Lee's importations aboard the ship *Lausanne*. But perhaps none of the differences would have begun to foam if it had not been for that ancient catalyst of unrest—economics.

Wherever a settler turned he felt the all-pervading power of the Hudson's Bay Company. To the French Canadians, long used to the firm's benevolent paternalism, the power was a comfort. To the Americans, however, it was an octopus. They began to wonder. If the Puget Sound Company became self-sufficient and no longer needed their wheat to fulfill its Russian contracts; if McLoughlin ever decided, for whatever reason, not to sell them ammunition or cloth or hardware, as he was already declining to sell livestock, what then would they do?

The obvious answer was to develop other arteries of trade. Opportunity arose in 1842 when brigs of the Massachusetts firm of Cushing and Company pushed up the Willamette to anchorage at the rapids below the falls and began bartering manufactured goods for pickled salmon, lumber, flour. To avoid McLoughlin's sharp eyes one entrepreneur opened a secret trading house in a cabin that purported to be a farm building. The Methodists established a store ostensibly for themselves, actually for everyone. They also led the way in building grist and sawmills that could supply goods needed for barter.

McLoughlin reacted as he had years before when Captain Dominis and other Yankee sea peddlers had invaded the Columbia. He lured the Indians' salmon away from the invaders with fancy prices; he either undercut or threatened to undercut the prices at which the settlers could afford to sell their lumber. To him it was simple business. He wanted to keep the trade of the region in the hands of his own firm, on the same fair terms he offered his own employees. But it did not work that way. Deeply resentful, the Americans became still more ready to support outsiders. And so one of George Simpson's long-standing fears was turned into reality: encouraged by the settlers in the Willamette, sea-borne adventurers more and more frequently stormed the company's once inviolable bailiwick.

Another, sharper conflict arose over the water-power rights of Willamette Falls. As noted earlier, ever since 1829 the company had been asserting shadowy claim to the site. Before going to London in 1838, McLoughlin had ordered timbers dragged to the riverbank for replacing a shanty destroyed by the Indians; but during his absence construction lapsed and two years later Alvin Waller of the Methodist mission asked if he might use the timbers for constructing a branch station that would bring salvation to the salmon fishers. McLoughlin had acquiesced. At the same time he carefully stated in writing his right to the riverbank and to "the small Island in the Falls . . . which I intend to claim when the Boundary line is drawn."

No local resident believed McLoughlin's protestations that he was acting for himself. They assumed he was fronting for the company because of United States laws that forbade corporations to acquire land in this country by pre-emption. Defeating such trickery perhaps seemed a patriotic duty to the Reverend Alvin Waller. In any case he and another mission member announced from the shelter of McLoughlin's logs that they were claiming for themselves, as private individuals, the riverbank and the island.

McLoughlin at once protested to Jason Lee. Lee evaded the issue, writing back that "a Citizen of the United States by becoming a Missionary does not renounce any civil or political right. I cannot control any man in these matters, though I had not the most distant idea when I stationed Mr. Waller there that he would set up a private claim to the land."

On the strength of this indirect green light from their superior, Waller and his associates formed a milling company and began building private homes. McLoughlin countered in December 1842 by platting, between the riverbank and the timbered bluffs to the east, a townsite which he named Oregon City. He compromised his position by buying off the Methodists with cash and choice lots in "his" town; but neither they nor their assigns stayed bought, and the maneuverings served only to make the quarrel more complex and bitter. Nor did McLoughlin help his stand by sounding sometimes as if he were acting for himself and sometimes for the Hudson's Bay Company, an ambivalence which in time would cause him as much trouble with his employers as with the Americans.

No sovereignty existed to give validity to any of these land claims. No arbiter could be called on to settle these or any disputes. So complete a vacuum was politically abhorrent, of course, and various bodies rushed in to fill it.

The first was Elijah White, whose arrival with the vanguard of the 1842 immigrants antedated the platting of Oregon City by only a few weeks. One of the '42 immigrants became McLoughlin's surveyor, another his lawyer, and most of them his clients: by spring they had built thirty houses on his townsite and so had established the first noncompany village in the Northwest. White very much wished to be their head man. When he called the settlers of the Willamette together to present his credentials as sub-agent to the Indians, he intimated that he possessed, as sole representative of the United States west of the Rockies, powers far more elastic than those ordinarily accruing to his position.

His listeners would have none of it. The immigrants with whom he had traveled too clearly recalled having hooted him out of the train's captaincy while on the trail, and the Methodists whom he had known earlier at the mission declined to be impressed by his new importance. But though they raucously grounded his political balloon, the question he raised remained aloft. Where did authority rest? What could the settlers do about ending their once Arcadian anarchy?

A debating society founded by mountain man Robert Newell spent the winter of 1842–43 arguing heatedly over whether it was more expedient to form an independent government at once or to wait for the United States to act. Other settlers fired off still another petition to Congress, this one bristling with malicious charges against McLoughlin and the Hudson's Bay Company.

More direct minds sought direct action. An opening was suggested by a farmers' meeting which assembled at Champoeg on February 2, 1843, to discuss means of controlling predatory animals. At this meeting a committee was appointed to look into the possibility of levying contributions from all the settlers—in effect, a common tax, which presupposes some sort of sovereignty—in order to pay bounties for wolves, bears, and panthers. The committee was instructed to report back at the home of Joseph Gervais, an ancient Astorian, on March 6; and it occurred to certain citizens that here was a wedge for a coup.

Quietly they gathered at Gervais' log cabin, and after the committee's resolutions concerning bounties had been approved, William Gray rose to his feet. (He was a member of the Methodist mission now, having left Whitman's Presbyterians the previous fall.) The settlers' flocks, he said, would henceforth be protected. But "how is it, fellow-citizens, with you and me, and our children and wives? Have we any organization upon which we can rely for mutual protection? . . . Now, fellow-citizens, I submit and move the adoption of . . . resolutions . . . that a committee be appointed to take into consideration the propriety of taking measures for the civil and military protection of this colony."

The resolutions were whooped through, the committee appointed. Its sole action turned out to be a recommendation that a provisional government be formed for Oregon. A general meeting of the settlers to vote on this recommendation was set for May 2, 1843, in, of all places, the grain warehouse of the Hudson's Bay Company at Champoeg.

The gathering was not well attended. Of the more than one hundred and twenty-five Americans living in the Willamette, only fifty or so showed up. Some of the absentees were simply indifferent. [1] Others stayed away because of hostility toward the Methodists, whom they suspected of trying to railroad the proceedings.

Approximately the same proportion of the French-Canadian population also appeared. They were an unwelcome threat, for their priest, on word passed down from the company, had coached them to vote against the proposed government. Their opposition was not unanimous, however. A few of the voyageurs who had come to the country thirty years before with the Astorians were pro-American. One or two others who had fled Canada during the abortive revolution of 1838 were anti-British on general principle. As a result the exact voting strength of the company bloc was a matter of uneasy conjecture to the Americans.

Apparently the Americans tried to confuse the Canadians by wording their resolution in such a way that a vote of "No" would bring affirmative results. There were quarrels and shouts and rappings for

[1] Among the indifferent were several disgruntled immigrants of 1842, who, not finding Oregon to their expectations, started south for California late in May under the leadership of Lansford Hastings. En route they met a group of California malcontents bound for Oregon. The parties traded curses about the regions each had left. Apparently the ex-Californians were the more vitriolic. Anyway, a large part of Hastings' group returned to the Willamette with their new friends. Hastings continued to California with the remnant, then went on east, wrote a guidebook, and in 1846 achieved infamy for his contributions to the tragedy of the Donner party in the Sierra Nevada.

order, and in the end the entire conclave may have boiled out into an open field for a final tally by heads. Lack of detailed records has resulted in apocryphal accounts, including one that has Joe Meek save the day by bellowing, "All in favor of the Report, and for an Organization, follow me!" It probably did not happen so dramatically; the decision probably did not tremble in the balance, as legend says, until Etienne Lucier, an Astorian and the district's first settler, crossed over to Meek's American line with a revolutionary fugitive, thus carrying the vote in favor of a provisional government fifty-two to fifty. In any event the Canadians withdrew in pique, and the Americans settled down to doing what they most likely would have done as a rump parliament even if they had been outvoted—naming still another committee, this one to draft a constitution for the proposed government.

The only lawbook available in Oregon at that time was the property of one James O'Neil, who had carried it west with him on Wyeth's 1834 expedition. The tome contained the ordinance setting up the old Northwest Territory, together with the Organic Law of Iowa. Being the only models available, these statutes became the basis of the Oregon constitution. There were a few startling departures from pattern, however. One was the eschewing of a governor in favor of an executive committee of three. Another was the abolition of taxes in the starry-eyed hope that the new government could be financed, like a church, through voluntary contributions.

Unmodeled also was Article IV, which declared that no private individual could hold claim to "extensive water privileges, or other situations necessary for the transaction of mercantile or manufacturing operations. . . . Provided that nothing in these laws shall be so construed as to affect any claim of any mission of a religious character, made previous to this time, of an extent not more than six miles square." The purpose of these discriminatory clauses was, of course, to freeze McLoughlin out of Oregon City and Willamette Falls, and at the same time to confirm the holdings of the Methodists to the tune of 23,040 acres.

Apparently the document was what the original settlers wanted. It was accepted by an overwhelming majority at a mass meeting on July 5, 1843, and an election of officers was scheduled for the following May, 1844.

The constitution did not prove to be what Applegate's men of '43 wanted, however. They looked it over almost as soon as they arrived, and clear legal minds among them quickly recognized several flaws. For one, the document drew no distinction between what was law and what was constitution. The three-man executive system was cumbersome, the scheme of financing through subscription ludicrous, the kowtowing to the Methodists unfair. Moreover, McLoughlin's generosity was having its effect. Although confirmed British-haters cursed him to the end, others began to wonder if the charges they had heard and read were accurate. One of the immigrants, M. M. McCarver, suggested that McLoughlin write him a letter answering the most damaging of the strictures, especially those that had originally emanated from Hall Kelley and Josiah Spaulding, and had been published as government documents. This McLoughlin did. Mc-Carver showed the letter around Oregon City. Coupled with the views of men like Jesse Applegate and Peter Burnett, it did much to soften hostility toward the company and, as a corollary, to raise questions in many minds about the constitution's discriminatory Article IV.

The Methodists, their position secured by Article IV, naturally wanted the clause maintained. But the temporal phase of their activities was falling under increasing fire, even from their own Missionary Board in the East. Various disgruntled members had taken home critical tales about Lee's performances, and Jason's careless bookkeeping had done nothing to reassure the head office. Finally the Board had decided to send out, by ship around the Horn, a man named George Gary to investigate the charges against Lee and, if need be, to supersede him.

Letters from the Board announcing Gary's assignment were carried to Lee by the immigrant train of 1843. Thoroughly upset, the raw-boned missionary determined to sail east and answer the charges in person. It was, for him, a fatal effort. Though protracted hearings held during the summer of 1844 largely exonerated him, his worn body collapsed and in March 1845, aged forty-one, he died without again seeing the land he had been so instrumental in settling. Perhaps it was just as well. Gary, the man dispatched to investigate the mission, soon concluded that the organization was no longer filling its purpose and should be dissolved. In June 1844 the farms, buildings, mills, store, goods—everything except the station at the Dalles—were sold, most of it going at bargain rates to former mission members. (McLoughlin did not share the bargain, however; he had to pay six thousand dollars to repossess lots he had given outright to the Methodists less than two years before in the contested claim at Oregon City.)

Knowledge that the mission was in disfavor with its own Board was in the air when the election of government officials was held during May 1844. This, together with a belief that the discriminatory constitution was largely the work of the so-called "Mission party," led to a resounding defeat at the polls of everyone associated with that organization. The men of '43, in short, wanted a new start under their own aegis. Of the legislators they elected, only Doc Newell and one other man had been in Oregon more than six months.

Energetically the new government set about remodeling the constitution by legislative acts which were not submitted to popula: vote—and hence were probably without force. Out went the discriminatory Article IV. Out went the three-headed executive committee, to be replaced at the 1845 elections with a single governor. Out went taxation by subscription; in its place was put a system so stringent that delinquent taxpayers lost their votes and right to be heard in court. In went a clause prohibiting intoxicating liquors. And in went a sweeping ban on Negroes.

The last act indicated the strength of the Southern farmers among the migrants. They hated not only the slaves who had made them economic misfits at home but all Negroes of any status. Shortly after arriving in Oregon they found apparent justification for the prejudice when two or three of the region's handful of free Negroes became embroiled with Indians in a confused brawl that brought death to two popular whites. Catching fire from the resultant indignation, the legislators passed a law which not only forbade the importation of slaves but also banished without exception all Negroes and mulattoes under pain of arrest and a flogging "once every six months until he or she shall quit the territory."

These and various minor items attended to, the legislators hung up their new broom and adjourned until December. After that time, they thought, their actions would be guided by word of the latest developments in the United States, as brought by the immigrants of 1844.

No conclusive information arrived, however. When the newcomers of '44 straggled wet and miserable out of the gorge, helped as usual by McLoughlin, all they could say was that tensions between Britain and the United States were more acute than ever. No solution about sovereignty had been reached; none might be without war. Meanwhile Oregon had no government except what it could provide for itself.

Critically the newcomers looked at the constitution as revised by the men of '43. Like their predecessors, they found it lacking; and once again, in travail and bitterness, Oregon set about trying to thresh a way out of anarchy.

Foremost among the newcomers' objections was the constitution's failure to establish jurisdiction over the Hudson's Bay Company. McLoughlin himself had talked the first legislators out of their tentative moves in that direction. But, snorted the newcomers, who was McLoughlin to say that a British firm was above the law or to set the Columbia as the boundary of the provisional government? Did he heed the boundary himself? Hardly. The Bay Company (or was it McLoughlin personally?) owned choice real estate in Oregon City on which it had already built, or was preparing to build, stores, warehouses, flour and sawmills. Yet the company declined to recognize the authority of the provisional government over these holdings or over the personnel who worked in them.

Meanwhile Americans were at last beginning to push north of the Columbia. Leader of the initial efforts was a thirty-year-old Kentuckian named Michael T. Simmons, completely illiterate but of persuasive talents which he had shown to good effect as one of the captains of the 1844 influx. Undeterred by McLoughlin's objections, he made an effort, in the winter of 1844–45, to reach Puget Sound. He failed, but the next summer tried again with another small party and this time succeeded. After a brief canoe exploration he picked a site for a claim on an open prairie near the southern tip of Budd Inlet, one of the complex of salt-water fingers that reach deep back into the beautiful hills at the sound's lower end. One attraction was the power of Tumwater Falls (from the onomatopoetic Indian word for rushing water—*tum-tum*). Another was Fort Nisqually at the tip of an inlet a few miles to the east.

Convinced the Budd Inlet region could be profitably developed (it later became the site of Olympia, capital city of Washington), Simmons hurried back to the cabin near Vancouver where his family was waiting—where, indeed, his wife in April had given birth to the first American child to be born north of the Columbia. Two single men and four more families joined him, among them that of George Bush, an elderly Quaker mulatto seeking to avoid the provisional government's new strictures against Negroes. Reluctantly McLoughlin gave the adventurers an order for supplies on Fort Nisqually and off they went, industriously chopping a sixty-mile ox-team road through the dense forest between Cowlitz Landing and Tumwater.

Under whose suzerainty did settlements north of the Columbia lie? English law gave officials of the Hudson's Bay Company the authority to try, in courts of their own establishing, misdemeanors committed in company territory and, in the case of felonies, to remand the accused to Canada for hearings. But would American citizens recognize any attempt to exert such authority?

The question was brought to a focus by Henry Williamson, an immigrant of 1844 who had joined Michael Simmons' abortive winter attempt to reach Puget Sound. After his return Williamson in February 1845 persuaded another recent immigrant to join him in a trespass on acreage directly claimed by the company. Within sight of Fort Vancouver itself the pair defiantly piled up a few logs in shape of a hut. On a tree above the shanty Williamson nailed a crude pre-emption notice that he was taking over the land.

McLoughlin ordered logs and sign removed. Williamson and his partner thereupon strode into the fort with demands that the claim be reinstated. When James Douglas, a justice of the peace under Canadian law, threatened the pair with arrest for trespass, they scorned him as lacking authority over American nationals and added dark threats of vigilante action to burn Fort Vancouver to the ground.

Probably it was bluff. But Douglas and McLoughlin had had too much experience with fire to accept that sort of bluff with equanimity. During the drought of the previous September a forest fire set by Indians to help their fall hunting and to stimulate the next year's grass had licked to the very edge of the stockade. Luck and frantic labor had finally checked the sea of flames, but after that experience one could not regard the fort's close-packed wooden buildings without shuddering at the thought of what might happen if another blaze were to be nudged along by something more purposeful than the caprice of the wind.

Hoping that the American spirit of fair play would recognize the company's rights in the matter of the Williamson trespass, McLoughlin and Douglas decided on a direct appeal to the settlers in the Willamette. A circular stating their side of the case was drawn up and distributed throughout the valley. Copies were sent to the three-man executive committee, still functioning until the spring elections should designate a single governor. That body returned a conciliatory reply, Williamson withdrew, and acrimony relaxed.

Nothing basic had been settled, however. Yet there had to be some sort of decision. Michael Simmons was pushing his explorations near the sound; others would inevitably follow; trespasses more serious than Williamson's were certain to result. With national sovereignty still in abeyance, what substitute could be found?

The solution derived was, in large part, the work of Jesse Applegate. Since his arrival in the fall of 1843, Applegate had spent each daylight hour and many a night one building a home, farming, surveying for his neighbors, and turning a neat profit speculating in a herd of California cattle. He did not want political office. But his neighbors thought differently. Without his knowledge they elected him to the legislature in the spring of 1845. Faced with the fact and objecting strenuously to some of the revisions his companions of '43 had made in the constitution, he agreed to serve.

Again the new broom swept vigorously. Out went the act excluding Negroes. (Later, during the agitations for statehood shortly before the Civil War, the ban would be revived.) In went a system of taxation less punitive toward delinquents. (Hard money was so scarce that wheat was accepted as legal tender; another act, in August, extended the acceptance to hides, tallow, beef, pork, lumber, and similar exportable goods.) And, at the insistence of Anglophobes like William Gray, in went an act specifically extending the jurisdiction of the provisional government north of the Columbia. In other words, the Americans were now directly challenging the authority of the Hudson's Bay Company.

McLoughlin's first reaction was to go on acting as if the provisional government did not exist. In Applegate's words, such a dichotomy "was simply organizing internecine war," and he set about healing the split. To obviate premature animosity from Gray's strong anti-British party in the legislature, he met secretly with McLoughlin during one of the factor's visits to the company's (or were they McLoughlin's?) holdings in Oregon City. Forcibly the American pointed out that, so long as ownership of the Northwest remained undetermined, the only recognizable sovereignty was that emanating from the people themselves—in other words from the provisional government. No landholdings, Applegate argued, could be maintained without the sanction of that government. Hence anyone could establish a claim on any unoccupied piece of ground anywhere, even at the very gates of Fort Vancouver, unless forestalled by a prior claim duly recognized by the provisional government. In other words, such trespasses as that committed by Williamson could be repeated at any time, unless the power of the provisional government forbade. And it was a power McLoughlin could hardly invoke without becoming a member of the government.

This exposition of the law might or might not have stood in international court. But it sufficed to do what Applegate wanted it to do;

it "caused the old Gentleman," he wrote his brother, "a night journey of 30 miles to consult his colleagues, and was the main cause of bringing them into the confederation."

Details had to be ironed out. To make the oath to support the provisional government palatable to British consciences, it was amended to include only such things as were "consistent with my duties as a citizen of the United States, or a subject of Great Britain." The company was not to be taxed on its crown-chartered operations, but only on the goods it sold to settlers. And finally, after an acrimonious wrangle in the legislature, it was agreed that the new county north of the Columbia was to be called Vancouver rather than Lewis and Clark. James Douglas of the Hudson's Bay Company was appointed one of the new district's justices of the peace; another, incongruously enough, was illiterate Michael Simmons, just then returning for his family in order to take it with him back to his new claim at Tumwater. And in order to make sure that Fort Vancouver was properly protected, nine loyal company men filed claim, under the provisional government, to nine pieces of ground embracing the company fields and orchards. Now, according to Applegate, there could be no trespass by Americans. Similar steps were projected to defend the choice lands of the Cowlitz and Nisqually farms.

With this recognition of its existence by the subjects of a foreign power, Oregon's homemade government at last achieved full sway. And to make it all legal, the oft-revised laws were at last submitted to and approved by the electorate.

In some respects it was a feat as astounding, politically speaking, as the more highly touted formation, four or five years later, of self-governing bodies by the California miners. No international tensions were at work in California. But war between the United States and Great Britain was a distinct possibility. While international diplomats exchanged stiff notes, while chauvinists in the United States Congress and the British House of Commons hurled inflammatory defiances, the men of Oregon, ignored by their governments, worked out a peaceable solution. It was done sometimes with quarrels made bitter by religious differences and by sectional hatreds brought from home. There were faultfindings, recriminations, visions, and revisions. It might have been chaos. Instead it turned out to be an order that was able to function, without sanction or money or power, until a stronger government finally got around to taking it over.

13. Decision

WHEN McLoughlin in August 1845 agreed to place the company's forts and farms under the jurisdiction of the provisional government, he was performing his last significant act in the Northwest. As far as the company directors were concerned both he and his fort had become anachronisms.

Lying just across the river from a growing American settlement, Fort Vancouver would be vulnerable indeed if war broke out with the United States—and James K. Polk had just been elected President on a platform demanding, among other aggressive items, "the reoccupation of Oregon." As a precautionary move, the company's annual supply vessels were ordered, for the first time in their history, to avoid the Columbia and unload their cargoes at Fort Victoria, the post which Black Douglas had built two years before at the southern tip of Vancouver Island.

McLoughlin, too, was about to be by-passed—with some reason, as has been previously noted. The revenues from the Columbia had dropped sharply. He was still disregarding instructions to close the post at San Francisco and would not be shocked into belated obedience until word of his son-in-law's scandalous suicide reached him in June 1845. The readjustments necessary to shift fur operations northward to Peter Skene Ogden in New Caledonia and to devote himself to the agricultural developments he himself had envisioned—these painful steps he seemed unwilling or unable to take. His annual reports, after paying only perfunctory attention to business, twanged wearisomely about Simpson's calloused treatment of his son's murder at Stikine and about his frustrated efforts to bring the killers to justice.

Meanwhile Douglas and other chief men at Fort Vancouver had been writing in alarm to Simpson about the huge sums in unsecured credit that McLoughlin had been advancing to the destitute American immigrants—humanitarian, yes; but, after all, the men in charge of the Columbia District would be held responsible for the losses. Moreover, Douglas added, McLoughlin was pouring thousands of pounds into the development of the holdings at Willamette Falls, or Oregon City. Since the region would almost certainly go in time to the United States, the expenditures seemed to Douglas and to Simpson an extravagant folly.

The exact status of the Willamette claims had never been clear. In Oregon City, McLoughlin acted as if he personally owned the property, but in his reports to Simpson he sometimes talked as if he was fronting for the company. In an extraordinary letter to the governor on March 20, 1845, he brought the ambiguity to an apex. He sent Simpson drafts totaling £4175. He said he was buying the claims from the company but added that he really did not mean the offer: he was too old to start a new venture and was taking on the property "to further the Interests of the Company and Extend British influence. . . . I find it absolutely necessary to do so to secure us and to prevent its [the real estate's] falling into the possession of others who would make use of the Influence it would give them to injure us." He hoped, he said, that he would not be allowed to suffer personally because of the patriotic purchase.

Blandly Simpson accepted the drafts as a bona fide offer and ordered all company real estate in the Willamette transferred to John McLoughlin.

A conclusion of deliberate malice on Simpson's part is inescapable. The company directors had just written the factor that his salary was to be cut by five hundred pounds a year and that henceforth he was to share management of the Columbia District with James Douglas and Peter Skene Ogden. If one more twist was necessary to make the discredited McLoughlin resign, this action concerning the claims would seem calculated to be it.

Certainly that is the way matters developed. Obediently McLoughlin absorbed the salary cut and the order to share management where once he had reigned alone. He consulted properly with Douglas, who was an old friend, about the propriety of joining the provisional government, and both of them signed the letters of August 14 settling the details.

Ogden, the third member of the new triumvirate, was not on hand to sign, having gone east some months earlier. By the end of August he was back, however, bringing with him what looked like still another of Simpson's insults—two inquisitive individuals named Harry Warre and Mervin Vavasour.

To McLoughlin, Warre and Vavasour were introduced as traveling sportsmen. In spite of natty clothes and fowling pieces, however, the pair were obviously after something other than wild game. They prowled about the fort making sketches and went up into the Willamette asking multitudinous questions about able-bodied males, supplies, politics, national sympathies, and other matters unrelated to hunting. But they did not consult McLoughlin. Stiffly the factor concluded that they were spies sent out by Simpson to check on his activities with the Americans.

Nor was Ogden fully candid. Hurrying to the mouth of the Columbia, he began work on a post that he said was for trade, though he must have known McLoughlin was too familiar with the land to swallow the tale. Then down from a British warship newly arrived in Puget Sound came a young lieutenant named William Peel. Peel, too, asked questions everywhere of everyone—but only casually of McLoughlin. The implications were obvious. Ogden was building a post that could be used as a military fort in case of war. Peel was gathering military information. But because McLoughlin had helped so materially in furthering American strength in Oregon, the British government was not sure of his loyalties and he was not taken into confidence. That, too, hurt.

Then came Simpson's letter selling him the Oregon City claims. In fury McLoughlin replied that he had not intended the offer, which had cost him well over twenty thousand dollars, to be taken seriously. Yet even as he wrote he realized the sale could not be abrogated. Feeling humiliated and cheated, he at last resigned his untenable position, as Simpson must have known he would. On January 4, 1846, he left the great fort he had built and moved up the Willamette to the growing city by the falls.

He was by no means destitute. For several years he would receive profits from his partnership stock in the Hudson's Bay Company. His reluctantly acquired Willamette sawmill he rented for a thousand dollars a year; the other Oregon City property, except for a grist mill he ran himself, he leased for comparable sums. But his heart was heavy. He had assumed as his private responsibility a large part of the debt owed to the company by the immigrants whom he had helped—debts which caused his countrymen, including snoopers Harry Warre and Mervin Vavasour, to suspect him as pro-American. In Oregon City, however, his long connection with the Hudson's Bay Company led the Americans to avoid him as pro-British. And so, as the crisis mounted, he became in this land to which he had devoted more than twenty years of his life a lonely old man without anchor, almost without country.

Henry Warre and Mervin Vavasour were indeed spies—but not, as McLoughlin assumed, sent by Simpson. Rather they were British army lieutenants acting on behalf of the British government, and their presence in the Northwest indicated the point to which relations between Great Britain and the United States had deteriorated.

By nature and by conviction England's Tory Prime Minister, Sir

Robert Peel, and his Foreign Secretary, Lord Aberdeen, were peace-loving men: for one reason, their free-trade dreams could not mature except in an atmosphere of international amity. Determined, therefore, to be patient, the two men at first chose to regard the uproar in the United States over Texas, California, and Oregon, and such antagonistic slogans as "Fifty-four Forty or Fight," as normal if regrettable phases of American election-year fever. To quiet Yankee cries for a Pacific port, the British went so far as to offer this country an enclave on Puget Sound. That being rejected, they suggested international arbitration. Again they were rebuffed. Shortly thereafter the newly elected American President, James K. Polk, declared in his inaugural address that the United States' title to Oregon was "clear and unquestionable." The British press roared in protest; and when Peel's Whig opponents in Parliament took up the cry, the Foreign Office decided that, although peace was wonderful, preparation for war was wisdom.

One immediate result was the delegation of Peter Skene Ogden to take back across Canada, in strictest secrecy, two lieutenants of engineers, Warre and Vavasour, whose mission was to examine the Northwest for "the practicability of forming military stations therein and conveying troops thither." Ogden himself was ordered to establish on the north side of the Columbia's mouth an ostensible trading post that could be quickly turned into a military fort.

As a more open gesture of defiance to the United States, the British Admiralty dispatched to Puget Sound during that tense summer of 1845 the fifty-gun warship *America*, to be followed later by the *Modeste*. By coincidence—or something more—the captain of the *America*, Sir John Gordon, was a brother of the Foreign Secretary, Lord Aberdeen. And on Gordon's staff was Lieutenant William Peel, third son of the British Prime Minister.

In order to obtain a firsthand military view of Oregon, Gordon sent young Peel overland from the sound to examine Fort Vancouver and the American positions in the Willamette Valley. By coincidence—or something more—Peel arrived in time to exchange views with Lieutenants Warre and Vavasour.

The engineers, who had exasperated Ogden with their toplofty airs during the transcontinental crossing, were pessimistic about defending the huge stretch of naked border between the United States and Canada. They doubted the feasibility of transporting any sizable body of troops across the passes, and questioned whether, in the case of conflict, the deficiency could be compensated for by a home militia composed of Fort Vancouver's gentle French Canadians.

Population figures, Lieutenant Peel had meanwhile learned, already favored the Americans. According to Sheriff Joe Meek's somewhat haphazard census, 1259 males and 851 females already inhabited the land south of the Columbia. Another immigration, reputed to be the largest yet, was on the way. Most of the approaching males, like those already in Oregon, would be frontiersmen, far better versed in handling guns than were the Bay Company's French Canadians. Furthermore, if American families could arrive overland in a matter of months, American troops could easily duplicate the movement.

This accumulated information young Peel dutifully took back to his captain at Puget Sound. Gorden, brother of a pacifist Secretary, had already decided that the wilderness he saw from shipboard was not worth fighting for, anyhow. Promptly he decided to dispatch Peel to London, where, as son of the Prime Minister, he was sure to make his report heard. Turning the dull job of watchful waiting over to the *Modeste* (and to the frigate *Fisgard*, due to arrive shortly), Gordon sailed to the Sandwich Islands. There he put Peel aboard a ship to Mexico with instructions that the lieutenant should cross the country as rapidly as possible and catch the first available transport to England.

None of this was known, of course, to the three thousand immigrants struggling across the continent toward crisis in Oregon. They anticipated trouble, for they had left Missouri while frontier jingoism was at white heat. They carried with them wild talk of war and also of exciting bills in Congress for promoting the settlement of the Northwest, even of a breathless proposal that a railway company, financed by land grants, be formed to build a steam-car route from lower Michigan to the Pacific.

The stimulation which these conjectures brought the immigrants soon wore off under the hammer blows of daily traveling. More so than its predecessors, the 1845 crossing was confused and ill prepared, fragmented by quarrels and by the need to spread far and wide for ample game and pasturage. One foolhardy section, deluded by the hope of avoiding both the Blue Mountains of eastern Oregon and the fearsome Dalles of the Columbia, left the main trail for a supposed short cut across the high sage plains east of the Cascades. Thirst, starvation, and mounting panic killed twenty or more of them before the survivors gave up the attempt and crawled weakly down the Deschutes

River to the Dalles, where they rejoined the caravans they had proposed to outdistance.

At the Dalles they were one more snarl in an already terrible congestion. Food was gone, rains threatened, and the only transport was a handful of Hudson's Bay bateaux and one or two ramshackle ferries put into operation by settlers already established. In despair a small group under Samuel K. Barlow broke away from the river and tackled the dense forests and precipitous ridges south of Mount Hood. Soon they had to abandon their vehicles and supplies. Snow caught them. Ragged and exhausted, riding their cows because there were not enough horses to go around, the wayfarers began a shambling race with death.

By the barest of margins they won. In the process they discovered something that had eluded earlier explorations by such veterans as Elijah White and Tom McKay—a pass by which a wagon road could be built across the Cascades.

If war developed, the matter would be vital. Britain controlled the river. The Indians at the portages, obedient to the Hudson's Bay Company, could paralyze travel through the gorge. Farther down the river, outside Fort Vancouver, rode the warship *Modeste*, shifted south from Puget Sound. Although her officers sought to allay American hostility by entertaining influential settlers at shipboard parties and dramatic productions, there was no mistaking the destructive power of those black cannon mouths.

To forestall possible strangulation, the provisional government in the spring of 1846 authorized Barlow to build a toll road along the route he and his party had discovered. The serpentine scratch he created would, for the next several decades, stand the hair of everyone who risked it straight on end. But it *was* usable; it did avoid the Dalles and the Cascades.

It was not enough, however. Other groups sought other routes, but the abysmal chasms and giant forests of the Cascades were too formidable. Only one party succeeded, the Old South Road Company, organized by a man named Levi Scott and by the Applegate brothers, Jesse and Lindsay. Motivated as much by the memory of the children they had lost at the Dalles as by the community's need for war-safe transport, the Applegates pushed with a dozen other men south out of the Willamette into the Umpqua and Rogue River valleys. Working southward and eastward from there, they did something which explorer John Charles Frémont had not been able to manage: they unraveled a way out of the mountains onto the bleak deserts of what is now northern Nevada. They then cut eastward toward the main Oregon Trail at Fort Hall. Indians killed one of them; thirst nearly strangled the rest, but an advance party at last broke through.

At Fort Hall, Jesse Applegate persuaded several travelers that the route he had just discovered was shorter and easier than the normal trail. They swung after him and soon wished they hadn't—through no fault of Jesse's. Heat, short feed, ill-judged stopovers, and quarrels boiling up out of overcharged nerves so delayed the party that winter rains caught them in the dense forests of southern Oregon. The rest of the way was a nightmare of mud and flooded streams. Every foot of the way the Applegates and their "road" were roundly cursed. Yet time would prove that a historic job had been done. Not only had a southern route into Oregon been found—one that would be increasingly improved and used—but also the lands south of the Willamette had been opened to settlement, a movement the Applegates themselves initiated two years later by clearing new farms for their families in the Rogue River and Umpqua valleys.

And still there was no news about what was happening in the East. During the summer the United States warship *Shark* put into the Columbia, but its commander could report only that the Pacific squadron was assembling farther to the south. This might imply anything: war with Mexico, war with England, war with both—or merely maneuvers. Still, the *Shark's* visit was a comforting counter to the *Modeste*, or would have been had not the American vessel embarrassed everyone by wrecking herself on the Columbia's bar, the second United States warship (Wilkes's *Peacock* was the first) to come a cropper at that treacherous passage. One bit of good resulted, however. The *Shark's* flag and cannon were salvaged and taken to the Willamette, to become the colony's first official emblem and armament.

And still there was no news. When the immigrants of '46 arrived, all they could say was that at the time of their departure Congress had been debating a resolution to notify England of the termination of the treaty of joint occupation. Passage of the resolution might be regarded in England as tantamount to a declaration of war. But no one knew, and the fall days dragged by in a welter of suspense.

Anything might have created an inflammatory incident. Fortunately nothing did; for back in Washington and London the once belligerent governments were deciding that they really did not want to fight each other after all.

By spring of 1846 war with Mexico over Texas had become inevitable, and Polk had decided that one conflict at a time was ample. Backing away from his party's cries of Fifty-four Forty or Fight, he let it be known that, since his predecessors had once agreed to accept the forty-ninth parallel as the northern boundary of Oregon, he would consider himself bound by their offer.

The Peel-Aberdeen government acquiesced. Young Peel's report—he had reached London via the Sandwich Islands and Mexico early in 1846—had suggested the difficulty of defending the Northwest against a determined attack. And why defend it? In Aberdeen's words the whole section, except perhaps for Puget Sound, was "a pine swamp." As for the sound, the Americans were justified in wanting a foothold there: they had no other first-class Pacific harbor, for Mexico still held San Francisco Bay and the Columbia's bar rendered that river all but unusable.

Furthermore, British Tories and British businessmen wanted peace, the former to push through Peel's sweeping reforms and the latter to enjoy the nation's recent upsurge of prosperity. Security prices crashed dismally at the mere threat that Palmerston's belligerent Whigs might take over the government and press toward war with the United States. Thus admonished, the Whigs softened their opposition and allowed Aberdeen quietly to inform the American Secretary of State that Polk's suggested boundary, the forty-ninth parallel from the mountains to the ocean, was acceptable. One face-saving compromise only was requested. When the line reached salt water, let it swing south through "the main channel" of the Straits of Georgia to Juan de Fuca and then west to the open sea. This ambiguously worded clause, destined in time to breed future quarrels, would leave all of Vancouver Island (and the Hudson's Bay post of Fort Victoria) securely in English hands.

The treaty was signed on June 15, 1846. No one bothered to notify the Northwest. Their first inkling arrived in a newspaper brought by ship from the Sandwich Islands. Though details of the settlement were lacking, celebrations swept the Willamette, to fade when later advice added that the Hudson's Bay and Puget Sound Agricultural companies had been confirmed in their possessions, choice lands which many an opportunist had been covetously eying. Nor were Douglas, Ogden, and the British traders any less shocked. If population was to determine sovereignty, as they had supposed (and as a continuing fiction still supposes), why should not their companies' thousands of cultivated acres and hundreds of farmers north of the Columbia have brought that section under the British flag?

Disgruntlement for Oregon's Americans increased as 1846 faded into 1847, as the new spring flowed into summer, and still no acknowledgement of their existence came from Washington—no official copies of the treaty, no governor, no territorial laws, nothing. Why? Having at last obtained the long-contested Northwest, did the United States not care enough about it to include it among the nation's other legally constituted territories? What of their land titles, their coinage, their courts, their navigational needs? In particular, what help could they expect in event of trouble with the increasingly restive Indians of the Rogue River Valley and the troublesome Cayuses athwart the immigrant trail east of the Cascades?

Actually, furious congressional debates born of the Wilmot Proviso concerning the extension of slavery had paralyzed all United States territorial organization. But the settlers of the Northwest could see only their neglect. They fumed and wrote memorials and finally, in the fall of 1847, sent to Congress a delegate named J. Quinn Thornton, who had come to Oregon the year before over Applegate's southern route and who never forgave Applegate for the suffering he endured.

Thornton's status was dubious. He was not elected by his constituents but had been appointed by Oregon's provisional governor. As an ex-member of the Methodist mission, Governor Abernethy was automatically suspect among a large segment of the population, and a great howl went up among his enemies about his highhanded avoidance of the democratic process. Before the argument could gain headway, however, a brutal tragedy drove it out of mind and belatedly did what nothing else had been able to achieve—shock the federal government awake to its responsibilities toward its farthest possession.

14. An Era Ends

BY THE close of 1845 the missions east of the Cascades were in danger of collapse, and Henry Harmon Spalding thought he knew why. It was the fault, he sputtered in an angry letter to his Board, of Tom Hill, "a most debassed infidel half breed Deleware, who has been some years in the Mts spreading his poison. . . . Perhaps 1000 have joined his party including 8 or 9 chiefs. They have abandoned all forms of worship."

Actually Tom Hill was a full-blooded Delaware. And he had reason for feeling poisonous. As a boy in the East, where he had learned to read and write and speak good English, he had seen his people despoiled of their homes and sent westward along another trail of broken promises. Tom's own form of escape had been to ride off to the Rockies. There, in 1834, aged twenty-three, he had joined Kit Carson's rollicking free trappers. Later he married a Nez Percé; and in 1839, when falling beaver prices broke up Carson's band, he went to live with his wife's people in a village of buffalo hunters at the head of the Missouri. Soon he assumed leadership. Even for a Delaware he was exceptionally tall and powerful. He was handsome; his black hair fell, when loosened, to the bend of his knees. And he had learned many useful things from the whites—different things from those being taught by the missionaries on the western side of the Rockies.

In 1845 his village crossed back over the mountains to their native land along the Clearwater. There Hill's virulence against the whites fastened itself on the missionary farms at Lapwai and Waiilatpu.

Many of the Nez Percés and the Cayuses were ready to listen to him. For nearly a decade now several of their tribesmen had sincerely endeavored to learn the white man's medicine. Warriors had stooped to such unnatural labor as hoeing in the fields and carrying logs on their backs for Spalding's cabin. They had cooped up their children in school. At times they had even suffered the hot-tempered Spalding (and, less frequently, Whitman also) to put them to the lash for peccadilloes.

None of it, as Tom Hill pointed out, seemed to do much good. In exchange for potatoes they had given up the zest of the annual buffalo hunt beyond the mountains. In worrying about their souls they had learned to fear hell.

This last dread had been intensified by the advent of the Catholics at the Hudson's Bay forts of Walla Walla and Colvile. As a teaching aid the Jesuits had evolved a pictorial "ladder," some versions of which were eight or ten feet tall and two or more feet wide. Transverse bars and colored dots represented the long ages of man's spiritual progress since the creation. Lateral branches of apostasy, notably Protestantism, were portrayed as leading to the everlasting flames of the Pit.

In order to counteract the impact of this visual demonstration, Henry and Eliza Spalding drew a terrifying six-foot ladder of their own. On it the road of Catholicism was the one that led to perdition. Quite naturally many of the Indians were confused and worried, seeing only the red fires of hell as a penalty for a mistake in choosing. Others grew cynical: why not worship according to profits? One

Nez Percé told Spalding that he would pray a whole year just for a coat and shirt. As for Tom Hill, he said that all white religion was nonsense.

He also said that the preachers were cheating the Indians in more material ways. Had not Samuel Parker promised, during his amazing solo trip through the mountains, that many benefits would flow to the Indians from allowing stations to be established on their lands? Parker had no doubt meant spiritual benefits, but Tom understood— or pretended to understand—something different. If one white man used another white man's land and wood and water, the user paid rent. But what rent were the missions paying?

Then there was the matter of the laws that had been imposed on the tribes during Whitman's famous ride to the East. These had come about after a Cayuse had tried to break into Narcissa's bedroom. Terrified, she had fled with a Hudson's Bay escort to the Methodist station at the Dalles, taking with her the half-breed daughters of Joe Meek and Jim Bridger and an orphaned boy whom she had adopted a short time before. While she was gone the mill at Waiilatpu had burned down. These outrages, together with reports of general restlessness among the Indians east of the Cascades, had led Sub-agent Elijah White to bustle across the mountains to enforce peace.

Always the United States had dealt with the Indian tribes as if they were individual nations. If no tribal government existed to treat with, one was imposed. In pursuit of this mischievous policy, Elijah White persuaded first the Nez Percés and later the more sullen Cayuses to elect a head chief and sub-chiefs (thereby creating intense jealousies), and then had made these chiefs responsible for enforcing a code of laws presented to the tribal councils by himself and by Tom McKay of the Hudson's Bay Company.

Under these laws death by hanging was prescribed as the punishment for murder or for the willful burning of a dwelling. Lesser crimes were to be punished by whippings administered by the chiefs. In the case of conflicts between whites and Indians, the guilty party would be punished by the agent—or so White promised.

Matters did not work out that way, however. Shortly after the adoption of the laws a party of Spokanes, Cayuses, and Walla Wallas suddenly decided to go to California and trade for cattle. At Sutter's Fort on the Sacramento a white man killed the truculent son of Chief Peu-peu-mox-mox, or Yellow Serpent, of the Walla Wallas. Indignation swept the tribes of the Columbia Basin. There was excited talk of sending an army of two thousand warriors to plunder California in revenge, a threat that created panic along the Sacramento and brought Elijah White hurrying back for still more conferences.

By fast talk White broke up the plans for the avenging army, which the erratic savages probably could not have formed in any event. But he did not punish the murderer of Peu-peu-mox-mox's son. To the resentful Indians his explanation that United States jurisdiction did not reach into Mexican California seemed pure subterfuge. Either the laws meant what they said or, as Tom Hill pointed out, the code was just another white man's cheat.

And finally there was the matter of the immigrants. The missionaries insisted that they had built their stations in the West to help the Indians. But the words sounded hollow when Whitman made his hurried ride to the East and then returned with the greatest number of whites the Indians had ever seen—just as though that were his purpose in going. The next year, in 1844, the doctor reinforced their suspicions by meeting the wayfarers with a pack-train load of supplies; and in 1845, Spalding added flour and vegetables from Lapwai. Yet the mission farms were supposedly for the Indians.

The Cayuses did reap some profits by trading food and game with the immigrants for clothing. But along with the gain went frictions. The Indians resented the littered campsites, the slain deer, the injured grass. They grew arrogant and often the whites responded with surprising meekness, for a man with a worn outfit and a frightened family was not eager for trouble. Contemptuously the Cayuses and the Indians at the Dalles began bullying small parties and stealing horses. In retaliation the whites seized replacement stock from unguarded Indian herds, and the bitterness grew.

The Nez Percés, who lived farther from the trail than did the Cayuses and Walla Wallas, were not often involved in these petty clashes. But Tom Hill made certain that his adopted tribesmen stayed aware of the broader implications. Look at the Willamette, he said. Its disease-ridden Indians had all but disappeared. How long before a similar decimation started here? How long before the destitute whites to whom Whitman and Spalding gave shelter each winter began staying permanently, as the doctor obviously hoped some would?

In the fall of 1845 the Cayuses invited Tom Hill to come to the Walla Walla Valley and talk to them. Getting wind of the visit, Whitman boiled up a huge kettle of mush and tallow and invited Tom and several Cayuse chiefs to dinner in the mission house—a conciliatory gesture the unbending Spalding had never made. Afterward Tom admitted that Whitman was a fair sort, and one can't help wondering what might have resulted if the acquaintanceship had developed.

Unfortunately it didn't. In January 1846, Peu-peu-mox-mox, the Yellow Serpent, led another party of Walla Wallas and related Cayuses to California on a trading and hunting trip. Tom went along, perhaps because he had somehow learned that Carson and several Delaware scouts were down that way with Frémont. When the Mexican War broke out, Hill enlisted at Sutter's Fort, being received into a company of white volunteers at the white man's pay of twenty-five dollars a month. (Peu-peu-mox-mox and nine of his Walla Wallas joined a company of Indian scouts at the Indian pay of six dollars a month.) Tom never returned. After fighting throughout the war with considerable dash, he drifted east into Kansas and died among his own people, the Delawares. But the words he had spoken stayed long in the minds of the Western Indians.

Peu-peu-mox-mox and his party remained in California until the summer of 1847. As they were starting home a deadly epidemic of measles swept their camp. In horror an advance emissary pushed ahead to the Walla Walla, bearing a long list of casualties. Soon wailing messengers were hurrying from village to village apprising the tribes of the fatal encounter with the white man's disease.

It was an ominous introduction to the four thousand or more persons who made up the migration of 1847. For when the wagons began straggling out of the Blue Mountains they brought measles with them. As a result more than half the Cayuse tribe died in conditions of unutterable filth and misery.

Whitman did what he could, though at the time his own affairs were devouring most of his time. He had just purchased the Methodist station at the Dalles, partly to keep the increasingly active Jesuits from getting it, and the transfer had to be put in order. He was involved in transporting equipment upriver for a new grist mill at Waiilatpu and in establishing a sawmill in the Blue Mountains. As usual, a number of destitute immigrants had congregated at his station. By the end of November he and Narcissa were providing for nearly sixty persons at Waiilatpu and for another dozen at the sawmill in the mountains.

Among the hangers-on was a half-breed French Canadian from Maine named Joe Lewis. Sensing the resentment of the stricken Cayuses for the whites, Lewis made capital for himself by whispering that the epidemic was part of Whitman's plot to steal the Indians' land by killing off the tribe. As proof, did it not seem strange that most of the whites whom the doctor treated recovered, whereas most of the Cayuses did not? Was the tribe turning into milk? What of the old custom that demanded a medicine man's life in forfeit for the death of a patient?

Some of the Indians still depended on the doctor for help, however. On Saturday, November 27, Whitman received a call from a lodge in the Umatilla Valley, thirty-odd miles to the southwest. He wondered whether he should go. Several of the people at the mission were sick, including three of the seven orphaned Sager children whom he and Narcissa had adopted. Besides, Indians were dying each day within sight of his own walls. These pressing needs demanded his presence at home. But a Catholic mission had just moved into the Umatilla and he feared its influence. Reluctantly he decided he would have to heed the call.

Spalding, who had recently journeyed down from Lapwai to deliver seventeen mule loads of grain and to put his daughter in the Waiilatpu school, went with him. As the two rode through the stormy night Spalding's horse fell, wrenching the rider's knee. Because of the injury he accepted, amicably enough, an invitation to spend the following night at the Catholic mission. Whitman, however, felt he must return straight home from his calls on the sick Indians. Borrowing a mule from the Catholics to replace his own jaded mount, he hurried off through the early November dusk.

Toward midnight he reached Waiilatpu. Narcissa was still up, watching Helen Meek and one of her adopted daughters, Louise Sager, both of them desperately ill. She seemed so exhausted that Marcus, who had had little enough sleep himself, sent her to bed and continued the vigil until breakfast. The meal finished, he went wearily outside to arrange for killing a beef. It was a dark, foggy day.

The butchering under way, he came into the kitchen where seventeen-year-old John Sager was winding twine. For a time Marcus napped in a chair. Then two Indians knocked at the door, asking for medicine. As he turned to fetch it one of them struck him with a tomahawk. He spun around to grapple with his assailant, and John Sager jumped for a pistol on the wall. The boy was shot dead. Whitman was dragged outside, still fighting, and dropped mortally wounded beside his doorstep. Simultaneously other Indians fell upon the men who were butchering the beef. Hearing the noise, Narcissa ran to a window. A musket shot shattered her arm.

For a time those inside the house held the Indians at bay. Then an emissary told them the building was to be burned and offered them safe conduct outside. Narcissa, who had fainted, was put on a wooden settee. A Mrs. Hayes and a man named Rodgers carried her through the door. As they appeared the Indians opened fire. Rodgers fell. Narcissa, struck by several bullets, rolled from the settee. An Indian seized her by the long golden hair that had so disturbed the mountain men at the gay rendezvous a dozen years before, lifted her, and beat her across the face with his quirt.

She was the only woman killed. Twelve males were massacred, however, and the two sick girls, Louise Sager and Helen Meek, soon died for want of attention. Six persons escaped, one of whom drowned in the Columbia River. Another, named Canfield, fled wounded through the hills to warn the station at Lapwai, a hundred and twenty miles away. The remainder—thirty-four children, eight women, and five men captured at the sawmill—were held as hostages. Some of the older girls were, in the euphemistic wording of the day, taken as wives by certain of the Indians. Otherwise there was little abuse, save for inadequate food and a continual, hideous fear about what was to happen next.

When word of the massacre reached Father Brouillet at the Catholic mission he set out with a single interpreter, an Indian, to see what he could do. With the suspicious Cayuses watching him, it was not much. He helped bury the mutilated corpses, offered solace to the bereaved, and through the interpreter pled with the Indians to shed no more blood. Then, with a son of one of the chiefs tagging along to keep an eye on him, he started back to Umatilla to intercept Spalding.

Just outside Waiilatpu he met the missionary, wild with anxiety about his daughter. Brouillet assured him the girl was alive and urged him to flee at once, for the chief's son had already galloped back to tell the others that Spalding was available.

Thanks to the early darkness and the fog, the would-be victim escaped and turned toward Lapwai. Unfortunately he fell into an exhausted sleep without hobbling his horse and the animal ran away. The remaining ninety miles he walked, foodless and tortured by his wrenched knee and ill-fitting shoes. On the sixth day he crept up to the bluffs overlooking his home. Indians were plundering it. For an agonizing few hours he thought that his family, too, had been massacred, but finally he reached a friendly Nez Percé who told him that Canfield's warning had arrived in time: Eliza and the mission workers had found refuge at the home of William Craig, a mountain man who had settled nearby with his Nez Percé wife. There Spalding joined them.

Loyal Nez Percés, many of whom were genuinely fond of Eliza Spalding, put a strong guard around Craig's farm. The protection was not all for the sake of the refugees, however. The Nez Percés, foreseeing violent reaction by the Oregon settlers, were evolving a bargain. Why couldn't the white prisoners held by them and by the Cayuses be used as a lever to persuade the big chiefs of Oregon— Governor Abernethy and the leaders of the provisional government —to come without troops to a peace council?

Runners were dispatched to ask the Cayuses what they thought of the idea. Spalding felt it was sound. Unbalanced by the terrors of the recent days, he even tried to further the plan by writing agitated letters to the Catholics at Umatilla and to William McBean, the Hudson's Bay trader at Fort Walla Walla, urging that they use their influence to keep troops away from the country. If war broke out, he said, his mission would be razed and his family slain. [1]

On receipt of the letter the Jesuits called a meeting of the Cayuse chiefs. By now the Indians were beginning to realize that the massacre might increase rather than lessen their difficulties, and the Nez Percé plan looked like an escape. Accordingly they said that they were willing to forget the deadly measles and the murder of Peu-peu-mox-mox's son if the Americans would forget Whitman's death and would not send troops into the region. They also asked that immigrants cease traveling through their lands.

At this point Peter Skene Ogden and sixteen heavily armed Hudson's Bay men arrived at Fort Walla Walla. Their coming was the company's reply to a messenger whom trader McBean had sent down the Columbia immediately on learning of the massacre. The man had reached Fort Vancouver the evening of December 6. Though the matter was essentially a problem for the American settlers, Douglas and Ogden had not wasted time going up the Willamette to Oregon City to consult with the provisional government. They knew the tempers of the Americans. The minute the news was released a punitive expedition would almost certainly set out; and in blind reaction the Indians might well kill any survivors yet alive at Waiilatpu. Indeed, anything white might fall under the savages' fury, including the company's undermanned posts beyond the mountains.

To rescue the living and to fortify Walla Walla, Ogden straightway

[1] The publication of this letter by the Catholics some weeks later put Spalding in a craven light in Oregon. His resentment perhaps explains in part the genesis of his later charges that the Whitman massacre was fomented by an unholy cabal of papists and the Hudson's Bay Company. Unhappily, many of the settlers were willing to believe him and the bitterness engendered persisted throughout the rest of the century.

hurried up the river. When there was no possibility of meddlers over-taking him, Douglas forwarded word of the Waiilatpu disaster to Governor Abernethy.

Ogden reached Walla Walla on December 19. Summoning the chiefs, he rejected all their efforts to bargain and said bluntly, "The company have nothing to do with your quarrel. If you wish it, on my return I will see what can be done for you; but I do not promise to prevent a war. Deliver me the prisoners to return to their friends, and I will pay you a ransom, that is all."

Such was the force of his character and of the company he repre-sented that he carried the point. In return for five hundred dollars' worth of shirts, blankets, guns, ammunition, flints, and tobacco—an expenditure never repaid to the company—the Cayuses handed over the captives at Waiilatpu. Runners were sent to Lapwai for Spalding's group, and early in January Ogden led the rescued, most of them still incoherent from the terror of their ordeal, down the river to the Willamette, there to remake their lives as best they could.

In the Willamette the settlers were reacting as furiously as Ogden and Douglas had anticipated. Within twenty-four hours a volunteer company of forty-five men had formed to march to the Dalles and occupy that strategic station against attack. With equal promptness the provisional government, which had little authority and less money, set about the frustrating task of raising and equipping an army of five hundred men.

In order to secure federal help the legislature decided to send Joe Meek overland to Washington. Physically, Meek was an obvious choice: thirty-seven years old, six feet tall, strong as a buffalo. An ex-mountain man, he knew every foot of the dangerous way. But what appealed even more to the lawmakers was the fact that Joe had served as a member of their own group, where he had allied himself with the anti-mission party against Governor Abernethy. Abernethy, it will be recalled, had appointed his own delegate to Congress, Jessy Quinn Thornton; and now Abernethy's opponents saw a heaven-sent opportunity to counteract Thornton's influence. For Joe Meek, in-credibly enough, was related to President Polk's wife and thus would be able to get into the White House itself.

Abernethy wanted the messenger to travel via the Sacramento, so that Joe could ask the military governor of army-occupied California for supplies, for whatever troops could be spared, and for a warship to patrol the Columbia. Meek, however, doubted the possibility of crossing the Siskiyou Mountains between Oregon and California in the dead of winter. [2] Besides, he was the legislature's messenger, not Abernethy's. He'd go the route they authorized, over the regular Oregon Trail, though it meant waiting for an escort of troops to clear a way through the land of the Cayuses.

With about as much efficiency as could be expected from an amateur government's first experience with war, the volunteer army began to assemble and move with its inadequate supply barges up the Columbia. At this point it occurred to the provisional government that if all the tribes of the interior were to unite against them the outnumbered soldiers would have bitten off far more hostility than they could chew. Manifestoes were thereupon issued declaring that this really wasn't a war but an expedition to capture the murderers of the whites slain at Waiilatpu. This curious ambivalence vastly annoyed the volunteers' fire-breathing colonel, who thundered that he had enlisted to fight, and resulted in explosive quarrels between him and a trio of peace commissioners traveling with him to mollify the enemy and to restrain undue zeal on the part of the troops.

The expedition caught no murderers. But the soldiers did serve their main purpose by preventing any general outbreak. They soundly whipped the Cayuses in the few skirmishes that developed; and in the process of marching back and forth across hundreds of miles of Indian territory they made a strong enough show so that the wavering tribes of the interior decided to listen to the overtures of the peace commission.

On the last day of February the marchers reached the burned ruins of Waiilatpu. There they reinterred the bones that wolves had dug from the shallow graves. What thoughts Joe Meek had about the half-breed daughter whom he had left with the Whitmans seven years before are not on record. But it is known that he cut from Narcissa's skull a lock of golden hair for a keepsake.

In early March a hundred soldiers escorted Joe and nine companions beyond Cayuse territory to the Blue Mountains. For added protection each envoy wore the respected Scotch cap and red belt of the Hudson's Bay Company. Weather, however, and not savages afforded the opposition. On the Bear River in southeastern Idaho the messengers

2 Meek was right in his estimate. When Abernethy realized the messenger was going to do things his own way, the governor dispatched stout Jesse Applegate southward with a party of sixteen experienced frontiersmen. Seven feet of snow in the Siskiyou Mountains forced them to abandon their horses. Carrying beds and food on their own backs, they tried to bull through on improvised snowshoes, could not make it, and turned back.

had to kill one of their horses for food and break out trail for the other animals on snowshoes woven from willow twigs, five or six laborious miles a day. Below-zero cold dogged them through Wyoming and out onto the plains. Along the lower Platte the weather warmed, but they had to travel at night for fear of the restless Sioux. Despite these handicaps they reached Missouri in early May, just as the first emigrant trains were striking out for the West.

On May 17, Joe was in St. Louis. He was dirty, whiskery, ragged. With an instinctive flair for the dramatic he decided to stay that way. Complete in greasy buckskins and blanket capote, he announced himself as "Envoy Extraordinary and Minister Plenipotentiary from the Republic of Oregon to the Court of the United States," and headed for the White House.

It was a sensational journey, well calculated to highlight the horror of the news he carried. Taking Meek at his own estimate as a character, the newspapers played up his melodramatic journey and then unlimbered their guns on Congress: if the lawmakers had not failed in their duty to organize and protect Oregon, the massacre might never have happened.

President Polk received his in-law immediately and the next day presented to Congress the eloquent memorial Joe had brought from the provisional government. Congress, however, was in no mood to be stampeded by rhetoric. The Oregon treaty with Great Britain and the victory over Mexico had abruptly increased the land area of the United States by fifty per cent. Organizing this vast domain would have been a nettlesome problem at best. In 1848 it was further snarled by the question of the extension of slavery. All summer the debate raged. Not until the Oregon bill was broken loose from those dealing with California and New Mexico was it finally passed and signed into law by Polk on August 14, 1848.

As marshal of the new territory President Polk selected Joe Meek. As governor he appointed Joseph Lane of Indiana. Wiry and handsome, gifted with a silver tongue and a world of physical courage, Lane had achieved a dashing reputation as a brigadier general in the Mexican War. Though his detractors scoffed that there was no profundity beneath all the glitter, even they conceded that he was a shrewd politician and a tireless worker. He needed to be tireless. Polk wanted Oregon Territory organized before the expiration of his term on March 4. But a fall crossing might mean snow in the mountains; accordingly Meek, with the Bear River drifts chill in his memory, proposed to the governor-designate that they avoid the snow by a long swing southward through the newly conquered provinces of Mexico.

Ten wagons escorted by twenty-five mountain men and soldiers carried the governor's entourage down the famed Santa Fe Trail. In New Mexico the party switched its baggage to pack mules, rode south along the Rio Grande almost to El Paso, then turned west through Tucson to the Colorado River, which they crossed on rafts made of bulrushes, their horses swimming behind. In Los Angeles they were caught up by incredible rumors of gold. In San Francisco the rush itself engulfed them. Scores of men whom Joe had last seen in Oregon were thronging the wharves with bags of gold dust, eager to return to their once poverty-stricken homes.

In company with several of these excited argonauts, Lane, Meek and the other officials sailed to the mouth of the Columbia. There head winds so delayed their ship that they switched to canoes. With the new governor and marshal taking their turns at the paddles, they toiled a hundred and twenty miles upstream to Oregon City. They were barely in time. On March 3, 1849, one day before the expiration of Polk's term, Joseph Lane formally declared Oregon to be a territory of the United States.

It was a significant change for the once orphaned land, but not so significant as the miracles soon to be wrought by the golden excitement in the south.

Book Four

THE PANGS OF ADJUSTMENT

1. The Magic Wand

THE overwhelming fact of the Oregon which Joe Meek had left in 1848 was her isolation. Almost nothing came overland into the territory except personal possessions, and most of these were worn out by the time the weary owners reached their promised land. Sometimes replenishment could be found at Fort Vancouver, sometimes at the stores set up on the lower Willamette by Yankee ship captains. But sometimes there was nothing at all. In 1848 the Hudson's Bay Company's annual supply brig was wrecked on the Columbia bar, and not a single independent trading vessel appeared that summer to relieve the pinch.

Clothing was a perpetual problem, with ill-fitting buckskin, canvas from discarded tents and wagon covers, and scratchy homespun from coarse local wool furnishing the most common materials. Cooking was done mostly in fireplaces, dishes were carved from wood, and everyday furniture was thrown together out of split cedar. Mothers doctored their families with herbs (teas of sage and tansy or poultices of onions or mustard), with whiskey (mixing in peppermint for an ointment for burns or salt for a gargle, and using it straight as a disinfectant), with superstition (rubbing bacon rind over a patient's body for scarlet fever), and with blithe disregard for elementary antisepsis (using cobwebs to stanch bleeding).

Tools were largely limited to what a man could swing with his own hands. Farms were consequently small. Laboriously the ground was cleared and the slash burned in the dry days after harvest, so that during late September the whole Willamette lay blurred under a dingy-copper, acrid-smelling haze of smoke. Wheat was the money crop, sown just before the winter rains and reaped the following summer with scythe and clumsy cradle. Flour was easier to ship than grain, and so mills sprang up wherever there was water power. If no mill was near, a man bagged his grain and hauled it over poor roads to the nearest river landing, there to load it on raft or barge or sail-rigged keelboat.

There was little currency. Small transactions were conducted by barter or by promises to pay in cattle, timber, or labor at some future time. Larger deals were based on warehouse receipts for stored wheat, the price of which steadily declined as the swelling numbers of immigrants began raising more grain than the Hudson's Bay Company could absorb. Still another drag on business was the erratic mail service. Letters were carried by private persons at prices based mostly on dickering. Although the United States Government belatedly scheduled a steamship run via the Horn, the first mail vessels were sidetracked by the gold rush and never reached Oregon.

Into this stultifying isolation there sailed, on July 31, 1848, the schooner *Honolulu*. Instead of bringing goods to the hungry community the captain purchased all the provisions he could lay hands on, plus every available pick, shovel, and crowbar. At first he said he was outfitting prospectors who were exploring for coal for the mail steamers, but after he had cornered the market he admitted the truth: an ill-favored immigrant named James Marshall, who had reached Oregon in '44 and a year later had drifted into California, had found gold at Sutter's mill on the American River.

Later ships confirmed the news and the stampede was on. Vessels touching at the Columbia were besieged for room; the cost of a deck passage, wherein a man fed himself and often slept between piles of lumber, soared from thirty to a hundred dollars. Stampeders unable to pay such prices hurried southward first with pack strings and then with wagon trains. Settlers from the newly opened Puget Sound region goaded their ox-drawn wagons back over the low divide to the Cowlitz River, loaded animals and vehicles on flatboats, disembarked on the south shore of the Columbia, and hurried in the wake.

That fall only nine out of twenty-three legislators appeared in the capital and the session had to be postponed for lack of a quorum. Newspapers ceased publication for want of printers, and acres of crops lay rotting in the laboriously cleared fields.

But it was worth it. Of the hundreds of thousands of rainbow chasers who poured into California from the entire world, the Oregonians fared best. They arrived early, while cream could still be skimmed. Those traveling overland helped to open and drain the virgin fields in the northern part of the state. By wintertime scores of them had filled their pokes with a thousand or five thousand or even ten thousand dollars' worth of dust. Married men in particular began drifting back home. Most of them traveled with another rainbow in their eyes. California was a gluttonous market for every kind of food, for every sort of lumber from shingles to pilings, for manufactured goods of any kind. The last items the Northwest could not supply, but the first two she could produce in plenty.

An estimated two million dollars in gold dust flowed into once moneyless Oregon during the early months of 1849. So did barrelfuls of Mexican and Peruvian silver dollars, imported to handle exchange. Instead of an occasional vessel tiptoeing across the Columbia's bar, more than fifty pushed into the river in 1849, with twenty tied up at one time in October waiting for cargoes that could not be supplied fast enough to meet the demand.

Ports with adequate facilities boomed—Portland, for a prize example. In 1846, Captain John Couch of Cushing and Company's trading firm grew tired of bucking the Clackamas Rapids below Oregon City, found a place lower down the Willamette River where deep water lay conveniently close to the bank, and said that here was the spot for oceangoing ships to unload. He took up a claim there, others moved in (one of the original town platters sold out for five thousand dollars' worth of tanned buckskin), and when the rush came they were ready. They built a covered wharf so that goods could be handled during the winter rains, lured in the Northwest's first steam sawmill in 1850, and the next year spent tens of thousands of farsighted dollars laying an all-weather road paved with planks to tap the rich farms of the Tualatin Plains. Meanwhile Oregon City, hemmed between rapids and falls, languished in spite of her water power. In 1851 she even ceased being the capital when the government offices were moved to Salem, partly through the machinations of the old mission party.

Although the territorial legislature continually memorialized Congress for help in road building, little was done and the rivers continued to be the vital highways of commerce. Steamers appeared, side-wheelers at first and then stern-wheelers, which were better adapted to the Western rivers. Shallow-draft boats that all but walked across sand bars pushed the head of navigation farther and farther up the Willamette, bringing prosperity to more and more towns. Restless pioneers could now move farther out and did. In 1849, Jesse Applegate and some of his road-blazing companions of '46 crossed from the Willamette into the grassy valleys breaking toward the Umpqua. In one of them, at the foot of a great bare knoll called Yoncalla, Jesse built pioneer Oregon's showiest home. But his brother Lindsay was still dissatisfied and pushed on almost to the California border before settling near present Ashland on a stream already named Applegate in memory of his having panned for gold there one day in 1848.

An inflationary spiral swept prices upward. Speculators reaped handsomely. Money jingled in the pockets of farmers and laborers, and their own demands for better goods increased the economic pressures. The provisional government decided to establish a mint. This Joe Lane properly declared unconstitutional as soon as he arrived, whereupon a private group coined fifty thousand dollars in five- and ten-dollar gold pieces to bring some sort of order to the chaotic money mess. It was not a profitable venture. The unalloyed gold coins proved to be worth about eight per cent more than their face value and soon disappeared from circulation.

So much energy so suddenly released needed the control of an energetic governor. Whatever his other faults, Joe Lane was that. An ardent Democrat and a personal friend of Polk's, he knew he would lose his job if the Whigs gained control in Washington. But instead of marking time until the election results reached him, he immediately summoned the legislature to deal with the tangled economy. He ordered the election of a delegate to Congress to replace Abernethy's private appointee, and told Joe Meek to take a census. In his corollary job as superintendent of Indian affairs, he hurried to the Dalles to talk to a delegation of discontented savages. They had scarcely been placated when he learned that Snoqualmie Indians had attacked the Hudson's Bay post of Fort Nisqually on Puget Sound, killing two Americans in the process. Lane rushed north, started the machinery going to apprehend the murderers, and then returned to meet a contingent of American troops just arrived by sea.

A military reservation had to be provided for the soldiers. Unfortunately the act creating Oregon Territory had done nothing about settling land titles. Where could barracks be put with an assurance that future litigation or Indian treaties would not displace them?

The lands of the Hudson's Bay and Puget Sound Agricultural companies offered a solution. The treaty with Great Britain had said that the intertwined firms were to be confirmed in their possessions, which seemed to imply sound title. James Douglas, moreover, had just shifted his headquarters from Fort Vancouver to Victoria, and part of the now unused acreage on the Columbia was open for sale. And so Vancouver Barracks, military headquarters of the Northwest, took shape on land once belonging to the fur company. A subsidiary post,

Fort Steilacoom, was built near Puget Sound on a meadow once claimed by the agricultural company.

Meanwhile another regiment was traveling overland from Fort Leavenworth. Cholera, desertions, and plain boneheadedness quickly thinned its ranks. In one injudicious attempt to run a raftload of supplies through the rapids at the Cascades, six soldiers were drowned and four or five tons of goods lost. An attempted land passage around Mount Hood resulted in heavy damage to worn wagons and exhausted stock. All told, the regiment reached its destination short seventy men, forty-six vehicles, and three hundred and fifty head of livestock. Living quarters at Vancouver not being ready for them, they were quartered in Oregon City, where they made themselves obnoxious with drunkenness and petty arrogance. During the winter more than a hundred deserted in a body to go to the gold mines. Governor Lane and a group of volunteers joined Colonel Loring in a pursuit that captured eighty of the defectors. Some of the remainder escaped in homemade canoes; others perished in the snowy mountains on the California border. When finally the obstreperous regiment was moved out of Oregon City in the spring, the relieved citizenry celebrated by burning down their noisome shelters.

The arrival of so many troops and the promises of a spring campaign so depressed the Cayuse Indians that they finally surrendered five of the actual Waiilatpu murderers, along with fifty horses to pay for their defense. Lane went up to the Dalles to receive the prisoners and made arrangements for their trial. Though unavoidably conducted in an atmosphere of supercharged emotionalism, it seems to have been a fair one. All five defendants were found guilty. Lane signed their death warrants and on June 3, 1850, they were officially hanged by the father of one of their incidental victims, little Helen Meek.

Joe Lane did not see the unhappy ending. By this time he knew that he was to be replaced as governor by a Whig appointee, John P. Gaines. Rather than be officially fired, he wrote out his resignation, to be effective June 18, 1850. Before the date arrived, the Rogue Indians in southern Oregon began acting up. Lane might justifiably have let the problem wait for his replacement but that wasn't his way. Immediately he headed south with an escort of fifteen whites and fifteen Klickitat Indians from a warlike people who had once inhabited the headwaters of the Cowlitz River under Mount Rainier but about 1840 had moved into the Willamette, elbowing aside the apathetic remnants of its original tribes.

The Rogues agreed to a council, apparently with secret intentions of seizing the white chief. But the Klickitats were too fast for them. At the first intimation of trouble Lane's Indians seized the Rogue chief and put a knife to his throat. During the moment's paralysis which this gave the chief's tribesmen, Lane walked boldly among them, striking the weapons from their hands. After that the Rogues talked turkey, though later events made results negligible. The victimized chief was so impressed by Lane's courage that he presented the ex-governor with a young Modoc prisoner to be his slave.

A Southern sympathizer, Lane saw nothing wrong with this. He took the boy along when he led his party on south to prospect for gold in the vast, canyon-split mountains below the Oregon-California border. He was still prospecting the following winter when an emissary reached him from the Oregon capital. Would Lane be willing to stand for election as Oregon's delegate to Congress in opposition to the mischief-making incumbent, Samuel Thurston?

Lane, to whom politics was the one real zest in life, said he would.

Even as he spoke, he must have known that he was letting himself in for the confusions, challenges, and recriminations that attend any period of violent adjustment. Oregon in the 1850s would be no exception. Sam Thurston, battening on trouble, had seen to that.

2. Assorted Frankensteins

AS DELEGATE from a territory, young Samuel R. Thurston, Oregon's first legally elected representative to the Congress of the United States, had no vote. But he could participate in debates, and on strictly territorial matters his voice possessed influence. Tirelessly Thurston used that voice—it was a glib one—in promoting one of the most significant and at the same time most mischievous bits of federal legislation connected with the early Northwest. This was the Donation Land Law, passed on September 27, 1850, to remedy a glaring omission in the original act creating Oregon Territory.

At the time of organizing the territory Congress had been at odds with itself over a basic land policy for the huge, unsettled acreage so recently added to the public domain. Originally the federal government had looked upon such lands as a source of revenue and had sold them at a relatively modest fee to interested settlers. Should this policy be continued? Should the Western states and territories be given a share of the proceeds—perhaps even the entire administration of the unoccupied lands within their borders? Or should the national government undertake to encourage Western migration by giving the land away free to prospective settlers?

Unable to reach a decision at the time of the original Oregon bill, the lawmakers contented themselves with declaring null and void all land laws of Oregon's provisional government but substituted nothing in their place. To the Northwest this was intolerable. They wanted their titles unclouded—and free.

Under Thurston's prodding Congress at length passed a stopgap measure based upon the abortive legislation which Senator Linn of Missouri had proposed a decade earlier. Under the terms of the bill each resident white or half-breed settler who was a citizen of the United States or who within a year declared his intention of becoming a citizen could receive 320 acres in his own name and, if married, another 320 acres in the name of his wife. Although designed to be temporary (the law applied only to the Northwest, was first scheduled to expire in 1853, and then had its life extended to 1855), the Donation Act was a long step toward establishing the nation's unoccupied territory as a free commodity, open to every citizen willing to work for it—a policy that culminated in Lincoln's Homestead Act of 1862.

The law was also the father of monsters. Sam Thurston was a demagogue. He had arrived in Oregon as recently as 1847, with both eyes and both ears open for the main chance. He saw the entrenched power of Abernethy's old mission party; he heard the rumbles which followed Henry Spalding's baseless charge that the Hudson's Bay Company and the Catholics had together been responsible for the Whitman massacre. These charges Thurston blatantly echoed in Washington. His particular target was John McLoughlin, former factor of the Hudson's Bay Company, a convert, in 1842, to Catholicism—and a claimant, against the leaders of the mission party, to the most valuable landholdings in Oregon City.

In an effort to strengthen his hold on the contested claim, McLoughlin had already declared his intention of becoming an American citizen. Ignoring this, Thurston inserted in the Donation Act a notorious clause which vested ownership of the island at Willamette Falls in a milling company that held title from the old Methodist mission. The same clause further declared that the rest of McLoughlin's unsold building lots were to be placed at the disposal of the territorial legislature, proceeds to be used for the founding of a university.

Even in Oregon City this was too much to choke down. McLoughlin was allowed by the legislature to live in his "forfeited" home; and after his embittered death in 1857 belated justice of a sort was done his legatees by returning to them all of the alienated property, save the island, on their payment of a thousand dollars to the uneasy beneficiary of the wrong, Willamette University.

Another pernicious feature of the Donation Act was its attempt to forestall speculation by declaring that title to lands taken under it would not mature until a man had completed four years' residence on his claim. [1] But what of lands already sold in such bustling townsites as Portland, Oregon City, and Salem? Ten years of litigation were necessary before the bill's sloppy wording on this point was finally cleared up.

The act even fostered the very speculative trends it professed to oppose. This came about through the provision granting an extra 320 acres to a man's wife, although Western congressmen surely knew that no individual family in that unmechanized day could possibly farm so much land. But what a man couldn't plow he could sell, once title matured; and in a frantic rush to cash in on the rosy future, girls as young as twelve and thirteen were wed to males old enough to be their grandfathers.

But the gravest injustice was, as usual, done to the Indians. The act said nothing about their titles. In theory these had already been extinguished by another measure which Thurston had pressed upon Congress. This prior law had empowered the making of treaties with every tribe west of the Cascade Mountains, whereby the Indians would sell their lands for useful annuities and would move to reservations on the eastern side of the mountains. The whites would then be free to claim the former Indian lands under the Donation Act.

Anson Dart of Wisconsin was appointed to effect the treaties. He was able and industrious, but shackled by inadequate funds and incompetent help (including Henry Spalding). He also found that the Indians did not see things as they were supposed to. They did not want to leave the mild climate of the ocean slopes for the deserts to the east. Their reluctance was intensified when the eastern Indians, knowing the coastal tribes to be riddled with veneral disease, promised to wipe out the proposed reservations.

Faced with the impasse, Dart decided to let the coastal Indians stay in compressed reservations on the western side of the mountains. Before the treaties could be ratified, however, settlers moved onto the reserves—generally in good faith, for the Donation Act implied that

[1] In 1853 the requirement was modified by allowing a man to buy the land, after two years' residence, for $1.25 an acre. This pre-emption feature, somewhat modified, also became a part of the 1862 Homestead Act.

MAP 4

The Routes of the Explorers, Early Forts, and Trading Posts of the Northwest

everything was open. They threw down the Indians' fences and huts, reduced the scanty game still further; their swine grubbed up the roots that were a main item of the red men's diet. Fortunately for the Willamette Valley, the Indians in that vicinity were too weak to do more than complain. But their objections, added to the counter-complaints of the settlers, led Congress to decline ratification of the treaties Dart had negotiated. Presumably this left land titles exactly where they had been before the start of the negotiations—in the hands of the Indians. As the settlers howled their anguish, Dart threw up his hands in despair and resigned.

All in all, times seemed ripe for challenging Thurston's handling of matters in Congress.

The moment Joe Lane's name appeared, his opponents objected that he was not a true Oregonian: he owned no property in the territory and, save for his adult son, had brought none of his family west with him. To quiet the first of the charges, Lane filed on a Donation claim in the Umpqua Valley near present Roseburg and then prepared for what promised to be a battle royal with Thurston. Issue was never joined, however. Thurston died at sea on his way home for the hustings, and after that Joe Lane was a shoo-in.

Before leaving for Washington the new delegate started south with forty or more miners to inspect his California gold properties. While he was on the road the Rogue Indians forgot the knife-at-the-throat treaty he had extracted from them the previous year and began attacking the Donation homesteaders moving onto their lands. By chance one-armed Phil Kearny, famed Indian fighter, was just then moving a small column of cavalry south to new stations in California. Kearny's troopers joined a motley group of volunteers mustered by Jesse Applegate; Lane rushed up with his small army of prospectors; and the combined force gave the Indians a thorough trouncing. His prestige burnished still higher by the victory, Lane took several sullen prisoners back to Oregon City and then sailed for the East.

Once again his military triumph proved illusive. As soon as Lane and the troopers had disappeared, the Rogues and their relatives—the Umpquas, the Shastas, the Klamaths, the Coquilles, and the Modocs—went right on pillaging. All told, thirty-six whites were killed and more wounded before winter rains brought a respite to the bloodshed. As usual, Indian casualties were incompletely recorded but beyond doubt soared far higher. And this was just the beginning. [2]

[2] Blood enough to be remembered, one would think. Yet the Indian wars of southern Oregon, though among the most ferocious of our pioneer annals, have been

The discovery of gold intensified the fury. Unaware of the smoldering threat, prospectors converged on the district from both sea and land. At first the sea approach was prompted by efforts to open supply routes into northern California. Vessels probed the sometimes risky mouths of the coastal rivers, unloaded exploring parties, and sent them up the south-trending canyons to see if roads could be opened to the interior. These scouts panned the gravel bars as they went. In the tributaries of the Rogue (and, for that matter, even in the sand of some of the ocean beaches) they found pay dirt. Meanwhile packers traveling between the Willamette and Sacramento had fallen into the way of refurbishing their stock in the meadows bordering the upper Rogue. To while away their time they, too, used their pans. And they, too, found gold.

By the spring of 1852 the rush was on. It slopped eastward across the mountains into the land of the Modocs. It reached southward into California across a still unsurveyed border whose location was so uncertain that some men cynically voted in both states yet refused to pay taxes in either. Its nominal center was the explosive town of Jacksonville, just west of present Medford, Oregon. But its real heart was an unguessable number of ill-defended tent and log-shanty camps scattered throughout the bewildering maze of canyons.

During the summer at least eighteen prospectors were killed by roving bands of savages. Posses of miners struck back, hanging various Indians for the murders, often without assurance that the victims were guilty. The Indians retaliated, the whites responded, the ill will spiraled.

The climax came in the fall. In 1852 the greatest flood of immigrants in Oregon's history poured down the trail from the East, stimulated by the glow of the Donation Land Law. The bulk of them followed the normal route over the Blue Mountains and down the Columbia. No small portion, however, were tempted by talk of gold to take the southern trail the Applegates had blazed six years before. They traveled in small sections, so that the Modocs were encouraged to begin a series of systematic attacks at Tule Lake, east of the Sierra and just inside the northern boundary of California. According to one set

largely forgotten. Part of the obscurity arises from the geography. In southern Oregon the coastal and Cascade mountain ranges merge in a convulsed jumble of forested peaks, deep canyons, and isolated grassy valleys. As a result the skirmishes that raged through them were as detached as they were brutal, a complexity of little wars rather than a clearly patterned, unified campaign. And, finally, the recriminations that followed the struggle were bitterly conflicting. Few fiction writers, to say nothing of Hollywood, have ventured to thread the labyrinth, and what would seem an almost inexhaustible source of melodrama thus remains largely unexploited.

of statistics, nearly a hundred men, women, and children died at intervals at Bloody Point, where a gaunt cliff crowded the wagon road close to the muddy shores of the lake.

When word of the outrages reached the settlements, volunteers stormed out of Jacksonville and Yreka. (The latter town was considered, in 1852, to lie in Oregon; accurate surveys eventually fixed it in California.) Leader of the Yreka contingent was hard-twisted Ben Wright, who wore his hair in glossy feminine ringlets about his shoulders, a quirk concerning which no one in the vicinity offered comment.

Wright's company, it is said, counted twenty-two mutilated bodies along the trail; the company from Jacksonville found another fourteen. Other rumored victims, mostly women and children, had vanished without trace.

With this as motivation the whites engaged the Modocs in a battle among the high tule reeds bordering the lake and killed at least thirty of them. The last of the immigrants were then escorted safely over the mountains. Wright, however, was not finished. Back to Tule Lake he went with eighteen die-hard companions.

What followed has been interpreted variously. According to Captain T. J. Cram, who investigated for the army's Department of the Pacific, Wright enticed forty-eight Modocs (other accounts go as high as ninety) into his camp "by means of a squaw" who promised the savages a peace council. After lulling the Indians' suspicions, the volunteers wantonly massacred forty of the defenseless red men, scalped them, and rode joyfully back to Yreka, waving their trophies at the muzzles of their rifles.

Not so, retorted C. S. Drew, adjutant of the 2nd Regiment of Oregon Mounted Volunteers, when Congress began to rumble over Cram's report. The Modocs were the ones who suggested the council through the squaw, intending to ambush the meeting. Wright, who knew their language, overheard their plotting and, being outnumbered five to two, "arranged his [plans] accordingly. Suffice it to say, the biters were bitten, hence the wails of a few pseudo-philanthropists and demagogues who pervert the truth . . . and then use their perversions to the disparagement of the volunteer service." [3]

Again winter brought a pause, but no end. When the mountains dried in the spring, the mutual murdering, raping, and raiding began

[3] This and other masses of conflicting testimony can be found in Cram's *Memoir*, House Ex. Doc. 114, 35th Congress, 2nd Session; Drew's *Account*, Sen. Misc. Doc. 59, 36th Congress, 1st Session; J. Ross Browne, special agent, *Report*, Sen. Ex. Doc. 40, 35th Congress, 1st Session; etc.—a staggering maze.

once more, a vicious summer, accounting, some figures insist, for approximately a hundred known white dead. Perhaps the sum is an exaggeration. But whatever the truth, it was bad enough.

By this time Joe Lane was back in the territory. He was governor again, having been appointed by President Pierce when the Democrats resumed control in Washington. Lane accepted the appointment, he says, as a personal tribute. He may also have considered the piquancy involved in returning to Oregon and booting out the man who had ousted him a few years earlier. In any event he took his family along this time, just so there would be no more objections on that account. For three days he functioned as territorial governor, then resigned and ran to succeed himself in Congress. Once again he was elected. And once again he found himself involved with the Rogues before he could journey back to the national capital.

On the resumption of hostilities he was appointed by his gubernatorial successor, George Curry, as brigadier general of the volunteer companies forming throughout the mining districts. Battle was joined in the murky light of forest fires set by the Indians. Among the first casualties was General Lane, shot through the arm. He put a crude bandage on the wound and kept going. Spotting him, the Indians called out that they would talk about peace if Lane and no more than ten more white chiefs would come to their camp, unarmed as an earnest of good faith.

Camp, it turned out, was an ancient tribal stronghold atop Table Rock, one of two huge cliff-girt mesas rising a thousand feet above the valley of the Rogue. Lane's fellow officers objected violently to going there, pointing out that if the Indians planned treachery there would be no way of forestalling it. Lane ignored them. One of his reasons was Joel Palmer. Palmer, Dart's successor as superintendent of Indian affairs for the territory, was trying desperately to formulate a new series of treaties that would suit both Congress and the Indians of the Northwest, and a conference on Table Rock looked like an opportunity to run a test case with Oregon's most troublesome band. Lane was not going to back out now. He did, however, take the precaution of demanding the son of one of the Rogue chiefs as hostage.

On the morning of September 4, 1853, Lane and Palmer and eight unarmed, unhappy officers rode as far up the slopes of Table Rock as their horses could travel. Dismounting, they scrambled the rest of the way over rocks and through brambles. On top of the mesa seven hundred warriors surrounded them. There was an ugly moment when a breathless runner arrived with word that a company of whites operating outside of Lane's command had broken the truce by tying an Indian to a tree and shooting him. Coolly, his wounded arm throbbing in its sling, Lane faced down the stir by promising punishment for the guilty men; and the tedious negotiations droned on.

In the end the Indians sold most of their Rogue River lands for sixty thousand dollars in useful merchandise to be paid in sixteen annual installments (less fifteen thousand withheld to compensate local settlers for the recent depredations). The treaty was novel in that it did not herd the Indians off their ancient domains to a new home in alien lands, as had been almost universally done in the East and as had been planned for Oregon. Rather, it let the savages retain full sovereignty over a "reserved" portion of their native homes, in this case near Table Rock, and granted them certain hunting and fishing rights even in the ceded portions.

This epochal agreement, and a similar one negotiated with the Umpquas, Lane took with him to Washington. Under his watchful eye the documents fared better than Dart's treaties had. Ratified by the Senate, they even became models for future Indian negotiations throughout the Northwest. But, as will be seen, they were no more effective than their predecessors in guaranteeing peace. Meanwhile, other mettlesome, if less bloody, adjustments were being called for far to the north.

3. Oregon's Rambunctious Stepchild

UNTIL California's hungry hands reached out toward the spectacular forests beside Puget Sound, growth north of the Columbia was negligible. Except for Fort Nisqually and the dwellings associated with the Puget Sound Agricultural Company, there was in 1848 scarcely a habitation other than the cabins clustered around Michael Simmons' grist and sawmills at Tumwater. A prognosticator probably would have looked on these as containing the seed of the future. Actually the germ lay three miles farther downstream, at the head of Budd Inlet, where a young epileptic named Levi Smith had built himself a shingle-roofed hutch, sixteen feet square, with a magnificent view of Mount Rainier to the east and of the Olympic Mountains to the northwest.

Smith was a personable young man. Among his many friends was Edmund Sylvester, who had first reached Portland on a Cushing and Company trading ship and who the next year, in 1846, had gone with

Smith to the sound in order to care for the epileptic during his seizures. The pair took up adjoining claims; each made the other his heir. Then, in 1848, Levi Smith was elected to represent his district in the Oregon legislature. As he was paddling along in a canoe to attend the session, convulsions gripped him. The canoe overturned, he drowned, and the claims at Budd Inlet became the sole property of Edmund Sylvester.

Shortly thereafter Sylvester joined the rush to California. He prospered, and late in the fall of 1849 in San Francisco he and three other young men purchased a tiny brig called *Orbit* in which to return to Puget Sound. Their intent seems to have been to secure a load of wharf pilings for the ravenous market within the Golden Gate.

They were forestalled by Michael Simmons. Simmons had just sold his Tumwater mills and claims and was looking for a way to invest the proceeds. Buying a controlling interest in the *Orbit* and her cargo, he sent her off to San Francisco with orders that her captain bring back enough general merchandise to start a store.

A store! To Edmund Sylvester that implied a town—and what better spot for the region's first town than his own tidewater claims at Budd Inlet? Quickly he erected a two-story building of logs and gave it, along with a pair of choice lots, to Mike Simmons, asking in return only that Mike open his store on the property. Simmons agreed. Sylvester thereupon named the embryo town Smithfield in memory of his dead friend. But the view of the Olympic Mountains was too dazzling for the prosaic name to stick. Soon the village was being called Olympia. (Two years later the mountain that dominated the eastern half of the panorama would furnish a name for another scattering of log houses on a bay some miles to the northeast—Tacoma, phonetic approximation of an Indian word for the overwhelming snow cone which explorer George Vancouver more than half a century earlier had called Rainier.)

Though vigorous, Olympia's young ambitions did not yet embrace two stores. When a competitor appeared in 1850 he was hustled off to the cabins growing up around the new army post of Fort Steilacoom. As a military installation, Steilacoom did not amount to much—a scant handful of soldiers quartered on land bought from the Puget Sound Agricultural Company—but its mere presence, together with the prompt hanging of the two Indians primarily responsible for the 1849 attack on Nisqually, served to pacify the local red men. Thus encouraged, the settlers began spreading out. Farms took root in the timber-free valleys of the glacial streams flowing northwestward from

Rainier and even on Whidbey Island, a fishhook of prairie land sprawling across the inland mouth of Juan de Fuca Strait. Yet for all the scattering, there could scarcely have been, in the summer of 1850, five hundred whites in the entire area.

Hoping to make the region easier to reach, storekeeper Simmons led a group of men eastward in a fruitless effort to chop out a wagon road over the Cascades and thence down the Yakima Valley to meet the Oregon Trail at Fort Walla Walla. He had private reasons for wanting the short cut. His aged mother, his married sister, Catherine Broshear, Catherine's husband, and her brother-in-law were due to arrive with the fall immigration; and Mike knew from experience how desperately hard was the Columbia gorge, to say nothing of the final pull up the Cowlitz to the Landing and then on through the bottomless mud and dense timber that separated the Columbia drainage from the sound. But the even denser timber of the Cascades turned the road builders back, and the newcomers had to struggle with the normal route.

Of Mike's family only Catherine Broshear appeared. In the sun-smitten valley of the Platte, cholera had killed her mother, her husband, her brother-in-law. Fortunately David Maynard, a doctor who had been summoned from another caravan to treat the dying, had taken over the team and wagon for her. As they had crept along the rest of the way through sand and mosquitoes and Indian scares, the lonely pair had fallen in love.

Simmons was deeply grateful—until he learned that Maynard had left behind him, in Ohio, a wife and a mountain of debts. Nor was the brother's protective outrage diminished when Maynard chopped a shipload of cordwood, sold it in San Francisco, and returned early in 1852 with a cargo of merchandise to open another store. His price cutting was the final affront. A delegation of Mike's friends called upon the interloper and suggested to him the advantages of moving his goods to the mouth of the Duwamish River in Elliott Bay, several miles to the north.

Maynard listened. He had already struck up a friendship with a visiting Duwamish chief named Sealth, or, as the whites pronounced it, Seattle, and so could count on the tribe's patronage. Additional trade would come from the sprinkling of settlers in the stream's upper valley (to everyone's confusion the farmers called their part of the Duwamish River the White), and from a new settlement located at the end of the promontory forming the southern side of Elliott Bay. Kissing Catherine a temporary good-by, Maynard began loading his stock of goods in Chief Seattle's long, graceful, black-painted canoes.

When he reached Elliott Bay he found three men already staking out claims between the Duwamish's marshy delta and the high clay bluffs to the north. Their names were Arthur Denny, Carson Boren, and William Bell. Originally they had been part of the settlement on the southern promontory of the bay, but during the winter, while cutting pilings for a tramp schooner, they had learned the handicaps of the spot: windy exposure, shoal waters, and nearly half a mile of beach between tide line and the nearest trees. Here on the north the roadstead was deeper, the timber handier. To be sure, the bordering hills were steep, but a man couldn't have everything.

They could have a store, Maynard said, if they would move their claims a mite northward toward the bluffs so that he could squeeze in beside the river. That way he would be close to the Indian village and to the salmon he hoped to pickle for export. Promptly the trio agreed.

Almost immediately they had to make another adjustment. Along came a man older than most in the district—he must have been forty or more—with solid shoulders, heavy features, and calculating eyes. He was Henry Yesler, from Maryland. The year before he had visited Portland, intending to cut lumber for the California trade, but the dangerous bar at the mouth of the Columbia had discouraged him. If the Puget Sound district proved better, he was prepared to move in with a steam sawmill.

A steam mill! Not even Olympia had that. Hastily the claim holders reformed their boundaries so that Yesler could have a narrow neck of land reaching from the waterfront back into the timber. There, at the rear of the other plats, his claim could balloon out and embrace as many acres of trees as the law allowed.

Satisfied with the proposal, Yesler went to San Francisco for his mill, leaving the others to build a long, open shed to house the machinery and a solid log cookhouse complete with the biggest fireplace in the region. They worked with a will. No doubt about it, a town was in the making here. Adopting Maynard's suggestion, they named it Seattle, after the tyee of the Indians who padded about, watching the proceedings with passive eyes.

By now the whole sound was booming. Between December 24, 1849, and July 22, 1851, San Francisco had been razed by no less than six fires, and at each rebuilding the demand for Northern lumber increased: for pilings, for ship spars, for the heavy squared timbers a man could hew with a broadax, for the sweet-smelling cedar shingles that practically anyone could rive with a froe during his odd moments. Increasing numbers of timber cutters meant increasing outlets for farm produce from the prairies along the inland river bottoms. In addition, coal was discovered near Bellingham Bay just under the border, and oysters at Budd Inlet and in Shoalwater Bay, where no fewer than a hundred and fifty men found employment digging mollusks to satisfy the whims of the nabobs beside the Golden Gate. One ship even came nosing into the sound looking for ice; when her captain reported home in disgust that the sound never froze, the quest was shifted to the glaciers of Alaska.

In spite of the good times, however, the population north of the Columbia still numbered, in 1851, fewer than two thousand, women and children included. One reason for the drag, according to the impatient boosters along the sound, was the neglect they suffered from the legislature. Dominated by Willamette farmers, that body was far less interested in their northern brethren than in the Indian troubles to the south and in their private feud with Lane's successor as territorial governor, phlegmatic John P. Gaines.

As part of the quarrel the legislators in 1851 declared Salem to be the capital of Oregon Territory. Gaines retorted with a declaration that Oregon City was the seat of government. In this stand the governor was supported by three Oregonians and by the two representatives from north of the Columbia, who saw no reason for dragging their tired bones another two score miles farther up the Willamette.

The five constituted themselves a rump parliament. Each day for nearly three weeks they solemnly came to order in the echoing governmental building. As sole member of the Upper House, Columbia Lancaster, from north of the river, declared himself in session, passed bills sent him by the Lower House, and dispatched memorials to Congress, praying that the federal government supply the needs denied his district by the aloof Willamette legislature.

No little truth was mixed with Lancaster's private comedy. Oregon Territory reached from California to Canada, from the coast to the Rockies—an enormous 350,000 square miles. Handicapped by the slow communications of the time, no single legislative body could possibly administer so much territory. The men from south of the Columbia admitted as much themselves. Jesse Applegate, while voicing a plea that United States territorial administration be overhauled so that local groups could elect their own governors, suggested a division of Oregon along the Columbia. The northerners added their bit by appointing Michael Simmons head of a committee to study the proposed split.

Upshot of the activity was a convention of northerners at Monticello, near the mouth of the Cowlitz River, in the fall of 1852. By now the northern population was edging toward the four thousand mark—quite enough, the rambunctious delegates felt, to justify their asking Congress to declare them a separate territory. They passed a memorial to that effect. A special committee carried the document to Salem to give it to Joe Lane for transmission to Washington and, incidentally, to lobby the Willamette legislature for a similar memorial in support of the division. David Maynard went along to Salem with the committee in quest of private aid. He wanted a divorce from his abandoned wife in Ohio, and in those days a decree could be obtained only through legislative action.

The Willamette lawmakers granted each request and added a lagniappe for Maynard in the form of an appointment as justice of the peace for newly created King County, embracing Seattle. The northern committeemen rode home to await congressional action, Maynard using his new freedom and influence to make peace with Mike Simmons and marry the widow Broshear.

The newlyweds had a hungry time of it. Few vessels called at Seattle that winter. Stocks of food dwindled, and when one high tide washed away a barrel of pork from the beach in front of Arthur Denny's cabin, the whole dismayed community turned out with torches to search the shore line for it. With spring, however, affairs throughout the sound picked up. More ships came, more mills. Among the latter was a new steam outfit built at Port Gamble on the western shore of the inland sea by A. J. Pope, W. C. Talbot, and P. J. Keller. They were an awesome trio with solid family backing in the prosperous lumber town of East Machias, Maine. They owned their own vessels and their own retail outlets in San Francisco. With their soundly capitalized Puget Mill Company they intended, so they implied, to import workers and machinery from Maine and to introduce the ways of big business to the virgin timberlands of the West.

Before the Port Gamble mill could saw its first log, even more exciting news arrived. Congress had created a northern territory named Washington (instead of Columbia, as the memorials had suggested) and had appointed as governor a man named Isaac Ingalls Stevens. Most exhilarating of all, Stevens was going to survey a route for a railroad on his way west to assume office.

A railroad from the East!
Let the Willamette match *that* if it could!

4. *"A Real Go-ahead Man"*

IN TWO respects Isaac Stevens personified the new territory he was to administer: neither of them ever suffered from modesty or from lack of ambition.

Born on March 25, 1818, in North Andover, Massachusetts, Stevens had been brought up by a humorless father who, among other disciplines, every morning plunged the lad fresh from bed into a hogshead of cold water. At the age of twelve Stevens ruptured himself pitching hay and for the rest of his life wore a truss that did not obviate moments of excruciating pain. After graduating from West Point at the top of his class, he entered the engineering corps. During the war with Mexico he was shot through the foot. The wound never healed properly. For years he had to wear a special shoe; on occasion the raw scar would fester afresh and expel fragments of bone. The part these two enduring agonies may have played in the outbursts that marred his later career has never been adequately weighed.

After the war Stevens was placed in the Coast Survey office, directly under A. D. Bache, one of the renowned scientists of the day. The young officer did a competent job of reorganizing the service and still had energy left for non-military politicking. In spite of a reprimand from the War Department, he stumped energetically for the election of General Franklin Pierce to the presidency. Shortly after Pierce's success Washington Territory was created. Stevens, just approaching his thirty-fifth birthday, asked Pierce for appointment as territorial governor, not, he said, in reward for services rendered but in recognition of the fact that no other candidate was so well qualified. He also had himself commissioned superintendent of Indian affairs for the district. In short, he hardly seemed lacking in confidence. And yet he was abnormally sensitive about his short stature; throughout his lifetime he would never allow himself to be pictured beside men who were taller than he.

Almost simultaneously with the governorship another job opportunity presented itself. This was the survey for a transcontinental railroad, fruit of the tireless efforts of Asa Whitney of New York. Bankrupted by the panic of 1837 and disheartened by the subsequent death of his wife, Whitney had gone to China in the early 1840s as the representative of several New York importing firms. There, within fifteen spectacular months, he amassed such a fortune that he never again had to engage in private business. From now on he could devote himself to a consuming hobby: a plan for putting still more of the Orient's trade into American hands by means of a transcontinental railroad that would eliminate the long and costly journey around the Horn.

The logical Pacific terminus for the road, Whitney decided after hearing from ship captains about the Columbia's bar, was Puget Sound. The logical way to finance the road, he said, was for Congress to grant the construction company a strip of land sixty miles wide along the right of way. This incredible acreage would be sold at low rates to settlers lured into the region by easy transportation, and when the last spike had been driven the completed railroad would become the property of the government.

For half a dozen years beginning in 1844, Whitney flooded Congress with memorials, lectured to any organization that would listen, wrote voluminously in the newspapers. The efforts had effect. Seventeen state legislatures and numerous private groups petitioned Congress to adopt the plan. Opposition, however, was equally strong. Whitney, whose interest in the project was completely selfless, was accused of a sinister plot to rob the public of a colossal empire. Others argued that the government, not private enterprise, should do the building. But the greatest furor arose over routes. Each section of the country sneered at its neighbors while extolling its own advantages. Slavery tensions complicated the issues: after the discovery of gold in California neither North nor South was willing to let the other tie itself by unbreakable steel rails to so potent a source of strength.

Just before the Thirty-second Congress expired, Senator Gwin of California offered a compromise. Let the different routes be surveyed so that debates could at least be based on more than conjecture. In March 1853, Congress complied by tacking onto the army appropriation bill an amendment authorizing the Corps of Topographical Engineers to spend a hundred and fifty thousand dollars examining five different routes between the forty-ninth and the thirty-second parallels.

Isaac Stevens, unembarrassed by his already full portfolio of jobs, asked to lead the northernmost survey. He not only landed the plum but in addition won from a Southern Secretary of War, Jefferson Davis, the fattest appropriation (forty thousand dollars) and the largest number of men (123) of any of the groups.

To prepare himself Stevens gulped down everything in print about the Northwest, consulted at length with George Simpson of the Hudson's Bay Company, sought out Oregon's delegate in Congress, Joseph Lane. To save time he decided to dispatch a party via the Isthmus of Panama to the Columbia so that it could explore the northern Cascades while he was examining the Rockies. As head of the Cascade explorers he chose another small man, twenty-seven-year-old George McClellan, who during the Mexican War had struck Stevens as "brave, intrepid, efficient, and devoted to duty"—an estimate the governor-designate would soon scale downward. A third party under Lieutenant Rufus Saxton was ordered to assemble supplies at Vancouver Barracks on the Columbia and with them establish a depot in the Bitterroot Valley, in what is now western Montana.

After starting part of his own supplies up the Missouri by keelboat, Stevens hurried to St. Paul, the eastern terminus of his survey. There an awed reporter, after watching him bring order to the confusion of baggage and ill-broken mules, declared that the governor was a "real go-ahead man." He needed to be. Though June was already at hand, he expected to examine a stretch of country two thousand miles long by two hundred and fifty wide and still reach his official chair in Olympia before snow flew.

By early September he was at Fort Benton in central Montana. Here he reassembled and reoutfitted his scattered parties of engineers before sending them forth once again to probe the Rockies for a suitable pass. He meant for them to do exactly as they were told. When one brash underling protested instructions he was told to follow orders or to be "shot down like a dog."

Stevens himself concentrated on what had by now become an obsession, the arranging of Indian treaties. As a model he adopted the history-making council of the plains tribes which Thomas Fitzpatrick, mountain man turned Indian agent, had conducted two summers before near Fort Laramie, in present Wyoming. At Fitzpatrick's council the Indians had agreed to allow transit rights to the whites and to stay within carefully delineated tribal boundaries, thus ending the incessant warfare that resulted from trespass on each other's domains.

Stevens hoped to make comparable history by winning tribal permission for a railway and by wooing into peaceful ways those Indians whom Fitzpatrick had missed, notably the Blackfeet and the Flatheads. To achieve this he scheduled, without authorization from the Indian Department, a great intertribal council for the summer of 1854. As his survey moved westward in '53, he prepared for the powwow by holding explanatory talks with every savage band he could reach.

The Indians, who had not the foggiest concept of steam cars, were inclined to be suspicious. Said one Assiniboin, "We do not understand it [the railroad], but I think it will drive away the buffalo." Equally foreign was Stevens' talk of amity and brotherhood. Ever since acquiring horses, the Flatheads, Nez Percés, Pend d'Oreilles, and the other mountain tribes had been joyfully swooping down onto the plains to hunt buffalo and scalp Blackfeet. Conversely, the Blackfeet every summer made sport by bursting through the high passes to raid the horse herds of the mountain tribes. An entire culture was built on those exhilarating skirmishes: dances, ceremonies, tribal migrations, folklore, storytelling. Still, the Indians agreed that it would do no harm to come to a council, especially since this eager little white man promised many presents and many good things to eat.

The advance conferences went so amiably that Stevens gained an inflated notion of his abilities as an Indian hand—a delusion which would have tragic impact on his future actions. In fact he made a great many bland assumptions that summer. By the time he reached Fort Benton he knew he could not complete the survey within the limits of the appropriation allowed him. Accordingly he wrote Jefferson Davis, saying that it would be a shame to suspend the work at this point, and sent another letter to the Indian Department asking authorization for the council he had been promising to the Indians as an accomplished fact. He then dispatched his parties toward the mountains as if their expenses were assured and turned his own course northward toward Canada to invite still more Indians to the big talk set for the following summer. After all, no word saying him nay could possibly arrive for several months.

He had not traveled far when a courier summoned him back to Fort Benton. Lieutenant Saxton, entrusted with establishing a supply dump in the Bitterroot Valley, had accomplished the task and then had ridden with a small party east across the Continental Divide to meet the westbound explorers. After consulting with Saxton, Stevens decided he would have to forgo his northern swing, abandon his slow wagons, and hurry ahead with a pack train in order to get out of the mountains before snow blocked the way.

Averaging a hard forty miles a day, the governor's train angled southwest and then west to the summit of the Divide at Cadotte's Pass. The men had now reached what Congress had designated as the eastern edge of Washington Territory. (Later the boundaries would undergo radical realignment and shrinkage.) Though drenched by a violent rainstorm, Stevens conducted an appropriate ceremony, then led the way down the Big Blackfoot River to the vicinity of present Missoula. Resisting a temptation to look for a rumored gold discovery (it was based on truth), the party next swung south up one of the West's loveliest valleys, the Bitterroot, to one of the storied spots of the northern Rockies—Fort Owen.

Fort Owen had started as the first Catholic mission in the mountains. A Flathead, it will be recalled, had been a member of the original delegation of Indians who had visited St. Louis in search of, so the whites believed, religious instruction. The initial response, however, had veered into the Oregon country and no missionary came among the Flatheads until later appeals elicited the enthusiasm of dark, intense Pierre-Jean de Smet of the Society of Jesus.

In 1840, De Smet rode as far as the valley of the Green River in present Wyoming with a motley crowd of fur men, independent Protestant missionaries, and the first wagon-carried families of western migrants, Joel Walker's party. There, at the final rendezvous of the expiring beaver trade, he met a handful of Flatheads and journeyed with them to a huge conclave of Indians assembled in Pierre's Hole, west of the majestic Tetons. Awed by his enthusiastic reception, the blackrobe celebrated Mass, taught the Lord's Prayer to the savages, baptized a few hundred, and returned to St. Louis, convinced that a great field awaited him.

The next spring, guided by Thomas Fitzpatrick, De Smet again journeyed west with another party of emigrants. In his own train were two more priests and three lay brothers, their scanty equipment loaded in four carts and a wagon. From Fort Hall they pushed due north over Lemhi Pass into the long north–south valley of the Bitterroot. A tumult of snow-wrinkled peaks reared on either side of the impressive trough, but the bottom lands were rich and mild. Delighted, the fathers erected a log chapel, named the spot St. Mary's, and began their work.

They needed help. Unable to get it from the struggling new Catholic missions in Oregon, De Smet journeyed to Europe and there obtained men and money not only for St. Mary's but for additional stations he hoped to establish throughout the northern Rockies. In the summer of 1844 he returned by ship with his reinforcements to Fort Vancouver. From there he worked his way up the Columbia to Fort Colvile and then overland to the Bitterroot, adding substance by his passage to Marcus Whitman's fears about the designs of the Papists on the Northwest.

With De Smet (who did not stay in the West) was Anthony Ravalli, destined through his unremitting labors to give his name to the Montana county which now embraces the Bitterroot. Ravalli taught the Indians to hoe and to pray. He built a grist mill and contrived saws out of old wagon tires. He never rested. But he failed, and in 1850 St. Mary's closed its doors.

Catholic sources blame several causes: harassment from raiding Blackfeet; the mission's inability to fulfill overenthusiastic promises made by De Smet; irreligious poisons spread by mountain men who resented the damper the priests put on their licentious ways with the Indians. No doubt all these things contributed. But the fundamental cause, similar to the one that troubled the Protestants, was the failure of the white man's medicine to live up to the Indians' expectations. In return for forswearing polygamy, easy divorce, their beloved gambling games, and especially the unrestrained dances that preceded their hunting trips and war parties, the Flatheads were offered a sedentary life based, without even the compensation of ceremony, on the hard work of agriculture. When novelty wore off they drifted back into their old ways, and St. Mary's closed for want of business. [1]

It was not a total loss. Just before its demise an ex-army sutler named John Owen wandered up from Fort Hall with his brother Frank. John, the dominant member of the pair, was short and fat. Black hair and a black goatee framed his broad, florid cheeks. Behind him rode a squaw hardly five feet tall. He called her Nancy. Despite her tininess Nancy could outwork many a white man with either a hoe or a pack mule. At night she was content to roll up in a blanket and sleep on the floor. Her husband was devoted to her.

Shrewd, merry, and self-educated to a surprising degree (he had an extensive library in his wagons), John Owen wanted to enter the Indian trade. He bought St. Mary's from the priests for three hundred dollars, added one or two buildings of his own, and surrounded the whole with a log palisade. Blackfeet kept raiding his horses, however, and in the fall of 1852 killed one of his workers. Disgusted, Owen withdrew among the Spokanes, where Spokane Gerry, educated at Red River, still held sway. There Lieutenant Saxton, bound from Van-

[1] Ravalli moved to the Coeur d'Alene mission on the river of the same name in Idaho. After helping build its chapel, he was shifted first to Colvile and then to California. During the gold rush of the 1860s he returned to Montana. Reopening St. Mary's on a new site, he labored for two more decades with an unflagging, selfless diligence that brought him the respect of whites and Indians alike.

couver to the Bitterroot with supplies, met the trader. Figuring that so many soldiers would dissuade the Blackfeet, Owen moved back to his fort and began the steady expansion which would make it, during the next twenty years, the social and commercial heart of western Montana. He was open for business when Stevens arrived on September 29, 1853.

By now the surveyor knew that the looping curves and tangled spurs of the Continental Divide could not be estimated within a matter of weeks. Accordingly he decided to establish a base called Cantonment Stevens a few miles upstream from Fort Owen and keep several parties working out from there as long as the weather allowed. One lieutenant, twenty-three-year-old John Mullan, was even detailed to stay all winter and keep measurements on the snowfall, a record of obvious import to a railroad. Unable to linger himself because of his duties as governor, Stevens pushed with a small party back down the Bitterroot to the Clark Fork. After crossing the mountains through a gap he called Stevens Pass, he paid a quick visit to the Coeur d'Alene mission, skirted the wooded hills bordering the lake of the same name, and followed the old fur trails to the ruins of Spokane House. There he heard from Indians that Captain McClellan of the Cascade survey had just reached Fort Colville, some eighty miles to the north. [2]

Though tormented by a flare-up of his old rupture, Stevens determined to visit his colleague at once. Accompanied by a single guide, he forced himself to keep going until he reached his destination at nine o'clock that evening. McClellan thumped his back, the post trader broached a keg of whiskey, the trader's wife cooked thick steaks in buffalo fat. It was a joyous reunion, lasting until the small hours; but the next day, hung-over and irritable from the pain in his abdomen, Stevens began to have his doubts about McClellan's work.

There were reasons for doubt. Little Mac had slighted every one of his assignments.

One was road building. Prodded by Lane, Congress had appropriated twenty thousand dollars to construct a wagon road from Fort Walla Walla over Naches Pass to Steilacoom—the short cut which Mike Simmons had tried unsuccessfully to open three years before. This job had been added to Stevens' long list of duties and in turn had been passed on by him to McClellan. At Vancouver McClellan decided he did not have enough men for both this and for surveying. He solved the difficulty by improperly awarding a few civilian con-

[2] By now a second *l* had crept inexorably into the second syllable of the fort's name.

tracts and from then on ignored the construction work, which was never done correctly. (He would spend the rest of his military career fretting about shortages of men, with incalculable cost to the North during the Civil War.)

His surveying was equally inadequate. He spent a leisurely three weeks at Vancouver Barracks assembling sixty-five men and a hundred and seventy head of livestock--far more than were either necessary or advisable for his purpose. Moving northward from Vancouver, he soon became entangled in the dense growth of firs and underbrush that blanket the moist western slopes of the Cascades. To gain mobility he crossed to the east where firs gave way to open forests of pine. Even there, however, he averaged a scant five miles a day as he worked northward, allowing his surveyors to pan for gold as they traveled. Short supplies finally led him to pare his forces. With the remainder he made a few perfunctory stabs up some of the streams, but he ran no lines and never crossed beyond the summit to see what the land on the west would be like. Much of the Divide he surveyed simply by looking at it from some convenient promontory.

On this basis he reported to Stevens that no feasible railroad pass existed between the Columbia gorge and the Canadian border.

This was a blow. Stevens had sold himself on the northern route—he could even visualize I. I. Stevens as head of the company [3]—but the Columbia gorge lay south of his jurisdiction. He needed a pass over the Cascades, and find it he would. Angrily he ordered McClellan to go back and do a decent job.

McClellan protested: his animals and equipment were too worn. A brisk fall of October snow gave weight to the argument, and reluctantly his superior gave in.

By different routes the two parties moved south to Fort Walla Walla. There Stevens, who arrived first, learned that Puget Sound settlers, annoyed by McClellan's neglect of their road, had voluntarily chopped out a passageway themselves. It did not amount to much. Nevertheless, so Stevens heard, a train of thirty-five wagons had managed to get across. Furthermore, according to Hudson's Bay traders and Indians, the recent snow had been no more than a normal October flurry and did not change their estimate that in any average year Naches Pass could be crossed with pack stock as late as December.

When McClellan came up, Stevens again ordered him into the mountains. Again Little Mac talked his way out of the assignment,

---

[3] A few years later he was one of the incorporators of the stillborn paper predecessor of the Northern Pacific.

which was given instead to Frederick Lander, the man whom Stevens had earlier threatened to shoot like a dog for questioning orders. Feeling the problem would now be attended to, the belated governor hurried on to Olympia.

Behind him Lander, who bore Stevens no love, heard that the immigrants risking Naches Pass had been forced by the snow to abandon their wagons. He consulted McClellan. Together they decided that under the circumstances it would be folly to attempt the survey.

Meanwhile Stevens had reached Olympia. He made appropriate speeches, summoned the legislature to meet in February, and ordered an election for a delegate to Congress (Columbia Lancaster won). He appointed as Indian agents Mike Simmons for the sound and A. J. Bolen for the Yakima country east of the mountains. Simmons, incidentally, needed the job. Illiterate, he had appointed a representative to handle his bookkeeping in the store and to conduct transactions in San Francisco. The fellow had absconded and now Mike was bankrupt.

Just as Stevens was about to start a canoe visit to the settlements along the sound, McClellan and Lander wandered in. Furious at their negligence (the rumor about the abandoned immigrant wagons was completely false), Stevens gave Little Mac peremptory orders to run a line without fail up the west slope of the Cascades. McClellan made a halfhearted attempt and said it wouldn't go: the snow was twenty-five feet deep in the mountains.

Almost immediately he had to eat the figure. Stevens had earlier sent word to Fort Walla Walla that Lieutenant Abiel Tinkham, leader of one of the parties that had stayed in the Rockies, should wind up his work by running a line over the Cascades from the east. Tinkham made the crossing in mid-January. He found seven feet of snow on the summit, rather than twenty-five, but said it lasted for so short a distance at that depth and was so light and dry in comparison to the compacted drifts of the Eastern states that in his estimate it "would cause very little detention to the passage of trains."

At this point Stevens and McClellan parted company. Yet when the time came to evaluate the several transcontinental surveys Jefferson Davis, after commending McClellan's capacity and resources, accepted his estimate of the northern route rather than Stevens'—or even rather than Lieutenant Mullan's. Mullan, who had stayed in the Rockies, found the snow so scant that in March he was able to bring a wagon across the roadless Continental Divide from Fort Benton to the Bitterroot. Obviously a train could do as well. (The winter of 1853–54, it should be added, was unusually mild in the Rockies.)

Possibly Davis' Southern leanings had something to do with his willingness to see the northern route belittled. Possibly, too, the Secretary of War was already prejudiced against Stevens because of the presumptuous way in which the governor had run up deficits. Curtly he protested the unauthorized drafts as they came in and wrote Stevens a blistering letter ordering all further operations stopped.

The letter reached Stevens late in February 1854. He reacted with characteristic impetuosity. Leaving his territorial secretary, Charles Mason, in charge of his office, he hurried via Panama to the national capital, hoping to secure the payment of the protested drafts and to gain permission for still more exploration. Then, too, there was the council with the Indians. Because of this emergency with Davis the meeting could not be held in the summer of 1854 as proposed. But surely the government would not cancel it entirely.

5. "I Wonder If the Ground Is Listening?"

IN WASHINGTON, D.C., Stevens was not able to win funds for completing his surveys. But he did secure thirty thousand dollars so that John Mullan, the lieutenant he had left in the Bitterroot Valley to check snowfall, could start locating a wagon road between the headwaters of the Missouri and the Columbia—inevitable precursor to any railway—and he did help the Northwest's delegates, Joseph Lane and Columbia Lancaster, obtain congressional appropriations for building other roads in their river-laced, forest-clogged districts. More gratifying to the governor's own interests were ten thousand dollars from the Indian Department for concluding his postponed council between the Blackfeet and the mountain tribes.

He was also shown the treaties which Joel Palmer had made with the Rogue and Umpqua tribes of southern Oregon. Would it be possible, he was asked, to put the Indians of Washington Territory onto similar constricted reservations so that their vacated hunting grounds might be opened for white settlement?

Blandly Stevens assured himself of infinite future trouble by saying yes.

When he headed back west via Panama he took with him his wife Margaret, their three daughters, and their twelve-year-old son Hazard. While crossing the isthmus, Margaret Stevens and the girls were stricken with Chagres fever. During their month-long convalescence in San Francisco, Stevens came into frequent contact with General John Ellis Wool, veteran of the War with Mexico and currently in command of the Department of the Pacific.

The two men did not take to each other. Wool's dislike congealed into hostility when Stevens, with characteristic brashness, publicly challenged one of the general's boasts about the battle of Buena Vista. A more diplomatic man would have reflected that if military operations ever became necessary in the territory of Washington they would have to be conducted under the supervision of General Wool's Department of the Pacific.

The last stretch of the journey to Olympia discouraged ailing Margaret Stevens almost to despair. All one drizzly day the family sat huddled in canoes as they were paddled up the Cowlitz to the log "hotel" at the Landing. A few cots in one small chamber were reserved for women; a battery of bunks in a larger dormitory served the men. The latter room was so packed with bewhiskered travelers in steaming wool shirts and mud-encrusted boots that the governor spent the night sleeping upright on a stool beside his wife—apparently she and the girls were the only female guests. Then on they went in a springless wagon beneath dripping firs and through mudholes that frequently bogged the vehicle down until more men could be summoned to pry it free. Two days of this brought them to a neck of land reaching into a gray bay. Down its center meandered one muddy street bordered by twenty rude houses and perhaps twice that many Indian huts. A scattering of canoes were drawn up on the beach; massive tree stumps stood everywhere. This was Olympia; this was home.

After opening the December session of the legislature, Stevens plunged into his treaty making, trying to persuade the multitudinous little bands of Puget Sound Indians to sell part of their holdings and move onto smaller reservations. Today it is fashionable to decry such robbery of the Indians. Actually, the pressures of the time considered, one wonders what other approach might have been taken. The hunting economy of the savages meant that intolerable amounts of productive land were going to waste. Teaching the Indians to get along with less ground while at the same time paying them for the acreage they relinquished seemed in the 1850s an eminently logical solution. To this end the government devoted more millions of dollars and far more energy than can be generalized under the word "robbery." That word should be reserved, rather, for the antics of the long list of gluttonous, incompetent, and dishonest subordinates who administered a basically sound policy.

Isaac Stevens as one of the policy's chief instruments deserves none of those adjectives. But he did embody other traits almost as harmful—haste, arrogance, and a maddening assurance that his view was always the right view. Expediency, another characteristic of the pioneer era, was personified in his two principal assistants, Michael Simmons and Benjamin Shaw. Anything to get the job done. As Shaw once said in describing his own talents, "I can get the Indians to sign their death warrants." He had no idea, of course, that future critics would take this metaphor literally. All he meant was that he knew how to manipulate primitive minds.

The first step was for him and Simmons and other local experts to meet with Stevens in the governor's Olympia office. There they drew rough maps of the areas occupied by the tribes of the sound area and then delineated the reservations they thought suitable. Next Simmons and Shaw would take several canoeloads of trinkets and food to a designated meeting ground. While runners assembled the natives for a preliminary briefing, workers cleared the space of brush and set up tents for the governor's party, which came sweeping in when all was ready.

The first council was held within the city limits of present Tacoma between December 24 and December 26, 1854. Though the Indians appeared in proud finery, Stevens wore the work garb of the district: red flannel shirt, trouser legs thrust inside his boots, a broad-brimmed black hat with his pipe held in its band. The Indians sat on the ground in concentric circles outside the evergreen arbor sheltering the white dignitaries. Standing before them, Stevens made an introductory speech sentence by sentence. Shaw translated into the Chinook trade jargon; Indian interpreters transformed that into native dialect. The gathering was then dismissed to talk over what had been said. The next day the proposed treaty itself was read and translated phrase by phrase.

There was considerable hesitation on the part of the Indians, most of it led by a Nisqually chief named Leschi. Leschi was part Yakima and made frequent trips across the Cascades to visit his inland relatives, who for some time had been discussing an attack on the whites. This talk Leschi had brought back to the sound, along with a terrifying notion of *polakly illeha*, the land of perpetual darkness (an echo, perhaps, of Alaska's long winter nights). *Polakly illeha*, so he said, was the reservation to which the whites intended to send the Indians when they signed the treaty.

The endless chattering annoyed Stevens. The weather was wretched and it may be that the old agonies in his abdomen and foot were troubling him again. It may even be that he drank too much, as George Gibbs, recording secretary of the conference, charged three years later (but not at the time). In any event pressure on the Indians increased. Gradually they were made to understand that the reservation was not to be located in the vague unknown but within the bounds of their own homelands—or at least within the lands of one of the neighboring tribes. There were arguments then over the location; each band wanted the reservation in its accustomed territory, and the objections of the losers could be overcome only by impossible promises that for all time they would be allowed to hunt and fish and dig roots in the old, familiar places. There were more promises of teachers, machine shops, livestock, and annuities in the form of useful goods. The Indians seem to have got exaggerated notions of what was being offered. Perhaps they simply misunderstood. Or perhaps there was a little loose talk on the part of the agents who were being goaded by Stevens to hurry up and get the thing finished.

On the third day the Indians began signing the treaty that was to alter their lives forever. When the document was filed, Leschi's signature, or mark, appeared with those of the other chiefs. Later he insisted, and Stevens' enemies made much of the contention, that the mark was fraudulent, that he had never approved the treaty. At this date the truth seems impossible to determine.

During the next six storm-lashed weeks Stevens traveled by schooner eight hundred miles throughout the sound and concluded three more treaties. A fifth council with the coastal Indians of the southwestern part of the state was broken up by a drunken chief, but Mike Simmons rectified matters by holding a special council of his own. Believing Indian affairs west of the Cascades were now in hand, Stevens in May shifted operations to the interior. Behind him he left nine thousand Indians glum with second thinking.

For a mess of pottage they had agreed to confine themselves to undesirable fractions of their former lands. Chiefs who had concluded the agreements found themselves unpopular. Some followed Leschi's lead and declared that their purported signatures were forgeries. Others insisted that they had not understood the terms, which is quite possible, for the Chinook jargon through which the negotiations filtered is a rudimentary language of no more than three or four hundred words. The more the Indians thought about it, the more it seemed to the hotheads among them that the treaties were exactly what the Yakimas and Klickitats beyond the mountains had predicted—a sly way of tricking them out of their holdings.

And now the white chief was off to treat with those Indians too. . . .

Stevens invited Joel Palmer, in charge of Oregon's Indian affairs, to attend the negotiations with him. There was no clear physical boundary between their territories. Although the Columbia served as far as its great bend to the north, the demarcation from there to the Rockies was the invisible forty-sixth parallel, a concept so abstract that there was no use even trying to explain it to the nomadic Indians, who wandered across it at will. Stevens thought it best, however, to stick to protocol and have the superintendents from both sides of the line on hand.

Palmer was reluctant. He was no coward—his negotiations in southern Oregon had proved that—but he knew how fierce was the disaffection among the interior tribes. Braving that ill will with no more than naked trust seemed to him recklessness beyond the call of an agent's duty. Finally, however, Stevens agreed to take along a small escort of soldiers from Fort Vancouver and at last Palmer consented.

The council—it developed into one of the most picturesque in the history of American Indian affairs—was held on lush meadows where the city of Walla Walla now stands. [1] On May 24, 1855, the Nez Percés arrived, two thousand strong. Naked, plumed, painted, astride belled and beaded horses that were smeared with vermilion and white clay, they swept by clashing their shields and chanting their songs. Afterward, on successive days, came the sullen Cayuses and Walla Wallas, the Umatillas, and the powerful Yakimas led by unfriendly Kamiakin. Others did not come at all: the Spokanes, the arrogant Palouses, and the outraged Klickitats, despoilers of the Willamette tribes, whom Palmer was sending back to their old homelands at the head of the Cowlitz.

An estimated five thousand arrived, mostly warriors but attended by enough squaws for housekeeping and thus, inevitably, by several children. For miles across the bottom lands their conical lodges rose beside cottonwood trees misty green with new leaves. For almost as

[1] Not to be confused with the site of old Fort Walla Walla (Wallula on today's maps), which stood thirty miles farther west where the Walla Walla River debouches into the Columbia.

far as the eye could reach their enormous horse herds grazed hills yet bright from the brief rains of spring.

By contrast the whites—scarcely a hundred of them—had erected a handful of tents for the commissioners and had placed a single home-made table of split pine logs under an arbor of boughs. The escorting soldiers occupied huts of branches draped with pack covers. A hastily erected log cabin sheltered the goods Stevens had brought along for presents. A huge mound of potatoes and a small herd of beef cattle furnished the wherewithal for future feasts. In the not unprejudiced words of Captain T. J. Cram, who later investigated the Indian troubles for General Wool's Department of the Pacific, the whole was "meagre . . . shabby . . . deficient in those points of show that are so well calculated to strike the fancy or command the respect of an Indian."

For nearly two weeks the talks dragged on, interspersed by banquets and, in the Indian camp, by noisy dances, horse races, and everlasting gambling. In their own way the savages could be crass enough. Their mystic feeling of kinship for the land they were being asked to re-linquish was not strong enough to close their ears to a good bargain. As one Cayuse put it:

"I wonder if the ground is listening? . . . The ground says, It is the Great Spirit that placed me here. The Great Spirit tells me to take care of the Indians, to feed them aright. . . . The Great Spirit in placing men on earth desired them to take good care of the ground . . . not trade it off except" (the Cayuse added) "you get a fair price."

He added further that he did not understand the treaty. For many of the Indians this was undoubtedly true. But some of the Nez Percés apparently understood it well enough to concoct a profitable bit of melodrama.

Leading actor in the show was the tribe's principal chief, known to the whites as Lawyer. He looked foolish, especially when wearing his favorite plug hat, to which he attached by means of colored bands of cloth a circlet of upright eagle feathers. But he knew enough to take advantage of the violent objections that most of the Indians were of-fering to everything the whites suggested.

Late one night he sidled up to Stevens with a warning that the In-dians were preparing an attack on the unsuspecting negotiators. The massacre could be forestalled, however. Lawyer would pitch his lodge beside the governor's tent, and the hostiles would then hold back lest their rush kill the Nez Percé chief and unite his powerful tribe against them in a war of vengeance.

Stevens agreed. And presto, no attack came. Cynics say none had been planned. Others, including Indians, say that the unfriendly tribes were really after Lawyer because of his playing up to the whites, and that the Nez Percé chief put his lodge where he did in order to save his own scalp. Whatever his motives, however, and whether or not an attack had been planned, from that night on Lawyer and his tribe were firmly established in Stevens' mind as the whites' most dependable allies.

This trust made Lawyer's next move completely easy.

After interminable speechmaking the assembled Indians agreed in principle to ceding to the United States something more than sixty thousand square miles of land, approximately equal to the combined areas of Pennsylvania and New Jersey. In return they were to receive annuities at the rate of about ten cents an acre, (later objected to in Congress as being too high), plus the usual shops and teachers to help the savages achieve more efficient modes of life. Bitter disputes then arose over the location of the territory the Indians were to reserve for themselves. Stevens wanted all the tribes placed on one large reserve within the Nez Percé homelands. His idea was that the friendly tribe would exert a beneficent influence over their more intractable fellows. The Indians, however, objected so violently to the amalgamation that the governor quickly modified his offer to three reservations: one in the Yakima Valley for the Yakimas, Palouses, and related tribes; another in eastern Oregon for the Cayuses, Umatillas, and Walla Wallas; and a third between the Snake River and the lovely Bitterroot Mountains for the sole use of the Nez Percés.

A confused and reluctant signing began. At that strategic juncture up dashed twenty Nez Percés headed by a venerable hero named Looking Glass. Word flashed around that the newcomers had heard of the council while hunting buffalo on the plains far east of the Rockies and that they had ridden hard all week in order to participate, only to find their homelands sold.

Dramatically Looking Glass denounced the signing. The Nez Percés recanted; the other tribes followed their lead. Then suddenly, two days later, Looking Glass capitulated. Mystified, Lieutenant Lawrence Kip wrote in the diary he was keeping of the council, "What he [Stevens] has been doing with Looking Glass since last Saturday, we cannot imagine, but we suppose savage nature in the wilderness is the same as civilized nature . . . and 'every man has his price.'" Captain Cram, checking matters later for General Wool, was even more suspicious. The entire show, he felt, had been manufactured so that the Nez Percés as a whole and the two chiefs as individuals could demand a better price for their surrender. If so, they succeeded. The boundaries of the proposed Nez Percé reservation were enlarged and Lawyer and Looking Glass were awarded salaries for governing the tribe (the last a fairly normal provision in Indian treaties).

The other tribes capitulated with equal abruptness. Their motive, according to investigator Cram, was treachery: "No disinterested witness to the proceedings believed that a single chief signed the treaty with the slightest possible intention of abiding by it." All they wanted was to get rid of the Nez Percés, lull the whites, and prepare for an uprising.

If there was treachery, neither Stevens nor the once hesitant Palmer detected it. Palmer went home and reported that all was well. Stevens, convinced that the tribes were placated, determined to ride on across the mountains with no more protection than a small group of Nez Percés chosen to represent their tribe in the council with the Blackfeet. Included in the entourage was mountain man William Craig, the Nez Percés' agent, who had served as an interpreter during the treaty making. The Nez Percés liked Craig so well that they let him keep his farm on Lapwai Creek, the only white man, under terms of the treaty, to be permitted inside the reservation.

In Montana the party concluded another treaty with the Flatheads and their relatives. Those Indians, too, added a delegation, and in full panoply the growing cavalcade crossed the Divide to the climactic meeting with the Blackfeet. In spite of delays occasioned by the laggard arrival of the treaty goods, the affair was a resounding success. The Nez Percés and Flatheads made what proved to be a permanent peace with their old enemies the Blackfeet; and for the first time the American government gained a workable understanding with those onetime scourges of the plains.

Gratified, Stevens turned toward home. On the evening of October 29, when he was thirty-five miles west of Fort Benton, a courier rode into his camp, so spent he had to be helped from the saddle.

His message was disastrous: from California to Canada the tribes were in arms.

6. Whose War Is This?

AS USUAL, the Americans misunderstood the workings of their own government. The treaties recently signed at Walla Walla by the Indians would not become operative until ratified by the United States Senate. But the Walla Walla council had scarcely adjourned when word spread that gold had been discovered near Fort Colville on the Columbia. Excited prospectors swarmed across the mountains. If they reflected at all about legal technicalities, they probably concluded that the signing of the treaties gave them every right to enter upon the "erstwhile" Indian lands.

The Yakimas fell upon the trespassers. There may have been outrages, as later charged—Indian women violated, Indian horses stoler. Or it may simply be that the restless savages found the small, ill-armed parties an irresistible temptation.

The survivors of one ambushed group fled back to Seattle with the alarm. Twenty-five-year-old Acting Governor Charles Mason, his pudgy humorless face worried behind its aureole of whiskers, called for volunteers. At approximately the same time (mid-September 1855) the Yakima agent, A. J. Bolen, determined to investigate. Reasoning that an escort of soldiers would attract rather than forestall resistance, he rode alone northward from the Dalles into the Yakima Valley. Three wild young braves slew him and tried to conceal the murder by burning his and his horse's bodies.

An Indian spy carried word of the killing to the Dalles. From the cantonment there Major Granville Haller marched against the Indians with eighty-four men and a howitzer. Another fifty men under Lieutenant W. A. Slaughter were ordered to cross Naches Pass from Fort Steilacoom and join Haller. The would-be squeeze play almost turned into a debacle. Several hundred Yakima warriors under Kamiakin killed five of Haller's men, wounded seventeen, captured his mules, and made him abandon his howitzer in a precipitate retreat. Warned in time, Lieutenant Slaughter escaped by a night march back across the mountains to Puget Sound.

Slaughter's retreat proved fortunate. Taking advantage of the dearth of troops in the sound area, the local Indians late in October killed nine settlers along the White River above Seattle. The survivors fled into the town, whose citizens hastily threw up blockhouses and fenced themselves off from land attack by a stockade. Then Slaughter unexpectedly reappeared to discomfit the Indians, and what might have been a general uprising dwindled off into sporadic hit-and-run clashes. One of the victims was Slaughter himself, shot through the heart one evening when he injudiciously exposed himself beside a campfire.

Well before this the Northwest had braced itself for a major campaign. Regular troops from Fort Vancouver began moving ponderously up the Columbia toward Yakima country. Both Mason of Washington and Governor George Curry of Oregon called for increased numbers of volunteers. As one of Curry's messengers galloped toward southern Oregon to seek enlistments among the miners, he was met by an agitated emissary bound northward to ask help from there. The Rogues and their neighbors had broken loose again.

The Rogue war was an intensification of vicious little conflicts that had culminated in August with some drunken Indians on the Klamath massacring ten or eleven miners. In revenge the whites shot, hanged, and threw into prospect holes twenty-five or so Indians—not the guilty ones, who had fled. The Indians struck back, and the war was on. Volunteers hurrying to the scene of conflict pounced in the dark on an unsuspecting village. At dawn they discovered that most of their twenty-three victims were old men, women, and children. Outraged, the Indians burned isolated farms and mines throughout the Rogue districts, killing at least sixteen settlers. On October 17 they capped the effort by surrounding a hamlet on Gallice Creek and with flaming arrows destroyed most of its cabins. The defenders were saved when volunteer troops arrived in the proverbial nick of time.

The messenger who overtook Governor Stevens in Montana gasped out an exaggerated account of as many of these details as he knew. He also added an urgent recommendation from officials in the settlements that Stevens not try to reach his office by riding west through hostile territory but that he retreat instead down the Missouri and journey home by way of Panama.

Stevens refused. Physical fear was no part of his make-up. More significantly, the treaties which were to make him famous had failed. Some compulsive offshoot of the trait that would not let him be pictured beside taller men now made him seek a spectacular reaffirmation of himself. Straight back through the enemy lands he dashed, over one pass so snowy that Indians crossing it a few days earlier had lost ten of their horses. Taking routes no one expected him to take, he caught first the Coeur d'Alenes and then the Spokanes by such surprise that they decided they had better not join the warring Indians after all.

Eighteen frightened miners had assembled for mutual protection not far from where Stevens held his conference with the Spokanes. He formed them into a militia company, complete with officers, called the Spokane Invincibles. Members of his own party organized under the name of the Stevens Guards. In retrospect it smacks of play acting, but at the time it was deadly serious. Plans were afoot, so the Spokanes warned, for the Yakimas and Walla Wallas to waylay the party; Peu-

peu-mox-mox himself had boasted that he would personally take the governor's scalp. Against these hundreds, perhaps thousands, of embittered warriors the Invincibles and the Guards could muster scarcely fifty rifles.

William Craig was sent ahead to Lapwai to assemble the Nez Percés. If the tribe was friendly they could help cut a way through enemy territory to the Dalles. If not—well, perhaps boldness would neutralize them, as it had the Coeur d'Alenes and Spokanes. Stripping equipment and supplies to a minimum, Stevens prepared to follow Craig on a fast dash through the sodden sleet of early December.

To the party's relief and mystification, they did not see a single Indian along the way. At Lapwai they learned why. Regular Army troops and a sprinkling of volunteers under bumbling Major Gabriel Rains had invaded the Yakima country in a fruitless campaign. The Indians easily slid out of the major's inept traps, but at least the sport had kept them occupied.

Peu-peu-mox-mox and his warriors had fared less well. Finding the Hudson's Bay Company's Fort Walla Walla abandoned, the Indians had joyfully burned it—inglorious end to the fabled landmark which Donald McKenzie had erected nearly forty years before. Belatedly worried by what they had done, the Indians then withdrew to their old homelands on the Touchet River, which flows into the Walla Walla from the north. There Oregon volunteers commanded by James Kelley caught up with them.

Under a flag of truce Peu-peu-mox-mox and half a dozen chiefs rode out to talk peace. Kelley gave his terms. Peu-peu-mox-mox sent one of his men to the village to tell the tribe what they must do. The other negotiators were held as hostages—by their own consent. In spite of this a great horde of Indians attacked. As the outnumbered volunteers edged away through the brushy defiles, the savages worked themselves into proper ecstasy by erecting on the hilltops tall poles bearing white scalps and dancing about them in a frenzy.

As the successive charges came, Peu-peu-mox-mox, though a hostage, howled exhortations to his warriors. During one desperate flurry Kelley ordered the Indian prisoners tied. Peu-peu-mox-mox protested: "No tie men; tie dogs and horses." The struggling savages were nevertheless dragged to the ground. When Peu-peu-mox-mox produced a hidden dagger, one of the volunteers hit him over the head with a gun barrel, killed him, and took his scalp—"a beauty," recalled one witness, "the hair about eighteen inches long, all braided in with beads and eagle feathers."

The battle, which ended in the defeat of the Indians, lasted four days. During that critical period, while every Indian in the vicinity was involved either as a spectator or a participant, Stevens crossed undetected to Lapwai.

Several hundred Nez Percés were assembled there. Most of them were friendly—or became so after learning of the Walla Wallas' defeat. Enrolling a gaily bedecked company as auxiliaries and appointing Craig their lieutenant colonel, Stevens hurried on to a temporary fort which the Oregon volunteers had established two miles above Whitman's old Waiilatpu mission (now occupied by two settlers as a Donation claim). There the governor was met with word that General Wool, in command of the Department of the Pacific, had appeared at Vancouver and was throwing more obstacles into the prosecution of the war—or at least the war as the settlers wanted it fought—than were the Indians.

John Ellis Wool was seventy-one years old. He had had a successful military career, beginning with the War of 1812. He was used to command and was solidified in the conviction that army methods were the only proper methods—an attitude almost certain to strike sparks from the equally flinty self-assurance of Isaac Stevens. The violent splinter wars of southern Oregon and northern California had persuaded Wool that the whites were often the chief aggressors and that the Indians needed the protection of his troops even more than did the settlers. He felt that the volunteer militia which the territorial governors threw into the field at the least sign of emergency were illegal and inefficient. He even believed that the emergencies were sometimes manufactured to provide pay checks for the volunteers and supply contracts for local merchants.

With these opinions firmly fixed, he set sail in November to see just what was happening in the Northwest. The trip northward from California did not improve his disposition. The weather was tempestuous. As the steamer was wallowing across the Columbia bar a boiler burst and the ship, laden with gunpowder, took fire. Fortunately a breaker hit the crippled vessel's stern and helped boost her over the bar into comparatively quiet water, where soldiers were able to extinguish the blaze.

At Vancouver, Wool learned that Governor Curry of Oregon, who knew the general's feelings about volunteers, had disobeyed regulations by refusing to put his home-mustered troops under command of the Regular Army officers. Infuriated, Wool ordered the Oregon volunteers disbanded. Curry declined—all by letter, for the two refused to meet in person. Meanwhile some Washington volunteers had arrived in Vancouver for mustering in. Wool ordered them home. Included in the number was a company recruited by former Indian agent Benjamin Shaw, commissioned a colonel by Acting Governor Mason, for the express purpose of rescuing Stevens. Nonsense, said Wool. Stevens should do as he had been told and come home via Panama.

All this was relayed to Stevens at the temporary fort on the Walla Walla by Shaw himself. For the time being, however, the governor swallowed his resentment. He had conceived a grandiose plan for a winter campaign, no small part of it based on the construction of a fleet of barges to master the Columbia's difficult supply routes. He dispatched a detailed outline of the scheme to Wool, but almost immediately an unprecedented cold wave turned the Columbia to ice as far as the mouth of the Willamette. Realizing his proposed operation would have to wait, Stevens started a chill ride for Olympia, intending to call on Wool en route.

The general must have known he was coming, but urgent messages from California led Wool to sail the evening before Stevens arrived. Considering himself insulted once again, the governor crossed to Olympia. There he threw himself energetically into defense measures that included removing all friendly Indians to the west side of the sound and erecting numerous blockhouses to ward off the unfriendly ones. The danger was acute. On January 26, 1856, Indians attacked Seattle itself, burning outlying houses but being driven off by cannon fire from a warship in the harbor and by the energetic presence of a company of marines.

In February, from California, Wool responded to Stevens' overexcited but now dormant plans for a winter campaign with unnecessary sarcasm. "You should have recollected," he wrote, "that I have neither the resources of a Territory nor the treasury of the United States at my command." Complacently he added, "Still . . . I think I shall be able to bring the war to a close in a few months, provided the extermination of the Indians, which I do not approve of, is not determined on, and private war prevented, and the volunteers withdrawn from the Walla Walla country." What he meant was that recent reinforcements by regular troops under Colonel George Wright at Vancouver and Lieutenant Colonel Silas Casey at Steilacoom would be quite sufficient to handle matters as they should be handled.

The letter and Wool's failure to call on him during a subsequent flying visit to the sound roused Stevens to a furious reply. In twenty-five hundred words of sonorous euphemisms he charged Wool with imbecility, inefficiency, untruthfulness, and wanton neglect of duty, especially in failing to let Stevens be rescued by Shaw's volunteers. If any faint possibility of co-ordinating the services had still existed, that letter ended it.

Co-ordination, heaven knows, was needed. The reason for Wool's second trip to Vancouver was the resumption, after the winter rains, of the wars in southern Oregon. On February 23 a concerted outbreak along the lower Rogue left more than sixty homes in ruins and thirty-one inhabitants dead, among them redoubtable Ben Wright (no kin to Colonel Wright), whose heart the Indians roasted and ate in order to absorb his courage. One hundred and thirty survivors, besieged for almost a month near Gold Beach, watched in wretched suspense as rescue ships failed in repeated efforts to effect landings through the heavy surf.

Agonized appeals from the settlers prompted Wool to start fresh troops north from California, south from Vancouver. In time the exigencies of the field brought their officers, against Wool's desires, into working with the volunteers, and by mid-July five years of frightful war in southern Oregon were at last over.

No such rapport was established in the north. In March, Colonel Wright, squat and fat and amiable, began the cumbersome job of moving his regiment toward Yakima country. A clog of supplies existed at the Cascades of the Columbia. Here goods had to be unloaded from the steamers and placed on a little wooden mule-drawn railroad for transfer to a pair of small stern-wheelers waiting at the upper end of the rapids. These two vessels thrashed through another forty miles of quiet water to the terrible chute of the Dalles. There land transport took over entirely.

There was a settlement at the lower end of the Cascades and another at the upper, with a blockhouse between, all on the northern bank of the river. The six-mile stretch was vital. A breaking of the Cascade portages would strangle operations in the interior. After Wright had heaved his forces through the bottleneck, however, he left a garrison of only nine men at the blockhouse.

Alert Kamiakin of the Yakimas promptly inveigled the Cascade Indians to join his tribe in a simultaneous attack on all three points. The blow failed by a whisker. The crew of one of the steamers at the upper end of the rapids managed to hold off the savages until the engineer got up enough steam for the vessel to churn up the river after Wright. Survivors of the attack at the lower Cascades fled to

Portland. Those who could not escape forted up, without water, either in the blockhouse or at Bradford's store at the upper Cascades. By the time Wright hurried back down the river and Lieutenant Phil Sheridan moved up, sixteen whites were dead, twelve wounded.

Warned by bugles of the soldiers' approach, the Yakimas fled, leaving their Cascade allies to pay for the failure. Wright hanged nine of them. And still he thought that Wool was correct, that the best way to deal with the Yakimas was through cajolery. He ordered George Curry once again to disband the Oregon volunteers in the Walla Walla country (Curry refused) and sent word to the Indians that he had arrived to treat as a friend, not to make war. Suspicious of so novel an approach, the Indians kept stalling until they could replenish their food stocks from the annual spring run of salmon and thus be ready for whatever happened. It turned out to be practically nothing.

In the meantime Isaac Stevens was working himself into still another altercation. On Muckleshoot Prairie east of Steilacoom on the sound lived certain French Canadians, former Hudson's Bay Company employees with native wives, whose farms seemed strangely immune to Indian attack. Stevens suspected the English company. He believed, for example, that its officials were encouraging the Indian attacks east of the mountains in order to keep Americans out and so gain control of the gold discoveries along the Columbia. [1] Equally ready to heed charges that the Muckleshoot French Canadians were informing the enemy about military movements, the Washington governor ordered the farmers to report to certain blockhouses, where they could be watched.

Five refused. Stevens imprisoned them in the Fort Steilacoom brig. This highhanded action annoyed various citizens who on behalf of the prisoners appealed for writs of *habeas corpus*. Stevens responded by declaring martial law, thus rendering the civil processes inoperative.

In defiance of the governor's edict, the chief justice of the territory, Edward Lander (no kin to the Lander whom Stevens had once threatened to shoot), opened court with the aid of a sheriff's posse and ordered Stevens arrested. Stevens had the marshal restrained by

[1] The view was not unreasonable. As early as 1852, Angus MacDonald, in charge of Fort Colville, knew that his men had found gold at several points along the Columbia and in Montana. He so notified his superiors, who warned him to keep the discoveries quiet. The company did not want to monopolize the strikes, however, so much as to forestall a rush of Americans that would ruin the fur trade—as indeed it had. And, officially at least, the company was not inciting the Indians.

force from serving the attachment and then retaliated by using his militia to arrest the judge and hand him over to Colonel Shaw of the volunteers for safekeeping. When Stevens further ordered the volunteers to close the courts, another justice called on the Regular Army to keep them open. Fortunately Lieutenant Colonel Silas Casey of the army was levelheaded enough to stall off an armed clash until Stevens' military commission could assemble and try the Muckleshoot farmers for treason.

The commission worked out a compromise. It upheld Stevens' right to declare martial law but denied themselves jurisdiction over trials for treason. The poor footballs of the uproar were then remanded to a civil court and freed for want of evidence.

Judge Lander, also released and bristling furiously, fined Stevens fifty dollars for contempt. Stevens rushed angrily to his office and, by virtue of the authority vested in him as governor, issued himself a pardon. This document, unique in the annals of American history, Lander refused to accept. Belatedly recognizing that popular sentiment was against him, Stevens then paid his fine under protest and sent to the President of the United States a passionate appeal for vindication. The reply, written by Secretary of War Marcy, was hardly what he expected: "The President . . . is induced . . . to express his distinct disapproval of your conduct."

By that time the Indians of the sound had been pacified, and Stevens was preparing to carry his mercurial energies back beyond the mountains.

An uneasy truce prevailed. The Yakimas had convinced Colonel Wright that they really meant no harm and, on Wright's so reporting, Wool had declared hostilities ended. In the Grande Ronde Valley of eastern Oregon, Shaw's volunteers made their peace by administering a sound drubbing to the Walla Wallas and Cayuses, and those Indians, too, seemed ready to settle down.

To Stevens the situation appeared ripe for another council. With an inadequate escort he visited the site of the first great Walla Walla council, hoping that this second effort would bring about the triumph he craved. But only the Nez Percés would talk to him, and as the dismayed governor started for home hostile Indians from several tribes (including a hundred or more disgruntled Nez Percés) swooped down on his flanks.

After a skillful withdrawal Stevens managed to reach Colonel E. J. Steptoe, who was camped eight miles away. Together they fought off the savages and Steptoe emerged converted: these Indians weren't friendly and the volunteers were better fighters than he had been led to believe. He said as much in a brisk letter that Colonel Wright forwarded to General Wool.

Wool retorted that Stevens had held the second council merely to reinflame hostilities. Once again he urged Congress not to ratify the treaties Stevens had negotiated the previous year. He also issued a proclamation closing the land east of the Cascade Mountains to settlers —but for some reason not to miners or to employees of established Hudson's Bay posts so long as the prospectors did not molest the Indians. He further ordered Wright and Steptoe to protect the savages by building a new Fort Walla Walla (forerunner of the modern city of the same name) on the site of Stevens' attempted council.

He overreached. So continuous a roar of protest about his actions had been going to Congress from the legislatures of Oregon and Washington that he was now replaced as commander of the Department of the Pacific by General N. S. Clarke. This brought no comfort to Stevens. Clarke rescinded none of Wool's orders. And the Washington governor was coming in for rebuffs of his own. He was replaced as superintendent of Indian affairs, and his legislature passed a resolution censuring him for his actions during the martial-law episode. Seeking vindication once again, Stevens resigned as governor and ran for delegate to Congress. In July 1857 he was elected by a decisive majority, and the next session of the legislature voted to rescind the censure.

During 1857 politics also absorbed Oregon. Although Congress had passed no enabling act authorizing self-government, the voters decided they were going to be a state anyhow. A constitutional convention was assembled in August and prepared a document that was quickly approved. Though Congress still ignored them, the people then proceeded to elect a full slate of officers. One of their senatorial designates was an ardent pro-slavery Democrat, former territorial governor and congressional delegate, Joseph Lane. It was a paradoxical choice, for the electorate had just overwhelmingly decreed that both slavery *and* free Negroes were to be excluded from the state. The latter restriction, incidentally, was not removed until 1926.

Though a senator at home, in Washington City Joe Lane was only a voteless delegate from a territory, as was Isaac Stevens. Joining forces, the two campaigned assiduously to steer Oregon's statehood bill through the sectional murk then beclouding congressional debates. By a narrow margin they succeeded. The vote in the House was

114 for admission, 103 opposed, and on February 14, 1859, President Buchanan signed the act. Oregon was now a state. [2]

At about the same time Stevens had the satisfaction of seeing the treaties he had concluded with the Indians four years earlier come up for renewed consideration. So far the documents had failed of Senate ratification because of General Wool's opposition, but in the West army opinion was being rapidly and forcibly revised.

The Indians of eastern Washington had not proved as amiable as Colonel Wright had anticipated. There were repeated clashes with miners; and after a group of prospectors at Colville late in 1857 petitioned for troops it was decided that Colonel Steptoe, in charge of new Fort Walla Walla, should march northward the following spring to give the savages a few words of fatherly advice.

Just before he started, the Coeur d'Alenes and Spokanes received infuriating word that a white man's highway was soon to be built through their lands. This was the Missouri-to-Columbia road for which Congress in 1854, at Stevens' behest, had allocated thirty thousand dollars. The long-delayed work had at last been intrusted to Lieutenant John Mullan with orders that he begin operations as early as he could in 1858. No one bothered to notify the Indians; their sole information was rumor. Nor did the Coeur d'Alenes and Spokanes think to ask the whites for details. They just got mad.

Steptoe was not aware of their rage. Supposing that his expedition would amount to little more than a practice march, he took only 158 men with him. Preparations were negligent. Antiquated arms were not replaced, and when his civilian packers found they lacked sufficient livestock to carry all the baggage, they evened matters by discarding several boxes of ammunition.

Friendly Nez Percés ferried the cavalcade across the brown flood of the Snake in canoes. As Steptoe resumed his northward march hostile Indian spies drifted unchallenged in and out of his lines. Some twenty miles south of the present city of Spokane a thousand or more warriors suddenly appeared in front of him. Their spokesman told Steptoe that they would not ferry the column over the Spokane River and that he might as well go home. Looking at their numbers, the colonel agreed.

Throughout that day and part of the next the Indians followed

[2] Oregon's eastern boundary, instead of being the Rocky Mountains, became what it is now. The lands shorn from her—the fat southern part of Idaho and a wedge of present Wyoming—were added to Washington Territory but remained there only until the gold rushes of the 1860s forced new realignments.

beside the retreating column, offering nothing more than jeers. Then, and the immediate cause is not traceable, long-range rifle fire began to crackle. The dragoons made angry little charges to dislodge the Indians from brush or trees. At each rush the Indians ran away, then returned to their sniping. The frightened animals of the pack train hampered maneuverability, and at dusk the troops found themselves pinned on the top of a steep hill. Baggage was arranged in bulwarks and the last ammunition issued—three rounds per man.

The soldiers were dead ducks and the Indians knew it. Victory dances began and the red sentries drifted away from their posts to join the fun. Some unknown hero among the besieged who knew Indian nature persuaded Steptoe to send out scouts to the south. No Indians. Abandoning guns, supplies, extra horses—even two mortally wounded men—the troops crept off through the dusk toward the Nez Percé ferry over the Snake, nearly ninety miles away. Incredibly they made it, thanks to an Indian quarrel over their abandoned loot.

A major disaster had been averted, but the blow to the army's prestige was devastating. Colonel Wright, who two years earlier had marched through the region declaring his friendly intentions, underwent a complete revulsion of feelings. When Catholic missionaries now failed to persuade the Spokanes and Coeur d'Alenes to accept his surrender terms, he moved up six hundred regulars to Fort Walla Walla, issued them brand-new, long-range repeating rifles, and began ruthless drills. Lieutenant Mullan, postponing his road work, hurried in to take charge of a company of Nez Percé auxiliaries. Privately Mullan hoped to get in a little surveying between fights and to that end took along a small cart for carrying his equipment. It was the only wheeled vehicle in the expedition. All else went by a pack train manned by a hundred mule skinners. This time there would be no dearth of ammunition.

The campaign was double-pronged. Inspired by the success of the Spokanes against Steptoe, the Yakimas had begun harrying parties of miners moving up the Columbia toward the new gold fields beyond the border. To teach them better, Major Garnett was sent through their lands with an additional three hundred men. Wright continued against the original miscreants.

The long-range rifles were too much for the Spokanes and their allies. Even by setting fire to the grass and creeping up under cover of the smoke, the savages could not come close enough for their inferior weapons to be effective. The last of the heart went out of them when Wright captured their main horse herd and spent two gory days slaughtering every animal.

As part of their surrender terms the tribes were forced to hand over for trial the individuals suspected of murdering whites or inciting the attack on Steptoe. The accused were given a summary trial and, if convicted, put to death. Garnett executed them by tying them to trees and shooting them; Wright by standing them in Mullan's cart, throwing a rope over a tree limb, and hanging them. The land was declared open for settlement and Wright further recommended that Stevens' treaties be ratified *in toto*.

With the go-ahead little man on hand to watch the vindication, the Senate complied on March 8, 1859. It was Stevens' last triumph. When his colleague Joe Lane campaigned for the vice-presidency of the United States as running mate of John C. Breckenridge, Stevens functioned as chairman of their national committee. Lincoln's victory ended their political careers. Lane retired to his farm near Roseburg, Oregon, unjustly vilified for his supposed complicity in a plot to form a new nation by splitting the Pacific coast states away from the East. Stevens joined the Union army, rising to the rank of major general. On September 1, 1862, aged forty-four, he was slain while rallying his men against Stonewall Jackson's advance after the second battle of Bull Run.

7. Exit Goliath

AS IT had the Indians, civilization toppled that other unique social organization of the wilderness, the Hudson's Bay Company. Squatters encroached on its lands; petty officials challenged its treaty-given right to move goods duty-free up the Columbia to its posts in New Caledonia. Rather than buck the tide, the company decided to sell its land claims and those of its subsidiary, the Puget Sound Agricultural Company, to the United States and withdraw its headquarters to the spot which James Douglas had selected in 1843 for just this contingency—Fort Victoria on Vancouver Island.

This island, the largest on the West coast of North America, was rented from the Crown for a token seven shillings a year. In return the company was obligated to establish a colony of emigrants from the United Kingdom, the theory being that stout settlements of Englishmen would prevent penetration by Americans and the consequent loss of more territory to the United States by what might be termed the Oregon method.

To free the proposed settlements from too much company interference, the Crown appointed an outsider, one Richard Blanshard, to be governor of Vancouver Island. This annoyed Chief Factor Douglas, grown autocratic with the years. By the simple process of making life miserable, he induced Blanshard to resign. The Crown then yielded to the company's London directors and appointed James Douglas governor. In theory Douglas was restrained by a council, but in practice restraint seldom occurred. The Black Scot named the council members himself, and all but one were employees of the company. When finally the ministry ordered the chief factor to institute an elected assembly, his rubber-stamp council set property requirements so high that a scant forty persons qualified to vote.

The only funds at the disposal of the new seven-man assembly were those deriving from liquor licenses. All other revenues (from land sales, from the newly discovered coal mines at Nanaimo) were collected by the company. By terms of the Crown grant the company deducted ten per cent of this income to compensate itself for running the colony and devoted the rest to administrative expenses. When the first assembly grew curious about these expenses Douglas withheld his books, as he was entitled to do under the wording of the grant.

There were few independent settlers around to protest his autocracy. Land terms were so onerous, in contrast to the liberal policy of the Americans just south of the border, that immigrants had little inducement to risk the long trip around the Horn. In 1858, after nine years as capital of the colony, Victoria had a population of scarcely five hundred, most of them servants or former servants of the company, and their numerous half-Indian progeny.

In his own eyes at least, Douglas had reason for looking askance at the workings of democracy. Oregon officials, bustling with their new self-importance, seized and sold for trespass a valuable British ship simply because its crew cut a few timbers from the unbroken forest beside Juan de Fuca Strait. The company vessel *Beaver*, with another ship in tow, was likewise confiscated for landing a single passenger at Nisqually before reporting to the port of entry at Olympia. In each case United States courts allowed the company twenty thousand dollars in damages; but other violations, particularly of the Puget Sound Agricultural Company lands near Nisqually and Cowlitz, went unpunished.

The Americans considered these lands fair game. The company paid no taxes on them, having been issued no patents by the United States Government. They occupied the choice prairie sections of a heavily timbered region. Most irritating of all, the French-Canadian squaw men who worked the farms for the company were suspected, rightly or wrongly, of being in secret league with the Indians during the uprisings of 1855–56.

According to one set of statistics, the company by 1853 had protested fifty cases of illegal squatting on its lands. By the end of the Indian wars it had lost to raiding white neighbors 6058 cattle and approximately the same number of sheep. When company managers grew outraged, they were ordered to swallow their wrath lest an inflammatory clash imperil the sale of the holdings to the United States.

Negotiations were difficult enough at best. The land claimed by the Hudson's Bay and Puget Sound companies south of the border (at Vancouver, Nisqually, Cowlitz, and the smaller forts of Walla Walla, Boise, and Hall) amounted to about twenty-three thousand acres, of which some three thousand were cultivated. Improvements, notably at Vancouver, were extensive. Figures about the worth of these lands and buildings and the common-law grazing rights in the surrounding countryside were enormously disparate. Isaac Stevens suggested $300,000. Angered by the livestock raids at Puget Sound, the destruction of Walla Walla by Peu-peu-mox-mox's Indians and the forced abandonment of Boise and Hall, the company countered with a staggering demand for $3,800,000. Second thinking in 1858 scaled this impulsive price down to $650,000; but before Congress got around to acting the Civil War intervened and all negotiations came to a stop.

Equally touchy was the boundary quarrel. By treaty the line followed the forty-ninth parallel "to the middle of the channel which separates the continent from Vancouver's Island; and thence southerly through the middle of said channel and of Fuca's straits, to the Pacific Ocean."

Unfortunately there were two channels, the Canal de Haro and the Strait of Rosario. Between them lay the idyllic and highly strategic San Juan Islands. Since these islands controlled the contiguous harbors of Victoria and Esquimalt as well as the approach to the Fraser River, James Douglas wanted his government to establish the Strait of Rosario to the east of the islands as the boundary. The Americans, on the

other hand, could obtain the islands by pushing the line westward
to the Canal de Haro.

Douglas moved first. In 1850 he set up a salmon-curing station on
San Juan, westernmost of the islands. Three years later he sent over
thirteen hundred head of sheep under a man named Charles Griffin.
Learning of this, the Washington legislature declared the islands attached to the territory's northernmost county, Whatcom. When the
company declined to pay taxes, the Whatcom sheriff seized thirty-
four rams and sold them at auction. Douglas dashed off a hot protest
to Stevens and asked damages to the amount of three thousand pounds.
Stevens bristled in return but was told by Secretary of State Marcy
to calm down while a joint commission of both governments studied
the problem. In 1857 the commissioners met on San Juan and with
elaborate politeness failed utterly to agree.

Meanwhile two home-grown woes were about to fall upon the
company. One was a parliamentary review of its affairs preliminary
to the scheduled renewal of its license in 1858. The other was the
discovery of gold on the Fraser River.

During the 1850s strong opposition to monopolies of all kinds had.
boiled up in England. Infant Canada, moreover (at that time consisting
only of the provinces of Quebec and Ontario), wanted to annex the
Red River colony and the plains of Saskatchewan, both of which lay
within the company's original enormous grant of Rupert's Land, as
the entire area draining into Hudson Bay was known. These two trends
combined in a merciless attack on the company during the review of
1857. When the parliamentary committee finally made its report on
the license, it was obvious that the once ironclad monopoly was about
to be softened.

Changes would have come in any event. Miners drifting northward
from the Colville discoveries in 1856 and 1857 turned up bits of gold
above the border along the Columbia, the Okanagan, the Fraser. Douglas tried to control the finds by buying all the dust produced, but
he could not control the spread of rumor. As excited talk flashed back
into Oregon and Washington, more and more miners crowded in. To
keep some sort of check on them Douglas boldly exceeded his authority (legally he was governor of Vancouver Island only) by issuing,
in January 1858, a proclamation stating that all mineral deposits on
the mainland belonged to the Crown and could be mined only under
license. These licenses, costing twenty-one shillings or about five dollars a month, were obtainable only at Victoria.

Three months later the deluge came. Douglas sent the gold he had been buying—several hundred thousand dollars' worth—aboard the company ship *Otter* to San Francisco for minting. Immediately the news got abroad. On April 20 the *Commodore* steamed north with four hundred and fifty excited prospectors—thus almost doubling Victoria's population. More ships followed. In June alone upwards of seven thousand persons sailed from San Francisco. By that time nearly three hundred raw lumber buildings had been hammered together on the meadows around Fort Victoria's stockade, and the price of choice building lots, sixty by one hundred and twenty feet, had soared from five dollars each to more than three thousand. Jealous Whatcom on the American side of the sound tried to cash in on the excitement by pointing out that it was closer to the Fraser River than was Victoria; but Whatcom could provide neither licenses nor adequate transport. Douglas' colony continued to reap the gain—and the headaches.

In the United States mineral on unclaimed land was free to whoever reached it first—except for Chinese, on whom most mining districts imposed special taxes. Douglas' licenses accordingly struck the immigrants as arbitrary and discriminatory, though actually the law applied to British citizens as well as to American "foreigners." In a resentful effort to avoid the fees, many stampeders by-passed Victoria and tried to sneak up the Fraser in Indian canoes, several of them drowning in the process.

To check them, Douglas stationed a warship at the mouth of the Fraser. (It seized sixteen unauthorized vessels in June alone.) To improve transport and to impose still further restraint on the miners, he gave to the Pacific Mail Steam Ship Company of California a charter to operate six vessels between Victoria and the head of navigation on the Fraser. The Pacific Company agreed to carry no unlicensed passengers and only goods belonging to the Hudson's Bay Company; in return the ship operators kept all proceeds save for two dollars per passenger, which sum was rebated not to the colony but to Douglas' company.

This was monopoly with a vengeance—and it was about run out. In England, Parliament declined to renew the company's exclusive trading rights west of the mountains. Douglas' restrictions in favor of the Hudson's Bay Company were disallowed, and on August 2, 1858, jurisdiction was placed in the hands of the new Crown colony of British Columbia.

Although the administration of British Columbia was designed to be distinct from that of Vancouver Island, Douglas was invited to be governor of both colonies, provided he severed every connection with the Hudson's Bay and Puget Sound Agricultural companies. He must have hesitated. For thirty-seven years the company had been his life. But he could go no higher in the firm than the chief factorship he already held, and his brief taste of civil authority had left him ambitious to make his mark in the British colonial service. The combined governorships, moreover, would bring him almost twenty-five thousand dollars a year—ten times the average salary paid by the United States to one of its territorial governors.

He accepted and on November 25, 1858, was inaugurated at New Fort Langley, two and a half miles upstream from the fur company's post of the same name. The ceremony was attended by as many ranking dignitaries as were available: Admiral Baynes of the Pacific Fleet; Colonel Moody in charge of a newly arrived company of Royal Engineers; gigantic Matthew Baille Begbie, the formidable new chief justice of the colony. A rainstorm washed out part of the formalities, and afterward Douglas returned directly to Victoria. British Columbia was to have its own capital—New Westminister, just surveyed by the engineers on the north side of the Fraser—but to James Douglas Victoria was home, and he would govern from there. His subordinates of course followed him, even those who had no business whatsoever on the island; and throughout his administration the Black Scot was accused of betraying British Columbia's interests either to the fur company or to the rival colony in which his home was located.

The charges seem unfounded. Meticulous, austere, and rigidly proud, Douglas achieved as aloof an impartiality as any man in such position could. He worked ceaselessly to improve transportation and establish law for the heterogeneous population of both territories. He toured the gold fields in person, appointed gold commissioners with police power to supervise all aspects of mining activity, and at the first rumor of disorder sent troops to the scene. Even toward his son-in-law, Alexander Grant Dallas, who succeeded him as factor of the Hudson's Bay Company, he was icily superior whenever the situation demanded.

The establishment of his iron rule was aided by a pause in the gold boom. Most of the first stampeders reached the Fraser in midsummer, just when melting snow in the mountains inundated the gravel bars. Disgusted both by the unexpected flood (they were used to spring runoffs) and by what they considered Douglas' cramping restrictions, the less patient of the men drifted home. Their bitter reports quickly changed the plans of many parasites who otherwise might have followed the scent of easy money to the new diggings and there made the governor's life much more difficult.

A fragment of the retrograde movement hung up on disputed San Juan Island. One of the disgruntled Americans, Lyman Cutler, planted a potato garden. On June 15, 1859, a pig belonging to Charles Griffin, the manager of the Hudson's Bay sheep farm, invaded the plot. Cutler shot the pig. Heatedly Griffin demanded a hundred dollars in damages and was told, unprintably, to chase himself. Since Victoria was less than twenty miles away, the company's chief factor, Alexander Dallas, decided to investigate in person.

Reports of what followed disagree. Dallas said that he merely remonstrated with Cutler, who grew abusive. Cutler said he was ordered to pay or be taken to Victoria for trial, a jurisdiction he refused to acknowledge. Whatever transpired, it was limited to words, and Dallas withdrew.

The Fourth of July arriving, the Americans on San Juan Island showed off their independence with a noisy celebration. By chance General William Harney, commander of the newly created Department of Oregon, landed that very day while on a tour of inspection. The settlers besought troops to defend their interests. As further justification they cited the fierce Haida Indians of the north, who in their huge canoes frequently raided the tribes of the sound for slaves and who two years before on nearby Whidbey Island had chopped off the head of a prominent resident named Colonel Isaac Ebey.

Harney, who felt San Juan would make a valuable naval station, decided that here was a way to force the issue over sovereignty. Returning to the mainland, he dispatched Captain George Pickett, soon to achieve fame at Gettysburg, with sixty men to occupy the island. They landed on July 27, 1859.

Douglas exploded. Off went three British warships and a detachment of troops with strange orders: dislodge Pickett yet avoid a clash. Pickett declined to co-operate. Though overwhelmingly outnumbered, he "nobly replied," in Harney's words, "that whether they [the English] landed fifty or five thousand men, his conduct would not be affected by it; that he would open his fire. . . ."

Good judgment rather than Pickett's defiance held the British commander offshore until Admiral Baynes, commander of the Pacific Fleet, could arrive. Baynes approved the restraint and told Douglas that he would not "involve two great nations in a war over a squabble about a pig." Pickett meanwhile apprised Harney of the growing concentration of British vessels, bristling now with 167 guns and 2140 men.

To oppose this formidable array, Harney ordered in 500 American reinforcements. Covered by fog, the troops managed to land. And still Baynes held back, though Douglas protested furiously at the intrusion.

By this time word of the trouble had reached Washington. In alarm the United States Government dispatched its biggest brass, Lieutenant General Winfield Scott, to investigate. Dryly Scott reported, "I found both Brigadier General Harney and Captain Pickett proud of their *conquest* of the island and quite jealous of interference. . . ." He interfered, nevertheless, chiding Harney officially and ordering Pickett's troops replaced by a token squad under a different officer.

The British called off their ships; Scott departed. Harney thereupon used a settlers' petition for help as excuse for sending Pickett back with more men, a foolishness that resulted in the general's abrupt recall. Nominal forces of each government thereafter held San Juan under joint military occupation until arbitration could be effected. In 1872 the islands were awarded to the United States. By that time the differences over the Hudson's Bay and Puget Sound Agricultural claims had also been settled, the United States paying four hundred fifty thousand dollars to the former, two hundred thousand to the latter.

During the year of the pig, 1859, mining along the Fraser declined —but only in contrast to the feverish expectations of '58: prospectors still managed to produce a million and a half in gold. More importantly, the searchers pushed deeper into the interior, opening new fields and creating new problems for Douglas, the most difficult of which was transportation to the towns at the upper end of the Fraser's thunderous canyons.

These fearful chasms Douglas avoided by mapping a road that left the river several miles below the mushroom camp of Hope and struck north through a series of lakes, streams, and portages, returning eventually to the main river at the raw camp of Lillooet. The miners themselves built most of the route during the summer of 1860, five hundred of them even putting up a bond of twenty-five dollars each as an earnest of good behavior and drawing their pay in merchandise.

The way had one drawback: the number of times freight had to be handled at the portages. With the discovery of the great Cariboo fields in 1860 and 1861, the frantic demand for supplies meant that an uninterrupted highway had to be developed.

Competition from the south helped speed the work. As had been true in California, Oregonians were among the first to reach the new diggings. As early as 1858, when the Yakima Indians were still on the warpath, enterprising Yankees had begun pressing inland up the Columbia with pack trains and herds of cattle, an enterprise stimulated in 1860 by a flurry of discoveries at Similkameen just north of the border. Among the leaders in the movement was erstwhile Indian Superintendent Joel Palmer, who first packed into British Columbia in '58 and in 1860 penetrated as far north as the Quesnel, where until his advent flour sold for $125 a barrel and tools were not available at any price.

It could be a long, hard trip. In 1861 teen-age Jack Splawn and two Indians helped a Major Thorp drive a herd of beef north past the long finger of Okanagan Lake and across the roaring Thompson River into the grassy hills around Cache Creek. When winter drew near the Indians vanished and the major had to attend to business at home. Jack was left with the cattle—but not alone. Mule skinners, many of them California Mexicans, moved into the grassy vales with their livestock and squaws, built a camp of log hutches, and settled down for the winter. The cold was intense. Jack's clothing was so inadequate that instead of riding out to check on his cattle he had to run to keep from freezing. For seventy days all he had to eat was beef. But finally spring and the major returned. On they went, into the wild tumbled hills of the Cariboo. All summer they herded the steers in such pockets of grass as they could find, driving a few head into the butcher shops as needed. When the next winter's first storm struck they killed the remaining animals, buried them in snow, sold the carcasses, and started for home, the major loaded with eighty-odd pounds of gold worth twenty thousand dollars.

All the fantasy of the early placer camps was there: short supplies, disappointment, rumor, and sudden dizzy strokes of luck; the grueling work of whipsawing lumber, digging shafts in compacted gravel, wading blue-lipped in the icy streams. It was lonesome. Even before the heyday of the Cariboo excitement, the Bishop of Columbia reported home to the Church of England that one of the colony's greatest lacks was that of suitable female companionship.

In response to his plea the Columbian Emigration Society was formed in London under church auspices to encourage "respectable females, neither afraid nor ashamed to work as domestic servants" to chance their fortunes in British Columbia. The first contingent of twenty, drawn from English orphanages, left in April 1862. Sixty more, heavily chaperoned, departed in June, followed in January by another thirty-six. Ages ranged from twelve to eighteen. The first age presumably was in the minority; one account describes the girls, who disembarked at Victoria two by two between a lane of eager spectators, as "more or less buxom, for they had been chosen with a desire to create a pleasing first impression." Nearly half of the arrivals were married almost at once, but, so clucks the same account, "a few were disappointments and the colony would have been better off without these."

To Americans, the most remarkable feature of the camps was their orderliness. From the beginning of Douglas' licensing system, the inpouring hordes knew that authority existed. They obeyed, some of them to their own amazement. The founder of the wild California town of Downieville was aghast at the docility. He said, so reported stern, far-ranging Judge Begbie from the forks of the Quesnel, that "they told me it was like California in '49; why, you would have seen all those fellows roaring drunk, and pistols and bare knives in every hand. I never saw a mining town anything like this."

Two and a half million dollars came out of the Cariboo in 1862, three and a half million in 1863. Disproportionate amounts of these sums were swallowed in freight charges. Importing a ton of goods from San Francisco, the closest supply center, cost sixteen hundred dollars, of which fourteen hundred was spent skirting the Fraser and winding from the mouth of the Quesnel eastward through the jagged mountains. Unless those prices were reduced, American packers working overland past Okanagan threatened to capture much of the commerce Douglas wanted to keep flowing through Victoria.

His answer was the most stupendous construction job in pioneer history, the famed Cariboo Road. Royal Engineers built the worst stretches, carving and blasting a heart-stopping path high along the precipices of the Fraser. Simultaneously private contractors hacked out clearance through the forests, laid corduroy across the swamps, hung suspension bridges above the glacial torrents. It cost a million and a quarter dollars. Potentially this was a ruinous debt for a wilderness province of perhaps twelve thousand permanent population. But Douglas financed the work with short-term bonds that he liquidated by levying (or allowing the contractors to levy as part of their payment) tolls so high the miners choked. Results were worth the treatment, however. Within two years the cost of freight from Victoria had dropped from about $1400 to $330 a ton—which was hardly cheap, except by comparison.

Before the final stretches of the road were completed Douglas' twin terms as governor expired. He refused reappointment. The Queen knighted him and as Sir James he retired with his half-Indian wife to a pillared mansion above the city born so suddenly from the trading post he himself had established only twenty years before.

The company for which he had originally built the post was about to retire also. Eastward, the colonies were going through the throes of confederation. British Columbia, which in 1866 had united with Vancouver, was invited to join the union. She hesitated. Between her and her Eastern sisters lay the towering granite of the Rockies and the wide reaches of Rupert's Land, still held by the Hudson's Bay Company. Commercial ties with Montreal and Toronto were non-existent; those with Puget Sound and San Francisco were life-blood.

The acquisition of Alaska by the United States in 1867 seemed to place British Columbia more firmly than ever in the Yankee embrace. Many Americans wanted to tighten the grip irrevocably by annexing both the Western colony and the central plains of Canada. One reason advanced in 1869 by the Senate Committee on Pacific Railroads for extending congressional favors to the Northern Pacific was the belief that completion of the route would seal "the destiny of the British possessions west of the Ninety-first meridian. They will become so strongly Americanized in interests and feelings that . . . the question of their annexation will be but a matter of time."

None of this was official. Nor did the United States Government itself ever encourage annexation talk, even when prodded by glowing suggestions that the country accept British Columbia in return for the *Alabama* claims against England. The agitation alarmed Canada, however. In return for confederation she offered to assume British Columbia's internal debts, maintain essential public services, pay the Western province an annual subsidy. Most importantly, she promised to build a Canadian railroad across the Rockies.

Politically at least, the way for such a transcontinental route was open. In 1869 the Hudson's Bay Company capitulated and sold to Canada, for three hundred thousand pounds, the bulk of Rupert's Land. Never again would a single company straddle the American continent, utter master of each destiny that fell beneath its shadow. The retreat which had begun so insensibly that day when Nathaniel Wyeth led Jason Lee onto the Oregon Trail was finished. British Columbia joined the dominion in 1871, and Canada, as well as the United States, stretched uninterrupted from sea to sea.

Book Five

EXTRAVAGANZA

1. Stampede

ON THE western slope of the Bitterroot Mountains, where a little stream tumbles down between the larger forks of Idaho's Clearwater River, an Indian was fishing for trout. As bait he used hellgrammite grubs, in whose gravelly shells he noted an occasional glint of yellow. Later on, when talking to an engaging old Indian trader named Elias Pierce, he remembered the color and chanced to mention it.

Pierce, who had learned prospecting in northern California and British Columbia, decided to look at the district. But when he endeavored to cross the reservation boundary with a small party in the spring of 1860 the Nez Percés ordered him back.

The opposition convinced him that gold must surely exist in the forbidden mountains. Hunting a guide who could spirit him past the watchful sentries, he paid a night visit to the lodge of old Timothy at Alpowa Creek. Timothy, one of Henry Spalding's first converts, liked the whites. But he was reluctant to offend his tribesmen by leading even a handful of them onto the reservation.

At this point his eighteen-year-old daughter Jane spoke up. She'd guide the interlopers, she said—and did, to a creek later called Oro Fino because of the flour-fine nature of its gold dust.

Short supplies soon forced the party out to the ramshackle hamlet growing up around the army's new Fort Walla Walla. More reluctance greeted their efforts to raise a grubstake. People were afraid of the Indians and of the mountain winter; and that fall only thirty persons risked pushing with the discoverers back into the diggings. Then in March 1861 one of the prospectors came out on snowshoes with a personal take of eight hundred dollars, good mining under winter conditions. More importantly, he reported that the Nez Percés apparently didn't mind a few whites digging in the steep, timbered canyons of the high country. To the Indians such territory was worthless; their concern lay in keeping plows out of their root grounds and pony meadows.

Bribery may have helped soften their opposition. According to one Nez Percé legend, money was seen passing between some of the whites and some of the chiefs. Be that as it may, on April 19 old Lawyer and forty-seven other Christianized, pro-white headmen signed an agreement stating that the area north of the Snake and of the South Fork of the Clearwater "is hereby opened to the whites in common with the Indians for mining purposes, provided, however, that the root grounds and agricultural tracts in said district shall, in no case be taken or occupied by the whites."

By this time the trail from Walla Walla was lined with pack trains and hurrying prospectors. Hard on their heels the steamboat *Colonel Wright* came thrashing up the Snake from the Columbia, looking for a suitable landing close to the mines. The best spot lay on the south bank, on the alluvial triangle between the Snake and the Clearwater where several Indians had established little grainfields and gardens. The agreement reaffirming the closure of this area was scarcely a month old. But surely the Indians would not object to a harmless boat landing and a single warehouse for storing goods.

Reluctantly the Nez Percés agreed. By October their fences had been torn down, their stock driven off; and a shack town of twelve hundred inhabitants—precursor of modern Lewiston—sprawled across the site.

By its very nature placer mining is the crudest form of exploitation —rush in, clean up, get out. The first men to reach a new strike generally profited most, whether from mining or from establishing townsites and stores. Hence the restless spread of would-be discoverers in all directions, the eager listening to rumor, the nervous stampede to each new gulch. To such men a paper closure of the Indian lands meant nothing. By summer Elk City had been established on the South Fork of the Clearwater, and heavily armed parties were pushing, in direct violation of the April agreement, onto the high, rolling benchlands above the canyon of the Salmon. There, in the peat bogs at the head of Meadow Creek, the searchers turned up the extraordinary deposits that gave birth to hectic Florence and its satellites.

Feeling in all sincerity that the Indians would be better off to recognize what could not be changed and to sell the violated lands for the highest price obtainable, several whites in 1863 prevailed upon the

Nez Percés to attend still another council. It was doomed from the outset. The mountain, non-Christian faction of the tribe, long accustomed to roaming in small bands under local leaders, had never been happy about having a single head chief for all Nez Percés, a concept imposed on them by Elijah White in 1843. The chieftainship of old Lawyer, with its apparent kowtowing to the whites, had done nothing to allay their hostility. And now Lawyer was cashing in again.

Under the terms of the proposed treaty most of the $260,000 offered for the violated lands would be spent in building up the agency and farmlands around Lapwai and Kamiah—home grounds of Lawyer's Christianized supporters.

Furiously the non-Christian bands rejected Lawyer. He decided nevertheless to go ahead with an agreement limited to his own followers—or so his supporters later insisted. The contention seems likely, for the reservation that he and his associates accepted was scarcely one tenth the size of the area originally allowed the tribe by the Stevens treaty of 1855. Even Lawyer could hardly have felt it was enough for the whole tribe; certainly those bands whose homelands were the lovely valleys of the Wallowa Mountains in extreme northeastern Oregon never believed that it was designed to hold them too.

Unfortunately the white negotiators seem honestly to have thought that they had dealt with the entire tribe. But since no gold was found in the Wallowas, no clashes would occur for several years to disabuse either party of its interpretation. By that time, as will be seen, rectification would be impossible.

The gold rush did not stop with Nez Percé territory. During the autumn of 1861 and again in 1862 restless groups roamed the gray sage deserts of eastern Oregon, motivated in part by a most durable will-o'-the-wisp: the lost Blue Bucket mine, supposedly stumbled across by a party of starved immigrants in 1845. Enrolled in one of these groups was young Moses Splawn, whose brother Jack was currently off in the distant Cariboo country, selling beef. Though several other parties, including one led by indefatigable Elias Pierce, made scattered strikes of varying degrees of richness throughout eastern Oregon, Moses Splawn's group had no luck. Discontent grew, and as the men neared the crossing of the Snake into present Idaho, Moses recalled another tantalizer almost as enduring as the tales of the Blue Bucket—Indian talk.

The year before, at Elk City and again near Florence, Moses had encountered an Indian who had told him that far southward, in a circular basin at the head of one of the creeks that form the Boise River, a man could find lots of this yellow dirt about which the whites grew so excited. Now Moses repeated the story.

It met with tempered enthusiasm. The Boise country lay within the range of the Bannack Indians, a marauding offshoot of the belligerent Snakes. In 1854, in the district Moses proposed to traverse, they had slain nineteen immigrants of the so-called Ward party. Unpunished, they kept up smaller raids during subsequent years, and in September 1860 completely shattered a train of eight wagons. Thirty-nine people perished in that attack—some fighting, a few simply vanishing, and five dying of starvation during their panicked flight afoot. The fifteen who survived did so largely by dint of eating the corpses of the perished. If Splawn wanted that kind of country, so declared most of the party, he could have it and welcome.

Seven of the group, however, decided to take the chance with him. As they traveled cautiously toward the Snake they recruited another small party of wanderers, only to have quarrels whittle the number back down to eleven. On Moore Creek, some forty miles north of present Boise, they found a circular, tree-rimmed basin that looked exactly as the Indians had said it would—exactly, indeed, as many mountain basins look.

Eagerly they dug shallow prospect holes. Just as a whoop of joy announced dazzling colors in one of the pans, the Indians attacked. A man named Grimes dropped dead. Rallying, the others beat off the savages, hastily buried Grimes in his own prospect hole, and fled.

The gold they showed in Walla Walla proved stronger than fear. Within months a reputed fifteen thousand people had poured into the basin. From there tendrils of the rush reached south across the Snake to the quartz lodes in the stark hills of the Owyhee country. In those almost trackless deserts the Bannacks and their despised relatives the Pah Utes would for years continue to bleed isolated habitations, but north of the Snake River the gold rush crushed the Indians. In 1863 the army established new Fort Boise forty miles up the Boise River from the old Hudson's Bay post of the same name. The climate was mild there and quickly a roaring supply and farm town grew up around the fort—far too populous and well armed a town for the Indians even to dream of attacking it. Anyway, their time had run out. Acting on anguished appeals from the Mormon hamlet of Franklin, in extreme southeastern Idaho, red-whiskered Patrick Connor and his California volunteers caught a camp of Bannacks beside the Bear River and in the below-zero cold of December slew 263 of the embattled warriors. Meekly then the remnants consented to settle down on the Fort Hall reservation just east of present Pocatello.

The western half of the Overland Trail was at last safe. So, too, was the long supply route from Salt Lake City northward to the spectacular new gold fields of western Montana.

Two names recur almost like a motif in any tale of early Montana history—the Stuart brothers, James and Granville, the first a year the elder. Wilderness-raised, they had gone overland to California with their father in 1852. He had already been there before, in '49, and one more rainy winter in the Sierra foothills sent him back to Iowa for good. The boys stayed, however—James twenty now, Granville nineteen. The next year, 1853, they nursed back to life a fever-wasted, destitute prospector named Rezin Anderson (they called him Reece) and after that the trio were inseparable. They went to Yreka together, and were there, almost on the Oregon border, when the Rogue River Indian wars broke out. For two years they fought and mined intermittently. Finally, in June 1857, they decided to go home.

They never got there. On Malad Creek in what is now southeastern Idaho, Granville became desperately ill. The party the partners were with went on; but James and Reece Anderson stayed with Granville during a seven weeks' convalescence.

Not far from their camp an old mountain man named Jake Meeks had set up a sort of swap shop where he traded fresh oxen and horses and odds and ends of supplies to westbound immigrants. One day James Stuart helped Meeks out of an ugly scrape with some passersby, and from then on Meeks was a frequent visitor at their camp. From him they learned of the lovely mountain valleys of western Montana where a scattering of former Hudson's Bay employees had settled with their little herds of livestock, coming south each summer to trade with the Mormons and with travelers on the Overland Trail. The brothers also heard that one François Finlay, a French-Canadian half-breed nicknamed Benetsee, had found traces of gold in the Deer Lodge Valley back in 1852 but had been told by the Hudson's Bay factor at Fort Connah to keep his mouth shut.

One more rumor . . . the Stuarts probably would not have heeded if the so-called Mormon war had not broken out just about the time Granville was ready to travel again. Federal troops started toward Utah, Brigham Young breathed defiance, and excited talk along the trail said that the Mormons were incarcerating as potential spies every gentile in the region. The Stuarts and Reece Anderson had no desire to winter in a Salt Lake City jail; when Meeks suggested they join him in the Beaverhead Valley of present southwestern Montana, they agreed.

There, where the Continental Divide arcs westward around the headwaters of the Missouri, they found a widely scattered colony of displaced trappers and half-breeds living with their squaws in skin tepees. Patriarch of the group was Richard Grant, who for years had run old Fort Hall for the Hudson's Bay Company. Grant was prosperous. He had a three-room log cabin and a herd of several hundred cattle, several hundred horses.

The mountain men knew there was gold in the district, but no one grew very excited about it—not even the Stuarts, in spite of their five years of chasing the will-o'-the-wisp in California. Indeed, they almost left Montana without turning over a pound of gravel—would have, if snow had not blocked their first attempt to get back over the passes to the south. Because of the delay they ran out of dried meat. To replenish the supply they went north, in April 1861, to the grassy benchlands of Deer Lodge Valley, so named because of a low butte shaped like an Indian tepee. Hot springs near its top and around its base attracted numerous deer—and hunters.

In the valley they found traces of Benetsee's old prospect holes. Idly they scratched up some color of their own. But their tools were inadequate, and when Blackfeet Indians stole several of their horses they decided to move on. During the next two years they were content to hang around the emigrant trail in southeastern Wyoming, swapping livestock.

North of them, meanwhile, a new route into the Northwest was being pushed through the timbered mountains. This was the wagon road which Lieutenant John Mullan had started to build between the Columbia and Missouri rivers in 1858 but which had been interrupted by the war with the Spokanes. Surveys he ran during that campaign convinced Mullan that he would need more money than he and Isaac Stevens had first envisioned. Hurrying east during the winter, he secured another hundred thousand dollars from Congress and in 1859 set vigorously to work.

From Walla Walla northward to Coeur d'Alene Lake the way was easy: a few streams to bridge and wooden markers to set out for showing directions. Beyond Coeur d'Alene, however, the workers ran into green-scummed swamps, dense forests, narrow canyons. An early winter pinned them in an ill-equipped camp. Livestock died; the men suffered from frostbite and the almost forgotten demon of scurvy.

None of it discouraged Mullan. In the spring of 1860 he obtained fresh animals from the Flathead Indians and pushed on across the Continental Divide to the American Fur Company's Fort Benton on the Missouri. He was proud of himself—"a monomaniac about his road," one diarist at Benton wrote. He calculated the route to be 624 miles long. Parts of it were barely passable (and would stay that way). Just the same, it was the first man-made crossing of the Rocky Mountains, harbinger of the steel rails he and Isaac Stevens had been dreaming of for seven years.

Congress had authorized the project as a military measure. Mullan now had to justify it by transporting three hundred recruits along it to the Pacific slope, thus saving the thirty thousand dollars that shipping them around the Horn would cost. As an initial step in the project, Pierre Choteau, Jr., of the American Fur Company built two specially designed, broad-bottomed stern-wheelers, and with the awkward craft ferried the soldiers and their supplies up the shallow Missouri to Fort Benton, farther than steamboats had ever gone before. At Benton the material was loaded into wagons, the soldiers marched, and Mullan hurried ahead to add a few improvements to his trace. One of his changes involved swinging from the Little Blackfoot River three miles south into Deer Lodge Valley, crossing Gold Creek almost where the Stuart brothers had dug their prospect holes two years before.

The troops had scarcely passed when the Stuarts and Reece Anderson reappeared, planning to winter in Deer Lodge with the little herd of cattle they had managed to acquire. A road! Inevitably immigrants would use it, so why bother going clear back to the Overland Trail next year? They could do their trading here. Settling beside the crossing, they built a cabin and fenced off a garden plot.

Prospectors began working nearby, and late the next spring the brothers finally took fire again. While Granville watched the ranch, James hurried with a party to Fort Benton to buy tools. Neither achieved much. Blackfoot Indians stole twenty-three of Granville's horses; and a drunken riverman searching through the hold of the supply steamer for alcohol set the boat afire. James came home without even a shovel. The best the brothers could do was send out an order by pack train to Walla Walla, 425 miles away, and hire two men with a saw to whipsaw some planks for their sluice boxes. By letter they urged their brother Thomas, mining in Colorado, to join them when they commenced work the following spring.

The winter started normally enough, routine chores and hunting trips broken by occasional gatherings at one cabin or another for the all-night poker games James so dearly loved or for a dance where Indian women and prospectors with handkerchiefs around one sleeve served as partners. Then in February there came an upheaval. James and a man named Powell ransomed a Snake squaw from some Flathead Indians who had just killed her husband. She was, James wrote in the joint diary he and Granville kept, "fair with red cheeks and brown hair and eyes and is evidently half white." Powell's Indian wife, furiously jealous, refused to have the woman around. That left it up to James: "As we have no cook it seems my lot to take her. . . . I might do worse. She is neat and rather good looking and seems to be of a good disposition. So I find myself a married man."

The change unsettled Granville (he was twenty-eight years old now), and in May he, too, found a Snake wife—"a fairly good cook, of an amiable disposition, and [important consideration among Indians] with few relatives." Her name was Aubony. Granville changed it to Ellen. For twenty-five years they lived together. Ellen bore him nine children, adopted two of James's, watched him become one of Montana's foremost citizens. [1]

In June, Thomas Stuart appeared with several "Pikes Peakers" from Colorado. Other immigrants drifted in. Most were drawn by the new Salmon River excitement in Idaho but weren't quite sure how to get there. The deep gorges and tortured mountains of central Idaho prevented direct approach from the east. A man either swung south along the Oregon Trail to Walla Walla and then in, or circled around north by the Mullan Road. Or he could start by the Oregon Trail and in eastern Idaho turn north to the Mullan Road. This northbound trail, which started at Salt Lake City, met the Mullan Road on the Stuart brothers' ranch. Inevitably a haphazard town grew up around their cabin. They called it American Forks, and the region around it was designated, in the summer of 1862, as Missoula County by the legislature in far-off Olympia.

James Stuart was elected county sheriff. His first job was running down a horse thief who proved so old and poor that the sheriff gave the fellow fifteen dollars and told him to keep going. His next job involved helping outside law men question three suspects who had holed up in American Forks. One resisted and was killed; one was arrested, tried, and hanged; the third was acquitted. About that same

[1] She died in 1887, a year after the worst blizzards the plains ever knew had bankrupted Granville's vast cattle ranch, seven years before President Cleveland appointed him United States minister to Uruguay and Paraguay.

time James sent east for medical books, instruments, and drugs. For the rest of his life he studied—a hobby strictly. Except in emergencies he treated only his friends, whom he never charged. Reminiscences say that he was competent.

The placers surrounding American Forks were mediocre, and when rich diggings were discovered due south at a place called Bannack, the camp moved over almost en masse. Leaving Reece Anderson to run the Gold Creek ranch, the Stuarts followed and set up a butcher shop which they supplied with their own beef.

The phenomenal success of the Bannack placers set prospectors to scouring the hills in every direction. In April 1863, James Stuart led a group of fifteen east toward the Yellowstone River. Another group was supposed to rendezvous with them at the mouth of the Beaverhead but missed connections. While trying to catch up, the smaller party was surrounded one dawn by Crow Indians. The savages stripped the whites of arms and horses and for three nights, while war drums beat, held them prisoner. Finally the prospectors were turned loose, given one ancient plug each to ride, and told to get out of Crow country fast. Warriors dogged their tracks to see that they obeyed. Uneasy under the surveillance, the whites shook off their watchers near the Madison River and fled into the hills, camping that night in a little gulch lined with alder trees. There, on May 26, 1863, while looking for a grassy place to picket their horses, two of the party, Bill Fairweather and Henry Edgar, made one of the great placer strikes of the American continent.

Intensely excited, the group went to Bannack for supplies. Each swore secrecy, but somehow the news leaked. Maybe it was just the shine of their faces. When they left Bannack two or three hundred men were at their heels, some trudging with packs on their backs, some leading burros, some riding. Halting after a time, the discoverers called a meeting and laid down the conditions under which they would reveal the diggings. The crowd agreed, Edgar pointed to the mouth of Alder Gulch, and the stampede was on. By the time James Stuart's party returned from weeks of fruitless prospecting and Indian fighting on the Yellowstone, the creek was staked solid from end to end— a ten-mile hodgepodge of shanties, tents, and sluice boxes. Granville and Reece Anderson came over from Bannack and joined James. He was chagrined. But probably the trio fared better than if James had found color. They opened a store.

One Confederate sympathizer suggested naming the gulch's principal camp Varina City after the wife of Jefferson Davis, but when the document bearing the name reached the nearest federal judge (in Idaho) he angrily struck it out. In its place he substituted Virginia City, an uninspired borrowing from the even more dazzling camp on Nevada's famed Comstock Lode. He should have been more foresighted. Within the next five years ten thousand Montanans would dig between thirty and forty million dollars' worth of gold from the gulch's coarse gravels and would give to our history the rawest saga of violence the West ever produced. Surely it was worth more than a secondhand name.

2. Law and Disorder

FORMAL government had a hard time overtaking the gold fields. The confused sprawl of the mountains complicated the confused and sometimes tragically funny efforts of the stampeders to impose order on their hectic affairs. Instability was the one staple. Before a new territory could be established or a new capital designated to meet the requirements of each booming strike, there were sudden shifts of population and fresh maneuverings for political preferment that wiped out each preceding attempt at organization.

In the beginning Washington Territory was responsible, from its capital at Olympia, for administering everything in the Northwest except Oregon. Peopled, the area became unmanageable, a geographic monstrosity sprawling eastward from the sound to the Continental Divide, from the Canadian border south to Utah. Olympian politicians wanted only enough of it to justify statehood when the time came. But before talk of statehood could grow even faintly serious, the Clearwater strikes pulled more people into northern Idaho than inhabited all of Washington west of the Cascades. At once a great cry went up to have the capital follow the population.

There was justice in the demand. Olympia's distance, as the Lewiston newspaper complained, with italics, "is between seven and eight hundred miles, interspersed with *huge forests, roaring rivers, and rocky shores of ice* with impassable barriers of snow. . . . One newly elected legislator *made his will,* settled all his worldly accounts, and bid his friends adieu—*perhaps forever!*"

Walla Walla, the raucous supply town that had grown up around the army post of the same name, felt she should be the new capital of Washington. Enough votes existed between there and the gold fields to swing the shift from Olympia—unless the gold-field votes could be diverted to something else. This could be accomplished, so reasoned the lumber and agricultural interests of Puget Sound, by slicing a new territory off the eastern side of Washington and locating its capital in the illegal town of Lewiston (illegal because no treaty ceding the spot to the United States had yet been ratified). Olympia would then remain the capital of a smaller, more manageable Washington centering on Puget Sound.

Lewiston promoters were of course happy to abet. Walla Walla, realizing that the proposed new territory would leave her dangling at the end of the inland deserts, subservient still to Olympia, fought vociferously. It was a forlorn battle, however, mostly because of William H. Wallace, Washington Territory's delegate in Congress.

Wallace was a political opportunist. Ever since his arrival on Puget Sound in 1853 he had been running for office, alternately defeated and elected. In 1861, after a one-month appointive interim as governor of Washington Territory, he had been sent to Congress and he wanted to keep the job. His hold in Washington was tenuous, however, and it occurred to him that he might be able to build stronger bonds in the new territory—especially if he were responsible for bringing that territory into existence.

He had two allies. One was the Oregon representative, whose Portland constituents felt their economic dominance of the mines would be increased by removing Olympia's unfriendly influence. The other was Congress itself. The Union believed that new territories could be used to offset Southern votes if and when the seceding states returned to the fold. More importantly, the Republicans were shoring up their national strength; and new territories meant new jobs for loyal party hacks. Accordingly, on March 3, 1863, the protests of Walla Walla notwithstanding, the Territory of Idaho was voted into existence. It was an even worse geographic monstrosity than its predecessor, for it included all of present Idaho, Montana, and Wyoming —an area one fourth larger than Texas. Its capital was Lewiston, awkwardly located on the extreme western border. The wall of both the Bitterroot Mountains and the Continental Divide lay between the capital and its eastern counties. Between it and the southern mines of Boise Basin and Owyhee was the abysmal gorge of the Salmon— the famed River of No Return.

The territory's obstetrician, William Wallace, was appointed by Lincoln as its first governor.

Actual organization lagged far behind paper creation. Wallace did not reach Idaho until late summer. He called for October elections and decreed that the legislative assembly elected then should meet in Lewiston on December 7. Having set the wheels to grinding, he resigned as governor and announced himself as candidate for Congress.

One of his campaign stunts was his cavalier treatment of Sidney Edgerton, the federally appointed chief justice. Edgerton hailed from the East, and Wallace knew the resentment of the territories at having outsiders sent in to manage their affairs. Supposedly, the best judicial district in a new territory was the right of the chief justice. But Wallace, while still governor, ordered Edgerton off to Bannack, in remote Montana, just to show that he too objected to "foreigners." The impact on the voters is problematical. In any event Wallace was elected to Congress, as he had schemed all along, and hurried east, leaving Idaho's administration in the hands of his incompetent secretary.

Until the legislature met there was little for the secretary to administer, for no laws had been codified. Whether or not the Washington code remained in effect during the interim was inconclusively debated. The question was academic, anyway: copies of the Washington code were unobtainable at such a distance.

The fluid population of the placer camps, the temptations bred by remoteness, and the ease with which a man could account for sudden wealth had always encouraged violence in the Western mining camps. In Idaho and Montana the evil was compounded by an influx of Civil War draft dodgers, deserters, and displaced guerrillas from Missouri and Kansas, many of them Confederate sympathizers ready to defy Union officials just on principle. Finding that no legally constituted bodies existed to investigate or punish, the hoodlum element grew more and more arrogant. A long series of crimes in Lewiston finally culminated in the wanton murder of a popular saloonkeeper named Ford, who dared object to the vandalizing of his establishment, and in the blatant robbery of a pack train coming in from Florence. Vigilantes met late in 1862, hanged two suspects, and spread a general warning for ruffians to clear out. The only real result was in a shift in the centers of trouble.

Some of the criminals moved south to Boise Basin; more crossed the mountains to the new diggings at Bannack. Among the latter was the most publicized badman of American mining-camp history, Henry Plummer.

Handsome, soft-voiced, and genial, Plummer had developed as a teen-ager in California an uncontrolled taste for other men's wives and other men's money. In Idaho he had uncovered further talents as an organizer. These reached fruition in Montana, where he knit together a gang so cleverly intertwined and so widespread that most of its members did not even dream how far it actually reached.

People instinctively liked Henry. Granville Stuart met him once on the road, invited him to the Gold Creek ranch, played poker with him all night (James lost twenty-two dollars), and repaired his broken shotgun for him. In Bannack, after a series of tumultuous brawls, in one of which he publicly gunned down a rival suitor for a current love, Plummer managed to drive the legally constituted sheriff out of the district and have himself elected in the man's place. When Virginia City boomed into prominence he extended his authority both as sheriff and as gang leader into that fabulous gulch as well.

Violence spread unchecked. Though few citizens seemed to have suspected Plummer as yet, they nevertheless welcomed Sidney Edgerton, exiled chief justice of Idaho, as a better promise of relief than was their own sheriff. Edgerton, however, had no machinery for setting up effective courts. Nor was he likely to get help from the distant capital at Lewiston; Governor Wallace had just departed from that town and the legislature would not meet until December. A better remedy, it was decided, would be to hurry an emissary to Washington, D.C., with a plea that Montana be given a government of her own. Because Edgerton had been a Republican congressman from Ohio and knew Lincoln personally, he was chosen to risk the winter journey. His supporters promised that during his absence they would collect evidence that could be used against the lawbreakers as soon as the territory he masterminded into existence began to function.

As matters developed, no one was content to wait so long. Edgerton had scarcely started east when outrage flared up over the finding of the frozen corpse of a young man named Thiebalt. Reconstruction of the murder indicated that he had been robbed of two mules and a little gold dust, wounded, and then wantonly dragged to death behind a galloping horse. A coldly furious posse placed the principal suspect, George Ives, on public trial. Wilbur Sanders, Edgerton's nephew, undertook the prosecution. Witnesses, a volunteer judge, and a jury of twenty-four men sat in wagons surrounded by some fifteen hundred shivering spectators. At sunset the case was given to the jury. Within an hour they were back beside the freshly lighted bonfire with their verdict: guilty. The crowd roared approbation. Ives was led under the light of a full moon to the scaffolding of a house under construction. There, while watchers swarmed onto adjoining roofs for a better view, he was hanged from a rafter.

Success fed on itself. Within days the famed Vigilante Committee of Montana had been formed—mob rule pure and simple for all its high-minded oaths, but defended ever since by Montanans as the only recourse possible under the circumstancs. Certainly these self-appointed defenders of civic virtue were effective. For some time their leaders had been quietly collecting the evidence they had promised Edgerton. The Ives affair pointed the way to still more data. On the basis of the information the aroused vigilantes made more sudden arrests, gleaned still more facts. As the appalling story grew, Plummer and his gang were tied definitely to no less than one hundred and two murders and an infinitude of lesser crimes. Faced with these staggering revelations, the vigilantes went swiftly to work. Within three weeks they banished eight persons from the territory and hanged twenty-four. Plummer was executed January 10, 1864, on a scaffold he himself had erected as sheriff for the hanging of a horse thief. Panicked survivors took to their heels, and a most subdued quiet prevailed when Sidney Edgerton returned from the East.

He had succeeded in his mission. On May 26, 1864, Congress took both Wyoming and Montana away from Idaho, leaving that territory with the idiotic boundaries it still possesses. Wyoming was returned (until 1868) to Dakota; Montana became an entity in its own right, with Sidney Edgerton its first governor. Organization suffered a lag similar to the one that had afflicted Idaho the year before: elections could not be held until October or the legislature meet until December. There was little lawlessness, however, even after the wild stampede of '64 to Last Chance Gulch, soon renamed Helena. Memory of the vigilantes was too acute.

The new territory had its troubles, nevertheless. No Eastern politician seemed willing to serve as territorial secretary. Since drafts could not be honored without the secretary's signature, Edgerton had to meet many of his office's initial expenses out of his own pocket. Discouraged by this and by the election of his political enemy, Andrew Johnson, to the vice-presidency, he resigned, and Montana had no executive head.

The legislature met anyway, in Bannack. By this time most of the population had migrated to Virginia City, and in February 1865 the legislature followed. Promptly Helena asserted *her* claims to be capital; after ten years of conniving, vote frauds, and general hullabaloo she won.

In the fall of 1865 a territorial secretary at last appeared and declared himself acting governor. He was a fantastic Irishman named Thomas Meagher. Sentenced several years earlier to life imprisonment in Tasmania for sedition in his native Ireland, he had escaped to New York. There he became a successful lawyer and during the Civil War had commanded a colorful brigade of Zouaves. He entered Montana with an escort of troops (the plains Indians were on the warpath) and thereafter used the soldiers, so his opponents insisted, as a personal bodyguard. He was continually at loggerheads with some faction or another. When he pardoned one notorious figure in spite of secret warnings from the vigilantes, that organization retorted by hanging the fellow on their own. In 1867, Meagher vanished from the deck of a river steamer at Fort Benton. His body was never found despite a standing reward of ten thousand dollars. Official reports say he fell into the river and drowned; unofficial whispers said that the vigilantes had grown tired of him.

Idaho, too, had governor trouble. Wallace's successor was Caleb Lyon of New York, who amazed his constituents with his polysyllabic rhetoric, his fastidiousness, and his insisting on formal dress for public functions. During his regime the Idaho legislature decided to shift the capital from Lewiston to more populous Boise. Lewiston objected. Obtaining an injunction forbidding the removal of the capital, the city fathers set a watch over Lyon to see that he stayed put. He proved more adroit than the posse anticipated. Shouldering a shotgun one January morning in 1865, he got into a canoe under guise of hunting ducks on the north bank of the Snake. In midstream he pretended to fall into the clutches of the current, which swept the canoe into Washington Territory. There he boarded a waiting carriage and journeyed not to Boise but to Portland. While taking his ease in the latter city he met, by chance, his incoming territorial secretary, a young Washington, D.C., clerk named DeWitt Smith, who had applied for the job in hopes of brightening his humdrum existence.

Lyon told Smith to disobey the Lewiston injunction and move the territorial seal and archives to Boise. Guessing the plot, the Lewiston posse shifted its vigilance to Smith—but without having benefited from experience. Smith lulled suspicion by pretending to ride horseback each day for his health. On one of his jaunts he picked up an escort of soldiers from nearby Fort Lapwai, seized the records, and spirited them south. A Lewiston mass meeting passed a resolution decrying the army's part and labeling the acting governor in print as a drunk, a lying thief, and an outlaw. A probate judge declared Smith's action illegal and ordered the records moved back to Lewiston. In rebuttal Boise appealed to the territorial Supreme Court, and there matters rested.

Boise was uncomfortable that winter. Heavy snows blocked the trails; food was scarce. In Idaho City, forty miles to the north, rioting miners started to loot the stores but were checked when the sheriff arrested their leader.

(That same month, February 1865, the price of flour in snowbound Virginia City jumped from $27 a hundred pounds to $160. Speculators were suspected of hoarding. By April the situation was so bad that the leading citizens formed a posse of five hundred armed men and with it searched every house in the city. Flour was dragged out of trunks, stables, haystacks, attics. The searchers gave each owner a receipt and then turned every pound into a central hall. There Granville Stuart gave each searcher a receipt in turn and made sure the totals checked. The next day the townspeople filed through the hall under guard, receiving twelve pounds for each person in a family at a price of thirty dollars per hundred. The money and the surplus flour were then prorated among the original owners, who were forbidden to sell above a set price unless they could produce written proof that they had paid more for the flour in the beginning. There were frantic complaints, but the highhanded measure stuck.)

In Idaho City there were repercussions. On May 18 members of the frustrated looters set fire to the town and burned down all but three of the public buildings. By this time Acting Governor DeWitt Smith was tired of adventure. "I have," he wrote his brother on May 20, "traveled hundreds of miles on horse back—over high mountains and along Indian trails, through Snow and rain—Sleet and ice—Swam rivers on horse back; and slept on the floor in log cabins where the Thermometer was Eight degrees below zero. I have been stiff and sore from riding, Suffered with Severe Colds, Sore throat & cough and had a shaking up generally."

To relieve his distress he took to drink. On August 19, 1865, he died in office. The next in line of succession, his good friend H. C. Gilson, entered office just long enough to steal thirty thousand dollars, with which he fled to Hong Kong.

In November Caleb Lyon drifted back, incredibly reappointed to a second term both as governor and as superintendent of Indian affairs. He passed the winter wandering around the Owyhee country looking for diamond mines, then resigned and went back to New York. When bookkeepers finally checked his expenditures as Indian superintendent, his accounts were found to be short by fifty thousand dollars. Congress ordered a belated investigation in 1875, but Lyon, who had whiled away the time writing a book on ceramics, died before he could be put on the stand.

Virginia City's excuse for vigilante action was that she had no other government; Boise's, that her government was corrupt. In 1866 morality sagged so low and criminals grew so brazen that masked committees took over and cleaned house by the customary hangings. This as usual frightened surviving outlaws into flight. Stability slowly returned, helped on its way by a Supreme Court ruling that Boise was the legal seat of government.

An even stronger stabilizing factor, in both Montana and Idaho, was the exhaustion of the placer beds and the gradual development of expensive quartz mills and deep-lode mines. Long-term capital investments and the growth of a working class dependent upon regular pay rolls brought increasing demands for order. There would be robbery still. But from now on most of it would be done by companies so carefully organized within the letter of the law that even the most determined committees of public safety could not reach them. Brigandage, in short, was just beginning to reach maturity.

3. How to Build an Empire

AS A taciturn young steamboat pilot first on the Mississippi and then on the Columbia, where he helped design the Western river's first stern-wheeler, John C. Ainsworth had learned to stay afloat among all kinds of snags and sandbars. But the reefs of finance, he discovered after acquiring a part interest in the *Carrie Ladd*, demanded even more alertness.

His problem hinged on geography, on the vast gap which the Columbia has torn through the Cascade Mountains. This vital stretch, the only deepwater entrance to the interior between Canada and Mexico, is sixty miles long. As a highway for commerce, however, the gap was marred, in Ainsworth's time, by boiling rapids at both its eastern and western ends.

The upper, or eastern, rapids were called the Dalles, a long gorge of dark basalt. Slantwise across the head of this gorge lay a reef terminating, at its southern extremity, in Celilo Falls, where Indians congregated to net the huge salmon that hurled themselves at the cataract on their way to the spawning grounds. Below the falls the river contracted into a space as narrow, in spots, as two hundred feet—"an agitated gut," wrote explorer William Clark in 1805, "swelling, boiling & whorling in every direction." Or as David Thompson put it six years later, "Imagination can hardly form an idea of the working of this immense body of water under such compression, raging and hissing as if alive."

To avoid the place an army freighter named Orlando Humason built in 1856 a wagon road that wound fifteen miles through basalt dikes and sand hills from Celilo Falls to the hamlet of The Dalles (the town has a capital *T*). For forty miles below The Dalles the water was quiet enough for steamers. Then came another series of rapids bracketing the lower end of Columbia gorge. Five or six miles long, these rapids were known by the same name as the mountains, the Cascades.

As at the Dalles, there were portages here also, mule-powered wooden tramways skirting both the north and south banks of the river. The tramway on the south, or Oregon, bank was owned by Colonel J. S. Ruckel and Harrison Olmstead; that on the north, or Washington side, by the Bradford brothers. Ruckel and Olmstead and the Bradfords each owned small steamers plying the quiet water between the Cascades and the Dalles. They had built the lower portages in order to feed freight to their competing steamers.

The Indian wars had set up a furious steamboat struggle over the army traffic moving upriver from Portland. John C. Ainsworth entered the competition with his *Carrie Ladd* in 1858, and after working harder than he ever had before he ended up deeper than ever in debt. This experience convinced him that the only way to stay alive as a boat owner was to hold freight rates up to a subsistence level. His initial attempt, made in 1859, was a loose pool arrangement among the rival steamboat owners called the Union Transportation Company. It did not work; the old jealousies were too deeply rooted.

That was his first lesson in economic piloting: where dollars were concerned, gentlemen's agreements were not enough. Effective control could be imposed only under one tightly knit company. And that would involve the whole river, not just part of it.

At The Dalles Ainsworth talked to shaggy, square-headed Robert R. Thompson. An immigrant of 1846, Thompson had made his first stake during the California gold rush and then had taken up a strategic land claim at The Dalles, where for a time he served as Indian agent. During the wars he and a man named Coe put a fleet of freight barges on the upper river and made enough money to build a steamer that they gratefully named the *Colonel Wright*. When Ainsworth approached him, Thompson was in the process not only of launching a second steamer named the *Tenino*, but also of acquiring Humason's portage road around the Dalles. Steamers and road made a formidable combination. Thompson, who quite frankly said his interests centered in a man named Thompson, knew it. To lure him into the proposed company, Ainsworth had to promise him one of the biggest blocks of stock, a down payment in cash, and a monthly salary as "consultant."

The bulk of the remaining stock went to the other portage owners, the Bradfords on the north bank of the Cascade rapids, Olmstead and Ruckel on the south. In return for granting Ainsworth's company exclusive rights to use the tramways, each portage owner was to receive one fourth of every freight charge levied on goods moving to The Dalles. Meanwhile, each was to retain full control of his own portage company. That was a mistake. To rule a river, as Ainsworth soon perceived, a man must rule everything on it, not just the boats.

After heated arguments, fourteen boat owners capitalized their conglomeration of steamers, barges, and landing facilities for an overblown $172,500. They named the combination the Oregon Steam Navigation Company; and although John Ainsworth's financial share was slight, his creative share was recognized by his election as president of the organization.

Operations began in January 1861. Winter was always a slack season, and spring promised nothing more than the driblets of freight bound for the mines around Colville and in far-off British Columbia, a little army traffic moving to Walla Walla, and a few adventurous settlers risking the newly opened valleys of the interior. And then, incredibly, the Idaho gold rush started. The number of passengers soared from an anticipated few hundred to more than ten thousand, freight to an unbelievable 6290 tons. Six months after the incorporation of the Oregon Steam Navigation Company its dazed stockholders split their original shares four for one and declared a five per cent dividend. By the end of the year each original five-hundred-dollar certificate had earned, in stock and cash, two hundred and forty dollars, a one-year profit of forty-eight per cent.

Robert Thompson, who now owned the portage road between The Dalles and Celilo Falls, sold it to the company. The directors spent a hundred thousand dollars buying oxen and wagons for the fifteen-mile haul around the rapids and then realized that wagons alone would not suffice. Early in 1862, Ainsworth hurried to San Francisco and located enough railroad rails to lay twenty miles of track. Though this was more iron than he would need at the Dalles, he borrowed enough money to purchase it all. Something was also going to have to be done about the bottlenecks at the Cascades.

Intensely jealous of each other, the rival portage owners at the lower rapids were trying to use the Oregon Steam Navigation Company to further their private interests. All through 1861 Ainsworth had tried to remedy his original mistake by offering to buy them out. They refused—until the usual Ainsworth luck came to his rescue again.

The series of floods that devastated much of the Northwest during December 1861 and January 1862 destroyed the Bradfords' wooden portage on the Washington side of the river. When spring came the surviving Olmstead-Ruckel portage on the Oregon side could not handle the rush of freight. To speed things up, the OSN (as the Navigation Company was called) bought them a steam locomotive to haul small flatcars over wooden rails sheathed with iron. Called the *Pony*, the locomotive consisted of a boiler five feet long resting on four drive wheels. A thin smokestack rose in the rear and an oversized steam dome bulged in the center. It was Oregon's first railroad. On its initial run all the company bigwigs assembled for a ride on its single open passenger car. Unfortunately, when the engine began laboring up the first grade, a belch of water and cinders from the stack drenched the celebrants.

The *Pony* was also a Trojan horse designed to topple the very portage company that it was ostensibly helping. The devious plan worked like this: first, the locomotive discouraged the Bradfords, who were glumly trying to repair their flood-ruined tramway on the northern bank. For twenty-eight thousand dollars they sold to the company. Instantly the OSN shifted the construction crews then at work on The Dalles—Celilo railroad to the north bank of the Cascades. As the workers began to lay the extra iron Ainsworth had bought in San Francisco, Olmstead and Ruckel realized that their *Pony* would soon be outclassed by a full-scale iron horse. Discouraged, they too sold out. The Oregon Steam Navigation Company now controlled the portages as well as the boats, and out of the maneuverings four men had emerged as the firm's dominant figures: Ainsworth and Thompson, and two Portland financiers, William Ladd and Simeon Reed. Under this big four the portage railroad on the north bank of the Cascades (the south-bank tramway was abandoned) and the one at the Dalles were completed at a cost of a million dollars—by a company which scarcely two years earlier had resorted to exaggeration to achieve a capitalization of $172,000. All of it was home-grown capital. This was unique; most Western monopolies were financed either in San Francisco or the East.

Meanwhile the hunger of the gold fields was stimulating agriculture. A steer that brought fifteen dollars in the overstocked Willamette was worth thirty-three dollars at Walla Walla. At once a new rush began for the illimitable acres of brown bunch grass east of the Cascades. Soon the drovers learned that the mountain trails were hard on the cattle. It was easier and more profitable to drive the herds to the head of the Cascade rapids (paying the portage roads for use of their bridges) and then load the animals on OSN steamers specially fitted for the run to The Dalles. In the first eight months of 1862 alone, forty-six thousand head of cattle moved upriver by boat, plus substantial numbers of horses, mules, hogs, and sheep.

Farmers soon followed, stimulated in part by the Homestead Act of 1862. The enormous numbers of livestock used around the mines for packing and freighting created an insatiable demand for the hay that could be grown in the lower valleys. Truck gardens sprang up as near the various mining centers as climate and water supplies allowed: at Boise, at Baker on Oregon's Powder River; in the lovely Grande Ronde; along the fertile valleys of the Walla Walla, the Umatilla, the Colville. But the big discovery had to do with wheat.

Wheat had, of course, long been the money crop of early Oregon, thriving in the moist climate of the Willamette. The early missionaries had found that it would also grow in the interior valleys, and Isaac Stevens had guessed that it might be dry-farmed on the hills as well. If so, here was one of the prodigious grainfields of America, unbelievable miles of volcanic topsoil stretching from the pine forests of Idaho west across the undulant Palouse country to the vast sagebrush plateaus within the Big Bend of the Columbia.

Who experimented first cannot be said. But the man who did more than anyone else to spread the word of the region's phenomenal growing powers was George Henry Atkinson. A Congregational missionary who had reached Oregon via the Horn in 1848 and had taken the lead in developing the young territory's schools, Atkinson hit on the happy phrase "Inland Empire" to designate the lands east of the Cascades and north of the Blue Mountains. He analyzed its soils. He pointed out that much of the region's scanty twelve inches of moisture comes as snow during winters and that only rarely were temperatures cold enough to kill the young stalks sprouting beneath the protective blanket. He rhapsodized about the cloudless glories of the warm spring days, the summer's rarity of hail. Everywhere he went he talked wheat, wheat, wheat. He wrote wheat, dreamed wheat, urged wheat. Personally he did not get a dime from it. He just liked to see wheat grow, its russets and ambers and golds filling a once empty world with the Biblical staff of life.

All this was grist indeed to the mill of the OSN. The company wanted the Inland Empire to develop, so that in time the volume of downriver traffic might equal that bound upstream to vanish in the gold fields. Ainsworth would even loan settlers money. But he saw no reason not to charge freight all it would bear, so that the farmers who at first had blessed the OSN as a life line soon joined other shippers in cursing it as a noose.

By 1865 the OSN flag rippled from eighteen steamers, many of them palace boats with elegant fixings; from a small navy of barges and towboats; from a fifty-thousand-dollar wharf at Portland and only slightly less modest facilities at The Dalles; from the portage railroads, from shops, and from huge white cracker-box hotels at the principal jumping-off points for the interior. Expenditures on all this ran, between January 1, 1862, and September 30, 1865, to slightly more than two million dollars. But the company could endure it. Gross revenues for the same period were just under five million.

Although the bulk of the revenue derived from traffic bound for the interior, the Columbia below Portland was not ignored. Freighters plied to Astoria; popular excursions were developed to the seashore. Only when it invaded the Willamette did the OSN encounter effective opposition in the form of another monopoly called the People's Transportation Company. After a nearly disastrous rate war, during which the Willamette group sent its boats onto the Columbia, the bruised rivals agreed to confine themselves to their original bailiwicks.

Competitors, to be sure, tried regularly to cut in on the Columbia's lucrative traffic. Those below Portland were crushed by rate manipulations; those above by the refusal of the portage railways to handle enemy freight at competitive prices. One group of San Francisco and British Columbia capitalists sought to break the strangle hold by building its own portage railroad. They secured the necessary charters from the Washington legislature, whose Puget Sound constituents were bitterly envious of the golden harvest which the OSN was pouring into Portland, and confidently entered the Columbia with one stern-wheeler and machinery for two more. The OSN took the involved legal battle that resulted to Congress, where the territorial legislation

MAP 5

The Mining Camps and Indian Settlements of the Northwest

CARIBOO COUNTRY
BRITISH COLUMBIA
RUCE
FRASER R.
COLUMBIA R.
THOMPSON R.
Lillooet
Kamloops
HEMLOCK
HELL'S GATE
OKANAGAN L.
KOOTENAY L.
Yale
Nelson
SIMILKAMEEN R.
Vancouver
Hope
OKANAGAN R.
Trail
Rossland
SAN JUAN ARCHIPELAGO
Metalline
SKAGIT R.
DIABLO DAM
Colville
Victoria
WASHINGTON
Kalispell
CHIEF
JOSEPH DAM
HEMLOCK
DOUGLAS
FIR
PINE
GRAND
COULEE DAM
Coeur d'Alene
Seattle
Kellogg
Burke
Spokane
Wenatchee
ROCK ISLAND DAM
Cataldo Mission
Wallace
Tacoma
Ephrata
Moses Lake
GRAY'S
HARBOR
Cle Elum
Olympia
BIG BEND
PINE
PALOUSE COUNTRY
MT. RAINIER
PRIEST RAPIDS DAM
Lapwai
Yakima
MT. ST. HELENS
Lewiston
OROFINO CR.
Kamiah
Astoria
MT. ADAMS
Walla Walla
Wallula
SPRUCE
BONNEVILLE
DAM
DALLES
DAM
COLUMBIA R.
McNARY DAM
WALLOWA
MTS.
JOSEPH'S
COUNTRY
Florence
Portland
The Dalles
SALMON R.
La Grande
MT. HOOD
HELL'S CANYON
DESCHUTES R.
Salem
WILLAMETTE R.
IDAHO
Baker
PINE
OREGON
PAYETTE R.
Eugene
Bend
Idaho City
Scottsburg
Boise
ARROWROCK
DAM
MALHEUR L.
HARNEY L.
Coos Bay
SNAKE R.
DOUGLAS
FIR
DONNER
UND
BLITZEN R.
Silver City
ROGUE R.
STEENS MT.
OWYHEE R.
KLAMATH L.
Jacksonville
KLAMATH R.
TULE L.
LAVA BEDS
Yreka
MT. SHASTA
CALIFORNIA
NEVADA

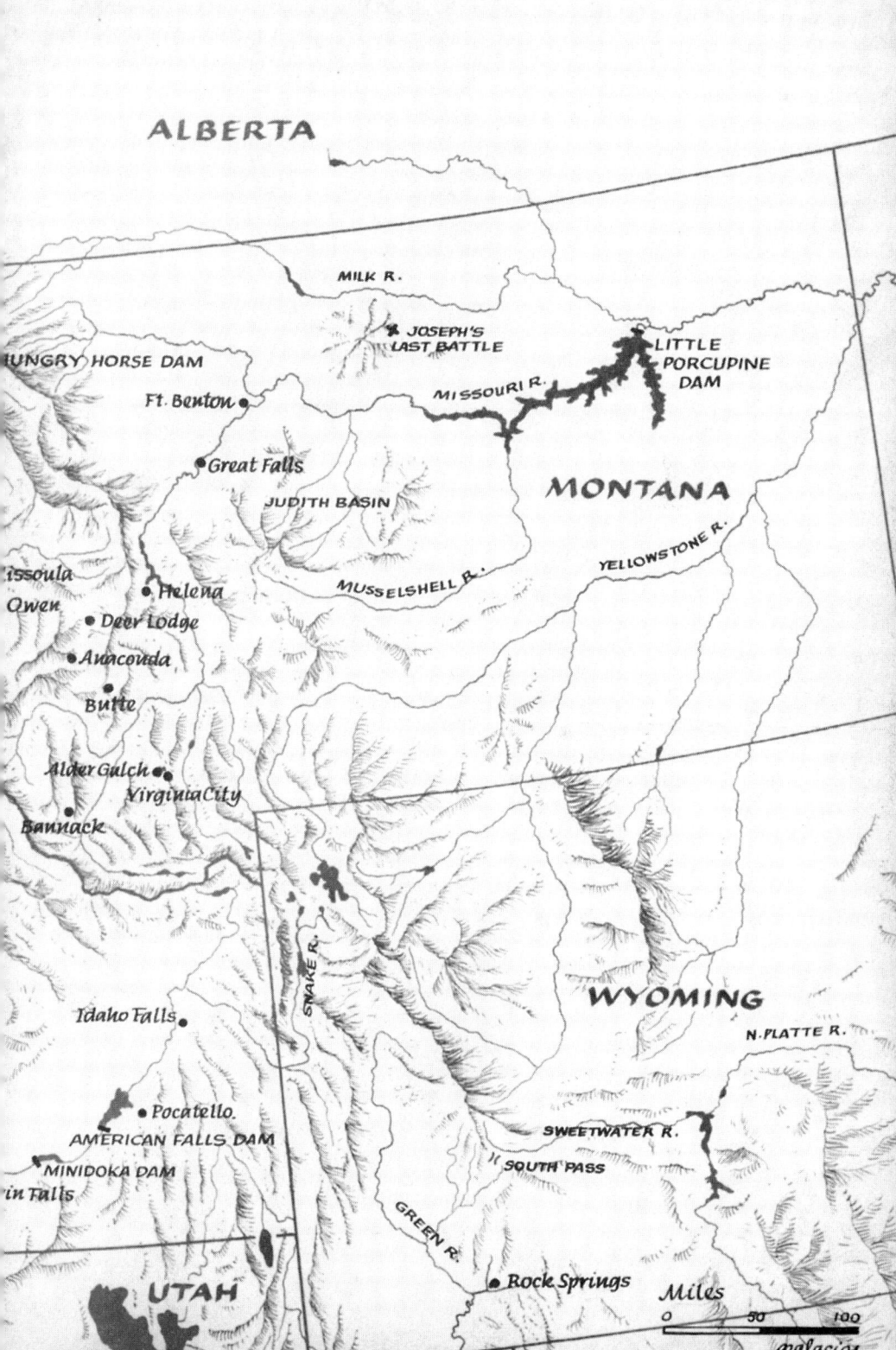

ALBERTA

MILK R.

JOSEPH'S
LAST BATTLE

LITTLE
PORCUPINE
DAM

HUNGRY HORSE DAM

Ft. Benton

MISSOURI R.

Great Falls

JUDITH BASIN

MONTANA

YELLOWSTONE R.

Missoula
Owen

Helena

MUSSELSHELL R.

Deer Lodge

Anaconda

Butte

Alder Gulch

Virginia City

Bannack

WYOMING

Idaho Falls

N. PLATTE R.

Pocatello

AMERICAN FALLS DAM

SWEETWATER R.

MINIDOKA DAM

in Falls

SOUTH PASS

GREEN R.

Rock Springs

Miles

UTAH

0   50   100

GREAT SALT L.

palacios

was disapproved. The would-be competitors thereupon sold their boats to the OSN and Simeon Reed exulted:

"Hereafter the Legislature of that [Washington] Territory will be reminded that there is a 'power above them.' " Whether he meant the Congress of the United States or the Oregon Steam Navigation Company is not clear.

At the upper river landings animal transport took over. As late as 1866, when Missouri River steamers were moving into Montana from the east and great wagon trains were creaking up from Salt Lake City on the south, the OSN supplied no less than six thousand mules with goods bound for the northern Rockies. Even camels were employed. Excited by the army's introduction of the alien beasts into the Southwest in 1856, a private firm brought over several head from Manchuria, selling them to bemused packers in Nevada, British Columbia, and Montana. They were not a success. They stampeded mules; their feet grew tender on the rocks; they were subject to unlikely accidents. In Montana, so runs one revered yarn, a hungry prospector stalked one down and slew it under the impression that it was a moose.

As fast as roads could be built, wagons took over from the mules. To the OSN directorate, there was anguish in some of the routes these huge land freighters followed. Portland was not yet a manufacturing city. Though her population increased tenfold during the gold boom of the sixties, she and the neighboring Willamette Valley produced, in addition to agricultural exports, only woolens, leather, and minor tools. The heavy machinery and fabricated goods used in the northern Rockies came either from St. Louis or from San Francisco.

The California trade traveled east over three routes: the old Overland Trail through Nevada; newer roads built across the mountains from the upper Sacramento Valley for the express purpose of capturing the Boise and Owyhee markets; or by coastal vessels to the Columbia, up the Columbia by OSN boat to The Dalles or Umatilla, and then along the Oregon Trail to Boise and even on to Fort Hall, where traffic destined for Montana turned north. The long lift over the Sierra offset the advantage which the routes through Nevada possessed in mileage. Meanwhile the Columbia route, though roundabout, offered the only waterway through the coastal mountains. In the eyes of the OSN this would have been a decisive consideration to California shippers—except for the machinations of one of the stormiest, most controversial, and highly colored robber barons of the West, Ben Holladay.

Holladay had begun freighting between Missouri and Utah with a shoestring outfit of surplus oxen and equipment that he bought from the army at the close of the Mexican War. He spread remorselessly. When the huge transportation firm of Russell, Majors and Waddell collapsed in 1862, Holladay took over. Within two more years he owned or controlled thirty-three hundred miles of stagecoach lines whose mail contracts alone grossed a million dollars annually. To keep in touch with the appropriate congressional committees, he eventually established one bronze and marble residence in Washington, another in New York City; his redheaded wife and their children he ensconced at White Plains in a mansion whose grounds were enlivened by a herd of buffalo and a narrow-gauge railway. There European counts would woo his daughters, but Holladay himself remained, under his broadcloth suits, a rough-edged frontiersman, six feet tall with a bushy black beard and an insatiable drive for empire.

In addition to his stage lines Holladay also had acquired, in the early sixties, a steamship line which he re-formed as the California, Oregon and Mexican Steamship Company. The fortnightly service from California to Portland and Victoria was abominable—and dangerous. In July 1865 the *Brother Jonathan* foundered off Crescent City with a loss of three hundred persons, including Colonel George Wright, hero of the Indian wars.

In the opinion of the OSN directorate, Holladay's wretched ocean line was the main reason that most San Francisco mining freight went inland over the Sierra rather than up the Columbia. They decided, accordingly, to establish their own coastal run, and sent an agent east to contract for a suitable vessel.

This aroused Holladay, who needed new ships anyway. In China he found one bargain, the *Oriflamme*, which he put on the Oregon run; and in New York he discovered a plum so ripe that it must have stunned even him. This was the 1500-ton *Continental*, a Civil War troopship which the government had optioned to one Asa Mercer for the purpose of transporting three hundred nubile maidens to the eager bachelors of Puget Sound.

The story of the Mercer girls is the Northwest's most enduring romance. Washington Territory during the 1860s was inhabited by a disproportionate number of unwed lumberjacks. When the whorehouse on the sawdust fill beyond Yesler's mill in Seattle imported white girls from San Francisco to replace its Indian squaws, the success was sensational, but it did not quiet the yearnings for a more stable form of home life.

Finally Asa Mercer decided to act. He had arrived in Seattle in

1861, fresh out of college, and had been employed to clear land for the still non-existent University of Washington. The next year he became the university's president. It was a rather hollow honor. The area as yet contained no scholars of college caliber and he first had to create his own student body by opening a preparatory school in a log building he erected with his own hands. As his pupils droned, he dreamed, stimulated no doubt by the recent importation of English females into British Columbia. The upshot was a trip to Boston. There he secured eleven young ladies, whom he took back to Washington. Enthralled, Seattle elected Mercer to the legislature. He served one term and then decided to repeat his triumphant importation on a grander scale.

An indeterminate number of Seattle bachelors backed him with subscriptions of three hundred dollars each. Relatives and friends entrusted him with other thousands of dollars for concluding business matters in the East.

It seems strange they should have. In retrospect, at least, Mercer's naïveté appears as total as his confidence. In his own words:

This was just at the close of the Civil War. . . . Hundreds of government vessels were lying idle and thousands of seamen were still on the payrolls, with bunkers overflowing with coal, at all of the government wharves. My thought was to call on President Lincoln, tell him of our situation, and ask him to give me a ship, coaled and manned, for the voyage from New York to Seattle, I furnishing the food supplies. Having sat upon Lincoln's lap [in Illinois] as a five-year-old and listened to his funny stories, and knowing the goodness of his heart, not a shadow of a doubt existed in my mind as to the outcome. . . .

He arrived in New York on April 17, 1865, two days after Lincoln's assassination. Undaunted, he went to Massachusetts and began drumming up trade just as if the vessel was still assured. He wrote such glowing letters home that the territory's bachelor population grew worried and appointed committees to prepare for the influx of females with housing, funds, and "articles to meet the immediate wants that must of necessity be pressing on their arrival."

In his quest for help Mercer eventually called on General Grant. What actually transpired cannot now be reconstructed. Mercer, however, seems to have derived a notion that Grant promised him free use of a 1500-ton steamer fully manned and coaled. But in the quartermaster's department the promise solidified into nothing more than an option to purchase the *Continental* for $80,000.

Although the price was an amazing bargain—the vessel had cost $240,000 to construct only two years before—Mercer might just as well have had an option on the moon.

And then somehow Ben Holladay learned of the arrangement and offered to take over the contract. As part of the consideration the stagecoach king contracted to carry five hundred passengers to Seattle at "a minimum price"—Mercer does not say how much. Nor does he say why he supposed he could round up five hundred fares, mostly feminine, for the long trip around the Horn to the then unknown lumber hamlet of Seattle. When sailing date arrived in January 1866 he had managed to produce scarcely one hundred. The quality was high, though. According to Mercer, "Never in the history of the world was an equal number of women thrown together with a higher average of intelligence, modesty, and virtue."

Such qualities were not calculated to impress Ben Holladay. He wanted quantity. For no more than a hundred passengers he would not sail the *Continental* beyond San Francisco and he would charge full price. To meet the fare Mercer had to misappropriate the last of the funds entrusted to him; and to get his maidens on from San Francisco to Seattle, he had to dispatch them in odd lots on such lumber schooners as became available. But at least he found himself a bride in his own cargo.

And Ben Holladay found a cheap ship.

Shortly afterward, at a cost of five times as much ($403,000, to be specific) the Oregon Steam Navigation Company acquired, also on the East coast, the steamer *Oregonian*. On December 24, 1866, she reached San Francisco. By that time Holladay was making the steamship business his principal effort. He had just sold his stage lines to Wells, Fargo for $1,500,000 cash and $300,000 in stock, and was buying up the vessels and franchises of every coastal competitor between Alaska and Central America. He warned the OSN that if the *Oregonian* entered his territory he would send ships onto the Columbia. This could develop into a most uncomfortable squeeze, since Holladay's erstwhile stage lines (he remained a director of Wells, Fargo) offered connections from The Dalles with every mining camp in the West. Steamers outside, wheels inland . . . Consoling themselves with the thought that at least they had forced Ben to improve service, the OSN sold its brand-new vessel at a sacrifice to a South American concern.

Other attempts at expansion proved equally expensive. One steamer built inland on the Snake to capture the trade of southern Idaho languished when overspeculation shut down most of the hopeful new quartz mills of Boise Basin. Other vessels churning across northern Idaho's Lake Pend Oreille and up the Clark Fork into Montana proved unable to compete with St. Louis trade moving up the Missouri. The minority stockholders began to grumble. Rather than argue, Ainsworth, Thompson, Ladd, and Reed in 1868 bought entire control of the company, then declared themselves a thirty-six per cent dividend as a Christmas present.

Even while congratulating themselves, however, they watched with considerable unease still another party of surveyors that had been sent from the East by the Northern Pacific Railroad. Was that paper organization going to catch fire at last?

The Northern Pacific, chartered in 1864, had been given the largest land grant ever awarded by Congress. From a broad strip along its right of way the company would receive for every mile of track it laid forty odd-numbered sections of land (25,600 acres) in each territory it traversed; and, in each state, twenty sections per mile. The only state involved, however, was Minnesota—unless the line should swing south into Oregon.

At first this southern dip seemed unlikely. The dread reputation of the Columbia bar had led Congress to specify a route from a point on Lake Superior to the deepwater harbors of Puget Sound, with nothing more than a branch line down the Columbia. Still, a surveyor could scarcely miss seeing that the lowest pass in the Cascades rose thirty-five hundred feet above salt water, whereas the Columbia gorge furnished a ready-made gap through the mountains. Whether these construction advantages would outweigh harbor facilities kept Portland and the cities of the sound on tenterhooks for years.

The OSN was not sure what it wanted. A line over the Cascades would ruin its monopoly but let it keep its steamers and a fighting chance to compete. A line down the river might end its existence entirely, but since its portage railroads controlled part of the right of way on each bank, its demise could be made costly to the slayer.

Or perhaps the problems would remain academic. Land grants in the wilderness produced little cash, and for years the Northern Pacific was unable to start construction.

Then in 1869 Jay Cooke began to show interest, and Ainsworth and his associates took alarm. They had reason. More than any other individual, Jay Cooke had financed the Union during the Civil War, by divining that vast reservoirs of capital lay untapped in the modest-income groups and that by adroit promotion and appeals to patriotism those vital dollars could be siphoned into circulation.

After the war Cooke turned his techniques to manufacturing and railroad bonds. The first overtures of the Northern Pacific he rejected, but in 1868 he went to Minnesota to look over certain properties he had acquired. There his imagination took fire: timber and water power in Minnesota, wheat in the Red River Valley, mines in the Rockies, harbors on the Pacific. The whole Canadian West might even fall to the United States if rails were to reach across the border and up the Saskatchewan toward the divide into the Cariboo.

He sent surveyors into the field. They came back enthusiastic. Construction problems in the Rockies would be less difficult than those already overcome by the Central Pacific in the Sierra. The land was not the arctic waste commonly envisioned, but a fertile paradise; Puget Sound, said one rhapsodic report, was "the Mediterranean of the Northwest."

The main line, added surveyor Thomas Canfield, should go down the Columbia—not on the north bank, where construction above The Dalles would be enormously expensive, but on the easier south side. This would lead into Oregon, a state, and reduce the land grants for that section. On the other hand, it would block any attempt by the Union Pacific to run a spur line up from Utah to Portland; it would facilitate building feeder routes into the growing agricultural regions of the Walla Walla, Grande Ronde, Umatilla, and Deschutes valleys of eastern Oregon; and it would guarantee that the rich trade of the Willamette would stay within the orbit of the Northern Pacific rather than drift south toward California.

Won by the reports, Cooke agreed in December 1869 to help finance the railroad by selling a hundred million dollars' worth of stock and a hundred million dollars' worth of bonds. His compensation was to be two hundred dollars in Northern Pacific stock for each thousand dollars' worth of bonds he sold. Also he was to receive the bonds at 88, netting for himself whatever they brought above that figure.

Revisions were secured from Congress authorizing a main line down the Columbia to Portland, then north through the Cowlitz Valley of Washington to a terminus on the sound, with an eventual branch line over the Cascades. Coppering his bets, John C. Ainsworth formed the construction company that was selected to lay track north from Kalama on the Columbia through the Cowlitz to—well, no one in authority would say just where. Real estate values around the terminus would soar. The directors of the Northern Pacific and of its construction company (not including Jay Cooke, who was merely the financial agent) wanted to cash in by secretly buying up the surrounding land.

Construction began in Minnesota and at Kalama in 1870. The Western end moved slowly, but in the East progress was rapid. For a year the directors of the OSN watched the giant strides and then decided that the time had come to reap. For five million dollars, half in cash and half in Northern Pacific bonds at a set price of 90, they sold to the railway the controlling interest in their boats (which would be useful for transporting construction materials), their portage roads, and their rights of way.

Cooke was meanwhile throwing all his vibrant imagination into pushing the public sale of the bonds. Following the accepted morality of the times, he spent nearly a million dollars to obtain good will among influential politicians and journalists; even Chief Justice Chase of the United States Supreme Court was inveigled into lending his name. Literature of such extravagant sorts flooded this country and Europe that soon the Northwest was being called Cooke's Banana Belt.

It did not work. Credit throughout the United States had been overstrained by the dizzy tarantella of speculation following the war. Interest rates were fantastic. Railroad bonds were being offered on every hand, secured by land grants so vast that the acreage could not possibly be sold, let alone brought into cultivation, for decades. Europe, once a sponge for American issues, had been turned resistant by the Franco-Prussian War and by unhappy experiences with fraudulent offerings.

Reeking scandals—the Tweed Ring, the Crédit Mobilier—had destroyed public confidence. In the Midwest the newly formed Grange was launching a furious attack on all railroads and demanding governmental control. Within the Northern Pacific itself (though not within Cooke's office) there was inefficiency and corruption. As rumors of it leaked out into the already shaky market, sales lagged and prices dropped. In a frantic effort to shore the crumbling structure, Cooke poured more and more of his own money into the rathole. His partners revolted, and on September 18, 1873, Jay Cooke and Company closed its doors, setting off a financial crash whose reverberations rolled around the entire world.

In the Midwest construction stopped at Bismarck, North Dakota. In the West, the builders barely managed to reach salt water at New Tacoma, a company-controlled real estate development on Commencement Bay, just outside of old Tacoma, hitherto an insignificant collection of cabins and sawmills. In fact there wasn't enough money to pay the last wages of the Western workers, and the angry crew started to tear up the rails before they could be pacified.

In its despairing attempts to meet its obligations, the Northern Pacific dumped onto the market the stock of the Oregon Steam Navigation Company which it had bought in at a price of 40 per share. Quickly the OSN quartet—Ainsworth, Thompson, Ladd, and Reed—recovered it, some as low as 13, most at 20. For the time being at least, their empire was once again secure in their hands.

4. "Coarse, Pretentious, Boastful, False and Cunning"

WHEN the Central Pacific in 1863 began its slow crawl eastward toward a junction with the Union Pacific, various would-be railroad kings at once grasped the profit possibilities inherent in constructing a feeder line to the Northwest. In October a group of these men incorporated the California and Columbia River Railroad Company. The next spring one of them led a surveying party northward into Oregon. His name was Simon G. Elliott, and he possessed more talent for corporate thievery than he himself yet knew.

In the still active gold town of Jacksonville, Elliott's party disbanded for want of funds. Before this, however, he had infected with the railroad virus a persistent Jacksonville optimist named Joseph Gaston. Gaston raised enough voluntary contributions for a party of Oregonians to finish the survey to the Columbia. The Californians and the Oregonians thereupon each besought Congress for federal aid in constructing the railway.

Congress moved slowly. Although a land subsidy bill was introduced into the Lower House in December 1864, it did not become law until July 1866. During the interim the original California and Columbia River group re-formed, with Simon Elliot left out in the cold. This new group, calling itself the California and Oregon Railroad Company, was designated by Congress as recipient of that part of the land grant lying within California. A trouble-breeding clause further added that a similar grant (twenty alternate sections of land for each mile of track constructed) should go to whatever Oregon company the Salem legislature specified.

Swiftly Joseph Gaston set up a company called the Oregon Central. Among its twenty incorporators were such men as Jesse Applegate,

Joel Palmer, and the big four of the Oregon Steam Navigation Company—Ainsworth, Thompson, Ladd, and Reed, who were interested in any development that might lead San Francisco freight toward their Columbia River steamers. With such men backing the company, the Salem legislature was easily persuaded to name the Oregon Central as recipient of the land grant. None of the grant's potential four million acres could be claimed, however, until twenty-five miles of track had been laid. In an effort to finance this crucial stretch, Gaston began soliciting subscriptions and trying to persuade the various counties through which the road would pass to guarantee interest on a small bond issue.

At this point Simon G. Elliott again appeared. Ejected by the Californians, he had borrowed two hundred dollars from a friend and had journeyed north to try his luck in Oregon. To the governor, to the Salem legislators, and to the directors of the Oregon Central he represented himself as the agent of the construction firm of Albert J. Cook and Company of Massachusetts, empowered to sign contracts for building the railroad. In actuality, no such firm existed.

The ordinary precaution of checking into Albert J. Cook and Company seems to have occurred to no one. But Joseph Gaston of the Oregon Central realized that construction contracts were the profitable end of railroading. He accordingly rejected Elliott's overtures and went on trying to raise money through personal persuasion. Unabashed, Elliott next proceeded to cut the Oregon Central Railroad from under Gaston's feet by playing on sectional jealousies. The more influential of the line's directors were from Portland and wanted the railroad to follow the west bank of the Willamette. Others, however, were from Salem, and these men cocked an appreciative ear when Elliott began speaking grandly of a railroad down *their* side of the river. Quarrels developed, the company split, and on April 22, 1867, the defectors incorporated themselves under the same name as the original group, the Oregon Central. To avoid confusion, Oregonians promptly began calling Gaston's original Oregon Central the West Side company and Elliott's offshoot the East Side company.

The East Siders brazenly proclaimed themselves the true heirs of the original Oregon Central and hence the rightful recipients of the federal land grant, as soon as they had built the necessary twenty-five miles of road. Unwilling to swim in such muddied waters, Applegate, Palmer, the OSN quartet, and others of Gaston's original backers now withdrew. Breathing fire, Gaston reorganized the West Side company without them, instituted court suits against the East Siders, and flooded every hamlet in Oregon with outraged circulars about Elliott's iniquity.

None of this ruffled Simon Elliott. Calmly he executed with the East Side company—their naïveté is almost incredible—a contract for the non-existent Albert J. Cook and Company to build a hundred and fifty miles of railroad, which as yet had not even been surveyed. Cook's—i.e., Elliott's—pay was to be five million dollars in twenty-year, seven per cent, first-mortgage Oregon Central (East Side) bonds and two million dollars in preferred stock, which the company issued on the strength of the land grant it hoped to get. A down payment of these bonds was given "Cook" in advance.

The contract safely in hand, Elliott forged an assignment of Cook's bonds to himself. He then hurried to San Francisco and there peddled several hundred thousand dollars' worth of the spurious paper by offering it at a huge discount. With the cash thus raised, he went to Boston and tried to buy equipment on the security of the construction contracts, which he had also assigned to himself. He managed to obtain four small locomotives and some machinery before copies of Gaston's circulars reached the East and choked off his credit. Resilient still, he shipped the locomotives around the Horn. By selling two of them to the Central Pacific he raised enough cash to begin grading his Oregon line—for apparently he intended to stay with the bluff until he had manufactured a real railroad from hot air.

His strategy, of course, was to set up a claim on the land grant by building twenty-five miles of track before Gaston's West Siders could beat him to it. The result was a strictly unofficial race—unofficial because the legislature had not yet said which Oregon Central was the rightful one. Speedy track construction might help persuade the lawmakers. So in April 1868, within two days of each other, the rivals broke ground on opposite sides of the Willamette at Portland. Since neither group possessed money enough to do more than start, the outcome probably would have been mutual exhaustion—if Ben Holladay had not appeared on the scene.

In San Francisco one of the purchasers of Elliott's bonds had sold the paper in turn to Holladay, who went to Oregon to check on what he had bought. Instantly he saw what Elliott had seen: a potential four million acres of federal land. All he had to do was take over the company and the Oregon legislature.

Neither proved difficult. Holladay controlled millions of dollars. To Elliott's impoverished East Siders he was an angel who had appeared just when they needed an angel most. To certain of the awed legislators he was the genial dispenser of more largesse than they had realized their jobs could command. In gratitude they found a technicality which enabled them to void their declaration that Gaston's original Oregon Central should be recipient of the federal grant and to substitute the East Side company in its place.

Congress, of course, would have to agree to the switch. To facilitate matters, Holladay hurried east. Gaston hurried after him, armed with a decision by the Oregon court that the East Siders had no right to the name Oregon Central. This was an inconvenience; Holladay had to reincorporate as the Oregon and California Railroad Company and then persuade Congress, over Gaston's vociferations, that despite the name change all was as it should be. Too busy to care very much, Congress accepted a compromise offered by one of Oregon's senators, George Williams, who later, if not then, was completely in Holladay's pocket. This suggestion made the construction race official: whichever company first built twenty miles of track should get the grant. Gaston's indigent West Siders seemed certain to lose; therefore they were granted a sop in the form of another grant contingent on their building a branch line from their road west to Astoria.

Gaston wanted more than a sop, however, and began flirting with Collis Huntington's Central Pacific. Huntington wanted a branch line from Nevada across southern Oregon into the Willamette, to head off competition from the Northern Pacific or from a possible Union Pacific branch from Utah to the Columbia. Gaston offered Huntington his West Side road as an outlet, if the Central Pacific would finance him in the race to capture the grant. It was an ingenious counterstroke, but when a bill authorizing the Nevada branch was introduced into Congress, Holladay's Senator Williams crippled it with such unworkable amendments that the Californians lost interest and withdrew.

To Gaston the blow was mortal. On the strength of the Central Pacific's support he had persuaded the construction firm of Reed and Company (headed by Simeon Reed and John Ainsworth of the OSN) to race Holladay in building those crucial twenty miles of road up the Willamette. But with the Central Pacific out of the picture, Reed and Ainsworth reneged. That ended Gaston. The West Siders sold everything they had, including the charter for the road to Astoria, to Holladay; and their once exuberant leader went to work for the victor as a traffic agent.

Promptly Holladay finished twenty miles of railroad on the east side of the Willamette. He thus captured the four hundred square miles of land that went with it and, more importantly, the right to claim twenty more square miles for each additional mile of track he laid. Actually this mere right was all he needed in order to embark on the sort of financial legerdemain then current throughout the United States. To a dummy corporation called the European and Oregon Land Company he conveyed these rights in return for the company's promise to pay for the land grant by 1889 at the rate of $1.25 an acre. The land company in turn would sell the holdings to settlers, if any, at the $2.50 per acre specified by Congress.

On the strength of the land company's promise, Holladay's railroad then issued millions of dollars in bonds, floating them in Europe through a San Francisco syndicate at far below par in order to raise cash in a hurry.

Holladay needed cash—and not just for completing his two railroads. He was building warehouses and a streetcar line in Portland. He had to remove the threat of steamboat competition on the Willamette by buying the nine vessels of the monopolistic People's Transportation Company. (These ships he incorporated with his coastal line as the Oregon Steamship Company, and on the basis of them issued still more stock and bonds.) He also had to redeem the old bonds issued by the Oregon Central (East Side) to pay for Elliott's abortive construction work. And he needed to get rid of Elliott himself, who resented being elbowed out of his creation and was beginning to fight back.

One of the involved lawsuits between the two men was scheduled to be heard in the United States District Court. Presiding judges were Matthew Deady of Oregon and Justice Stephen Field of the United States Supreme Court. In September 1871, so it is charged, Holladay gave Field four hundred shares of stock in the European and Oregon Land Company. Such gifts to public men were by no means rare during that era; Chief Justice Chase of the Supreme Court was simultaneously accepting favors from Jay Cooke. Still, this gift was even balder than most: if Elliott won the suit, the value of the stock would depreciate; if Holladay won, it would certainly rise.

Field sent a hundred shares to his colleague, Judge Deady. Deady returned it, thus announcing himself as Holladay's enemy. [1] Such enmity promised embarrassment, for Holladay was tampering with the makers of the law as well as with its defenders.

1 What eventually transpired about the gift—or bribe—is unknown and perhaps academic; before the cross suits and appeals were finished, neither Holladay nor Elliott was in a position to profit, and the small judgments which each man won from the other in the different actions brought the victor little more than personal satisfaction.

His senator, George Williams, had failed of re-election in 1871, but, being a loyal party man, had been appointed by President Grant as Attorney General of the United States, an office Williams filled with singular incompetence. An Attorney General was a useful tool to have, of course, but Holladay wanted a senator even more. To get one, he needed to dominate the state legislature, which in those days elected United States senators. This dominance he achieved by seeing to it that hand-picked candidates were sent to Salem. Some of the legislators were assured their seats by an outright purchase of the electorate and by multiple voting. The grateful legislators then paid for their seats by chosing as senator one John H. Mitchell, who openly declared, according to his opponents, "Whatever is Ben Holladay's politics is my politics; and whatever Ben Holladay wants, I want."

Mitchell's opponents produced other accusations. The man's real name, they said, was Hipple. In 1860 he had deserted his wife and two children in Pennsylvania. In Oregon he had assumed his mother's surname of Mitchell. Remarrying without benefit of divorce, he fathered six more children and built up a lucrative law practice. His imposing physique and rolling oratory were useful political assets. But bribery was even better.

The United States district attorney for Oregon, A. C. Gibbs, ordered an investigation of the election of the legislators. A Holladay sheriff selected the grand jury. It refused to return any indictments. At Gibb's behest, Judge Deady dismissed the group and ordered another jury impaneled. Mitchell, or Hipple, now took alarm and asked Attorney General Williams to replace Gibbs with a more complaisant prosecutor.

Williams wanted Mitchell in the Senate. He, Williams, had just been nominated by Grant to succeed Salmon Chase as Chief Justice of the Supreme Court, but there was doubt about the confirmation. Part of the Senate's opposition stemmed from Williams' incompetence, part from the antics of his wife, Kate.

Kate Williams, then in her mid-thirties, was a handsome, bold, and intensely ambitious woman. Presuming that her husband was as good as in his robes, she took to lording it over the wives of mere senators. The women carried their pique to their husbands. Thus inspired, some of the men began questioning a peccadillo which, in the free-wheeling Grant era, they might otherwise have overlooked: through her husband's connivance, Kate Williams had bought a carriage and livery for her servants out of the contingent fund of the Department of Justice.

Williams, in short, needed Mitchell's vote in order to be confirmed as Chief Justice. To get it he replaced Gibbs with an attorney who did not prosecute the bribery charges. But the very blatancy of the maneuver cost more than it gained. Such a roar of protest arose throughout the country that Williams' nomination was withdrawn. That seemed to exhaust Congress' righteousness, however. Mitchell was seated without even a perfunctory investigation of his election or of the charges about his personal life—charges he all but admitted in 1874 by belatedly divorcing his first wife and legally changing his name. [2]

Holladay had his senator. But it was not enough. Even in boom times the Willamette Valley's seventy thousand people could not support a steamship company and two railroads. And the mid-1870s were not boom times. The same depression which broke Jay Cooke drove Holladay's far less substantial bonds lower and lower.

The bulk of the bonds had been floated in Germany, and now the worried investors sent an agent to America to investigate. He found construction on the Oregon and California stopped at Roseburg, on the Oregon Central (West Side) less than halfway to Astoria. Both distances were shorter than Holladay's reports had indicated. So were the visible resources of the country. And, finally, the land grants held by the dummy European and Oregon Land Company were obviously not being used for the benefit of the railroads.

When these facts were reported to the German bondholders they called for advice on a former countryman whose knowledge of finance had come almost entirely from books. But at least he could speak English.

He had been born Heinrich Hilgard in Bavaria, son of a distinguished jurist. Estranged from his father, he had changed his name to Henry Villard and, aged eighteen, fled to America. Readily mastering the new language, Villard became, before he was thirty, one of his adopted country's top journalists, famous for his reports on the Colorado gold fields and, during the Civil War, for his work as a front-line correspondent. After the war he married the spirited daughter of abolitionist William Lloyd Garrison and became the secretary of the American Social Science Association, a job which entailed close theoretical study of corporate structures. Failing health sent him to Germany for recuperation, and there he was prevailed

[2] In 1905, after three more intermittent terms in the Senate, John Mitchell was convicted on land-fraud matters. He died while an appeal was pending. The Senate, which thirty years earlier had not bothered over charges of fraud in his election, now declined the normal courtesy of sending a representative to his funeral.

upon to become a member of a protective committee established by the worried purchasers of Holladay's Oregon and California Railroad bonds.

In 1874 he sailed to New York to meet Holladay. Antipathy was immediate. Henry Villard was fastidious. Holladay, shiny with diamonds and heavy watch chain, was, to use Villard's own description, "illiterate, coarse, pretentious, boastful, false and cunning." In the frail little German the blustering six-foot frontiersman met his match. Villard ordered him to liquidate the European and Oregon Land Company and return the land grant to the Oregon and California Railroad. Squirming and unhappy, Holladay also agreed to remit all future railroad receipts to a representative of the bondholders.

To check personally on what receipts might be expected, Villard went to Oregon. He liked what he saw, installed a man to keep an eye on Holladay, and returned to Germany with hopeful reports. Almost at once, however, Villard's representative was cabling desperately from Portland that Holladay refused to keep his promises.

Back to Oregon Villard went. On February 29, 1876, he stripped Holladay not only of the Oregon and California, but of Oregon Central (West Side) and the Oregon Steamship Company as well. Adroitly he then persuaded Holladay's numerous and not very compatible creditors to install one man as manager of all three companies—that man to be Henry Villard.

It was Villard's conviction that development of the transport firms must go hand in hand with development of the country. Accordingly he set up immigration bureaus in Boston (a populous port of entry), in England, and in northern Europe. To divert settlers from California he established other bureaus in Topeka and Omaha, heartland of the Union Pacific. To meet competition on the coast and recapture the San Francisco–Portland trade for the Oregon Steamship Company, he spent large sums of money repairing the decrepitude into which Holladay had let the line fall.

The railroad creditors protested. In their opinion the money should have been spent pushing the railroad on through the difficult mountains of southern Oregon, so that title to still more land could be perfected. The criticism annoyed Villard, who by then was feeling his oats. Because of his success with Holladay, another group of disgruntled German bondholders had employed him to look into the tangled affairs of the Kansas Pacific. During the course of the complex negotiations Villard had outmaneuvered those redoubtable wolves of Wall Street, Jay Gould and Sidney Dillon of the Union

Pacific, and had emerged with the beginnings of a personal fortune. Rather than argue matters of policy with his erstwhile employers, he jockeyed the bondholders of all three Oregon concerns into selling out to him at bargain prices. By 1879 Holladay's shattered empire was once more under the absolute control of a single man.

It was a heady feeling and demanded more. Before the ink was dry on the contracts, transcontinental dreams of his own were glowing behind Henry Villard's austere, calculating eyes.

5. The Bones of Their Mother

LURED by the propaganda of Ben Holladay's land promoters, wheat farmers poured into the Willamette and the valleys south of it in such numbers that the annual exports of grain from those districts leaped from 28,000 tons in 1870 to 44,000 tons in 1873. Eastward, in the Walla Walla Valley, similar spectacular increases convinced one optimist that the region could even support a railroad of its own—one of the strangest little roads ever built (but no stranger than the legends that have grown up around it).

Its promoter was Dr. Dorsey Syng Baker, a non-practicing medical man who had settled in Walla Walla at the beginning of the Idaho gold rush and had prospered modestly first as a merchant and then as one of the founders of the first bank in Washington Territory. This bank's total deposits on January 1, 1870, amounted to $17,223.50, a figure that leads one to think the settlers acted wisely the next year when they voted down a bond issue that proposed to raise three hundred thousand dollars for building a railroad thirty-two miles long from Walla Walla to the OSN boat landing at Wallula.

Disagreeing with the majority, Dorsey Baker determined to build the road from his own pocket and from private borrowing. In December 1871 he went to Pittsburgh and for forty-four hundred dollars bought a tiny seven-and-a-half-ton locomotive that he shipped around the Horn. (Legend says he also purchased one thousand plug hats to pay Indians for carrying the dismantled engine over the Columbia portages, a yarn that ignores the existing portage railroads of the OSN.) Logs for crossties and for wooden stringers to use as rails were floated down the Yakima River from the Cascade Mountains and boomed across the Columbia to a sawmill near Wallula. Actual laying of the wooden track began late in 1872, with Baker hovering anxiously over every crew, insisting on rigorous economy.

(Legend says that he used hog lard as lubricating oil for the locomotive and saved flour by making the cooks in the boardinghouses brush off the bugs they picked from the flour bins.)

Before ten miles of track had been built, the wooden rails were wearing out under the weight of the construction cars pulled by the little locomotive. So Baker had the stringers covered with strap iron. (Legend says he covered the rails with wet rawhide which shrank as hard as iron as it dried—but during storms stretched out again and grew too slippery for traction. Another tale adds that one winter starving timber wolves put the road out of commission by eating up the leather sheathing.)

It took Baker three years, from 1872 to October 1875, to build the thirty-two miles; and although during 1874 he hauled five thousand tons of freight between Wallula and the slowly advancing railhead, he was about broke. He might not have made the last six miles at all if a committee of Walla Walla citizens had not raised a subsidy of twenty-five thousand dollars. (Legend says he highjacked them into it by threatening to stop at Whitman's old Waiilatpu mission and build a rival town of his own there.) He needed help. His strap iron was wearing out, and to save the road from material dissolution he had just ordered sixty-five thousand dollars' worth of steel rail from England.

Until the rail arrived, a ride on the Walla Walla and Columbia River Railroad was an adventure. Rolling stock consisted of the little engine, a flatcar or two, and a narrow passenger coach with wooden benches running lengthwise of the car. Occasionally an end of strap iron would spring loose under the wheels and jab up through the floor. This transfixion not only alarmed the passengers but also halted the train until the crew could cut the coach loose with sledge hammers and cold chisels.

Still, it was a train. The OSN thought highly enough of it to buy it in 1878 for $321,123. And it was symptomatic. The Northwest was filling up. Those Indians who believed they could roam at will because they had not signed treaties committing themselves to reservations soon learned the whites did not agree.

The first clash came with the Modocs of southern Oregon. In 1864 a treaty had attempted to place the tribe with the related Klamath Indians on a reservation west of Klamath Lake; but the Modocs hated their neighbors and soon a group of them, denying they had signed the treaty, moved back to their old homes along Lost River near the California border.

Their leader was a chief called Captain Jack. By and large Jack was favorably disposed toward the whites. He restrained overt hostility and in 1869 let Alfred B. Meacham, superintendent of Indian affairs for Oregon, persuade him to return to the reservation on the promise that the Klamaths would be forced into friendliness. The Klamaths declined to co-operate, however, and soon the Modocs marched back to Lost River, saying that they had listened to the whites for the last time.

The settlers along Lost River, it should be noted, had grievances of their own. Many of the Modocs preferred to live by begging rather than working; when handouts failed, the savages prostituted their women in order to raise money for obstreperous drinking bouts. The whites complained so bitterly about the Indians that finally, in the fall of 1872, Superintendent T. B. Odeneal, Meacham's successor, sent out troops to herd the red men back where the settlers thought they belonged.

The Modocs refused to go. One of them pulled a gun, a soldier tried to disarm him, and the fight was on. When it was over, ten troopers and three or four civilian volunteers lay dead. Only two Modocs were killed, one of them a woman.

Knowing the whites would send reinforcements, the Modocs crossed the California border to the lava beds south of Tule Lake, a congealed inferno of glass-sharp ridges, intersecting trenches, and labyrinthine caves. En route to this almost impregnable stronghold, Captain Jack's followers behaved themselves. Not so those under a brave named Hooker Jim. Blood-maddened, they slew thirteen white men on their wild gallop through the valley.

All told, fifty-three warriors and a somewhat larger number of women and children found refuge in the tortured stone. At dawn on January 17, 1873, four hundred soldiers attacked through the fog. The lava shredded their clothes and skin. They heard the bang of guns, the whine of bullets. But they never saw an Indian. When retreat sounded, nine troopers were dead, thirty were wounded. Not a Modoc was scratched. Rejoicing, the Indian women stripped the corpses and dragged up sagebrush for a victory fire.

A thousand reinforcements poured in under General Edward Canby. In Washington, however, the old Wool belief that settlers generally caused Indian wars still prevailed. Out came orders for a peace commission to treat with the Modocs. The commission members, after various changes, consisted of ex-Superintendent Alfred

Meacham as chairman; General Canby; a Methodist preacher named Eleazer Thomas; and one LeRoy Dyer.

After weeks of inconclusive parleys the Indians, very puffed up at having stalled off what seemed to them the entire United States Army, decided to frighten the pusillanimous government into granting their terms by murdering the commissioners. At first Jack opposed the idea, but the others put a woman's bonnet and shawl on him and shamed him into complying. Even so, the plan was not unanimously approved and secret warnings were sent to the commissioners through Toby Riddle, the Modoc wife of the whites' interpreter.

General Canby pooh-poohed Toby's agitated report. Eleazer Thomas, who had been anticipating the advent of Easter by praying fervently for peace, said that faltering now would betray want of faith. Meacham was convinced the Indians meant trouble but felt that as chairman of the group he was duty-bound to go along. He and Dyer violated the armistice terms by slipping single-shot derringers into their coat pockets.

On Good Friday, April 11, 1873, accompanied by Toby and Frank Riddle, the four went to the council tent, situated on an open flat between the army camp and the Modoc stronghold. Only a few Indians were there. After some rambling talk Jack suddenly drew a concealed revolver, shot Canby through the head, and then held the general's twitching shoulders to the ground while another Indian cut his throat. Another concealed gun dropped Thomas. Meacham, wounded, jumped behind some rocks with his derringer while Toby flung herself on his attackers in an effort to protect him. Frank Riddle fled. The Indians, who liked Riddle, did not fire at him but concentrated on Dyer, scampering away beside him. Both men escaped.

Meacham fired his lone shot and then fell, five bullets in him. One of the Indians began to scalp him. Toby fruitlessly threw rocks at the man, then cried that soldiers were coming. Frightened, the Modocs ran back into the lava. Incredibly, Meacham lived. By the time the war was over he was up and around.

It was not an easy victory. Slipping undetected from cave to cave, the Modocs survived repeated artillery bombardments. They pounced on stragglers. Twenty-four of them caught three times their number of white soldiers between two ridges, killed thirty-two and wounded seventeen. But they could not defeat shortages of ammunition, food, and water. Late in May the defections began. By June all had been captured. For the murders of Canby and Thomas, four were hanged, including Captain Jack; two more were sentenced to life imprisonment. The rest of the tribe was exiled to Indian Territory in what is now Oklahoma. In southern Oregon, relatives and friends of more than a hundred dead and injured whites felt that the punishment was too light.

Farther to the north other whites were growing increasingly annoyed with the attitude of a minority of the Nez Percés. Various small bands of the tribe, it will be recalled, had declined to sign the 1863 treaty setting up the small reservation on the Clearwater. Not having signed it, they refused to be bound by it. To the whites this was absurd. The will of the majority should prevail, and had not most of the Nez Percés settled as specified near Lapwai and Kamiah? Why, then, should this stubborn minority be allowed to graze huge herds of cattle and horses without restraint across the best range land and set up their tepees on choice agricultural tracts?

Inevitably there were clashes. Taking advantage of the Indians' nomadic ways, a white squatter would throw down some family's ramshackle fences during its absence and build a cabin on the site. Indian drovers were challenged over range rights. Others were victimized simply because they were Indians.

The Nez Percés seldom retaliated. They knew they could not count on justice from white juries. Of twenty-eight murders of Nez Percés committed during the 1870s only one resulted in the indictment of a white man. Nor did the Indians dare strike back outside the law, fearing that if they did troops would be sent against them and they would lose what few rights they still had.

Largest of the non-treaty bands was that led by one of Spalding's early converts, Old Joseph. Size was relative, however. The group numbered scarcely sixty males, many of them polygamous. As a homeland these sixty families claimed a million high, grassy acres in northeastern Oregon, an idyllic triangle bounded around its northern apex by the deep canyons of the Snake and Grande Ronde rivers and on the south by the granite peaks of the Wallowa Mountains. Old Joseph thought he had saved this lovely country for his people at the Walla Walla council of 1855. When the whites tried, in Joseph's opinion, to repudiate their promises, he angrily destroyed the New Testament Spalding had given him and in place of the white man's religion embraced the new messianic Dreamer cult which was forming among the Indians of the Columbia plateau.

Founder of the Dreamer faith was a medicine man named Smohalla, member of a small offshot of the Nez Percés who dwelt near Priest Rapids on the middle Columbia. He was a hunched, aggressive little man with bright eyes in a huge round head. Once another Indian had beaten him so severely in a fight that afterwards Smohalla had been afraid to go home. Instead he wandered for five years down through California into Mexico and back across Arizona and Utah.

Returning finally to his own people, he told them that he had been sent from the dead by the Great Spirit Chief to lead the Indians back to their old ways. Revelations, he said, came to him through dreams (perhaps in epileptic trances). To foster similar trances among his followers, Smohalla added to their native, hypnotic ritual of drums and dances other ceremonial forms he had picked up from the Catholic missions and among the Mormonized Indians of Utah—kneeling, chanting, bell ringing. Compellingly eloquent, he preached that cataclysmic eruptions of nature and an overwhelming resurrection of all dead Indians would exterminate the whites and restore the land to its original owners.

Because farming and mining were symbolic of white civilization, Smohalla attacked the pursuits bitterly:

My young men shall never work. Men who work cannot dream, and wisdom comes to us in dreams. . . . You ask me to plow the ground? Shall I take a knife and tear my mother's bosom? Then when I die she shall not take me to her bosom to rest. You ask me to dig for stone. Shall I dig under her skin for her bones? Then when I die I cannot enter her body to be born again. . . .

Something of this mystic feeling of kinship for the land was in Old Joseph's words when the dying chief in 1871 summoned his thirty-one-year-old eldest son to him and said, as Young Joseph later reported the conversation:

"A few more years and the white men will be all around you. They have their eyes on this land. My son, never forget my dying words. This country holds your father's body. Never sell the bones of your father and mother. . . ."

For a brief time it seemed that Young Joseph might be able to hold out. In 1873, President Grant set aside part of the Wallowa country as a hunting reserve for the entire Nez Percé tribe, but reaction in the Northwest was so opposed that in 1875 the order was rescinded. Meanwhile the cleavage between the heathen non-treaty Indians and the Christianized treaty group on the Clearwater reservation was growing deeper and deeper. The Dreamers scoffed at their fellows for embracing a religion that tried piously to reform the red men but apparently did nothing about the shocking immorality of the white riffraff in Lewiston and in the rowdy mining camps along the Salmon. They laughed at the shoddy annuity goods which the reservation Indians received under the treaty. And they sorely tried the patience of the Nez Percé agent, an earnest Presbyterian named John Monteith, by luring his charges off on yearlong buffalo hunts beyond the Rockies or shorter trips to the root grounds, absences that interrupted the education of the children and the routine agriculture of the parents.

A steady stream of complaints about these difficulties and about the growing number of clashes with the whites finally led the government, in November 1876, to send a commission to the Lapwai agency to investigate. Its recommendations were, first, that the Dreamer preachers "be removed from further contact with the roving Indians," and, second, that the non-treaty group be settled on the reservation within a reasonable time, peacefully if possible, but by force if necessary.

The non-treaty Indians appealed. More conferences followed. At one of them a Dreamer named Toohulhulzote spoke so fiercely against the recommendations that General O. O. Howard, one of the commissioners and commander of the Department of Oregon, lost patience and arrested him. To the Indians it was an outrageous indignity. They grew sullen. Howard, completely exasperated, then ordered them to gather up their livestock and be on the reservation within thirty days.

For Joseph's band it was an impossible ultimatum. Their herds were scattered far and wide through the Wallowa mountains; the streams they would have to cross were swollen with spring floods. But troops were nearing the country. Rather than risk a clash, Joseph persuaded his followers to try to comply.

Many animals were lost during the hasty roundup. Still more perished in a desperate fording of the flooded Snake. The Indians were in an unhappy mood when they stopped to rest and to hold conferences with other non-treaty bands beyond the Salmon, not far from Grangeville.

On the afternoon of June 13, 1877, one of the visitors, Wal-lait-its of White Bird's band, and two friends set out to kill the settler who three years earlier had murdered Wal-lait-its' father. They did not find the man they wanted. But they did find and kill four other whites against whom their band bore grudges. A fifth, wounded, managed to escape.

When word of the bloodshed reached the Indian camp, Joseph and the other chiefs were away, butchering beef. The restraint of the chiefs missing, seventeen more braves, some from Joseph's band, joined the original three. Fired by captured whiskey, they killed fifteen more settlers, maltreated a few women, and plundered several buildings.

Many of the Indians, frightened by the prospects of retribution, tried to disassociate themselves from the outbreak by fleeing to the agency at Lapwai. But most of the camp—the total number of warriors probably never reached two hundred—felt that the time had come to make a stand. Joseph and his brother decided to stay with them. In confusion and fear the camp moved south to White Bird Canyon, there to prepare for the soldiers they knew would follow.

Their first success was as phenomenal as that of the Modocs. With a cost of only two casualties to themselves the Indians killed thirty-three soldiers. A few days later on the Clearwater they fought off four hundred of General Howard's troops and then withdrew across Lolo Pass toward the Bitterroot Valley. Though Joseph seems not to have directed the actual battles, his was the over-all strategy that was finally adopted: a thirteen-hundred-mile retreat to Canada, where the band hoped to join Sitting Bull's Sioux, who had fled across the border after the Custer massacre. To manage, Joseph would have to impose on his volatile Indians a discipline almost unheard of in savage crises.

The first test came on the Bitterroot. There General Gibbon, moving north from Fort Missoula, caught the Indian camp, women and children as well as warriors, by complete surprise. It is a measure of Joseph's leadership that in spite of crippling losses the Nez Percés rallied without panic and drove Gibbon back with heavy casualties. When Howard's reinforcements arrived shortly afterward the Indians demoralized the new attack by stampeding the column's pack mules.

Next they tried to hide their true destination by veering south into Yellowstone Park. In good order they dodged Colonel Sturgis, hurrying in from the east, and turned north, fighting off attacking Crows as they went. But they could not outrun the telegraph. Apprised of Joseph's new course, General Nelson Miles intercepted him within a day's march of the border. Miles paid, though. Fifty-three of his men were killed or wounded on the first charge. Then snow began to fall. Artillery bombarded the unsheltered Indians, Howard arrived to add to the impossible odds, and after five days of hopeless skirmishing, Joseph sent an emissary to the whites:

"I am tired of fighting. Our chiefs are killed. . . . It is cold and we have no blankets. The little children are freezing to death. My people, some of them, have run away to the hills and have no blankets, no food. No one knows where they are. [A hundred or so, mostly wounded, reached Sitting Bull's camp.] . . . My heart is sick and sad. From where the sun now stands, I will fight no more, forever."

It had been his understanding that if he surrendered his people would be returned to the Idaho reservation. They never were. After seven desolate years in the unfamiliar climate of the Midwest, where malaria reduced the bands by half, the remnant were sent to the Colville Reservation in northern Washington.

At least two thousand troops accoutered with all the aids of civilized murder had opposed the fleeing Nez Percés. Though burdened with their women and children and equipped with outmoded weapons, the Indians nevertheless killed 126 of the enemy, wounded 140 more. It was almost a victory—or so it seemed to one of General Howard's Indian scouts, Buffalo Horn of the Idaho Bannacks. Leaving Howard after a quarrel over some horses, Buffalo Horn traveled among the Indians of southern Idaho and eastern Oregon, preaching the vulnerability of the whites and saying that if the red men united they could once more become masters of the country.

By the spring of 1878 he felt ready to strike and with two hundred warriors started west from Idaho to join the Piutes, raiding as he went. Volunteer troops caught up with the band in the Owyhee country, and in the bloody melee that followed Buffalo Horn was mortally wounded. At this some of his would-be conquerors melted away, but the rest pushed on toward the high sage deserts of southern Oregon.

It is a vast, gray, silent land, home of lean coyotes and swift black-tailed jack rabbits. At first it looks desolate, but California cattle growers, driven from their state's great central valleys by the inexorable spread of the wheat farmers, had recently discovered the nutritive quality of the dry-looking rye grasses and of the rippling white sage.

Pioneers among these ranchers were W. B. Todhunter and John Devine. In 1869 they settled on Whitehorse Creek under the grim escarpment of Steens Mountain. On their barn they put a weather vane shaped like a horse (it is still painted white every year) and to carry out the motif Devine, dressed like a Spanish don, rode his vast range astride a white horse ablaze with silver trappings.

North of Steens Mountain, on Donner und Blitzen River (christened by troops camped there during a thunderstorm) was the barony of Frenchglen, named for its owners, Hugh Glenn and Peter French.

Glenn, master of fifty-five thousand acres of farm land in the Sacramento Valley, was the wheat king of California. But he wanted cattle too, and in 1872 sent his diminutive son-in-law, Pete French (five feet five, one hundred and thirty pounds) into Oregon to find suitable range.

The ranch Pete developed filled the Blitzen Valley down to the marshy shores of Harney and Malheur lakes, noisy with the din of uncountable flocks of avocets, killdeers, ducks, geese, grebes, and stately white herons that one day would be almost exterminated for their plumes. Into this treeless waste Pete French imported lumber a hundred and fifty miles from the Blue Mountains to build corrals, bunkhouses, barns, and a broad-fronted mansion for his wife, who one day packed up and left him, apparently to Pete's unconcern.

When the Bannacks came raiding, Pete helped form a volunteer company of cowboys that joined the pursuing troops from Idaho. The Indian strength had increased materially. Though Chief Winnemucca's Nevada band of Piutes held back, the rest of the tribe had joined the hostilities, bringing their number to more than two thousand, almost half of them warriors. White troopers and cowboys numbered fewer than three hundred. But no Captain Jack, no Joseph led this undisciplined gang of Indians. A surprise attack by the whites on Silver Creek, north of the lakes, wounded the new chief, Egan, and sent his warriors fleeing north toward a scheduled junction with still more allies, the Umatillas.

Just short of the Umatilla reservation, troops under General Howard whipped the Bannacks and Piutes again. The Umatillas thereupon underwent a change of heart. In return for the whites' promise of an amnesty for their contemplated war, they arranged a treacherous conference with the wounded Egan. During the talks they slew him and thirty of his principal men.

The Indian army disintegrated. The Piutes crept home; the Bannacks started in small groups back toward Idaho, hoping to mingle unobtrusively with those of their tribesmen who had stayed peacefully on the Fort Hall reservation. Along the way some of them fell in with the so-called Sheepeaters, renegade Indians from several tribes who had holed up in the jumbled mountains of central Idaho. Reinforced, the Sheepeaters began raiding isolated mines along the Weiser and Payette rivers. Their picayune successes served only to call attention to them; and during the summer of 1879, in a campaign whose most formidable opponent was nature, not Indians, the army routed them out and put them on a reservation.

It was the Indians' last spasm. The illimitable acres they had used so uneconomically were now the unchallenged possession of the invaders. Whether the new owners would prove better managers of the land's great bounty and thus justify the agonies of the change remained to be seen.

6. The Railroad Rush

THOUGH willing to risk dizzy financial spins, Henry Villard wanted the economic apparatus on which he performed to be solidly braced. Such anchorage the government helped provide in the late 1870s by resuming specie payments and promising to retire the deflated greenbacks of the Civil War. Everywhere business picked up; and as the dust of the Indian uprisings began to settle Villard saw signs that the Northwest was ready to share the general prosperity.

His immigrant bureaus were sending more and more settlers into the territory served by his Willamette railroads. Other farmers, attracted by the cheaper land of the interior, were moving up the Columbia in such numbers that in 1877 the Oregon Steam Navigation Company felt justified in launching its largest palace boat, the *Wide West*, 236 feet of white elegance. Yet immigrants found the route painfully roundabout—west to San Francisco, north to Portland, and then east or south again to reach one's destination. Surely the time had come for more direct connections with the East.

Settlers of the Inland Empire had additional grievances. The produce of their plateaus might be limitless, they thought—if only transportation were developed. Livestock, for instance. The plains of Montana and Wyoming were crying for cattle and sheep. At first the demand had been supplied by Texas longhorns, but the Wyoming Cattlemen's Association looked with disfavor on the tick fever introduced by the Southern cattle. Oregon cattle were tick-free. Moreover, they carried the strain of choice animals driven west by the early pioneers and hence were of better quality than the longhorns.

The drift back east began quietly in the late 1870s. Several small herds had reached the Wyoming plains before the Cheyenne *Sun*, on February 15, 1879, grew excited over the Oregon plans of one G. A. Searight. "The greatest cattle driving enterprise of the age," cried the paper, ". . . destined to overshadow and eclipse any scheme of like character yet undertaken. It is proposed to proceed to northeastern Oregon, and drive and escort a horde [sic] of about five thousand cattle from the Pacific Slope. . . ."

On March 4, the day Searight's twenty-seven cowboys left Cheyenne to the strains of a brass band, the *Sun* let its readers know the full magnitude of what was being done:

The expedition which left Cheyenne today was composed almost exclusively of Texans—young men who have spent years on the trail between Texas and Kansas. They regard this trip as equal to two trips to Texas, and as many of them will be absent on the trail nearly two years their farewells to friends were of a serious nature. They go over the Union Pacific to Ogden, Utah, where they will require six weeks of steady traveling to reach Baker City, and about one month's time to get the herds road-branded. . . . The time required to make the trip is seven or eight months for fat beef cattle, and twenty months for cows and young cattle. . . .

Searight's herd was immediately followed by more, bigger, and faster ones. The numbers of migrating sheep kept pace. In August 1882, so reported the Cheyenne *Daily Leader,* "There are now 100,000 head of cattle and 200,000 head of sheep being driven from Idaho, Oregon, and Nevada, eastward."

Montana was receiving her share as well. By 1880 the Deer Lodge and Beaverhead valleys, beef centers for the mining camps, had been filled to overflowing. Searching for virgin range, Granville Stuart, backed by bankers Andrew Davis and Samuel Hauser, formed the famous DHS brand and moved across the hills into Judith Basin, southeast of Great Falls. When Stuart's herd arrived the only other animals visible were ponderous buffalo, skittering antelope. Three years later not a buffalo remained. Hundreds of thousands of cattle (many from Texas) competed for the last big stand of "free grass" in the country. Rustlers preyed unchecked—until the summer of 1884, when a group called Stuart's Stranglers, remembering Plummer's demise in Virginia City, took over from the indifferent law and cleaned house.

As long as ample feed existed beside the trails, many of the Northwest's migrating herds would continue to move on foot. But men who foresaw shortages in grass or who wanted mobility enough to seize advantageous marketing conditions grew discontent. Why didn't someone build a railroad?

The wheat ranchers of the Inland Empire were meanwhile having their own problems with transport. Save for Dr. Baker's thirty-two-mile road, the rivers were their chief highways. Sometimes the rivers were hard to reach. From Lewiston to its junction with the Columbia, the Snake flowed between steep bare hills that were dangerous and difficult to negotiate with loaded wagons. Beginning in 1879, long wooden pipes were laid from the plateau tops to the steamboat docks and the wheat was dumped in golden floods down the conduits, but from there on problems remained unsolved. At the docks the wheat had to be sacked, an additional expense. It had to be shifted from boat to train and back again at each of the portage railroads. Sometimes there were no boats. Harvest season coincided with the low water of autumn, and the flat-bottomed stern-wheelers of the OSN often hung up on sand bars. Or else the river froze while the grain was still on the docks.

In spite of these handicaps, the wheat was of such high quality that at Portland it could be transferred to sailing vessels and sent around the Horn to Liverpool, there to compete successfully with grain from anywhere in the world. The trade, starting with a single vessel in 1867, attracted eighty-one tall, lean four-masted windjammers in 1880. Though respectable, the figure was far below California's record. Part of the reason for the lag, so boosters in the Northwest thought, was the lack of a railroad to break the clog along the river.

The citizens of Puget Sound were even more disconsolate. When the Northern Pacific by-passed established towns to locate its terminus at New Tacoma, Olympia and Seattle each tried to tilt with the windmill by building railroads through community effort. Olympia started first. Led by the governor, a holiday crowd on April 7, 1874, began shoveling out a grade for an eighteen-mile spur to the Northern Pacific tracks at Tenino. Enthusiasm soon faltered, however, and the job was not finished until a private contractor took over in 1878.

Seattle was more ambitious. Instead of a spur, she proposed to have a railroad of her own, the Seattle and Walla Walla, running over Snoqualmie Pass to the grainfields and perhaps transcontinental connections in the eastern part of the territory. On May 14, 1874, cannon fired, steam whistles blew, and men, women, and children began to dig. By fall, interest and money were waning, but a fortunate discovery of coal induced private capital to carry on until, by 1877, about twenty-four miles of track had been completed.

One small coal field would not lift the road across the Cascades, however. Additional financing through land grants suggested itself, of course, but a decade of flagrant abuses had led Congress to abandon that form of subsidy. Hunting for an alternative, Western promoters pounced on the fact that the Northern Pacific had laid no rail since Jay Cooke's failure in 1873. Congress, the promoters argued, would therefore be justified in declaring the road's grant forfeited, and in parceling out the reclaimed acreage among local companies that would guarantee construction in their respective areas.

The Northern Pacific, which had been reorganized in 1875 under energetic Frederick Billings, resisted vigorously. Billings' ally in Congress, Senator Windom of Minnesota, beat down one after another of the forfeiture bills introduced by Oregon and Washington representatives. To allay hostility in the sound region, the company in 1877 pushed a line east from Tacoma, letting people assume it was going to cross the Cascades. But when the iron reached still another coal discovery on the Puyallup River, some thirty miles away, it halted. Billings had no money yet for the sort of construction job the people of the sound desired. Wouldn't anyone, the frustrated citizens asked each other in despair, build the railroad they needed?

Meanwhile Henry Villard, after elbowing Holladay aside, had in February 1879 taken over complete control of the Oregon railroads. In June the fastidious little German came to Seattle, looked over the coal mines of the Seattle and Walla Walla Railroad, and without more ado purchased them, along with two colliers for transporting the coal to Portland. (A little later he would buy the Seattle and Walla Walla Railroad as well.)

Ample fuel had become important to Villard. His friendly enemy, Jay Gould, was then involved in the manipulations that would produce the hydra known as the Gould System. As part of his devious machinations, Gould suggested that if Villard built a line through the Columbia gorge the Union Pacific might lease the trackage as its main outlet to the sea, rather than continue using Collis Huntington's Central Pacific. Villard agreed. To gain control of the rights of way through the gorge, he gave Ainsworth, Reed, and associates $110,000 for an option on the Oregon Steam Navigation Company. By the time Villard got back to New York with the option, however, Gould's pursuit of bigger game had swirled him on out of the Union Pacific. Huntington scowled at the road's new directorate; obediently they backpedaled on the Columbia proposal; and there Villard stood, holding his option.

Completely resilient, he formed the Oregon Railway and Navigation Company. It consisted of his Willamette railroads, the Oregon Steamship Company—and the OSN, whose 40,000 shares of stock he purchased half with cash furnished by his friends and half with bonds and stock of the new Oregon Railway and Navigation Company, a form of spontaneous generation common to the railroad juggling of the day. The purchase gave the OR & N (as the Oregon Railway and Navigation Company was inevitably called) not only a right of way down the south bank of the Columbia through the gorge but also brought with it control of Dr. Baker's remodeled strap-iron phenomenon to Walla Walla. Feeders could be pushed at will into the wheat and livestock country. The OR & N might even mature Villard's transcontinental dream by invading Utah or Wyoming and forcing its own junction with the Union Pacific. Or it could gain the same end by crossing Idaho to link with the Utah and Northern, which was then building north from Salt Lake City toward the burgeoning copper mines of Butte.

Construction to fill in the gaps along the Columbia and link Portland directly with Walla Walla began in 1880. Almost simultaneously a dismaying complication arose: the Northern Pacific, which Villard had discounted as negligible, began to move again.

Frederick Billings had raised forty million dollars. Arrogant with that new muscle, his roistering construction crews established a base camp in the hamlet of Ainsworth at the junction of the Snake and Columbia rivers, and from there drove northeast toward Lake Pend Oreille and eventual junction in the Rockies with other crews laying track across the Montana plains. Meanwhile, Billings was contemplating two possible routes from Ainsworth on to the Pacific—down the north bank of the Columbia or over the Cascade Mountains to the sound.

The north-bank prospects did not worry Villard. The upheaved terrain on that side of the river above the Dalles would make construction costs prohibitive; and below the Dalles the OR & N could impose the right of way of the now defunct OSN portage road at the Cascade rapids. But a crossing of the Cascade Mountains in Washington was something else. Though expensive, such a line would make available the superior harbor facilities of the sound. Furthermore, under the terms of its original grant, for each mile of track the Northern Pacific built, it could claim 25,600 acres of some of the best timberland in the United States.

Hoping to counter these attractions, Villard offered to save the Northern Pacific millions of dollars in construction costs by letting them use the OR & N tracks through the gorge. All he wanted in return was Billings' promise not to build either down the Columbia's north bank or across the Cascades.

Billings was happy enough to lease the OR & N tracks for the time being but was vague about the future. The only way to be safe, Villard decided, was to gain control of the Northern Pacific. Through friends he quietly bought as much of his rival's stock as his private resources could afford. It was not enough. On February 11, 1881, accordingly, he wrote a letter to fifty-five of the country's leading businessmen, saying he wanted eight million dollars. He did not reveal his reason but merely promised an accounting by May 15. In perhaps the most extraordinary gesture of confidence in financial history, he was given the eight million dollars for his famous "blind pool." But it was not enough either. He postponed the accounting until June 24 and asked for twelve million more. With the twenty million dollars thus raised, Villard purchased control of the Northern Pacific, ousted Billings, and voted himself in as president.

As a holding company to operate both the OR & N and the Northern Pacific he established, on July 15, 1881, the Oregon and Transcontinental. The peace that the Oregon and Transcontinental tried to impose on its restless subsidiaries was bound to be uneasy. Essentially they were competitors. The Union Pacific, for example, had decided to build into Oregon after all and was pushing a subsidiary, the Oregon Short Line, northwest from Granger, Wyoming. The OR & N was hurrying southeast to meet the Short Line at Huntington, on the Idaho-Oregon border, and an uncomfortable possibility arose that the Union Pacific would maneuver some arrangement whereby it could use the OR & N tracks all the way to Portland, to the Northern Pacific's detriment. On top of that, the bondholders of the Willamette railroads were clamoring for Villard to build toward California and a junction with still another transcontinental, the Southern Pacific. To the minority stock- and bondholders of the Northern Pacific so many possible ententes with competitors augured poorly for future health. As yet, however, they could do nothing except keep their fingers crossed.

Ignoring their long faces, Villard set vigorously to work to develop the country for the benefit of everyone. The immigration bureaus he had established in connection with his Oregon railroads now joined hands with state and territorial promotion bureaus and with the aggressive agencies Billings had already set up for the Northern Pacific. The effect was immediate. On November 7, 1881, the San Francisco *Chronicle* growled jealously, "It is not the blindness of immigrants to the natural attractions of California, but the industry of the Oregon agents that robs us of the laboring thousands that seek our shores."

In America, nationwide publicity was assured by subsidizing newspapers, especially foreign-language ones; by taking influential journalists on elaborate tours; and by flooding with Northwestern literature any section of the country that experienced a crop failure. In England, 831 local agents distributed Northern Pacific pamphlets; another 124 spread the tidings through northern Europe.

White-topped wagons thickened as never before on the unrailed sections of the overland route. Each month during 1882 another twenty-eight hundred hopeful settlers moved up the Columbia. Busy locators escorted the new arrivals out to potential farms; and in Spokane Falls the influx was so great that the city had to build a large immigrant house to shelter the bewildered homeseekers while they searched out their mites of promised land.

Meanwhile the western construction crews of the Northern Pacific had driven from Lake Pend Oreille through the dense forests along the Clark Fork to meet the track layers twisting over the Continental Divide in Montana. The junction came in early September 1883 on the north bank of the Deer Lodge River, sixty miles west of Helena near present Garrison. To celebrate the occasion Villard steamed westward on a special train with General Grant, the German minister to the United States, and the governors of all the states and territories through which the line ran. Appropriately, someone remembered to invite aging John Mullan. Various Indian chiefs were also present to re-enact the ceding of their various lands to the Great White Father.

Workers tore up nine hundred yards or so of track for the ceremony and built a long platform beside the gap. The notables assembled, a brass band struck up a tune, and in twenty minutes a special crew relaid the missing iron. Grant made a speech; Villard made another and tapped the golden spike with a sledge hammer. On the train rolled, bedecked with evergreen boughs and flags, through towns delirious with welcome to climax in Portland: louder bands, longer parades, brighter bunting.

On the face of things there was reason to celebrate. Public land offices could scarcely keep up with new registries. Cattlemen had a rail outlet to the Northern plains and within a year would have another one via the Short Line and Union Pacific to Cheyenne, Denver, and Omaha. The sawmills whining and smoking along the Columbia could at last ship their produce to the treeless parts of the interior. The odorous salmon canning industry, which had begun in 1866 when two boats produced a pack of 4000 cases, had reached its zenith with 1700 boats furnishing 630,000 cases. The Butte mines were booming;

the Coeur d'Alenes were beginning to show promise. Success, as usual, fed on itself. New manufactories and service industries had to be established to care for the new population, and the cities of the Northwest were embarking on a decade of the fastest growth, in terms of percentages, that they would ever know.

In spite of these things, worry thinned the smile with which Henry Villard greeted each new welcoming committee. Construction prices had exceeded estimates. At the same time he had had to keep his promises to the investors in his blind pool by declaring high dividends out of his shrinking treasury. New bonds could be issued only on the strength of land-grant titles perfected by satisfactory track completion; and the government, wary because of previous chicanery by other roads, was moving slowly. By October 1883, just after the Portland celebration, the Northern Pacific's operating deficit had reached nine and a half million dollars; its bonded indebtedness stood at sixty-one million. Stock prices collapsed, and on January 4, 1884, Villard was forced to resign from all his companies. Shattered in health and fortune, he went to Germany to try to recuperate both.

Different presidents assumed control of the Northern Pacific (Robert Harris) and of the Oregon and Transcontinental and its subsidiary, the Oregon Railway and Navigation Company (Elijah Smith). Promptly the antagonistic concerns fell into a feud abetted by jealousies long smoldering between Portland and the cities of Puget Sound.

Soon the policy conflicts grew so sharp that the Northern Pacific determined to build its own line up the Yakima Valley, penetrating the Cascades to Tacoma by a tunnel two miles long under Stampede Pass. The contract for the bore, second largest in the United States, was awarded in January 1886 to Nelson Bennett, who with his brother Sidney was already at work laying rails between the Columbia and the little town of Yakima. A time clause demanded completion of the tunnel within twenty-eight months. To save every second the Bennetts had to start lifting donkey engines, sawmills, pipe, compressors, air drills, construction locomotives, and tons of food supplies up eighty-seven miles of roadless mountain to an altitude of twenty-eight hundred feet during the dead of winter. After a frantic struggle with snow, trees, canyons, and waterfalls, they made it. By the beginning of April men were at work inside both the east and west headings of the tunnel. It was well they started when they did. The herculean job was finished only seven days ahead of the deadline.

Behind them the track crawled slowly across the rich, baked soil of the Yakima Valley. When the chief real estate owners in the town of Yakima (population four hundred) asked exorbitant prices for a depot site, the Northern Pacific laid out a rival town four miles away and bribed Yakima's principal hotel operator to migrate to their village by transplanting his two-story frame structure free of charge. Soon all Yakima was following, light buildings on great trucks pulled by forty or fifty mules, larger ones ponderously tipsy on big, slow-moving iron rollers. It was very pleasant for the Northern Pacific: instead of buying building space, the railroad was now selling it.

In 1887 a temporary track had been laid over Stampede Pass and trains run into Tacoma. The next year the tunnel was completed. That same year C. W. Griggs and his son Everett, noting the depletion of the forests of the Great Lakes region, bought eighty thousand acres of timberland from the Northern Pacific, founded the St. Paul and Tacoma Lumber Company, and in 1889 built the first mill in Washington Territory designed to cut timber for carriage by rail rather than in the lumber schooners that until then had monopolized the trade.

To strike back at the Northern Pacific, the Oregon and Transcontinental, which controlled the OR & N, leased the latter's tracks through the Columbia gorge to the Union Pacific. At about the same time the OR & N divested itself of Holladay's and Villard's Oregon and California through the Willamette; the Southern Pacific picked up the road and in 1887 completed construction to California. Meanwhile, down at the Columbia's foaming mouth army engineers were commencing work on a prodigious stone jetty designed to tame the river's fearsome bar. That long-range improvement, together with the rail connections, should have guaranteed Portland's stature as the Northwest's leading harbor—if her railroads were used to full capacity.

They were not likely to be. With the shortsightedness typical of the railroad economics of the era, the OR & N, like the OSN before it, charged inland shippers all the traffic would bear. The price of wheat, however, was declining steadily—from $1.43 a bushel in 1874 to $.86 in 1885. It took a seer of no particular magnitude to predict that farmers caught in the squeeze would desert the OR & N in droves and use the rival Northern Pacific if that railroad offered lower rates. [1]

[1] As events developed, a very slight rate differential served the NP well. In 1886, the year before the Cascade crossing was opened, Portland exported 6,037,000 barrels of flour; in 1889, the year after the Stampede Tunnel was completed, the figure dropped to 3,470,000 barrels. During the same period Puget Sound's exports of flour jumped from 272,000 to 2,297,000 barrels. Later Portland recaptured some of the lost volume (5,600,000 barrels in 1894) but the rate of recovery did not match the growth of exports from the sound (4,211,722 barrels in 1894). Figures on wheat exports tell the same story.

To the Oregon and Transcontinental, parent of the OR & N, the answer seemed to lie not in reducing the rate through the gorge but in having the Northern Pacific maintain an equally high scale on its Cascade line. To achieve the hope, the Oregon and Transcontinental would have to have a voice in Northern Pacific policy making. As heirs of half of Villard's old empire, the Oregon and Transcontinental held approximately one quarter of the outstanding Northern Pacific stock, but had nevertheless been kept off the railroad's board of directors. Determined to force a way in, the Oregon and Transcontinental recklessly bought sixty thousand more shares of Northern Pacific securities. All this did was to empty her treasury. Desperately she turned to her founder, Henry Villard, and asked if he could bail her out with German money.

Villard raised the sum and as agent for the German investors returned to the Northwest in 1887. The Northern Pacific, already feeling the strain of building across the mountains and remembering how Villard had absorbed them in 1881, tried to insure his good will by electing him to its board also.

Villard did his best to work out freight and territory divisions that would please everyone—the OR & N, the Oregon and Transcontinental, the Union Pacific, the Northern Pacific. Regional jealousies and personality clashes were too thorny. The Union Pacific abrogated its agreement with the OR & N and a wild jockeying for supremacy began. Duplicating lines took off in every direction; injunctions and counterinjunctions flew as fast as the picks and shovels.

During the strife a new competitor approached from the East— James Jerome Hill and a collection of slowly accreting local lines that in 1890 took on the name of Great Northern Railway.

Canadian-born, blinded in one eye by a boyhood accident, Hill had landed in St. Paul at the age of eighteen as clerk for a steamboat company. He had a powerful physique: a great arching chest, a craggy head, a tangle of beard that soon turned iron gray. He was intensely ambitious. In 1872 he set up, with a Canadian partner, a shipping firm of his own—the Red River Transportation Company—and began plying boats between the United States and Fort Garry in Canada, as Winnipeg was then known. He grew fast. When a short line called the St. Paul and Pacific went broke in the mid-seventies, he raised more Canadian money to whisk it from under the reaching fingers of the reorganized Northern Pacific. Vigorously he extended his new acquisition northward (shortly he would change its name to the St. Paul, Minneapolis and Manitoba), and in December 1878, at Pembina, hooked onto a branch of the new Canadian Pacific—for which line his Red River Transportation Company had been hauling millions of dollars' worth of construction materials purchased in the United States.

His Canadian connections led Hill on into the Canadian Pacific itself, just then gathering forces to cross the plains and mountains to the Western sea. (Construction in British Columbia was already under way. When Hill joined the board of the Canadian Pacific, Andrew Onderdonk of California, financed by a syndicate that included Simeon Reed of the old OSN, had seven thousand men chewing a way through the Fraser River canyon. Although Onderdonk utilized the bed of the Cariboo wagon road wherever possible, his laborers still had to bore fifteen tunnels, pile up huge fills and trestles, hang by ropes to the cliff faces while blasting millions of tons of rock down into the seething river. It was the kind of work Onderdonk had seen Chinese crews perform successfully for the Central Pacific in the Sierra, and accordingly he proposed to import thousands of coolies of his own into British Columbia. Reaction was violent. In the federal House a British Columbia delegate proposed a resolution that "no man wearing his hair more than five and one-half inches in length be deemed eligible for employment" upon the Canadian Pacific Railroad. Onderdonk retorted, "You must have this labor or you cannot have the railway," and calmly brought in the Chinese despite continuing opposition. [2])

On Hill's advice, the proposed route of the Canadian Pacific was moved farther south to check possible excursions across the border by the Northern Pacific. To locate the new route through the Rockies and the jumbled Selkirks, he hired an American, short, profane, long-bearded A. B. Rogers. To build the track, he imported another American, massive William Van Horne. The job they did was epochal. In 1885, Van Horne broke through the Selkirks to join Onderdonk at Eagle Pass. On November 7 the last spike (of ordinary iron) was

[2] The West coast's long antipathy toward the Chinese began in the placer mines. Since the yellow men labored patiently and lived cheaply, they often succeeded where white men could not or would not. Many mining camps excluded them until the ground had been thoroughly worked, then sold the claims to them for reworking. On the lower Columbia they were denied fishing privileges but were employed at starvation wages for the undesirable work inside the canneries. The national government's Chinese Exclusion Act of 1882 did not pacify rabble rousers. In 1885 mobs murderously attacked Chinese camps at the coal mines near Rock Springs, Wyoming, and in hop fields east of Seattle. That same year the Orientals were driven out of Tacoma and their quarters burned. In Seattle, after months of unrest, 196 of them were forcibly hustled aboard a steamer bound for San Francisco and riots nearly engulfed those left behind before a Home Guard and the territorial militia could restore order.

driven before a small gathering of chilled dignitaries and workmen. Called on for a speech, Van Horne spoke a single sentence: "All I can say is that the work has been well done in every way." The conductor called, "All aboard for the Pacific," and the train rolled on toward Port Moody at the head of long, narrow Burrard Inlet, just north of the Fraser. Harbor facilities at Port Moody proving inadequate, track was extended in 1887 to a small collection of sawmills and shacks called Granville. To the sad confusion of Vancouver Island and Vancouver, Washington, Van Horne arbitrarily rechristened Granville as Vancouver, simply because he liked what he had read about the English explorer of the same name. Within a year the new town's population had jumped from a few dozen to seven thousand.

Well before this, in 1883, James Hill had resigned from the Canadian Pacific to build a competing railroad of his own just south of the border. He moved cautiously, reaching feeders into every fertile nook in the Northern plains and stimulating immigration even more assiduously than Villard had. Since he was in no rush to perfect land-grant titles—he had no land grant—he was not tempted into shoddy construction work or hastily chosen gradients.

Foot by foot his engineers searched for shorter lines and easier climbs than those followed by the rival Northern Pacific. In December 1889, John F. Stevens, who had helped A. B. Rogers unravel the mountains for the Canadian Pacific, set out with a lone Indian to find the key pass which better-equipped parties under Isaac Stevens (no relative) had missed nearly half a century before. This was Marias Pass on what is now the southern boundary of Glacier National Park. In the bitter cold his guide collapsed. Stevens pushed ahead on foot and at evening found the gap. The thermometer stood at forty below. To keep from freezing the lone surveyor built a fire but could not keep it going. Tramping out a runway, he spent the night walking back and forth, back and forth. He suffered no ill effects. It was not so with his former boss, A. B. Rogers, who that same year died as the delayed result of a horseback fall suffered while searching out an economical way for Hill's railroad to pierce the Coeur d'Alene Mountains between Montana and Idaho.

The Northwest, particularly the Inland Empire, watched Hill's approach with joy. Here, perhaps, was a way to end the discriminatory freight rates from which they suffered.

To placate the big wholesale firms of the coast and to enable them to do the jobbing for the interior, the Union Pacific and the Northern Pacific carried goods to Portland or Tacoma more cheaply than to inland points, even though the freight went straight through the inland stations on its way to the coast. Spokane, for example, paid $2.00 on writing paper that was laid down on the coast for $1.17; $1.81 on steel rail as against $.81 at tidewater. Relief had been denied by the new Interstate Commerce Commission on the plea of the railroads that in shipping to the coast they had to meet competition by water. But perhaps a new railroad's hunger for business would help end the discrimination.

On February 11, 1892, Spokane citizens thronged to the Auditorium Theatre to hear Jim Hill expound his case. He wanted a free right of way through the heart of the city so that he could buck the already established Northern Pacific and Union Pacific. In return for the land he promised to locate his shops nearby. More vaguely he mentioned rates. Aglow with excitement, the city fathers gave him what he wanted. In time they got the shops. But not the rates. As the Spokane *Review* pointed out immediately after the Auditorium speech, "At saying one thing and conveying another Mr. Hill is adept." Forty-nine more years were to pass before the Inland Empire at last achieved freight treatment comparable to that enjoyed by the coast cities.

Seattle, humbled at being served by only an indifferent Northern Pacific branch line from Tacoma, would have liked to greet Hill even more handsomely than had Spokane. She could not, however. The approaches to the city were largely controlled by a local concern called the Seattle, Lake Shore and Eastern; and in 1890 the Northern Pacific had bought the road, not so much to help Seattle as to keep Hill from using the line to gain access to the sound.

The move did not bother Hill. He incorporated a subsidiary called the Seattle and Montana to build thirty-three miles north to Everett. Entry into Seattle was secured across the tide flats and made usable by a broad earth fill. Meanwhile, Hill's locating engineer, John Stevens, found a way up the Wenatchee River to a low pass over the Cascades and on down the Skycomish to Everett. Connections were made early in 1893 and Great Northern trains rolled unimpeded into Seattle.

By this time Hill had ceased to worry about his transcontinental rivals. A nationwide panic was settling on the land and he doubted if either the Union Pacific or Northern Pacific would survive. In their struggle to dominate the lower part of the Columbia Basin they had grievously overbuilt their competing branch lines. Furthermore, the Union Pacific had just overstrained itself to buy control of the OR & N. The Northern Pacific, still groggy from the expenses of the Cascade tunnel, was faced with the need to replace some of the track so hastily laid through the Rockies in 1883. Under the circumstances the quickening slump in the grainfields and in the silver mines of the interior was almost certain to be disastrous. James J. Hill could quite likely win the entire Northwest by biding his time. Panic or no panic, it was an exhilarating prize to contemplate.

7. Mineral Boom—and Bust

GRIZZLED and solitary, Andrew J. Prichard in November 1878 wandered afoot over the Mullan Road from Montana westward onto the South Fork of Idaho's Coeur d'Alene River. As Prichard walked he brooded over the ills which, in his mind, had disjointed his world: soulless corporations, concentrated wealth, and the dehumanizing, mechanical monsters of the Industrial Revolution. If ever he found money he would fight these evils. His weapon was ready, a loose organization of utopian freethinkers called the Liberal League. But poor. As poor as he, Andrew Prichard, was.

At the mouth of one of the heavily timbered gulches that ran down into the South Fork of the Coeur d'Alene River from the mountains to the north he dug into the gravel and unearthed traces of gold. In accord with his liberal propensities he gave the claim as radical a name as he could then devise, the Evolution. But he had no opportunity to exploit it. He was broke and winter was coming on. Drifting on down the river, he passed the famous wooden church of the Cataldo mission and crossed Fourth of July Pass to the new army post at the northern tip of Coeur d'Alene Lake. He found a few odd jobs in the vicinity, then moved on to Spokane Falls, a hamlet of nine families where the Spokane River roared over the reefs below Havermale Island. At Spokane, Prichard entered into a contract to supply logs to a little water-powered sawmill. But he kept thinking of the Evolution. The next fall, when cold weather threatened to close the river and the sawmill, he went back to the mountains. He had one silver dollar in his pocket, some food, and tools enough for building a cabin.

During snowstorms he dreamed utopias and wrote letters to fellow members of the Liberal League. During good weather he scratched around the gravel of the nearby creeks. For two years he barely managed to stay alive. Discouraged, he decided, late in 1881, to look at the far side of the mountain that reared steeply behind his cabin. It was an arduous trip, precipitous and brush-tangled, but on the tributaries of the North Fork of the Coeur d'Alene River he found gravel bars loaded with coarse gold. Feverish with excitement, he stayed there panning until heavy snows ran him back to his cabin on the South Fork.

Somehow the news leaked. Early in the summer of 1882 a handful of men showed up at the Evolution and, according to one story, frightened Prichard into guiding them across the mountains. Dazzled by what he showed them, the group was unwilling to spend time journeying outside to register their claims, but kept mining as long as the weather permitted.

This gave Prichard opportunity to mature his own plans. Earnestly he wrote to correspondents in the Liberal League:

I have made discovery of a gold-bearing country that will give employment to at least 15,000 to 20,000 men. . . . There are two good and natural townsites where will be built cities representing thousands in less than two years. . . . I would like to see as much of this go into the hands of the Liberals as possible, and also see them build a city where they can have their own laws and enough of this vast mining region to support it, which they can do if they will go at it cool and work together.

The next spring, 1883, he tried to go at it cool by obtaining powers of attorney from freethinking colleagues and filing claims for them in absentia. In August, assuming apparently that the League was protected, Prichard decided to reveal his find. With a companion he entered a newspaper office in Spokane Falls and dropped onto the editor's desk a buckskin bag containing four pounds of gold nuggets.

Instantly the story became grist for a publicity pamphlet issued by the Northern Pacific, just then preparing to link its lines in Montana. Jubilantly the broadside concluded its panegyric by declaring, "Such is a brief sketch of the Coeur d'Alene mines, which surpass in richness and volume the most fabulous quartz and placers ever discovered . . . they are inexhaustible, and although thousands may work them, there will still be room for thousands more."

By October the thousands were pouring in. Westerners came by the Northern Pacific and its stagecoach connections to the ramshackle town adjoining the army's Post Coeur d'Alene. At Coeur d'Alene they swarmed aboard a little steamer which chugged down the serpentine lake to the Coeur d'Alene River and turned up this to the landing near the Cataldo mission. There the prospectors could rent horses for the ride to the diggings.

Travelers from the east left the train at Thompson Falls, approximately where David Thompson had built Saleesh House three quarters of a century earlier, and struggled on across forty miles of rough mountain trail. East or west, they had a rough winter. Freight could reach them only by hand-drawn toboggan or dog team. The tents and drafty cabins of Eagle City were built on foundations scratched out of snow four feet deep. After such experiences the impatient prospectors of Eagle (and of Murray, founded a few months later on the second of Prichard's "good and natural townsites") were not inclined to honor the stakes of the absent freethinkers. The notices that Prichard had posted for them were torn down, the claims jumped; and nothing remained to the Liberal League but lawsuits.

For whatever comfort it was worth, the gravels would not have supported their cities for very long. In two years "the most fabulous quartz and placers ever discovered" grudgingly gave forth a scant three quarters of a million dollars. But before the boom collapsed it drew into the Coeur d'Alene Mountains several prospectors who were able to recognize other minerals than free gold.

In the spring of 1884 some of them crossed back toward the South Fork. At once they began coming across blowouts of a lead ore similar to that which in Colorado was associated with silver. During the summer several claims were filed, and knowledge of them was in Noah Kellogg's mind when he was sent forth from Murray the following year with instructions to look for gold.

Noah Kellogg was an unemployed carpenter sixty years old. He had been grubstaked, partly to get rid of him, by a building contractor named Origen Peck in association with a retired doctor from the British navy, one John Cooper. Included in the twenty-odd dollars' worth of supplies that the pair bought for Kellogg was a three-dollar donkey.

Kellogg lost the burro on the South Fork side of the mountains and was presumably carrying his samples of lead-silver ore on his own back when he returned to Murray. He got no sympathy from his patrons. Cooper and Peck wanted gold and on seeing his offerings showed him the door. But if Peck and Cooper weren't interested in what he had, others were. Kellogg secured a partner named O'Rourke and a fresh grubstake from saloonkeepers Harry Baer and Dutch Jake Goetz.

On the way back to the South Fork, Kellogg and O'Rourke found and used the lost burro. Legend says the jackass promptly strayed again, this time into Milo Gulch, and that while the prospectors were searching for it they stumbled onto a magnificent outcrop of ore. Elaborations on the theme add that the donkey itself discovered the outcrop and was staring transfixed at its silver sheen when the searchers arrived. Or perhaps the prospectors had left the donkey in camp and were simply following up a quartz lead in the manner of their craft when they spotted the lode.

In any event the two men found, near the site of modern Kellogg, one of the fabulous silver mines of the world, the Bunker Hill & Sullivan. For more than seventy years dividends from its sprawling shaft heads and smelters have topped a million dollars annually; during recent decades it has ranked as the greatest single lode-mine producer of lead and zinc in the United States. At that, it is only slightly more dazzling than some of its neighbors. Of the ten leading silver producers in the United States, six are crowded into a twenty-mile stretch along the South Fork of the Coeur d'Alene River.

The spot where the donkey stopped (if it was the donkey) lay within four miles of Prichard's original Evolution claim. And it guaranteed for Idaho all of the industrial pangs that Prichard had hoped to forestall.

The pangs came later, however. The first impulses were to find some way of sharing the plum. On the strength of their original grubstake (and the donkey) Cooper and Peck sued for and won from the district court an interest in the mine. Outraged, Kellogg and his second set of backers appealed to the territorial Supreme Court. While the litigation was pending, Simeon Reed of the old OSN came up from Portland with millions of dollars to invest—but not in properties paralyzed by litigation. Hastily the disputants resolved their difficulties. Cooper and Peck were bought out for seventy-six thousand dollars, a fair return, it would seem, on a three-dollar jackass. The others then extracted close to a million from Reed, three hundred thousand of it going to the once unemployed carpenter, Noah Kellogg.

The same year that Reed's syndicate made the purchase and started developing the property (1887), an Eastern railroader named Daniel Corbin laid a narrow-gauge railway down the Coeur d'Alene River to the head of navigation at the old mission. From there steamboats carried ore on down the river and across the lake to the town of Coeur d'Alene, where a spur track connected with the Northern Pacific. Business was so good that within one year the Northern Pacific bought Corbin out. Abandoning his narrow-gauge tracks, it built its own line across the mountains from the east. This left a vacuum in the west which was promptly filled by the OR & N, that is to say, by the Union Pacific. Its tracks met the Northern Pacific's at the town of Wallace, deep in an evergreen-shaded hollow from which three canyons radiated like spokes. Within a space of seven miles along the northern spoke the mine towns of Gem, Frisco, and Burke were plastered in tiers to precipitous slopes swept nearly every winter by avalanches. Burke, home of the huge Tiger-Poorman workings, was so cramped between its mountain walls that the hotel and mills were built over the railroad; lesser shops have to raise their awnings when a train goes by.

Eastward in Montana, where the town of Butte lay hard against the rolling backbone of the Continental Divide, fortune was going through an even dizzier whirl. There was silver in Butte also. During the 1870s it attracted, among others, two men whose feuds would rack the territory for decades—William Andrews Clark and Marcus Daly.

Clark arrived first. Wiry, ambitious and niggardly, with a shock of wavy hair and whiskers like a terrier, he made his first money placer mining at Bannack in 1863. Confidently he risked the gains and his neck freighting winter supplies up from Salt Lake City at speculative prices. The venture succeeding, he branched out and in 1869 established a wholesale merchandising and banking business in the little town of Deer Lodge, thirty-odd miles from Butte.

During occasional business trips to the neighboring town he grew convinced that a man who understood ore reduction could turn the region's shallow prospect holes into rich producers. Quietly he secured a few options. And then, in 1872, aged thirty-three, William Andrews Clark hied himself to New York City for a year's study in the newly opened Columbia University School of Mines. Out of the book learning (and some fancy sleight of hand which cost a man named Farlin a good silver mine) came Butte's first successful roasting mill.

A small rush started. Among the new arrivals was Marcus Daly, scouting for Salt Lake City promoters. An Irish immigrant, Daly had learned practical mining over a pick and shovel first in California, then in Nevada. He proved his nose for ore by finding the Ontario mine in Utah for George Hearst of San Francisco and for Hearst's lawyers, Lloyd Tevis and swart James Ben Ali Haggin, son of a Kentucky barrister and a Turkish refugee's daughter. After that success Marcus Daly, almost totally uneducated, was sought after as a mining engineer.

After examining prospects around Butte, Daly suggested to his principals the purchase of the Alice silver mine and took a share of it himself. Four years later, in 1880, he grew interested in the nearby Anaconda. When his Salt Lake partners refused to go along he sold them his interest in the Alice for thirty thousand dollars and with that sum purchased the neighboring property. Then he went to San Francisco to see Hearst, Tevis, and Haggin. Remembering the Ontario, they gave him thirty thousand dollars for a three-fourths interest in his new acquisition. So Daly had his purchase price back, plus one fourth of whatever he turned the mine into.

He leased Clark's smelter and commenced operating the Anaconda as a silver property. The deeper he went the more copper he encountered. These cuprous intrusions had long disturbed Butte's silver seekers. But the country's new electrical industry was creating stronger markets, and Daly told his partners they just might have a killing in sight if they went after the red metal on a large enough scale.

Hearst was reluctant, fearing that the new Lake Superior copper mines with their high-grade ore and water transport could not be bucked. The Anaconda had no coal, no coke, no water for a smelter. It wouldn't work.

Daly said he could make it work. The territory's new railroads would bring in coal; the mountains were full of wood for additional fuel; he'd find water. Secretive little Ben Ali Haggin believed him. He swung over the other partners, and Daly shut down the Anaconda for a thorough remodeling.

The sudden closure mystified the camp. With Daly's connivance word got around that the vein had pinched out. The surrounding mines took fright; he bought them at bargain prices. Then he began installing a three-compartment shaft and huge engines capable of lifting hoists twenty-five hundred feet. Butte's mystification increased: everyone knew the Anaconda was scarcely four hundred feet deep. Had Marcus Daly lost his mind?

Twenty-six miles to the west he located a smelter site with ample water. Clark was after the same site for a silver-reduction plant. Daly outmaneuvered him and the enmity that had been slowly generating between their antithetical natures—Clark elegant, pale, frigid; Daly crude, florid, jovial—sparked white hot.

Daly's partners poured four million dollars into the smelter and a contiguous town named Anaconda. In September 1884, Daly began operations. Other Butte mine owners, Clark included, fell over themselves to follow suit. Alarmed, the Lake Superior mines sought to crush the upstarts by cutting prices. Butte retorted by intensifying production: in 1885 the Anaconda alone turned out thirty-six million pounds of copper, the other Butte mines thirty-two million. The total production of seventeen Lake Superior mines during the same period was seventy-seven million pounds.

Again the Lake mines cut prices. Though one of the worst winters the Rockies would ever know was on hand, Daly closed his plant for overhauling. When he reopened in the spring of 1887 capacity had doubled and he could produce copper three quarters of a cent cheaper per pound than before the closure. That year Butte's production far outstripped Lake Superior's. That year, too, a French syndicate tried to corner the world's copper by offering mines everywhere thirteen cents a pound for their entire output, planning obviously to boost retail prices when control was complete. Daly wanted to hold out, but Haggin, tired of the war with the Lake mines which had reduced prices to ten cents a pound, agreed to go along.

They were wild, high days. Any miner who wanted work could find it in Butte. They poured in by the thousands. So did the parasites who preyed on them, the merchants who supplied them. The earth rumbled with never ending explosions; the sun shone blood red through stinking clouds of sulphur fumes that withered vegetation as far as the eye could see. But who cared about vegetation? Everyone had money.

Butte and Coeur d'Alene—those were the principal fever centers. There were others. In Washington the Old Dominion mine, discovered the same year as the Bunker Hill & Sullivan, turned Colville from a hamlet of two stores and a brewery into a sturdy city. East of Colville other finds sent temperatures soaring all along the lower Pend Oreille River into British Columbia, where the Toad Mountain silver mines near Kootenay Lake boomed Nelson into prominence. Other lodes, untested yet, turned up in the Slocan district beyond Nelson and at the headwaters of Trail Creek, just west of the Columbia and only six miles north of the international boundary. To make these potential millions of dollars tributary to Spokane, Dan Corbin, creator of the narrow-gauge railway into the Coeur d'Alene, in 1889 laid new track through Colville and on toward a projected smelter at Northport, just south of the border.

Farmers drawn into the Northwest territories by the railroads and miners by these sudden bursts of mineral discovery swelled population to the point that Congress could no longer ignore demands for statehood. During the eighties the efforts had been blocked by Democrats fearful of new Republican votes, but with the election of Benjamin Harrison to the presidency in the fall of 1888, Congress capitulated. The Dakotas, Montana, and Washington were authorized to hold constitutional conventions during 1889. Feeling left out, Idaho and Wyoming summoned their own conventions without congressional authority.

Disasters plagued the territories during the deliberations. Great fires gutted the entire business districts of Seattle and Spokane and the small town of Ellensburg in the Yakima Valley. In Montana, on May 4, the huge Anaconda smelter burned to the ground. That same year the French syndicate which had been trying to corner the market collapsed and the price of copper plunged to seven and one half cents a pound. Frightened bankers who had loaned the syndicate thirty-three million dollars proposed to dump its huge stocks on the open market. To forestall a world-wide metal collapse, Anaconda joined the powerful Calumet and Hecla mines at Lake Superior in warning the foreigners to dribble out their copper slowly over the years or the Americans would cut everyone's throat by flooding the market with five-cent copper. The bluff worked. Prices steadied. Daly rebuilt the Anaconda smelter and had it back in operation by September.

With equal ardor Spokane and Seattle built imposing new brick and stone edifices on the ashes of its old wooden structures; and the dizzy dance went on. Business had been good—or at least had seemed good—throughout the eighties and optimists glowed with a mystic feeling that statehood (achieved by Montana and Washington in November 1889, by Idaho and Wyoming in July 1890) would somehow make it better.

Statehood also sparked the Clark-Daly feud into a raucous free-for-all.

With so many millions in his pocket that money no longer salved his ambition, William Andrews Clark ran as a Democrat for one of Montana's two new Senate seats. In those days senators were chosen by the state legislatures, but unfortunately for Clark, exuberant Montanans had elected *two* legislatures, one Democratic and one Republican. Each sent senators to the national capital. Congress seated the Republicans and Clark was sent back to Butte, his humiliation in no wise lessened by the hoots of Marcus Daly's subsidized newspaper in Anaconda.

About this same time Anaconda decided it would like to be the capital of the new state. Other cities shared the aspiration. Helena, wishing to retain the seat of government, objected vociferously. Buffeted from all sides, the politicians decided on a primary election to be held in 1892; the two cities leading that race would then hold a runoff in '94.

Daly obviously supported Anaconda. Clark forsook Butte, where he was unpopular, and backed Helena. He then complicated the issue by running for the Senate seat that fell open in 1892. Results were mixed. His town led Anaconda in the capital balloting, but his senatorial hopes were crushed after a vicious fight in the legislature. Once again Daly's paper crowed in delight, heralding the defeat as a sign "that the majority of the legislature is honest and that a seat in the United States Senate cannot be bought."

Seared by the insults, Clark vowed that Anaconda would never become the capital. He poured a reputed two and a half million dollars into the fight. Daly countered with a mere four hundred thousand. (Daly was having other troubles. The panic of '93 was shaking copper prices; moreover, George Hearst had died in 1891; his estate had thrown his Anaconda stock onto the market, and outsiders were raiding the once tightly knit corporation.) But what Daly denied in cash he made up for in vigor. When a drunk was jailed in Helena for shouting on the street, "Hurrah for Anaconda," Daly rushed over on a special train loaded with lawyers and sprang the man on a writ of habeas corpus. Miners liked that kind of gesture.

It was not enough, however. Helena carried the election by two thousand votes. Exhilarated citizens dragged Clark's carriage by ropes through the winding streets and jammed the auditorium twelve thousand strong to hear his victory speech. His feelings touched, he provided free liquor for all and touched off one of the greatest mass drunks in history. And now *his* paper had a chance to crow: "This election is . . . the Waterloo of the most tyrannical corporation [i.e., Anaconda] that ever attempted to crush out the independence of the people. . . ."

But if the citizens of Helena were riding high, the rest of the land was not. Bewilderingly, devastatingly, the sheen had gone from the hopes which statehood was supposed to have polished still brighter.

Despite its booming mines, large segments of the Northwest's economy had felt the effects of the doldrums that for several years had been creeping across the country. The fierce winter of 1886–87 that destroyed the overcapitalized ranches of the high plains ended the export market for Oregon cattle. Wheat prices sagged lower and lower, until the cost of shipping a bushel of grain three hundred miles equaled what the farmer received for it in the market.

Debtors (and one of every four farms in the Northwest was mortgaged in 1890) believed that the low per capita circulation of money was largely responsible for the debacle. Demands for currency inflation centered more and more stridently on silver. This agitation the Republicans withstood until the advent of their new brethren from the recently admitted states of the West. The fledgling senators, entering into what seemed a treacherous alliance with the more radical Democrats in Congress, helped force the passage of the Sherman Silver Purchase Act of 1890. Under its terms the government was forced to buy four and a half million ounces of the white metal per month, paying for it with notes redeemable in either gold or silver coin. This of course accorded with the desires of Western mineowners but was diametrically opposed to the thinking of conservative Republicans elsewhere.

In spite of the drastic medicine, prices continued to decline. Even silver, which for a few months rose under impact of the Sherman Act from $.84 to $1.05 per ounce, soon declined again, touching $.78 in 1893. Meanwhile the huge mines of the Coeur d'Alenes were chewing deeper and deeper into the earth; in time some of the shafts would reach from elevations of nearly four thousand feet to depths a thousand feet below sea level. Such operations required elaborate machines —expensive machines—and for the first time the Northwest began to feel what Andrew Prichard had feared a decade before: the dislocations of the Industrial Revolution.

Workers proud of skills that once had made them the equal of any neighbor in the hurly-burly mining camps now felt themselves relegated to inferior status as the slaves of some mechanized Frankenstein. Management seemed to grow increasingly impersonal as more and more capital flowed in from the outside. New York financiers, for example, gained control of the mighty Bunker Hill & Sullivan, while at the same time the Northern Pacific and Union Pacific absorbed the local rail lines.

Because of their fears the workers in the Coeur d'Alene listened sympathetically to union organizers from Butte and in 1889 formed a federation called the Coeur d'Alene Executive Miners' Union. To counter it the operators formed the Mine Owners' Protective Association.

The union promptly demanded improved wage and hour conditions. The owners, worried by the steady drop in lead and silver prices, resisted. There were further troubles over the collection of hospital fees and the deliberate favoring of non-union workers. Matters came to a head in 1892, when the mines closed down, ostensibly because of a dispute with the railroads about freight rates. In time the owners won concessions from the railways, but instead of passing on part of the savings to the workers they insisted that the drop in metal prices forced them to reopen their plants at lower wage rates than ever.

Infuriated, the union called a strike. Defiantly the Protective Association imported a trainload of scabs to the Frisco mine, halfway between Wallace and Burke. On July 10 pitched battles outside both Frisco and Gem killed five men and wounded sixteen or more. While the bullets were flying, unionists slipped up the hill above the Frisco, dropped a case of dynamite down the penstock, and blew the mill to pieces. The dazed non-unionists then surrendered and were loaded into boxcars for deportation.

More scabs were captured at the Bunker Hill & Sullivan when the unionists threatened to blow up the concentrating plant unless the management gave in. During the exodus that followed, a brutal melee developed at the steamboat landing near the old mission. Two unarmed strikebreakers were killed; others caught before they could run into the hills or jump into the river were beaten and robbed.

The mines reopened with the help of militia sent in by the governor, but the bitterness continued. In 1899 it exploded again. Enraged by the refusal of the Bunker Hill & Sullivan to recognize their union, a thousand strikers razed the mine's huge concentrating plant, killing two men in the process—"a giant picnic," said Harry Orchard, who helped with the dynamiting. Again there was martial law, imposed this time by Governor Frank Steunenberg, and again the wholesale arrests and highhanded incarceration of unionists in boxcars and unsanitary bull pens left a smoldering bitterness. In 1905 it vented itself in a final spasm of fury when Harry Orchard was hired to assassinate Steunenberg by means of a crude bomb wired to his gatepost.

As the panic of '93 spread, a special session of Congress repealed the Sherman Silver Purchase Act. The white metal skidded to sixty-three cents an ounce; every silver mine and mill in Butte and many of those in the Coeur d'Alene shut down. Banks collapsed. At Port Townsend on Puget Sound the eerie silence of desertion settled over a city built for the several thousand people necessary to man the streetcar systems, nail factory, and dry dock promulgated on hopes that the Union Pacific would turn the spot into a salt-water rival of

Seattle and Tacoma. But the Union Pacific failed; Port Townsend died. The Northern Pacific joined the company of the drowning, and Henry Villard's railroad days were at last ended forever.

Various ills were blamed for the disasters. The railroads, once welcomed as shining knights that would slay the dragon of steamboat monopolies, had turned themselves into villains through their very success. For as soon as the ships were driven off the Columbia the carriers set up rate structures and service facilities to suit themselves, whereupon a great cry arose to bring the steamers back. But there was no way for the boats to compete successfully with the railroad through the Columbia gorge until canals were built around the Dalles and the rapids at the Cascades. In the drear months of '93, Congress heeded the uproar with appropriations to build a three-thousand-foot ditch at the Cascades. In '96 it was opened with elaborate fanfare, but stayed little more than a gesture so long as the far more difficult stretch at the Dalles remained untouched.

Land frauds were excoriated with equal bitterness. There was reason. In the high deserts of the Inland Empire and south into Oregon, speculators were wont to put boats on wheels and have the craft pulled through the sagebrush. They would then solemnly swear they had boated through the district and would claim the land they wanted under various swamp-act provisions. Much of this "swamp" land went to politicians—a hundred thousand acres to Governor Thayer of Oregon, for instance.

Still more acreage was absorbed by the fraudulent entries of cattle and sheep ranchers, who righteously insisted that they were forced to be dishonest by the very nature of the government's land laws. Geared to the small farms of the East, these acts allowed no legal means whereby a man could obtain enough government land in semiarid regions for grazing profitable numbers of livestock. "Profitable numbers" was, of course, an elastic phrase. Pete French, to care for his gigantic herds, expanded his Blitzen River outfit south of Malheur Lake to a block of territory seventy-five miles long by thirty wide, with a fenced lane through the middle of it so that lesser mortals could go to town. There were objections. During the course of one of the arguments, on the day after Christmas, 1897, little Pete French, king of the Oregon cattlemen, was shot and killed by an angry settler.

Around Puget Sound the lumber companies bucked the land laws by similar means for similar reasons. The Timber and Stone Act of 1878, for example, would sell to individuals (but not to corporations) 160 acres of government land that was unfit for cultivation. This was not enough land to justify the sawmills and heavy machinery necessary to handle the giant trees of the coastal mountains, once cutting had retreated beyond the water line. So the companies rounded up gangs of their own employees, of sailors temporarily in port, and of wandering derelicts, took them into the woods, and had them make entry on pre-selected sites. The "homesteaders" were then ferried by the shipload to land offices. Here they registered their claims, then stepped outside and for the price of a night on the town sold the holding to a waiting company agent.

The companies created more anger by holding these lands in reserve. Timber for immediate needs was purchased from individual loggers who as often as not simply helped themselves from the public forests. It was easy enough. Surveys were incomplete; enforcement offices were inadequately staffed. And if a man was apprehended he could avoid prosecution by paying a fine that generally did not equal his profits.

As the depression deepened, protests against all these things gathered fury and were finally caught up in the nationwide fervor known as Populism. Part of Populism's appeal—and it rang an exhilarating call in the West—was for the inflationary free and unlimited coinage of silver. Sensing the potency of the demand, William Jennings Bryan stole the Populists' thunder by turning the silver issue into an emotional catchall involving patriotism, morals, and the sanctity of the home. With it he prevented the disintegration of the Democratic party and largely because of it carried, during the presidential election of 1896, every state of the West save California and Oregon. Oregon he lost by a scanty 2117 votes. Populous Multnomah County (Portland) made the difference, thanks to the blatant purchase of votes by the frightened Republican machine.

Oddly, the defeat in Oregon achieved more lasting reform than did the Populist-Democratic victory in Washington. In the latter state the triumphant "Poplocrats" fell into such bickerings among themselves that progressive legislation was largely forestalled until well after the turn of the century. But Oregonians, sickened at last by the long stench of corruption, put teeth into their registration laws and started the drive toward the once sensational "Oregon system" of the initiative and referendum.

Silver, however, was a dead issue. Prices were riding up again on the flood tide of new gold discoveries throughout the world. Among the greatest of these, and one that funneled its magic vitality almost exclusively through the Northwest, was the Klondike. Buoyed by the surge, even wilder extravaganzas were in the making.

8. One More Merry-go-round

SAN FRANCISCO nabobs, feeling the need of ice, imported a shipload of it from Alaska in 1852 at a cost of seventy-five dollars a ton. The extraordinary price started a boomlet. Freezing ponds were built near Sitka and Kodiak, and Alaska's first railways (to strain the word) were constructed for carrying the product out to the wharves.

During the operations ship captains noted other possibilities: the fur trade of the panhandle, held by the Hudson's Bay Company under a leasing agreement with the Russian-American Fur Company; the enormous seal herds that congregated in the Bering Sea; the teeming fisheries off the serrated coasts. The upshot was that after the Civil War Secretary Seward offered the Russian minister seven million dollars for the Northern icebox and then tossed in a lagniappe of two hundred thousand dollars to extinguish any "privileges, franchises, grants, or possessions" ceded by the Russian-American Fur Company to "any associated companies"—in other words, the California ice carriers and the Hudson's Bay Company.

In place of the British and Russian monopolies came the Alaska Commercial Company of San Francisco, which in 1869, for an annual fifty-five thousand dollars, obtained from the United States Government an exclusive right to kill seals *on* certain islands in the Bering Sea. Apparently the company did not know how easily seals could be killed in the water, for nothing was said about pelagic, or open sea, hunting.

During the eighties the omission rose to plague the licensees. American, Canadian, Russian, and Japanese hunters tagged the migrating herds as they moved toward the breeding grounds, ruthlessly killing males and females alike. In 1883 a few of the unlicensed sealers dared penetrate the Bering Sea itself. At once the Washington lobbyist of the Alaska Commercial Company protested to the Revenue Department. A cutter was dispatched to seize the intruders. To make life easy for the government, the company prepared a brief for the United States district attorney in Alaska to follow in prosecuting the offenders, and another for the judge to use in assessing penalties.

Prodded by angry shipowners in Victoria, where the sealing fleet of some fifty vessels was an item of no little economic importance, the British and Canadian governments challenged the right of the American Treasury Department to confiscate sealers operating as much as fifty miles from land. The United States retorted that the purchase from Russia made the area north of the Aleutians in effect a closed sea and, besides, as owner of the seal herds it had a right to protect them from uncontrolled depletion.

When the measured acidity of diplomatic notes accomplished nothing, the quarrel was referred, in 1892, to arbitration. The tribunal denied America's right to extend its jurisdiction beyond the three-mile limit; and after considerable huffing and puffing the United States compromised $1,250,000 in damage claims for $473,151. Far more significant was the tribunal's statement that natural resources did need conservation. Out of this awareness eventually came historic agreements by Russia, Japan, Great Britain, and the United States to outlaw pelagic sealing and restrain the hunting on land. So far as sealers were concerned, the era of jungle economics was over.

During these same years, by contrast, the inland parts of the continent were experiencing their most violent spasms of exploitation—the gold rush to the Klondike, the copper wars in Butte, the lumber stampede to the evergreen forests of the Northwest.

There had been minor gold excitements in the North ever since the gaudy days of Cariboo. In 1881 the golconda mines of Juneau were discovered. A few years later the rich gravels of the Upper Yukon brought a population of some six hundred to Fortymile just inside the Canadian border; in 1893 another eight hundred flocked to Circle City on the American side of the line.

Then, in August 1896, word sped down the river of fantastic strikes in a section called Klondike. Alaskan sourdoughs poured into the overnight town of Dawson. Because the frozen streams did not allow washing the gravel laboriously dug during winter, the ice-stiff earth was stacked in piles to wait for spring. The delayed harvest passed all belief. A Californian named Barry washed out $130,000 in a few weeks. A man named Dismore garnered $24,480 in one day. Frank Phiscator, wearied of digging after he had shoveled up $100,000, sold half his claim for $1,333,000. (Figures as usual do not include those who netted just blisters.)

Barry, Phiscator, and other fortunates took the first boats they could catch back to the States, the *Excelsior* of the Alaska Commercial Company and the *Portland* of a rival concern. The *Excelsior* docked at San Francisco on July 15, 1897. The sight of happy prospectors staggering down the gangplanks with suitcases full of gold left ship reporters too stunned to take full advantage of the story. But the wire services prepared the way for the *Portland*, due at Seattle two days later. A journalist caught the ship in the sound and in a burst of inspiration calculated her cargo not in dollars but in weight —a ton and a half of gold. The vision of such a cool yellow heap shook the imagination of a depression-weary land and started a frantic scramble of raw greenhorns for one of the harshest regions on earth.

Voices rose in warning. The manager of the Alaska Commercial Company, which stood to profit as much as anyone, declared, "I regard it as a crime for any transportation company to encourage men to go to the Yukon this fall. . . . It will be impossible to get enough provisions through to supply the demand. The Seattle people who are booming the steamship lines may be sincere, but a heavy responsibility will rest on their shoulders should starvation and crime prevail in Dawson City next winter. . . ."

No one paid any attention, least of all the Seattle people. They wanted to be entrepreneurs for this bonanza. San Francisco might call herself the mining capital of the Pacific slope. Portland might boast of being the Northwest's largest city. Victoria and Vancouver might caution that the Klondike fields lay within Canada and that goods purchased in America would be subject to duty on crossing the border. But Seattle was the logical outfitting point—or so said an overwhelming barrage of publicity developed by the Chamber of Commerce.

The drive worked. Gold seekers by the thousands poured into the city, jammed its hotels and stores, paid hungrily for its entertainment, stimulated its infant industries. There seemed to be no end. Before the bloom could fade from the Klondike, another rush started to Nome, where gold could be dug right from the sands of the beach. While that excitement was still at its height another surge washed toward Fairbanks. And when the treasure began flooding back, most of those glittering tens of millions of dollars poured through Seattle.

The city grew lustily. To flatten her steep hillsides and make room for still more multistoried commercial buildings, engineers turned gigantic hydraulic hoses on the mountaintops, sluiced them down to workable grades, and piled up the detritus on the tide flats—room for additional extensions. The shipyards expanded until in 1904 they were capable of launching both the battleship *Nebraska* and Jim Hill's freighter *Minnesota*, reputedly the fastest merchant ship afloat. In 1910 the census made official what everyone knew anyway: Seattle had displaced Portland as the most populous city in the Northwest.

The spectacular developments of the Klondike overshadowed the otherwise remarkable mines in southern British Columbia: lead-silver at Slocan, Kimberly, Nelson; gold at Trail; huge deposits of low-grade copper at Grand Forks. All these were conveniently near the border. In spite of the Canadian Pacific's hurried new east-west crossing over Crowsnest Pass in the Rockies, the bulk of the Canadian mining trade flowed south to Spokane, already battening on her wheat, her cattle, and the reviving mines of the Coeur d'Alene.

Eastward, atop a fume-stripped mountain of copper, Butte roared with undiminished vigor. When business had started to gasp during the panic of '93, William Clark and Marcus Daly had imported (in rivalry, not in conjunction) keg upon keg of gold coins. Revived by cash transfusions of more than a million dollars, the copper camp and her satellites straightway roared back to their rowdy ways.

By 1900 these mining centers were no longer classifiable as towns. They were cities. The 30,470 souls living within Butte's sulphurous limits made her the largest metropolis in Montana; Spokane's 36,848 inhabitants represented a hundredfold jump in twenty years; Seattle with 80,671 residents was twice the size of her neighboring rival, Tacoma. Such growth invited the conservatism of cities: cautious financing, cultural refinements, churches, ordered homes. Yet the mining rushes on which the cities waxed strong inevitably fostered recklessness and irresponsibility. The result was a painful civic schizophrenia best epitomized, perhaps, by the long struggle each city had over "box houses."

A box house was a combination saloon and variety theater. The basic design consisted of a crude stage at one end of a main auditorium sprinkled with sawdust and dotted with tables. Surrounding the area, and often elevated onto a gallery, were small cubicles. Each cubicle possessed a door in the rear end through which refreshments could be passed; and in front was a screen which enabled the room's occupants to watch the main floor and the stage without being seen themselves. To promote the sale of drinks young ladies hired by the establishment "hustled" the boxes, although the cubicles were often equipped, so declared the *Spokesman-Review* of Spokane in an outraged editorial, with "couches which permit of immorality in its most depraved form." The girls also circulated among the tables on the main floor, and every so often assembled on the stage for song-and-dance routines with traveling vaudeville performers.

Among untallied dozens of box houses, a trio achieved distinction of sorts: the Coeur d'Alene in Spokane, the Comique in Butte, the People's in Seattle. The owner of the last named, John Considine, once grew annoyed at Seattle's chief of police over a charge that he, Considine, had provided an abortion for a seventeen-year-old employee. By putting on pressure in the right places Considine had the chief removed from his job. Later he killed the disgruntled lawman in a spectacular gunfight on the streets and was acquitted. He was a consummate showman. To lure customers away from his rivals, Considine promoted fancier and fancier entertainment, charging a basic ten-cent admission fee and making up the difference in his bar. From this activity sprang what was one of the nation's first popular-priced vaudeville circuits, enormously successful until a Greek named Alexander Pantages came down from the Klondike and beat Considine at his own game.

Classiest box house of all was Spokane's Coeur d'Alene, lovingly created by Dutch Jake Goetz and Harry Baer. Goetz and Baer were the saloonkeepers of Murray, Idaho, who gave Noah Kellogg his second grubstake during the search for the Bunker Hill & Sullivan mine. Out of their gamble the pair had realized almost a quarter of a million dollars.

Jake, an ebullient soul, liked to see people enjoy themselves. When he married in Murray in 1887, he nailed handbills to trees for miles around, inviting everyone to the ceremony. The streets were gay with Chinese lanterns; dynamite caps were distributed for fireworks. The wedding procession was a torchlight parade led by the Murray unit of the national guard, the hose companies of the surrounding camps, and a cornet band in full regalia. After banqueting in Murray's Louisville Hotel, most of northern Idaho danced the night away as guests of the beaming bridegroom.

With the fortune made from their grubstake, Dutch Jake and his more retiring partner, Harry Baer, built a box house in Spokane. Almost immediately it was destroyed by the great fire of 1889. The partners reopened in a tent, soon expanded to a three-story structure housing a trio of bars, a restaurant, bowling alleys, theater and Turkish bath. Jake insisted that the Coeur d'Alene was a high-toned place. The bars refused liquor to minors and to patrons who already had had too much. Moreover, any miner down on his luck could always get a meal and a place to sleep.

When the Spokane newspaper retorted in 1901 that the Coeur d'Alene was "a department store of vice and immorality," Jake was hurt. In rebuttal he opened his largest barroom for religious services by three of the city's leading ministers, who took up their stand, according to the *Spokesman-Review*, "under a large picture of 'Satyr and Nymphs,' . . . a remarkable example of the nude in art.

"Mingled with the hymns of salvation and message of religion [the paper continued] were the clink of glasses, the maudlin utterances of tipsy men, the noise of shuffling feet, the hurrying to and fro of waiters with the calls of 'one stein,' 'one egg sherry,' 'one gin fizz and four whiskey cocktails,' 'ham and eggs.' . . . Free Bibles were distributed to those who asked for them as long as the supply lasted. . . . 'Dutch Jake' apparently was as pleased with it all as a boy with his first pair of red top boots."

After two decades of success the Coeur d'Alene, yielding to the onslaughts of civic virtue and state prohibition, turned itself into a law-abiding hotel. Its long retreat into respectability, however, was delayed, as was the case with many another box house, by corrupt alliances with local police and politicians. Seattle in particular achieved a fetid sort of distinction under Mayor Hiram Gill, who was finally defeated in a recall election, then switched coats and got himself voted back into office as a reform candidate! But it remained for Butte to show how far corruption could really be spread.

Villain of the piece—or hero, in the eyes of thousands of copper miners—was Frederick Augustus Heinze. A graduate of the Columbia University School of Mines, Heinze first arrived in Butte in 1889, aged nineteen. He seemed older. He was assured, gracious, muscular, flamboyant, and in the opinion of many women, handsome.

Even as a teen-ager Fritz Heinze saw that untrained Butte was dangerously wasteful in its ways. This carelessness the boy determined to turn to his own account. Back to New York he went to study smelting and to build up contacts by means of an editorial job on the *Engineering and Mining Journal*. Fortified by his studies and by fifty thousand dollars inherited from his grandmother, he returned to Butte in 1892. He was twenty-two years old. Through lease and purchase he acquired several small mines that he quickly developed into paying properties. He built his own reduction plant, installing in it a new leaching process discovered by a Butte miner, and soon halved the prices charged by the huge competing smelters of William Clark and Marcus Daly.

To expand further Heinze would eventually have to buck one or the other of those formidable rivals. That meant money—millions of it.

In the rapidly expanding mines of Rossland, just north of the British Columbia border and seven miles up Trail Creek from the Columbia River, he found his opportunity. Purchasing a townsite at the mouth of Trail Creek, he began constructing, in October 1895, a plant that eventually grew into the largest non-ferrous smelter in the British Empire. His initial contract was for treating seventy-five thousand tons of gold and copper ore from the burgeoning Le Roi mine.

Spokane interests, notably Daniel Corbin, took alarm. Until Heinze's appearance Rossland ores had been traveling by wagon and steamboat to the smelter at Northport, just south of the border. To keep the ore moving south, Corbin built his Red Mountain Railway into Rossland. Heinze countered by mortgaging his Butte properties for a million and a half dollars and building the narrow-gauge Columbia and Western. One branch of the Columbia and Western ran from Trail up to Rossland. Another branch extended north to Robson, where his freight cars could pick up smelting limestone brought by boat down the Arrow Lakes from Nakusp. This railroad, aided by labor troubles inflicted on the American smelter by the new Western Federation of Miners, ended Northport. But Corbin, as usual, emerged unbruised: he sold his railroad to Hill's Great Northern.

While construction on the Columbia and Western was in progress, Heinze visited Ottawa and Victoria, lavishly entertaining legislators both of the Dominion and of British Columbia. Openly he declared that he was seeking cash subsidies from the federal minister of railways and land grants from the province so that he could extend the Columbia and Western to the ocean. Perhaps it was a bluff, but after noting that Heinze's smelter had just blown in its fifth furnace, the directors of the Canadian Pacific decided against playing poker with that much power. Instead, they got rid of Heinze by purchasing both his railroad and his smelter. [1]

Heinze, twenty-eight years old, now had the millions he needed. Back to Butte he went, prepared to split the copper camp wide open.

His wedge was the so-called "apex law" of mining. This mischievous bit of legislation allowed the owner of an apex, or the point where a vein comes closest to the surface, to follow that vein any distance within the prolonged end lines of his claim, even though he entered adjoining property in the process. In Butte's fractured, displaced earth it was difficult to tell where veins apexed or to determine which tendrils of ore were true extensions of any given lode. Heinze "ex-

[1] The latter ballooned into the giant Consolidated Smelting and Mining Company and turned Trail into one of British Columbia's leading industrial cities.

perts" could swear to almost anything and be right—if a complaisant judge was hearing the case. And in one of the district courts Heinze had just such a judge: tobacco-chewing, semiliterate, cunning William Clancy.

Brazenly Heinze's miners followed what Heinze said was an apexing vein into property owned by Boston interests. Suits and injunctions flew. While lawyers droned above ground, Heinze kept on extracting hundreds of thousands of dollars' worth of ore below. Then high on Butte's denuded hill his sharp eye discovered an even more dazzling opportunity: a triangle of unclaimed ground only a few feet long on each side. Seizing it, he blandly said that on this infinitesimal piece of real estate there came to an apex the veins of each adjoining mine, the mighty Neversweat, St. Lawrence, and Anaconda properties of Marcus Daly and associates.

Anaconda, to use the generic name, was in the process of selling out to Standard Oil. Knowing that the combined resources of both giants would be instantly devoted to crushing him, Heinze decided he would need to control more district courts than just the one presided over by William Clancy. Electing the judges he wanted involved a foray into politics. That in turn threw the ambitious youngster—Heinze was still only twenty-nine—into the frosty embrace of Daly's dedicated enemy, William Clark.

Clark needed an ally. In his mania for recognition, the icy little millionaire had stooped to political immoralities beyond parallel, had endured rebuffs beyond belief. Twice he had been defeated in his bids for office, once when he ran for territorial delegate for Congress, again when he tried to become senator. The defeats merely increased his determination, and in 1898 he set about electing to the legislature men who would be committed to sending him to Washington. It was harder than he thought. Daly's machine controlled the Democratic party (Clark, too, was a Democrat); and although Clark's campaign committee spent $139,000 (never audited), as opposed to some $7000 by Daly, they were able to send to Helena fewer than one quarter of the votes necessary. Undeterred, Clark then proposed the outright purchase of as many legislators as were necessary to achieve a majority.

Balloting began in January 1899. During one acrimonious session a legislator named Fred Whiteside waved aloft thirty bills of one thousand dollars each which he charged had been offered to him and to three other men for their votes. Daly's newspapers howled corruption; Clark's organs retorted that the whole thing was a conspiracy to discredit their candidate. A grand jury threw out Whiteside's charges on the basis of insufficient evidence. Simultaneously Clark's henchmen dug up other evidence that Whiteside's own election had been achieved through a fraudulent vote count. In self-righteous horror, Clark's paper called Whiteside "a masculine strumpet, a political bawd, a well paid harlot of a conscienceless gang," and demanded that he be unseated. He was. A Clark man took his place and the buying went on. In eighteen days, so it was charged, Clark spent $431,000 and in the end secured the seat he so desperately wanted.

Daly retaliated by financing a committee that protested the election before a Senate investigating body. After hearing three months of testimony the senators decided that Clark's election should be nullified. Before the action became official Clark hastily resigned. This of course left one of Montana's senatorial seats vacant. With incredible callousness Clark next lured Montana's governor out of the state and had the obedient lieutenant governor appoint him, Clark, to the empty Senate chair. Outrage was so vocal, however, that he made no attempt to go to Washington. Instead, he allied himself with Heinze and set about securing the vacant seat by an "honest" election in 1900.

By this time Daly, sick and near death, had negotiated for thirty-nine million dollars the sale of Anaconda and certain other Butte properties to Henry Rogers and William Rockefeller of the Standard Oil Company. A new trust called Amalgamated Copper was formed out of the purchase and capitalized at seventy-five million dollars. Similar stock watering took place shortly thereafter when Amalgamated absorbed the Boston companies which were fighting Heinze and on the basis of five million dollars' worth of property boosted Amalgamated's capitalization to a dizzy $155,000,000.

Fighting this huge combination turned Heinze into an astute, spellbinding demagogue. First he and Clark made themselves heroes to the miners by instituting the eight-hour day in their workings and by challenging Amalgamated, which employed far more men, to follow suit. Then Heinze, a fluent orator, took to the stump with lurid pictures of what would happen if Standard Oil should, through Amalgamated, fix itself leachlike upon Montana:

"My fight against Standard Oil is your fight. . . . If they crush me tomorrow they will crush you the day following. They will cut your wages and raise the tariff in the company store on every bite you eat and every rag you wear. They will force you to dwell in Standard Oil houses while you live, and you must be buried in Standard Oil coffins when die. . . ."

The tactics won. On election day Clark secured the legislature he needed to send him to the Senate, Heinze the judges who would decide the apex cases his way. And then, in a final, unbelievable double cross, Clark sold his properties to Amalgamated, leaving Heinze to fight on alone.

He made a spectacular battle of it. His miners, sometimes tangling physically with the enemy in their noisome tunnels, continued to steal Amalgamated ore below ground so that their Robin Hood could continue his expensive legal fight on the surface. Standard soon found a way to sober the rank and file, however. In October 1903, Amalgamated closed every mine, smelter, coal field, lumber camp, and store it owned in Montana. This meant that four out of every five wage earners in the state faced winter without work. The glamor went from Heinze then, in spite of the famous day when he held fifteen thousand sullen people at bay with a dramatic speech from the courthouse steps in Butte. Pressured by angry petitions from thousands of frightened homes, the governor yielded to Amalgamated's insistence that he call a special session of the legislature to pass "fair-trial" laws that would end Heinze's control of the judiciary.

The boy wonder quit then—not without profit. After long dickering he sold his holdings to Amalgamated for ten and a half million. Going to New York, he tried to found a rival copper trust, juggled with banks, failed, and helped precipitate the panic of 1907. Montana meanwhile lay quiescent under the absolute suzerainty of a single corporation, an economic domination from which the state has not yet fully emerged.

Butte's tangled struggle was of only academic interest to railroader James Jerome Hill. Whoever won, his railroads would still haul the bulk of the camp's—and of all the Northwest's—ore and machines, lumber and coal.

The depression of '93 had, as he foresaw, bankrupted his rivals, the Union Pacific and the Northern Pacific. Although the Great Northern's bid in 1895 to assume control, as a corporation, of the Northern Pacific, had been blocked on anti-trust grounds by the courts, no law existed to prevent Hill, his ally J. Pierpont Morgan, and their associates from buying Northern Pacific stock as individuals. This they did, securing not quite a majority but enough to let them so manipulate policies that the Northern Pacific became in effect a second track for the Great Northern.

To secure traffic for both roads, Hill either built or bought spur lines into the mining fields of British Columbia. He lured thousands of overoptimistic dry farmers into eastern Montana and encouraged wheat growing throughout the Inland Empire. He fostered apple orchards in the Wenatchee and Yakima valleys of Washington until production was measured not by the carload but by the trainload; he saw the cattle business of the interior revive as beef steers traveled his roads across the mountains to slaughterhouses on the populous coast. He helped persuade the Orient to buy flour, steel rails, and cotton; in emulation of the Canadian Pacific's successful Asian trade he launched the Great Northern Steamship Company (which, because of government regulations, never quite achieved what he wanted it to).

The most significant of his efforts had to do with stimulating the lumber industry. Times were ripe. The first forest reserves, predecessors of the present national forests, had been formed in 1891. They spread quickly, limiting the unrestrained cutting of timber on public lands. At the same time the timberlands of the Great Lakes region were nearing exhaustion. Of necessity the lumber business had to seek new footholds.

Vigorously Hill advertised the Northwest as against the pinelands of the South. One feature of a parade held in St. Paul to celebrate the completion of the Great Northern was a monster log of Douglas fir pulled by twenty horses. Shortly thereafter he reduced rates on lumber shipped from Puget Sound to Minneapolis. At first the effect was limited. The best markets in the Midwest were south of Minneapolis, beyond reach of the Great Northern; and in any event the depression years following '93 prevented rapid expansion. But when crop prices picked up in the Midwest, so would the demand for lumber.

To make ready, Hill began gathering in every acre of trees on which he could lay hand. Some of his methods were devious. For example, settlers beside a Dakota railroad long since absorbed by the Great Northern had been given clear titles to their property by land agents, unaware that the vanished railroad once had been awarded a land grant by Congress. Suddenly the Great Northern started eviction proceedings. The courts upheld the move, and in pain the astonished farmers appealed to the government for relief. In embarrassment Congress offered Hill his choice of equal amounts of government land elsewhere. Piously he consented to accept sixty-five thousand acres in the Northwest. By strange coincidence, his timber cruisers had just selected those very acres as the best timberland available in the state of Washington.

The Forest Lieu Act of 1897 opened the way for a similar swap. Under the act's terms the possessor of acreage within the bounds of the new Forest Reserves could exchange his property for equal amounts of land outside the reserves. Thousands of acres of Northern Pacific grant land lay above timberline on the bald peaks of the Cascades. These peaks were inside the forest boundaries, and so Hill was entitled to exchange the glaciated boulders for ranks of unreserved Douglas fir.

In 1900 the maneuvers paid off: he sold nine hundred thousand acres of Northern Pacific grant land to the Weyerhaeuser Timber Company of St. Paul for six dollars an acre. The stampede was on now. Lumber barons and lumberjacks swarmed in droves through the fir and pine forests of the Northwest. Sawmills went up by the hundreds. Washington's annual cut of lumber soared from one billion to four billion feet. Lake Coeur d'Alene turned into a monster millpond as booms of logs jostled down the rivers to the whining mills on the lake shore. Speculators went wild. Why not? One tract of Idaho land that sold for $240,000 in 1901 brought $2,500,000 in 1909.

To further his grip on the lumber markets of the Midwest, Hill in 1910 enlisted J. P. Morgan's help in acquiring control of the farm country's most prolific railroad, the Burlington. This aroused the new head of the Union Pacific, E. H. Harriman, who had also wanted the Burlington, and triggered the last of the great railroad wars.

In a frenzied stock manipulation that almost shook Wall Street apart, Harriman and his bankers just missed seizing control of the Northern Pacific. That road, it will be recalled, used the tracks of the OR & N, a Union Pacific subsidiary, to roll through the Columbia gorge to Portland. In order to break loose from so uncertain a dependence, Hill now projected the Spokane, Portland and Seattle down the river's tumbled north bank. It cost him thirty-five million dollars and endless legal battles with the paper railroads Harriman incorporated to contest the right of way. In the end Hill won—but he also had to let the Union Pacific into Puget Sound.

Contrary to expectations, the war brought no joy to the wheat farmers of the Inland Empire. They had already formed the Open River Association in an effort to bring steamboats back to the Columbia and thus force a reduction in freight rates. When rates stayed up during the railroad struggle, the association persuaded the government to build a canal eight miles long around the rapids at the Dalles.

While the work was going on they put their own boats to churning the Columbia above the Dalles, used a state-financed railroad as a portage around the falls, and below the Dalles hired the steamers of the Regulator Line—which, oddly enough, belonged to James J. Hill. Hill did not mind abetting the canal, since it annoyed Harriman. Furthermore, he did not believe that water competition would have enough over-all effect to be serious. He was right. The canal, opened finally in 1915, never lived up to the expectations of its promoters.

More annoyance for Harriman came when the Great Northern decided to build up the Deschutes River, east of the Cascades, and sneak into California the back way. This was the preserve of another Harriman road, the Southern Pacific, and response was instantaneous. Neck and neck the competing crews raced along opposite sides of the Deschutes River, harassing each other with dynamite blasts, mysteriously rolling boulders, faked telegrams. Long wagon trains dragged supplies through the deserts and down the canyon's rocky sides. Farmers with strategic homesteads found their holdings worth more than even delirium could have predicted. Finally the key spot fell to Harriman, and he brought Hill to a stop at the hamlet of Bend. Not for twenty more years would the Great Northern make connection with the Western Pacific in California and so gain entry into San Francisco.

The rails made Bend another lumber center, its population jumping from five hundred to five thousand in a decade. It was lumber, as well as an outlet to the Orient, that persuaded the Chicago, Milwaukee and St. Paul road to stretch tracks across the mountains to Tacoma, bringing the Northwest a fourth transcontinental line that it did not need.

Lumber—and more lumber! In tight, high-towering phalanxes, evergreen, ever murmurous, the stupendous forests of the Northwest sprawled across the Rockies, skipped the deserts of the interior, and then marched in thickening ranks to the very brink of the sea. Blanketing the tangled mountains of northern Idaho was the largest stand of white pine in America. In the dry air of the eastern Cascades rose hushed cathedral aisles of ponderosa pine, laced with picture-book shafts of sunlight. Nurtured by moister weather near the sea, the firs and cedars towered, three hundred, almost four hundred feet high. It was the noblest forest in the United States, and the richest. In one Douglas fir alone, its sinewed trunk reaching ninety feet to the first thick branches, was lumber enough to build four ordinary five-room bungalows.

Except near the water's edge, where the first lumber tugs plied, trees so huge were beyond the mastery of the early settlers. With the coming of the twentieth century, however, technology began its attack. Shay-geared locomotives wound deep into the mountains for giant logs whisked through the air by the intricate cableways of the high-lead system invented in 1911. Mills grew, bandsaws snarled, ships came. It was one more explosive outburst of the hungry energy that had built—and simultaneously despoiled—America. Those furious surges had left cities in their wake, docks and railyards, factories, fat barns, homes. But they also gnawed down the forests, gulped the grass and the minerals, turned prairies to dustbowls, dispossessed the Indians even of their last reservations.

As late as 1909 seven hundred thousand acres of the Flathead, Spokane, and Coeur d'Alene Indian lands were thrown open for home-steading. Frantic thousands of applicants hurried in to register their names at Kalispell and Missoula, Montana; at Coeur d'Alene and Spokane. Some of the seekers died as dead, if not as romantically, as their pioneering predecessors: two trains loaded with would-be home-steaders collided outside Coeur d'Alene, killing fourteen and injuring seventy-four. When the final lottery was held there were nearly three hundred thousand entries for about four thousand claims. An esti-mated three million dollars were spent on train fares alone; many of the disappointed paid out in their quest sums that in any real estate office would have purchased better farms than the lottery offered. But this was the golden West. This was something for nothing—if you grabbed soon enough and were lucky enough.

Seven hundred thousand acres! Thirty years earlier there had been millions upon millions. The merry-go-round was running down. The miles of grass, the forests that reached beyond seeing, the fish of the rivers, even the rivers themselves—like the seal herds of the Bering Sea—were not inexhaustible. If future generations were to see the bounties that had lured their parents to the farthest frontier, a new spirit would have to walk the land.

Book Six

FOR THESE BLESSINGS

1. The Trees

FIRE was an enemy all lumbermen could apprehend. They might disagree about associations to control prices and production; quarrel with their workers about hours and wages; rail against the national government concerning forest reserves; bicker with the states about taxes. But when a gale-driven crown fire raced toward their property lines through trees three hundred feet high, they found unanimity. Here was a monster everyone should fight.

It had not always been so. The trees of the densely wooded sections of America loomed as obstacles to agriculture. Fire was a tool "to let in sunlight and air," to remove cover the Indians might use for attack, or to provide a firebreak against an uncontrolled blaze sweeping through the surrounding woods. The Indians as well as the whites fired the underbrush (and, inevitably, the trees) to facilitate hunting and to improve grass. If this "planned" burning got out of hand, no matter. Some later settler would be thankful for the clearing.

Fort Vancouver of the Hudson's Bay Company was almost destroyed by a forest fire in 1844. In the dry summer of 1868 smoke along the coast was so dense that ships in Puget Sound navigated by compass, and ocean steamers for weeks could not see clearly enough to grope a way across the Columbia bar. In Jacksonville, Oregon, the paper editorialized plaintively, "It is very common for parties going into the mountains to set the whole country on fire. This we think very wrong. It not only kills the timber but also fills the valleys full of smoke, thereby rendering it very unhealthful."

As settlement spread, so did destruction. In 1902 scattered blazes east of Portland devoured scores of farms, mills, and even little towns. Across the river in Washington, in the box corner where the Columbia bends north, the damage was more appalling. Glumly the Tacoma paper reported on September 16:

Thirty-eight bodies were found today in the Lewis River valley, indicating that the devastation there by forest fires was worse than supposed. . . . The burned district was settled by five hundred prosperous farmers, who lost all they had. . . . One hundred and forty sections of the finest timber in Cowlitz County were destroyed. [1]

The report stirred Ray Stannard Baker, a visiting journalist, to indignation in *Century Magazine:* "There seems no way to stay this criminal wastefulness and loss, the very robbery of coming generations; there is no concerted action, no thought for the future. While the fire burns, the people talk, as at the burning of a neighbor's barn; the newspapers agitate: but with the first rain the fires are forgotten until another year."

Mr. Baker was wrong. One man was doing more than talk. He was tall, somber George Long, manager of the huge holdings which the Weyerhaeuser Timber Company was accumulating throughout Washington, Oregon, and the Idaho panhandle. Many of the seven hundred thousand acres blackened by the so-called Yacolt burn of 1902 were Weyerhaeuser acres.

Aroused, Long helped devise and push through the shocked Washington legislature the Northwest's first effective forest-fire legislation. He persuaded neighboring landowners to establish patrols, pooling men and equipment and sharing the cost on a pro rata basis. For advice in formulating prevention and suppression programs he turned to Gifford Pinchot's infant United States Forest Service.

In spite of Pinchot's tireless crusading for improvement, there was in 1903 little other than advice that his department could offer. For one thing, his six clerks and six foresters functioned under the Department of Agriculture, but the forest reserves were administered by the Department of the Interior. The latter had no foresters and was committed to the idea of protecting its timberlands from everything, including legitimate use.

In 1905, helped by the exposure of the notorious Oregon land-fraud cases, Theodore Roosevelt persuaded Congress to transfer the national forests to the Department of Agriculture and to add muscle to Pinchot's Bureau of Forestry. National and state conservation committees were formed to mold public opinion. Yet all the groundwork did not

[1] The account is not entirely accurate. Revised figures indicate that sixteen people died in the Lewis Valley, another eighteen or nineteen in widely scattered communities along the western slope of the Cascades. And the farmers were not prosperous. They were stump ranchers living on cutover land purchased from the lumber companies. The soil, laced with roots and poisoned with tree acids, was in the main suited only to growing trees, as hundreds of hopeful purchasers learned to their sorrow.

prevent a furious outcry when Roosevelt in 1909 added 148,000,000 acres to the swelling national forests. Prodded by their angry constituents, Senators Hayburn of Idaho, Carter of Montana, and Mondell of Wyoming fought back by opposing Pinchot's requests for higher appropriations to run his expanded domain.

During the course of the debates Hayburn delivered himself of a classic sentiment: fires were Providence's way of clearing the land for homesteaders. Just how thoroughly fire could clear the land the senator's home town of Wallace, Idaho, was soon to learn.

The summer of 1910 came hot and dry to the Northern Rockies and the pine foothills of eastern Washington. At first this seemed desirable. Snowfall the previous winter had been heavy. In late February avalanches roaring into the mining town of Burke, Idaho, crushed twenty-one persons. On March 1 another slide tossed two Great Northern trains into a canyon of the eastern Cascades with a loss of more than one hundred lives.

Under the spring sun the moisture soon vanished. Fires began to erupt, first in British Columbia. The towns of Whitewater and McGuigan disappeared; near Nelson two hundred miners and their families lost every possession. In July lightning from dry thunderstorms spread the destruction through northern Idaho and western Montana. Everywhere there was smoke, oozing over the ridges, flowing down the canyons.

Employment agencies at Butte and Spokane sent three thousand temporary fire fighters, mostly riffraff, into the woods. More efficient help was recruited from lumber camps, ranches, mines, railroad crews. On August 8, President Taft authorized the use of troops.

Communications and supply problems for so many widely scattered men were almost insoluble. It is a rough, wild country. In 1910 there were few trails, fewer roads; only a spidery handful of telephone and telegraph lines paralleled the railroad tracks. Pack trains and messengers on horseback had to feed and inform the ill-trained thousands.

Clumsily, almost blindly, the crews were shifted from one danger point to the next. New fires broke out faster than old ones could be contained. By August 19 the maps in the headquarters office of District One at Missoula (which supervised the forests in western Montana, northern Idaho, and northeastern Washington) were freckled with pins indicating three thousand minor blazes, ninety major ones.

On August 20 the holocaust came. A dry gale shrieked up from the southeast. Small blazes merged into big ones, the big ones into infernos. Crown fires raced through the treetops at seventy miles an hour. After them came the solid mass of the ravenous ground fires. Balls of gas exploded in crimson bursts. The roaring wind uprooted trees, toppled flaming snags in a rage of sparks. Whirlwinds laced with embers danced ahead, scattering new fires miles in advance of the booming front.

Trapped men burrowed into sandspits beside the streams or crouched in the pools with blankets over their heads. They screamed and sang and prayed. Some went mad; a few killed themselves. Eyes were blinded by smoke; flesh grew puffed and raw. Survivors stumbling to the creeks for a drink found the steaming water acrid with lye from the ashes and foul with dead fish.

No one knows how many ranch buildings and animals, how many sawmills, mine structures, and prospectors' camps were destroyed. Railroad ties burned out; rails buckled in the heat. The new Chicago, Milwaukee and St. Paul line lost sixteen bridges from 120 to 775 feet long. The construction towns of Taft and Deborgia, the hamlets of Haugan and Tuscor were wiped out. Backfiring and wind shifts saved the Idaho lumber camps of St. Joe and St. Maries, where residents fled across pontoon bridges into the knee-deep muck of the sloughs, but though their lives were saved the resources on which they lived were gone.

Most of the Coeur d'Alene mining camps were able to hold the enemy out of the streets. But not Senator Hayburn's home town of Wallace. The fire burst over the encircling ridges on the evening of August 20. A vast roar filled the ways. Embers and cinders rained on the housetops; the hills were a seething mass of crimson. Rescue trains tolled their bells, blasted their whistles. In panic the refugees streamed toward the depot with such possessions as they could carry. A hundred or more homes burned in Wallace that fearful evening. But twice that many were saved by the desperate labors of a company or two of Negro troops and by the men and women who refused to leave.

Among those who stayed was Mrs. Edward Pulaski. Her ranger husband was somewhere in the hills above town directing a crew of fifty fire fighters. Hoping against all the evidence of her senses, Mrs. Pulaski spent the night with several other frightened wives on the tailing flats of one of the mines. On Sunday she returned through smoking rubble to her home. It had been spared. Shortly she saw two blackened, limping scarecrows leading a blinded man toward her. The blinded one—eventually he recovered part of his vision—was her husband. He had taken his crew (except for one man killed by a falling snag) and two horses into a mine tunnel. He had hung a blanket over the tunnel mouth and for as long as he could stand had kept it soaked with water. Finally, like everyone else inside, Edward Pulaski fainted from smoke and gas. After the fire passed, he revived, as did most of his crew. Not all, however. Five men and both horses were dead.

All told, the blaze killed eighty-five fire fighters, ranchers, and miners. Another hundred and twenty-five men were missing—vagrants, mostly, who had signed up for temporary employment and then ran away in the confusion. And three million acres of the best white pine in America had been lost.

There had been—and would be—more deadly forest fires in America.[2] But this one, coming during an awakening public interest in conservation, brought immediate results. Pinchot got the appropriations he wanted. Congress passed the Weeks Act, donating money for fire protection to states that would match the funds. It was modest enough at first. Montana and Idaho received $10,500 each, Oregon and Washington $10,000. (That same year Washington's fire budget was raised to $75,000.) In 1924 the Clark-McNary Act greatly expanded the funds available for co-operative fire-control efforts by federal, state, and private agencies. On more and more hilltops lookout towers rose on their spindly legs. Trails and roads and telephone lines, supplemented later by radio, threaded an increasing cross-stitch through the green blanket. Year by year technology added its improvements: mechanized brush smashers, fire plows and power saws for clearing firebreaks; huge aluminum tankers for water and four-wheel-drive vehicles for equipment and men; airplanes and helicopters lumbering along with water bombs and with spectacular smoke jumpers for parachuting into inaccessible terrain.

This was the easily visible effort. Other ills were more insidious and less easily mastered. The lumber market has always been excessively sensitive. A drought or crop failure in the Midwest will, through lessened demand, immediately depress prices. Favorable conditions, on the other hand, lead to overproduction. After the San Francisco earthquake and fire of 1906, for example, mill operators met the anticipated rise in demand with such a flood of boards and beams that

[2] The 1871 Peshtigo holocaust in Wisconsin burned 1,125,000 acres, killed 1500 people. An 1894 fire at Hinckley, Minnesota, swept 160,000 acres, killed 418 persons. In 1918 the lumber town of Cloquet, Minnesota, was gutted with a loss of 400 lives.

prices collapsed instead of soaring. Always there were scores of small "gyppo" outfits hanging around the fringes, ready to start cutting the instant the market strengthened. Still other companies were often driven during periods of depression to add to the chronic overproduction by cutting excessive quantities of wood in order to meet tax bills or high interest charges.

These unstable economics created what was perhaps America's most unstable and violent labor picture. Employers insisted that the marginal nature of their operations precluded such folderol as safety appliances and showers, toilets, and clean bunkhouses in the camps, to say nothing of high wages. (Actually wages in the Northwest lumber industry, though low, were consistently above the national average for lumber workers.) Moreover, the nature of their help enabled the operators to resist demands for improvement. Many of the lumberjacks were Scandinavians, largely inarticulate. Many were migrants, restless, reckless, improvident, irresponsible. Another transitory element were neighboring farmers working for a stake and with little interest in future conditions. The public, too, was apathetic, partly because of excesses committed by a rowdy minority of workers who on paydays roared through colossal debauches on Seattle's skidroad; in Erickson's vast bar, 684 feet long, in Portland; or in the red-light dives of Gray's Harbor.

The shingle weavers were the first to organize. After years of indifferent success they endeavored, under an American Federation of Labor charter, to extend their coverage to all millworkers and woodsmen. But in 1914 their union lost both a strike and, on the political front, an initiative measure for an eight-hour day. Disheartened by the defeats, members drifted away, leaving a vacuum that the notorious Industrial Workers of the World rushed in to fill with a mighty thunderclap of violence.

The IWW—the Wobblies—had formed in 1905 with the blessings of the radical Western Federation of Miners. They were dedicated to roughshod force. Workers were to "take possession of the earth and machinery of production and abolish the wage system." Any tactic that worked was good. "The question of 'right' and 'wrong'," proclaimed Big Bill Haywood, "does not concern us."

One favorite tactic was the "free-speech fight." Wobblies swarmed into whatever towns the leaders decided were offensive. By defying ordinances against street gatherings and demonstrations, they had themselves jailed in such numbers that civic machinery broke down. An early leader in these clogging maneuvers was auburn-haired

MAP 6

The Waterways, Dams, and other Natural Resources of the Northwest

CARIBOO COUNTRY

BRITISH COLUMBIA

COLUMBIA R.

THOMPSON R.

FRASER R.

Lillooet

Kamloops

HELL'S GATE

OKANAGAN L.

KOOTENAY L.

Yale

SIMILKAMEEN R.

Nelson

Vancouver

Hope

OKANAGAN R.

METHOW R.

Rossland

Trail

SAN JUAN ARCHIPELAGO

Metalline

Victoria

SKAGIT R.

WASHINGTON

Colville

Kalispell

Seattle

Coeur d'Alene

Spokane

Kellogg

Murray

Cataldo Mission

Burke

Wallace

Tacoma

Cle Elum

BIG BEND

GRAY'S HARBOR

Ft. Steilacoom

Olympia

PALOUSE COUNTRY

MT. RAINIER

Pierce City

Yakima

Lapwai

MT. ST. HELENS

Lewiston

OROFINO CR.

Astoria

MT. ADAMS

Ainsworth

Walla Walla

Komiah

Wallula

Elk City

CASCADE

COLUMBIA R.

Florence

Portland

PORTAGE

The Dalles

WALLOWA MTS.

SALMON R.

DESCHUTES R.

La Grande

JOSEPH'S COUNTRY

MT. HOOD

WILLAMETTE R.

Salem

Baker

IDAHO

OREGON

HELL'S CANYON

Eugene

Bend

PAYETTE R.

Scottsburg

Idaho City

Boise

Coos Bay

MALHEUR L.

SNAKE R.

HARNEY L.

ROGUE R.

DONNER UND BLITZEN R.

Silver City

STEENS MT.

OWYHEE R.

Jacksonville

KLAMATH L.

TULE L.

KLAMATH

LAVA BEDS

Yreka

MT. SHASTA

NEVADA

CALIFORNIA

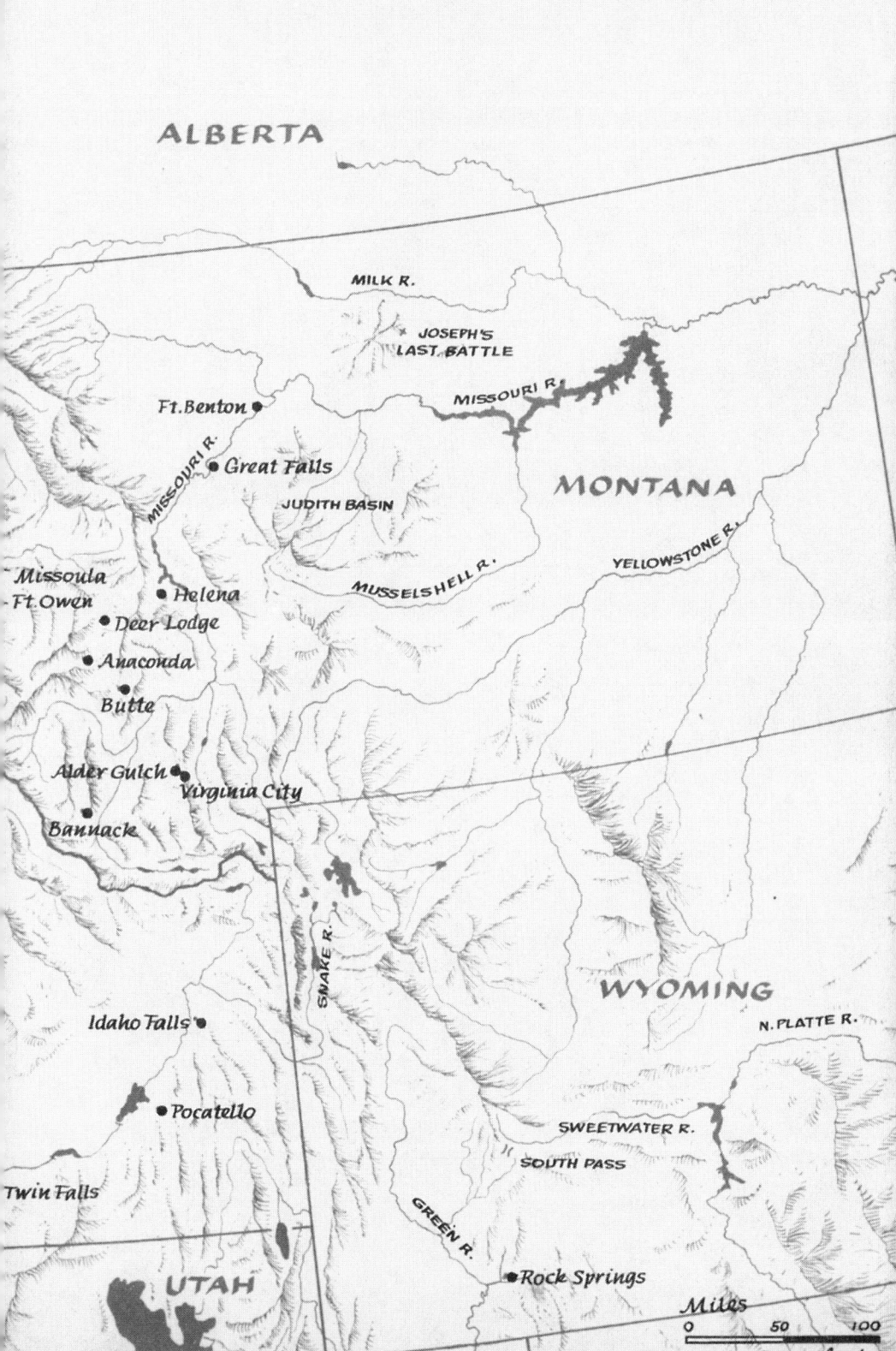

ALBERTA

MILK R.

JOSEPH'S
LAST BATTLE

MISSOURI R.

Ft.Benton

Great Falls

MONTANA

JUDITH BASIN

YELLOWSTONE R.

Missoula
Ft.Owen

Helena

MUSSELSHELL R.

Deer Lodge

Anaconda

Butte

Alder Gulch

Virginia City

Bannack

SNAKE R.

WYOMING

Idaho Falls

N. PLATTE R.

Pocatello

SWEETWATER R.

SOUTH PASS

Twin Falls

GREEN R.

Rock Springs

Miles

0   50   100

UTAH

GREAT SALT L.

palacios

Elizabeth Gurley Flynn. Called Gurley (most of her followers naturally thought it was Girlie), she was nineteen years old and reputedly beautiful. In 1908, clad in broad sombrero and red neckerchief, she led a "raid" that completely inundated Missoula, Montana. After the town gave up and released the mob they flowed joyously on, by boxcar, to Spokane.

Yowling, jeering, Gurley still in the lead, the invaders turned the streets into an uproar. Hundreds were arrested. In jail they went on a hunger strike and refused to cut wood for their stoves, though it was winter. The city let them shiver. This resulted in wild charges of inhumanity: "Four hundred men and women of the ranks of labor . . . on the bare floors of a jail, slowly starving . . . thirty days of torture." After three months everyone got tired of the performance. The prisoners were released and promised to leave town after the local union had been granted the right of assembly and of distributing IWW literature.

These were opéras bouffes. Not so was the free-speech fight that bloodied Everett, Washington, in 1916. There the IWW threw itself uninvited into a strike of the AF of L shingle weavers. When police broke up the initial demonstrations by the Wobblies, an additional two hundred and fifty "orators" were called in from Seattle. Warned by a Pinkerton detective, the Everett sheriff met the invaders at the dock with an armed posse. Someone started to shoot. In ten minutes five Wobblies and two possemen were dead. Fifty more were wounded.

The Wobblies insisted that none of them had carried a gun and that the casualties resulted from the cross fire of the scattered posse. Seventy-four of the radicals were nevertheless arrested for murder. No solid evidence against them was ever unearthed. As a result the first man tried was acquitted and the other defendants were released.

The Wobblies might have capitalized on the public sympathy they enlisted during the Everett "massacre." Instead, they immediately alienated support by their tactics during the First World War. Hoping to take advantage of the tight labor market and of the unprecedented demand for wood brought about by the conflict, the AF of L and IWW together closed nearly every lumber mill on the West coast.

Popular pressure and appeals to patriotism soon drove most of the AF of L men back to work. The IWW followed suit reluctantly but harassed operations with slowdowns, disobedience, and general obstructionism. To combat them the government, under Colonel Brice Disque, promoted the Loyal Legion of Loggers and Lumbermen.

Called the 4L and directed by an executive council composed of equal numbers of employers and employees, the Loyal Legion used anti-German propaganda and ringing appeals to patriotism to recruit members. It achieved the eight-hour day and brought improved conditions to the logging camps. But the IWW charged, and many workers believed, that the 4L was loaded in favor of the operators. As a result much of its appeal vanished with peace.

Because of all these things the IWW by war's end was associated in the mind of the Northwest with anti-Americanism. Rabble rousers plagued the union. In Centralia, Washington, on Armistice Day, 1919, an American Legion parade led by the president of a lumber company charged the hall of the local union, intending to wreck it. Rifle fire met them. Three Legionnaires were killed, several wounded. Frenzied, the mob completely destroyed the building, emasculated one IWW member, and in a raid on the jail that night mistakenly lynched a man they did not want.

On vague evidence eleven Wobblies were charged with murder. A change of venue shifted the trial to Gray's Harbor. Even there the atmosphere was completely unfriendly to the defendants. Troops patrolled the courthouse against demonstrations by the union but allowed Legion members to attend the trial in uniform. Torn between doubts that the accused were guilty and the emotions seething around them, the jury tried to compromise with a weak, ridiculous verdict finding two of the eleven defendants guilty of murder in the third degree. Either the killings had been cold-blooded and premeditated—first-degree murder—or the accused were innocent. Angered, the judge ordered the jury to try again. This time seven defendants were found guilty of second-degree murder, two were acquitted, and one was declared insane.

Though justice had been ill served, the Wobblies had violated popular opinion too often to profit. They still advocated sabotage with lurid posters of spitting black cats in wooden shoes (sabots); they still called wildcat strikes in isolated camps; they still preferred violence to arbitration. But their day was done. Partly because of their lack of restraint, unionism throughout the Northwest lumber trade languished until 1933. That year the National Industrial Recovery Act stimulated a fresh drive toward organization that culminated in the great strike of 1935. It was confused and bitter. No agreement existed among the workers about aims or methods. Although they resented furiously the use of the National Guard against them in several cities, they grew even more rancorous over their own internecine struggles for power. The tensions were heightened by the entry of the CIO into the picture, and for years distrust and uncertainty were the chief characteristics of unionism in the lumber mills and logging camps.

The same NRA lumber code that fostered labor organization in the 1930s carried, in its famous Article X, provisions committing the industry to good forestry practices as defined by the "theorists." Various other forces combined to help the conservation idea take hold. The Works Progress Administration and the Civilian Conservation Corps, whatever their faults, did leave improvements for all to see by planting seedlings, thinning overcrowded stands, checking tree diseases and soil erosion, building access roads, and creating new recreational facilities. Publicists found good copy in bewailing, often to excess, potential timber famines and greedy lumber barons.

Under impact of these forces popular opinion became aggressive. During the depths of the depression, for example, the people of Oregon voted ten million dollars' worth of bonds to reforest the area gutted by the huge Tillamook fire of 1933—"one of the great human achievements in engineered conservation," according to William Greeley, Chief Forester of the United States.

Professional conservationists were likewise experiencing a change of opinion. Once they had fought to have every forest protected, no matter what its age. Gradually, however, they had learned that a mature forest is a static forest and that the clearing away of ripe or overripe trees is one way to hasten growth. The moist lands of the Cascades, they learned further, can regrow forests with almost frightening vigor if given a chance.

From these facts developed the idea of sustained-yield lumbering, that is, the cutting of no more trees than the forests themselves can replace each year. In an effort to show how the program might work the Department of the Interior, set up, under its Bureau of Land Management, practice units on three million acres of revested land grants in Oregon. (Originally the land had been awarded to Ben Holladay's old Oregon and California Railroad. Because Holladay's successor, the Southern Pacific, had violated certain technical terms of the grant, the government recaptured the unsold portions of the land in 1916.)

Since the annual cut available on the grant lands was small, an operator who won cutting privileges was expected to flesh out his harvest with lumber from his own private holdings—holdings over which the government now demanded supervisory rights. Complaints were instantaneous. Lumbermen with limited private lands cried out that the act favored large companies. Concerns that did win contracts complained against what they called the arrogant officiousness of the rangers who invaded their camps and tried to tell them how to run their businesses. Because of these objections and a general feeling that the government was far too interested in putting more and more acreage under bureaucratic control, the sustained-yield program has experienced rough sledding. When the Forest Service endeavored to extend the plan to the national forests in general, only one lumber company during the 1940s was willing to work out a long-range, hundred-year program. Whether matters will change as the grant administration develops new practices to overcome the objections still remains to be seen.

The lumbermen were not being merely obstructionists. They believed they had a better plan than the sustained-yield program for staving off timber depletion. This was the tree farm.

The idea was not new. As long ago as 1911, George Long of the Weyerhaeuser Timber Company had urged the citizens of Washington's Chehalis Valley to reseed cutover lands in order to maintain their economy. Two obstacles, however, militated against the move. First, an overnight fire might destroy the work of years. Secondly, the tax situation did not favor the slow process of growing trees.

Counties needing revenue assessed timberland on the value of the trees, not on the value of the land. This seemed unfair. A farmer, for instance, was not taxed on his corn crop; so why should a lumberman year after year be assessed on the harvest value of a crop of trees that could be reaped only once?

Results were predictable. Marginal operators logged off their timber in a hurry and let the cutover land revert to the counties in lieu of delinquent tax bills. Nor were the men who held their lands willing to increase their bills by planting trees. Years of compromise were necessary before a solution was worked out to alter the situation yet not completely dislocate county finances in the process. Like most compromises, the measures have not won wholehearted approval. But at least they are an attack on the problem. At the same time fire-prevention tactics have developed to the point where lumbermen at last feel justified in risking the long-term investment necessary to grow saw logs from seeds to maturity.

The first attempt was made by the Weyerhaeuser Company in 1941 on its Clemons tract of 120,000 acres near Gray's Harbor. To gain public support and to prevent careless burning by trespassing hunters and berry pickers, some publicist hit on the shrewd idea of calling the area a tree farm. Attractive signs calling it that were posted about the land's perimeter. The Joint Committee on Conservation of the Northwest's two lumber associations liked the idea and worked out a definition: A tree farm is an area devoted "to the continuous production of forests crops . . . protected from fire, insects, tree disease, and excessive grazing."

Within sixteen years—that is, by the beginning of 1957—the idea had spread to ninety-five hundred tree farms in forty-four states. These farms can be of any size, from wood lots on up to tracts of hundreds of thousands of acres. The trees, in the Northwest at least, are seldom planted by hand. Rather, seed trees are left by the loggers, either in scattered ranks or in solid blocks according to the variety being restored, and these parent trees do the work. Occasionally the process is hastened by seeding from airplane or helicopter, after the tract has first been poisoned to eliminate seed-eating squirrels and mice. Only when seeding for some reason proves inadequate are nursery trees set out by planting machines that have increased tenfold the results once obtained by arduous hand methods.

Research by both the government and private industry has been intensified. New uses of wood have been discovered—plywood, film, plastics, pressed fuels, pulp and cellulose products to the number of five thousand. Equally rapid has been the progress in silviculture. Faster-growing, disease-resistant strains of trees, better methods of pest control and ground preparation, scientific thinning, and a horde of other carefully developed practices are helping the forests in their own sturdy efforts to restore themselves.

Results have been phenomenal. Despite an enormous increase in consumption, America in 1952 for the first time in decades produced more wood than she used. This is not yet true in the Northwest, where old trees still constitute the primary supply. But it can be true. For surely, Northwesterners say, they can carry to a triumphant conclusion the trends they themselves were so instrumental in launching.

2. The Fish

ALL told, according to the estimates of recent investigators, the prehistoric Indians who thronged to the Columbia system during the salmon runs probably garnered with their spears, seines, reed baskets, and primitive dip nets a harvest of no less than eighteen million pounds of fish each year.

The figure becomes impressive—and alarming—when contrasted to the haul of modern fishermen. Today's power boats, floating gill nets, modern trolling rods, and scientific traps can produce from the Columbia in an average year only about fifteen million pounds of salmon.

At first there seemed no limit to the swarms of huge Chinooks and the smaller, redder bluebacks (called sockeye salmon on the Fraser River and in Alaska). During the peak years of the 1880s and 1890s the Columbia River canneries packed as many as 630,000 cases during the annual runs, each case consisting of forty-eight one-pound tins. Between Portland and the mouth of the river twenty-five hundred boats competed for the scaly harvest. Men fought and connived for choice spots in which to place their nets or the huge, creaking fish wheels which, revolving like water wheels, could fill a scow with flopping salmon while the owner simply sat back and watched. Teams of horses driven shoulder-deep into the water dragged deep-pouched seines onto the beaches. Canneries lurched out over the river on odorous piles. The town of Astoria, center of the Columbia fishing industry, climbed higher and higher up its steep green hills, its streets crowded with the pigtailed Chinese who prepared the fish for the cans and with the blocky Swedes and Finns who more and more monopolized operations on the river.

Better ways to catch fish were continually devised. Shortly after the turn of the century power boats and power winches for handling bigger nets began to churn the river. Simultaneously the Iron Chink invaded the canneries—an awesome contraption that in one minute could cut the heads, tails, and fins off sixty sockeye salmon, then with rotating knives and brushes disembowel and clean the fish as well.

Mechanization demanded high capitalization. This in turn started a cycle of heavier and still heavier fishing. Competition forced the canneries to utilize the less tasty silver salmon and chums. To beat each other to the runs, trollers ventured into salt water beyond the river mouth and intercepted their quarry with hook and line. Yet, though effort increased, the total harvest continued to decline.

Foreseeing future impoverishment in the industry, the states of Washington and Oregon began to impose regulations. At first the laws were haphazard; until 1909, for instance, there was no uniformity in closed seasons. Each year, however, co-operation increased; regulations became more stringent. And still the annual take declined, until today the Columbia produces scarcely a third of the fish it once yielded in such abundance.

A further threat appeared with the building of dams. In 1931 a private power company threw a concrete block across the river at Rock Island, Washington, near the mouth of the Wenatchee. In 1938 the government's Bonneville Dam tamed the Cascade Rapids, and on paper others took form.

Fortunately the first two dams, Rock Island and Bonneville, were relatively low and could be circumvented by fishways. Three ladders, or sequences of artificial cascades connecting steplike pools, were constructed at each dam. They did not work perfectly. Occasionally the salmon were badly bruised as they hurled themselves at the ladders in their blind compulsion to reach their native grounds, there to create new life and then die. On the way downstream the fingerlings suffered in riding over the spillways or through the turbines. More insidious was the delay occasioned as the fish searched for the ladders. Each dam, studies indicate, holds back the run for two or three days, and when salmon are ready to spawn, any slowdown increases mortality.

The completion of Grand Coulee Dam, which was far too high for fishways, blocked off eleven hundred miles of spawning grounds on the upper Columbia. To compensate for this loss a bold experiment was tried. Salmon migrating toward the upper river were trapped as they climbed the fishways at Rock Island Dam. Half of these fish were transplanted by tank truck to the four major tributaries between Rock Island and Grand Coulee (the Wenatchee, Entiat, Methow, and Okanogan rivers). The hope was that salmon, after being forcibly taken where they would not go of their own accord, would nevertheless spawn on the new grounds. And if adult salmon could not be transplanted, perhaps their progeny could be. Half of the salmon trapped at Rock Island were stripped of eggs and milt and the artificially spawned eggs were placed in a hatchery on the Wenatchee. The fingerlings thus raised were then distributed to the various tributaries.

Five years later, in 1947, when the normal life cycle of the planted salmon should draw the fish back to their new homes, the counters at Bonneville Dam totted up the greatest run yet tallied in the ladders. Some of these fish, moreover, were salmon which had been marked as fingerlings upon being released on the new spawning grounds. Northwestern news presses clattered with human-interest stories. Man could restore as well as destroy.

The most spectacular recovery was among the bluebacks, or sockeyes. Grand Coulee had almost exterminated them, for prior to the building of the dam they had reproduced principally in the lake-fed tributaries of the upper river. Only 11,000 of them, it is estimated, entered the Columbia in 1945. Five years later the figure soared tenfold: between 1950 and 1956 the number varied between a low of 178,000 and a high of 320,000. It sounds good. But long-term graphs made up of many factors show signs that the bluebacks, and the other species as well, are again starting a downward trend.

New threats rise faster than old ones can be eliminated. More and more hydroelectric dams are humming not only on the main river but on the tributaries. Power has drawn industry, including the enormous plutonium plant at Hanford. The waste of the factories is added to the sewage discharge of a rapidly expanding population. During the low water of fall, for example, salmon are completely blocked by Portland's gross pollution from entering a once favorite stream, the Willamette. Lumbering adds its problems. Log jams block the smaller creeks; water temperatures soar disastrously in deforested areas; floods silt the spawning grounds. Sport fishing, meantime, has had a phenomenal increase in popularity.

Strenuous efforts are being made to meet the complications. In 1948, Oregon, Washington, and Idaho signed with the federal government a co-operative agreement whose main aim is to make available new spawning grounds in place of old ones no longer usable. Potential breeding streams blocked by natural obstacles are studied carefully to determine whether they present conditions favorable to reproduction. If so, the blockading rapids or falls are circumvented by building concrete fishways. Sometimes the mere clearing of a channel is enough. In 1950, for example, the removal of 170 log jams and 32 beaver dams from the Clatskine River opened up twenty-three miles of new spawning area.

Stocking and maintaining these new grounds call for more and larger hatcheries. Fingerlings, it has been discovered, survive better if held until the spring of their second year, the year of their migration to the sea. This increases feeding costs and adds strain to their rearing ponds. Defenses have to be set up against disease; diet studies must be conducted. Hand in hand go experiments in selective breeding to improve size and color.

Somehow it seems ironic that in this struggle to preserve the salmon nothing has been done to save the Indian fisheries. One by one industrialization or dams have closed the teeming salmon grounds that so amazed the first explorers—the basalt reefs at Willamette Falls, the island-studded cascade at Spokane, the foaming rocks at Kettle Falls where David Thompson watched the huge fish fall helplessly into basket traps shaped like pots.

As these fisheries closed, increasing numbers of Indians, some from as far away as Montana and California, converged each autumn on the volcanic islands and jutting rocks that surrounded Celilo Falls at the head of the Dalles. By the Stevens treaties of 1855, Celilo, like the other Columbia fisheries, had been guaranteed to the Indians forever. Only a man with at least one quarter Indian blood in his veins could fish there. Favorable spots where rickety wooden platforms could be rebuilt each fall out over the roaring torrent passed from father to son. Commercial fish buyers, mostly whites, built cable cars from the bank to the islands, hoping that the grateful Indians would in turn sell their produce to the producer of the convenience. A few fancy cars were powered by gasoline motors, though most were drawn by hand. Often the swaying vehicles were so overloaded with men and fish that they sagged into the foam.

Once arrived at his station, each fisher secured himself by a rope around his waist. Generally he fished blind, sweeping his long-handled net swiftly down the current in hope of encountering a salmon coming up. Frequently he encountered more than one. Cases are on record of a man earning a thousand dollars a day during the brief autumn runs. Catches worth a hundred dollars a day were common. No small part of the success rose from the Indians' privilege of fishing when the river was closed to whites. During these closed seasons the red men were supposed to dry their catch for home consumption, not sell it commercially. This edict they violated with impunity by selling the fish one by one to wide-eyed tourists who stopped by to see what was going on.

The building of the Dalles Dam in the 1950s drowned the Celilo fishery. Before the end came investigators were sent to the falls to see just what the Indians might be losing. To their amazement, the whites found that the dip-net fishers at Celilo accounted for three quarters of all the salmon taken above Bonneville Dam. (The biggest harvest, of course, is below Bonneville.) All told, the commercial value reached about seven hundred thousand dollars a year, for which compensation was proffered. No attempt was made, obviously, to weigh in dollars the ancient culture which ended when the falls were inundated. But at least the Indians did not have to face the death of the salmon runs, an eventuality still possible on the Columbia, in spite of vigorous efforts to forestall it.

Elsewhere restoration work has been more spectacular. The first break-through occurred in the vast halibut banks between the mouth of the Columbia and the Bering Sea, a larder that in 1907 ranked as one of the major fisheries of North America. Then came the usual story, overfishing that in little more than a decade reduced the catch from sixty-five to twenty-two million pounds per year.

Alarmed, Canada and the United States in 1924 appointed a commission to study means of saving the industry. The committee worked cautiously, delving for years into musty company records, government files, and the logs of fishing vessels. Sixteen thousand halibut were tagged and released. Eggs were scooped up and examined, all on the theory that adequate regulation of the fish would depend on a thorough understanding of their habits.

Out of the piling statistics emerged the unsuspected fact that halibut are divided into distinct "races" and that each race stays within fairly well defined localities. Blanket regulations covering the whole industry would therefore not suffice, and each area would have to be managed as an individual entity. Strictures were first imposed in 1932 and varied subsequently as continued scientific studies dictated. Increases began at once. In 1954 and again in 1955 the monetary return to the fishing fleet amounted to three and a half million dollars more than the total value of the catch in the unregulated year of 1931. Conservation, it would seem, can indeed be made to pay.

Under the rigorous supervision of the United States Fish and Wildlife Service a threatened depletion of the salmon fisheries of Alaska was likewise averted and a continuous supply assured for the refrigerated "mother" ships that each spring sail north with hordes of attendant fishing vessels and for the four thousand workers flown to the canneries by the annual "salmon airlift." So marked was the success that hope was raised that even the "doomed" Fraser might be restored.

Because of innumerable high lakes at the sources of its tributaries, the Fraser was once the greatest sockeye salmon stream in the world. Beginning late each spring and continuing through the fall, unguessable millions of fish poured through the Strait of Juan de Fuca. Some turned aside into Puget Sound and the rivers of Washington, notably the Skagit. Most of them, however, followed favorite routes through the San Juan Islands and up the Strait of Georgia to the multiple mouths of the Fraser.

The San Juan Islands lie in American waters. Swarms of Washington fishermen located the salmon runs, ambushed them with traps and seines. Motor trolling developed after 1912, with a single boat setting out as many as twelve lines and thirty hooks motivated by powered reels. Canadian fishermen, angered by the interception, clamored for control. Washington fishermen retorted that the real danger to the industry was the Canadian custom of fishing the river too close to the spawning grounds.

A major disaster in 1913 should have ended the quarrel. By that time it was known that the life cycle of a Fraser River sockeye salmon is four years. Fishermen had noted, furthermore, that the Fraser sockeye had mysteriously established what is called a "quadrennial dominance." For three years the runs would be normal. Then, on each fourth year, an extra surge of productivity took place, so that the return of these fourth-year fish resulted in a catch greater than the harvests of the three preceding years combined.

Hudson's Bay Company records reaching back to 1822 showed that this dominance had prevailed for almost a century. The year 1913 was no exception. Fishermen that year expected, and reaped, a bountiful crop—2,392,815 cases of choice sockeye salmon, compared to a normal-year average of about 500,000 cases. But they did not rejoice. Even as they hauled in the fish they heard of a terrifying circumstance which made them fear the riches could never be repeated.

North of Hope, at the narrows called Hell's Gate, a thunderous cascade of boulders had been dynamited into the river that spring by workers building a railroad. Just as the salmon began to reach this obstruction, summer floods poured down the canyon. The narrows became a maelstrom. A seething mass of fish jammed up for ten miles below the Gate, hurling themselves in vain at the torrent. Either they were battered to death or were so bruised that they gave up and drifted back to whatever quiet water they could find and there died without spawning.

Fishermen braced themselves for a major shrinkage. Their dread was borne out: within eight years the great quadrennial pack had dropped from more than 2,000,000 cases to a puny 143,000.

Bewilderingly, the other runs were shrinking as well. The last of the Hell's Gate obstruction was removed in 1915, and the normal runs should have continued their average of 500,000 or more cases. But by 1929 the normal-year take had dwindled to a miserable 90,000. The loss to the fishing industry of Canada and the United States, so economists have recently calculated, has amounted to more than one billion dollars.

Almost immediately after the 1913 disaster demands arose for international control of the Fraser and its approaches, but unfortunately the fishermen of the two nations could not agree on methods. Not until after they had been faced with the phenomenal restoration of the halibut banks and the example of Alaska did the quarrelers resolve the differences and in 1937 sign a belated treaty, establishing the International Pacific Salmon Fisheries Commission.

Following the precept of the halibut investigators, the salmon commissioners made haste slowly. Two full sockeye cycles were studied (it took eight years) before the first regulations were promulgated. During this time the committee's fishery experts learned that the sockeyes are subdivided, somewhat like halibut, into "races." That is, salmon born in the same stream stick together and there is almost no interbreeding between the various stock. This meant that once a race of fish had been exterminated, as the Quesnel River race had been exterminated by the 1913 blockade, it could not be replenished by voluntary migrants from other streams.

The different races, it was further learned, migrate at different times. The variation is determined by the need of the fish to reach their spawning grounds when water temperatures are at a chilly optimum, between forty-five and fifty-five degrees Fahrenheit. If these varying migrations reach Hell's Gate, constricted by its railroads, during periods of high water, mortality soars. And for some years this unhappy coincidence was exactly what had been occurring.

The first problem thus became one of assuring the fish safe passageway through Hell's Gate during flood time. A model of the canyon was built at the University of Washington. Using data revealed by experiments with the model, engineer Milo Bell in 1945 and 1946 hung, with considerable difficulty, two concrete fishways on the canyon cliffs, so that the salmon could use these when high water roared through the Gate. (A third and still higher way was added in 1952.) Results were spectacular. The run in 1943, before the fishways were built, was estimated at 141,000 salmon. The same cycle in 1951 soared to 1,671,500 fish.

This was only part of the problem. The varying times of the migrations indicated that closed seasons on fishing would have to be imposed at carefully calculated intervals, so that some spawners from every race could reach their home grounds—yet not in such numbers that they would overpopulate the beds. The timing and placing of these intermittent closures proved extraordinarily difficult. For one thing, the salmon must pass through two hundred miles of heavily fished waters before they even reach the Fraser; for another, the commission is obligated by treaty to see that both the Canadian and United States fleets receive equal amounts of the catch.

Each year new formulas are devised for closing the different areas —and each year they are upset by unanticipated changes in the number of fishing boats, in the areas covered by the vessels, or in the efficiency of their gear. Still, by compiling statistics every twenty-four hours and ordering emergency closures or extensions of the open times as needed, the commission has achieved uncanny success, particularly in distributing the harvest. Between 1946 and 1956 the Canadians caught 18,423,459 salmon; the Americans, 18,008,749. Certain key runs in 1952 and 1953 were maintained by means of emergency edicts. But occasionally there are misses. In 1955 certain of the races were too heavily exploited before the shifting circumstances were detected, and as a result future years of the cycle are almost certain to suffer.

Meanwhile the commission has been trying to restore river systems left barren by the blockades of 1913 and subsequent years. Both fingerlings and eggs have been transplanted. For some reason not yet understood, the transplantation of fingerlings has succeeded in only one case out of ten. Eggs placed in gravel beds carefully prepared to duplicate the conditions of the spawning grounds from which they were taken have fared better.

Predictions are risky. Still, circumstances and time have favored the Fraser fisheries over those of the Columbia. Lumbering and the demands for irrigation water are not likely to create as grave problems on the Canadian river as they have on the American. There has been more opportunity to brace for problems of sewage, industrial waste, and hydroelectric dams. As usual, men will have what they want. If they desire the salmon keenly enough, it is just possible that, in spite of the inroads of civilization, scientific conservation may be able to continue its dramatic work and lift the Fraser back to its pre-eminent place as the world's greatest fishing stream.

3. The Water

ON EITHER side of the baked, sun-wasted soil of the Northwest's huge inland plateaus the mountains rise cool and wet. No other spot in arid America is so favorably situated for irrigation. To the west the Cascades capture as much as nine *feet* (not inches) of precipitation annually. To the northeast and east the Rockies sweat their vast ice fields into the Columbia, send the Clark Fork pouring into

Pend Oreille Lake, start the turgid Snake on its horseshoe sweep through southern Idaho.

Water everywhere—but the bulk of it lies at the bottom of canyons far too deep for a lone man's strength to master. Numbly the first settlers plodded on through the chocolate dust to the moister lands of the coastal belts.

Here and there, of course, spots existed where a single shovel could do the job. The Yakima Indians of central Washington learned in prehistoric times to scratch little ruts out of the river that bears their name. The French-Canadian servants of the Hudson's Bay Company, prodded by George Simpson's edict that they grow more potatoes, brought shallow ditches to the trading posts. Marcus Whitman dug an ambitious canal ten feet wide at Waiilatpu. Seeing how well his crops did when watered, his Cayuse neighbors appropriated what they needed from his canal—after all, stealing was easier than digging ditches of their own.

Community effort was introduced by the Mormons of southeastern Idaho. As population increased, corporations were formed to bring still more water from the streams. The more conservative of these companies earned their profits by selling water rights and furnishing maintenance service on the canals. A more dazzling scheme was for the incorporators of an irrigation firm to buy up great amounts of dry sagebrush at a song, water the land, and cash in by selling it at greatly enhanced prices.

Both plans became entangled with the land policies of the federal government. The Desert Land Act of 1877 allowed a settler 640 acres (as opposed to the normal homestead allotment of 160) if he undertook to irrigate eighty of his acres. The act produced only a handful of Rube Goldberg water wheels, wooden pipes, flumes, and ditches; for as even a congressman should have guessed, a project potent enough to wet eighty acres was far beyond the resources of the average individual. As a result the Desert Land Act, like the Swamp and Timber acts, was used primarily as one more fraud for concentrating land in the hands of a few energetic "barons."

To remedy matters and to help quiet cries raised throughout the agricultural West by the depression of '93, Congress in 1894 passed the Carey Act. This measure allowed the government to grant to a state (or territory), upon application, one million acres of public land if the state supervised the reclamation of those acres during the ensuing ten years. Actual development of the grant land could be turned over to private corporations if their plans were approved by a state administrative agency. Unfortunately, boondoggling, political jockeying, poor engineering, and sloppy administration gave most Carey Act projects a bad name. Save in Idaho, relatively little land was applied for. In that state, however, 868,000 acres were eventually brought into production.

The greatest shackle on development was the chaos of water rights. In the early days a man or company obtained a claim simply by posting notice of intention to divert so many inches of water. Unsupervised, this led into fantasy. In eastern Oregon enough water was claimed to turn entire counties into lakes—if the water had existed. Men with homesteads adjacent to streams howled in anguish when settlers above them whisked the water out of its natural bed to a fertile bench far removed from the creek valley. The owners of potential farms increased the vociferation on discovering that they were blocked off from water by the paper rights of speculators who probably would never utilize the moisture they claimed.

Slowly and painfully the settlers groped for some way out of the impasse. From their surveys emerged figures that showed in black and white what everyone knew anyway: stream flow, on which ultimate settlement of the conflicts must be based, was extremely variable. No solution was possible which did not stabilize the creeks by impounding water during flood stages and releasing it during drought. The bigger the reservoirs, the more claims could be satisfied—and the higher the cost.

Corporations were formed to build the necessary dams and ditches but often found that they had bitten off more than they could chew. In 1883, for example, Eastern capitalists conceived the idea of bringing canals down from the Idaho mountains to placer bars near the mouth of the Boise River. The project would be made self-liquidating by selling water to farmers whose holdings the ditches traversed en route. The gold from the gravel bars, washed out during non-irrigating seasons, would be sheer profit.

The first step was to claim 150,000 inches of water from the Boise River, more than the stream carried at normal flow. [1] Work started with shovels, horse scrapers, and hope. These resources failing, contracts were awarded to a professional construction firm. Work went faster then—and more expensively. Soon the irrigating company could not pay its bills, and the construction firm found itself owning ditches

---

[1] That was just the beginning. By 1898, one hundred and fifty claimants had asserted rights to 6,361,800 inches of Boise River water. In September of that same drought-stricken year the river flowed 35,000 inches.

it did not want. It unloaded onto farmers' co-operatives. Pinched first by the panic of '93 and then by a severe drought at the end of the decade, the farmers spent most of their time in litigation and hand-wringing.

Similar misadventures throughout the West led to insistent demands that the federal government do more than simply give away land which mocked the recipient's hopes. This in turn led to the New-lands Act of 1902, legislative parent of the behemoth of the Western scene, the Reclamation Service (since 1923, the Bureau of Reclamation). In theory at least, the service was to make its projects self-liquidating by means of long-term charges against the lands reclaimed.

Eagerly the Boise co-operatives petitioned the new fairy godfather for help. The Service obliged—its first venture in the Northwest. Results were inspiring. One notable feature was Arrowrock Dam, 1100 feet long and a soaring 354 feet tall, for years the highest in the world. Staring upward at so massive a structure, bemused spectators began to wonder if it might not be possible to build bigger dams across bigger rivers, perhaps even the torrential Columbia.

Elsewhere in the Northwest the infant Reclamation Service encountered opposition. Some of its proposed developments were blocked by exorbitant costs. Other plans were upset by ranchers who owned the best reservoir basins or by private irrigation companies who claimed the water of the streams. Of these controversies, the most bitter was the one that raged up and down the fertile but gaspingly dry Yakima Valley in central Washington. Even yet it is not dead history. Arguments used there are still being heard today, half a century later, beside certain dam sites along the Snake.

The Yakima River runs from the Cascade Mountains southeast to join the Columbia at Richland. Its principal tributary is the Naches, which heads at no great distance from the gargantuan bulk of Mount Rainier and meets the parent stream near the spot to which the Northern Pacific Railroad had lured the town of Yakima in the 1880s.

Even before the advent of the railroad, private irrigation companies had learned that water would boost the value of land from ten to fifty or more dollars an acre. This attractive speculation was by no means lost on the Northern Pacific, which had land in plenty to sell and was certain to benefit from any increase in population. Eventually, after helping various companies with publicity and occasional dollars, the railroad joined with the lower valley's most aggressive group to form the Northern Pacific, Yakima and Kittitas Irrigation Company.

Although a resplendent valley-long program was produced on the drafting boards, actual construction boiled down to the Sunnyside canal just south of Yakima city. It was ambitious enough: a main ditch eight feet deep and sixty-two feet wide at the top. When twenty-five miles had been shoveled out, local residents were invited to attend, on March 26, 1892, the dedication of what the company called "the beginning of the most important system of irrigating canals in America." Bands played; anvils boomed. Miss Dora Allen swung a bottle of champagne against the valves and declaimed to the rush of waters, "Flow on, thou liquid savior of our land!"

Within a year the panic of '93 had stopped the shovels. The company collapsed, then reorganized in 1900 as the Washington Irrigation Company. By 1902 seven hundred miles of main ditch and laterals were watering thirty-six thousand acres. Other companies expanded with equal fervor, until fertile Yakima proclaimed that four fifths of all the irrigated acres in the state of Washington lay within her borders. [2]

At this juncture the Reclamation Act was passed. One of its ardent supporters was Senator Wesley Jones, resident of Yakima. Although private enterprise had succeeded marvelously in his district, Jones felt that the government could do still better—and invited the engineers of the Reclamation Service to conduct a survey. This threatened invasion of their domain caused a frantic scramble among the private companies to appropriate every water right in sight, especially those appertaining to the deep, cold, glacial lakes in the Cascades, where small dams could create large reservoirs. In their wild jockeying, the companies grew wroth at each other as well as at the government. One group even dynamited a dam another one had put across the outlet of Lake Cle Elum; and by 1905 far more water had been claimed than the Yakima and its tributaries could possibly produce.

Dismayed by the uproar, the Reclamation Service withdrew. This brought about a dilemma. In those days the organization's work was financed by the sale of public lands, and by law it was required to spend at least fifty-one per cent of these proceeds in the states where the sales were made. The only projects the Service's engineers could find in Washington, save at Yakima and a modest program at Okanogan, were far too expensive for its resources. Yet it was legally obliged to spend the money it had.

Realizing this, Senator Jones prevailed on the Reclamation engineers to reconsider the Yakima plan. He also began lining up valley

[2] The boast needs some qualification: Washington, with less than one quarter of one per cent of her lands under water, at that time ranked last among the irrigating states.

support against the private companies. In fresh alarm the Northern Pacific and the Washington Irrigation Company tried to push through the state legislature a bill which would have frozen the federal government out of the strategic storage lakes in the mountains. This effort failed. Another defeat came when the state, complying with the advice of the Reclamation Service, set up a commission to adjudicate the conflicting water claims and scale them down to an amount approximating what the river could produce.

The downgrading was painful to the claimants, but most of them accepted it. When certain recalcitrants refused to go along, local merchants subscribed $23,000 to buy their land and then voluntarily relinquished the disputed water rights. The trend, in short, was running strongly in favor of federal development. Sensing this, the Washington Irrigation Company suddenly offered to sell to the Reclamation Service its canals, but not its lands, for $640,000. At first the government gagged at the price but in 1906 acceded, opening the way for an elaborate network of canals which today serve nearly half a million acres, one of the largest irrigation projects in the nation.

Eastward across the Columbia from the Yakima country lies an enormous area called the Big Bend. The name derives from the fact that the erratic Columbia bounds the land boxlike on the north, west, and south. On its eastern edge are rolling wheat farms, slanting a golden streak from Walla Walla northward through the Palouse Hills to the pine forests near Spokane. These were—and are—enormously productive farms. Their promise had led latecomers to drift on westward from the Palouse Hills to try to find similar farms in the Big Bend. Hundreds of thousands of scabbed, eroded, lava-baked acres were put under fence, around the hamlets of Quincy and Ephrata, and near the shallow waters of Moses Lake.

At first the farms succeeded, thanks to the beneficent ability of the volcanic soil to sponge up and store throughout the years even the rarest drops of moisture. After a few seasons of wheat growing, however, the earth was dehydrated. In the Palouse Hills the moisture could be restored by letting fields lie fallow for a year or two, but in the Big Bend the rainfall was not adequate for even that.

The stubble dried. Gray-spirited farmers abandoned their homesteads to the gray desert. The jack rabbits came back, the rattlesnakes, the dry whisper of wind under the unbroken blue of the fiery skies. Not far to the west, meanwhile, in climatic conditions almost identical, the Yakima bloomed with cash crops more valuable than roses. North of Yakima, at Wenatchee, irrigation systems fostered by Jim Hill's Great Northern Railroad pushed the value of apple lands up toward a thousand dollars an acre. Surely the Big Bend could do as well— if only some way of bringing water could be devised.

Yearning eyes looked down at the Columbia, cool-flowing at the bottom of a canyon almost a thousand feet deep. The river had not always been so inaccessible. During the ice age, when the stream had been much larger than it is now, a glacial dam had forced it from its bed due south through the heart of the Big Bend. To break a way through the basalt the water had carved out a huge trench some fifty miles long, from two to six miles wide, and in places more than six hundred feet deep. At one spot the incredible torrent had plunged over cliffs a mile and a half wide, perhaps the biggest waterfall the world had ever known.

Eventually the ice dam melted; the shrunken river resumed and deepened its former course. High and dry now, the great ditch it had carved ran from nowhere into nowhere, stark, silent, awesome. Who named it Grand Coulee is unknown. Fur traders were calling it that in 1814 when Alexander Ross, gaping at its "columns, pillars, battlements, turrets, and steps above steps," declared it to be "the most romantic, picturesque, and marvelously formed chasm west of the Rocky Mountains . . . the wonder of the Oregon."

What the river had done once, perhaps it could be made to do again. A Big Bend real estate agent named Laughlin MacLean proposed in 1892, while farmers were still coming into the country, to use the Grand Coulee not only for irrigation but as "a first-class ship canal." There were, he admitted, difficulties. A dam a thousand feet high, as MacLean estimated it, would be necessary to lift the Columbia to the level of its onetime bed. The smelting city of "Northport will then be in the bed of a huge lake, but it will make a metropolis of Coulee City." Such a lake, he might have added, would also drown a large part of southern British Columbia, to which Canada might conceivably have objected. But such matters did not bother Mr. Mac-Lean. Neither did the problem of financing: "With the rich placer mines that will be exposed in the dry bed of the present channel, there will be plenty of capital. . . . It is surely a grand enterprise."

A few ungentlemanly hoots greeted the words, and the grand enterprise lay dormant until 1918. That year it was revived by a pair of dusty residents of Ephrata, William Clapp and James O'Sullivan, and given publicity by indefatigable Rufus Woods of the Wenatchee

World, who considered himself spokesman for most of central Washington.

The revived proposal contained no mention of placer beds. To preclude international complications, the new dream suggested limiting the dam to whatever height would back up the lake no farther than the Canadian border. The water would then be lifted the rest of the way into the Coulee by huge pumps powered by electricity generated at the dam itself.

Proponents of this scheme became known as "the pumpers."

That same year, 1918, a Yakima Valley irrigation expert named E. F. Blaine came up with an equally grand enterprise. His scheme was to bring water to the Big Bend through a gigantic system of canals, tunnels, and siphons from a dam one hundred and thirty miles away on the Clark Fork River at Albeni Falls, Idaho. Spokane businessmen were instantly interested, for Blaine's brobdingnagian ditch would pass close to their city. During the non-irrigating season of winter, when local water supplies for generating power were short, the imported flood could be used to turn private dynamos in the city.

Proponents of this scheme became known as "the gravity men."

Instantly an issue was joined which still causes tempers to grow short and memories to rankle. Basically, the controversy was an inevitable extension of the public works-private enterprise quarrel that had troubled Yakima a few years earlier. Only federal funds were ample enough to build either Big Bend system. In either case the water produced would be used to develop privately owned farms which, to be sure, were supposed eventually to pay for the water provided them. But were only farms to be favored? Might not other private industries legitimately receive benefit from the expenditure of public money on natural resources? If so, how much voice should these industries have in determining the policy of the public works?

Generally speaking, the pumpers represented the view that the reclamation of public lands was a legitimate field for public expenditures but that the fostering of private power corporations was not. The gravity men took the contrary stand that if the government went into the business of producing power, as it would have to if Grand Coulee were built, the move would constitute an unwarranted interference with the rights of private enterprise. Forestalling Grand Coulee in favor of the gravity system from Albeni Falls became, in some ears at least, a rallying cry for proponents of free enterprise.

The early rounds went to the gravity men. A Columbia Basin Commission appointed by the state spent a hundred thousand dollars on surveys and recommended the dam at Albeni Falls. Pump proponents ridiculed as far too low the cost estimate presented by the commission. The Reclamation Service supported the figures of the pumpers, who were further heartened when a Seattle engineering firm brought in a report favoring Grand Coulee.

At this point someone suggested an impartial arbiter. General George Goethals, builder of the Panama Canal, was approached. He asked a fee of twenty-five thousand dollars. When the Columbia Basin Commission could afford only fifteen thousand, Spokane businessmen met the balance. Goethals, after admitting that the Grand Coulee idea had merit, placed his blessing on the gravity plan. Spokane crowed. The frustrated pumpers, some of them, muttered darkly that the general was far too obliging to bite the hand that paid him.

The gravity men's next step was to mold congressional opinion. A Columbia Basin Irrigation League was formed to prepare national publicity, to take visiting congressmen on sight-seeing trips, to set up a lobby in the national capital. The poverty-stricken pumpers of the Big Bend had no such resources to employ. But they were not without support, especially in Idaho and Montana.

The gravity plan envisioned getting its necessary storage capacity by increasing the size of Pend Oreille Lake in Idaho and Flathead Lake in Montana. In both sections prosperous farms and towns would be inundated for the benefit of Washington citizens. This aroused considerable animosity. Idaho went so far as to pass a law that would make the Pend Oreille reservoir virtually impossible. Angry gravity men muttered darkly that pumpers from the Big Bend were behind the dastardly move.

Meanwhile Senator Jones of Yakima had adroitly maneuvered into a river and harbor bill authorization for the army's Corps of Engineers and the Federal Power Commission to conduct a nationwide survey of the irrigation, navigation, flood control, and power potentials of all major United States rivers. Because this authority appeared in House Document 308 of the 69th Congress, first session, the habit grew of referring to the anticipated report in cryptic Americanese as "Army three-oh-eight."

The 308 surveys on the Columbia lasted from 1928 until 1931. As the time neared for the publication of the highly secret document, the Columbia Basin all but perished with suspense.

Army 308, when released, was ten inches thick. That part of it dealing with the Columbia recommended many things—but not the

Pend Oreille gravity system. Such a system, the engineers said, would cost more even than a dam at Grand Coulee 550 feet high and 4300 feet long, equipped with twelve of the biggest pumps ever conceived to lift water the remaining 280 feet to the canyon rim. Furthermore, said the report, the Grand Coulee system could be largely paid for by selling surplus power, as the gravity system could not be. And finally Grand Coulee would cause no interstate bickering with Idaho and Montana.

By this time the paralyzing depression of the 1930s had gripped the nation. Grand Coulee and another dam which the Corps of Engineers recommended at the Cascade Rapids (to be called Bonneville Dam) became the footballs of politics. Franklin Roosevelt promised the Northwest both dams during his campaign for the presidency, but after his election only Bonneville was authorized. Roosevelt's belated reasoning: Coulee's estimated cost of four hundred million dollars would overburden the shrunken economy and would bring too much additional cropland into production at the very time the New Deal was destroying agricultural surpluses.

At this, Senator Clarence Dill of Washington, according to his own not exactly self-effacing reminiscences, went raging into the White House. Just what were the people of the Northwest going to think of this broken promise?

The Great Compromiser "picked up the long yellow cigarette holder on his desk . . . looked at me and said, 'Let's build a low dam . . . make some cheap power for a few years and when the depression is over, we can finish the dam and start the irrigation project.'"

It was a crumb. Under general supervision of the Bureau of Reclamation bedrock was grouted, power machines began moving dirt, job hunters began lining up at the employment agencies. But it was poor food for the Big Bend, even though Dill promised that the dam's foundations were being laid in such a way that the structure's height could be increased in the vague future. Then they'd get their water —maybe.

The long-dried Big Bend did not want water in the future. It wanted it now. When Roosevelt, his family, and Secretary of Interior Harold Ickes visited the site in the summer of 1934, the route of their motor caravan was lined with strident banners crying, "We want the high dam."

That and what Ickes was shown in the stark gorge of the Columbia made him see, so he wrote later, "with the eyes of understanding. When I got to Ephrata, I was committed in my own mind to the high dam." Jim O'Sullivan, Rufus Woods, and the scarred veterans of the long fight redoubled their pressure. Western congressmen fell into line, and in June 1935 the Bureau of Reclamation was ordered to forget the low dam and start work on the high one.

Within another year 7789 dam builders were on the job. Concrete poured in at the rate of more than twenty tons each minute, until ten and a half million cubic yards of it shone whitely between the sun-scoured hills. In 1940 a cataract 850 feet wide foamed over the spillway. A lake destined to be 151 miles long was backing up toward the Canadian border. Publicists strained their imaginations to invent comparisons which would show how big this thing is: four United States Capitol buildings could be placed inside the dam; the four largest ocean liners in the world could be lined up on its top with room to spare; each of its generator rooms is more than twice the size of Yankee Stadium; its spillway . . . but perhaps it is enough just to say that Grand Coulee is, excepting possibly the Great Wall of China, the largest single thing ever built by the hand of man.

A gigantic monolith in the middle of the desert—as useless, its opponents chanted, as the pyramids of Egypt. Who, one sarcastic congressman demanded, was going to buy all that power? Jack Robinson Rabbit?

Circumstances soon answered him.

There is, it would seem, a tide in the affairs of nations also. On October 4, 1941, power was delivered from the first of Coulee's mammoth generators. Two months later, on December 7, 1941, Japanese aircraft bombed Pearl Harbor. By early 1942 demands for electricity had become so exacting that a power pool was set up under the Bonneville Power administration to bring together and then distribute for maximum efficiency every kilowatt produced between Puget Sound and eastern Montana, between the Canadian border and Salt Lake City. Aircraft factories, aluminum factories, fabricators of all kinds sprang up wherever the transmission lines could reach. And then, early in 1943, there began pouring onto a desolate flat farther down the river the fifty thousand people needed to build and operate a plant whose deadly purpose only a handful of them guessed —the giant plutonium works at Hanford.

That was who bought the power.

Since the war the Bonneville Power Administration, under which the complex electrical distribution is managed, has raised a host of uneasy questions. The efficient central grid which it established during the war saved millions of barrels of oil and millions of tons of coal at a time when those commodities and the transportation facilities to handle them were desperately short. But how far should efficiency reach in peacetime?

For example, the Power Administration does not run the increasing number of dams being built everywhere in the basin. But it is concerned with getting its power as cheaply and in as uniform supply as possible, if for no other reason than that it is obligated to pay for the multimillion-dollar transmission systems that it has erected. Should it therefore have a right to dictate how water should be stored and released in the dams which regulate its power supplies—even if its orders conflict with the demands of flood control and irrigation? If not, who does determine priorities?

How social should its administrative philosophy be? By law the Power Administration is required, in selling its power, to give preference to public systems: municipal light and power plants, for instance. To expand its market, should it, in direct competition with private enterprise, foster rural co-operatives and public utility districts? Should it continue its research into the development of new industries through electrical power and then, on the basis of its findings, voice itself about the location of new plants, with all that this implies to civic planning? Should it, armed with its billions of kilowatts of power, concern itself with management? With labor policies? Or (to load the question another way) should the Northwest be allowed to grow haphazardly, as the expediencies of the moment suggest?

Similar questions agitate other prospective developments in the Columbia Basin. During the late 1940s the Corps of Engineers was busy revising and expanding its 308 report into a "Main Control" plan involving vast dams on every tributary. Talk of so much water is generally dry enough to frighten away popular interest. But in May 1948 heavy rains and high temperatures east of the Cascades flushed torrents of melting snow down the streams. Bonners Ferry on the Kootenai, Wallace on the Coeur d'Alene, Lewiston on the Snake, Wenatchee, Yakima, and dozens of smaller towns were ravaged by flood. At Vanport, across from Portland, dikes crumbled and an avalanche of water poured almost without warning through a city of eighteen thousand people, tossing houses like chips. Fifty-two lives were lost throughout the basin, thirty-eight thousand homes were destroyed, and groggy calculators estimated that a hundred million dollars' worth of damage had been done.

After that experience people read with quickened interest the revised 308 report which the Corps of Engineers issued a few months after the disaster. What the army said about flood control made sense. Or did it?

The Department of the Interior jumped into the act with *its* ideas. Since then the competing Bureau of Reclamation and the Corps of Engineers have come up with plans for no less than 405 power, flood control, irrigation, navigation, recreation, anti-pollution, and fishery proposals that blanket every stream in the Northwest. Several of the plans conflict; many overlap. As one single example: both bureaus have surveyed the same dam site in Hell's Canyon of the Snake at a cost of $250,000 each—after which private industry sent in its crews.

Two dozen or more state and federal agencies go separate ways with what are essentially related problems of lumbering and soil erosion, irrigation, salmon restoration, and everything else remotely connected with water. Would it not be more efficient to unify all this under a single Columbia Valley Authority modeled after TVA? Or is such colossal power to be safely entrusted to any one agency? The very thought of it gives shivers to the people in the Flathead Valley of Montana. They know that raising the height of the Kerr Dam a mere seventeen feet would improve the efficiency of the entire Columbia storage system, and consequently it is a project urgently recommended by the planners. But the development would also drown one of the loveliest sections of farmland in the mountain West. Who is entitled to pass such a sentence?

As long as we are asking questions, try this one: What happens to these grandiose plans if the Canadians decide to do what they have gently mentioned in the past—divert the upper Columbia through a relatively short tunnel into the watershed of the Fraser?

During the war, when emphasis shifted to power and after that to flood control, the water-starved people of the Big Bend sometimes wondered whether the original purpose of Grand Coulee had not been forgotten. Gradually, however, priorities were restored and work began on a complex of storage reservoirs and canals which ultimately will bring more than one million acres under cultivation, a farm paradise capable of supporting, so its boosters contend, a population of at least one hundred thousand people.

As the various blocks are opened, applicants for land are chosen by the drawing of lots. Homesteads range from ten to one hundred and sixty acres each. It is rich, fat land, eminently suited to intensive cultivation. But it is not cheap land. A man needs several thousand dollars to bring his farm into production, and he profits most by raising specialized crops that he could not have marketed from so remote a place before the days of rapid transport—dairy products, asparagus, choice fruits, and the like.

The water began to flow, finally, in 1952. To publicize the event, a board of agricultural examiners selected from a nationwide horde of applicants the family of a man named Donald Dunn to be the recipients of a free farm—or, rather, a free area of sagebrush. But that seemed picayune. So local labor unions, businessmen, and neighbors from around Moses Lake agreed to put onto the plot everything the Dunns would need—and put it there in a hurry.

At midnight a bomb went off, signalizing the beginning of the stunt. Under floodlights three hundred workers swarmed out to erect a home, barn, and outbuildings. Thirty-four tractors rumbled onto the sagebrush, the land levelers first and then the disks, drills, and harrows. By noon half of the farm's eighty irrigable acres had been planted. Water came an hour or two later. At sunset Governor Bowman milked a cow in the new barn. By dark Donald Dunn, his wife, and two children stood blinking inside a completely furnished new seven-room home, still not quite sure what had happened to them.

A publicity stunt, to be sure. But a symbol, too, compressing a century's hopes down into a few hours. For always the far corner of our land has been a region big with promise.

It still is.

BIBLIOGRAPHIC NOTE

Inevitably, there exists an enormous literature covering the two centuries of history of the Pacific Northwest. One of the most valuable bodies of that literature is the hundred-odd volumes into which are bound the publications of the Oregon, Washington, and Montana historical societies. My chief reliance has been on those publications and, in so far as they appear in print, on the journals and reminiscences of actual participants in the scenes described in the text. In bringing coherence to this heterogeneous collection I have, of course, depended heavily on the work of those regional historians whose names appear below.

This bibliography, in spite of its apparent size, does not pretend to be exhaustive, but rather indicates those several books and monographs which I found most useful and which I feel will give the curious reader more detailed information about whatever phases of the Northwest's colorful history he may like to explore still further. As an additional aid, the references have been broken down according to topic. Obviously there is considerable overlapping. Long titles, particularly of periodical articles, are occasionally abbreviated.

Generally speaking, the publication date following a book is that of the edition I used, not necessarily the date of original issue. Since the historical quarterlies are bound into volumes by year, I have limited identification to year only. Further space saving comes from employing the following abbreviations:

AHR   - American Historical Review
BCHQ - British Columbia Historical Quarterly
CHR   - Canadian Historical Review
HSM   - Contributions to the Historical Society of Montana
OHQ   - Oregon Historical Quarterly
PHR   - Pacific Historical Review
PNQ   - Pacific Northwest Quarterly
WHQ - Washington Historical Quarterly

1. HISTORIES OF THE WEST

Billington, Ray A. *Westward Expansion*. New York, 1950———. *The Far Western Frontier*. New York, 1956
Caughey, John W. *History of the Pacific Coast of North America*. Los Angeles, 1933
Ghent, W. J. *The Early Far West*. New York, 1931
Graebner, Norman A. *Empire on the Pacific*. New York, 1955

Riegel, Robert. *America Moves West*. New York, 1956
Schafer, Joseph. *The Pacific Coast and Alaska*. Philadelphia, 1904

II. STATE AND REGIONAL HISTORIES

Andrews, Clarence L. *The Story of Alaska*. Caldwell, Ida., 1935
Bancroft, Hubert H. *History of Alaska; History of British Columbia; Native Races*, Vol.1; *History of the Northwest Coast*, 2 vols.; *History of Oregon*, 2 vols.; *History of Washington, Idaho, Montana*. San Francisco, 1886–1890
Burlingame, Merrill G. *The Montana Frontier*. Helena, 1942
Carey, Charles H. *A General History of Oregon*. 2 vols. Portland, 1935
Clark, Robert C. *History of the Willamette Valley*. 3 vols. Chicago, 1927
Fuller, George. *A History of the Pacific Northwest*. New York, 1931
Gates, Charles M. *Readings in Pacific Northwest History*. Seattle, 1941
Gray, W. H. *A History of Oregon, 1792–1849*. Portland, 1870
Hailey, John. *The History of Idaho*. Boise, 1910
Holbrook, Stewart. *The Columbia*. New York, 1956
Howard, Joseph K. *Montana, High, Wide and Handsome*. New Haven, 1943
Howay, F. W. *British Columbia*. Toronto, 1928
Howay, F. W., Sage, W. N., and Angus, H. F. *British Columbia and the United States*. Toronto, 1942
Hutchinson, Bruce. *The Fraser*. New York, 1950
Johansen, Dorothy, and Gates, Charles M. *Empire of the Columbia*. New York, 1957
Lockley, Fred. *History of the Columbia River Valley* . . . Chicago, 1928
MacFie, Matthew. *Vancouver Island and British Columbia*. London, 1865
Meany, Edmond S. *History of the State of Washington*. New York, 1909
Morgan, Murray. *The Columbia*. Seattle, 1949
Morton, Arthur S. *A History of the Canadian West to 1870*. London, 1939
Tompkins, Stuart R. *Alaska*. Norman, Okla., 1945
Winther, Oscar O. *The Old Oregon Country*. Stanford, 1950———. *The Great Northwest*, rev. ed. New York, 1955
Wright, E. W., ed. *Lewis and Dryden's Marine History of the Pacific Northwest*. Portland, 1895

III. EXPLORATIONS BY SEA

Augur, Helen. *Passage to Glory*. New York, 1946
Cook, James, and King, James. *Voyage to the Pacific Ocean*. Vol. 3. London, 1784
Denton, V. L. *The Far West Coast*. Toronto, 1924
Golder, Frank. *Russian Expansion on the Pacific*. Cleveland, 1914
Howay, F. W., ed. *Voyages of the "Columbia" to the Northwest Coast*. Boston, 1941
Jewitt, John. *Narratives of Adventures and Sufferings*. New York, 1815
Laut, Agnes. *Vikings of the Pacific*. New York, 1905
Manning, W. R. *The Nootka Sound Controversy*. Washington, 1905
Marshall, James, and Marshall, Carrie. *Adventures in Two Hemispheres*. Vancouver, B.C., 1955

Meares, John. *Voyages . . . to the Northwest Coast of America*. London, 1790
Morison, Samuel. *The Maritime History of Massachusetts*. New York, 1921
Ogden, Adele. *The California Sea Otter Trade*. Berkeley, 1941

IV. EXPLORATIONS BY LAND

Bakeless, John. *Lewis and Clark*. New York, 1947
Brebner, John B. *The Explorers of North America*. New York, 1933
Burpee, L. J. *The Search for the Western Sea*. 2 vols. Toronto, 1935
DeVoto, Bernard. *The Course of Empire*. New York, 1952——, ed. *The Journals of Lewis and Clark*. New York, 1953
Mackenzie, Alexander. *Voyages . . . to the Frozen and Pacific Oceans*. Toronto, 1927
Tyrrell, John, ed. *David Thompson's Narrative . . .* Toronto, 1916
White, Catherine, ed. *David Thompson's Journals . . .* Missoula, 1950

* * *

Elliott, T. C., excerpts from and comments on Thompson's Journals in WHQ, 1917, 1918, 1919, 1920, 1925.
Morton, Arthur S., on David Thompson in CHR, 1936, 1937
David Thompson and Jeremy Pinch: OHQ 1937, 1938, 1939

V. THE ENGLISH FUR TRADE

Barker, Burt, ed. *Letters of Dr. John McLoughlin . . . 1829–32*. Portland, 1948
Bryce, G. *The Remarkable History of the Hudson's Bay Company*. New York, 1900
Caywood, Louis R. *Excavations at Two Fort Okanogan Sites*. San Francisco, 1954——. *Final Report, Fort Vancouver Excavations*. San Francisco, 1955
Davidson, Gordon. *The North West Company*. Berkeley, 1918
Dunn, John. *The Oregon Territory and the British North American Fur Trade*. Philadelphia, 1845
Garth, T. R. *Archaeological Explorations at Fort Walla Walla*. Vancouver, Wash., 1951
Holman, F. V. *Dr. John McLoughlin, the Father of Oregon*. Cleveland, 1907
Innis, Harold A. *The Fur Trade in Canada*. New Haven, 1930
Lewis, William, and Phillips, Paul, eds. *The Journal of John Work*. Cleveland, 1923
MacKay, Douglas. *The Honourable Company*. Indianapolis, 1936
Maloney, Alice. *Fur Brigade to the Bonaventura*. San Francisco, 1945
Merk, Frederick. *Fur Trade and Empire*. Cambridge, Mass., 1931
Montgomery, Richard. *The White-Headed Eagle: John McLoughlin*. New York, 1934
Morton, Arthur. *Sir George Simpson*. Portland, 1944
Rich, E. E., ed. *The Letters of John McLoughlin . . . 1825–46*. 3 vols. Toronto, 1941–44,——,
 ed., *Peter Skene Ogden's Snake Country Journals*. London, 1950
Ross, Alexander. *The Fur Hunters of the Far West*. 2 vols. London, 1855
Sage, Walter N. *Sir James Douglas and British Columbia*. Toronto, 1930

Simpson, Sir George. *Overland Journey Around the World*. Philadelphia, 1847
Wallace, Stewart, ed. *Documents Relating to the North West Company*. Toronto, 1934

*   *   *

Atkin, W. T. "The Snake River Fur Trade, 1816–24," OHQ, 1934
Lamb, W. Kaye. "The Advent of the Beaver," BCHQ, 1938——.
    "The Founding of Fort Victoria," BCHQ, 1943
Maloney, Alice. "The Hudson's Bay Company in California," OHQ, 1936
Merk, Frederick. "Snake Country Expedition, 1824–25," OHQ, 1934

VI. THE AMERICAN FUR TRADE

Alter, J. Cecil. *James Bridger*. Salt Lake City, 1925
Chevigny, Hector. *Lord of Alaska*. Portland, 1951
Chittenden, H. M. *The American Fur Trade of the Far West*. 2 vols. Stanford, Calif., 1954
Cox, Ross. *Adventures on the Columbia*. 2 vols. London, 1831
DeVoto, Bernard. *Across the Wide Missouri*. Boston, 1947
Ferris, Warren. *Life in the Rocky Mountains*. Denver, 1940
Franchère, Gabriel. *Narrative of a Voyage to the Northwest Coast of America*. Cleveland, 1904
Irving, Washington. *The Adventures of Captain Bonneville*. New York, 1883
    ——. *Astoria*. New York, 1895
Morgan, Dale. *Jedediah Smith*. Indianapolis, 1953
Osborne, Russell. *Journal of a Trapper*. Portland, 1956
Pilcher, J., and Ashley, W. *Report on the Hudson's Bay Company* . . . Sen. Doc. 29, 21st Congress, 2nd Session, 1829
Pilcher, Astor, Cass, et al. *Report on the Fur Trade* . . . Sen. Doc. 90, 22nd Congress, 1st Session, 1831
Porter, Kenneth. *John Jacob Astor*. 2 vols. Cambridge, 1931
Rollins, Philip, ed. *The Discovery of the Oregon Trail*. New York, 1935
Ross, Alexander. *Adventures of the First Settlers on the Oregon*. Cleveland, 1904
Skinner, Constance. *Adventurers of Oregon*. New Haven, 1921
Smith, Arthur H. D. *John Jacob Astor*. Philadelphia, 1929
Townsend, John K. *Narrative of a Journey* . . . Cleveland, 1905
Victor, Francis Fuller. *The River of the West*. Hartford, 1871
Wyeth, John B. *Oregon*. Cleveland, 1905
Young, F. G., ed. *The Correspondence and Journals of Captain Nathaniel J. Wyeth*. Eugene, Ore., 1899

*   *   *

Eaton, Clement. "Nathaniel Wyeth's Oregon Expeditions," PHR, 1935
Howay, F. W. "The Loss of the Tonquin," WHQ, 1922
Morison, Samuel. "New England and . . . the Columbia River Salmon Trade," OHQ, 1927

VII. MISSIONARY ACTIVITIES

Blanchet, F. N. *Historical Sketch of the Catholic Church in Oregon.* Portland, 1878

Brosnan, Cornelius. *Jason Lee.* New York, 1932

Chittenden, H. M., and Richardson, A. T. *Life, Letters, and Travels of Pierre-Jean de Smet.* 4 vols. New York, 1905

De Smet, Pierre-Jean. *Letters and Sketches, 1841–42;* and *The Oregon Missions, 1845–46.* Cleveland, 1906

Drury, Clifford. *Henry Harmon Spalding.* Caldwell, Ida., 1936——. *Elkanah and Mary Walker.* Caldwell, Ida., 1940——. *Marcus Whitman, M. D.* Caldwell, Ida., 1937

Elliott, T. C. *The Coming of the White Women.* Portland, 1937

Gay, Theresa. *Life and Letters of Mrs. Jason Lee.* Portland, 1936

Lee, Daniel, and Frost, Joseph. *Ten Years in Oregon.* New York, 1844

Marshall, W. I. *Acquisition of Oregon and . . . Whitman,* 2 vols. Seattle, 1911

Palladino, L. B. *Indians and Whites in the Northwest.* Lancaster, Pa., 1922

Parker, Samuel. *Journal of an Exploring Trip Beyond the Rocky Mountains.* Ithaca, 1844

Whitman, Narcissa. *Journal.* Oregon Pioneers Association Transactions, 1890
——. *Letters.* Oregon Pioneers Association Transactions, 1893

* * *

Blue, George. "Green's Missionary Report on Oregon, 1829," OHQ, 1929

Drury, Clifford. "Gray's Journal of 1838," PHR, 1938

Haines, Francis. "The Nez Percé Delegation to St. Louis in 1831," PHR, 1937

Lee, Jason. "Diary," OHQ, 1916

O'Hara, Edwin. "De Smet in the Oregon Country," OHQ, 1909

Oliphant, J. Orin. "George Simpson and the Oregon Missions," PHR, 1937

Reilly, Louis. "Father Ravalli, Pioneer Missionary," *The Catholic World,* 1927

Shaeffer, C. "The First Jesuit Mission to the Flathead Indians," PNQ, 1937

VIII. THE OREGON TRAIL AND THE BEGINNING OF SETTLEMENT

Allen, Miss A. J. *Ten Years in Oregon: The Travels and Adventures of Dr. Elijah White and Lady.* Ithaca, 1850

Applegate, Jesse A. *Recollections of My Boyhood.* Roseburg, Ore., 1914

Bell, James. *Opening a Highway to the Pacific.* New York, 1923

Brown, Jennie. *Fort Hall on the Oregon Trail.* Caldwell, Ida., 1932

Burnett, Peter. *Recollections . . . of an Old Timer.* New York, 1880

Edwards, Philip. *Diary of the Great Cattle Drive . . . in 1837.* San Francisco, 1932.
——. *Sketch of the Oregon Territory.* Liberty, Mo., 1842

Farnham, Thomas J. *Travels in the Great Western Prairies.* Cleveland, 1906

Ghent, W. J. *The Road to Oregon.* New York, 1929

Hastings, Lansford. *The Emigrants Guide . . .* Princeton, 1932

Hulbert, A., and Hulbert, D. *The Call of The Columbia.* Denver, 1934——. *The Oregon Crusade.* Denver, 1935——. *Where Rolls the Oregon.* Denver, 1933

Johnson, Overton, and Winter, William. *Route across the Rocky Mountains.*
     Princeton, 1932
Lenox, Edward. *Overland to Oregon.* Oakland, 1904
Newell, Robert. *Memorandum.* Manuscript, University of Oregon.
Paden, Irene. *The Wake of the Prairie Schooner.* New York, 1943
Palmer, Joel. *Journals of Travels . . . 1845-46.* Cleveland, 1907
Powell, Fred W. *Hall J. Kelley on Oregon.* Princeton, 1932
Rucker, Maude Applegate. *The Oregon Trail and Some of Its Blazers.* New
     York, 1930
Slacum, William. *Memorial.* Sen. Doc. 24, 25th Congress, 2nd Session, 1837
Tobie, H. E. *No Man Like Joe.* Portland, 1949

* * *

Applegate, Jesse. "A Day with the Cow Column," OHQ, 1900
Applegate, Lindsay. "The Applegate Route . . . 1846," OHQ, 1912
Burnett, Peter. Letters, OHQ, 1902, 1904
Galbraith, John. "Early History of the Puget Sound Agricultural Company,"
     OHQ, 1954
Nesmith, James. "Diary . . . 1843," OHQ, 1906
Powell, Fred. "Hall Jackson Kelley, Prophet of Oregon," OHQ, 1917
Scott, Leslie. "Indian Diseases as an Aid to . . . Settlement," OHQ, 1928
Tobie, H. E. "From the Missouri to the Columbia," OHQ, 1937
Young, F. G. "Ewing Young and His Estate," OHQ, 1920——. "The Oregon
     Trail," OHQ, 1900

IX. THE PROVISIONAL GOVERNMENT AND THE OREGON QUESTION

DeVoto, Bernard. *The Year of Decision: 1846.* Boston, 1943
Dobbs, Caroline. *Men of Champoeg.* Portland, 1932
Greenhow, Robert. *History of Oregon and California.* Boston, 1847
Howison, Lieutenant N. M. *Report on Oregon in 1846.* House Doc. 29, 30th
     Congress, 2nd Session, 1848

* * *

Barry, J. Neilson. "The Champoeg Meeting . . . ," OHQ, 1937
Bradley, Marie. "Political Beginnings in Oregon," OHQ, 1908
Clark, Robert. "Last Steps in Forming a Provisional Government," OHQ, 1915
Holman, F. V. "The Oregon Provisional Government," OHQ, 1912
Merk, Frederick. "British . . . Propaganda and the Oregon Treaty," AHR,
     1934——. "Oregon Pioneers and the Boundary," AHR, 1924
Pike, C. J. "Petitions of the Oregon Settlers," OHQ, 1933
Scott, Leslie. "Modern Fallacies of Champoeg," OHQ, 1931——. "Oregon's Pro-
     visional Government," OHQ, 1929
Shafer, Joseph. "British Attitudes toward Oregon," AHR, 1908——. "Letters of
     Sir George Simpson, 1841-43," AHR, 1911——. "The Oregon Pioneers
     and American Diplomacy" in *Essays in American History,* 1910——.
     "Warre and Vavasour," OHQ, 1909

Shippee, Lester. "The Federal Relations of Oregon," OHQ, 1918, 1919
Thomas, R. B. "Truth and Fiction of the Champoeg Meeting," OHQ, 1929
Van Alstyne, R. W. "International Rivalries in the Pacific Northwest," OHQ, 1945
Young, F. G. "Finances of the Provisional Government," OHQ, 1901

X. TERRITORIAL DAYS

Denny, Arthur. *Pioneer Days on Puget Sound.* Seattle, 1908
Greer, T. T. *Fifty Years in Oregon.* New York, 1912
Hancock, Samuel. *Narrative.* New York, 1927
Leighton, Caroline. *Life at Puget Sound . . . 1865–81.* Boston, 1884
Meeker, Ezra. *Pioneer Reminiscences of Puget Sound: The Tragedy of Leschi.* Seattle, 1905
Prosch, Thomas. *David S. and Catherine T. Maynard.* Seattle, 1906
Settle, Raymond, ed. *The March of the Mounted Riflemen.* Glendale, 1940
Splawn, A. J. *Ka-mi-akin, the Last Hero of the Yakimas.* Portland, 1944
Stevens, Hazard. *The Life of Isaac Ingalls Stevens.* 2 vols. Boston, 1900
Winthrop, Theodore. *The Canoe and the Saddle.* Reprint, Portland, n.d.

* * *

Bagley, C. B. "Mercer Immigration, Two Cargoes of Maidens," OHQ, 1904
Chaffee, E. B. "The Clash Between North and South Idaho over the Capital," PNQ, 1938
Cohn, Samuel. "Martial Law in Washington Territory," PNQ, 1936
Ellison, Joseph. "Designs for a Pacific Republic," OHQ, 1930
Engle, Flora. "Story of the Mercer Expeditions," WHQ, 1915
Galbraith, John. "The British and Americans at Fort Nisqually, 1846–59," PNQ, 1950
Gray, Mary. "Settlement of the Claims . . . of the Hudson's Bay Company," WHQ, 1930
McKay, Charles. "History of San Juan Island," WHQ, 1907, 1908
Murray, Keith. "A Governor's Place in History," PNQ, 1955
Wells, Merle. "Clinton DeWitt Smith, Secretary of Idaho Territory," OHQ, 1951——. "The Creation of Idaho Territory," OHQ, 1951

XI. INDIANS

Brady, Cyrus T. *Northwest Fights and Fighters.* New York, 1909
Browne, J. Ross. *Indian Wars . . .* House Ex. Doc. 38, 35th Congress, 1st Session, 1858 (Also Sen. Ex. Doc. 40, 35th Congress, 1858)
Cram, T. J. *. . . Memoir of the Department of the Pacific, 1855–57.* House Ex. Doc. 114, 35th Congress, 2nd Session, 1859
Defenbach, Byron. *Red Heroines of the Northwest.* Caldwell, Ida., 1935
Drew, C. S. *Account of . . . the Indian Wars in Oregon.* Sen. Misc. Doc. 59, 36th Congress, 1st Session, 1860
Glassley, Ray. *Pacific Northwest Indian Wars.* Portland, 1953
Haines, Francis. *The Nez Percés.* Norman, Okla., 1955
Hodge, F. W., ed. *Handbook of American Indians.* Washington, 1907

Howard, O. O. *My Life and Experiences.* Hartford, 1907——. *Nez Percé Joseph.* Boston, 1881

McWhorter, L. V. *Hear Me, My Chiefs!* Caldwell, Ida., 1952

Mullan, John. *Topographical Memoir of Col. Wright's Campaign.* Sen. Doc. 32, 35th Congress, 2nd Session, 1859

Ronan, Peter. *Historical Sketch of the Flathead Indian Nation.* Helena, 1890

Swan, J. G. *The Northwest Coast.* New York, 1857

Victor, Francis. *The Early Indian Wars of Oregon.* Salem, 1894

Wellman, Paul. *The Indian Wars of the West.* New York, 1954

* * *

Coan, C. H. ". . . Federal Indian Policy in the Pacific Northwest, 1849–52," OHQ, 1921

Haines, Francis. "Nez Percé and Shoshone Influence . . . ," *Greater America,* Berkeley, 1945——. "Problems of Indian Policy," PNQ, 1950——. "Tom Hill, Delaware Scout," *California Historical Quarterly,* 1946

Hare, W. H. "Chief Joseph's Own Story," *North American Review,* 1879

Prosch, Thomas. "The Indian War in Washington," OHQ, 1915

XII. TRANSPORTATION

Albright, George L. *Official Explorations for the Pacific Railroad.* Berkeley, 1921

Bryan, Enoch. *Orient Meets Occident.* Pullman, Wash., 1936

Frederick, J. V. *Ben Holladay: The Stagecoach King.* Glendale, 1940

Gibbon, John M. *Steel of Empire.* Indianapolis, 1935

Hedges, James B. *Henry Villard and the Railways of the Northwest.* New Haven, 1930

Holbrook, Stewart. *James J. Hill.* New York, 1955——. *The Story of American Railroads.* New York, 1947

Jackson, W. Turretine. *Wagon Roads West.* Berkeley, 1952

Josephson, Matthew. *The Robber Barons.* New York, 1934

Mills, Randall V. *Railroads down the Valleys.* Palo Alto, 1950——. *Stern-Wheelers up the Columbia.* Palo Alto, 1947

Moody, John. *The Railroad Builders.* New Haven, 1921

Oberholtzer, Ellis. *Jay Cooke.* 2 vols. Philadelphia, 1907

Quiett, Glen C. *They Built the West.* New York, 1934

Reigel, Robert. *The Story of Western Railroads.* New York, 1926

Reports of Explorations . . . for a Railroad . . . to the Pacific Ocean, Vols. I and XII. Washington, D.C., 1855–60

Smalley, E. V. *History of the Northern Pacific Railroad.* New York, 1883

Villard, Henry. *Memoirs.* 2 vols. Boston, 1904

Villard, Oswald G., ed. *The Early History of Transportation in Oregon.* Eugene, Ore., 1944

* * *

Baker, W. W. "The . . . Walla Walla and Columbia River Railroad," WHQ, 1923

Boyd, William. "The Holladay-Villard Transportation Empire," PHR, 1946

Brown, Arthur. "Promotion of Emigration to Washington Territory," PNQ, 1945

Clarke, S. A. "The Oregon Central Railroad," OHQ, 1906

Elliott, T. C. "The Dalles-Celilo Portage," OHQ, 1915

Ellis, David. "The Oregon and California Land Grant," PNQ, 1948

Ganoe, John. "The . . . Oregon and California Railroad," OHQ, 1924

Gaston, Joseph. "The Genesis of the Oregon Railway System," OHQ, 1906——. "The Oregon Central Railroad," OHQ, 1902

Gill, Frank. "Oregon's First Railway," OHQ, 1924——, and Johansen, Dorothy. "A Chapter in the History of the Oregon Steam Navigation Company," OHQ, 1937, 1938

Gillette, P. N. "The Oregon Steam Navigation Company," OHQ, 1904

Howard, Addison. "Captain John Mullan," WHQ, 1934

Johansen, Dorothy. "The Oregon Steam Navigation Company," PHR, 1941

Meinig, Donald. "Wheat Sacks out to Sea," PNQ, 1954

Mills, Randall V. "A History of Transportation in the Pacific Northwest," OHQ, 1946

Overmeyer, Philip. "Attorney General Williams and the Chief Justiceship," PNQ, 1937——. "George B. McClellan in the Pacific Northwest," PNQ, 1941

Poppleton, Irene. "Oregon's First Monopoly—the OSN Co.," OHQ, 1908

XIII. MINING

Dimsdale, T. J. *The Vigilantes of Montana*. Norman, Okla., 1953

Glasscock, C. B. *The War of the Copper Kings*. New York, 1935

Greenough, W. Earl. *The First 100 Years, Coeur d'Alene . . .* Mullan, Ida., 1947

Langford, N. P. *Vigilante Days and Ways*. Boston, 1890

Mullan, John. *Miners and Travelers' Guide . . .* New York, 1865

Philips, Paul, ed. *Forty Years on the Frontier . . . the Journals and Reminiscences of Granville Stuart*. 2 vols. Cleveland, 1925

Quiett, Glenn C. *Pay Dirt*. New York, 1936

Siringo, Charles. *A Cowboy Detective*. Chicago, 1912

Stoll, William T. *Silver Strike*. Boston, 1932

Stuart, Granville. *Montana as It Is*. New York, 1865

Trimble, William. *The Mining Advance into the Inland Empire*. Madison, Wis., 1914

Jim Wardner of Wardner, Idaho by Himself. New York, 1900

Works Progress Administration. *Copper Camp*. New York, 1943

*   *   *

Edgar, Henry. "Journal," HSM, 1900

Lewis, William, ed., James Watts, "Experiences of a Packer . . . during the Sixties," WHQ, 1928, 1929

Stuart, Granville. "Life of James Stuart," HSM, 1876

Toole, Kenneth Ross. "The Anaconda Copper Mining Company . . . ," PNQ, 1950——. "When Big Money Came to Butte," PNQ, 1953

Underhill, W. M. "Historic Bread Riot in Virginia City," WHQ, 1930
Winner, Dorothy. "Rationing during the Montana Gold Rush," PNQ, 1945
Woody, F. H. "A Sketch of . . . Western Montana," HSM, 1896

XIV. NATURAL RESOURCES

Coman, Edwin, and Gibbs, Helen. *Time, Tide and Timber*. Stanford, 1949
Craig, Joseph, and Hacker, Robert. *The History . . . of the Fisheries of the Columbia River*. Washington, D.C., 1940
Greeley, William B. *Forests and Men*. New York, 1951
Holbrook, Stewart. *Burning an Empire*. New York, 1944
Jensen, Vernon. *Lumber and Labor*. New York, 1945
Lillard, Richard G. *The Great Forest*. New York, 1947
Morgan, Murray. *The Dam*. New York, 1954
Spencer, Betty G. *The Big Blowup*. Caldwell, Ida., 1956
Sundborg, Gus. *Hail, Columbia*. New York, 1954

* * *

Baker, Ray Stannard. "The Great Northwest," *Century Magazine*, 1903
Boening, Rose. ". . . Irrigation in the State of Washington," PNQ, 1918, 1919
Buchanan, Iva. "Lumbering and Logging in Territorial Days," PNQ, 1936
Coulter, Calvin. ". . . National Irrigation in the Yakima Valley," PNQ, 1951
Cox, John H. "Trade Associations in the Lumber Industry," PNQ, 1950
Dill, Clarence C. "Congress, Impressions Before and After Going." Typescript, n.d., Eastern Washington Historical Society, Spokane
Greeley, William B. "It Pays to Grow Trees," PNQ, 1953
Harding, Bruce. "Water from Pend Oreille," PNQ, 1954
"Men, Mills and Timber." Weyerhaeuser Timber Company. Tacoma, 1950
Rabestraw, Lawrence. "Uncle Sam's Forest Reserves," PNQ, 1953

* * *

Annual Reports of the International Pacific Salmon Fisheries Commission, New Westminster, B.C., 1937–1956, esp. Thompson, William, "Effect of the Obstruction at Hell's Gate on the Sockeye Salmon of the Fraser River," 1945
Biennial Reports of the Fish Commission of Oregon. Portland, 1951–1957
Publications of the International Pacific Halibut Commission. Seattle, 1936–1955

XV. RECENT ECONOMICS AND LABOR PROBLEMS

Chaplin, Ralph. *Wobbly*. Chicago, 1948
Freeman, Otis, and Martin, Howard. *The Pacific Northwest*, rev. ed. New York, 1954
McKinley, Charles. *Uncle Sam in the Pacific Northwest*. Berkeley, 1952

* * *

Tobie, H. E. "Oregon Labor Disputes, 1919–23," OHQ, 1947

XVI. LOCAL AND MISCELLANEOUS

Bailey, Robert. *River of No Return.* Lewiston, Ida., 1935

Bird, Annie. *Boise: The Peace Valley.* Caldwell, Ida., 1934

Binns, Archie. *Northwest Gateway.* New York, 1941

Dunbar, Seymour, and Phillips, Paul, eds. Major John Owen, *Journals and Letters*, 2 vols. New York, 1927

Dyar, Ralph. *News for an Empire.* Caldwell, Ida., 1952

Fargo, Lucille. *The Spokane Story.* New York, 1950

Holbrook, Stewart. *Far Corner.* New York, 1952

Kane, Paul. *Wanderings of an Artist.* London, 1859

Lugrin, N. *The Pioneer Women of Vancouver Island.* Vancouver, B.C., 1928

McArthur, Lewis A. *Oregon Geographic Names.* Portland, 1952

Morgan, Murray. *Skid Road.* New York, 1951

Rollensen, John. *Wyoming Cattle Trails.* Caldwell, Ida., 1948

Warren, Sidney. *Farthest Frontier.* New York, 1949

Wilkes, Charles. *Narrative of the United States Exploring Expedition*, Vols. IV and V. Philadelphia, 1845

Index

Aberdeen, Lord, and Oregon dispute, 252, 256

Abernethy, Gov., 257; and Joe Meek, 265–66

Across the Wide Missouri (De Voto), 155

Adams, Thomas, 193, 196, 199

Adventure (schooner), 42, 43, 47

Adventures on the Columbia (Cox), 142, 157

Ainsworth, John C., and Northern Pacific, 354; and OSN, 345–49, 352, 353, 357; as steamboat owner, 343–44

Alaska, acquired by U.S., 325; islands off, 40; Russian fur trade in, 83; Spain takes over, 15–16

Alaska Commercial Company, and seals, 400; on settlers, 402

Aleutian Islands, 11, 19, 103; sea otters, 13–14

Aleuts, Russian exploitation of, 13–14

Amalgamated Copper, 408

American Board of Commissioners for Foreign Missions, 157, 165, 174, 175, 215, 219; Whitman visits, 223

American Federation of Labor, 420–21

American Forks, 334

American Fur Company, 83, 156, 166

American Society for Encouraging the Settlement of the Oregon Territory, 142, 143

Anaconda (city), 394

Anaconda (mine), and Daly, 392–99; and French syndicate, 393, 394; and Heinze, 407

Anderson, Reece (Rezin), at Gold Creek, 335; and Stuart brothers, 331, 333

Applegate, Charles, 229

Applegate, Jesse, and Abernethy, 226n.; Great Emigration of, 228–37; and Gaston, 356; and Old South Road Company, 254; on Oregon constitution, 242, 247–48; on settlers, 227; in Umpqua Valley, 271; withdraws from West Side Company, 357

Applegate, Lindsay, 229, 235–36; in Cali-

fornia, 271–72; and Old South Road, 254; and Oregon caravan, 224

Astor, John Jacob, 54, 99; career of, 82–84; efforts of to supply Astoria, 102; and restitution of Astoria, 108; settlements of, 88–90; and Treaty of Ghent, 109

Astoria, 32, 96, 97; Astor's efforts to supply, 102; British take, 105; North West Company occupies, 104; settlement of, 88; threat to, 99

Astorians, 84–92; expeditions of, 94–98; and Indians, 100–1; and North West Company, 98–106; and *Tonquin*, 92–93

Athabaska district, 53–54, 55, 117; Pass, 86, 91, 110, 113, 121

Atkinson, George Henry, and wheat, 347–48

Attoo, 36, 37, 39; desertion of, 40, 42

Baer, Harry, 389–90, 404

Bailey, Dr. William J., 164–65, 187–89, 201

Bannack Indians, gold discovery on lands of, 330; raids of, 373

Bear River, 113, 126, 161; valley of, 99

Beaver (trading ship), 90, 97, 101, 103, 171–72

Beaver, Rev. Herbert, 179–80

Beaver pelts, and trade war, 136–37

Benetsee, 331, 332

Benton, Thomas Hart, 114, 115

Bering, Vitus, 8–12

Billings, Frederick, reorganizes Northern Pacific, 377; and Villard, 378–79

Black, Capt., 105, 108

Blackfeet Indians, 69, 70, 75, 94, 123, 124, 126; peace treaties, 303; and Stevens, 289–90

Blanchet, Father, 190, 207

Blue Mountains, 96, 106, 113, 128

Boise, as capital, 340–43; as fort, 162–63, 330

Boise River, gold near, 330; irrigation canals in, 435–36

Boit, John, 39, 43, 47–48; on Columbia River, 45–46; journal of, 40–46

Bonneville, Benjamin de, 148n., 152, 168, 182
Bonneville Dam, 442; and salmon, 427–28
Bonneville Power Administration, 443–45
Box houses, 403–5
Bradford brothers, 344–46
Bridger, Jim, 167, 169, 218
British Columbia, 97, 114, 131; as crown colony, 319–20; political dilemma of, 325. See also New Caledonia
Bromfield Street Church, 153, 158–59
Broshear, Catherine, 283, 286
Broughton, Lt. W. R., 43, 48, 122
Bryant, William Cullen, 6, 399
Bulfinch's Harbor, 44
Bunker, Hill & Sullivan, 390, 396–97
Burlington Railroad, 411–12
Burnett, Peter, 224, 228, 235
Burns, Jane, 107–8
Butte, mining fortunes in, 391; prosperity in, 403

California, British posts in, 203; Drake in, 2, 3; gold rush to, 270 ff.; Hudson Bay Company penetrates, 134; trade routes from, 349
California and Columbia River Railroad Company, 356
California, Oregon & Mexican Steamship Company, 350
California and Oregon Railroad Company, 356
Canada, boundary of, 91; ceded to England, 53; early growth of, 318, 325; expeditions to, 5; Napoleon's designs on, 64
Canadian Pacific Railroad, 91; east-west crossing, 403; and Heinze, 406; and Hill, 384
Carey Act, 434–35
Cariboo, settlement of, 323–24
Cariboo Road, 324
Carmichael, Lawrence, 183–88
Carson, Kit, 145; and Tom Hill, 257, 261
Carver, Jonathan, 6, 43, 56
Cascades, 96; canal built at, 398; portages at, 344; wagon trail across, 254
Casey, Lt. Col. Silas, 308, 311
Cattle, drives of, 184–86, 229, 235, 374–75; importance of in Northwest, 190
Cayuse Indians, 113, 156; and measles epidemic 261; and Nez Percé peace plan, 264; Oregon army subdues, 266, 273; and settlers, 260
Celilo Falls, 97, 343, 344; Indian fisheries at, 429
Central Pacific Railroad, 359; and Union Pacific, 356
Champoeg, 183, 240–42
Charbonneau, Toussaint, 66, 67

Chase, Salmon P., 355, 360, 361
Chatham (tender), 43, 48
Chicago, Milwaukee & St. Paul, 412, 418
Chinook Indians, 72–73, 88, 165, 170, 179; jargon of, 298, 299
Clapp, William, 439–40
Clark, William, 55–56; expedition of, 65–76; journal of 71–74
Clark-McNary Act, 419
Clarke, John, 97–101, 104
Clarke, William Andrews, buys legislative seats, 407–8; and Daly, 392–94, 407–8; and Heinze, 407–9; runs for Senate, 394–95; sells out, 409
Clatsop, Fort, 52, 73
Clatsop Indians, 73
Clayoquot Sound, 26, 39, 40, 42, 43
Clearwater River, 71, 74, 95, 98, 99, 169
Coeur d'Alene, as mining center, 393; mission at, 293
Coeur d'Alene Executive Miners' Union, 396–97
Coeur d'Alene Indians, and Stevens, 305–6; and Steptoe, 313–14
Columbia, 23ff.; as first American ship to circumnavigate globe, 36
Columbia Basin Commission, 441
Columbia Basin Irrigation League, 441
Columbia Department, 107–9, 114 ff.; changes in, 249–51. See also Astoria; George, Fort.
Columbian Emigration Society, 323–24
Columbia River, Astor's right to, 83–84; debate over, 245–46; Gray's discovery of, 45; Great Bends of, 86; lands north of, 246; Lewis & Clark explore, 72; steamboat traffic on, 343 ff.; Thompson reaches, 77, 91
Columbia and Western Railroad, 406
Colvile, Andrew, 117, 154
Colvile, Fort, 122, 136, 194; gold near, 304
Cook, Capt. James, 16–20, 44, 56; journal of, 21–22
Cooke, Jay, 353–55, 360, 362, 377
Coolidge, David, 25, 34
Corbin, Daniel, 390, 393; and Heinze, 406
Couch, Capt. John, 197n., 271
Cox, Ross, 142, 157
Craig, William, 218, and Nez Percés, 303, 306, 307
Cram, Capt. T. J., on Stevens' Indian Council, 301–3; on Tule Lake ambush, 279
Crew, C. S., on Tule Lake ambush, 279
Crooks, Ramsay, 94–97, 97n.
Cuadra, Juan Francisco, 15–16, 21, 46–48
Curry, Gov. George, calls for volunteers, 305; and Gen. Wool, 307–8; and Col. Wright, 310

Dallas, Alexander Grant, and Douglas, 320; and Griffin-Cutler dispute, 321

Dalles, The (city), 344

Dalles, the (rapids), 91, 137, 138; canal around, 411; Clark on, 343–44; Oregon emigrants at, 253–54; portages at, 344; settlements in, 192, 193, 200; Thompson on, 344

Dalles Dam, and Indian fisheries, 429

Daly, Marcus, and Anaconda, 392–99, 408; and Clarke, 392, 395, 407–8; and fight for state capital, 395; and Ontario mine, 391

Dart, Anson, and land treaties, 276–77

Davis, Jefferson, and Stevens, 288, 290, 295–96

Desert Land Act of 1877, 434

DeVoto, Bernard, 155

Discovery (sloop), 16, 17, 20, 43, 48

Disque, Col. Brice, and the 4L, 421–22

Dobbs, Arthur, company of, 5, 12

Dolly (schooner), 90, 93, 105

Dominis, Capt., 137, 143, 150, 157

Donation Land Law, 274–77

Dorion, Marie, 74, 96, 106

Dorion, Pierre, 94, 106

Douglas, James, 178, 201; Alaskan expedition of, 202–3; California expedition of, 203–4; and Cariboo Road, 324; character of, 320; in command, 215; and criticism of McLoughlin, 249–50; and death of McLoughlin's son, 213–14; and discovery of gold, 318–19; and dispute over boundary, 317–18; and Fort Vancouver, 246; as governor, 319–25; and Hudson Bay Company, 315; knighted, 325; in Oregon government, 248

Douglas, Capt. William, 27–37

Drake, Sir Francis, 1, 2, 3, 7, 21

Dreamer cult, the, 368–70

East India Company, 20, 27, 62, 83, 109

East Side Company (Oregon Central Railroad), 357–60

Edgerton, Sidney, 338–40

Edwards, Philip, 186–87, 193, 226

Eells, Cushing, 195, 215, 234

Elliott, Simon G., 357–60; and California & Columbia River Railroad, 356

England, American colonies war with, 21; dispute about Northwest Passage in, 16; as dominant force in North America, 5–6; and Spanish claims to Nootka, 34 ff. *See also* Great Britain

Ermatinger, Francis, 151–53, 160; Flathead brigade of, 194

European and Oregon Land Company, and Holladay, 360, 362; and Villard, 363

Finlay, Jacques (Jocko), 81, 87

Fire, destruction wrought by, 415–16; in Northwest, 417–19

Fisgard (frigate), 253

Fisk, Dr. Wilbur, 157–58, 170

Fitzpatrick, Thomas, Indian treaties of, 289; and De Smet, 291

Flathead Indians, 70, 91, 98, 101, 152–63, 167, 168; brigade of, 194; peace treaties of, 303

Flathead Post, 124–28, 152

Florez, Viceroy, 31, 33, 37

Florida, 6, 64; U.S. purchases, 115

Floyd, John, 114–15

Forest Lien Act of 1897, 410–11

Franchère, Gabriel, 93–94, 105

Fraser, Simon, 77; expedition of, 79–81; on Mackenzie, 79–80

Fraser River, 47, 59, 61, 80, 104, 131; discovery of gold on, 318–19; as salmon stream, 430–31, 433; transportation problems, 322. *See also* Tacoutche-Tesse

Freemen, 123–24

Frémont, John Charles, 230–33

French, Peter, 372–73, 398

French Canadians, 123, 126, 128, 150, 151; and Oregon self-government, 241–42

French Prairie, 151, 162

Friendly Cove, 26, 27, 31, 32, 34, 35, 42, 46, 49

Forty-ninth parallel, as boundary, 204, 317–18

Fuca, Juan de, 4–6; Strait of, 5, 14, 17, 25, 26, 44

Furs, Chinese reaction to, 20; importance of to Bering's men, 11; importance of in Siberia, 7–8; King on, 20–21; trade, 19, 36, 53

Funter, Robert, 29–33

Gaines, John P., 273, 285

Gale, Joseph, 205–6

Gantt, John, 231, 233

Gaston, Joseph, 356–59

George, Fort, 80, 105, 107, 115, 121, 122, 125. *See also* Astoria

Gerry, Spokane, 155, 194, 292

Gertrúdis (sloop), 33, 35. *See also North West America*

Gervais, Joseph, 193, 240–41

Goethals, Gen. George, 441

Goetz, Dutch Jake, 389–90, 404–5

Gold, in California, 270 ff.; effect of discovery of on Indians, 278; on Fraser River, 318–22; in Klondike, 399–401

Golden Hind (Drake's ship), 1, 2, 7

Gordon, Sir John, 252–53

Grand Coulee Dam, history of, 439–43; purpose of, 427–28; and salmon, 427–28

Grange, the, 355

Grant, Pres. Ulysses S., and Nez Percés, 369; and Northern Pacific Railroad, 380

Gray, Robert, 24–37; and Cuadra, 46–47; discovers Columbia River, 62; second expedition of, 39–47

Gray, William, 176–80; fired, 219, 221–22; at Lapwai, 194–95, 215; and Oregon self-government, 241

Great Britain, accepts 49th parallel boundary, 256; in dispute over Oregon, 250 ff.; and Hudson's Bay Company, 182; in Northwest, 225; Northwest claims of, 115–23, 130; at war with U.S., 91

Great Northern Railway, and Hill, 383, 409; and Southern Pacific, 412; and Union Pacific, 411

Great Northern Steamship Company, 410

Griffin, Charles, 318, 321

Gurley (Elizabeth Gurley Flynn), 420–21

Hall, Fort, 161, 163, 165, 170, 173, 176, 177, 193, 221

Hanna, James, 26, 49

Harney, Gen. William 321–22

Haro, Gonzalo López de, 30, 31

Harrison, Pres. Benjamin, 394

Haswell, Robert, 24, 25; log of, 30

Hastings, Lansford, 221, 241n.

Hearst, George, and Daly, 391, 392, 395

Heceta, Bruno, 15, 21, 25, 46; river of, 17

Heinze, Frederick (Fritz), and apex law, 406–7; builds railroad, 406; career of, 405; and Clarke, 407; fights Standard Oil, 408–9

Helena, as Montana's capital, 340, 395

Henry, Alexander, 53, 54, 83

Henry, Alexander, the younger, 104, 104n.; journal of, 107

Henry, Andrew, 78, 94

Henry, William, 86

Hilgard, Heinrich. See Villard, Henry

Hill, James Jerome, and Burlington Railroad, 411–12; buys into Northern Pacific, 409; and Great Northern Railway, 383–85; and lumber industry, 410–13

Hill, Tom, 257–61

Hipple. See Mitchell, Sen. John

Holladay, Ben, 349–50; lawsuits against, 360; and Mercer, 352; and Oregon Central, 358–60; in politics, 361; as robber baron, 360; and steamships, 352; and Villard, 363–64

Hope (brig), 39n., 40, 46

Howard, Gen. O. O., and Bannacks, 373; and Nez Percés, 370–72

Hudson, Capt. Thomas, 31, 34, 35

Hudson's Bay Company, 5, 53, 54, 62; Americans challenge, 247; California settlement, 203; combines with North West Company, 114; demotes Mc-

Loughlin, 249–51; dispute with U.S., 317–18; feud with North West Company, 109–14; fur trade, 400; and Great Britain, 182–84; loses trading rights, 319; and Oregon constitution, 245; and Russian-American Fur Company, 198; sells out, 325; settlers' opinion of, 225, 238; withdraws to Fort Victoria, 315

Hunt, Wilson Price, 94–106

Idaho, divided, 340; early violence in, 338; statehood, 394; as territory, 337

Indian council, at Walla Walla, 300–3

Indian fisheries, 428–29

Indian lands, homesteading on, 413

Indians, aid Mackenzie, 57–59; and Astorians, 100–1; and Christianity, 153–54; debauchery of, 81–82; Fitzpatrick's treaties with, 289; and Gov. Lane, 272–74; and Gray, 25, 42, 44–45; Kendrick's treatment of, 41–42; lack of success in domesticating, 218 ff.; and land treaties, 276–77, 280–81; Ledyard's impression of, 17–18; and massacre of Whitmans, 262–63; Palmer's treaties with, 296; religious dilemma of, 258–59; and resentment of settlers, 260; Spaulding's report on, 220; Stevens' treaties with, 289–90; and U. S. Government, 259, 297–98, 304, 307, 313; in Willamette Valley, 191–92

Industrial Workers of the World (IWW), 420. See also Wobblies

Ingraham, Joseph, 33, 47; as captain of the Hope, 39n., 40, 46

Inland Empire, 347–48

International Pacific Salmon Fisheries Commission, 432–33

Iphigenia Nubiana, 27–37

Iroquois Indians, 83, 85, 87, 110, 112, 125, 154

Isaac Todd, 99, 101–8

Ives, George, 339–40

Jefferson, Thomas, 22, 54–55; as President, 52; purchases Louisiana, 63; as Secretary of State, 38–39

Jessaume, René, 66, 67

Jewitt, John, 49–52, 73

Jones, Sen. Wesley, and land reclamation, 437–38; and irrigation survey, 441

Joseph, Old, and Nez Percés, 368–69

Joseph, Young, 369–72

Juan Fernandez Island, 29, 32, 105

Kamchatka, 20, 22; peninsula of, 8–12

Kamiah, mission at, 195, 215

Kamiakin, Chief, 300, 304, 309–10

Kansas Pacific Railroad, 363

Keith, James, 108 ff., 136

Kelley, Hall Jackson, 141–48, 157, 164, 182

Kellogg, Noah, 389–90
Kendrick, John, voyages of, 24–43, 47
King, Lt. James, 20–21
Klamath Indians, 277; and Modocs, 365–66
Klickitat Indians, and Gov. Lane, 273–74
Kootenae House, 78, 79
Kootenai River, 81, 82, 87; Thompson explores, 79
Kootenay Indians, 77, 98, 101
Kullyspell House, 81, 87

Ladd, William, and OSN, 346, 353, 357
Lady Washington. See Washington
Laframboise, Michael, 145, 146
Lake Superior mines, 392–93
Lancaster, Columbia, 285, 295–96
Lane, Joseph, as congressional delegate, 277, 280–81; as governor of Oregon, 267–68, 272–74; and Oregon statehood, 312–13; and petition for Oregon split, 286; retirement of, 315; and Rogue Indians, 277, 280–81; second term as governor, 280; and Stevens, 289, 296, 312
Langley, Fort, 122, 131, 132, 134, 136
Lapwai, mission at, 180, 193–95, 215, 218; closed, 219; reopened, 223; warned of Indians, 263
Lark (astor ship), 102, 103, 106
Last Chance Gulch. See Helena
Lausanne (charter ship), 199–201, 220
Lawyer, Chief, and discovery of gold, 327–29; and Stevens, 301–3
Lee, Anna Maria (Mrs. Jason), 193
Lee, Daniel, 158, 162, 168, 192; at Dalles, 193, 200
Lee, Jason, Board investigates, 243; death of, 243, expansion plans of, 191–200; missionary work of, 147, 153, 158–63; settlements of, 200–1; and Wilkes, 206; and Willamette debate, 239–40
Ledyard, John, 16–19, 21–22, 54; heirs of, 23 ff.; and Jefferson, 63
Lewis, Meriweather, 63–64; early life of, 65–76; expedition of, 65 ff.; journal of, 66–73. See also Lewis and Clark
Lewis and Clark, 32, 52; expedition of, 65–76, 83
Lewiston, town of, 337; as capital, 341
Liberal League, and Prichard, 387–89
Linn, Sen., and bills for Oregon Territory, 196, 220, 225, 230
Long, George, and forest-fire legislation, 416; and tree farms, 424
Loriot (brig), 181, 182–86
Louisiana, 6, 64; purchase of, 39, 63
Lovejoy, A. L. 221–23
Loyal Legion of Loggers and Lumbermen (4L), 421–22
Lucier, Étienne, 193; and Oregon self-government, 242

Lumber industry, economics of, 419–20; in Northwest, 410–13; organization of, 422–23; and sustained-yield lumbering, 423–24; and tree farms, 424
Lydia (brig), 51–52; fails to meet Lewis and Clark, 73, 74
Lyon, Caleb, as governor, 341, 342–43

Mackenzie, Alexander, 55, 64, 66, 114; Arctic trips of, 55–56; explorations of, 48 ff.; Fraser on, 79–80; journal of, 62; knighted, 63; second expedition of, 56–61
Mackenzie, Roderick, 55, 57–61
Manifest Destiny, 141, 226
Maquilla. See Maquinna
Maquinna, 28, 42, 44; massacres Boston crew, 49–51
Martínez Don Estévan José, 30, 31, 41–42, 49; claims Nootka, 34; expedition of, 31–39; theft of spoons from, 15
Mason, Charles, 296, 304, 305, 308
May Dacre (brig), 158, 160, 162, 164
Maynard, David, 283–84, 286
McClellan, George, 289, 293–95
McClellan, Robert, 94, 95, 97, 97n.
McDonald, Finan, 78, 81, 87, 90, 124
McDougal, Duncan, 84, 88, 89, 93, 99–106
McGillivray, Douglas, 66, 67n.; and Thompson, 77
McKay, Alexander, death of, 119; explorations of, 57 ff., 84, 90, 92, 93
McKay, Marguerite Wadon, 119
McKay, Thomas, 119 n., 160–62, 193
McKenzie, Donald, explorations of, 84, 93–101, 103–6, 110–13, 123, 161
McLeod, Alexander, 133, 134
McLoughlin, John, on agriculture, 189–90; aids Great Emigration, 236–37; and American settlers, 245; and American trappers, 136–39; and Applegate, 247–48; and Rev. Beaver, 179–80; and California expansion, 203; and Columbia, district, 118 ff.; and Douglas, 202–3; and Fort Vancouver, 122, 246; on fur trade, 172–73; and Hudson's Bay Company, 249–51; and Indians, 131–33; and Kelley, 146–48; and Lee, 192; loses position, 215; and North West Company, 118–20; and Northwest settlers, 149, 152, 162, 163, 170, 178; and Oregon constitution, 242–43; and Puget Sound Agricultural company, 198–99, 201; and Simpson, 209, 211–12, 249; and Slacum, 182–85; and Thurston, 275–76; and trade monopoly, 238; and Varney, 208–9; vindicates son's death, 213–14; and Willamette Falls claims, 239–45, 249–51
McLoughlin, John, Jr., 202, 204; murder of, 211

McTavish, Donald, 107
McTavish, John George, 91–92, 97, 99, 101, 102
McTavish, Simon, 62, 66
Meares, John, 26, 28, 29, 34, 36, 44, 47, 56; *Memorial* of, 37–39; *Voyages* of, 39, 44
Meek, Joe, 174, 217; census of, 253; and daughter, 218, 263; and Oregon self-government, 242; Washington commission of, 265–68
Menzies, Alexander, 43, 61
Mercer, Ada, and Mercer girls, 350–52
Methodists, in Oregon, 191–97, 242–43
Mexico, 4, 6, 14, 116, 127; and Texas, 182; war of, 261, 267. *See also* New Spain; Spain
Miller, Joseph, 94, 97, 97n.
Mine Owners' Protective Association, 396–97
Mining, apex law of, 406–7; violence in camps of, 336, 338–40
Missions, importance of, 153–62, 191–92, 196–97
Missouri River, 99; basin of, 64; headwaters of, 126; upper, 68
Missouri-to-Columbia road, 313
Mitchell, Sen. John H., 361–62
Modeste (warship), 252, 253, 255
Modoc Indians, 277; and gold rush, 278; and Klamath Indians, 365–66; retreat of, 366–67; punishment of, 367–68; at Tule Lake, 279
Mojave Desert, 145
Mojave Indians, 133, 138
Monroe, James, and Monroe Doctrine, 115; on *status quo* doctrine, 108
Montana, achieves statehood, 394; as territory, 340
Mullan, John, and Indian uprisings, 314–15; and Missouri-to-Columbia road, 313, 332–33; and Stevens' survey, 293, 295–96

National Industrial Recovery Act, and lumber industry, 422
New Albion, 3, 17. *See also* California
New Caledonia, 79, 90, 104, 114, 116, 131. *See also* British Columbia
Newell, Robert "Doc," 217; on Oregon government, 240; and wagons, 218, 220
Newlands Act of 1902, 436
New Spain, and Russian exploitation, 14. *See also* Mexico; Spain
Nez Percés, The (Haines), 155
Nez Percé Indians, 91, 98, 152–63, 167, 168; bloodshed of, 370; and discovery of gold, 327–29; peace of with Blackfeet, 303; peace plan of, 264; protect Spaldings, 264; and Steptoe, 313; and Stevens, 301–3, 307; and Tom Hill, 258, 260; villages of, 71–74, 111; and Walla Walla

council, 368–70
Nez Percé, Fort, 111, 113, 124, 128, 138
Nipissing Indians, 85, 87
Nisqually, Fort, 138, 190, 192, 201
Nootka Island, 15, 17–19, 22, 26, 54; abandoned by Spain and England, 49
Nootka Sound, 17, 21, 22, 26, 27, 31; Spain claims, 34–46
Nootka Sound Convention, 38
Northern Pacific Railroad, under Billings, 378; buys out Corbin, 390; buys out local lines, 396; charter of, 353; and Coeur d'Alene mine, 388; fails, 355–56, 398; Harriman almost seizes, 411; and Hill, 383–87; and Jay Cooke, 354–55; junction of, 380; lumber on land of, 410–11; reorganized, 377; Villard buys, 379; and Yakima Valley line, 381–82
Northern Pacific, Yakima, and Kittitas Irrigation Company, 436–37
Northwest, boom for statehood in, 393–94; Indian uprisings in, 304–5; and panic of 1873, 395–99; Spanish claims to, 115; weather of, 2
North West America (sloop), 29–37
North West Fur Company, and Astor, 84 ff.; and Astorians, 97–101; buys Pacific Fur Company, 105; combines with Hudson's Bay Company, 114; and Hudson's Bay Company, 53–55, 75–77; and Mackenzie, 62; and Treaty of Ghent, 109; and XY Company, 66, 67n.
Northwest Passage, 1, 3, 8, 16 ff., 44
NRA lumber code, provisions of, 423

Ogden, Peter Skene, 122, 125–29; builds post, 251–52; in command, 215, 249–50; journal of, 127–29, 138–39; rescues captives, 264–65; and Russian-American Fur Company, 198–200
Okanogan, post at, 96, 97, 101, 121
Okanogan River, 91, 93, 131
Olmstead, Harrison, 344–46
Oregon, constitution of, 242–48; effect of gold rush on, 271; feud over capital of, 285; Haswell's impression of, 24–25; isolation of, 269–70; missions in, 191–200; and petition for entrance into U.S., 192–93, 196–97, 220; politics in, 237–48; proposed split of, 285–86; self-government in, 248; settlement of, 141 ff., 223–37; statehood of, 312–15; as territory, 267–68
Oregon and California Railroad, 359–63; Southern Pacific buys, 382
Oregon Central Railroad, land grant to, 357; East Side Company of, 357–60; and Gaston, 356; West Side Company of, 357–59
Oregon City, capital removed from, 271; dispute over, 249–51; founding of, 239–

45; rump parliament meets at, 285. *See also* Willamette Falls

Oregon Provisional Emigration Society, 197, 199

Oregon Railway and Navigation Company, 377 ff.; and Hill, 386; and Northern Pacific, 378–79; policy conflicts in, 352; and Villard, 381

Oregon Short Line, 379

Oregon Steamship Company, 360, 363

Oregon Steam Navigation Company (OSN), and Ainsworth, 345–46; and animal transport, 347, 349; buys Walla Walla Railroad, 365; competitors of, 348; and Holladay, 352; launches *Wide West*, 374; minority stockholders bought out, 353; and Northern Pacific, 355–56; and Oregon Central, 357; and Villard, 381

Oregon system, 399

Oregon and Transcontinental, buys into Northern Pacific, 383; policy conflicts in, 381; and Villard, 379–81, 383

Owen, Fort, 291–93

Owhyhee (brig), 136, 137, 150, 157

Pacific Fur Company, 84, 101; sold to North West Company, 105

Pacific Northwest, 1, 5; claims to, 130 ff.; Drake's impression of, 2; Spain takes possession of, 15. *See also* Northwest

Pacific Ocean, 21; rights to, 1; role of in trade, 54; Russia's drive to, 7–16; search for water passage to, 5–6

Palmer, Joel, in British Columbia, 323; Indian treaties of, 296; and Stevens' Indian council, 300–3; at Table Rock, 280; withdraws from West Side Company, 357

Parker, Samuel, 165–72, 177, 178

Peace of Paris, terms of, 6, 53

Peace River, 56–58, 61, 62, 77, 131; Canyon, 57

Peel, Sir Robert, 252, 256

Peel, William, 251–53, 256

Pelly, Gov. J. H., 190–91

Pelly, Kootenay, 155

Pend Oreille, gravity system, 441–42

Pend Oreille Lake, 81, 82, 87

People's Transportation Company, Holladay buys, 360; and OSN, 348

Pérez, Juan, 17; explorations of, 14–15, 31

Peu-peu-mox-mox, death of, 306; and son's murder, 259–60; second trip of, 261

Piegan Indians, 75, 78; and Thompson, 82, 85

Pierce, Elias, 327–29

Pierre's Hole, 148, 169; Indian conclave at, 291

Pilcher, Joshua, 135–36, 142–43

Pinchot, Gifford, 416–19

Pittman, Anna Maria, 188. *See also* Lee, Anna Maria

Plummer, Henry, 338–40

Polk, Pres. James K., and Oregon, 249, 252, 256, 267–68

Pond, Peter, 53–55, 83

Portland, freight war in, 382; settlement of, 271

Possessory rights, attraction of, 210, 224–25; lack of in Vancouver, 316

Prentiss, Narcissa, 166, 168. *See also* Whitman, Narcissa

Prevost, Comm. James B., 108, 111

Prichard, Andrew J., and Coeur d'Alene mine, 387; and Liberal League, 387–89

Puget Mill Company, 286

Puget Sound, 47, 116, 130, 132, 134, 137, 204; American settlers in, 245–46

Puget Sound Agricultural Company, 198–200, 315, 316; Red River emigrants desert, 238

Puget Sound Indians, 92; and Stevens, 296–97

Quesnel, Jules, 80

Rae, William Glen, tragedy of, 202, 204, 214

Railroads, congressional favors to Northern Pacific, 325; urgent need for, 375 ff. *See also* names of railroads

Reclamation Act, 437–38

Red Mountain Railway, 406

Red River, 109–10; colony at, 210; and emigrants to Willamette Valley, 238

Red River Transportation Company, 383–84

Reed, John, fate of, 106; and McKenzie, 94–97; and trappers, 98–101

Reed, Simeon, buys Bunker Hill and Sullivan mine, 390; and Canadian Pacific, 384; and Gaston, 359; and OSN, 346, 349, 353, 357

Regulator Line, and Hill, 411–12

River of the West, 6, 43, 60, 60n.

Rocky Mountain Fur Company, 153, 160

Rogue Indians, and Gov. Lane, 273–74, 277, 280–81; Palmer's treaties with, 296; war of, 305

Rogue River Valley, settlements in, 254–55

Roosevelt, Pres. F. D., and irrigation dams, 442 ff.

Roosevelt, Pres. Theodore, and forest conservation, 416

Ross, Alexander, 97, 113, 122, 124–26; journal of, 107n., 111, 112

Ross, Fort, abandonment of, 198; Russian post at, 84, 190

Ruckel, Col. J. S. 344–46

Rupert's Land, 318, 325

Russia, and Alaska, 115; and Astor, 83–84, 97, 102; and Ogden, 138; in Siberia, 7 ff.; treaty of with China, 7–8

Russian-American Fur Company, 190; agreement of with Hudson's Bay Company, 198; and Astor, 83–84; and Hudson's Bay Company, 400

Sacajawea, 67–69

St. Louis, Indians visit, 155; trade route from, 143, 148, 151, 153

St. Paul, Minneapolis and Manitoba Railroad, 383

St. Paul and Pacific Railroad, 383

Salem, Oregon, 163; as capital, 271, 285

Salish Indians, Thompson on, 81. *See also* Flathead Indians

Salmon, 72, 87; industry, 424–33; trade in, 139, 143

San Francisco, founding of, 14; under Mexican rule, 116

San Idlefonso, treaty of, 64

San Juan Islands, 132; dispute over, 321–22; and salmon fishing, 430–31; strategic importance of, 317–18

San Roque River, 15, 25. *See also* Columbia River

Saxton, Lt. Rufus, and Stevens' survey, 289, 290, 292

Scurvy, Cook's treatment for, 16; treatments for, 39

Seals, pelagic hunting of, 400–1

Sea otter, exploitation, 12–14, 17–21; extermination of, 136; trade, 23, 27, 40, 49, 54

Seattle, as gold town, 402–3; great fire in, 394; settlement of, 283–84

Seattle, Lake Shore and Eastern Railroad, 386

Seattle and Montana Railroad, 386

Seattle and Walla Walla Railroad, 376–77

Selkirk, Lord, 109, 114

Shaw, Benjamin, and Indians, 298, 308; and Stevens, 311

Shepard, Cyril, 170, 188, 191, 197; death of, 201

Sherman Silver Purchase Act of 1890, 396–97

Siberia, explorations in, 7–8; Ledyard in, 22

Silver spoons, 18, 31, 34. *See also* Nootka

Simmons, Michael, and Indians, 295, 298, 299; in Oregon self-government, 248, 286; and sister, 283, 286; and Tumwater Falls, 245–46, 281–82

Simpson, George, on California expedition, 203; crosses continent, 209–10; and Hudson Bay fur trade, 114, 116–24; and

Indians, 154–55; journal of, 120; letter of, 190–91; and McLoughlin, 209, 211–14, 249–51; and McLoughlin, Jr., 202; on Oregon missionaries, 197–98; and Puget Sound Agricultural Company, 198–200; and Stevens, 289; visits Columbia, 130–39; and Wyeth, 150–52

Slacum, William, 193, 196; and Lee, 182–86; and McLoughlin, 181

Smet, Pierre-Jean de, and Fort Owen, 291–92; mission of, 222

Smith, Asa, fired, 219; at Kamiah, 195, 215

Smith, DeWitt, 341–42

Smith, Jackson & Sublette, 133, 135, 143

Smith, Jedediah, 142, 193; and Ogden, 125–27; testimony of, 135–36; at Vancouver, 133–36

Snake Indians, 69, 111–13, 123–26; brigade of, 123, 125, 138; exploitation of, 110, 129

Southern Pacific Railroad 379, 382

South Sea Company, 27, 62

Spain, claims of to Northwest, 34 ff., 115; holds Nootka, 41; and Louisiana, 64; rights of in Pacific, 1

Spalding, Eliza, 173 ff., 257–58

Spalding, Henry Harmon, fired, 219; at Lapwai, 194–95, 215; and Nez Percé peace plan, 264; reinstated, 223; rescued, 265; and Tom Hill, 257–58; trip with Whitman, 262; and Waiilatpu massacre, 263; and Whitman, 173–81, 234

Spaulding, Capt. Josiah, 199, 201, 204; report of on Indians, 220

Splawn, Jack, and Cariboo, 323

Spokane, great fire in, 394; mining trade in, 403

Spokane, Portland and Seattle Railroad, 411

Spokane Indians, and Stevens, 305–6; and Steptoe, 313–14

Status quo ante bellum, doctrine of, 108; renewed, 130

Steptoe, Col. E. J., 312–14

Stevens, Isaac Ingalls, and boundary dispute, 318; Columbia route of, 308; as delegate, 312; early career of, 287–88; family of, 296–97; as first governor, 286; and Gen. Wool, 307–9; and Indians, 289–90, 296–303, 315; and Indian uprisings, 305 ff.; and Muckleshoot farmers, 310–11; and Oregon statehood, 312–13; retirement of, 315; and second Indian council, 311–12; survey of, 289–96

Stevens, John L., 385–86

Stewart, Sir William, 160, 164, 167, 174

Stikine, Fort, 202; disaster at, 212–14

Stuart, David, 84, 88; and Astor, 92, 93, 96–98, 101

Stuart, Granville, 331, 342

Stuart, James, 331; in Deer Lodge, 333; as sheriff, 334

Stuart, John, and New Caledonia, 80, 90, 104, 131

Stuart, Robert, 84; and Astor, 88, 89, 93, 96–98

Sublette, William, 148, 148n., 151, 160

Tacoutche-Tesse, 59, 62, 79. See also Fraser River

Thompson, David, 66, 154; early life of, 76–77; expeditions of, 81–82, 84–88, 90, 92; map of, 76; in northern Saskatchewan, 75–79

Thompson, Robert R., and OSN, 344, 345, 353, 357

Thorn, Capt. Jonathan, 89–90, 92

Thornton, J. Quinn, 257, 265

Thurston, Samuel R., 274, 275–77

Timber and Stone Act of 1878, 398–99

Tonquin (Astor ship), 84, 89, 119, 146; destruction of, 92–93

Tree farms, 424–25

Tshimakain, mission at, 195, 215, 219, 234

Tudor, Frederic, 143, 173 n.

Turner, John, and Oregon settlers, 135, 164, 187, 193

Umpqua Indians, 277; Palmer's treaties with, 296

Unalaska Island, 14, 19, 31

United States, 28, 38, 39; boundary of, 91; and Columbia River, 45; and Northwest, 137, 142–43, 204; Oregon claims of, 151; settles Oregon border, 256; war of with Great Britain, 91

U. S. Bureau of Forestry, 416

U. S. Fish and Wildlife Service, 430

Union Pacific Railroad, absorbs local lines, 396; and Central Pacific, 356; fails, 398; and Hill, 383–87, 411–12; and mines, 390–91

Union Transportation Company, 344

Vancouver, Capt. George, 43, 48, 61

Vancouver, Fort, 122, 128, 132–33, 135–38, 146, 149, 170, 173, 177, 178; abandoned, 211–12

Vancouver Island, 5, 14, 26, 47, 90, 92; Cook's discovery of, 17

Victoria, Fort, effect of gold rush on, 319; founding of, 212

Villard, Henry, bankrupt, 381; and Billings, 378–79; buys Northern Pacific, 379; immigrant bureaus of, 374, 379–80; investigation of, 362–63; and OR & N, 377; and Oregon and Transcontinental, 383; outmaneuvers Holladay, 363–64; retires, 398

Voyage to the Pacific Ocean, A (Cook), 34, 54

Voyages Made in the Years 1788 and 1789 from China to the North West Coast of America (Meares), 38, 44

Wagon, use of, 175–76, 218, 226–27, 233, 234–35

Waiilatpu, 180, 193; closed, 219; as emigrant haven, 233; massacre at, 262–63; Meek returns to, 266; meeting at, 221–22; progress at, 215–16, 218; reopened, 223

Walker, Joel, 216–17, 291

Walla Walla, Fort, 149, 162, 170, 171, 177, 193; gold discovered near, 327–28; Indians burn, 306, 313–14. See also Nez Percé, Fort

Walla Walla, Indian council at, 300–3; treaties of, 304

Walla Walla and Columbia River Railroad, 364–65

Walla Walla Indians, in California, 259, 261

Waller, Rev. Alvin F., 201; and McLoughlin, 239

Washington (sloop), 23–26, 28, 30, 34, 35, 40, 47; refitted as brig, 41

Washington, achieves statehood, 394; as territory, 286, 336

Washington Irrigation Company, 437–38

Water rights, federal development of, 437–38; history of, 435–36

Weeks Act, 419

Western Federation of Miners, 406, 420

Western Pacific Railroad, 412

West Side Company (Oregon Central Railroad), 357–59, 363

Weyerhaeuser Timber Company, and development of tree farms, 424–25; and forest fires, 416; and Hill, 411

Wheat, and Atkinson, 347–48

White, Dr. and Mrs. Elijah, 188, 201; and Indians, 220–22, 240, 259–60

Whitman, Marcus, advises settlers, 226; and Frémont, 230–31; and Great Emigration, 231–34; and Indians, 234, 260–61; and measles epidemic, 261; as missionary, 166–73; murder of, 262–63; treks East, 222–23; wagon travel of, 174–81; at Waiilatpu, 194, 215–19

Whitman, Narcissa, 173–81, 215

Whitney, Asa, 287–88

Wilkes, Lt. Charles, visit of, 204–9

Willamette Falls, 147; McLoughlin's claims in, 249–51; settlement of, 192; water rights to, 239–45. See also Oregon City

Willamette Valley, 90, 93, 97, 101, 110; agriculture in, 189–90; mission in, 160; plans to colonize, 139, 141, 147, 150

William, Fort, 91, 110–13, 162, 173

Williams, Sen. George, 359–62

Wobblies, the, 420–21

Wool, Gen. John Ellis, and Indian wars, 309–12; northwest trip of, 307–8; and Stevens, 297

Wright, Ben, murdered by Indians, 309; at Tule Lake, 279

Wright, Col. George, 308–10; drowned, 350; and Indian uprisings, 311–15

Wyeth, Nathaniel, 138–39; at Fort Hall, 160 ff.; and Kelley, 143; and McLough-

lin, 147; trip west, 148–53

Wyoming, achieves statehood, 394; as part of Dakota, 340

XY Company, 63, 66, 67 n., 77

Yakima Indians, attacks of, 304; and Wright, 311

Yakima River Valley, irrigation controversy in, 436–38

Young, Ewing, and Kelley, 145–48, 164, 173; and still, 183–86, 193; will of, 206–7